Bevan an

The Inves

A Guide t 101 785 168 9 **nal**

Investigat

ONE WEEK LOAN

- 9 APR 2008

D1354323

Bevan and Lidstone's
The Investigation of Crime:
A Guide to the Law of Criminal Investigation

Third edition

by

Denis Clark

Senior Lecturer in Criminal Justice Studies, Centre for Police Research and Education, School of Social Science, University of Teesside

 LexisNexis®

United Kingdom	LexisNexis UK, a Division of Reed Elsevier (UK) Ltd, Halsbury House, 35 Chancery Lane, LONDON, WC2A 1EL, and 4 Hill Street, EDINBURGH EH2 3JZ
Argentina	LexisNexis Argentina, BUENOS AIRES
Australia	LexisNexis Butterworths, CHATSWOOD, New South Wales
Austria	LexisNexis Verlag ARD Orac GmbH & Co KG, VIENNA
Canada	LexisNexis Butterworths, MARKHAM, Ontario
Chile	LexisNexis Chile Ltda, SANTIAGO DE CHILE
Czech Republic	Nakladatelství Orac sro, PRAGUE
France	Editions du Juris-Classeur SA, PARIS
Germany	LexisNexis Deutschland GmbH, FRANKFURT and MUNSTER
Hong Kong	LexisNexis Butterworths, HONG KONG
Hungary	HVG-Orac, BUDAPEST
India	LexisNexis Butterworths, NEW DELHI
Ireland	LexisNexis, DUBLIN
Italy	Giuffrè Editore, MILAN
Malaysia	Malayan Law Journal Sdn Bhd, KUALA LUMPUR
New Zealand	LexisNexis Butterworths, WELLINGTON
Poland	Wydawnictwo Prawnicze LexisNexis, WARSAW
Singapore	LexisNexis Butterworths, SINGAPORE
South Africa	LexisNexis Butterworths, Durban
Switzerland	Stämpfli Verlag AG, BERNE
USA	LexisNexis, DAYTON, Ohio

© Reed Elsevier (UK) Ltd 2004
Published by LexisNexis UK

A CIP Catalogue record for this book is available from the British Library.

ISBN 0 406 95742 8

Printed and bound in Great Britain by CPI Bath
Visit LexisNexis UK at www.lexisnexis.co.uk

Preface

Criminal investigation is a process of interlocking activities influenced by cultural and psychological considerations, regulated by law. It has never been more complex, with a myriad of legal and practical issues besetting the investigator. The Second Report of the Shipman Inquiry (2003), which mirrored many of the criticisms contained in the Stephen Lawrence Inquiry (1999), relating to flawed police investigations and a lack of adequate documentation, serve as painful antidotes to complacency. While the process must always be viewed holistically, this book deals with the law only.

Since the previous edition there has been unprecedented growth in the legislation and common law that investigators must be aware of. In addition to this growth, the 'police family' has been extended and there has been an upsurge in the number of state investigators. Indeed at the time of writing the new agency to deal with organised crime had just been announced with the suggestion that the government were considering lowering the standard of proof for certain offences.

The Human Rights Act 1998 is a most significant influence on the law of criminal investigation - an influence seismic in its impact on the actions of police and public authority investigators. There is now a statutory requirement to comply with human rights principles and the courts must take account of the jurisprudence of the European Court of Human Rights. It is against this background that the Government's proposals must be seen and many of the changes have been influenced by the Act as much as by crime control concerns.

A survey of some of the changes in this edition illustrates the increasing complexity of the law of criminal investigation.

There has been a major revision of the Police and Criminal Evidence Act 1984 Codes of Practice which took effect from 1 April 2003. The prosecution's requirement to disclose its case was set out in the Criminal Procedure and Investigation of Offences 1996 and has been recently considered by the House of Lords in the context of public interest immunity. Measures to protect vulnerable witnesses were the subject of the Criminal

Justice and Youth Evidence Act 1998. The Crime and Disorder Act 1998 gives new powers to combat disorder. Three criminal justice Acts, including the Criminal Justice Act 2003, have been passed containing provisions to deal with a range of issues, including disclosure and evidence. Additional measures to combat terrorism were contained in the Terrorism Act 2000 and the Anti-Terrorism Crime and Security Act 2001. Following on from a report by the Cabinet Office, the huge and complex Proceeds of Crime Act 2002 that established the Assets Recovery Agency and gave new, stronger powers of asset confiscation was enacted. The Police Reform Act 2002 has created the 'designated investigator' and given a broad range of powers to civilians. Surveillance is now regulated by the Regulation of Investigatory Powers Act 2000.

This edition takes account of all these developments, with the principal focus on powers of investigation. It was prepared by Denis Clark who has updated and rewritten the text while retaining its original style. It provided an opportunity to renew an old friendship with Ken Lidstone who supported and encouraged the author much more than he will appreciate.

I continue to encourage criminal justice professionals, police officers and non-police investigators to contact me (denis.clark2@btopenworld.com) with any problem or query. I particularly appreciate the contributions of students on the MSc Criminal Investigation and Covert Human Intelligence courses, as well as colleagues, Alisdair Gillespie, Alf Magrs and Alan Doig at Teesside University. A special note of thanks goes to the following: John Atha of West Yorkshire Police, Kevin Kealy, Larry Warburton, formerly of Lancashire Police, Bob Barnes of the National Crime Squad, David Crinnion, formerly of the Metropolitan and British Transport Police Forces and Dianne Squires of Lincolnshire Police, all of whom made helpful comments during work on the material.

My thanks must also go those concerned in the production of the book: the editorial staff at LexisNexis and Judy Flynn at Teesside University whose organisational skills have been much valued. My family, especially my wife, Elizabeth, Margaret Clark, Jean, Adrian and Valerie Bell will always have my gratitude for their selfless support, while Rebecca Jane Clark, aged eight months, has some responsibility for my failure to meet the original publishing deadline.

The law is as stated at 28 April 2004.

Denis Clark

The Centre for Applied Socio-Legal Studies
University of Teesside
Middlesbrough TS1 3BA

Contents

7   Treatment and questioning of persons in police detention   383

Table of statutes

Paragraph numbers in **bold** type indicate where the Act is set out in part or in full

Table of cases

1 Introduction

1.1 The theme that runs through the development of investigative powers in England and Wales has been the desire to protect the liberty of the individual from the arbitrary use of power and the need to ensure that the state has sufficient powers to enforce the law effectively and efficiently. Many of the provisions now on the statute book are available to other state agencies and it is no longer appropriate to view the police as having a monopoly on the use of investigative powers. Growth in investigative powers has been exponential, so too the expansion of those who may exercise them. Regrettably, this has not resulted in simplification, but rather the need to be aware of a diversity of legislative and common law sources of power.

1.2 The trend began in 1986 with the passing of the Police and Criminal Evidence Act 1984, which emanated from the Royal Commission on Criminal Procedure, appointed in 1978 to consider, inter alia, 'the powers and duties of the police in respect of the investigation of criminal offences and the rights and duties of suspects and accused persons, including the means by which they are secured'. This statute remains preeminent in providing the legal landscape against which investigative powers are exercised. This despite amendments to it brought about by a series of Acts affecting the criminal justice system as well as the Criminal Justice and Public Order Act 1994 which provided for inferences to be drawn from silence in certain circumstances. Hard on its heels was the Criminal Procedure and Investigations Act in 1996, the purpose of which was to place a statutory duty on the prosecutor to disclose its case against reciprocal obligations on the defence.

1.3 At about the same time the United Kingdom became increasingly aware of its vulnerability to human rights challenges. A number of high profile cases in the European Court of Human Rights highlighted gaps in the legislative framework that needed urgent attention. The Human Rights Act 1998 became law in October 2000, providing new rights based approach to investigative powers. It was however too late to prevent the impact of cases on the right of silence, access to a solicitor and the calling into question of the ex parte public interest immunity procedures. Amendments to the

Criminal Justice and Public Order Act 1994 were hurriedly passed in the Youth Justice and Criminal Evidence Act 1999, although this was primarily intended to implement the recommendations of 'Speaking up for Justice' (1998), the Report of the Home Office Interdepartmental Group on the Treatment of Vulnerable or Intimidated Witnesses in the Criminal Justice System.

1.4   Legislation on the use of covert human intelligence sources, intrusive surveillance, interception of communications and other state invasions of privacy was passed in the Regulation of Investigatory Powers Act 2000. A complex piece of legislation lacking coherence, with oversight and supervision from two commissioners – the Interception and Surveillance Commissioners. For those who operate the legislation it has represented significant challenges, not least because the draft codes were being used to regulate operations while still subjected to revision. It appears the process is now bedded in among a great deal of confusion as to the meaning of terms such as proportionality and uncertainty as to the limits of aspects such as the activities of covert human intelligence sources.

1.5   Public Interest Immunity has been considered on a number of occasions by the European Court of Human Rights and recently by the House of Lords in *R v H and C* (2004), to the extent that it can no longer be said that the courts must employ a balancing of competing rights but rather the right to disclosure is tipped more towards the defendant. The common law has also expanded the abuse of process doctrine to the point that where entrapment takes place it is likely the prosecution will be stayed. The impact that this will have on the effectiveness of covert policing remains to be seen.

1.6   The Police Reform Act 2002 has expanded the police family – the concept of the office of constable must be re examined in its wake. International terrorism has necessitated two new Acts – the Terrorism 2000 Act and the Anti Terrorism, Crime and Security Act 2001. A continuing emphasis on recovering the assets of illegal entrepeneurism has justified the consolidation and addition of confiscation provisions in the monumental Proceeds of Crime Act 2002. There are a variety of new measures in the Criminal Justice Act 2003 and the modern day recognition of global crime has brought about the Criminal Justice (International Co-operation) Act 2003.

1.7   The scheme of this edition is similar to that of previous editions but with human rights legislation considered in Chapter 2 and placed in context elsewhere in the book. Chapter 3 takes account of the changes in stop and search powers influenced by the MacPherson Enquiry (1999). Chapter 4 deals with powers of entry and search modified as they are by the 'sift and seize' amendments to PACE. The increase in the number of offences for which there is a power of arrest is detailed in Chapter 5. Detention, identification procedures and questioning are the subjects of Chapters 6 to 8.

1.8   Chapter 9 deals with surveillance powers, principally contained in the Regulation of Investigatory Powers Act 2000. There is of course, much greater reliance on both technological and forensic investigative techniques and the additional powers to take samples are included where appropriate in the text.

1.9   Account has been taken of the numerous decisions of the courts which impact on investigative powers, many of which have developed through burgeoning litigation in the civil courts. The text emphasises the importance of the lawful exercise of investigative power, this is no straightforward task and the law of criminal investigation, like so many areas of the law, calls for rationalisation and codification.

1.10   The style of referencing, as with previous additions, avoids footnotes and cases have only been given their dates in the text. A complete list of cases and their citations is found in the Table of cases. References to the Articles of the PACE Northern Ireland Order follow references to PACE 1984, eg '(s 1, Art 3)'.

2 The regulation of criminal investigation

2.1 This chapter is divided into two sections. Firstly there is an outline of the process of criminal investigation and, secondly, key concepts and definitions are described. In the first part there is a broad overview of the elements of investigation together with an outline of the legal aspects which regulate the process. Criminal investigation is not just the province of the police: a multiplicity of investigative agencies have a range of powers, some of which were previously conferred only on holders of the office of constable, but now made available to police staff by the Police Reform Act 2002 and to the investigative arms of a number of public authorities through the Regulation of Investigatory Powers Act 2000. The second section consists of common legal concepts and definitions which regulate and influence the investigative process. This section sets out human rights considerations and also the threshold requirements which provide the legal basis for the exercise of powers. It should be seen as a route map in the sense that many of the terms are common to the law of criminal investigation and they will be referred to throughout the text. Finally there is a discussion of the law relating to the exclusion of evidence because of its importance to the investigative process.

THE PROCESS OF CRIMINAL INVESTIGATION

2.2 Criminal investigation is the process undertaken to establish whether an act, intention to act or omission may be labelled a crime and, if it is, the collection of evidence to determine those responsible and how they will be dealt with in the criminal justice system. There are two broad categories of investigative process, namely 'reactive' and 'proactive investigation'. To these categories should be added a third area of activity, that of intelligence gathering of the type which is collected as part of preventative strategies but which is ostensibly subject to similar legal controls. All investigation consists of the gathering of information and, for policy reasons, investigators seek to separate that which they label '*intelligence*' from that which they label '*evidence*' – it is because of these tensions that the third category which could be appropriately labelled, 'preventative intelligence gathering' has emerged. The categories are frequently interchangeable and should be viewed as overarching styles comprising a range of investigative techniques and strategies.

Reactive investigation

2.3   The traditional style of investigation is reactive; this consists of a search for evidence following an allegation of, or discovery of circumstances which amount to, a crime. Primary focus is on identifying the suspects. It follows a basic sequence:

- Crime scene preservation and examination – a systematic examination of the location and vicinity for trace evidence, marks, items of property and so on which may have evidential value
- Search for witnesses – obtaining witness accounts from victims and people who may have knowledge of issues relating to the crime
- Information evaluation – consultation of data in information systems, matching witness accounts and analysis of available evidence.

2.4   This demand led style of investigation combines the skills of the historian with the scientist – experts may be used such as crime scene specialists, forensic scientists and psychologists. It is heavily reliant on accurate information and its effective analysis. If suspects are identified the techniques involve may become proactive in the sense that the investigator employs strategies which are associated with the style of proactive investigation.

Proactive investigation

2.5   This style of investigation has been the guiding principle behind work on serious crime. The Audit Commission's (1993) Report sought to influence the police and other investigative agencies to focus their attention on criminals rather than crimes. It operates on the basis that investigation should be intelligence-led making use of information from informants and profiling techniques such as crime pattern analysis. Systematic evaluation of information takes place and leads to more efficient use of resources; investigative effort is put into activities such as surveillance and undercover operations. In recent years the emphasis has moved towards the recovery of the financial benefits of crime.

2.6   Proactive investigation has proved to be particularly effective in dealing with terrorism and organised crime. Its effectiveness is dependent on the secrecy of its methods – this creates a tension between fair trial rights and the public interest in keeping those methods secret.

PREVENTATIVE INTELLIGENCE GATHERING

2.7 This category has emerged under such influences as the Crime and Disorder Act, the Sex Offenders Act 1997 and, more recently, the Laming Enquiry into the death of Victoria Climbie (2003) and the murders of Jessica Chapman and Holly Wells in Soham, Cambridgeshire, with the failures in data sharing which resulted in the Bichard Inquiry (*The Times*, 18 December 2003). It represents a category of investigation whereby information is gathered and stored for public protection. In essence it is a recognition of the importance of information in terms of public protection and a consequence of the legislation which encourages multi-agency solutions to crime and disorder.

THE REGULATORY FRAMEWORK

2.8 The diagram on the next page sets out the principal sources which make up the framework of criminal investigation. Investigators must have a detailed knowledge of all these sources because each source has an influence on, and regulates the process of criminal investigation. There are a number of other sources, of lesser importance, which must also be taken into consideration. Data protection and freedom of information legislation, practice directions, the Code for Crown Prosecutors, Attorney-General's Guidelines, charging standards as well as the internal policies of organisations with investigative powers must all be taken into account.

Principal sources which regulate the process of criminal investigation

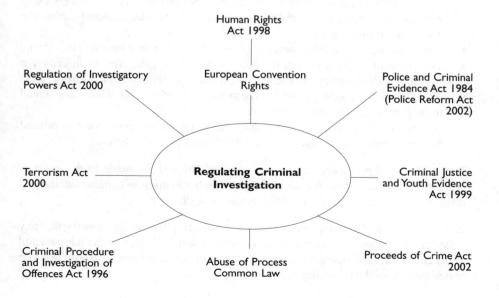

Human Rights
Act 1998

Regulation of Investigatory
Powers Act 2000

European Convention
Rights

Police and Criminal
Evidence Act 1984
(Police Reform Act
2002)

Terrorism Act
2000

**Regulating Criminal
Investigation**

Criminal Justice
and Youth Evidence
Act 1999

Criminal Procedure
and Investigation of
Offences Act 1996

Abuse of Process
Common Law

Proceeds of Crime Act
2002

THE INTEGRITY OF THE INVESTIGATIVE PROCESS

The disclosure regime

2.9   No matter what strategies are used in the investigative process, the public interest lies in compliance with the law. Criminal investigation consists of policy making and specific actions as part of a staged process. The investigation is regulated by the requirement to maintain accurate records and, in due course, to be accountable to the courts if a prosecution takes place. It is essential that investigation is conducted ethically and investigators approach their task in a methodical and scientific manner. This is recognised by the courts.

2.10   The judges developed a common law duty for the prosecution to disclose the evidence which it has at its disposal to the defence in an effort to achieve a fair trial for an accused person and to achieve 'equality of arms'. It is now the subject of a statutory regime set out in the Criminal Procedure and Investigation of Offences Act 1996 (CPIOA 1996) and supplemented by a Code of Practice issued under the Act. Application of the disclosure provisions is set out in s 1(3) which states that Part I of the Act applies where no criminal investigation has begun before 1 April 1997. 'Criminal investigation' is defined in s 1(4) as follows:

> 'an investigation which police officers or other persons have a duty to conduct with a view to it being ascertained whether (a) a person should be charged with an offence, or (b) whether a person charged with an offence is guilty of it.'

2.11   The requirements of the Act are:
- A statutory duty is placed on the police (other investigation agencies charged with the duty of investigating criminal offences must have regard to the Code's provisions) to record and retain information and material gathered during the course of an investigation
- The prosecution inform the defence of the information they intend to use at trial
- The prosecution must inform the defence of certain categories of information which they do not intend to use at trial (primary prosecution disclosure)
- The defence have a duty to inform the prosecution of the case which they intend to present at trial (defence disclosure)
- Defence disclosure triggers off a duty on the part of the prosecutor to present further material to the defence (secondary prosecution disclosure).

2.12   There are provisions in the Act for application to be made to the court in circumstances where there is a dispute about whether to disclose certain material and there are sanctions laid down for defence failure to disclose.

2.13   The Code of Practice makes the investigator responsible for ensuring that any information relevant to the investigation is recorded and retained, whether it is gathered in the course of the investigation or generated by the investigation. The duty to retain material includes the following categories:

1. Crime reports, including crime report forms, relevant parts of incident report books and police officer's notebooks
2. Final versions of witness statements
3. Draft versions of witness statements where their contents differ from the final version
4. Interview records (written or taped)
5. Expert reports and schedules
6. Any material casting doubt upon the reliability of a confession
7. Any material casting doubt on the reliability of a witness.

2.14   The investigator must draw to the prosecutor's attention any material which might reasonably be considered capable of undermining the prosecution case and, after the disclosure by the defence, must look again at the material, in the light of the defence statement, and draw to the prosecutor's attention material which might reasonably be expected to assist the defence. Section 32 of the Criminal Justice Act 2003 has amended s 2 of the CPIOA to make the test for primary disclosure an objective one. Additionally the CJA has extended the onus on the defence to provide a more detailed statement of defence and made provision to allow the police the opportunity to interview defence witnesses (A Code of Practice will have to be drawn up before these measures can be implemented). The responsibilities on the investigator to ensure full disclosure cannot be understated.

2.15   Sensitive material will frequently be gathered during the course of an investigation. This is information which the investigator believes is not in the public interest to disclose. Examples of which are material relating to national security, material given in confidence, material relating to informants and undercover officers. These types of information must be included on a separate schedule.

Provisions applicable to witnesses

2.16   An accused person may not be called as a witness in criminal proceedings except upon his own application (Criminal Evidence Act 1898, s 1).Otherwise a witness is competent if he may lawfully give evidence and compellable if he may lawfully be required to give evidence. The general rule as to competence is that all persons are competent to give evidence, subject to two exceptions. Section 53 of the Youth Justice and Criminal Evidence Act 1999 ('YJCEA 1999') provides that all persons are competent to give evidence in criminal proceedings unless it appears to the court that a person is not able to:

(i) understand questions put to him as a witness, and
(ii) gives answers to them which can be understood; or
(iii) is a person who is charged in criminal proceedings (who will not be competent to give evidence for the prosecution.

2.17   It is for the court to determine whether a witness is competent to give evidence whether it is raised by a party to the proceedings, or by the court of its own motion

(YJCEA 1999, s 54). The party calling the witness is required to satisfy the court that, on a balance of probabilities, the witness is competent to give evidence. In determining the question of competency the court must treat the witness as having the benefit of any directions under s 19 (special measures) which the court has given or proposes to give in relation to the witness, expert evidence may be received on the question and the determination takes place in the absence of the jury (if there is one). A witness may not be competent because he is prevented by reason of mental illness or drunkenness, if it is contended that a witness is in either category the judge must rule as to competence. A deaf and dumb person is competent if he is able to understand the nature of the oath and he may be examined through an interpreter and if a dumb person is able to write he may write down his answers. Children under 14 are not permitted to give sworn evidence (YJCEA 1999, s 55(2)). In order to test the ability of a child to give intelligible testimony the court should watch any video-taped interview with the child of ask questions of the child, or both.

2.18   Section 80 of PACE provides that the wife or husband of a person charged in the proceedings shall be compellable to give evidence on behalf of that person. The wife or husband of a person charged in the proceedings shall be compellable as follows:
(a)   to give evidence on behalf of any other person charged in the proceedings but only in respect of any specified offence with which that other person is charged; or
(b)   to give evidence for the prosecution but only in respect of any specified offence with which any person is charged in the proceedings.

2.19   An offence is specified if:
(a)   it involves an assault on, or injury or a threat of injury to, the wife or husband or a person who was at the material time under the age of 16;
(b)   it is a sexual offence alleged to have been committed in respect of a person who was at the material time under that age; or
(c)   it consists of attempting or conspiring to commit, or of aiding, abetting, counselling, procuring or inciting the commission of, an offence falling within paragraph (a) or (b) above.

Special measures directions in the case of vulnerable and intimidated witnesses

2.20   Chapter I of Part II of the YJCEA 1999 contains special measures which are derived from the recommendations of 'Speaking up for Justice', the Report of the Interdepartmental Working Group on the Treatment of Vulnerable or Intimidated Witnesses in the Criminal Justice System (Home Office, 1998). The Act allocates special measures to witnesses on the basis of need, predicated on the classification of witnesses as those who are vulnerable as a result of the personal characteristics of youth and incapacity and those who are likely to suffer undue fear or distress if they give evidence in the traditional manner. In respect of witnesses in the first group the special measures which may apply are: screening the witness from the accused, giving evidence by live link, ordering the removal of wigs and gowns while the witness testifies, giving evidence in private (in sexual cases and cases involving intimidation), video recording of evidence in chief, cross-examination and re-examination, examination through intermediary and the provision of aids to communication. Witnesses eligible only by reason of fear or intimidation do not have the last two measures made available to them. Special measures apply to both prosecution and defence witnesses but not to an accused person.

Age and incapacity

2.21   Those witnesses under 17 at the time of the hearing are eligible for special measures by reason of age (YJCEA 1999, s 16(1)(a)). Witnesses who may qualify on the grounds of incapacity fall into two categories, firstly, those suffering from mental disorder or otherwise having a significant impairment of intelligence and social functioning (s 16(2)(a)). The court may find that a witness comes into these categories without first considering any views expressed by the witness (s 16(4)). Mental disorder is defined by the Mental Health Act 1983, s 1(2) to mean mental illness, arrested or incomplete development of mind, psychopathic disorder and any other disorder or disability of mind. The second set of witnesses who qualify on the grounds of incapacity are witnesses with a physical disability or disorder (s 16(2)(b)). Eligibility in relation to both types of incapacity arises only where the court considers that the quality of evidence given by the witness is likely to be diminished by reason of the incapacity if no assistance is provided.

Fear and distress

2.22   Special measures are also available to witnesses if the court is satisfied that the quality of evidence given by the witness is likely to be diminished by reason of fear or distress 'in connection with testifying in the proceedings' (YJCEA 1999, s 17). It is therefore necessary to show the causal link between the fear of distress and the prospect of giving evidence in the proceedings. This may be established because of the nature of the crime, through fear of confronting the witness or due to the embarrassing nature of the evidence he must give. A number of circumstances must be taken into account by the court in deciding eligibility (s 17(2)); these include the nature and circumstances of the offence and other matters which include:

(i)   social and cultural background
(ii)   ethnic origin
(iii)   domestic and employment circumstances
(iv)   religious and political beliefs; and
(v)   any behaviour towards the witness by the accused or those associated with him, including anyone else likely to be an accused or a witness in the case.

2.23   Complainants in respect of sexual cases are presumed eligible under s 17 but can inform the court that they prefer not to be regarded as eligible for special measures if they so wish. Sections 16 to 27 and 31 to 33 of the YJCEA 1999 dealing with special measures came into force on 24 July 2002: Youth Justice and Criminal Evidence Act 1999 (Commencement No 7) Order 2002 (SI 2002 No 1739). For a detailed account of these provisions see Birch and Leng (2000).

THE IMPACT OF HUMAN RIGHTS ON CRIMINAL INVESTIGATION

The emergence of human rights jurisprudence in UK law

2.24   Until recently, the general approach to protecting rights in the UK was to think of liberty or freedom. The doctrine of parliamentary sovereignty and the lack of a written constitution or bill of rights have enabled Parliament to encroach on freedom (Gearty (1995)). A naïve British society has been complacent about the lack of entrenchment and the protection of fundamental freedoms. Instruments which have been assumed to protect important rights such as Magna Carta and the Bill of Rights Act 1689 can be appealed or amended by statute and in any event, protected the interests of powerful groups. The essential tradition has been one of recognising negative freedoms.

2.25   As the state gradually expanded in the nineteenth century some of these negative freedoms were removed to secure improved quality of life (economic and social rights) for the worst off in society. The process continued in the twentieth century with the development of new tribunals to implement new social rights rather than to protect liberties. Scepticism of the ability of politicians to protect freedom has grown exponentially as the state has grown and the executive has become more powerful with the possibility of challenge diminished by party discipline. This particularly so at times of national emergency (Gearty (1995)).

2.26   After the Second World War as the UK has signed up to a number of international instruments debate has emerged as to the scope of particular rights and freedoms and the best way of protecting them. Rights consciousness has gradually developed influenced by the UK's closer association with European institutions. This closer association with the Council of Europe and the European Communities and Union has exerted a fundamental impact on the place of rights in legal and practical thought in the UK.

2.27   The UK acceded to the European Convention on Human Rights in 1953, but it was not until 1966 that victims were able to petition the Commission. Since then the UK has frequently had to defend itself against charges of infringing Convention rights and has often changed domestic law to give effect to decisions of the European Commission and Court of Human Rights.

2.28   By the mid-1990s the UK was becoming increasingly rights-conscious. Judges influenced by ECHR and other developments in the common law world were beginning to recognise convention rights. In parallel with this change of judicial attitude the European Union was giving a higher profile to fundamental rights in ways which had the capacity to affect national law directly. It was only a matter of time before the Bill of Rights debate, reactivated by Lord Scarman in the 1974 Hamlyn Lectures, became unstoppable. Attempts to improve human rights protection were introduced by politicians from a range of political standpoints and, in 1993, the Labour Party adopted the policy of incorporating convention rights into UK law. In October 2000 the Human Rights Act 1998 became law.

The effect of human rights law on domestic law

2.29 The Human Rights Act 1998 incorporates the rights and freedoms set out in the European Convention on Human Rights into UK law. As such it marks the beginning of a new era for the protection of human rights in the UK. Domestic courts had increasingly accepted the legitimacy of referring to the convention but, in the view of the Government, incorporation was necessary.

2.30 The HRA 1998 does not make decisions of the European Court and Commission of Human Rights binding in domestic law but it does include a strong provision in relation to the interpretation of Convention rights. Section 2(1) requires

'that any court or tribunal determining a question in connection with a Convention right must **take into account**, inter alia, judgements, decisions, declarations, and advisory opinions of the European Court of Human Rights'.

It is clear that s 2 was intended to require courts to take account of Strasbourg decisions regardless of the identity of the respondent state.

2.31 The convention's approach to the protection of human rights is an increasingly important part of domestic law; fundamental to its operation is that the safeguards must be interpreted so that they are 'practical and effective' not 'theoretical or illusory' (Starmer, 1999). A consequence of this approach is that there are both explicit and implicit rights contained in the convention.

Public authorities

2.32 The primary focus on the Convention rights is on public authorities. HRA 1998, s 6(1) states:

'It is unlawful for a public authority to act in a way which is incompatible with a convention right'

2.33 Although some bodies are clearly public authorities such as government departments, local authorities, the police, the Inland Revenue and others who have no private function, the Act does not define public authority.

2.34 There are other bodies who may exercise private and public functions who are subject to the duty to comply with convention rights in respect of their public function only. Whether a body is a public authority will have to be decided on a case-for-case basis, suffice to say that most of the powers which are referred to in this text are exercised by public authorities whose duties under s 6(1) are clear.

2.35   It is common ground that there are three principal levels of rights under the Convention. First, there are absolute rights, such as those under Art 2 (right to life) and Art 3 (right not to be subjected to torture or inhuman or degrading treatment). Derogation from these rights is not permitted under any circumstances. Secondly, between the absolute and qualified rights are those contained in Arts 5 and 6 which declare the rights most frequently raised in criminal proceedings. Thirdly, there are qualified rights: those under Arts 8-11, where the right is declared and then interference with it is permitted in certain circumstances. The practical difference between these categories of rights is that restriction in the public interest can be justified, but only on the grounds expressly provided for within the texts of the articles themselves. According to the case law a limitation or restriction on these rights can only be justified in the following circumstances:

1.   The limitation or restriction must be 'prescribed by law', the requirements of which are the law must be adequately accessible and it must be formulated with sufficient precision to enable individuals to regulate their conduct. The Privy Council in *de Freitas v Ministry of Agriculture* (1999) said that the fundamental issue under consideration is the principle of legal certainty (per Lord Clyde).
2.   The limitation or restriction must be in order to pursue a legitimate aim, ie one of the aims specifically listed in the article.
3.   The limitation or restriction must be necessary in a free society. This means in respect of the third category of rights it must be shown that the limitation or restriction fulfills a pressing social need and it is proportionate to the aim of responding to that aim.
4.   The limitation or restriction must not be discriminatory. In issue is if differences in treatment have no objective and reasonable justification.

2.36   Every exercise of an investigative power must therefore be shown to be lawful in pursuit of a legitimate aim, necessary and proportionate to the end which is sought to be achieved. Necessity is not defined in the Convention but has been interpreted as not synonymous with 'indispensable' but not as flexible as 'ordinary, useful or desirable' (*Silver v United Kingdom* (1983)). Proportionality occupies a central position in the exercise of investigative powers; it is considered a vehicle for conducting a balancing exercise and it balances the nature and extent of the interference against the reasons for interfering. A number of questions must be considered:

1.   Would it have been possible to achieve the legitimate aim by a less intrusive means? (*Campbell v United Kingdom* (1993))
2.   Does the interference deprive the right-holder of the very essence of the right? (*Rees v United Kingdom* (1987))
3.   Is the right of sufficient importance in the circumstances to warrant particularly strong reasons being required to justify any interference? (*Jersild v Denmark* (1994))

4. Does the interference cause harm to the right-holder which is serious enough to outweigh any benefit which that interference might achieve through furthering a legitimate aim? (*Dudgeon v United Kingdom* (1982))
5. Are there sufficient safeguards against abuse? (*Klass v Germany* (1978))

2.37 The elements of proportionality were formulated by the House of Lords in *R (Daly) v Secretary of State for the Home Department* (2001) as follows:

- that the objective of the interference is sufficiently important to justifying limiting the right;
- that the measures designed to meet the objective are rationally connected with it;
- that the used means to impair the right is no more than is necessary to accomplish the objective; and
- that the interference does not have an excessive or disproportionate effect on the affected individual.

2.38 Fordham and de la Mare provide an excellent analysis of how the UK should approach the concept of proportionality. The principle of proportionality, they argue, is at the heart of the European legal order and is increasingly recognised as a key component of the rule of law. Their analysis is clearly applicable to the state's exercise of investigative powers and the following is extracted from 'Identifying the Principles of Proportionality' (Fordham and de La Mare in Jowell and Cooper (2001)).

Proportionality under the HRA 1998: suggested rules

2.39
1. Before deciding to make any measure which may restrict one of the Convention rights, there are *key questions* which a public authority should address. It should *ask* whether there is a pressing need in these respects:
   Q1 Is the measure adopted to pursue a legitimate aim?
   Q2 Can it serve to further that aim?
   Q3 Is it the least restrictive way of doing so?
   Q4 Viewed overall, do the ends justify the means?
2. It should *consider*: (a) what competing interests are at stake; (b) what weight should be given to those competing interests; (c) whether any of them can properly take precedence over another.
3. The authority should only adopt the measure if, having asked and answered the key questions, the authority considers that the measure is (a) a justified thing to do and (b) the right thing to do.
4. The authority should record its assessment of all these matters for future reference. Often, it will be appropriate to make immediate disclosure of the reasoning with communication of the measure.
5. If a measure is adopted without assessing these matters, the authority will usually be well-advised to reconsider afresh whether the measure is appropriate.

6.   If the authority is challenged under the HRA 1998, it will have the burden of explaining to the Court, by way of *evidence*, on what basis (by reference to the key questions) the measure is justified.

7.   In order to test the justification for the measure, the Court will often be assisted by evidence of a broader picture than usually available in litigation.

8.   Only rarely will it be necessary to probe evidence by way of cross-examination and disclosure. If the Court is not satisfied by the evidence presented by the public authority the authority' s onus is not discharged and the Court can strike down the measure and/or order it to be reconsidered afresh.

9.   The first task of the Court is to ask whether the authority addressed its own mind to the key questions and, if not, order that the measure be reconsidered afresh.

10. The second task of the Court is to ask whether the public authority has shown an objective justification for the measure, by means of justified answers to the key questions.

11. In applying that test of justification, the Court asks whether it considers that the measure was (a) a justified thing to do, but *not* whether it considers that the measure was (b) the right thing to do.

12. In applying the justification test, the Court should ask itself what height of intensity should be applied in relation to the key questions. The best way to approach this is by asking what width of 'margin' (latitude) should be afforded to the authority.

13. The width of the margin (and so height of intensity) should not be set by 'reading across' analyses of the 'margin of appreciation' in Strasbourg case-law, though such cases are helpful in identifying relevant factors influencing *relative* width.

14. The width of the margin generally depends on the nature of: (a) *the right infringed* (how fundamental?); (b) *the objective pursued* (how compelling?); (c) *the measure and decision-maker* (what status?); and (4) *the context of the dispute* (how sensitive?).

15. In some special high intensity cases there will in effect be no margin, and only one justified answer. In some special low-intensity cases there is a wide margin and the Court is effectively asking whether the measure is reasonably open to the public authority. In most cases, there will be a margin but not a wide one. The Court is effectively asking whether there was a pressing social need such that the measure is objectively justified.

RELEVANCE OF THE RIGHTS TO CRIMINAL INVESTIGATION

2.40   The following articles will be discussed in terms of their relevance to the investigative process:

- Article 2 – right to life
- Article 3 – right to freedom from inhumane and degrading treatment
- Article 5 – right to liberty
- Article 6 – right to a fair trial
- Article 8 – right to privacy and family life.

Article 2 – the right to life

2.41

(1) Everyone's right to life shall be protected by law. No one shall be deprived of his life intentionally save in the execution of a sentence of a court following his conviction of a crime for which this penalty is provided by law.

(2) Deprivation of life shall not be regarded as inflicted in contravention of this Article when it results from the use of force which is no more than absolutely necessary:

    (a) in defence of any person from unlawful violence;

    (b) in order to effect a lawful arrest or to prevent the escape of a person lawfully detained;

    (c) in action lawfully taken for the purpose of quelling a riot or insurrection.

2.42 Article 2 ranks as one of the most fundamental provisions of the Convention from which no derogation is permitted, even in times of national emergency. Its provisions must be strictly construed, and any deprivation of life must be subjected to 'the most carefu l scrutiny' (*McCann, Savage and Farrell v UK* (1997)). Consequently there is a positive obligation on the police to take reasonable steps to protect potential victims from a real and immediate threat to their lives which is attributable to the actual or threatened criminal acts of a third party (*Osman v United Kingdom*). This also means that the state is under an obligation to conduct an effective official investigation into alleged breaches of the right to life. The authorities must act of their own motion and cannot leave it to the next-of-kin to initiate a complaint or take proceedings. The investigation must be independent, thorough and prompt, and must be capable of leading to the identification and, where appropriate, the punishment of those responsible. There must be a sufficient element of public scrutiny of the investigation or its results to ensure accountability and the next-of-kin must be involved to an extent necessary to safeguard their legitimate interests: *Jordan v United Kingdom* (2002).

2.43 In the context of criminal investigation Art 2 places a duty on the state to conduct an effective, efficient and independent investigation where death results from actions of the state, the duty extends beyond the police to the prison authorities and others. The extent to which this places a duty on the state to investigate unlawful killings which do not involve its agents is controversial. The police have a duty at common law to keep the peace and positive obligations towards victims under the European Convention on Human Rights (see De Than JoCL 67 (165)).

Article 3 – prohibition of torture

2.44

No one shall be subjected to torture or to inhuman or degrading treatment or punishment.

2.45 In order to constitute a violation of Art 3, the treatment or punishment complained of 'must attain a minimum level of severity': *Ireland v United Kingdom*. The threshold is relative and will depend on the' sex, age and state of health' of the victim (*Campbell and Cosans v United Kingdom*). The law must provide adequate protection for individuals against the infliction of inhuman or degrading treatment by other private individuals.

2.46 Article 3 potentially arises in the context of conditions of detention, the taking of intimate samples and the questioning of suspects.

Article 5 – the right to liberty

2.47

(1) Everyone has the right to liberty and security of the person. No one shall be deprived of his liberty save in the following cases and in accordance with a procedure prescribed by law:
   (a) the lawful detention of a person after conviction by a competent court;
   (b) the lawful arrest or detention of a person for non-compliance with the lawful order of a court or in order to secure the fulfilment of any obligation prescribed by law;
   (c) the lawful arrest or detention of a person effected for the purpose of bringing him before the competent legal authority on reasonable suspicion of having committed an offence or when it is reasonably considered necessary to prevent his committing an offence or fleeing after having done so;
   (d) the detention of a minor by lawful order for the purpose of educational supervision or his lawful detention for the purpose of bringing him before the competent legal authority;
   (e) the lawful detention of persons for the prevention of the spreading of infectious diseases, of persons of unsound mind, alcoholics or drug addicts or vagrants;
   (f) the lawful arrest or detention of a person to prevent his effecting an unauthorised entry into the country or of a person against whom action is being taken with a view to deportation or extradition.
(2) Everyone who is arrested shall be informed promptly, in a language which he understands, of the reasons for his arrest and of any charge against him.
(3) Everyone arrested or detained in accordance with the provisions of paragraph (1) (c) of this Article shall be brought promptly before a judge or other officer authorised by law to exercise judicial power and shall be entitled to trial within a reasonable time or to release pending trial. Release may be conditioned by guarantees to appear for trial.
(4) Everyone who is deprived of his liberty by arrest or detention shall be entitled to take proceedings by which the lawfulness of his detention shall

be decided speedily by a court and his release ordered if the detention is not lawful.

(5) Everyone who has been the victim of arrest or detention in contravention of the provisions of this Article shall have an enforceable right to compensation.

2.48   Article 5(1)(a) to (f) provides an exhaustive definition of the circumstances in which a person may be lawfully deprived of his liberty and is to be given a narrow construction (*Winterwerp v Netherlands*).

2.49   In addition to falling within sub-paras (a) to (f), any detention must be: (a) 'lawful' ; and (b) carried out 'in accordance with a procedure prescribed by law'. These terms refer to conformity with national law and procedure, and it is therefore in the first place for the national authorities, notably the courts, to interpret and apply the law (*Wassink v Netherlands* (1990)). In particular the term 'lawful' has been held to require that the domestic law on which the detention is based must be accessible and precise (*Amuur v France (1996)*). In *Steel v United Kingdom*, the Court held that domestic law governing arrest and detention for breach of the peace was 'formulated with the degree of precision required by the Convention' . Cf *Hashman and Harrup v United Kingdom* (bind over to be 'of good behaviour' failed to give any reliable indication of what would constitute a breach of the order).

2.50   The second limb of Art 5(1)(b) is the legal basis for powers of temporary detention exercisable by the police without reasonable suspicion, such as the power to detain for the purpose of verifying ownership of a vehicle). Powers under Sch 7 of the Terrorism Act 2000 are justified under this limb – ie the stop is carried out to secure the performance of a legal obligation ie the obligation to provide information and submit to a search (*McVeigh, O'Neill and Evans v United Kingdom* (1981)), so to the powers of senior officers to give a blanket authority to stop people of vehicles in a specified area for three purposes. These are combatting terrorism, preventing violence between gangs in public and catching fleeing offenders. Article 5(1)(c) authorises arrest on reasonable suspicion of having committed a criminal offence. The arrest must be for the purpose of bringing the person concerned before the 'competent legal authority' which in England and Wales is a magistrates' court. The words 'reasonable suspicion' mean the existence of facts or information which would satisfy an objective observer that the person concerned may have committed the offence (*Fox, Campbell and Hartley v United Kingdom, Murray v United Kingdom and O'Hara v United Kingdom* (2002)).

2.51   Article 5(2) requires that an arrested person be provided with the reasons for an arrest. The detained person must be told 'in simple, non-technical language that he can understand, the essential legal and factual grounds for his arrest so as to be able, if he sees fit, to apply to a court to challenge its lawfulness' (*Fox, Campbell and Hartley v United Kingdom*).

2.52   The exercise of a power of arrest must therefore have lawful authority, be exercised in a non-arbitrary and non-discriminatory manner and be based on reasonable suspicion that the person has committed, is committing, or is about to commit an offence.

2.53   Article 5(3) guarantees the right of an arrested person to be brought before a judge or other judicial officer 'promptly' after an arrest. The detention regimes in PACE and the Terrorism Act are thought to meet the requirements of this article but the ECHR has not set abstract time limits and it is unlikely to do so.

Article 6 – the right to a fair trial

2.54

(1) In the determination of his civil rights and obligations or of any criminal charge against him, everyone is entitled to a fair and public hearing within a reasonable time by an independent and impartial tribunal established by law. Judgment shall be pronounced publicly but the press and public may be excluded from all or part of the trial in the interest of morals, public order or national security in a democratic society, where the interests of juveniles or the protection of the private lives of the parties so require, or to the extent strictly necessary in the opinion of the court in special circumstances where publicity would prejudice the interests of justice.

(2) Everyone charged with a criminal offence shall be presumed innocent until proved guilty according to law.

(3) Everyone charged with a criminal offence has the following minimum rights:

(a) to be informed promptly, in a language which he understands and in detail, of the nature and cause of the accusation against him;

(b) to have adequate time and facilities for the preparation of his defence;

(c) to defend himself in person or through legal assistance of his own choosing or, if he has not sufficient means to pay for legal assistance, to be given it free when the interests of justice so require;

(d) to examine or have examined witnesses against him and to obtain the attendance and examination of witnesses on his behalf under the same conditions as witnesses against him;

(e) to have the free assistance of an interpreter if he cannot understand or speak the language used in court.

2.55   Article 6(1) guarantees the general right to a fair trial and is to be given a broad and purposive interpretation (*Moreiva de Azvedo v Portugal*). In considering whether the rights of the defence under Art 6 have been respected, the European Court of Human Rights will have regard to the proceedings as a whole, including appellate proceedings, and may consider whether or not the appellate proceedings have rectified any defect which arose at the first instance hearing (*Adolf v Austria*). The minimum guarantees set out in Art 6(3)(a) to (e) are specific aspects of the general right to a fair trial and are not therefore. exhaustive. The relationship between Art 6(1) and (3) 'is that of the general to the particular'; accordingly, a trial could fail to fulfil the general conditions of Art 6(1), even though the minimum rights guaranteed by Art 6(3) are respected (*Jespers v Belgium*). In *Brown v Stott* (2001), Lord Bingham observed that whilst the overall fairness of a criminal trial cannot be compromised, the constituent rights comprised, whether expressly or implicitly, within Art 6 are not themselves absolute. Lord Hope stated in Brown and Stott that a three-stage test was required in determining the question of incompatability with Art 6:

(i) Is the right which is in question an absolute right, or is it a right which is open to modification or restriction because it is not absolute?

(ii) If it is not absolute, does the modification or restriction which is contended for have a legitimate aim in the public interest?

(iii) If so, is there a reasonable relationship of proportionality between the means employed and the aim sought to be realised?

2.56 In *R v A (No 2)* (2002), Lord Steyn observed that it was well-established that the right to a fair trial in Art 6 was absolute in the sense that a conviction obtained in breach of it cannot stand. The only balancing permitted was in respect of what the concept of a fair trial entails; account could be taken of the familiar triangulation of interests of the accused, the victim and society. In that context proportionality had a role to play.

2.57 The application of Art 6(1) is limited to circumstances in which there is a 'criminal charge'. In considering whether proceedings are 'criminal' for the purposes of Art 6, the European Court will be guided by the classification applied by the relevant state, such a classification being the starting point (*Engel v Netherlands* (1976)). It will also look at the nature of the offence, whether the offence applies to a specific group or is of general application (*Ozturk v Germany* (1984)) and the possible penalty (*JJ v Netherlands* (1998)). The last factor is of particular importance (*Brown v Stott* (2001)). This means that proceedings that are classified as regulatory or disciplinary may still fall within the definition of 'criminal charge'. The criminal provisions of Art 6 have no application to proceedings under either s 1 (anti-social behaviour orders) or 2 (sex offender orders) of the Crime and Disorder Act 1998: *Jones v Greater Manchester Police Authority* (2002). The right to a fair trial involves observance of the principle of 'equality of arms' under which the defendant in criminal proceedings must have 'a reasonable opportunity of presenting his case to the court under conditions which do not place him at a substantial disadvantage vis-à-vis his opponent': *Neumeister v Austria*. The principle of equality of arms under Art 6(1) overlaps with the specific guarantees in Art 6(3), though it is not confined to those aspects of the proceedings. For example, it will be a breach of the principle where an expert witness appointed by the defence is not accorded equal treatment with one appointed by the prosecution or the court: *Bonisch v Austria*.

2.58 The importance of compliance with the jurisprudence of Art 6 cannot be overstated. It has been considered by the court in the context of evidential admissibility, the privilege against self-incrimination and, more recently, non disclosure on the grounds of public interest immunity has come under scrutiny.

Evidence

2.59   The Convention itself contains little specific reference to the rules of evidence in criminal proceedings. Most evidential issues arise in the context of the presumption of innocence in Art 6(2), or in relation to Art 6(3)(d) which provides the right for each defendant to examine witnesses. In general, the assessment of evidence is within the appreciation of the domestic courts, and it is not open to the European Court of Human Rights to substitute its own view of the facts for an assessment which has been fairly reached by an independent and impartial court. The Court may only interfere where there is an indication that the domestic court has drawn unfair or arbitrary conclusions from the evidence before it. However, the admission of certain types of evidence may render the trial as a whole unfair. There is no absolute requirement to exclude illegally obtained evidence, but the use of such evidence may give rise to unfairness on the facts of a particular case (*Schenck v Switzerland*) *X v Germany*. In *Khan v United Kingdom* (2000) the Court stated:

'It is not the role of the court to determine, as a matter of principle, whether particular types of evidence – for example, unlawfully obtained evidence – may be admissible or, indeed, whether the applicant was guilty or not. The question which must be answered is whether the proceedings as a whole, including the way in which the evidence was obtained, were fair. This involves an examination of the unlawfulness in question and, where violation of another convention right is concerned, the nature of the violation found.'

It was held that the admission of evidence obtained by means of a listening device in breach of Art 8 did not automatically render the proceedings unfair. The police had acted compatibly with Home Office guidelines; that the incriminating statements had been made voluntarily and without inducements; and that the 'unlawfulness' in issue related solely to the absence of a statutory basis for the surveillance. However, the discretion to exclude evidence under s 78 of PACE did not provide an adequate remedy since prior to the enactment of the Human Rights Act 1998, the national courts had not had jurisdiction to rule on the substance of the applicant's Art 8 complaint or to grant appropriate relief if the complaint was well-founded (see *R v Khan (Sultan)* (1997)). *Khan* was followed in *PG and JH v United Kingdom* (2001), where the court found breaches of Art 8 in relation to the use of a covert listening device under the Home Office guidelines, and in relation to the covert recording of suspects' conversations in the police station for the purpose of voice pattern comparison, but nonetheless held that the admission of the resulting evidence at trial was compatible with Art 6. The voice samples, which in themselves contained no incriminating admissions, were to be regarded as analogous to bodily samples or other items of real evidence.

2.60   In *R v X, Y and Z*, the Court of Appeal held that the domestic courts should attach 'considerable importance' to any breach of Art 8 in determining an application to exclude evidence, but that it would remain necessary to engage in the exercise of reviewing and balancing all the circumstances of the case. In *R v P* (2002) Lord Hobhouse observed that the decision in *Khan v United Kingdom*, was consistent with the House of Lords' judgment in *R v Khan (Sultan)*, and that the admissibility of unlawfully obtained evidence was to be determined by reference to Art 6 and s 78 rather than Art 8. The admission of evidence obtained as a result of maltreatment with the aim of extracting a confession will inevitably violate Art 6: *Montgomery v HM Advocate* (2000).

Entrapment

2.61   Where issues of entrapment and agents provocateurs arise the right to a fair trial will be violated where police officers have stepped beyond an 'essentially passive' investigation of a suspect's criminal activities and have 'exercised an influence such as to incite the commission of the offence': *Teixeira de Castro v Portugal* also *Lüdi v Switzerland*. In *R v Looseley; A-G's Reference (No 3 of 2000)* (2002), the House of Lords gave guidance on the application of Art 6 to cases of alleged entrapment. By recourse to the principle that courts have an inherent power and duty to prevent abuse of their process, the courts would ensure that executive agents of the state do not misuse the coercive law-enforcement functions of the courts and thereby oppress citizens of the state. Entrapment was an instance where such misuse may occur. It was simply not acceptable that the state, through its agents, should lure its citizens into committing acts forbidden by the law and then seek to prosecute them for doing so. The role of the courts was to stand between the citizen and the state and make sure this did not happen. A useful guide to identifying the limits of acceptable police conduct was to consider whether the police did no more than present the defendant with an unexceptional opportunity to commit a crime. The yardstick was, in general, whether the conduct of the police preceding the commission of the offence was no more than might have been expected from others in the circumstances. If that was the case, then the police were not to be regarded as inciting or instigating crime. Since they did no more than others might be expected to do, they were not creating crime artificially. However, the provision of an opportunity to commit crime should not be applied in a random fashion, or used for wholesale virtue-testing. In general, the greater the degree of intrusiveness involved in a particular technique, the closer would the court scrutinise the reason for using it. On this, proportionality had a role to play. The ultimate consideration was whether the conduct of the law enforcement agency was so seriously improper as to bring the administration of justice into disrepute. The use of proactive techniques was more likely to be necessary, and hence more appropriate, in some circumstances than in others. The secrecy and difficulty of detection and the manner in which the particular criminal activity was carried on were relevant considerations, but the gravity of an offence was not, in itself, sufficient justification. The police were required to act in good faith. In general, it would not be regarded as a legitimate use of police power to provide people not previously suspected of being engaged in a particular criminal activity with the opportunity to commit crime. The only proper purpose of police participation is to obtain evidence of criminal acts which they suspect someone is about to commit or in which he is already engaged. It is not to tempt people to commit crimes in order to expose their bad characters and to punish them. However, a pre-existing reasonable suspicion of the particular individual who has committed the offence would not always be necessary. The police might, in the course of a bona fide investigation into suspected criminality, provide an opportunity for the commission of an offence which is taken by someone to whom no suspicion previously attached. In deciding what was acceptable, regard was to be had to the defendant's circumstances, including his vulnerability. In general, the defendant's predisposition to commit an offence or previous criminal record would be irrelevant, unless linked to other factors grounding a reasonable suspicion that the accused is currently engaged in the criminal activity alleged.

Self-incrimination

2.62   The right to a fair trial includes 'the right of anyone charged with a criminal offence ... to remain silent and not to contribute to incriminating himself': *Funke v France*. In *Saunders v United Kingdom*, the Court considered that the admission in evidence at the applicant's trial of transcripts of interviews with inspectors of the Department of Trade and Industry violated Art 6(1) since at the time of the interrogation the applicant was under a duty to answer the inspectors' questions, a duty which was enforceable by proceedings for contempt. The Court described the right to silence and the right not to incriminate oneself as generally recognised international standards which lay at the heart of a notion of a fair procedure under Art 6. The latter right presupposed that the prosecution in a criminal case must prove its case without resort to evidence obtained through methods of coercion and oppression in defiance of the will of the accused. In this sense the privilege against self-incrimination was 'closely linked' to the presumption of innocence. The protection against self-incrimination, as it was understood in *Saunders*, was relevant only where the prosecution sought to introduce evidence obtained by powers of compulsory questioning in the course of a criminal trial. Under the Human Rights Act 1998 it would be incumbent on a judge to consider whether Art 6(1) required the exclusion of such evidence. Article 6 did not, however, prevent the use of compulsory questioning powers during the investigative phase of an inquiry. Notwithstanding the decision in *Funke*, the Court had drawn a clear distinction in *Saunders* between questioning during the course of 'extra-judicial inquiries' and the use of the material thereby obtained in a subsequent criminal prosecution.

2.63   In *Brown v Stott* (2001), it was held that the admission of answers obtained pursuant to powers of compulsory questioning under s 172 of the Road Traffic Act 1988 was compatible with Art 6 as interpreted in *Saunders*. In contrast to the position in *Saunders*, s 172 provided for the putting of a single simple question rather than prolonged interrogation and the penalty for non-compliance was moderate and non-custodial. Section 172 was a proportionate response to the problem of maintaining road safety, which did not involve improper coercion or oppression. In *Heaney and McGuinness v Ireland* (2001) it was held that a criminal prosecution for withholding information in connection with an alleged act of terrorism was incompatible with Art 6 since it destroyed the 'very essence' of the privilege against self-incrimination.

2.64 Different considerations apply to rules permitting the drawing of adverse inferences from the silence of the accused under interrogation or at trial. In *Murray v United Kingdom*, the Court found that the provisions of the Criminal Evidence (Northern Ireland) Order 1988 (SI 1988 No 1987), as applied to the facts of that case, did not constitute a violation of Art 6(1). The Court emphasised that the independent evidence of guilt was strong, and that the Northern Ireland legislation incorporated a number of safeguards: in particular the adverse inferences had been drawn by a judge, sitting without a jury, whose decision was recorded in a reasoned judgment which was susceptible to scrutiny on appeal. In *R v Birchall* (1999), the Court of Appeal recognised that the application of ss 34 and 35 of the Criminal Justice and Public Order Act 1994 in a jury trial could lead to violations of Art 6(1) and (2) unless the provisions were the subject of carefully framed directions. In *Condron v United Kingdom* (2001), the European Court of Human Rights held that the direction given to the jury had failed to strike the balance required by Art 6. In particular, the jury should have been directed, as a matter of fairness, that if the applicants' silence at interview could not be attributed to their having no answer, or none that would stand up to cross-examination, then no adverse inference should be drawn.

The prosecution's duty of disclosure

2.65 In *Jespers v Belgium* the Commission held that the 'equality of arms' principle imposes on prosecuting and investigating authorities an obligation to disclose any material in their possession, or to which they could gain access, which may assist the accused in exonerating himself or in obtaining a reduction in sentence. This principle extends to material which might undermine the credibility of a prosecution witness (para 58). Non disclosure of evidence relevant to credibility may also raise an issue under Art 6(3)(d): *Edwards v United Kingdom*. The Court in *Edwards*, specifically left open the question whether the rules of public interest immunity in England and Wales conform to the requirements of Art 6. In *Rowe and Davis v United Kingdom*, the Court held that whilst Art 6(1) generally requires the prosecution to disclose to the defence all material evidence for or against the accused, considerations of national security or the protection of vulnerable witnesses may, in certain circumstances, justify an exception to this rule. Any departure from the principles of open adversarial justice must however be strictly necessary, and the consequent handicap imposed on the defence must be adequately counterbalanced by procedural safeguards to protect the rights of the accused. Where the prosecution had withheld relevant evidence on public interest immunity grounds, without first submitting the material to the trial judge, the requirements of Art 6 were not met; and the resulting defect could not be cured by submitting the material to the Court of Appeal in the course of an appeal against conviction. In *Fitt v United Kingdom*, and *Jasper v United Kingdom*, the Court held, by a majority of nine to eight, that there was no violation of Art 6 where the material in question had been submitted to the trial judge under the ex parte procedure established in *R v Davis, Johnson and Rowe*. Where a judge, considering the admissibility of certain evidence held an ex parte hearing during which he put questions to a witness that the witness had previously declined to answer in open court on grounds of public interest immunity, the procedure adopted did not violate Art 6: *PG and JH v United Kingdom* (2002). The Court of Appeal has held that the procedure for ex parte public interest immunity applications is unaffected by the case law summarised above: *R v Davis, Rowe and Johnson (No 2)* (2000); *R v Botmeh and Alami* (2002). Subsequently the House of Lords have considered public interest immunity in *R v H and C* (2003) in the light of the European Court's judgment in *Edwards and Lewis v United Kingdom*: see para 9.13–9.15, post.

Article 8 – the right to private and family life

2.66

(1) Everyone has the right to respect for his private and family life, his home and his correspondence.

(2) There shall be no interference by a public authority with the exercise of this right except such as is in accordance with the law and is necessary in a democratic society in the interests of national security, public safety or the economic well-being of the country, for the prevention of disorder or crime, for the protection of health or morals, or for the protection of the rights and freedoms of others.

2.67   The concept of private life is broadly defined: *Niemietz v Germany*, It includes not only personal information, but an individual's relationships with others, including (in certain circumstances) business relationships.

2.68   The right to respect for a person's home includes the right to peaceful enjoyment free from intrusion: *Lopez-Ostra v Spain*. The concepts of a person's home and private life may, in some circumstances, extend to professional or business activities or premises: *Niemietz v Germany, Chappell v United Kingdom*. Correspondence includes both written communications and telephone calls: *Klass v Germany, Malone v United Kingdom*. It will also extend to modern means of electronic communication provided the person concerned can reasonably expect that his communications will be private.

2.69   A criminal prosecution constitutes an 'interference by a public authority' for the purposes of Art 8(2): *Dudgeon v United Kingdom, Modinos v Cyprus*. The mere threat of a prosecution may be sufficient if it directly interferes with private life: *Norris v Ireland*. The following have all been held to constitute interferences with the right protected by Art 8: searches of private or business premises (*Funke v France Chappell v United Kingdom*); searches of motor vehicles (*X. v Belgium*); temporary seizure of personal papers (*X v Germany*); intrusive surveillance (*Klass v Germany, Khan v United Kingdom* (2000); security vetting (*Hilton v United Kingdom*); the compilation and disclosure of criminal records (*Leander v Sweden*); photographing suspects or detainees (*Murray v United Kingdom, McVeigh, O'Neill* and *Evans v United Kingdom*); unless carried out in a public place, such as during the course of a demonstration (*Friedl v Austria*),the publication (although not the taking) of photographs of a private individual (who was not participating in a public event) which were taken in the street (*Peck v United Kingdom* (2003)); a refusal to permit a detained person to contact his family (*McVeigh, O'Neill and Evans v United Kingdom*); the disclosure of confidential information about the medical condition of a witness (*Z v Finland*); the disclosure by police or social services to a third party of an allegation concerning the sexual abuse of children (*R v Local Authority and Police Authority in the Midlands, ex p LM* (2000).

2.70   Article 8(2) sets out the circumstances whereby an interference with the right to private and family life will be justified . Activities are justified provided it can be shown that:

- the interference is in accordance with the law (*Halford v United Kingdom* (1997));
- it is for one of the purposes specified in Art 8(2); and
- the interference is necessary and proportionate.

2.71   In *R (S) v Chief Constable of South Yorkshire; R (Marper) v Chief Constable of South Yorkshire* (2003), it was held that the provision in s 64(1A) of PACE, which permits the retention of fingerprints or samples following acquittal or discontinuance was not incompatible with Art 8. Assuming that Art 8 was engaged, the provision pursued a pressing social need and was proportionate to the prevention of crime. In *R v Pearce* (2002) it was held that the principle that children and unmarried partners were compellable witnesses, whilst spouses were not, involved no breach of Art 8. In so far as compulsion to give evidence was an interference with the right to respect for private and family life, it was justified under Art 8(2) as necessary for the prevention of crime.

2.72   In *McLeod v United Kingdom*, the Court held that the common law power of entry to prevent or deal with a breach of the peace (which is expressly preserved by s 17(6) of PACE), was 'defined with sufficient precision for the forseeability criterion to be satisfied'. The Court nevertheless found a violation of Art 8, where two police officers had entered the applicant's home in her absence to assist her ex-husband to remove items of property. There was no risk of a breach of the peace in fact and the officers had failed to take adequate steps to establish that the husband had a lawful right of entry.

2.73   Intrusive surveillance constitutes an interference with the rights protected by Art 8: *Klass v Germany, Malone v United Kingdom*. It can in principle be justified in the interests of national security or for the prevention of crime, and provided it is 'in accordance with law' . The term 'in accordance with law' has a special meaning in this context. The law must give an adequate indication of the circumstances in which, and the conditions under which, such surveillance can occur: *Malone v United Kingdom*. The rules must define with clarity the categories of citizens liable to be the subject of such techniques, the offences which might give rise to such an order, the permitted duration of the interception, and the circumstances in which recordings are to be destroyed: *Huvig v France,Kruslin v France.* There must, in addition, be adequate and effective safeguards against abuse: *Klass v Germany, Malone v United Kingdom.* Whilst it is desirable that the machinery of supervision should be in the hands of a judge, this is not essential providing the supervisory body enjoys sufficient independence to give an objective ruling: *Klass v Germany.*

THE POLICE AND CRIMINAL EVIDENCE ACT 1984: THEMES AND DEFINITIONS

2.74   The Police and Criminal Evidence Act 1984 (PACE) became law on 1 January 1986. Prior to that date the law governing police (and some other investigative agencies) powers for the investigation of crime was unclear and antiquated. The Act placed police powers on a statutory footing and as such represents a most significant influence on the investigator. A number of common themes and definitions are used throughout the statute and these will now be discussed.

Codes of practice (ss 66, 67, arts 65, 66)

2.75   In spite of the considerable detail in its sections and Schedules, PACE is largely an outline of the law. For practical implementation, it must be supplemented by Codes of Practice and Regulations (see post). These add some operational flesh to the legislative skeleton. There are six Codes of Practice:

Code A   The Exercise of Powers of Stop and Search,
Code B   The Searching of Premises and Seizure of Property,
Code C   The Detention, Treatment and Questioning of Persons by the Police,
Code D   The Identification of Persons Suspected of Crime,
Code E   Tape-recording of Interviews with Suspects,
Code F   Video-recording of interviews.

2.76   The Codes had, until recently, to be approved by the resolution of both Houses of Parliament (s 67(3)-(5)) – the affirmative resolution procedure – and could be updated from time to time (subject to the same parliamentary procedure) (s 67(7)). The Criminal Justice and Police Act 2001, s 77 has now given the Home Secretary power to issue amendments for up to two years for trial purposes subject only to the negative resolution procedure. This procedure has weakened parliamentary control over the Codes and combined with the new procedure for developing and amending the codes appears to be a retrograde step in terms of the liberty of the individual. A Home Office/Cabinet Office Joint Review of PACE suggested that the consultation process which takes place to develop and amend the codes should be limited to those representing chief constables and police authorities and anyone else '*the Home Secretary thinks appropriate*'; the Criminal Justice Act 2003 has amended s 67 (4) to give effect to this procedure. Section 67(11) provides that the Codes shall be admissible in evidence in criminal or civil proceedings, and if any provision appears relevant to any question arising in the proceedings it shall be taken into account in determining the question. The word 'shall' indicates that once the judge takes the view that a breach of the Code was relevant to any question in the proceeding he is obliged to take it into account (*R v Kenny* (1992)). The third, revised, edition which incorporates all five (as there were then) Codes came into force on 10 April 1995 after much consultation. They seek to be 'clear and workable guidelines for the police, balanced by strong safeguards for the public' (Foreword to the 1995 Codes). In *R v Ward* (1993) the Court of Appeal held that in deciding whether to exercise the discretion to exclude evidence under s 78 of PACE, the Court could have regard to the current Codes of Practice. In part, the Codes paraphrase some of the Act's provisions and in this way the frequently complex provisions in the Act are explained in a lucid fashion. It follows that the language used in the Codes is looser than that used in the statute. It is important therefore to distinguish between parts of a Code which merely repeat the statute and those which supplement it. The former parts are not the authoritative version. As to the latter, the Codes frequently supplement the Act in very important matters. Indeed, one of the issues regularly discussed during passage of the PACE Bill was whether items properly belonged to the Bill or to a Code. In this context the language employed in the Code assumes a greater significance. Since it bestows additional rights on the citizen and imposes extra duties on the police, it ought, it is suggested, to be interpreted more rigorously than the descriptive parts. However, a further distinction can be drawn. There are some parts of the Codes which are both supplementary to the Act and mandatory (see the conditions of detention, para 7.238, post) and those which are supplementary but advisory. The Code of Practice on Stop and Search is the best example of the latter. By tackling the elusive concept of 'reasonable suspicion' it inevitably contains a larger measure of guidance than instruction.

Scope

2.77 The Codes of Practice are primarily directed to the police but they also extend to those other officials who are similarly charged with the investigation of offences (s 67(9)), eg commercial investigators employed by a company to investigate possible crimes committed by its staff (*R v Twaites* (1990)). However, whether a person is 'charged' with this duty is a matter of fact to be decided in each case (*R v Bayliss* (1993), *Joy v FACT* (1993)). Thus a store detective may be (in *Bayliss* there was no clear evidence about the terms of employment and scope of their duties so the Court of Appeal declined to interfere with the trial judge's decision that he was not bound by the Code of Practice); on the other hand an investigator employed by the Federation against Copyright Theft is (*Halawa v FACT* (1995)). An inspector employed by the Department of Trade and Industry under the Companies Act 1985 to investigate a company's affairs has been held, surprisingly, not to be a person so charged for s 67(9) purposes (*R v Seelig and Spens* (1991)). In the Home Office's view an immigration officer investigating the status of an entrant is also not 'charged' (though the officers are instructed to abide by the relevant Code procedures and an immigration Code of

Practice incorporating them has been issued). Similarly, RSPCA officials have agreed to abide by the Code (*RSPCA v Eager* (1995)). In *R v Smith (WD)* (1994) it was held that a Bank of England supervisor, whose task it was to ensure that the standards required for authorisation as a bank by the Bank of England are maintained, was not a person 'charged with the investigation of offences etc' within s 67(9) (the Bank of England has a special department to deal with the investigation of fraud and the charging of offenders). In *Dudley Metropolitan Borough Council v Debenhams plc* (1994) an entry to premises by trading standards officials was held to be subject to Code B and in *R v Tiplady* (1995) it was accepted that they are subject to Code D. In *R v Stewart* (1995) it was argued that the entry by electricity company officials executing a warrant of entry to premises was subject to Code B and s 16 of PACE. However, in the latter case, as in others whether or not the particular persons come within s 67(9) is not conclusive for the Code 'also enshrines certain principles of fairness . . . which may have a wider application'. That means that the principles underlying the Code may be of 'assistance' when considering the exercise of the general discretion to exclude evidence under s 78 whether or not the person is bound by their terms.

2.78   By s 113 the Secretary of State for Defence may by order direct that any part of PACE, relating to the investigation of offences or to detained persons, shall apply to investigations under the Army Act 1955, the Air Force Act 1955, or the Naval Discipline Act 1957. Section 113 required him to issue codes of practice to govern those who conduct these inquiries (ie officers charged with the task of investigating offences under those Acts). (See SI 1986/307 and SI 1989/2128.) Unlike s 67, breach of a Code will by itself involve legal liability as regards proceedings taken under one of the Forces Acts, but, like s 67, a breach does not per se involve liability under the general criminal or civil law. The Codes are admissible in evidence in all proceedings, and a court-martial, the Courts-Martial Appeal Court and Standing Civilian Court can take account of it.

2.79   Codes of Practice have become popular in recent years as a method of conveying the finer details of the parent Act. Their legal effect is varied. In some areas a breach of it can be used in evidence at legal proceedings, whereas in others it is merely a consultative document. The Codes of Practice passed by Parliament under PACE and 1989 NI Order are a form of delegated legislation, similar to the Immigration Rules passed under the Immigration Act 1971. But, whereas the latter bind the immigration appellate authorities, the Codes do not bind the courts. Their effect is as follows. First, breach of a Code does not of itself lead to legal liability for the transgressor (s 67(10)). However, if relevant to any question arising in the proceedings a court must take a breach into account in determining that question; for example, in deciding whether to admit evidence against an accused in criminal proceedings (ss 76 and 78, arts 74 and 76), or in determining the guilt or civil liability of a police officer or of any other person governed by the Code. A breach of a Code does not have to be acted upon by the court. Indeed, it is highly unlikely that a court will pay anything more than fleeting attention to breaches of minor aspects of the Codes. On the other hand, the courts regard many Code provisions as important safeguards for the citizen and treat transgressions of them as 'significant and substantial' and as warranting the exclusion of evidence (see *R v Walsh* (1989) and other cases discussed at para 8.153, post). The principal category here is the procedures in Code C covering the questioning of suspects and the recording of interviews (see further paras 8.32). Second, a breach of a Code is a ground for a complaint against the police under Part IX of the Act and may also lead to disciplinary proceedings against the offending officer, for breach of a Code is a disciplinary offence (s 67 (8)); unless the principle of 'double jeopardy' applies, which in essence prevents an officer being punished twice for the same conduct. The Codes are divided into sections and at the end of most are Notes for Guidance. The latter (unlike Annexes to the Codes) are not regarded as provisions of a Code (see para 1.2 to each Code). They clearly enjoy an inferior status. However, it is highly arguable that some Notes for Guidance deserve inclusion in the body of the Code and vice versa; see, for example, Code A, Note IE (stop and search of juveniles). (The former Code C, Note 11A (definition of an interview) is now part of Code C as 11.1A.) In other words some Notes will attract stricter judicial attention than others.

2.80   Various sections of PACE and other legislation permit the Home Secretary to promulgate regulations (eg specifying 'recordable offences' for the purpose of fingerprinting under ss 27 and 61, dealing with the police complaints procedure). The Codes of Practice are supplemented by Home Office Circulars along with force standing orders and procedural instructions.

Reasonable suspicion

2.81   There must be safeguards to protect members of the public from random, arbitrary and discriminatory searches. Clarification of powers will help but the principal safeguard must be found in the requirement for and stricter application of the criterion of reasonable suspicion.' (Royal Commission 1981, para 3.24-25)

2.82   The criterion of reasonable suspicion or, more properly, of reasonable grounds to believe or suspect, is the legal threshold for the exercise of almost all the coercive powers available under PACE and other relevant legislation and for the non-coercive powers contained in PACE such as delaying the detained person's right to consult with a solicitor. Magistrates and senior police officers who may authorise the exercise of certain powers must also be satisfied that there are reasonable grounds to believe that the exercise of those powers is justified. In the absence of reasonable grounds to believe or suspect, the exercise of those powers is not permitted and any consequential interference with the liberty of the individual is unlawful. The importance of the criterion cannot therefore be overstated.

'Believe' or `suspect'

2.83   Two formulations of 'reasonable grounds' are used in PACE and NI Order. (A) Reasonable grounds to believe is used, for example, in respect of:

(a) the issuance of warrants to search premises (s 8, Art 10);

(b) the issuance of orders or warrants to produce or search for evidence held in confidence (Sch 1);

(c) the issuance of orders or warrants to detain a person without charge (ss 42, 43 and 44, arts 43, 44 and 45);

(d) entry to premises without a warrant to arrest persons or recapture them (s 17, Art 19);

(e) the search of persons or premises following an arrest (s 32, Art 34);

(f) the seizure of evidence found in consequence of a search of premises (s 19, Art 21), or persons (s 32, Art 34);

(g) authorising detention in police custody (s 37 (3), Art 38 (3));

(h) the intimate search of persons in police detention (s 55, Art 56);

(i) the power to delay informing someone of the fact of arrest (s 56, Art 57);

(j) the power to delay access to a solicitor (s 58, Art 59).

The Criminal Justice and Public Order Act 1994 provides a number of powers which may be authorised or exercised by particular police officers if that officer reasonably believes that statutory requirements are satisfied:

(k) the authorisation by a superintendent or above of the power to stop and search persons or vehicles under the CJPOA 1994, s 60;

(l) the power of the senior officer present to direct trespassers on land and therefor the collective purpose of residing there for any period to leave the land (CJPOA 1994, s 61);

(m) the power of a superintendent or above to direct that persons making preparations for, gathering to attend or attending an unauthorised rave to leave the land and remove vehicles (CJPOA 1994, s 63);

(n) the power of a superintendent or above to authorise a constable to enter on to land in order to ascertain whether an unauthorised rave is to take place or to exercise the power under s 63 (above) (CJPOA 1994, s 64);

(o) the power of a uniformed constable to stop a person and to direct him not to proceed in the direction of a gathering which is the subject of a direction under s 63 (above) (CJPOA 1994, s 65);

(p) the power of the senior officer present to direct that a person who is committing, has committed or intends to commit the offence of aggravated trespass leave the land (CJPOA 1994, s 69);

(q) the power of the chief officer of police to apply to the local council to prohibit (in the case of the Metropolitan and City of London Police the power of the Commissioner to prohibit) trespassory assemblies (Public Order Act 1986, s 14A added by the CJPOA 1994, s 70);

(r) the power of a constable in uniform to stop persons and to direct that they do not proceed in the direction of a prohibited trespassory assembly (the Public Order Act 1986, s 14C added by the CJPOA 1994, s 71).

In addition, whenever a power is conditional upon the offence being a serious arrestable offence (as defined by s 116 and Sch 5, Art 87 and Sch 5, see para

2.97, post), the person who is to exercise the power must have reasonable grounds to believe that the offence is a serious arrestable offence.
(B) Reasonable grounds to suspect or reasonable suspicion, on the other hand, is used, for example, in respect of:

   (a) the power to stop and search a person or vehicle (s 1(3), Art 3 (3));
   (b) powers of arrest under ss 24 and 25 (Arts 26 and 27) and in respect of the powers of arrest preserved by Sch 2 and all statutory powers of arrest created since PACE came into force;
   (c) search of premises following an arrest for an arrestable offence (s 18, Art 20) (cf s 32, where a search of premises following an arrest for any offence requires reasonable grounds to believe).

2.84 Occasionally there is a dual formulation; for example, in s 4 (Art 6) (the setting up of road blocks) there must be reasonable grounds for believing that the offence is a serious arrestable offence; and for suspecting that the person sought is, or is about to be, in the area in which the vehicle is to be stopped.

2.85 The different formulations seek to impose a higher threshold for those powers which require the existence of reasonable grounds to believe and it is no coincidence that those powers involve the invasion of a person's privacy, his continued detention or delay in the exercise of one of his rights or the decision to authorise powers which will interfere with the rights of the citizen and involve decisions which can be taken after mature reflection. In contrast, those powers which are exercised most frequently, and often without the luxury of mature reflection, for example, stop and search and arrest powers, are conditional upon the existence of reasonable grounds to suspect. This is a much lower standard than reasonable grounds to believe. In legal theory the latter standard requires something close to certainty. In *Johnson v Whitehouse* (1984), Nolan J, speaking of the requirement of a reasonable belief as the threshold to the requirement of a breath test under the road traffic legislation, said:

> 'The greater force of the word "believe" is an essential part of the law and the request for a breath test . . . can only be justified if there are reasonable grounds for believing – in the full sense of the word – that the person was the driver of the vehicle.'

2.86 In *Baker v Oxford* (1980) the Divisional Court also accepted that there was a distinction between 'believe' and 'suspect' but did not indicate what it was. However, in argument it had been suggested that 'suspect' implied an imagination that something exists without proof, whereas 'believe' implied an acceptance of what was true. As Lord Devlin put it in *Hussien v Chong Fook Kam* (1970), 'suspicion in its ordinary meaning is a state of conjecture or surmise where proof is lacking: I suspect but I cannot prove'.

2.87 It is not necessary to have substantial proof before one can be said to *'believe'* but the existence of a belief implies that there is more information available which turns conjecture or surmise into an acceptance that something is true. In the offence of handling stolen goods the mental element is 'knowing or believing' that the goods are stolen. In *R v Hall* (1985) it was said:

> 'A man may be said to know that goods are stolen when he is told by someone with first-hand knowledge (someone such as the thief or burglar) that such is the case. Belief, of course, is something short of knowledge. It may be said to be a state of mind of a person who says to himself: "I cannot say I know for certain that these goods are stolen but there can be no other reasonable conclusion in the light of all the circumstances, in the light of all I have heard and seen." '

2.88   If, therefore, there are 10 steps from mere suspicion to a state of certainty, or an acceptance that something is true, then reasonable suspicion may be as low as step two or three, whilst reasonable belief may be as high as step nine. In the main, those powers in PACE for which the threshold requirement is a reasonable belief can be exercised in the comparative calm of the courtroom or police station or where the facts necessary to reach that state of mind are readily available and there is time to consult them. These circumstances justify the use of the higher standard. Those powers for which reasonable suspicion is required are, in the main, exercisable in the street in circumstances which may not permit of mature reflection. The exercise of those powers is none the less a serious infringement of the liberty of the citizen and affects the greatest number of people. It is therefore imperative that the criterion be strictly applied if it is to be a safeguard against the arbitrary exercise of police powers. The criterion of reasonable suspicion in the context of stop and search powers and powers of arrest is considered in the relevant chapter (para 3.18 and paras 5.16-5.27, post); here it is considered more generally. There are always two issues in determining whether there is reasonable suspicion or, more correctly, reasonable cause to suspect: first, whether the constable had suspicion; and second, if so, whether it was reasonable suspicion.

2.89   In *Siddiqui v Swain* (1979) the Divisional Court said '. . . the words "has reasonable cause to suspect" [or believe] import the requirement that the constable in fact suspects [or believes] . . .'. That suspicion derives from his own observation or from information supplied to him from other sources. However, though this is a subjective requirement, the question is not answered by the constable's assertion that he in fact suspected. There must be objectively verifiable facts which led him to suspect that the person had committed the offence in question. It may be that his conclusions from those facts are not reasonable: there is then suspicion but not reasonable suspicion. The two issues are therefore not entirely separate. The judge or jury may determine that the absence of any reasonable grounds for the suspicion means that the constable did not in fact suspect. This is similar to the defence of mistaken belief in the general criminal law. If a defendant says that he was labouring under a mistake of fact and therefore held a particular belief, he must be judged on the facts as he believed them to be (the subjective approach). However, if there are no reasonable grounds for such a belief, the jury may well conclude that the defendant did not in fact hold that belief (*DPP v Morgan* (1976); *R v Williams (Gladstone)* (1987)). The question whether a constable actually suspected is therefore not answered by his assertion that he did. If there is no reasonable basis upon which he could have suspected, the judge or jury may conclude that he did not in fact suspect. The above applies also to the question whether a constable reasonably believed. More facts are necessary to sustain a belief but if there are no such facts or there is no reasonable basis for such facts, it may similarly be concluded that he did not hold the belief asserted. The facts may be sufficient to justify a suspicion and even a reasonable suspicion, but where reasonable belief is required that is not enough.

'Reasonable'

2.90 The adjective *'reasonable'* imports an objective standard and requires facts and circumstances which would lead an impartial third party to form the belief or suspicion in question. In a civil action arising out of the exercise of a power which requires a reasonable belief or suspicion, the question whether there were reasonable grounds will be decided by the judge, as it will in the rare criminal cases in which the question arises (cf *Herniman v Smith* (1938)). In forming that belief or suspicion the person is not constrained, as is a court, by rules of evidence. Consequently, inadmissible evidence may be taken into account; for example, hearsay, the previous character of the accused, including any previous conviction, or information from an informant. The hearsay or information must itself be reasonable and the constable must be satisfied that it is true, or possibly true, depending on whether the standard is 'believe' or 'suspect'. An anonymous telephone call would satisfy neither standard and reasonable steps must be taken to verify that information. How far the person should go in seeking verification also depends upon whether the standard is reasonable grounds to believe or to suspect. (See the discussion at para 5.16 of the need to make further inquiries. It is argued that such inquiries are necessary to establish reasonable suspicion (or belief) but not when reasonable suspicion (or belief) exists and the discretion to exercise a power is available. One may then make further inquiries before acting but one need not do so.) Clearly the latter standard will be satisfied by taking fewer steps than will the former. Informants are a regular source of information giving rise to a reasonable belief or suspicion. How much verification is necessary will depend in part upon the type of information, and in part upon the credibility of the informer. The more often the informant gives credible information the greater his credibility and the fewer steps which need to be taken to verify it, though much will depend on the nature of the information and of the informant. It has been suggested that information from a principal or accomplice in the crime cannot be the basis of reasonable cause to believe or suspect (*Isaacs v Brand* (1817)). If this was the ratio of that case, which is doubtful, it cannot in modern times be good law. As with the case of one party to a crime giving evidence against another party, one must be aware that the person has, or may have, a purpose of his own to serve and take appropriate steps to verify the information: see *James v Chief Constable of South Wales* (1991) where the court said that information derived from an informant should be treated with considerable reserve. However, the supplier of drugs or seller of stolen goods can often provide more reliable information than those who are not involved and who have a better reputation. Where the information comes from fellow police officers, a constable may be justified in acting on it without any verification. For example, constable A hears a crash of glass at 2am. He turns a corner to see a shop window broken and a youth running away. He communicates this information, together with a description of the youth, to his radio operator who in turn passes it to all constables in the area. At 2.05am constable B sees D, who answers the description, running from the direction of the incident. Constable B has reasonable grounds to suspect that:

(a) an arrestable offence (criminal damage and/or theft) has been committed; and

(b) D has committed it.

He may then arrest him under s 24(6) of PACE (Art 26(6) of the NI Order) (see para 5.31, post). Note that the constable is under a duty to tell D why he is being arrested, in effect to state the reasonable grounds justifying the arrest.

2.91   The above discussion applies to the other requirements of reasonable grounds to suspect or believe (or a similar formulation) whether contained in PACE or Order or other statutes. For example, an application for a search warrant under s 23(3) of the Misuse of Drugs Act 1971 requires 'reasonable ground for suspecting that any controlled drugs are unlawfully in the possession of a person on any premises . . .'. In such a case the applicant must have a reasonable ground for the suspicion and the magistrate must be satisfied that there is such a ground and that it is reasonable.

Reasonableness in the exercise of the discretion to exercise a power

2.92   If there is a reasonable cause to suspect (or believe) which then justifies the exercise of a power, the constable generally has a discretion (an executive discretion as opposed to judicial discretion) as to whether to exercise it. This is imported by the word 'may'; for example, 'may arrest', 'may stop and search'. Where there is reasonable cause to suspect that stolen or prohibited articles will be found on a person or in a vehicle, in practice the choice is not between obtaining the person's consent or exercising the power, rather one should seek to exercise the power with the co-operation of the suspect; it will seldom be the case that the discretion to stop and search should not be exercised. Where there is reasonable cause to suspect an offence and an offender the choice will be between proceeding by summons or arresting – this is an exercise of discretion. It should not be confused with the obtaining of a person's consent to some action in respect of him or his property. If there is no legal power to do the act, one must obtain consent before it can be done (see further para 2.93). In all cases in which a constable exercises his discretion, it must be exercised reasonably in accordance with the principles laid down in *Associated Provincial Picture Houses Ltd v Wednesbury Corpn* (1948). 'Unreasonableness' in this context means acting in a way in which no sensible policeman would act, or acting so absurdly that he 'must have taken leave of his senses' (Lord Scarman, *Nottinghamshire County Council v Secretary of State for the Environment* (1986)). Not unexpectedly the courts have been slow to find that the police have contravened this principle. In *Holgate-Mohammed v Duke* (1984) the House of Lords held that a constable had not acted unreasonably (and therefore unlawfully) by arresting a person, in respect of whom there was reasonable suspicion, simply because he believed that he would be more likely to confess and tell the truth while in custody; similarly in *Ward v Chief Constable of Avon and Somerset Constabulary* (1986) discussed at para 5.08, post.

Consent and powers

2.93   Consent is one of the most important and effective 'powers' in the armoury of the police. The limitations, either express or implied, on police action which are laid down by statute or the codes of practice do not apply where the consent of the individual or bodies concerned is obtained. As indicated in Chapter 4, research suggests that almost a third of searches carried out without a search warrant were recorded as being undertaken with consent. Material which under Part II of PACE (Part III of the PACE (NI) Order 1989) is excluded from police access, can be obtained with the consent of the person in possession. PACE and Order provide for the voluntary attendance of persons at a police station 'to assist police with their inquiries'. This gives the police a period of 'detention' which is in most respects the same as that following arrest but without the time limits imposed by the Act and Order. Code C, which deals with the treatment of persons detained, is concerned in the main with persons in custody at police stations. Though Note of Guidance 1A stipulates that those attending voluntarily be treated with no less consideration than those in custody, and points out that there is an absolute right to legal advice or to communicate with others outside the police station, the volunteer does not get the protection of an independent custody officer overseeing his stay in the police station. No custody record is opened because he is not in custody and while Code C 3.21 and 3.22 requires that he be arrested if the officer decides that he is not to be allowed to leave, that he be cautioned if suspected of an offence, and informed of his right to free legal advice and given a notice explaining this right, it is left to the investigating officer, rather than the custody officer. Thus, consenting to assist the police places the volunteer in a position of vulnerability which can be, and is, taken advantage of by some police officers.

2.94   Some of the protections for the arrested person in a police station are only available on request, for example the right of access to a solicitor. The person in police detention may by signature on the custody record indicate that he does not want such protection, and if he does so indicate, he is clearly in a more vulnerable position. Provisions in the 2003 Code C seek to ensure that:
(a)   the detainee is made aware of his rights and, in particular, that legal advice is free; and
(b)   consent to waive rights is informed and free.
Nevertheless, the incentive to seek consent or voluntary attendance is clear. The constable is able to act in circumstances in which a statutory power could not be exercised or, if such a power could have been exercised, the limitations imposed on statutory powers no longer exist, the safeguards against abuse are weaker and the paperwork which accompanies the exercise of statutory powers or formal procedures is reduced or eliminated.

2.95   There is a body of evidence indicating that the concepts of consent and voluntariness are being used with increasing frequency, and in many cases being abused because the person is not freely consenting or volunteering but is in truth submitting to authority. Concern about the use of 'consent' in the context of stop and search powers has resulted in amendment to the Code of Practice to the effect that a person may no longer be searched unless there are reasonable grounds or the search is authorised by a senior officer. (see para 3.67) The reliance on consent and voluntary co-operation has been justified as being consistent with the aims of PACE and with the concept of policing by consent (see paras 4.78-4.83, post). It is, however, consistent with neither. PACE attempts to achieve a balance between police powers and individual liberty. It contains effective controls to limit the circumstances in which a police power may be exercised and the manner in, and the extent to, which it is exercised. Consent avoids such limitations. Two particular issues are raised: first, the true meaning of consent; and second, whether consent is being improperly used as an alternative to the exercise of a power. These are discussed in Chapter 4 in the context of consent to enter and search premises (paras 4.78-4.83) but the principles considered there apply to the exercise of all police powers.

Other threshold requirements to the exercise of particular powers

2.96

'. . . circumstances may arise requiring the application of a power which of its nature would be unacceptable in the normal run of cases: intimate personal searches, the taking of certain body samples [see now amendments to PACE by the CJPOA 1994] prolonged detention or detention without allowing access to legal advice. In assessing whether such powers should be available and the special safeguards to be applied to them if they are, we concluded that account must be taken of the effectiveness of the power in investigating the offence concerned and of the importance that society places upon bringing those suspected of it to trial. The seriousness of the offence is, accordingly, a critical consideration.' (Royal Commission on Criminal Procedure, 1981, para 3.5)

Consequently Parliament, in PACE, decreed that the police can only exercise certain powers if there are reasonable grounds to believe that the offence for which the person is arrested and detained, or in respect of which the power is to be exercised, is a 'serious arrestable offence'. Other possibly less intrusive powers can only be exercised in respect of 'recordable offences'. This is not so much a matter of protecting the citizen, rather it is concerned with administrative convenience, for example the creation of national records of fingerprints and DNA profiles.

Powers exercisable if a 'serious arrestable offence'

2.97

s 4 (Art 6)   Road checks s 8 (Art 10) – The issue of search warrants by magistrates

s 9 (Art 11) and Sch 1	The issue of an order for production of, or warrant to search for, special procedure material
s 42 (Art 43)	Authorisation by a superintendent or above of the continued detention of a person
s 43 (Art 44)	The issue by a magistrates' court of a warrant of further detention
s 44 (Art 45)	The extension by a magistrates' court of a warrant of further detention
s 56 (Art 57)	Delay in notifying someone of the person's arrest
s 58 (Art 59)	Delay in permitting access to legal advice

2.98 The limitation on the exercise of these powers followed the recommendation of the Royal Commission. It concluded that the exercise of the powers must be warranted by the specific circumstances of a particular case and must be capable of immediate challenge and subsequent review. 'Only thus can adequate safeguards be provided against the arbitrary and indiscriminate use of such powers' (Royal Commission 1981, para 3.10). The reasonable belief that an offence is a serious arrestable offence is an essential precondition to the exercise of the above powers. It follows that the exercise of these powers in respect of an offence, which is not reasonably believed to be a serious arrestable offence, is unlawful. Consequently, the interference with the liberty of the citizen will be a tort, and/or a defence to a criminal charge arising out of a failure to comply with a constable's instructions or to a charge of assaulting or obstructing a constable in the execution of his duty. For example, the authorisation by a superintendent of continued detention beyond 24 hours will be a false imprisonment if the offence is not a serious arrestable offence. In contrast, if a serious arrestable offence is not involved, then delay in notifying someone of the arrest or in permitting access to a solicitor is not tortious, but it can be taken into account in considering the admissibility of any confession (see ss 76 and 78 (Arts 74 and 76), discussed in paras 8.101-8.172, post).

Meaning of 'serious arrestable offence'

2.99 The Royal Commission recommended that the exercise of the above powers be limited to 'grave offences' but could only produce a very imprecise definition of what that meant. The Government preferred the term 'serious arrestable offence'. This is based upon the concept of 'arrestable offence' defined in s 24 (Art 26, discussed in paras 8.101-8.172, post). That definition incorporates all the most serious offences and a number of offences which can be serious because of their circumstances and their consequences. The definition of a 'serious arrestable offence' follows a similar pattern and is based on a proposal made by the Law Society that certain arrestable offences should always be regarded as serious, whilst others should be serious only if they satisfy one or more criteria. Statutes passed since PACE have added to or amended the original definition. These changes are taken account of in the following discussion.

2.100 Serious arrestable offences fall into four categories:
(A) Offences which are always serious arrestable offences

(1)   Treason
(2)   Murder
(3)   Manslaughter
(4)   Rape
(5)   Kidnapping
(6)   Incest with a girl under the age of 13 (under 14 in NI)
(7)   Buggery with a person under the age of 16
(8)   Indecent assault which constitutes an act of gross indecency
(9)   Any of the offences mentioned in paras (a) to (f) of s 1 (3) of the Drug Trafficking Act 1994

(s 116(2)(a)- (c) as amended by Sch 1, para 9, DT Act 1994 (Art 87))

(1)   Explosive Substances Act 1883, s 2 (causing an explosion likely to endanger life or property)
(2)   Sexual Offences Act 1956, s 5 (intercourse with a girl under the age of 13) (NI Criminal Law Amendment Act 1885, s 4 (intercourse with girl under 14))
(3)   Firearms Act 1968, s 16(possession of firearms with intent to injure) (Firearms (NI) Order 1981, Art 17)
(4)   Firearms Act 1968, s 17(1) (use of firearms or imitation firearms to resist arrest) (Firearms (NI) Order 1981, Art 18 (1))
(5)   Firearms Act 1968, s 18 (carrying firearms with criminal intent) (Firearms (NI) Order 1981, Art 19)
(6)   Road Traffic Act 1988, s 1 (causing death by reckless driving) (Road Traffic (NI) Order 1981, Art 139 (1))
(7)   Taking of Hostages Act 1982, s 1
(8)   Aviation Security Act 1982, s 1 (hijacking of aircraft)
(9)   Criminal Justice Act 1988, s 134 (torture) (added by s 170, Sch 15 of the Criminal Justice Act 1988)
(10) Road Traffic Act 1988, s 1 (causing death by dangerous driving; s 3A causing death by careless driving when under the influence of drink or drugs)
(11) Aviation and Maritime Security Act 1990, s 1 (endangering safety at aerodromes) and
(12) AMSA 1990, s 9 (hijacking of ships) and
(13) AMSA 1990, s 10 (seizing or exercising control of a fixed platform)
(14) Channel Tunnel (Security) Order 1994 No 570 (Art 4 Hijacking of Channel Tunnel trains and Art 5 (seizing or exercising control of the the tunnel system)
(15) Protection of Children Act 1978, s 1 (indecent photographs and psuedo- photographs of children) (added by the CJPOA 1994, s 85 (3))
(16) Obscene Publications Act 1959, s 2 (publication of obscene matter) (added by the CJPOA 1994, s 85 (3))

(s 116(2)(b), Art 87(2)(b); Sch 5, Part II as amended)

(B) All other arrestable offences are serious arrestable offences only if their commission leads to, or is intended to lead to, or is likely to lead to, any of the following consequences:
(1)   Serious harm to the security of the state or public order

(2) Serious interference with the administration of justice or with the investigation of offences or of a particular offence

(3) The death of any person

(4) Serious injury to any person

(5) Substantial financial gain to any person, and

(6) Serious financial loss to any person

(s 116(3) (a) and (b), and (6) (Art 87 (3) (a) and (b))

(C) An arrestable offence which consists of making a threat is serious if carrying out the threat would be likely to lead to any of the consequences mentioned in (B) above.

For example, threatening to kill, contrary to s 16 of the Offences Against the Person Act 1861, or blackmail contrary to s 21 of the Theft Act 1968, if the demand is likely to lead to substantial gain and serious financial loss

(s 116(4) (Art 87 (4)).

2.101 There was little disagreement during parliamentary debates on the seriousness of offences falling into category (A). However, some concern was expressed during the third reading of the Bill in the House of Lords over the offence of indecent assault which constitutes an act of gross indecency. It was feared that this would be used by the police in order to harass homosexuals. However, the Government minister made it clear that this was not the intention. The offence of committing an act of gross indecency under s 13 of the Sexual Offences Act 1956 (as amended by s 144 (3) of the Criminal Justice and Public Order Act 1994) is punishable by a maximum of five years' imprisonment (and therefore an arrestable offence) only if one man is over 21 and the other is under 18; otherwise the maximum penalty is two years' imprisonment.

'The terms "assault" and "gross" in relation to the indecent act which it involves, taken together pick out the range of activity in relation to the sexual abuse of young people which brings these offences into the category which justifies the use of reserved power.' (House of Lords Debates, 19 October 1984, col 1236)

2.102 Category (C) offences are likely to prove the most difficult to identify. Terms such as 'serious harm', 'serious interference', 'serious injury', 'serious financial loss' and 'substantial gain' do not lend themselves to precise definition. Some assistance is provided by s 116(8) (Art 87 (8)) which states that injury includes 'any disease and any impairment of a person's physical or mental condition' (see *R v Miller* (1954) where 'bodily harm' was held to include the inducement of a hysterical or nervous condition). Rape is a serious arrestable offence under s 116(2)(a) (Art 87(2)(a)) and Sch 5, Part I, but lesser assaults which affect the victim's mental condition can be a serious arrestable offence. Determining whether a financial loss is a serious loss requires consideration of the circumstances of the particular loser. Section 116(7) (Art 87 (7)) makes this clear by stating that:

'Loss is serious . . . if, having regard to all the circumstances, it is serious for the person who suffers it.'

2.103 There is no similar provision in respect of financial gain which suggests that an objective test applies. Thus, theft of £1,000 from a bank with assets of several millions will not be a serious financial loss to the bank, whereas theft of the same amount from an impoverished widow clearly would be. Whether the theft from the bank is a serious arrestable offence will therefore depend on whether £1,000 is a substantial financial gain to the thief. This is to be judged by the standards of ordinary reasonable people. In *R v McIvor* (1987), the theft of 28 dogs, owned collectively by a hunt and worth in total £800, was not a serious arrestable offence, the loss not being serious to the collective owners. In *R v Smith (Eric)* (1987), the Walsall branch of a nationwide chain of stores selling electrical equipment was robbed of two video recorders, worth £400 each, and £116 in cash. The learned Recorder doubted whether the loss of goods and cash totalling £916 was a serious loss to such a large company and thought the gain to the two robbers involved was not necessarily substantial. Quaere, in determining whether the gain to the person is substantial, the fact that the proceeds were shared between the participants is to be taken into account; eg in *Smith* (above) the two robbers would have each received property and cash valued at £458. If four men steal £4,000 from a branch of a nationwide chain of bookmakers, the loss to the bookmakers will not be serious and the gain to the individual thief may not be substantial if the proceeds are shared equally. Though s 116(6)(e) (Art 87(6)(e)) uses the singular 'any person', in this context the singular includes the plural (Interpretation Act 1978, s 6(c)) suggesting that the total proceeds is the determinant.

Multiple offences

2.104 In determining whether the financial loss is serious or the gain substantial, offences must be considered individually. Thus D may have committed a series of burglaries and stolen property worth £50,000 in total. That in itself does not make the burglaries serious arrestable offences. The loss or gain in respect of each burglary must be considered in isolation and, while some will be serious arrestable offences, others may not. For example, burglary 1 of a house in the stockbroker belt in which property valued at £3,000 was stolen, may not be a serious loss to the occupier. Burglary 2 of a modest cottage, owned by a retired couple and in which half that amount was stolen, probably will be a serious loss to them. £3,000 will probably be seen as a substantial gain to the burglar so that both burglaries will be serious arrestable offences. On the other hand, if only £1,000 is stolen from a rich stockbroker it will probably not be a serious loss to him, nor a substantial gain to the thief.

2.105 The following examples indicate the application of the category (C) criterion, bearing in mind that the offence must first be an arrestable offence.
(a) D, a civil servant, takes a copy of a document marked 'secret' which he believes discloses malpractice by a Government minister. He passes it to a newspaper. It may be an offence under the Official Secrets Act 1989. These are arrestable offences, even though punishable by only two years' imprisonment (s 24(2) and Sch 1 of PACE), Art 26(2)(c) discussed in para 5.32, post). The Government, who are 'the

sole judges of what the national security requires' (*The Zamora* (1916)), describe the disclosure as 'causing serious harm to national security'. The offence may then be a serious arrestable offence (s 116(6) (a), Art 87 (6) (a)).

(b) D approaches jurors and offers them money to bring in a not guilty verdict. This is an offence at common law of attempting to pervert the course of justice and an arrestable offence under s 24(1)(b) (Art 26(1)(b)). Such conduct is always a serious interference with the course of justice and will therefore be a serious arrestable offence (s 116(6)(b), Art 87(6)(b)).

(c) D is driving his motor car at a normal speed through a town centre. He is momentarily distracted by a shop window display and fails to see a pedestrian crossing the road. The pedestrian dies from injuries inflicted when the car struck him. D is guilty of, at most, driving without due care and attention contrary to s 3 of the Road Traffic Act 1988. Although the offence has led to the death of a person, it is not an arrestable offence and cannot therefore be a serious arrestable offence (s 116(6)(c), Art 87(6)(c)).

(d) D sets fire to his factory intending to claim on his insurance. He does not warn the night watchman, his intention being that the watchman should discover the fire and raise the alarm. The watchman is asleep and is severely burnt. D has committed arson contrary to s 1(2) of the Criminal Damage Act 1971. It is a serious arrestable offence in view of the consequences (s 116(6)(d), Art 87(6)(d)).

(e) D and others hijack a bullion van and steal gold bullion worth £1 million. It is robbery (s 8 of the Theft Act 1968), involves a substantial financial gain to D and the others, and is a serious financial loss to the owners of the bullion (s 116(6)(e) and (f), Art 87(6)(e) and (f)).

(f) D steals £1,000 from a bank with assets of £12 million. This is a serious arrestable offence only if it is a substantial gain to D, because the loss of £1,000 can hardly be described as a serious loss to the bank. On the other hand, if force or threat of force is used, it will be a serious arrestable offence, regardless of the amount stolen, if serious injury is caused or is the intended or likely result (see s 116(6)(d), Art 87(6)(d) and para 2.19, post).

'Is intended or is likely to lead' to any of those consequences

2.106   This phrase would bring within the ambit of 'serious arrestable offence' attempts, conspiracies and other inchoate offences which involve arrestable offences and which are intended, or are likely, to produce any of the consequences listed in s 116(6) (Art 87(6)). For example, murder is always a serious arrestable offence under category (A) and attempted murder is also always such an offence under category (C). Conspiracy to commit treason will similarly always be a serious arrestable offence under category (C) because it is always intended, or is likely, to result in serious harm to the security of the state. Armed robbery, attempted armed robbery or a conspiracy to rob in which violence or firearms are to be used, will be serious arrestable offences because these offences either result in serious injury to persons, or are intended or likely to do so, or will result, or are intended, or likely to, result in substantial financial gain and serious financial loss. 'Likely' suggests a balance of probabilities, more than a 50–50 chance, and whenever firearms are carried or violence is contemplated, there is a 'likelihood' that serious injury or death will be a consequence. Thus, almost every offence which the police, or the general public, would describe as serious, will be a serious arrestable offence under this definition. (NB possession of firearms with intent to injure, to resist arrest, or with criminal intent, are arrestable offences under s 116(2)(b) (Art 87(2)(b)))

2.107   It should be noted that the fact that the offence is defined as a serious arrestable offence does not mean that the powers available will be exercised. In some cases the reasonable belief that the offence is a serious arrestable offence is one of a number of requirements. Even if the theft of £50 from an old age pensioner is a serious arrestable offence, the police are unlikely to invoke the extended powers of detention or to delay access to a solicitor. It is even less likely that magistrates could be persuaded to issue a warrant of further detention. However, if there are reasonable grounds to suspect that the offender in such a case is, or is about to be, in an area, a road check under s 4 (Art 6) may be authorised. This may not be what the Royal Commission or the Government intended, but it is a consequence of the definition of serious arrestable offence together with the minimal requirements for the setting up of road checks.

Recordable offence

2.108   Section 61 of PACE (Art 61 of the NI Order) permits the taking of the fingerprints of a person (over 10 years of age) without consent who has been charged with, or has been told that he will be reported for, a recordable offence. This category of offence is defined in the National Police Records (Recordable Offences) Regulations 1985 (SI 1985/1941 as amended by SI 1989/694) and includes all offences punishable by imprisonment and a small number of non-imprisonable offences. Code D, Note of Guidance 3A, states that:

> 'The recordable offences to which this code applies at the time when this code was prepared, are: any offences which carry a sentence of imprisonment on conviction (irrespective of the period, or the age of the offender or actual sentence passed); and non-imprisonable offences under:
> – s 1 of the Street Offences Act 1959 (loitering or soliciting for the purposes of prostitution); s 43 of the Telecommunications Act 1984 (improper use of public telecommunications system);
> – s 25 of the Road Traffic Act 1988 (tampering with motor vehicles);
> – s 1 of the Malicious Communications Act 1988 (sending letters etc with intent to cause distress or anxiety); and
> – s 139(1) of the Criminal Justice Act 1988 (having an article with a blade or point in a public place).'

(If convicted of a recordable offence fingerprints may also be taken without consent and if given a custodial sentence they will be taken while in prison custody.)

2.109 The result is the routine taking of fingerprints from almost all those arrested and detained at a police station who are charged with or reported for an offence. Those who are convicted of an arrestable offence but who have not been in police detention or given a custodial sentence may be required to attend a police station to have their fingerprints taken and arrested for this purpose if they do not comply. The purpose of taking fingerprints post-conviction is to enable the police to build up a data bank of fingerprints for purposes of comparison in the investigation of other offences. A similar regime now exists in respect of the taking of non-intimate samples. Under the original s 62 of PACE (Art 63 of the NI Order) the police only had the power to take an intimate sample from a person, even when he consented, if he was suspected of being involved in a serious arrestable offence. Similarly under s 63 (Art 63), the taking of a non-intimate sample without consent could only be authorised if the person was reasonably suspected of being involved in such an offence. The Royal Commission on Criminal Justice recognised that DNA profiling is now a powerful diagnostic technique and so helpful in establishing guilt or innocence that they recommended that the police be allowed to take non-intimate samples without consent from those arrested for serious criminal offences and that the relevant DNA sample be retained for subsequent use for the purposes of a frequency database.

2.110 The Criminal Justice and Public Order Act 1994, ss 54-56 (Arts 10-12 of the Police (Amendment) (NI) Order 1995), amend ss 62 and 63 to permit the taking of non-intimate samples without the person's consent when that person is charged with or reported for a recordable offence as defined above in relation to the taking of fingerprints, subject to the provisions of s 63 (3) (he is in police detention and a superintendent authorises it) thus putting the taking of non-intimate samples broadly on a par with the taking of fingerprints (see Chapter 7 for a detailed discussion of the amended law).

Reasonable force (s 117, Art 88)

2.111 Section 3 of the Criminal Law Act 1967 (Criminal Law Act (NI) 1967, s 3) provides that anyone may use such force as is reasonable in the circumstances to prevent crime, or in effecting or assisting in the lawful arrest of offenders, suspected offenders, or persons unlawfully at large (the use of force in order to effect an arrest is discussed in para 5.164, post). Not only must the use of force be reasonable but it must also be proportionate. However, PACE (1989 Order) gives constables a number of powers which do not fall within s 3 of the 1967 Acts in that they are not used in the prevention of crime or in effecting an arrest, for example the power to search a person, or to take his fingerprints. These powers would be useless against the obdurate or hostile person who refuses to co-operate. They must therefore be backed by the application of force and s 117 (Art 88) bestows a general power to use 'reasonable force, if necessary' in relation to any coercive power under the Act (Order). The word 'reasonable' limits the amount of force by requiring objective facts which in turn justify the application of the degree of force. 'Necessary' imports a similar limitation but also means that other non-coercive means have been used in an attempt to exercise the power or that these other means are likely to fail. This suggests that a reasonable explanation should be given, if practicable, to the person against whom the power is to be exercised. Thus, in *Brazil v Chief Constable of Surrey* (1983), it was held that, where a person is to be searched at a police station following an arrest, there is a duty to state the reasons for that search. Section 54(5) (Art 55(5)) gives effect to that decision (see para 7.26, post), but it is submitted that the principle underlying it, that no coercive power should be exercised without, where practicable, giving reasons, is of general application. If such reasons are not given, then the exercise of the power is unlawful and, it is submitted, the use of force is not 'necessary'.

2.112 Three factors flowing from the use of the words 'reasonable' and 'necessary' deserve special emphasis. First, the amount of force used must be related to the purpose for which the power is to be exercised. Whilst in the context of arrest or the prevention of crime lethal force may be used to prevent a serious crime or the escape of a dangerous offender, many of the powers to which s 117 (Art 88) relates can never justify the use of such a degree of force. For example, the taking of a person's fingerprints would not justify the use of a degree of force sufficient to break that person's fingers. Second, the context in which many of the powers will be exercised (at the police station) suggests that there will usually be sufficient constables at hand to subdue a person effectively without the use of a high degree of force (see *Sturley v Police Comr* (1984), discussed in para 5.164, post). Third, the use of excessive or unnecessary force, though unlawful and likely to form the basis of acquittal ((1995) Times, 15 June); acquittal of police officers following the death of Joy Gardner, an illegal immigrant, on the basis that the force used to restrain her was excessive and therefore unlawful, will not necessarily affect the lawfulness of the power being exercised. Thus, for example, excessive force used to effect a lawful arrest will not render the arrest unlawful (*Simpson v Chief Constable of South Yorkshire Police* (1991) discussed in para 5.126, post). Similarly, the use of excessive or unnecessary force in order to gain entry to premises in order to carry out a search under ss 17, 18 or 32(2)(b) (Arts 19, 20 or 34(2)(b)) will not render the entry a trespass, but will expose the constable to an action for assault and/or damages.

Delegation of duties (s 107)

2.113 Throughout PACE there are powers which can only be exercised by, or on the authority of, a superintendent (eg denial of access to legal advice (s 58), intimate searches (s 55)) or an inspector (eg search after arrest (s 18), review of detention (s 40)). To avoid the situation where there are no available officers of the requisite rank, s 107 provides that a chief inspector shall be treated as holding the rank of superintendent if:

(a) he has been authorised by an officer holding a rank above the rank of superintendent to exercise the power or, as the case may be, to give his authority for its exercise; or

(b) he is acting during the absence of an officer holding the rank of superintendent who has authorised him, for the duration of that absence, to exercise the power or, as the case may be, to give his authority for its exercise. (Section 107(1) as amended by the Police and Magistrates' Courts Act 1994, s 44, Sch 5, Part II, para 35.)

2.114 Section 107(2) further provides that for the purpose of any provision of PACE or any other Act under which a power is exercisable only by or with the authority of an officer of at least the rank of inspector, an officer of the rank of sergeant shall be treated as holding the rank of inspector if he has been authorised by an officer of at least the rank of chief superintendent to exercise the power or, as the case may be, to give his authority for its exercise.

2.115 This provision links up with the procedure for permitting a junior officer to 'act up' during the temporary absence of a more senior officer (eg when the latter is on annual leave or is attending a training course or is sick). Since this 'acting' senior officer is not in fact promoted to the higher rank, he could not exercise the accompanying powers were it not for s 107.

2.116 It should be noted that s 107 refers only to powers (highlighted above). There are duties under PACE which are placed on an inspector and s 107 does not apply to the delegation of that or any other duty. It is arguable that the authorisation to act in the higher rank includes all the duties of that rank, whether imposed by statute or otherwise. In any event the undertaking of a duty by an acting inspector is unlikely to be the subject of legal challenge, whereas the exercise of a power by an officer not of the rank required by statute, or the authorisation of its exercise, is very likely to be challenged as clearly unlawful. Section 107 solves the problem of powers and there may in practice be no problem as regards duties. An acting inspector should therefore have no qualms about undertaking the duties of an inspector. Apart from s 107(1)(b), which is limited to the duration of the superintendent's absence, there is no time-limit on the length of an authorisation under s 107.

Application of the Act (ss 113, 114)

2.117 PACE is predominantly concerned with the powers of constables, though in relation to arrest the powers of the citizen are also dealt with. 'Constable' refers to the ancient office of that name which can be traced back to 900 AD. Despite the fact that police forces are creatures of statute, they are, in essence, simply a number of constables, whose status derives from the common law, organised together in the interests of efficiency. Whilst there are different ranks and there is a tendency to refer to the lowest rank as constable, all ranks are constables. Whenever this, or any other Act, refers to a 'constable' it is therefore referring to all police officers. The hallmark of a constable is his attestation as a constable. Every member of a police force maintained for a police area and every special constable appointed for such an area must, on appointment, be attested as a constable by making the appropriate declaration before a justice of the peace. Until he does so, he has no more authority than an ordinary citizen. After attestation, he has all the additional powers and duties of a constable. Under the Police Act 1964, s 19, a member of a police force, that is a police force maintained for an area under that Act, has all the powers and privileges of a constable throughout England and Wales ' [and the adjacent United Kingdom waters]', the bracketed words being added by s 160 of the Criminal Justice and Public Order Act 1994 (and see the extension for cross-border enforcement of warrants of arrest and other arrest powers discussed below, para 2.42). 'Powers' in this context includes powers under any enactment, whenever passed or made and such powers may be exercised in the adjacent waters whether or not the enactment applies to UK waters, defined as 'the sea and other waters within the seaward limits of the territorial seas (Police Act 1964, s 19(5A) as added by the CJPOA 1994, s 160). Special constables have such powers and privileges only within the police area for which they are appointed and in areas contiguous to such areas.

2.118   Other statutory police forces, such as the British Transport Police, the Atomic Energy Authority Police and the Ministry of Defence Police, and any special constables appointed to such forces, have all the powers and privileges of a constable but their jurisdiction is limited by the statute which creates them: see the Atomic Energy Authority (Special Constables) Act 1976, s 3 and the Ministry of Defence Police Act 1987, s 2. The jurisdiction of the British Transport Police was extended by the Transport Police (Jurisdiction) Act 1994 which amends the British Transport Commission Act 1949, s 53 and repeals the Railways Act 1993, s 132(5). The Act extends the jurisdiction of the British Transport Police and enables them to act as constables in England and Wales in, on and in the vicinity of premises of any subsidiary of the British Railway Board and anywhere in England and Wales in matters connected with or affecting any of the Board's subsidiaries or a police service user or their undertakings. The Act also makes transitional provision to ensure that British Transport Police constables appointed before the amendments came into force on 1 April 1994 have the same jurisdiction as those appointed after that date.

2.119   There are other bodies sometimes called 'police' but their members are not constables, eg parks' police. They are simply citizens wearing a uniform and do not have the powers of a constable. Similarly, persons employed by local authorities to 'police' communities are simply citizens in uniform with no police powers. As a further complication, some governmental agencies such as Customs and Excise and immigration officers are given statutory powers of search and arrest in connection with the investigation of offences within their particular area of duty, but they again are not 'constables'. As to the armed services see para 2.120, post.

Application to armed forces (s 113)

2.120   PACE, s 113(1) allowed the Secretary of State (for Defence) to direct by statutory instrument that any provision of PACE relating to the investigation of offences, or the detention of persons, should apply, with appropriate modifications, to the investigation of offences under the Army and Air Force Acts 1955, and the Naval Discipline Act 1957. Codes of Practice have also been issued.

Application of the Act to Customs and Excise (s 114)

2.121   Customs and Excise officers investigate crime and deal with the public in much the same way as the police, albeit in respect of a limited number of offences created by Customs and Excise Acts. Their powers derive, in the main, from those Acts. To ensure the thorough and adequate investigation of offences (which may often be serious in terms of the quantity and kind of goods involved and the potential loss to the Exchequer) it was thought right that the police powers provided by PACE and the appropriate constraints on those powers should apply equally to officers of Customs and Excise. Section 114(2) allowed the application, by Treasury Order, of any provision of PACE relating to the investigation of offences, or to the detention of persons, to officers of Customs and Excise, subject to appropriate modification and certain exceptions. However, the application can only relate to matters for which Customs and Excise have statutory responsibility. This was achieved by a series of statutory instruments in 1985.

The Police Reform Act 2002

2.122   Arising from the White Paper *Policing a New Century: A Blueprint for Reform* (Cm 5326) the purpose of the Act was:

- to free up police time for their core functions by making more effective use of support staff including 'detention officers', 'escort officers' and 'investigating officers' acting as scenes of crime officers;
- as part of the drive to tackle crime more effectively, the Government intended that police forces could employ specialist investigating officers to combat specialist crime in areas such as finance and information technology;
- to provide additional capacity to tackle low-level disorder and help reduce the public's fear of crime. The Act enables chief officers to appoint suitable support staff as 'Community support officers 'who will be given powers sufficient to deal with minor issues.

2.123   The Act enables chief constables to designate suitably skilled and trained civilians employed by their police authority who are under the chief constable's direction and control to exercise powers and to undertake duties in carrying out specified functions (s 38). Designation for civilians falls into four categories – community support officer, investigating officer, detention officer or escort officer. Chief Constables and the Director General of the National Criminal Intelligence Service and the National Crime Squad are given the power to designate 'investigating officers' . A person cannot be designated unless the chief officer is satisfied that he is (a) a suitable person to carry out the functions for which he is designated and (b) is capable of effectively carrying out those functions. Designated officers are required to comply with the relevant PACE Codes of Practice.

2.124   The following is an extract from the Home Office Circular detailing the powers of civilians designated under the Act:

Investigating Officers (support staff only)

1.   Part 2 of Sch 4 contains a range of powers to support designated investigating officers. For example, powers of entry, search and seizure, powers to obtain search warrants, to seize evidence and to apply to a judge for access to special procedure or excluded material will support the work of designated investigating officers in specialist areas such as the investigation of financial and Information Technology crime. Powers to enter and search premises following arrest will be particularly relevant to the work of Scenes of Crime Officers. The powers to arrest for further offences which may come to light during interview and the power to warn a person being interviewed about the consequences of any failure to account for their presence at a particular place will support designated investigators in the interviewing process.

2.   Designated investigating officers have a power to use force to enter any premises. However, this power can only be exercised in the company, and under the supervision, of a constable, or for the purposes of saving life or limb or preventing serious damage to property.

3.   A suitably designated investigating officer will be able to exercise some or all of the following powers:

   •   Search warrants
        Apply for and be issued with a search warrant, and to seize and retain things for which a search has been authorised under s 8 of PACE (PACE). The use of force to enter any premises can only be used if the designated person is in the company, and under the supervision, of a constable. The provisions of ss 15 and 16 of PACE which contain safeguards covering the process of applying for a search warrant, the contents of the warrant and the way in which the warrant should be executed extend to warrants dealt with by designated persons. The provisions of s 20 of PACE which extend the power of seizure to computerised information apply as does the protection from seizure to legally privileged material under s 19(6) of PACE. Sections 21 and 22 of PACE impose the same obligations on designated persons in relation to providing records of seizure, providing access to or copies of seized material and retaining seized material as apply to constables.

   •   Access to excluded and special procedure material
        Obtain access to special procedure or excluded material under s 9 of PACE by making an application to a circuit judge under Sch 1 to PACE. The provisions of s 20 of PACE which extend the power of seizure to computerised information apply to material seized under Sch 1. The

protections and obligations under ss 19(6), 21 and 22 of PACE apply to material seized by or produced to a designated person under these provisions.

- Entry and search after arrest

  Use the powers under s 18 of PACE to enter and search any premises occupied or controlled by a person who is under arrest for an arrestable offence and to seize and retain items further to such an search. The use of force to enter any premises can only be used if the designated person is in the company, and under the supervision, of a constable. The designated person may conduct such a search before the arrested person is taken to a police station and without obtaining authority of an inspector if the presence of the arrested person in necessary for the effective investigation of the offence. Standard PACE protections and obligations under ss 19 (6), 21 and 22 are extended to material seized by a designated person under these provisions.

- General power of seizure

  When lawfully on any premises, exercise the same general powers to seize things as are available to a constable under s 19 of PACE. The designated person may also make use of the power to require, in certain circumstances, the production of electronically stored material in a form in which can be taken away. Once again, standard PACE protections and obligations apply.

- Access and copying in the case of things seized by constables

  Act as the supervisor of any access to seized material to which a person is entitled, to supervise the taking of a photograph or seized material or to photograph it themselves under s 21.

- Arrest at a police station for another offence

  Arrest a detained person for a further offence under s 31 of PACE if it appears to the designated investigating officer that the detained person would be liable to arrest for that further offence if released from their initial arrest; the consequences of failure to account for certain objects, marks etc under s 36 of the Criminal Justice and Public Order Act 1994 apply to such arrests.

- Power to transfer persons into custody of investigating officers

  When a designated investigating officer is given custody of a detained person in the police station, the custody officer' s responsibilities are transferred and they will have to ensure that the person in their lawful custody is treated in accordance with PACE and the relevant PACE codes of practice.

- Power to require arrested person to account for certain matters

  Question an arrested person under ss 36 and 37 of the Criminal Justice and Public Order Act 1994 about facts which may be attributable to the person' s participation in an offence. Eg the person's presence at a particular place at a relevant time or the presence of potentially incriminating objects such as marks. They may also warn the suspect about the capacity of a court to draw inferences from a failure to give a satisfactory account in response to questioning.

- Extended powers of seizure
  Use powers available to constables under Part 2 of the Criminal Justice and Police Act 2001 (not yet commenced). These are additional powers of seizure so that where a designated person has been provided with a specific power of seizure and is exercising it on premises is compromised by the sheer bulk or complexity of the material to be searched through, that material can be moved elsewhere for sifting, subject to a range of detailed safeguards.

Detention officers (support staff and contracted out staff)

1. The powers available to designated detention officers, both police authority employed and contracted out personnel concern the handling of persons in custody. While this is an area in which police support staff are increasingly involved, these powers will broaden the scope for support staff within the custody suite and give their work a clear foundation in law.
2. A suitably designated detention officer will be able to perform some or all the following functions:

Attendance at police station for fingerprinting

- Require certain defined categories of persons who have been convicted in relation to recordable offences to attend a police station in order to have their fingerprints taken under s 27 (1) of PACE.
  - Non-Intimate searches of detained persons
    Conduct a non-intimate search of persons detained at a police station or elsewhere and seize items found during such searches under s 54 of PACE in the same circumstances as constables can. The restrictions on the scope of the search and seizure and the circumstances in which searches can be carried out apply to designated detention officers as they do to constables.
  - Searches and examination to ascertain identity
    Carry out a search/examination under s 54A in order to find identifying marks or determine the identity or persons detained at police stations and to photograph any mark.
  - Intimate searches of detained persons
    Conduct an intimate search of a detained person under s 55 (6) of PACE in the same very limited circumstances as constables.
  - Fingerprinting without consent
    Take fingerprints without consent in the same circumstances as a constable can under s 61 of PACE and discharge the duty to inform a person from whom an intimate sample has been taken that the sample may be the subject of a speculative search against existing records.

- Warnings about intimate samples
  Discharge the duty under s 62 (7A) (a) of PACE to inform a person from whom an intimate sample has been taken that the sample may be the subject of a speculative search against existing records.
- Non-intimate samples
  Take non-intimate samples without consent in the same circumstances as a constable can under s 63 of PACE and inform the person from whom the sample is to be taken of any necessary authorisation by a senior officer and of the grounds for that authorisation by a senior officer and of the grounds for that authorisation; inform the person that a non-intimate sample may be the subject of a speculative search against existing records.
- Attendance at police station for the taking of a sample
  Require certain defined categories of persons who have been charged with or convicted or recordable offences to attend a police station to have a sample taken under s 63A(4) of PACE
- Photographing persons in police detention
  Photograph detained persons under s 64A of PACE and require the removal of face coverings/face paint if necessary.

Escort officers (support staff and contracted out staff)

3. The powers available to designated escort officers, both police authority employed and contracted out personnel, allow them to transport arrested prisoners to police stations, to escort detained persons from one police station to another and other locations specified by the custody officer.
4. Suitably designated escort officers will be able to perform some or all the following functions:
   - Power to take an arrested person to a police station
     Take a person arrested by a constable to a designated police station as soon as practicable unless the person is working in an area not covered by such a station and it appears that it will not be necessary to hold the suspect for more than 6 hours; delay removal to a police station if the arrestee is required elsewhere for immediate investigative purposes.
   - Escort of persons in police detention
     On the authority of a custody officer, escort detainees between police stations or between police stations and other specified locations. Where the custody officer transfers a detainee to the escort officer under these provisions, the escort officer becomes responsible for ensuring that the detainee is treated in accordance with PACE and the relevant PACE Code of Practice.
5. In the exercise of both these powers a designated escort officer is treated as having that person in their lawful custody, under a duty to prevent their escape and entitled to use reasonable force to keep that person in their charge. They also have the same power that a constable has under s 54(6A)

and (6B) to carry out a non-intimate search of a person and to seize or retain anything found on that search. Restrictions on the scope of the search and seizure and the circumstances in which searches can be carried out apply to designated escort officers as they do to constables.

How the powers can be used

6.   Concern has existed for some time both within and outside the police service about the amount of time police officers spend at the police station dealing with prisoners and associated paperwork. Arresting officers generally deal with their own prisoners from the point of arrest through to transportation back to the station, evidence gathering, interviewing, documentation and file preparation. Although support staff are already employed in supporting the police in many of these areas, their involvement has been limited owing to lack of necessary powers. In many areas they can only perform functions in the company of another constable. The powers in the Police Reform Act allow chief officers to deploy support staff more flexibly in support of their police officer colleagues.

7.   Taking the three groups of support staff in turn, the following are examples of how powers might be used:

(a)   Designated **investigating officers** have a range of search, seizure and retention powers available to them which will enable them to undertake searches of premises without having to be accompanied by a constable. Currently, a specialist IT expert might be called upon to accompany a police officer to premises to advise on where to look for relevant evidence held on a computer. Their role however is limited effectively to that of an adviser with no powers to search or seize. If such a person were designated as an investigating officer they would be able to enter and search premises and search for relevant material. The use of force to enter any premises can only be used if the designated person is in the company, and under the supervision, of a constable.

(b)   At present **Scenes of Crime Officers** (SOCOS) who are often civilian employees do not have the right to enter premises or seize property as evidence unless they have the consent of the owner/occupier. If a SOCO attended a crime scene and discovered property within the premises which was of interest to the police, they would not be able to seize it, but would have to rely on a constable to revisit the premises to seize it later, at which point it might well have been removed.

Most of the work SOCOS is carried out on the basis of consent and thus they are normally able to conduct their business effectively without the need for formal powers. However in order to operate effectively in some circumstances they must be accompanied by someone with constabulary powers.

If a SOCO is a designated investigating officer they will have the necessary powers to enter and search premises and seize material when consent or cooperation is not forthcoming, to enable them to carry out an examination of the crime scene and preserve evidence which might otherwise be lost. The use of force to enter any premises can only be used if the designated person is in the company, and under the supervision, of a constable.

(c) A further example of how the designated investigating officer powers might be used is in relation to the **interviewing** process. Currently a civilian statement taker/interviewer would have to request a constable to exercise the power to arrest at a police station for a further offence under s 31 of PACE and powers to require arrested persons to account for certain matters such as the presence of an object, substance o mark or their presence at a particular place. A designated officer who was conducting an interview would be able to exercise these powers themselves.

(d) Designated **detention** officers have a number of police powers which will support the work of the custody officer, particularly in identifying the suspect. They will be able to undertake non-intimate searches of suspects even where consent is withheld, take fingerprints and non-intimate samples without consent, search and examine suspects for identifying marks and take photographs of suspects, using reasonable force if necessary. Currently these powers can only be undertaken by support staff with the consent of the suspect and consequently a constable has to be called upon to support staff where consent is withheld.

(e) The powers of **escort** staff to transport arrested persons or prisoners are currently limited so that where a suspect is not co-operating a police officer will have to accompany the escort staff in the transportation of the prisoner. A designated escort officer will have powers to use reasonable force to prevent the suspect escaping and to search the person for harmful or dangerous articles.

The extended powers mean that once an arresting officer has arrested a suspect, instead of having to return to the station to process the suspect they will be able to hand them over to a designated escort officer who can carry out the transportation and booking in procedure at the police station themselves.

EXCLUSION OF EVIDENCE

2.125 There are two reasons why improperly obtained evidence may be excluded from the trial:

(a) The first stems from the proven or likely unreliability of the evidence. The clearest example of this arises with confessions. It lay behind the previous principle of voluntariness and is now explicitly stated in s 76(2)(b) of PACE (NI Order, r 74(2)(b)).

For example, if the police have offered an inducement, or made a threat, to a suspect in order to obtain a confession from him, there is a strong probability that the confession will be untrue. This reliability principle is discussed in paras 8.48-8.54, post, but it is important to note that much of PACE (Parts IV and V) and three Codes (on Detention etc, Identification and Tape-recording of Interviews) are concerned with what happens at the police station. Breaches of many of these provisions can lead to unreliable confessions or to the accused at least raising the issue at his trial in the hope of raising a reasonable doubt. Police officers must therefore be made aware of the need to comply with the Codes' provisions. The exclusion of unreliable evidence (and quite possibly the collapse of the prosecution case) can act as a deterrent to police misconduct.

(b) The second reason for excluding evidence rests upon fairness to the accused. The idea is that, if the police break the law, they should not be allowed to profit from their wrongdoing by securing a conviction. The evidence which they have obtained unlawfully should be excluded at trial even if the evidence is true. This type of exclusionary rule can be strict (ie all illegally obtained evidence is always excluded) or discretionary (ie exclusion depends upon a variety of factors). The United States has been the clearest exponent of the former, whilst Scotland is an example of the latter. English common law accepted but has rarely enforced a discretionary exclusionary rule and, with the exception of the breathalyser legislation, rejected a strict rule. As to a discretionary power to exclude evidence, for many years English courts insisted that they had such a discretion. Lord Goddard uttered the classic statement in *Kuruma v R* (1955):

> 'the judge always has a discretion to disallow evidence if the strict rules of admissibility would operate unfairly against the accused . . . if, for instance, some admission of some piece of evidence, eg, a document, had been obtained from a defendant by a trick, no doubt the judge might properly rule it out'.

His successors, Lords Parker (in *Callis v Gunn* (1964)) and Widgery (in *Jeffrey v Black* (1978)) produced dicta to similar effect. However, with one exception (*R v Payne* (1963)), the courts consistently refused to exercise this discretion so as to reject real, as opposed to confessional, evidence, even in the face of clearly illegal conduct by the police. Thus, in *Jeffrey v Black* (1978):

> 'the simple unvarnished fact that evidence was obtained by police officers who had gone in without bothering to get a search warrant is not enough to justify the justices in exercising their discretion to keep the evidence out' (Lord Widgery).

(See also *R v Mackintosh* (1982), a case involving a blatant disregard for the Judges' Rules.) In reality, the obiter dicta of Lord Goddard in *Kuruma v R* (1955) forged a myth that judges possessed, and would use, a discretion to exclude evidence which had been improperly obtained. Later Lord Chief Justices fostered the myth but were careful not to apply its message. The House of Lords in *R v*

Sang (1979), however, rejected Lord Goddard's statement. Instead, Lord Diplock observed:

> '(1) A trial judge in a criminal trial has always a discretion to refuse to admit evidence if in his opinion its prejudicial effect outweighs its probative value.

> (2) Save with regard to admissions and confessions and generally with regard to evidence obtained from the accused after commission of the offence, he has no discretion to refuse to admit relevant admissible evidence on the ground that it was obtained by improper or unfair means.'

2.126 The first rule is well established. Evidence of disposition, previous convictions and reputation is normally irrelevant and is for that reason inadmissible. However, even when evidence is deemed relevant and prima facie admissible, 'there should be excluded from the jury information about the accused which is likely to have an influence on their minds prejudicial to the accused which is out of proportion to the true probative value of admissible evidence conveying that information' (Lord Diplock). The second rule is also aimed at securing a fair trial for the accused. Thus, admissions and confessions are excluded because confessions, which have been obtained by oppression or in circumstances in which they are likely to be unreliable, are suspect and should not be given in evidence. The House of Lords refused to accept that the courts had a further role to play in disciplining the police by excluding non-confessional evidence which has been obtained 'improperly or unfairly'. This ruling accepted the reality that, whilst the courts had frequently agreed with Lord Goddard's statement, they had regularly refused to accept the disciplinary role. See, for example, the refusal of the House of Lords to exclude evidence obtained by trespassing on property and planting a listening device (*R v Khan Sultan* (1994)) and a similar refusal to exclude evidence obtained by tapping a pay phone inside a police station (*R v Ahmed* (1995)). See also Williams and *O'Hare v DPP* (1993) – insecure vehicle apparently loaded with cigarettes left in a high crime area in order to catch would-be thieves and *R v Christou and Wright* (1992) – a jewellery shop operated by police to catch thieves and handlers. These cases emphasise that the common law is not concerned with how the evidence was obtained but with how it is used at trial and its effect upon that trial. Real evidence such as drugs or stolen goods speaks for itself, and such relevant evidence may operate unfortunately for the accused but not unfairly.

THE DISCRETION TO EXCLUDE UNDER PACE, s 78 (PACE ORDER, ART 76)

2.127 During the passage of PACE through Parliament, Lord Scarman tabled a detailed amendment to the Bill in the Lords which gave the courts the power to exclude evidence obtained by illegal, improper or deceptive conduct on the part of the police. The Government were then forced into accepting the need for an exclusionary rule but watered it down. Thus, the Lords' detailed amendment was replaced by the looser terms of what is now s 78. The former was rejected because:

(1) it would unnecessarily punish the police;
(2) it would lead to lengthy trials within trials as to the admissibility or otherwise of the evidence;
(3) the Government's proposal was 'simple and clear in form, yet suitably flexible' (Home Secretary, House of Commons Debate, 29 October 1984, col 1014).

2.128 In the context of this book, argument (3) is of most relevance, for it is not at all clear what this opaque section means. It reads as follows:

'(1) In any proceedings the court may refuse to allow evidence on which the prosecution proposes to rely to be given if it appears to the court that, having regard to all the circumstances, including the circumstances in which the evidence was obtained, the admission of the evidence would have such an adverse effect on the fairness of the proceedings that the court ought not to admit it.

(2) Nothing in this section shall prejudice any rule of law requiring a court to exclude evidence.'

(Since s 78 (Art 76) has been used mainly in the field of confessions, it is considered in detail in Chapter 8. To avoid repetition the main points and the non-confession areas will be mentioned here.)

GUIDANCE: POINTS ON s 78

2.129 Section 78 (Art 76) is directed solely at the trial stage.

'The purpose of excluding evidence should not be disciplinary. It should be to avoid evidence being adduced which if adduced would lead to an unfair trial.' (Home Secretary, House of Commons Debate, 29 October 1984, col 1012)

Thus though s 78 is concerned with 'the circumstances in which the evidence was obtained' the central concern is with the effect of the evidence and the manner of its obtaining upon the fairness of the trial. However, the section has proved to be a mischievous and unpredictable weapon wielded to protect the accused and to assert the authority of the court over its own proceedings. No matter what the judges may say to the contrary, one inevitable consequence of exclusion is to discipline the police by rejecting evidence which they have improperly obtained which often leads to the acquittal of the defendant (occasionally judicial irritation is openly expressed, *eg R v Canale* (1990) and more recently *R v Weerdesteyn* (1995)).

2.130 The court has a very wide discretion to exclude evidence, ie it can do so 'if it appears to the court . . .'. It follows that the burden of persuading the court or judge to exclude the evidence lies on the defence (*Vel v Owen* (1987) in contrast to the position under s 76 (2) where it is on the prosecution.

2.131 Section 78 (Art 74) is to be construed widely after considering all the circumstances and the courts have refused to confine it by firm rules. This gives considerable scope for the defence to raise it. Indeed the number of cases in which the section is raised indicates that defence counsel are very alert to it.

2.132 'Including the circumstances in which the evidence was obtained' is sufficiently open-ended to cover breaches of PACE, Codes of Practice and all other laws, the unreasonable exercise of discretionary powers, deception or tricks. The more significant the breach, the more likely it is that s 78 will be exercised. However, the key to s 78 (sometimes, it would appear, overlooked, or glossed over, by the courts) is not the fact of a breach, but the 'adverse effect on the fairness' of the trial. That link has to be established.

2.133 In the confessions area, it is suggested that s 76(2)(a) (dealing with oppression) was intended as a statement of principle and of what kind of police conduct is regarded as beyond the pale; s 76(2)(b) is then concerned with the mainstream of any criminal justice system viz whether the confession is reliable. The wording of s 76(2)(b) 'anything said or done which was likely, in the circumstances . . . to render unreliable any confession' means that occasionally something will be said or done of which the courts disapprove but which is not likely to render the confession unreliable (eg *R v Mason* (1987) where D was deceived into believing that police had positive evidence of his guilt). Section 78 is then available to deal with that situation but was intended to deal mainly with the non-confession area and with police conduct or other circumstances of which a court disapproves (eg unfair identification methods; see (f) below). The Court of Appeal has taken a very different path. Section 78 has in many cases usurped the role intended for s 76(2)(b) being used as the main weapon in regulating how the police obtain confessions. There are, however, signs that greater attention is being paid to the actual words of the section. Thus in *R v Oliphant* (1992) the Court of Appeal said:

> 'It is important, in deciding the admissibility of evidence under PACE, not to be diverted by other decisions of the court, often on different facts, from considering the statutory language.'

The Court also appears to be seeking to curb the tendency to use s 78 to exclude confessions by suggesting that once the confession satisfies the test for admissibility under s 76(2), prima facie, its admission would not have an adverse effect on the fairness of the trial – see *R v Weeks* (1995) and *R v Campbell* (1995) (see further paras 8.145).

2.134 Outside confessions, s 78 has been used in the following areas (precise categories cannot be delineated since the section is of a flexible nature and the courts are unwilling to confine it so).
(i) Identification issues. The law places great store by the accurate identification of suspects; it is therefore rightly suspicious of mistakes or improprieties in the identification procedures (see further para 7.66, post). Section 78 can thus be employed to ensure fairness to the accused (see *R v Nagah* (1990); *R v Conway* (1990); *R v Britton and Richards* (1989); *R v Gall* (1989); *R v Grannell* (1989); *R v*

Ladlow (1989); *R v Gaynor* (1988); *R v O'Leary* (1988); *R v Quinn* (1990); *R v Brown* (1991); *R v Samms, Elliot and Bartley* (1991); *R v Martin and Nicholls* (1994); *R v Knowles* (1994); *R v Quinn* (1995), *R v Allen* (1995); *R v Hickin* (1996); *R v Johnson* (1996); *R v Macmath* (1997); *R v Wait* (1998); *R v Jones and Nelson* (1999); *R v Sangarie* (2001); *R v Miah* (2001)).

(ii)   The section has been argued, largely unsuccessfully, in the context of alleged entrapment by the police and Customs and Excise (ie whether D has been tricked or unfairly trapped into committing an offence): *R v H* (1987); *R v O'Connor* (1986); *R v Gill* (1989); *R v Harwood* (1989); *R v Katz* (1989); *R v Ali* (1991); *R v Edwards* (1991); and cf the facts of *DPP v Wilson* (1991); *Williams and O'Hare v DPP* (1993); *R v Christou and Wright* (1992); *R v Smurthwaite and Gill* (1994); *Ealing London Borough v Woolworths plc* (1995). But see *R v Looseley* (2001) and *A-G's Reference (No 3 of 2000)* in the context of abuse of process, para 2.135 post .

(iii) Somewhat doubtfully the failure to conduct a stop and search properly justified the exclusion of evidence found on the basis that it may render any subsequent trial unfair, in that if it had been properly done, D might have given an explanation which would have reduced the eventual charges brought against him: *R v Fennelley* (1989).

(iv)   Improprieties in the breath-alcohol procedures in road traffic cases may be unfair to the accused at trial (see *Matto v Wolverhampton Crown Court* (1987)).

(v)   If D cannot properly challenge the evidence brought against him in court, it may be unfair to admit it: *R v Quinn* (1990).

(vi)   The section was argued, alongside the common law discretion, in *R v Khan (Sultan)* (1994) in an attempt to persuade the court to exclude evidence obtained by trespassing and planting a listening device to the wall of a house – not unfair within the section. Similarly in *R v Ahmed* (1995), evidence obtained by tapping a telephone within a police station; *R v Bailey and Smith* (1993); *R v Parker* (1995) – both covert taping of suspects in cells; *R v Effik* (1994) and *R v Cadette* (1995) – covert taping of telephone conversations. In all cases the reliability of the evidence was beyond doubt and in none was the police conduct considered such as to justify exclusion at common law or under s 78. In *R v Sargeant* (2001) the defendant confessed after he was confronted with an illegally recorded telephone transcript, although the law lords considered the judge was right to admit the confession the conviction was unsafe under s 78.

(vii) The section has been used to exclude other forms of evidence which are the province of the general law of evidence and will not be considered in this book.

Section 82(3) (Art 70(3)) preserves the common law discretion to exclude evidence. As *R v Sang* (1980) indicated, the discretion is limited. It retains very much a residual and sparse role, and the courts' marked reluctance in pre- PACE days ever to exercise it continues as *R v Khan (Sultan)* (1994) demonstrates. Additionally there is very little that can be done at common law which cannot be done under s 78 (see *Matto v Wolverhampton Crown Court* (1987)) and, so far as real evidence is concerned, the courts are unlikely to exclude under s 78 in circumstances when they would not have done so at common law. See for example

R v Stewart (1995) – no exclusion of evidence of meter tampering, which was there for all to see, even if there were breaches of PACE and Code B. In *Chalkley and Jeffries* (1998) the Court of Appeal held that s 78 did not widen the common law and the criteria for judging unfairness were the same as under the common law. However this view was rejected in *Loosely* (2001) and *A-G's Reference (No 3 of 2000)* when the law lords made clear that the discretion under s 78 is a broad one.

ABUSE OF PROCESS

2.135   At common law judges have a discretion to stay a prosecution on the grounds that it constitutes an abuse of process (*Connelly v DPP* (1964)). Dennis (*The Law of Evidence*, Sweet and Maxwell, London, 2002) considers the doctrine belongs more to the realm of criminal procedure than criminal evidence but concedes that there is some overlap between the functions of the abuse of process doctrine and s 78 of PACE. In *Ex p Bennett* (1994) the House of Lords held that the court has jurisdiction to stay proceedings and order the release of the accused when the court becomes aware that there has been a serious abuse of power by the executive. The court can refuse to allow the police or prosecuting authorities to take advantage of such an abuse of process by regarding it as an abuse of the court's process. Lord Griffiths, at p 62 stated, that the courts cannot,

> 'contemplate for a moment the transference to the executive of the responsibility for seeing that the process of law is not abused. The judiciary should accept a responsibility for the maintenance of the rule of law that embraces a willingness to oversee executive action and to refuse to countenance behaviour that threatens either basic human rights or the rule of law'.

2.136   In *Bennett* the defendant claimed he had been forcibly abducted and brought to this country to face trial in disregard of extradition laws. Lord Steyn in *R v Latif* (1996) confirmed that the same principle applied in entrapment cases. The court may stay the relevant criminal proceedings and the court may exclude evidence under s 78. The development of this remedy overtakes *Sang* and is a consequence of reinforcement by the Human Rights Act 1998. It is unlawful for the court, as a public authority, to act in a way which is incompatible with a Convention right.

2.137   Entrapment is not a substantive defence but it may deprive a defendant of the right to a fair trial embodied in Art 6. The grant of a stay, rather than the exclusion of evidence at the trial, should normally be the appropriate response in a case of entrapment (*R v Looseley* (2001)). Exclusion of evidence from the trial may have the same effect in practice as an order staying the proceedings because there may be little evidence other than that of undercover officers. A prosecution founded on entrapment would be an abuse of the court's process.

2.138   A decision whether to stay criminal proceedings as abuse of process is distinct from a determination of the forensic fairness of admitting evidence but the practical effect is also the symbolic enforcement of the court's integrity.

2.139   The judicial response to entrapment is based on the need to uphold the rule of law. A defendant is excused because the police have behaved improperly. In *Latif* and *Shahzad* the House of Lords were asked to rule that it was an abuse of process for customs officers to lure an organiser in the heroin trade into the jurisdiction so that he could be arrested and tried for being concerned in an illegal importation of heroin. The argument was rejected by Lord Steyn who held that the judge had been entitled to find Shahzad was an organiser in the heroin trade who took the initiative in proposing the importation. The conduct of the undercover customs officer,

> 'was not so unworthy or shameful that it was an affront to the public conscience to allow the prosecution to proceed. Realistically, any behaviour of the customs officer was venial compared to that of Shahzad'.

2.140   In *Looseley*, the House of Lords considered two undercover police operations directed against drug dealers. Both involved purchases of drugs by police officers and the House gave guidance on the limits of entrapment. The court decided that a defendant predisposed to commit a crime of the same or a similar type, should opportunity arise, could be entrapped. If the defendant lacked such a predisposition, and the police were responsible for implanting the necessary intent that could be repugnant to the integrity of the trial process and an abuse of process. In identifying the limits to the types of police conduct which in any set of circumstances are acceptable a useful guide is to discover whether the police did no more than present the defendant with an 'unexceptional opportunity to commit a crime'. Lord Nicholls quoted from the Canadian case of *Ridgeway v R* ((1995)) finding guidance in the words of McHugh J:

> 'The State can justify the use of entrapment techniques to induce the commission of an offence only when the inducement is consistent with the ordinary temptations and stratagems that are likely to be encountered in the course of criminal activity. That may mean that some degree of deception, importunity and even threats on the part of the authorities may be acceptable But once the state goes beyond the ordinary, it is likely to increase the incidence of crime by artificial means.'

2.141   His Lordship went on to explain that there were other factors to be taken into account when assessing the degree of police impropriety. Providing an opportunity to commit a crime is intrusive to a degree and should not be applied in a random fashion and used for 'wholesale virtue-testing' without good reason. The language of human rights principles is used,

> 'The greater the degree of intrusiveness, the closer the court scrutinises the reason for using it. On this, proportionality has a role to play. Ultimately the overall consideration is always whether the conduct of the police or other law enforcement agency was so seriously improper as to bring the administration of justice into disrepute.'

2.142   If the formulation of a prosecution would,' affront the public conscience' (*R v Latif* (1996) at 112 per Lord Steyn),or 'conviction and punishment would be deeply offensive to ordinary notions of fairness' (*Nottingham City Council v Amin* (2000) at 1076 per Lord Bingham CJ), the court would find there had been an abuse of its process and order a stay. Circumstances of relevance would include the nature of the offence, the secrecy and difficulty of detection and the motive for the police operation. The police must act in good faith and not as part of a malicious vendetta against an individual or group. Particularly significant is the nature and extent of police participation in the crime and the greater the inducement held out by the police and the more forceful or persistent the police overture, the more readily a court may conclude that the boundaries have been overstepped.

2.143 In contexts other than entrapment the interplay between the power to exclude evidence and the abuse of process doctrine is less clear. Where the prosecution sought to adduce evidence obtained by telephone tapping carried out abroad in *R v Auila* (1998) the Court of Appeal rejected defence submissions that the evidence should be excluded under s 78, and as an alternative, an argument that the use of the evidence would be an abuse of process. Evidence obtained by telephone tapping in this country is inadmissible by statute (Regulation of Investigatory Powers Act 2000, s 17 formerly Interception of Communications Act 1985) however in the country where the tapping occurred it was lawful and the Court rejected the arguments that it was unfair or that its use would offend against any fundamental principle of justice.

2.144 The doctrine of abuse of process continues to develop; in the context of the exclusion of evidence there are two alternatives: either it has no application to the exclusion of evidence and is concerned only with other matters going to the issue of whether the prosecution should be proceeded with at all; or the doctrine has a residual role to play in the case of serious pre-trial impropriety. In *R v Sutherland* and *R v Finch* the views of both trial judges was that where there was serious impropriety the prosecution should be stayed.

3 Stop and search powers

INTRODUCTION

3.1   Prior to the Police and Criminal Evidence Act 1984 (PACE), the police had no general power to stop and search persons or vehicles for stolen goods or other unlawful articles. Some areas of the country (notably London under s 66 of the Metropolitan Police Act 1839) offered such a power in relation to stolen goods and there were, and still are, a motley collection of powers covering specific articles such as prohibited drugs, firearms, crossbows, wild plants, badgers and birds' eggs (see the list in Annex A to the Code of Practice, A, which deals with the Exercise by Police Officers of Statutory Powers of Stop and Search). The absence of a general power meant that the stopping of a person without his consent was technically a false imprisonment and the search was an assault, whilst the search of a vehicle was a trespass – the stopping possibly being permitted under the road traffic legislation (see para 3.45, post). Apart from risking a civil action in such circumstances, the police officer would step outside his duty and could lose the protection of s 89 (2) of the Police Act 1996. In practice, these risks were more theoretical than real and did not prevent widespread stopping and searching with the express or tacit consent of the person. Moreover, the few powers available nationally, such as s 23 of the Misuse of Drugs Act 1971, could be stretched to justify a general search of the person, since the courts were prepared to admit relevant evidence even though it was seized during an illegal search. In this context, Part I of PACE introduced no radical change but, in essence, legalised existing police practice.

3.2   The arguments in favour of a general stop and search power were threefold. First, though the success rate may vary, stops and searches inevitably bring to light crime. In London, for example, the power was seen as an immensely valuable method of crime detection, as more than 700,000 recorded stops in London in 1981 appeared to indicate (see The use, effectiveness and impact of police stop and search powers, Willis (Home Office 1983)).

3.3   Second, a successful stop and search detects and clears up crime in one action and may lead to detection of others; for example, a person found with housebreaking tools automatically contravenes s 25 of the Theft Act 1968 and may well then admit to having committed burglaries. Such a power of stop and search can, it was argued, be a valuable contributor to the success rate of a police force (see Willis, op cit).

3.4   Third, the possession of proscribed weapons and articles can only be properly detected by a stop and search, since they can be readily concealed about the person or in a vehicle. Yet, under the previous law, a lawful search for them was only possible after an arrest and that arrest in turn was hedged by restrictions.

3.5   The Royal Commission on Criminal Procedure (1981) accepted these arguments, believing:

> '… that people in the street who have committed property offences or have in their possession articles which it is a criminal offence to possess should not be entirely protected from the possibility of being searched.' (Report, para 3.17)

3.6   It was satisfied, on the basis of figures suggesting a 12 per cent arrest rate in the Metropolis (Royal Commission, Law and Procedure Volume, para 26 and Appendices 2 and 3) that the availability of stop and search powers was of use in the detection of crime and recommended that a uniform stop and search power be made available for the whole of England and Wales, firmly based upon reasonable suspicion and subject to strict safeguards on the exercise of such power. Part I of PACE (Part II of the NI Order) endorsed part of that recommendation. It empowers the police to stop, detain and search persons and vehicles for stolen and prohibited articles (ss 1 and 2, Art 3); and to set up road blocks in certain circumstances (s 4, Art 6). There are provisions for the written recording of stops and searches and road blocks (ss 3 and 5, Arts 4 and 5) and a Code of Practice supplements PACE. Unfortunately for the purposes of exposition and understanding, PACE does not provide the full picture. Although it provides the principal stop and search power, it does not, as the Royal Commission (1981) had suggested, provide the sole one. There are other statutory authorities, some of which differ in scope from the PACE power. The list of such authorities includes the Firearms Act 1968, Misuse of Drugs Act 1971, and the Terrorism Act 2000 (see Code A, Annex A for a list) and is enlarged as and when Parliament sees the need to tackle a particular problem. For example, in 1987 the Government became 'increasingly anxious about the habitual carrying of knives in public' (Home Secretary, Hansard vol 125, col 684). Within months the carrying of certain blades and sharply pointed articles was made an offence and the police were given a power to stop and search for them (Criminal Justice Act 1988, ss 139, 140, see below, para 3.24). Similarly, the concern about the use of crossbows led to the power contained in the Crossbow Act 1987. Subsequently concern over the use of guns and knives, and in particular their use against unarmed police officers, has led to the introduction of a power to authorise the stop and search of persons or vehicles within a prescribed area for a 24-hour period in order to prevent incidents of serious violence in that area (s 60 of the Criminal Justice and Public Order Act 1994, discussed below, para 3.25). Amendments to the Prevention of Terrorism (Temporary Provisions) Act 1989 to stop and search persons or vehicles for articles which could be used for the purposes of terrorism were introduced following terrorist bombings in Warrington and the City of London. These powers are now contained in ss 43-46 of the Terrorism Act 2000. All the existing stop and search powers are set out in the Appendix to Code A together with a brief indication of their scope.

THE EFFECTIVENESS OF STOP AND SEARCH POWERS

3.7 Historically the use of stop and search has been a sensitive issue for police-community relations. The Scarman Report (1981) was critical of the use made by the Metropolitan Police of stop and search powers under Section 66 of the Metropolitan Police Act 1839 (since repealed) as contributing to the Brixton disturbances. Claims that stop and search powers were used excessively against ethnic minorities were regularly made pre-PACE (see Willis, *The Use and Effectiveness and Impact of Police Stop and Search Powers* (1983); Smith and Gray, *Police and People in London* (PSI 1983)). During the 1990s, following the publication of ethnic monitoring under s 95 of the Criminal Justice Act 1991, there has been closer scrutiny of stop and search statistics. In 2002-03 895,300 persons and/or vehicles were stopped and searched under PACE powers and 50,820 stop/searches were made in anticipation of violence, some 13 per cent of those searched were arrested (Ayres,Murray and Fiti 'Arrests for Notifiable Offences and the Operation of   Certain Police Powers' (2003)).

3.8 The collection and interpretation of this data is by no means unproblematic: there are wide variations in recording practices between forces, there may be reluctance by some officers to record all stops and procedures have not always been reliable. Notwithstanding these difficulties the data indicates over-representation of ethnic minorities in the stop and search figures.

3.9 More recently, the MacPherson Inquiry into the death of Stephen Lawrence recommended changes to the recording and monitoring of all stops and stop and searches (Recommendations 61-63). The inquiry found that discriminatory operational practices were responsible for a loss of public confidence in policing particularly in the black community.

3.10 In response to the Report of the MacPherson Inquiry , the Home Office's Policing and Reducing Crime Unit was commissioned to carry out a programme of research on stops and searches. ("Police Stops and Searches: Lessons from a Programme of Research Series Papers 127-132). This extensive research informed the process of updating Code A and many of its recommendations have been progressed by Police Forces. In identifying legitimacy as the focus of the research the programme examined and recommended statistics to address:

- police trust and confidence
- legality, and
- effectiveness.

Readers who wish to peruse the research in detail will find it at   :http://www.homeoffice.gov.uk/rds/policerspubs1.html

The following represents a summary of the recommendations.

Public trust and confidence

3.11   The primary threats to public confidence are the following:
- disproportionate rate of stops and searches of those from minority ethnic backgrounds
- poor management of encounters by police officers; and
- inadequate explanations by officers to those stopped or searched.

Recommendations
(i)   improve supervision of searches
(ii)   identify ethnic biases in search practice
(iii)   effective targeting of stops and searches at crime problems
(iv)   improve handling of encounters between police officers and the public
(v)   raise public awareness of police powers and their rights
(vi)   involve the community to achieve support for policing activities
(vii) improve monitoring and record-keeping
(viii) measuring disproportionality
(ix)   review searches not requiring grounds including 'voluntary' searches.

Legality

3.12   The main threats to legality were identified as:
- searches which take place without reasonable grounds
- the use of generalisations and negative stereotypes as a basis for suspicion
- problems obtaining informed consent for 'voluntary' searches
- non-recording of searches.

Recommendations

The recommendations were:
(i)   clarifying PACE Code A
(ii) training guidance on the meaning of reasonable suspicion.

Effectiveness

3.13   Threats to the effectiveness of searches include:
- poor grounds for suspicion
- inaccurate and less up-to-date information or intelligence
- failure to utilise good intelligence; and
- a performance quality which emphasises quantity rather than quality.

Recommendations

The recommendations were:
(i)   making the best use of intelligence
(ii) improving the reliability of suspect descriptions
(iii) improved supervision of searches
(iv) monitoring arrest quality.

3.14   Fitzgerald's (1999) study of stop and search in London reported that use of the power has a 'significant effect on preventing crime, both directly and indirectly'. She suggests 'that the power is valuable and the public want the police to use it'. In reaching these conclusions however the research identified a number of problems:

- being searched makes it significantly more likely that someone who has been stopped by the police will end up dissatisfied with the encounter;

- black people stopped by the police are more likely to be searched. So searches exaggerate the extent to which black people are stopped by the police relative to whites. At the same time searches increase black people's level of dissatisfaction with stops;

- searches are beginning to impact on young Asians without previous criminal records who are coming to the attention of the police in larger than average groups;

- yet some of the searches which are creating these problems may not be justifiable in terms of PACE and more may simply be unnecessary – including searches which produce arrests;

- at the same time, it would be possible significantly to boost the numbers of arrests which come from legitimate searches since the justifiable use of power is elastic. The number of searches could increase considerably without making any difference to the arrest rate;

- but extending the use of the power would increase the number of members of the public generally who are inconvenienced by being searched. More specifically, it would amplify the disproportionate impact of the power on black people; and it seems certain also to increase the proportion of young Asians with criminal records – largely through arrests for possession of small amounts of cannabis;

- in deciding to what extent the power should be used, therefore, some decision is needed about where the balance should be struck between the crime-related gains and the possible community-related damage.

3.15   Significantly the research continues to demonstrate that the experience of being searched is associated with reduced confidence in the police and this contributes to lower levels of confidence in the police among those from minority ethnic groups.

3.16   The important point to note is that, apart from two exceptions (see para 3.34), the requirements in ss 2, 3 and 5 of PACE and the Code of Practice apply to all stop and search powers, including that under s 60 of the 1994 Act and the provisions of the PTA 1989. This means, inter alia, that annual police force reports must contain a record of the stop and search powers exercised during the year. The number of recorded stops and searches under PACE and other legislation increased from a modest 109,800 in 1986 to 946,120 in 2002 and the arrests correspondingly increased from 18,900 to 114,300 The consequential charge and conviction rates are not known but would have been much less. The reasons for stop and search were: stolen property (320,900) and drugs (363,100). Offensive weapons accounted for 62,600 searches and going equipped to steal 93,200, there were 9,900 searches for firearms and 45,500 classified as 'other', ie under the miscellaneous terrorism, wildlife conservation, aviation security, customs and excise and sporting events provisions.

3.17   The steady growth in the exercise of stop and search powers reflects an initial 'softly softly' approach and an increasingly proactive approach to the high level of burglaries and violent crimes. There is, however, a high price to be paid for the 13 per cent 'success rate' in the exercise of stop and search powers: 87 per cent of those stopped and searched were wrongly suspected and this may have created much antagonism against the police (see para 3.7-3.15 ante). Claims that stop and search powers are used excessively against ethnic minorities have been regularly made pre-PACE (see Willis, *The Use and Effectiveness and Impact of Police Stop and Search Powers* (1983); Smith and Gray, *Police and People in London* (PSI 1983)). Such claims continue to be made and are now supported by Government figures (Hansard Vol 250, Written Answers 1 Dec 1994, col 842), which suggest that ethnic minorities are over-represented in the stop and search figures: for example 42 per cent of those stopped in the Metropolis were black or Asian, although they comprise only 16 per cent of the population. A similar pattern appears in other areas with a large ethnic minority. It is however, not statistically valid to draw conclusions of discrimination from data of this kind (see Fizgerald et al, *Policing for London* (Willan, 2002)).

PRINCIPLES GOVERNING STOP AND SEARCH

3.18   The new code requires officers to use the powers in a non-discriminatory and responsible manner. If they discriminate on the grounds of race, colour, ethnic origin, nationality or national origin their actions are unlawful under the Race Relations (Amendment) Act 2000 (para 1.1). They must be responsible in their approach, having regard to the dignity of the person stopped and intrusions on liberty must be brief, presumably the restriction must be only that which is necessary in order to exercise the power.

3.19   It is also suggested that unless these principles are adhered to the use of the powers may be drawn into question and their effectiveness in detecting and preventing crime may be undermined.

3.20   Whereas previously accountability principles were set out in the notes for guidance, these are now contained in the main code, para 1.3 states that non compliance with these principles may draw the use of the power into question.

3.21   Significantly, the new codes sets out the justification for the power as,

'The primary purpose of the stop and search powers is to enable officers to allay or confirm suspicions about individuals without exercising their power of arrest.'

It goes on to state that,

'Officers may be required to justify the use or authorisation of such powers, in relation to both individual searches and the overall pattern of their activity in this regard to their supervisors or in court.'

3.22 By including this language in the code rather than in the notes for guidance the message to officers is clear. Not only does the code point out that abuse of the powers is likely to be harmful to police-community relations but also that misuse of the powers can lead to disciplinary action.

3.23 It is no longer permissible to search a person with his or her consent unless a legal power exists. This amendment was introduced to deal with the concerns articulated by ethnic minorities and to remove the ability of the police to circumvent the requirements of reasonable suspicion. Just because there is a power to search does not mean that officers should not seek to gain cooperation and para 3.2 confirms that cooperation must be sought in every case even if the person initially objects to the search.

'the co-operation of the person to be searched should be sought in every case, even if he initially objects to the search. A forcible search may be made only if it has been established that the person is unwilling to co-operate (eg by opening a bag) or resists ...' (Code A, para 3.2)

3.24 In other words if the person objects to a statutory search, further attempts to obtain his co-operation should be made before resorting to the use of reasonable force.

3.25 An essential precondition for the exercise of the stop and search power, except that under s 60 of the CJPOA 1994, is that the constable must have reasonable grounds for suspecting that he or she will find stolen or prohibited articles (s 1 (3) of PACE, Northern Ireland Order 1989 Art 3(3)).

3.26 A constable does not have the power to stop a person in order to find such grounds . This concept of reasonable suspicion (discussed more fully in paras 2.81–2.92, ante)is inherently imprecise and will, as the Code of Practice puts it (para 2.2) depend on the circumstances in each case:

'There must be an objective basis for the suspicion which is based on facts, information and/or intelligence which are relevant to the likelihood of finding an article of a certain kind or in the case of searches under section 43 of the Terrorism Act, 2000 to the likelihood that the person is a terrorist.'

3.27 The point was strikingly made in the first version of the Code of Practice (1985) which stated that the level of suspicion for stop and search must be no less than that required for arrest without warrant.

3.28 Despite being dropped from later versions this remains true and properly observed, is a formidable constraint on the exercise of stop and search powers. It must therefore be more than mere suspicion, a hunch or an instinct.

3.29 A person may not be detained in order to find grounds for a search, nor may a refusal to answer questions provide grounds. A citizen is under no obligation to answer questions (*Rice v Connolly* (1966)). Although such refusal may increase the constable's suspicion and where a police officer has an encounter with a member of the public, without detaining them against their will, reasonable grounds for suspicion emerges, the officer may search the person even though no suspicion existed when the encounter began. (para 2.11)

3.30 The Code makes clear that personal factors such as a person's race, age, appearance or previous convictions cannot be used alone or in combination with each other as a reason for searching a person. Thus generalisations or stereotypical images that certain groups or categories of people are more likely to be involved in criminal activities cannot, without more, amount to grounds justifying stop and search. In order to carry out a search the constable must have:

- reliable supporting intelligence or
- information of some specific behaviour by the person concerned or
- some level of generalisation stemming from the behaviour of a person.

3.31 Paragraph 2.4 states that reasonable suspicion should normally be linked to accurate and reliable intelligence or information describing an article being carried, a suspected offender or a person who has been seen carrying an item of property known to have been recently stolen from premises in the area. Targeting searches in a particular area at specific crime problems is said to produce a number of benefits. These include increased effectiveness, minimising inconvenience to law-abiding members of the public and helps in justifying the use of searches both to those who have been searched and to the general public.

3.32 What this means in practice is that the constable is required to exercise the power sparingly and that reasonable suspicion requires a higher threshold than in the past. 'deal conditions' exist when a number of factors come together; for example where accurate and up-to-date intelligence or information exists and officers are well-informed about crime patterns. (para 2.5)

3.33 However para 2.6 appears to contradict these principles in that it is suggested that

> 'where there is reliable information or intelligence that members of a gang habitually carry knives unlawfully or weapons or controlled drugs, and wear a distinctive item of clothing or other means of identification to indicate their membership of the group or gang, that distinctive item of clothing or other means of identification **may** provide reasonable grounds to stop and search a person.'

3.34   On the one hand officers are advised that a range of factors cumulatively are preferable in establishing reasonable suspicion and then on the other it is suggested that merely *wearing distinctive clothing or other means of identity which indicates membership of a gang* whose members habitually carry weapons or drugs may be sufficient. The note for guidance (note 9) states,

> 'other means of identification might include jewellery, insignias, tattoos or other features which are known to identify members of the particular gang.'

The potential for mistakes in the exercise of this power is great and is compounded by vague guidance.

3.35   Does this mean that Hells Angels or members of Combat 18 are to be searched every time they come into contact with the police? It is submitted that the use of the word 'may' requires more than just information and the wearing of insignia and that the prudent officer would require some more specific information or intelligence than that suggested in para 2.6.

3.36   Where an officer has reasonable grounds to suspect that a person is in 'innocent possession' of a stolen or prohibited article for which he or she is empowered to search, the officer may stop and search that person even though there is no power of arrest. This appears somewhat superfluous but is presumably essential because consensual searches are no longer permissible.

3.37   In all circumstances where an officer who has reasonable grounds for suspicion detains a person in order to search he or she must inform the person that they are being detained for the purpose of search. Before commencing the search the officer may ask questions which may remove the necessity to search. The person must be informed that the grounds no longer exist, no search may take place and the person must be told that, in the absence of any other lawful power to detain, they are free to leave. It should be noted that reasonable grounds for suspicion cannot be provided retrospectively by such questioning (para 2.9).

3.38   Paragraph 2.11 adds a new provision in respect of searches following 'encounters'. It is recognised that police officers will come into contact with people in the ordinary course of their duty and reasonable grounds to justify a search will emerge during such encounters, even though no grounds existed when the encounter began. The person must be informed as soon as the officer decides that he intends to carry out a search in these circumstances. A case which illustrates the potential problems for this provision is *Samuels v Metropolitan Police Comr* (1999, CA) the point at which the officer developed grounds to search was scrutinised. This was a civil action for damages by the defendant who had forcibly resisted an officer who wished to search him for suspected possession of a prohibited article. The defendant's appeal was allowed because there were no grounds to conduct the search when the officer stopped him and the fact that he walked away without answering the officer's questions did not provide grounds for the search.

THE POWER TO STOP

3.39   Concern expressed by the police over what they believed to be an increase in attacks on police officers by persons using guns, knives and other dangerous weapons, coupled with a belief that the requirement of reasonable suspicion needed for a s 1 PACE search was too restrictive, led the Home Secretary to introduce what is now s 60 of the Criminal Justice and Public Order Act 1994. It is essentially a compromise. It permits a stop and search of vehicles and pedestrians for offensive weapons or dangerous implements, which can be carried out under s 1 only if there is reasonable suspicion that such weapons are being carried, without the need for reasonable suspicion, but limits the use of such powers by purpose, locality and time.

3.40   Section 60(1) provides that where an officer of the rank of inspector or above reasonably believes that:
(a)   incidents involving serious violence may take place in any locality in his police area, and that it is expedient to give an authorisation under this section to prevent their occurrence,
(b)   persons are carrying dangerous instruments or offensive weapons in any locality in his police area without good reason
then he may authorise powers in a specific locality and for a specific period which must not exceed 24 hours. The power permits any constable in uniform to stop and search any pedestrian and any vehicle, their drivers and passengers for offensive weapons or dangerous instruments. The period does not have to be the full 24 hours and lesser periods will suffice. However, if the threat persists after the 24-hour period has been authorised, then an officer of or above the rank of superintendent, who believes it is expedient to do so, may extend the period for a further 24 hours. The superintendent must have regard to any offences which have or are reasonably suspected to have been committed which are covered by the activity which is authorised. Before the power is authorised the officer must be satisfied that there is an objective basis to suggest that either people are known to be carrying knives or dangerous instruments in the area or that serious violence is predicted in the future and the code note 11 refers to such matters as intelligence or such information as a history of antagonism between particular groups or previous incidents of violence at or connected with particular events or locations. This power has been used for example in relation to threats of racial violence, one example being after the bombing in Brixton (when 39 people were injured in a racially motivated bomb explosion: see *The Guardian* (30 April 1999)) and is frequently used in areas of London and other cities where there have been an outbreak of shooting incidents. The authorising officer must decide what reasonably constitutes a locality and note 13 of the code states that in deciding this the officer

'may wish to take into account factors such as the nature and venue of the anticipated incident, the number of people who may be in the immediate area of any possible incident, have access to surrounding areas and the anticipated level of violence. He or she should not set a wider area than he believes is necessary for the purpose. Where an officer authorises this power and is below the rank of superintendent he must take steps to notify a superintendent as soon as practicable.'

It is to be noted that only one extension is permitted and therefore further use of the power requires fresh authorisation (note 12). The authorisation and any extensions must be in writing and in circumstances where it is not possible to authorise in advance it must be recorded in writing as soon as practicable.

3.41 In the course of a search under these powers if a constable discovers a dangerous instrument or an article which he has reasonable grounds for suspecting to be an offensive weapon he may seize it. Significantly the section also creates an offence of failing to stop or to stop a vehicle when required to do so by a constable exercising his powers under this section. The offence carries a penalty on summary conviction of imprisonment for a term not exceeding one month or to a fine not exceeding level three on the standard scale or both. A new s 60AA provides powers to require the removal of disguises and where officers are exercising their powers under s 60 or powers authorised under s 60AA(3) they may require the removal of items wholly or mainly worn for the purpose of concealing identity and to seize such items where the officer believes that the person intends to wear them for this purpose. It is to be noted there is no power to stop and search for disguises and the power may only be used where an authorisation has been granted under ss 60 or 60aa. If a person fails to remove an item worn by him or her when required to do so by a constable in the exercise of this power then an offence is committed for which there is the same penalty as for the offence of failing to stop when required to do so under the section. There is no doubt that an officer exercising powers under ss 60 and 60AA do not exercise powers in accordance with the PACE (*DPP v Avery* (2002)).

Persons

3.42 The power to stop and search can be directed against persons of any age (except the Crossbows Act 1987, s 4 (Crossbows (NI) Order 1988, r 6) which applies to persons under 17 reasonably suspected of carrying a crossbow capable of firing a missile or parts thereof). PACE does not contain a specific power to stop persons for the purpose of a search, but there is a power under s 1(2) (Art 3(2)) to detain a person for the purpose of such a search and the power to use reasonable force to do so (see para 3.105, post). This contrasts with the other statutory powers of search (eg s 47 of the Firearms Act 1968; s 23 of the Misuse of Drugs Act 1971), which give a power to stop as does the power under s 60(4) of the CJPOA 1994. Some give a power to detain as well, and others leave the detention power to be implied. Therefore, the power to detain arises, expressly or impliedly, whenever the constable proposes to conduct a search under PACE or any other Act which authorises the search of persons without an arrest. If the reasonable grounds to suspect possession of stolen or prohibited articles arise before the person is stopped, the power to detain arises at the time the person is stopped. However, persons are often stopped by the police simply to inquire about their movements or to seek other information. In these circumstances it is clear that, since there is no general power to stop citizens, still less to detain them, for this purpose (see *Donnelly v Jackman* (1970), *Collins v Wilcock* (1984)), there is no obligation on the citizen to stop when requested to do so by a constable unless the constable has decided to exercise his power to search. This will be apparent from the information which, under s 2 (Art 4), he must convey to a person before he proceeds to a search. It must be remembered that these Notes for Guidance are not part of the Code A (para 1.2) and their breach need not incur the penalty of the exclusion of evidence under s 78 of PACE (Art 76).

3.43   Section 1 of PACE (Art 3) merely authorises the search for, and seizure of, stolen or prohibited articles. There is no need to show that the person was aware of the article or of its nature. For the purposes of prosecution, however, it may well be necessary to establish that the person satisfied the complex requirements of 'possession'. For example, 'possession' in the context of the offence of possession of prohibited drugs has been held to include a mental element which requires knowledge that one has the substance. Thus, in *Lockyer v Gibb* (1967), Lord Parker LCJ said:

> 'If something were slipped into your basket and you had not the vaguest notion that it was there at all you could not possibly be said to be in possession of it.'

3.44   In *Warner v Metropolitan Police Comr* (1969), the House of Lords held that, where a drug is in a container of some kind, D may possess the container knowing there are contents, but not 'possess' the contents where he is mistaken as to the nature of those contents and not merely their quality. The purpose of these decisions is to avoid the conviction of someone upon whose person, or in whose car or premises, prohibited drugs are found but who was unaware of their presence. Since no offence is created by s 1 of PACE (Art 3 of the Order), an offensive weapon slipped into a person's pocket without his knowledge would entitle a stop and search under s 1 (Art 3), but would not necessarily be sufficient 'possession' for the offence under s 1 of the Prevention of Crime Act 1953 or s 139 of the Criminal Justice Act 1988. (See para 3.52-3.55, post, for a discussion of possession of stolen or prohibited articles.) In cases of 'innocent possession' Code A, para 1.7A provides that where a police officer has reasonable grounds to suspect that a person is in innocent possession of a stolen or prohibited article or other item for which he is empowered to search, the power of stop and search exists despite the absence of a power of arrest. However, the officer is then encouraged to obtain the person's co-operation in the search for the article instead of resorting to the use of force.

Vehicles

3.45   A constable in uniform already has a power under s 163 of the Road Traffic Act 1988 to require the driver of a vehicle to stop, but there is considerable doubt whether that power can legitimately be used for non-road traffic purposes (see *Hoffman v*

Thomas (1974)). In *Steel v Goacher* (1983) the Divisional Court held that the stopping of a vehicle may be justified under the general common law duty of the police to prevent criminal activity, subject to there being reasonable grounds to suspect such activity. The power to stop a vehicle may therefore derive from the common law. However, the Government took the view that 'the police have power under the Road Traffic Act to stop a vehicle without qualification as to purpose' (Government Minister House of Commons, Standing Committee E, 13 December 1983, col 339 but one may note that s 60(4) of the CJPOA 1994 seems to contradict this by conferring a power to stop persons and vehicles to search for weapons and dangerous instruments). On this view, s 1(2) (Art 3(2)) of PACE is concerned with the powers to detain a stopped vehicle (thereby clarifying *R v Waterfield and Lynn* (1964) and confirming *Lodwick v Sanders* (1985)) and to search it. The alternative and, it is submitted, preferable view is that s 163 is confined to stops for road traffic offences and that s 1(2) (Art 3(2)) of PACE permits a constable in uniform to detain a vehicle for the purpose of a search and, by implication, to require that the vehicle be stopped. On this latter view, the power under s 163 is unaffected by s 1(2) (Art 3(2)) and the powers will often be used in conjunction with each other. If the constable uses s 163 and the motorist fails to stop, an offence under the Road Traffic Act 1988 is committed. If he uses the s 1 power, a charge of obstruction under s 89 of the Police Act 1996 would be possible. Whichever view is preferred, the drafting of Part I of the Act remains unclear, for though it is headed as 'Powers to stop and search', remarkably no specific power to stop persons or vehicles is mentioned, save in relation to s 4 (Art 6) (road checks) and s 6 (Art 8) (statutory undertakers). As regards the other statutory powers of search, some bestow an express power to stop persons or vehicles (s 60(4) of the CJPOA 1994, see para 3.67, post) or vehicles (Firearms Act 1968, Misuse of Drugs Act 1971, Sporting Events (Control of Alcohol etc) Act 1985), whilst others are silent on the matter and the above discussion is relevant.

3.46 'Vehicle' includes vessels, aircraft and hovercraft (s 2(10), Art 4(11)). A 'vessel' includes 'any ship, boat, raft or other apparatus constructed or adapted for floating on water' (s 118(1), Art 2(2)). No further definition was considered necessary because 'one would know a vehicle when one saw it' (Minister of State, Standing Committee J, 14 December 1982, col 52). As the case law on other Acts illustrates, this is too simplistic a view. Apart, obviously, from motor vehicles (cf s 185 of the Road Traffic Act 1988, s 136 of the Road Traffic Regulation Act 1984) the term includes trams, bicycles, horse-drawn carts, handcarts and perambulators. Significantly, s 185(1) of the Road Traffic Act 1988 defines a 'trailer' as 'a vehicle drawn by a motor vehicle' so that where, for example, a caravan is drawn by a motor vehicle, two vehicles are involved. An empty poultry shed drawn by a tractor is a vehicle (*Garner v Burr* (1950)), as is an office hut towed by a motor vehicle (*Horn v Dobson* (1933)) and a movable stall on wheels (*Boxer v Snelling* (1972)). In Boxer it was said that where there is no statutory definition of 'vehicle' the determination of a borderline case depended not only on the construction and nature of the contrivance but also the circumstances of its use. It is thus a question of fact in each case. For horse-drawn vehicles, the horse is likely to be seen as part of the vehicle but, where ridden, the Act (like the Road Traffic Acts but unlike the Wildlife and Countryside Act 1981, s 19, which refers to 'anything that the person may be using') makes no reference to 'animal'. In some rural areas a horse might still be regarded as a 'vehicle' in line with Boxer's reference to the individual circumstances; however, if 'vehicle' is interpreted, as it was in Boxer, according to the *Shorter Oxford English Dictionary*, as 'a means of conveyance provided with wheels or runners for the carriage of persons or goods', then articles carried on the animal, for example in saddlebags, cannot be the subject of a stop and search.

3.47   A hovercraft is a motor vehicle for some road traffic purposes and if used on a road may be stopped by a uniformed constable. Searching of stationary aircraft is implied by s 2(10) (Art 4(11)) but can only apply to aircraft landing or parked in public places as defined by s 1(1), (4) and (5) (Art 3(1), (4) and (5)). Other statutory powers of stop and search do not define 'vehicle' but clearly an aircraft qualifies and, since most of these powers can be exercised anywhere, the aircraft need not be parked in a public place (eg a search under the Misuse of Drugs Act 1971 of a plane landing on a private airstrip or field). A constable or specified airport official has the power to stop and search aircraft at specified aerodromes for firearms, explosives and other dangerous articles (s 13 of the Aviation Security Act 1982), whilst a constable can board and search aircraft for anything stolen or unlawfully obtained (s 27 of the 1982 Act). Under s 163 of the Customs and Excise Management Act 1979, Customs and Excise officials (and constables) have the power to stop and search vehicles, vessels and aircraft for goods in respect of which they suspect excise offences are being or have been committed. Section 163(3), which applies the section to aircraft, imposes a limitation on the exercise of the stop and search power which 'shall not be available in respect of aircraft which are airborne'.

Vehicles as premises

3.48   The wide definition of a vehicle can include many forms of mobile homes, such as touring or gypsy caravans, caravanettes and houseboats. If such vehicles are travelling or are situated in 'public places' (as defined and explained by s 1(1), (4) and (5), Art 3(1), (4) and (5) – see paras 3.86-3.87, post), eg lay-bys and temporary mooring berths, they can be stopped and searched on reasonable suspicion under s 1 (Art 3). It is arguable that caravans, houseboats and the like, which remain on a permanent site, cease to be 'vehicles' for the purposes of s 1 (Art 3) and, in any event, such sites may not fall within the ambit of public place as defined by s 1(1) (Art 3(3)). It should be noted, however, that vehicles also qualify as 'premises' for the purpose of searches under PACE (s 23, Art 25) eg entry and search in order to make an arrest (s 17, Art 19) or after an arrest under s 18 or 32 (Art 20 or 34). An important implication of this broad definition of 'premises' is that the wide powers of seizure under s 19 (Art 21) (general power of seizure whilst on premises) can be exercised during a lawful stop and search. Thus, when vehicles are searched under s 1 (Art 3), evidence of any offence can be seized if it is necessary to prevent its concealment, loss, damage, alteration or destruction (s 19(3), Art 21(3)), even though the power of seizure for s 1 is limited to 'stolen or prohibited' articles (s 1(6), Art 3(6)). If, on the other hand, the stop and search is exercised unlawfully, any evidence thus obtained may be excluded (see further para 2.125, ante).

Unattended vehicles

3.49 By implication from s 2(6) of PACE (Art 4(7)) a constable may search an unattended vehicle under the PACE or other statutory powers. He can use reasonable force to do so (s 117, Art 88). The vehicle must, of course, be in a 'public place' and, while that is widely defined (s 1(1), s 1(5), Art 3(1), (5)) excludes the possibility of a person's vehicle being searched while parked on a drive in his garden or in a yard or other premises occupied with, and used for the purpose of, a dwelling. Section 1(5) (Art 3(5)) only applies, however, to vehicles belonging to those residing in such premises or parked there with the consent of the resident. If, for example, D, who resides elsewhere, were to park his car on P's driveway without his consent, the vehicle could be searched, assuming that there are reasonable grounds to suspect that it contains stolen or prohibited articles. (As to the procedure to be followed after the search of unattended vehicles, see para 3.114, post.)

'Anything which is in or on a vehicle' (s 1(2)(a)(ii), Art 3(2)(a)(ii))

3.50 The stop and search power extends to 'anything in or on a vehicle'. This clearly includes such inanimate items as a toolbox or luggage in the boot or on a roof rack. It does not, however, include persons who are in the vehicle. If they are to be searched, there must be reasonable grounds to suspect that they, as opposed to the vehicle itself, are in possession of stolen or prohibited articles. The distinction is far from academic. For example, the police may have information that a youth, whose description fits D, has threatened someone with a bayonet which he carried in the boot of his car. Some hours later D is seen driving his car and carrying three passengers. There would be reasonable grounds to search the vehicle and D, but not the three passengers unless there are further grounds for suspicion such as D being seen to pass something to a back-seat passenger.

THE OBJECT OF THE SEARCH

3.51 As already noted, s 1 of PACE (Art 3) merely allows the police to search for evidence of offences, viz the possession of stolen or prohibited articles or blades. Reasonable suspicion that the articles are stolen (para 3.52) or prohibited (para 3.55) or blades (para 3.66) is sufficient to authorise seizure (s 1(3) and (6), Art 3(3) and (6)). The mere finding of them and/or the person's response to inquiries will suffice to give rise to reasonable suspicion of an offence and an arrest or summons may follow. Prosecution will then depend on the circumstances and terms of the relevant statute.

Stolen articles

3.52   In the absence of a definition, it must be assumed that 'stolen' bears the same meaning as that given to 'stolen goods' in the Theft Act 1968 (Theft Act (NI) 1969), since any offence resulting from the possession of a stolen article will be an offence under the 1968 Act. Under s 24 of that Act, stolen goods:

(i)   need not have been stolen in England or Wales;

(ii)   cover not only the original property but also any other property representing it either directly or indirectly. Thus, if D1 steals goods and sells or exchanges them to D2, both are in possession of stolen goods;

(iii)   includes those obtained by deception or blackmail.

3.53   The decision of the House of Lords in *R v Gomez* (1993), which removes the distinction between theft and obtaining by deception, means that, with the exception of land, 'stolen' must now include obtaining by deception so that any dishonestly obtained property is within the ambit of a s 1 stop and search.

3.54   Possession will usually be evidence of one of the offences under the Theft Act 1968 (as regards 'unwitting possession', see para 3.65, post).

Prohibited articles

3.55   These fall into three types:

(a)   offensive weapons (s 1(7)(a), Art 3(7)(a)) and a person who has with him in a public place any such weapon may be guilty of an offence under s 1 of the Prevention of Crime Act 1953;

(b)   articles for theft etc (s 1(7)(b)), the carrying of which may constitute an offence under s 25 of the Theft Act 1968 (see 3.20, post); and

(c)   articles made, adapted or intended for use in criminal damage which may constitute an offence under s 3 of the Criminal Damage Act 1971.

Offensive weapon

3.56   This is defined in s 1(9) (Art 3(10)) as:

'any article ... made or adapted for use for causing injury to persons ... or ... intended by the person having it with him for such use by him or by some other person'.

3.57   The definition is identical to that in s 1(4) of the Prevention of Crime Act 1953 (as amended by the Public Order Act 1986) and reference can be made to case law on that Act. There are three categories.

(i)   'Articles made for causing injury' – The question here is whether the article is an offensive weapon per se, ie that its purpose (of causing injury) is so patent as to require no elucidation to a court. Examples are a bayonet, cosh, telescopic truncheon, a police officer's truncheon (unless legitimately carried, see *Houghton v Chief Constable of Greater Manchester* (1987)), a knuckleduster (dicta in *R v Petrie* (1961)), a flick knife (*R v Simpson* (1983)), sword stick (*R v Butler* (1988)), and a rice-flail (*Copus v DPP* (1989)). They clearly include firearms and there is thus an overlap with the stop and search power under s 47 of the Firearms Act 1968. Injury in s 1(9) may be interpreted to include shock and alarm (in *R v Miller* (1954) actual bodily harm in s 47 of the Offences Against the Person Act 1861 was held to include an hysterical and nervous condition resulting from an assault on the basis that injury to the state of a man's mind is serious bodily harm). If not, a search for imitation firearms must be justified under the 1968 Act. Explosives are not specifically mentioned. They qualify as offensive weapons in this category if made up as a bomb, but otherwise qualify as category (iii) weapons (see below). In so far as the article is sharply pointed or has a blade exceeding three inches, there is also an overlap with the stop and search power supplied by the Criminal Justice Act 1988, s 140 (see para 3.66, post).

(ii) 'Articles adapted for use for causing injury' – Again the question is whether the article is offensive per se. They would include a chair leg studded with nails, a peaked-cap with razor blades embedded in the peak, a sharpened comb, a deliberately broken bottle or glass. 'Adapted' implies a deliberate decision to change the character of the article to make it suitable for the purpose of causing injury (cf *Maddox v Storer* (1963)). If D were to knock over a milk bottle while backing away from a would-be assailant and then picked up the broken bottle he would not, it is submitted, have 'adapted' the bottle for use for causing injury and, whether or not it is an offensive weapon, will depend on the intent with which D has it with him, for it may then fall within the third category.

(iii) 'Articles intended to cause injury' – The purpose of category (i) and (ii) weapons is self-evident and the prosecution needs only to prove possession of them in a public place. In this category, however, it must go further and show that the carrier intended to use the weapon to cause injury (eg a washing-up liquid bottle filled with acid, cf *R v Formosa* (1990) where the bottle could not qualify as a designed or adapted weapon under the Firearms Act 1968, but could fall within the category (iii) under discussion). It is here that the greatest practical difficulties may arise, for almost all articles are capable of becoming an offensive weapon, from a car jack to a drum of pepper. The facts of each case will of course vary and much may depend upon the citizen's explanation to the police. Thus, in *Buckley v DPP* (1988) the police relied upon the facts that a machete (not offensive per se) wrapped in newspaper had been hidden in the car, and his story that he used the machete to cut grass (though other garden tools in the car were not hidden) was unbelievable. In contrast, in *Southwell v Chadwick* (1986) it was held that a machete in a sheath and a catapult were not offensive weapons per se and the Crown would therefore have to disprove D's explanation that he used them lawfully to kill squirrels to feed wild birds which he kept. Moreover, for the purposes of the Prevention of Crime Act 1953 the intention must be to cause injury to others and not to oneself (*R v Fleming* (1989)); thus, if the same view is taken of s 1(9) of

PACE (Art 3(10)) and the police are told that D has set off to commit suicide and they intercept him, removal of his weapon would have to be justified on the constable's common law duty to preserve the peace and not the s 1 stop and search power. It follows that if a constable stops a car for the purpose of a search under PACE, assuming reasonable grounds for suspicion, and finds in the boot various tools, car jack, handle, etc, these would not be prohibited articles unless there is some evidence of an intent to use them to cause injury to others. If D were driving to P's house intent on assaulting P with the car jack, and somehow the constable knew this, the car jack would then be a prohibited article, an offensive weapon. But in such a case the constable already has a power to arrest D in order to prevent the commission by him of an offence with that weapon, and a power to search the person and car following the arrest (ss 25 and 32 of PACE, Arts 27 and 34). The s 1 power therefore adds nothing to the constable's powers in such a case. Moreover, unless a constable can see the article or has some specific information about the person, vehicle or circumstances, he will not have the necessary reasonable suspicion to employ s 1 (Art 3). The reasonable suspicion must arise beforehand, and justify the search. The search cannot be justified afterwards when articles are discovered. It is highly likely therefore that in practice persons will be stopped either at random or on a lesser suspicion than 'reasonable grounds to suspect', based on surrounding circumstances and the constable's experience, for example, of football 'hooligans'.

Articles carried for self-defence

3.58   It has been held that it is not a reasonable excuse for carrying an offensive weapon that it is carried for self-defence unless the person shows that there was an 'imminent, particular threat affecting the particular circumstances in which the weapon was carried' (*Evans v Hughes* (1972) and see also *A-G's Reference (No 2 of 1983)* (1984)). Thus, in *Malnik v DPP* (1989) D possessed a rice-flail because he feared that X would become violent when asked to return some property. This was held not to be a reasonable excuse. It is the policy of the law to discourage citizens from embarking on such expeditions when the risk of violence is obvious. D should call the police instead. Anti-rape sprays, some of which are offensive weapons within categories (i) and (ii), can never, it seems, be lawfully carried since they are carried with intent to cause injury, even though the intent is conditional upon being attacked. CS gas, Mace sprays and electric stun guns the size of a cigarette packet which are carried by many American women, are clearly offensive weapons. If the woman is in fact attacked, the use of the spray might be seen as reasonable self-defence under s 3 of the Criminal Law Act 1967. Even security guards employed by the various security firms are not lawfully entitled to carry truncheons or weapons as a matter of routine (*R v Spanner* (1973)), nor are taxi-drivers who carry coshes in their cabs (cf *Patterson v Block* (1984)). Similarly, a shopkeeper or store detective can be searched, at least when on the public side of the counter. If he is behind the counter, the power to search will only arise if he is still in a 'public place' as defined in s 1(1) (Art 3(1)). In *Anderson v Miller* (1976), a firearm placed under the counter was held still to be within a public place for the purposes of the Firearms Act 1968 and a similarly broad interpretation would be possible under the 1984 Act (see further para 3.89, post).

3.59 The phrase 'or by some other person' in s 1(9) (Art 3(10)) of PACE is clearly intended to authorise the search for and seizure of an offensive weapon which is carried by a person who has no intention to use it himself but which he is carrying for someone who has. If, therefore
(a) D1 and D2 are together, and
(b) D2 knows that D1 has a weapon with him for D2's use for causing injury, and
(c) D2 has immediate control over it in that he can call for it when he wants to use it,

3.60 then D1 can be searched under PACE and D2 would have the weapon 'with him' for the purpose of prosecution under the Prevention of Crime Act 1953 (*R v Byast* (1955); *R v Webley* (1967)). In such a case D1 cannot be charged jointly with D2 since the offence under the 1953 Act requires that the person who has the article with him must intend to use it for causing injury. However, he could be charged with aiding and abetting D2 in the commission of the offence. Section 1(7)(b)(ii) (Art 3(7)(b)(ii)) similarly goes further than s 25(1) of the Theft Act 1968 (s 24 of the Theft Act (NI) 1969), which refers to articles which D 'has with him', by including within the definition of 'prohibited articles' articles carried by D1 for use by D2. As with s 1(9) this permits the searching of D1 when he is reasonably suspected of carrying a prohibited article for someone else's use. In some cases the parties will be jointly engaged in the criminal enterprise so that both may be arrested even though only one carried prohibited articles.

Housebreaking implements etc

3.61 Section 1(7) and (8) of PACE (Art 3(7), (8)) combine the words of s 25(1) and (3) of the Theft Act 1968 (Theft Act (NI) 1969) in defining a prohibited article as an article made or adapted for use in the course of, or in connection with, or intended for use in:
(i) burglary;
(ii) theft;
(iii) an offence under s 12 of the Theft Act 1968 (Theft Act (NI) 1969) (taking motor vehicle or other conveyance without authority); or
(iv) an offence under s 15 of that Act (obtaining property by deception).

3.62 Possession of such an article is an offence under s 25 of the Theft Act (s 24 of the 1969 Act) and the stop and search power is intended to facilitate the detection of such an offence. As has been seen (para 3.19), s 1(7)(b)(ii) (Art 3(7)(b)(ii)) goes further than the offence under s 25 of the 1968 Act (s 24 of the 1969 Act) by including articles carried by a person with the intention that some other person should use them. (NB: the NI Order also refers to r 172 of the Road Traffic (NI) Order 1981. This contains the offence of taking a motor vehicle, trailer or pedal cycle without consent. Section 12 of the 1969 Act refers only to 'other conveyances'.)

3.63   Although s 1(7)(b) of PACE (Art 3(7)(b)) and s 25(3) of the 1968 and 1969 Acts use the phrase 'made or adapted', there are few articles which are made for the criminal purposes set out in the Act. More often, articles which are made for legitimate purposes are used for illegitimate ones, eg skeleton keys, picklocks, jemmies. In each case the important question is the use for which the article is intended rather than whether it is made or adapted for a particular purpose. Some articles, such as skeleton keys, call 'for explanation by the accused' (Criminal Law Revision Committee, Eighth Report, para 151) and the absence of an explanation together with the circumstances of possession will normally arouse reasonable suspicion and may amount to evidence from which a court or jury can infer the necessary criminal intention (s 25(3) of the Theft Act 1968 and see now s 36 of the Criminal Justice and Public Order Act 1994 which permits proper inferences to be drawn from a failure to account for possession of objects).

3.64   There are, however, many more articles in daily legitimate use which can be lawfully employed within s 1(7)(b) (Art 3(7)(b)) but for which the intention to use them unlawfully will be extremely difficult to discern. For example, gloves, credit cards which can be used to open certain locks or obtain property by deception (*R v Lambie* (1982)), sellotape which may be used to prevent noise when glass is broken and sandwiches or bottles of wine which may be used to cheat one's employer by selling one's own goods rather than his (obtaining by deception: *R v Rashid* (1977); *R v Doukas* (1978)). There may be circumstances in which a constable could have reasonable suspicion for s 1 (Art 3) purposes, for example, a person seen wearing gloves on a hot summer's evening in a darkened alleyway. In the more normal course of events, however, the wearing of gloves could not justify such a suspicion. It follows that if the stop and search powers are to be used widely, the police will have to resort to a random selection or to a lesser standard of suspicion, followed by the discovery of an article, arrest and interrogation in order to prove the criminal intention. Again, the initial stop and search may be justified in fact, but not in law.

Possession in the context of the relevant offences

3.65   As was earlier indicated (para 3,43, ante), s 1 of PACE (Art 3) is not dependent upon the person 'possessing' an article but, in the context of the particular offence arising from seizure of the stolen or prohibited articles, a narrower and more complex question of proving 'possession' is called for. In particular, possession may be interpreted as requiring knowledge that the article is in one's possession (cf *Lockyer v Gibb* (1967) and *Warner v Metropolitan Police Comr* (1969), ante).

(i)   Unwitting possession of stolen goods – s 22 of the Theft Act 1968 states that a person handles stolen goods if, knowing or believing them to be stolen, he dishonestly receives the goods (receiving is the relevant form of handling in this context though there are many other forms). It is for the prosecution to prove knowledge or belief. 'Knowing' requires actual knowledge that the goods are stolen while 'believing' implies that there would be such knowledge unless D deliberately closed his eyes to the circumstances. Thus, it is perfectly proper for the judge to direct a jury that they may find that D knew or believed the goods to be stolen because he deliberately closed his eyes to the circumstances (*R v Pethick* (1980); *R v Griffiths* (1974); *R v Grainge* (1974)). It follows that in a case of 'unwitting possession' the stolen goods can be the object of a search under the s 1 (Art 3) power and may be seized, but no offence of handling is committed.

(ii) Possession of a prohibited weapon or blade – Section 1 of the Prevention of Crime Act 1953, s 25 of the Theft Act 1968, s 139 of the Criminal Justice Act 1988 (blades) and s 3 of the Crossbows Act 1987, use the phrase 'has with him' rather than 'has in his possession' and it may be that the former bears a narrower meaning than the latter. For 'possession' can include articles which are at home or elsewhere but still in 'possession' of the person, while 'has with him' can relate only to those articles immediately to hand. This is in fact the distinction drawn between the offence under s 16 of the Firearms Act 1968 (Firearms Act (NI) 1969) (possessing a firearm with intent to endanger life) and s 18 of that Act (having with him a firearm with intent to commit an indictable offence). Under s 18 mere possession, for example having the firearm at home intending to commit an indictable offence in the future, is not sufficient, he must have the firearm with him while in the course of committing the offence; whereas under s 16 such possession with intent to kill is sufficient. As for possession under s 1 of the Firearms Act, the strict view in Warner, above, has been adopted: see *R v Waller* (1991). 'Has with him' has also been interpreted as a narrower form of possession requiring knowledge that the person has the article with him (*R v Cugullere* (1961) and see *R v Russell* (1985)). Such an interpretation is, it is submitted, more in keeping with the mischief at which the statutes are aimed. However, in the context of unlawful possession of drugs, the Court of Appeal in *R v Martindale* (1986) has refused to follow this view and has held that a person remains in possession of articles even if he has forgotten about them (eg an offensive weapon in a car's glove compartment or boot which the driver knowingly put there some years ago but has now forgotten about). This view has been persuasively challenged (see [1986] Crim LR 737). Certainly unwitting possession (in the sense of an article secretly dropped into a person's handbag or pocket) is insufficient. Whichever view (*Russell* or *Martindale*) is accepted, the important point is that such questions do not matter for the purposes of stop and search under s 1 of PACE.

Articles which have a blade or are sharply pointed

3.66 This is the fourth category of article for which the police can stop and search under PACE. By virtue of s 139 of the Criminal Justice Act 1988 it is an offence to carry in a public place any article 'which has a blade or is sharply pointed' (except for a folding pocket knife with a blade of less than three inches). Unlike the Prevention of Crime Act 1953, there is no need for the prosecution to establish that the weapon is offensive per se or is intended to cause injury. Instead the burden lies on the defence to show a 'good reason or lawful authority' for carrying the article (eg as a sportsman, as part of a national or religious costume, a chef with his knives en route to work, a carpenter). To assist in the detection of this offence, s 140 of the 1988 Act added to PACE a power for a constable to stop and search for such articles (Art 3(2)(a)(iii) and (9) of the NI Order). Examples are a Stanley knife, butterfly knife, carving knife, push dagger, handclaw, footclaw, blowpipe, sharpened comb and knitting needle. They obviously overlap with offensive weapons prohibited by the Prevention of Crime Act 1953 (see para 3.56, ante). The matter is important when it comes to charging the individual since (a) the maximum penalty is higher under the 1953 Act, and (b) the prosecution has the easier task in court if it uses the 1988 Act (see above); but at street level the same problem confronts the constable, that is, unless he is exercising the s 60 CJPOA 1994 power, discussed below, he must have reasonable suspicion that D has with him an offensive weapon (1953 Act) or prohibited blade (1988 Act) before he can stop and search D. Rarely will there be such clear information as to satisfy that requirement.

POWERS TO STOP AND SEARCH FOR OFFENSIVE WEAPONS AND DANGEROUS IMPLEMENTS (CRIMINAL JUSTICE AND PUBLIC ORDER ACT 1994, s 60)

The authorisation

3.67   Concern expressed by the police over what they believed to be an increase in attacks on police officers by persons using guns, knives and other dangerous weapons, coupled with a belief that the requirement of reasonable suspicion needed for a s 1PACE Act search was too restrictive, led the Home Secretary to introduce what is now s 60 of the Criminal Justice and Public Order Act 1994. It is essentially a compromise. It permits a stop and search of vehicles and pedestrians for offensive weapons or dangerous implements, which can be carried out under s 1 only if there is reasonable suspicion that such weapons are being carried without the need for reasonable suspicion, but limits the use of such powers by purpose, locality and time.

3.68   Section 60(1) provides that where a superintendent or above (or a chief inspector or inspector if there is a reasonable belief that violent incidents are imminent and no superintendent is available (sub-s (2)) reasonably believes that:
(a)   incidents involving serious violence may take place in the locality; and
(b)   it is expedient to do so to prevent their occurrence,
he may authorise the exercise of the stop and search power provided by sub-s (4) at any place within a specified locality for a period not exceeding 24 hours. This period may be extended for a further six hours if the authorising officer or a superintendent thinks it is expedient to do so, having regard to offences which have, or are reasonably suspected to have, been committed in connection with any incident falling within the authorisation (sub-s (3)). It is clear from sub-s (1) that the period authorised may be less than 24 hours but the wording of sub-s (3) makes it clear that six hours can only be added to the period authorised originally. Thus if the authorisation is for 12 hours it can be only be continued for a total of 18 hours. If the circumstances which justified the original authorisation continue beyond that time there seems to be no reason why

a fresh authorisation cannot be given. In practice, if there is doubt about the period required, it may be tempting to authorise 24 hours and call the operation off if the circumstances no longer warrant the exercise of these powers. However, Code A 1.8 adds a requirement that the period authorised shall be no longer than appears reasonably necessary to prevent, or try to prevent, incidents of serious violence. For example, where serious violence may be anticipated before, during and after a football match an authorisation may cover a period some hours before and after such a match. Any authorisation must be given in writing and signed by the authorising officer. It must specify the locality in which and the period during which the stop and search powers are exercisable and any extension must also be given in writing. Where it is not practicable to give the authorisation or extension in writing, it must be recorded in writing as soon as it is practicable to do so.

The stop and search power

3.69 Subsection (4) confers on any constable in uniform power:
(a) to stop any pedestrian and search him or anything on him or carried by him for offensive weapons or dangerous implements;
(b) to stop any vehicle and search the vehicle, its driver and any passenger for offensive weapons or dangerous implements.

('Vehicle' includes a caravan as defined in s 29 of the Caravan Sites and Control of Development Act 1960 (sub-s (11)) and the section also applies (with necessary modifications) to ships, aircraft and hovercraft (sub-s (7)).)

3.70 'Dangerous instruments' means instruments which have a blade or are sharply pointed; 'offensive weapon' has the same meaning as in s 1(9) of PACE 1984, discussed in paras 3.66, ante (sub-s (11)).

3.71 One may note, that unlike the s 1 power, a constable in uniform has a specific power to stop persons and vehicles; there is no need to rely on s 163 of the Road Traffic Act 1988 in order to stop a vehicle. Failure to stop or to stop the vehicle is an offence under sub-s (8), considered below.

3.72 As indicated earlier, this power may be exercised without the need for any suspicion, reasonable or otherwise. Subsection (5) states that:

'A constable may, in the exercise of those powers, stop any person or vehicle and make any search he thinks fit whether or not he has any grounds for suspecting that the person or vehicle is carrying weapons or articles of that kind.'

3.73 This only applies to the power to search for offensive weapons and dangerous instruments under s 60(4) of the 1994 Act. The apparent width of the phrase 'any search he thinks fit' is limited by Code A 1.5 which applies the provisions of Code A to searches under s 60. Code A 3.5 restricts searches in public to a superficial examination of outer clothing. This paragraph restates s 2(9)(a) of PACE which states that the power under s 1 (and now s 60) does not authorise a requirement to remove more than an outer coat, jacket or gloves but implies that there is a power to require more clothing to be removed in private, eg a police van or police station if nearby. It is, however, arguable that there is no such power, certainly not in PACE, though it may be done with consent. A more extensive search than is permitted by s 1 of PACE or s 60 above should be carried out at a police station following an arrest. The danger is that under s 60 there may be no reasonable suspicion to justify an arrest and the phrase 'any search he thinks fit' may be seen as justifying a more extensive search in private. Even if this is so the purpose of the search must be borne in mind. Weapons of violence are hardly likely to be concealed about the person in places where the 'pat down' search will not reveal them. This search power may operate alongside the s 1 of PACE, or other statutory powers of stop and search. The manner and extent of the search should be the same whichever power is relied upon, the only significant difference being the need for reasonable grounds to suspect possession of whatever is to be searched for under PACE and other statutory powers, but not under s 60.

3.74   Section 60(6) of the 1994 Act provides a power to seize dangerous implements or articles found following a search which are reasonably suspected to be offensive weapons. Subsection (12) makes it clear that this power is in addition to, and not in derogation of, any existing power. Thus within the authorised period and locality the s 1 power, and all the other stop and search powers, apply subject to reasonable suspicion, alongside the s 60 power, whereas outside the authorised period and locality all the other powers are available while the s 60 power is not.

3.75   Unlike the s 1 power a person who fails to stop or (as the case may be) to stop the vehicle when required to do so by a constable in the exercise of this power commits an offence punishable on summary conviction by imprisonment for a term not exceeding one month or a fine not exceeding level 3 on the standard scale or both. There is no power of arrest but the power to arrest under s 25 of PACE will be available if a general arrest condition is satisfied, eg the person refuses to give his name and address (see para 5.62, post).

3.76   As mentioned above, this power could be used as part of the policing of certain football matches and relieve the police of the difficulty imposed by the requirement of reasonable cause to suspect that particular persons are carrying prohibited articles etc. However, there must be reasonable cause to believe that incidents involving serious violence may take place on the occasion of the particular match. This is a higher threshold than reasonable cause to suspect, and the adjective 'reasonable' imports an objective standard which in this context will require a recent record of serious violence among the supporters of the particular football club or clubs (see para 2.90, ante).

Information and records

3.77   Sections 2 and 3 of PACE and Code A 2.4, 3 and 4 set out the procedure for the conduct of all searches, the information which a constable must take reasonable steps to give to the driver of any vehicle to be searched (but not the passengers) and to any pedestrian and the records to be made after the search. These provisions apply to a s 60 search and are discussed at paras 3.100 to 3.104, post. Section 60(10) of the 1994 Act (and Code A 4.7) expressly state the entitlement of the driver of a vehicle stopped to a written statement that the vehicle was stopped under the section if they apply for such a statement within 12 months of the date of the stop. A pedestrian may similarly obtain such a statement within 12 months of being stopped and searched. The wording of s 60(10) suggests that such a statement must be supplied whether or not the vehicle is searched, whereas the pedestrian is only entitled to such a written statement if he is stopped and searched. Code A 4.7A suggests the reverse: that the driver of a vehicle is entitled to a written notice that they have been stopped under s 60 within 12 months of the vehicle being searched, rather than stopped as s 60(10) states; while the pedestrian may obtain such a notice if he is stopped, not stopped and searched as s 60(10) states. Code A, Note of Guidance 4C makes it clear that the s 60(10) written statement means a record that the person or vehicle was stopped under s 60. The object is, it seems, to entitle those stopped under the s 60 power to a written notice confirming this. If either a vehicle or a pedestrian is stopped and searched under any statutory power this will be recorded on the national search record. The s 60(10) requirement would appear to be in addition to the entitlement to a copy of the national record of the search under s 3(8) of PACE and Code A 2.6, but Code A 4.7 states that it may form part of a national search record (so that both requirements are contained in the same document) or it can be supplied as a separate document which, in the case of a vehicle, can be required if it was stopped under s 60, though not in fact searched.

PREVENTION OF TERRORISM – POWER TO STOP AND SEARCH PERSONS AND VEHICLES: TERRORISM ACT 2000, ss 43-46

3.78   Section 43 (1) of the Terrorism Act 2000 empowers a constable to stop and search a person whom he reasonably suspects to be a terrorist to discover whether he has in his possession anything which may constitute evidence that he is a terrorist. The search under this section must be carried out by someone of the same sex.

3.79   Section 44 of the Terrorism Act 2000 provides a more random power provided it is authorised by the appropriate senior police officer.

3.80   Section 44 (1) confers on any constable in uniform power:
(a)   to stop any vehicle (which includes ships, aircraft , hovercraft , train or vessel (s121);
(b)   to search any vehicle, its driver or any passenger for articles of the kind which could be used for a purpose connected with the commission, preparation or instigation of acts of terrorism as defined above;
(c)   to stop any pedestrian and search anything carried by him for articles described above.

3.81   Section 45 (1)(b) provides that a constable may stop any vehicle or person and make any search he thinks fit whether or not he has any grounds for suspecting that the vehicle or person is carrying articles of the kind referred to (see the similarly worded s 60(5) of the CJPOA 1994 discussed at para 3.72 above).

3.82   Where it appears to a commander or above in the Metropolitan or City of London Police, or an assistant chief constable or above in other forces, that it is expedient to do so in order to prevent acts of terrorism, he may give an authorisation that the powers to stop and search vehicles or persons conferred by this section shall be exercisable at any place within his areas or a specified locality for a specified period not exceeding 28 days (s 46)

(a)   While the authorisation under s 46(2) may last up to 28 days, the person giving the authorisation is required under s 46(3) to inform the Secretary of State as soon as is reasonably practicable. If the Secretary of State does not confirm or substitute an earlier period of authorisation within 48 hours the authorisation ceases to have effect after 48 hours. The Secretary of State may also cancel the authorisation at any specified time (s 46(6)). This provision introduces an element of political control into the exercise of what is after all a sweeping power. Notwithstanding the failure of the Secretary of State to approve the authorisation the lawfulness of the initial period of 48 hours is not called into question (s 46(4)(b)).

(b)   Though the powers may be exercised 'at any place within his locality or a specified locality' this must mean any place or locality where the police officer is lawfully entitled to be.

3.83   Authorisation must be in writing and signed by the authorising officer (s 44(5)). The driver of a vehicle (but not a passenger) and any pedestrian stopped under this section are entitled to a written statement that the vehicle or they were stopped under this section if they apply for one within 12 months of the date of the stop (s 45 (6) and Code A 4.7A). Code A 1.5 applies the provisions of that Code to stops and searches under this section. It follows that requirements of ss 2 and 3 of PACE, information and records, apply to this power, but if the inquiries are linked to the investigation of terrorism the constable need not give his name, but he shall give his warrant or other identification number and the police station to which he is attached.

3.84   One may note the following.

(a)   There is a specific power to stop vehicles and persons. A failure to stop or (as the case may be) to stop the vehicle; or the wilful obstruction of a constable in the exercise of these powers is an offence (s47(1), punishable on summary conviction to imprisonment for a maximum of six months or a level 5 fine or both. No power of arrest is provided but s 25 of PACE provides such a power if an arrest condition is satisfied. In *R v Redman* (1994) the Court of Appeal held that there was a common law power of arrest for obstruction of the police in the execution of their duty where its nature was such that it actually caused, or was likely to cause, a breach of the peace, or was calculated to prevent the lawful arrest of another. This may provide an additional or alternative power of arrest in such circumstances.

(b)   The driver of a vehicle and any passenger may be searched and s 44(2) permits the search of a pedestrian and anything carried by him

'Those new powers will help to safeguard the public against the dual threats of vehicle bombs and small devices carried by individual terrorists.' (Hansard, Common, 11 January 1994, col 30)

In *R v Lucien* (1995) it was held that s 78(2) of the Customs and Excise Management Act 1979, which authorises the search of 'anything carried with' a person entering or leaving the UK, meant carried by sea, air or train, and permitted the search of the shoes of a passenger arriving at Gatwick by train. The court pointed out that there are specific powers to search the person's clothing and warned against using s 78(2) of the CEMA 1979 instead of those specific PTA powers.

3.85 Section 57(1) of the Terrorism Act 2000 creates an offence of possessing any article in circumstances giving rise to a reasonable suspicion that the article is in the person's possession for a purpose connected with the commission, preparation or instigation of acts of terrorism. It is a defence for the person to prove, on the balance of probabilities, that at the time of the alleged offence the article was not in his possession for the purposes of terrorism. However, if he and the article were both present in any premises (and 'premises' includes a vehicle: s 121 Terrorism Act 2000); or the article was in premises occupied or habitually used by him other than as a member of the public, the court may accept the fact proved as sufficient evidence of his possessing that article at the time unless it is further proved (by him) that he did not at that time know of its presence in the premises, or if he did know that he had no control over it. The offence is an arrestable offence within s 24 of PACE being punishable on indictment by up to ten years' imprisonment or a fine or both, and on summary conviction up to six months' imprisonment or a fine not exceeding the statutory maximum or both. Section 58 sets out the offence of without lawful authority or reasonable excuse (proof of which lies on him) collecting or recording information or possessing any record or document likely to be useful to terrorists in planning to carry out any act of terrorism as defined above, eg a list of the names and addresses of Government ministers. This too is an arrestable offence punishable to the same extent as the offence under s 57(1).

VENUE OF THE STOP AND SEARCH

3.86 Unfortunately for ready understanding, the statutes which bestow a power of stop and search vary in terms of the place where the power can be exercised. The Annex to the Code of Practice usefully notes the differences. Thus, it will be seen that, for example, the Terrorism Act, the Badgers Act and the Misuse of Drugs Act can be used anywhere (eg assuming reasonable suspicion, a constable can enter a private wood to investigate badger-baiting and search suspected persons for evidence such as badger tongs; a constable lawfully in a house can search the occupants). This second example shows that, even if a stop and search can be exercised anywhere, the constable must be at that place lawfully (having been invited there, present there with implied permission to investigate an offence, lawfully there under another police power, eg a warrant). Some of the statutes allow a stop and search at any place other than a dwelling-house and give the constable the right to enter that place (Wildlife and Countryside Act, Deer Act, Crossbows Act) eg he could enter outbuildings on reasonable suspicion that unlicensed wild birds are being kept or birds' eggs are being hoarded. The Firearms Act power is confined to a public place, except where a constable reasonably suspects that a person is carrying a firearm with criminal intent or is trespassing with a firearm. In the latter case he has the right to enter any place (s 47(5) (s 39(6) of the NI Act)). Section 1(1) of PACE (Art 3(1)) achieves much the same result by permitting the exercise of the stop and search power:

'(a) in any place to which at the time when he proposes to exercise the power the public or any section of the public has access, on payment or otherwise, as of right or by virtue of express or implied permission; or

(b) in any other place to which people have ready access at the time when he proposes to exercise the power but which is not a dwelling'.

3.87   (a) clearly encompasses a public place, as used in the Firearms Act, and simple examples are all roads, footpaths, subways, recreation grounds, supermarket car parks, public transport, civic buildings such as a museum, cinemas, shops, public houses, restaurants, night-clubs, banks, public conveniences or lavatories in shops. Section 35(2) of the Highways Act 1980 permits the local highway authority or district council to enter into agreements with those who own or have an interest in land on which a building is, or is proposed to be, situated for the provision of ways over, through or under such buildings, to be dedicated as public rights of way. These will normally be maintained by the appropriate authority who may make byelaws governing the conduct of those using the walkways and the times at which they are open to the public. Such walkways, identifiable by the display of such byelaws and opening times, fall within s 1(1)(a) (Art 3(1)(a)). Many cities and towns have local Acts giving powers similar to those of the Highways Act 1980. Where, under the provisions of such local Acts, a footway or place is declared to be a walkway, city walkway or pedestrian way, such areas qualify for s 1(1)(a) (Art 3(1)(a)). Byelaws may be made in respect of local Act walkways and the display of these, together with opening times where appropriate, may assist in recognition. The definition is similar to that used in the Prevention of Crime Act 1953 and *Knox v Anderton* (1982) suggests that a landing and staircase in a block of flats qualify. It is identical to the definition used in the Public Order Act 1986 and similar to that in the Public Order Act 1936. Cases under the latter are still relevant. Thus, a tennis court at Wimbledon (*Brutus v Cozens* (1973)) or a football ground (*Cawley v Frost* (1976)) are public places, but not a shop's car park when the shop is closed (*Marsh v Arscott* (1982), and cf *Sandy v Martin* (1974), a road traffic case involving a pub's car park). This last case is most questionable in the context of stop and search since many shop car parks today are easily accessible to the public after shop hours and may be used as short cuts or as meeting places, but they will fall within the next paragraph. Clearly distinguishable is the fenced and locked car park.

3.88   Under s 60 of the CJPOA 1994 the authorisation permits the exercise of the stop and search power conferred by that section in 'any place within that locality', and s 44 of the TA 2000 refers to 'an area or at a place specified in the authorisation'. As indicated above this must mean any place where the constable is lawfully entitled to be.

3.89   The scope of s 1(1)(b) (Art 3(1)(b)) is more uncertain. It is aimed at places adjoining those already covered by s 1(1)(a) (Art 1(1)(a)). For otherwise a person in a public place, for example, a shop, could avoid a stop and search by the simple expedient of moving to a private part of the premises, for example, a courtyard at the rear of the shop. The key to s 1(1)(b) (Art 3(1)(b)) is whether 'people' as opposed to 'the public or any section of the public' (in s 1(1)(a), Art 1(1)(a)), have 'ready access to the place'. Under the Public Order Act 1936, the speedway track or similar track between a football pitch and the spectator area was held to be a 'public place' even though the public were not permitted access to it. The Divisional Court considered the premises in their entirety. The fact that the public were not permitted access to certain areas did not exclude them from being a 'public place' (*Cawley v Frost* (1976)). Considering an identical definition of 'public place' in the Firearms Act 1968, the Divisional Court held that a shopkeeper who kept a firearm under the counter of his shop had a loaded firearm in a public place for the purposes of s 19 of that Act, notwithstanding that the public were not permitted access to that side of the counter (*Anderson v Miller* (1976)). Both places can qualify under s 1(1)(b) (Art 3(1)(b)). Indeed, places with 'ready access' to people are capable of extremely broad interpretation. They can cover all areas into which a person can move with little difficulty, eg unlocked doors leading to storerooms in a shop or to toilets for the staff, or doors marked 'private' but which are unlocked. They could easily include accessible gardens attached to private dwellings.

3.90   However, to avoid undue invasion by the police on to such property, s 1(4) and (5) (Art 3(4) and (5)) makes it clear that the police can only search persons or vehicles in the curtilage of a dwelling-house if they believe that the person or vehicle is trespassing. The subsections do not therefore give a general power to enter what are private premises. But, by authorising a search of trespassers, they ensure that the police will be acting lawfully towards the person searched or the owner of the vehicle searched. It is still possible, however, for a person to evade a search by going on to premises owned by a relative or friend. He can claim to be there with the express or implied consent of the occupier and, since the premises are not a public place and the constable has no power of entry vis-à-vis the occupier, the constable must leave if required to do so by the occupier (unless of course he can claim some other power of entry, see Chapter 4). Section 1(4) and (5) (Art 3(4) and (5)) require 'reasonable grounds for believing' that the person or vehicle is not lawfully on the premises. This is a high standard to satisfy and the fact that, for example, the occupier of a house is not the registered owner of a car parked on his drive would be insufficient on its own to justify a search.

Examples

3.91   These examples presuppose that, with the exception of exercise of the s 60 CJPOA 1994 power, the constable has reasonable grounds to suspect that stolen or prohibited articles or blades will be found.

(1) A vehicle is seen parked at an address, other than that of its owner. It is parked in a driveway at the side of a private house. The constable should inquire of the householder whether it is parked with his permission. If it is, the constable cannot search it. If no householder appears, the constable can only search the vehicle under the s 1 power if he has:
   (a) reasonable grounds to believe it is not lawfully parked there; and
   (b) reasonable grounds to suspect that stolen or prohibited articles may be found in it.
(2) If a vehicle is parked in the drive of a house which has been converted into an office, the building is not a dwelling, and s 1(5) (Art 3(5)) is irrelevant and a search may take place.
(3) D is sitting on his front lawn which abuts on to a public footpath. There is no fence and ready access can be gained from the path. He is in possession of a bayonet which he uses for gardening. The police cannot enter and search D.
(4) D is seen in someone else's garden putting a flick knife in his pocket. Police can enter and search D (see the facts of *R v Hunt* (1992)).
(5) D is seen on a country estate, the grounds of which are open to the public. Section 1 (Art 3) may be used.
(6) D is seen in the enclosed and private garden of the country estate. Section 1 (Art 3) may be used if s 1(4) (Art 3(4)) is satisfied.
(7) A vehicle is seen in the courtyard of a shop, above which is situated a residential flat. The constable should make inquiries to see if s 1(5) (Art 3(5)) applies (whether the vehicle is there with the permission of the flat occupier) before the vehicle can be searched.
(8) A National Front meeting is to be held in a local hall. Various groups have threatened to break it up and it is reasonably believed that incidents of serious violence may occur in that locality. A superintendent authorises the exercise of the stop and search powers under s 60(4) of the CJPOA 1994 for a period of 12 hours covering the period before and after the meeting within a radius of two miles from the meeting place. A constable in uniform may stop and search any pedestrian or vehicle, its driver or passengers for offensive or dangerous weapons whether or not there are reasonable grounds to suspect that they are being carried.

PUBLIC PLACE IN THE OFFENCE-CREATING ACT

3.92 The offence under s 25 of the Theft Act 1968 (s 24 of the NI Act 1969) is committed if D has with him a housebreaking implement 'when not at his place of abode'. It follows that possession anywhere other than at his place of abode is an offence. However, the Prevention of Crime Act 1953 contains a narrower definition of 'public place' than that in s 1(1) (Art 3(1)) of PACE. It might be argued that since the PCA 1953 definition does not, for example, include walkways, the police may search for and seize an offensive weapon possessed in a walkway but that the possessor commits no offence under the PCA 1953. There are two answers to this argument. First, whether or not a place is a 'public place' within the PCA 1953 is a question of fact and it would be open to a court to hold that a walkway is a public place. Second, the court may draw the reasonable inference that if D had the article in a place which is not a public place within the PCA 1953, and is not his home, he must have carried it to or from such a place through public places (*R v Mehmed* (1963)). Thus, by either route an offence is committed. As for unlawful possession of a blade, this offence is committed in a 'public place' (s 139 of the Criminal Justice Act 1988) and is defined, non-exclusively, in similar terms to s 1(1)(a) (Art 3(1)(a)) of PACE.

SEARCH AS A CONDITION OF ENTRY TO PUBLIC PLACES

3.93   Football grounds and night-clubs, and similar places of public entertainment, fall within s 1(1) (Art 3(1)) of PACE and the other statutory powers of stop and search. However, searches of persons entering them need not be carried out under statute, for it is open to the organisers of such events to require those entering the premises to submit to a search as a condition of entry. Such a search may take place inside the premises or at the entrance and may be conducted by employees of the organisation or uniformed constables. In such a case the constables are not then exercising their statutory powers and none of the safeguards or requirements of ss 2 and 3 (Arts 4 and 5) of PACE applies. The sanction for refusal to submit to such a search is refusal of entry. If, however, one does submit and stolen or prohibited articles are found, an offence may be committed and an arrest may follow. Where the search is preceded by the information required by s 2 (Art 4), it will indicate that the constable is exercising a statutory power and a refusal to comply can then result in reasonable force being used to detain the person and conduct the search; resistance to the officer could lead to a charge under s 89 Police Act 1996.

INVOLUNTARY PRESENCE IN A PUBLIC PLACE

3.94   The fact that a person is not aware that he is in a public place or that he is in a public place involuntarily is no bar to a s 1 (Art 3) search and is unlikely to be a defence to a charge of possession of a prohibited article. In *Winzar v Chief Constable of Kent* (1983), D was carried from a hospital and arrested on the forecourt for being found drunk in a highway. Goff LJ held that the fact that his presence on the highway was momentary or involuntary was immaterial, the offence having been created to deal with persons who were drunk in public places. Similarly an unconscious person could be searched for drugs under the Misuse of Drugs Act 1971 or an intoxicated person for an offensive weapon under s 1 (Art 3) of PACE.

PROCEDURE

3.95   The principal safeguard against abuse of the stop and search power should be the requirement for, and strict application of, reasonable suspicion. However, the difficulties of defining reasonable suspicion and the fact that in many circumstances it will not be possible 'reasonably' to suspect possession of prohibited articles (particularly where they only become prohibited articles when possessed with a particular intent) mean that the principal safeguards in practice must be the duties imposed by ss 2 and 3 (Arts 4 and 5) of PACE on constables exercising stop and search powers. Section 2 (Art 4) applies before a search and s 3 (Art 5) afterwards. They apply to all stop and search powers (other than searches of vehicles conducted by statutory undertakers (as to which see para 3.150, post), searches under the Aviation Security Act 1982, s 27(2), and in Northern Ireland searches under the TA 2000, s 15 thus including, for example, the Misuse of Drugs Act 1971.

3.96 It must be emphasised that these duties only arise if a constable intends a stop and search under a statutory power. He can still try to stop a person or vehicle and ask questions but may not conduct a search without the person's consent. The duties of ss 2 and 3 (Arts 4 and 5) arise if he needs to rely on the statutory powers.

A constable in uniform

3.97 With the exception of the power under s 60 of the CJPOA 1994 and that under the new s 44 the Terrorism Act 2000, which can only be exercised by a uniformed constable, the stop and search powers can be exercised by both uniformed and plain-clothed officers, but note that only a uniformed officer can exercise the power under s 163 of the Road Traffic Act 1988 to stop vehicles. The exercise by plain-clothed officers can clearly pose difficulties if the officer does not identify himself quickly and the citizen resists the officer's instructions. It will normally be an offence of wilful obstruction to refuse to stop for a constable who proposes, on reasonable suspicion, to exercise stop and search powers, or an offence of resisting or assaulting the constable if the person physically resists. An honest but mistaken belief that the person seeking to stop you is not a constable is a good defence to a charge of wilful obstruction under s 51(3) of the Police Act 1964 (*Ostler v Elliott* (1980)), but not to a charge of assault (*R v Forbes and Webb* (1865)). In *R v Williams (Gladstone)* (1987) it was held that a mistaken but honest belief is sufficient to justify the use of reasonable force in self-defence; the reasonableness of the belief is only relevant to the question of whether that belief was held, and not to the question of guilt or innocence (see further para 5.174 post).

Section 2(1) (Art 4(1))

3.98 Once a person or vehicle has been detained under any stop and search power, the constable need not proceed with the search if he subsequently discovers that:
(i)   no search is required, eg his reasonable suspicion is eliminated after a conversation with the suspect; or
(ii) a search is impracticable, eg where a disturbance develops and he must turn his attention elsewhere.

3.99 Paragraph 2.3 of the Code makes an important point here. Reasonable suspicion must exist before the stop. It cannot be retrospectively generated by the person's reaction to preliminary questioning or by his refusal to answer questions, though, of course, the constable's pre-existing reasonable suspicion will often be confirmed and heightened by the person's reaction.

THE DUTY TO INFORM THE SUSPECT (S 2(2) AND (3), ART 4(2))

3.100 Once a constable has decided to proceed with a search, he must take reasonable steps to bring to the attention of the person to be searched or of the person in charge of the vehicle (s 2(5)), the matters mentioned below. This duty should reduce the dangers of arbitrary use of s 1 (Art 3) powers for, first, the need to articulate one's reasons for action acts as a restraint. Second, the person to be searched is less likely to react aggressively if the constable's purpose is explained to him. The duty is thus a statutory elucidation of what is good police practice. 'Reasonable steps' in s 2(2) (Art 4(2)) take account of the situation where the person to be searched is incapable of understanding the constable's instructions, eg through intoxication or language difficulties. The phrase requires the constable to establish, if practicable, whether a person accompanying the suspect can act as interpreter (see Code, para 3.11). It can also permit the constable to search once he has tried in slow and clear terms to communicate with the person. The importance of compliance with this duty of informing the suspect lies in the possibility that a court will use s 78 (Art 76) of PACE to exclude evidence obtained from a stop and search unless the constable can prove that he supplied the information (*R v Fennelley* (1989)). The duty to inform does not apply in relation to the search of unattended vehicles, or to searches of vehicles by statutory undertakers (s 6, see para 3.71, post; which are so frequent and well established as to make such explanations impracticable and unnecessary) and to searches under s 27(2) of the Aviation Security Act 1982 (searches of persons and aircraft at designated airports for certain cargo). Apart from these exceptions, a constable cannot conduct a search until he has taken reasonable steps to inform the citizen of the following matters.

(1) The duty to furnish documentary evidence that he is a constable – This duty only applies to plain-clothed officers who seek to search the person or vehicle. 'Documentary evidence' avoids the confusion which might follow from a hasty and mumbled identification and refers to an officer's warrant card. On the other hand, the speed with which a warrant card and the other duties below can be addressed to a person does not mean that the person will comprehend the information. Good policing and the requirement of 'reasonable steps' in s 2(2) (Art 4(2)) demand that care be taken in the provision of such information and that the citizen be given adequate opportunity to assimilate it before the constable proceeds to the search.

(2) The duty to give his name and that of the police station to which he is attached – Outside Northern Ireland there is no duty to give the number of the constable because different police forces use different numbering systems and this was felt

to endanger clarity. Confusion could still arise when a force has officers bearing a common name who are attached to the same police station. The additional requirement to state the number would remove this possibility. When an officer is investigating terrorism, there is no duty to state his name (Code A, para 2.4). Instead he should give his warrant or other identification number.

(3)   The duty to state the object of and grounds for undertaking the search – Research studies conducted on the exercise of stop and search powers all indicate a high level of antagonism and resentment if the reasons for the stop and search are not explained (Wiley and Hudick (1980) (USA); Brown (1980) (Australia); Butler and Tharme (1981); Manning and Butler (1982) and Willis (1983) (England)). Thus, it is both legally (see *R v Fennelley* (1989)) and socially necessary to comply with these duties. There is, of course, no duty to state precisely the object of the search. Indeed the constable will seldom know this with any precision but he should indicate whether the object is to search for stolen goods, offensive weapons, housebreaking implements, drugs, etc. It is submitted that a statement that he is searching for 'stolen or prohibited goods' is too imprecise for compliance with the section. The grounds for undertaking the search appear to mean the grounds giving rise to reasonable suspicion and will invariably indicate the object of the search (if the stop and search is under s 60 of the CJPOA 1994 or s 44 of the Terrorism Act 2000 the grounds would be the authorisation under the section but here too the object of the search, offensive weapons or dangerous instruments in the case of s 60, or articles which could be used for the purposes etc of terrorism under s 44, would be stated). For example, a constable is informed by the manager of a shop that a youth, who is described, has just attempted to purchase goods with a stolen credit card. The constable sees a youth answering that description in the vicinity soon afterwards. He should then, having stated his name, state that he proposes to carry out a search for a stolen credit card (the object of the search) because a youth answering his description has just attempted to purchase goods at a nearby shop with a stolen credit card (the grounds for undertaking it). Similarly, if reliable information has been received that a youth was seen waving a dagger or selling drugs, that would give rise to reasonable suspicion that the described youth was in possession of an offensive weapon or prohibited drugs. Thus, except for s 60 searches or s 44 Terrorism Act 2000 searches, the two duties go together in that the reasonable suspicion tends to identify the article to be searched for.

(4)   The duty to inform the person searched, or person using the vehicle searched, that a written record will be made of the search and that the person can obtain a copy of that record – This requirement is designed to prevent the arbitrary exercise of stop and search powers, particularly since the falsifying of the reasons for a search is a disciplinary offence. Working against this deterrent is the fact that there is often pressure on constables to exercise stop and search powers either to demonstrate to supervisors that they are doing their job, or to increase 'productivity' by detecting offences or simply to gather 'intelligence' about persons abroad at particular times (Willis (1983) p 15). If this happens, abuse is

bound to occur and could lead to further abuse such as falsifying the reasons for the stop and search. Thus, the surest safeguard against abuse lies in the proper supervision, by senior police officers, of the exercise of the power, both out of concern for the individual, and out of concern for the long-term credibility and effectiveness of the police.

3.101 The duty under s 2(3)(d) (Art 4(2)) does not in fact arise if it appears to the constable that it will not be 'practicable' to compile a record of the stop and search (s 2(4), Art 4(5)). The most obvious example of this is the stopping of large numbers of people, eg football crowds or motor cyclists, visiting a seaside resort on a Bank Holiday, or potential suspects following a murder or rape. The argument runs that it is not practicable for a constable in the hurly-burly of football supporters to compile a record of each stop and search on the spot and even less so to compile them later at a police station. Three answers may be given to this argument.

3.102 First, in some cases, such as football matches, persons can be searched as a condition of entry, in which event ss 2 and 3 do not arise.

3.103 Second, the strictures of the Code of Practice on the meaning of 'reasonable suspicion' make it clear that the police cannot search hundreds of people just because of the officer's previous experience with that type of person. Under the s 1 power reasonable suspicion must exist against each person before he is searched. The power under s 60 of the CJPOA 1994 (considered above in para 3.68) is in part a recognition of the problems faced by the police in policing large numbers of persons, some of whom are intent on violence. When authorised, the power may be exercised without the need for reasonable suspicion. If this power can be authorised it may reduce the temptation to 'stretch' the s 1 power in order to search large groups, some of whom may be bent on violence.

3.104 Third, it may be that the constable is called away urgently to deal with other matters in which case he can still tell the person that he will make a record of the brief search later at the station.

REASONABLE FORCE

The constable

3.105 Section 117 (Art 88) of PACE permits a constable to use 'reasonable force if necessary' to detain or search a person or vehicle. Without such a provision the power under s 1 would be useless against the uncooperative citizen. What is 'reasonable force' is a matter of fact and degree depending on the circumstances, in particular the amount of resistance offered by the citizen. In most cases the force used will be little more than the taking hold of an arm to prevent the person running away. As the resistance mounts so the degree of force to meet it will increase and this may merge into an arrest for assaulting, resisting or wilfully obstructing the constable.

The citizen

3.106   If the constable has no reasonable suspicion, or if he fails to carry out the duties imposed on him by ss 2 and 3, he is acting unlawfully and not within his duty. English law permits a citizen to use reasonable force against a constable, or anyone else, who is acting unlawfully against him (s 3 of the Criminal Law Act 1967 and Criminal Law (Northern Ireland) Act 1967). The fact that the citizen knows that he is innocent is not a ground for resisting if the constable has reasonable suspicion. Since it is almost impossible to check on the reasonableness of that suspicion at the time, it would be most unwise to assume that the constable is acting unlawfully. Compliance followed by complaint is the best course. If, however, resistance is resorted to, the force used must be reasonable, and whether or not it is will depend on the degree of force used by the constable (see the discussion in paras 5.174 post in the context of resisting arrest).

EXCESSIVE FORCE

3.107   If either the constable or the citizen uses excessive force, a charge of common assault or of some aggravated assault will lie depending on the force used and the injury caused. If the constable is not acting in the execution of his duty, a charge under s 89 of the Police Act 1996 cannot be brought against the citizen, but the fact that the constable is acting unlawfully is not a defence to a charge of assault arising from the use of excessive force by the citizen.

DETENTION FOR THE PURPOSE OF A SEARCH

3.108   Section 2(8) (Art 4(9)) provides that a constable may detain a person or vehicle for such time as is reasonably required to permit a search to be carried out either at the place where the person or vehicle is first detained or nearby. How long a period of detention is required depends on what is being searched for and whether the search is of a person or a vehicle. As is implied by the restrictions on the removal of clothes (s 2(9), Art 4(10)), the search of a person in public is to be confined to a 'pat down' of the body and search of pockets and similarly accessible areas of clothing such as waistbands of trousers and socks. There is no requirement in PACE that females only be searched by females, though a male officer searching a female suspect would be well advised to confine the search to pockets of clothing and handbags, and the Code of Practice, para 3.5, requires a search to be undertaken by an officer of the same sex if it involves more than a superficial examination. In these circumstances, a search of a person for a small article will seldom take more than ten minutes while a search for a larger article will take less time. On the other hand, if the person is carrying a rucksack, bed roll and similar equipment the search may take considerably longer. Similarly a search of a vehicle could take a considerable amount of time, particularly if the article sought is small (eg prohibited drugs) and the vehicle, which could include a caravan or houseboat, is large and full of other articles. What is reasonable is then a matter of fact and degree in the particular circumstances. Detention beyond what is reasonable in the circumstances will be unlawful.

'THERE OR NEARBY' (s 2(8), Art 4(A))

3.109 The search may be carried out either at the place where the person or vehicle is detained or nearby. A similar provision was contained in s 8(1) of the Road Traffic Act 1972 in the context of breath tests. This too was held to be a matter of fact and degree in all the circumstances of the case. Appellate courts will, since it is a question of fact, generally regard themselves as bound by findings of fact by magistrates and in *Arnold v Chief Constable of Kingston-upon-Hull* (1969) the High Court refused to disturb a finding that a police station one-and-a-half miles away was not 'there or nearby'. In *Donegani v Ward* (1969) the Divisional Court similarly refused to disturb a finding that 160 yards from the scene of the stop was not 'there or nearby'. The purpose of the stop and search restriction of 'there or nearby' would appear to be twofold. First, to prevent the stop and search power being used as a device to persuade a person to go to a police station, thus creating a form of 'back door' arrest; and second, to permit a limited degree of flexibility so that searches may take place in less public positions such as shop doorways or a police van if close at hand, thus avoiding embarrassment where possible (see also the Code of Practice, para 3.5). The ready proximity of such positions means that in practice 'nearby' should mean a very restricted area. Above all, the Code of Practice requires (para 3.1) that every reasonable effort be made to reduce embarrassment to the minimum.

LIMITATIONS ON THE EXTENT OF THE SEARCH

Persons

3.110 Section 2(9) (Art 4(10)) does not authorise a constable to require a person to remove any part of his clothing in public other than an outer coat, jacket or gloves (or headgear in Northern Ireland). Thus, hats and shoes are excluded (though an officer can feel under a hat or, if it falls off, he can search it). This, together with the 'there or nearby' requirement in s 2(8) (Art 4(9)), emphasises the limited nature of the search under s 1 (Art 3). It is not intended to be a 'strip' or 'intimate' search: a strip search should only be carried out following arrest and at a police station, while an intimate search can only follow arrest for an offence, be of a person in police detention and must be justified and authorised in accordance with s 55 (see Chapter 7, post). In *R v Hughes* (1994) the Court of Appeal held that forcing a person to spit out a drug which he had concealed in his mouth was not an intimate search within s 55, there being no physical intrusion into a body orifice, in this case the mouth. Such an interpretation is no longer necessary because s 59 of the Criminal Justice and Public Order Act 1994 redefines an intimate and non-intimate search. A search which consists of the examination of a person's mouth is now a non-intimate search (the new definition is to be found in s 65 of PACE rather than formerly in s 118).

3.111 Section 2 (Art 4) applies to the exercise of any stop and search power. Two points should be noted, however. First, s 2(9)(a) (Art 4(10)(a)) applies only to a constable who proposes to 'require' the citizen to remove clothing. The latter may of course consent to a more thorough search (this must be informed consent which requires that the person knows that he can refuse, see para 3.04). Second, s 2(9) (Art 4(10)) refers only to the removal of clothing 'in public'. It is therefore argued by some that the constable can remove more clothing (eg shirt, hat, shoes) if a private place can be found nearby such as a police van (see Code A 3.5) and many constables believe they can go further and require a strip down to underwear in such a private place. There is, however, no express power to conduct a more thorough search of the person prior to arrest. The person can consent to a more extensive search but if an extensive or strip search of the person is needed, and those under section 23 of the Misuse of Drugs Act 1971 frequently require a more intimate search, he should, it is submitted, be arrested (the reasonable grounds to suspect possession of prohibited drugs or other articles to be searched for also justifies arrest for an offence), and the search conducted at a police station under s 54 or s 55 (Arts 55 and 56) (see para 7.28 post, for the rules governing strip searches). In this respect Code A 3.5, which suggests that 'a more thorough search (eg by requiring a person to take off a T-shirt or head gear)' may take place out of public view, conflicts with Code C, Annex A(B) 9 which defines a 'strip search' as 'a search involving the removal of more than outer clothing' and which, by implication, should take place only in a police station following arrest for an offence and detention (the definition is in Code C and such a search must be recorded in the custody record (Annex A (B) 12) and, according to para 10, may only take place if it is considered necessary to remove an article 'which a person should not be allowed to keep ...'. For discussion of an identical provision in the context of search on arrest, see para 5.157 post.)

Vehicles

3.112 There is no limit to the extent of a search of a vehicle other than the limit on the period of detention to 'such time as is reasonably required to permit a search to be carried out' (s 2(8), Art 4(9)). As with search of persons, the search is not intended to be a 'strip' search involving the removal of panels. Such a detailed search would require garage facilities and the virtual 'arrest' of a motor vehicle. It is suggested that this can only be achieved following the arrest of the person in charge of the vehicle and the search of the vehicle xunder s 18 (Art 20), s 32 (Art 34) ('premises' in these sections (articles) includes a vehicle, see s 23 (Art 25)).

SEIZURE

3.113 A constable may seize articles which he has reasonable grounds to suspect are stolen or prohibited (s 1(6), Art 3(6)). As to the seizure of other articles, if he is searching a vehicle, a vehicle qualifies as premises (s 2, Art 25) and thus the wide powers of seizure under s 19 can be invoked (ie seizure of evidence of any offence is allowed if the evidence would otherwise be destroyed etc, see para 4.73, post). If he is searching a person, s 19 does not apply. In that case he must arrest the person and can then seize the evidence of other offences under s 32 (Art 34). The provisions relating to the citizen's access to articles seized and held by the police (s 21, Art 23) and to the police powers to retain such articles (s 22, Art 24) apply to all stops and searches (see para 4.139, post).

DUTIES TO BE CARRIED OUT AFTER SEARCH (s 2(6), Art 4(7), CODE A 4.8 AND 4.9)

Unattended vehicles

3.114   Where an unattended vehicle or something in it has been searched, the constable must leave a notice containing the information mentioned in s 2(6) (Art 4(7)). This is a sensible requirement, for if duplicate keys are used to enter the vehicle the owner may have no other indication that it has been searched. A record must be made and a copy made available to the owner if requested (see s 3 (Art 5)). A record of what has been seized needs to be included. The reference to compensation for any damage caused (eg a forced window) serves to alert the owner to the funds set aside by each police force for the compensation of vehicle owners (s 2(6)(c), Art 4(7)(c) and Code A 4.9). The notice should, if practicable, be placed inside the vehicle (s 2(7), Art 4(8)). But if, for example, a lorry's trailer is searched and the constable cannot get into the cab to leave the notice without damaging it, the notice must be left outside the vehicle, normally under a windscreen wiper. Code A 4.10 and the law of negligence require that a vehicle should be left secure wherever possible.

Records (s 3(1), Art 5(1))

3.115   Where a constable has carried out a search under s 1 or any other stop and search power:
(1)   he shall make a record of the search in writing unless it is not practicable to do so (s 3(1), Art 5(1));
(2)   if a constable is required by sub-s (1) to make a record but it is not practicable to do so on the spot, eg his presence is urgently required elsewhere or the weather is very bad, it must be completed as soon as practicable after the search (s 3(2), Art 5(2)).

3.116   These subsections can be read as meaning that where large numbers of persons are searched, eg football supporters, or in a situation of public disorder, no record need be made at all because the constable is not then required by sub-s (1) to do so and therefore sub-s (2) does not apply. This is the interpretation adopted by Code A 4.1 and it may well be correct. However, such large-scale searches can rarely, if ever, be justified under s 1 (Art 3) given the requirement of reasonable cause to suspect that a particular individual is carrying stolen or prohibited articles or blades. Even when there is no requirement of reasonable suspicion, as in searches conducted under s 60 of the CJPOA 1994, which can only be exercised in circumstances of impending serious violence which imply potentially large numbers of searches, records must be made of at least the power under which the vehicle was stopped or the stop and search of a pedestrian was made if under s 60 (s 60(10) discussed at para 3.68, ante). It follows that rarely, if ever, will a situation arise in which it is not practicable to make the record required by sub-s (1).

3.117   The record is compiled on a pro-forma document, called the national search record. A separate record must be completed for each search conducted. However, if a person and vehicle are searched for the same reason, one record will suffice (Code A 4.5). What happens if the vehicle and all its passengers (eg a coach, or minibus) are searched? Code A 4.5 states that if a person is in a vehicle and both are searched, and the object and grounds are the same, only one record need be completed. If more than one person in a vehicle is searched, separate records for each search of a person must be made. If only a vehicle is searched the name of the driver and his or her self-defined ethnic identity must be made, unless the vehicle is unattended.

Name of person searched

3.118   Section 3(3) (Art 5(3) and Code A 4) provides that the record shall include the name of the person searched if it is known to the constable and of course the constable can ask for the name. But there is no power to require the name nor to detain a person to find out his name; so, where the name is unavailable, the constable must include a description of the person (s 3(3), (4), Art 5(3), (4)). It is, perhaps, indicative of the mistrust of the police that the request for the name and address of a person stopped is liable to antagonise the person more than the stop and search itself. However, names and addresses of persons abroad at night have long been a source of intelligence and when crimes are committed in the area the list of such persons is a useful starting point in the investigation. The police have then to weigh the usefulness of such intelligence against the antagonism likely to result from a request for names and addresses. The record should note the person's ethnic origin. The new code emphasises the importance of accurate monitoring. Officers should record the self-defined ethnicity according to the categories used in 2001 census question listed in Annex B. Respondents should be asked to select one of the five main categories and then a more specific cultural background.

3.119   The ethnic classification should be coded using the above coding system. The record also contains an additional 'not stated' box but should not be offered as an explicit alternative. This is clearly a controversial area requiring a sensitive approach from police officers. The purpose of obtaining data on ethnicity is to,

'obtain a true picture of stop and search activity and to help improve ethnic monitoring, tackle discriminatory practice , and promote effective use of powers'

3.120 If the person stopped gives what appears to be an incorrect answer – the example given in the code is a person who appears to be white states that they are black! – the officer should record the response that has been given. The officer's own perception of the ethnic background of every person stopped must be recorded using the PNC/Phoenix classification system. If the 'not stated' category is used the reason for this must also be recorded.

3.121 Where the search is of a vehicle the note must include a description of the vehicle (s 3(5), Art 5(5)) including its registration number (Code A 4.3(iii)) if it has one. The constable can, where motor vehicles are concerned, exercise Road Traffic Act powers to require the name and address of the driver, but not of passengers, and can discover the name and address of the registered keeper via the Police National Computer. In this respect motorists are more vulnerable than pedestrians.

3.122 The record shall also:
(a) state the object of the search; the grounds for making it; the date and time; the place where it was made; details of anything found; details of any injury or damage caused; and
(b) the identity of the constable making it and each constable involved in the search, except in relation to terrorism investigations when his warrant or other identification number and duty station will suffice (Code A, para 4.4).

Obtaining a copy of the record

3.123 When a copy of the record made under s 3 PACE is made at the time of the search the officer must immediately give a copy to the person who has been searched (Code A para 4.2).

3.124 The person searched, or the owner or person in charge of the vehicle searched, may obtain a copy of the written record if he asks for one before the end of a period of 12 months beginning with the date on which the search was made (s 3(7), (8), (9), Art 5(8), (9), (10)). It should be noted that the constable is under a duty to tell the citizen of his right to a copy if a record is to be made (s 3(3), (4), (6), Art 4(2), (3), (4)). The phrase 'asks for one' (s 3(7)) includes a written request. It will be seen below that failure to comply with s 3 (Art 4) or s 60(10) of the 1994 Act is much less likely to be visited by any sanction than other breaches of Part I.

3.125 The duty to make a written record does not apply to the detention and search of vehicles under the Aviation Security Act 1982 (searches for cargo) or by constables employed by statutory undertakers, for example, the search of a vehicle leaving the premises of British Rail by a constable of the British Transport police or leaving a port by the port police force. Such a duty was felt to be unduly burdensome given the frequency of such searches.

THE EFFECT OF A FAILURE TO COMPLY WITH ss 2 AND 3 (Arts 4 AND 5)

3.126   The Act does not provide an express penalty for a failure to comply with these provisions, but three sanctions may arise. First, the constable will be acting unlawfully and will expose himself to a civil action. Second, the court may exercise its power under s 78 (Art 76) to exclude evidence obtained by an unlawful stop and search. Third, the constable's conduct can be the subject of a complaint which may lead to disciplinary action. These are considered in Chapter 2 but here the following points may be noted.

Civil action

3.127   In *Christie v Leachinsky* (1947) the House of Lords held that where a constable arrests a person on reasonable suspicion of an arrestable offence, or of any other crime which is arrestable without a warrant, he must, in ordinary circumstances, inform the person of the true grounds for arrest. A failure to do so will normally render the constable liable for false imprisonment and/or assault. In the context of arrest, this decision was given statutory force by s 28 (Art 30) of PACE and is discussed more fully in paras 5.56-5.64, post. In the context of stop and search, *Pedro v Diss* (1981) equated detention for the purposes of a search under s 66 of the Metropolitan Police Act 1839 with arrest and held that the failure to inform the person of the reasons for the stop and search meant that the constable was not acting in the execution of his duty for the purpose of s 51 of the Police Act 1964. Thus, a charge of assaulting the constable under s 51 failed. It follows that the constable is also liable for false imprisonment and/or assault. Since the duty to state the object of the search and the grounds for undertaking it are statutory duties (s 2(3), Art 4(4)), the courts will clearly adopt a similar stance under PACE. They may perhaps go further by holding that a failure to carry out any of the duties in s 2 (Art 4), will render the constable liable for false imprisonment and/or assault. Substantial damages, however, are unlikely to be forthcoming if, for example, a constable fails to give his name but carries out his other duties under s 2 (Art 4). As regards s 3 (Art 5), however, there is no civil action available to cater for a failure to compile a record.

Exclusion of evidence

3.128   If the possible unlawfulness or impropriety of a stop and search is raised before the trial court, the court has the power under s 78 (Art 76) to exclude evidence obtained thereby if its reception would adversely affect the fairness of the proceedings (for a detailed discussion of s 78 (Art 76), see para 2.125 ante). Much is likely to depend on the gravity of the impropriety and of the offence. A more serious breach is the failure to show that the citizen has been informed of the reasons for the stop and search and one Crown Court has registered its disapproval by excluding the subsequent evidence (*R v Fennelley* (1989)). But in *R v McCarthy* (1996) Crim LR 918 the defendant was convicted of conspiracy to supply cannabis. Some two weeks before her arrest the car she was travelling in was stopped on the pretext that it was a *'routine'* stop. The car had in fact been stopped in the course of a drugs operation because her companion had been observed to take a package from a third person. A package containing £50,000 in cash, but no drugs, was found. The companion stated it was to buy a Mercedes car and they were allowed to continue. At the trial it was argued that this evidence should be excluded under s 78 because of the pretence employed by the officer and the breaches of s 2(2) and (3) of the Act. The Court of Appeal allowed the evidence, finding there was no bad faith or significant or substantial breach of the Code. It is difficult to agree with the Court's view that the deceit was not a substantial breach but the admission of the evidence could not have adversely affected the fairness of the trial. Clearly in cases of this type to provide suspects with full information could jeopardise an operation but the risks of having the evidence excluded would have to be weighed carefully in the balance.

Complaints against the police

3.129 The operation of stop and search powers should be closely monitored by each police force. Though of little practical use to the individual, this method of accountability may have some effect on the future exercise of stop and search powers. The Code of Practice for stop and search powers is of far greater importance, for a breach of the Code is a breach of discipline and can therefore be the subject of an official complaint under Part IX of PACE.

ROAD CHECKS

3.130 Under s 163 of the Road Traffic Act 1988 (Road Traffic (NI) Order 1981, Art 180), a constable in uniform can require the driver of a vehicle to stop but uncertainty surrounds the purposes for which this power can be employed (see para 3.45, ante). To clarify matters, s 4 of PACE (Art 6) permits the police to use s 163 in order to set up road checks, or in more conventional parlance, road blocks, in certain, defined circumstances. A 'road check' means the obstruction of a road in order to stop:
(a) all vehicles passing along it; or
(b) vehicles selected by any criterion (s 4(2), Art 6(2)).

3.131 Road checks are set up by all police forces from time to time, and in particular in the event of a major crime in the area or the escape of a prisoner. Under s 4 (Art 6) a police officer of at least the rank of superintendent may authorise in writing a road check in the following circumstances.
(1) A road check may be authorised if the officer has reasonable grounds to believe that a person has committed a serious arrestable offence (as defined by s 116 (Art 87), see paras 2.13-2.20, ante) and reasonable grounds to suspect that he is, or is about to be, in the area covered by the road check (s 4(1)(a), (4)(a), Art 6(1)(a), (4)(a)). This has proved to be the most used ground for road checks (see figures below).

Simple examples are an alert following a murder or bank robbery. The reasonable cause to suspect that the murderer or bank robbers are in the area will, in the first instance, arise from the report of the crime and this may then result in several road checks being set up to cover all exits from the scene of the crime or escape, each being justified by the same reasonable grounds for suspicion. Reports that the car or person wanted has been seen in the area will also often justify road checks in that area. In these circumstances, there will generally be a greater opportunity to assess the credibility of witnesses but even in such cases the dangerousness of the person sought must be a factor to be taken into account in assessing the need for road checks. It follows that in such cases a lower level of reasonable suspicion will be relied upon.

(2) A road check may be authorised if there are reasonable grounds for believing that witnesses to a serious arrestable offence are likely to be traced (s 4(1)(b), (4)(b), Art 6(1)(b), (4)(b)). For example, at the end of a football match a fan is stabbed to death. Departing vehicles may be stopped in the hope of finding witnesses to the crime. A child is murdered at about 4pm. On subsequent days motorists are stopped around that time in case regular travellers may have spotted something on the day of the crime. It should be noted that the superintendent's reasonable belief in s 4(4)(b) (Art 6(4)(b)) refers to the nature of the offence, whereas in the other categories it refers to the likelihood that the relevant person will be found. Potentially, therefore, this category may be over-used, viz the officer may authorise a check if he thinks that witnesses of serious arrestable offences may be found. Common sense, resources and adverse publicity (eg following the annual reports of chief officers, see para 3.70, post) are the safeguards against random or trawling exercises or checks set up, for example, to 'raise the public's awareness of crime'. If the police wish to seek witnesses to a road accident (not a serious arrestable offence), section 163 of the Road Traffic Act 1988 gives the power to stop vehicles for a road traffic purpose.

(3) A road check may be authorised if there are reasonable grounds for believing that a person is intending to commit a serious arrestable offence and reasonable grounds for suspecting that he is, or will be, in the area covered by the road check (s 4(1)(c), (4)(c), Art 6(1)(c), (4)(c)). For example, the police have information that a large sale of drugs is to take place in the area but cannot identify the place of the transaction and thus hope to catch the participants beforehand. Cases of such specific advance information will be exceptional. More usual will be the general knowledge that a particular area has a high level of particular crimes, eg burglary, and the reasonable belief that, by stopping vehicles and possibly searching them under s 1 (Art 3), a number of criminals are certain to be caught. The potential for misuse of this power is illustrated by:

(a) the broad scope of 'serious arrestable offences' (see paras 2.97-2.107, ante);
(b) the fact that vehicles may be stopped by 'any criterion' (s 4(2), Art 6(2)); and
(c) the fact that 'intending to commit' in s 4(1)(c) (Art 6(1)(c)) can refer to an earlier stage of preparation than an attempt or conspiracy, the latter already being 'offences'.

The availability of resources and the policy of good policing in what may be a very sensitive area of policing are the real safeguards against misuse. The possibility of civil actions or the lodging of a complaint are more remote sanctions.

(4) A road check may be authorised if a person unlawfully at large is reasonably suspected to be, or about to be, in the area (s 4(1)(d), (4)(d), Art 6(1)(d), (4)(d)), eg an escaped prisoner or inmate of a psychiatric hospital; X escapes from a prison in county A and is thought likely to try to contact his family in county B. Both police forces can employ s 4(1)(d) (Art 6(1)(d)).

Setting up a road check in an emergency

3.132 Section 4(3) (Art 6(3)) requires that a police officer of at least the rank of superintendent authorise the setting up of road checks (cf the Royal Commission which had recommended the rank of assistant chief constable, Report, para 3.32). However, s 4(5) (Art 6(5)) provides that a police officer below that rank may authorise a road check if any of the conditions specified in s 4(1) (Art 6(1)) is satisfied, and it appears to him that a road check is required as a matter of urgency. The authorisation need not be in writing. In most police forces it is the officer in charge of the operations room who will initiate the road check in response to a reported serious crime or escape. That officer may not be of superintendent rank and may not be able to contact a superintendent or above in situations where seconds count. If a road check is authorised in such circumstances, it must be recorded in writing, a superintendent or above must be informed as soon as is practicable (s 4(6), (7), Art 6(6), (7)) and the latter may then authorise its continuance (s 4(8), Art 6(8)) or discontinuance, in which event he must record in writing the fact that the road check was set up, and the purpose of it (s 4(9), Art 6(9)).

The authorisation

3.133 Every authorisation (including an emergency one under s 4(5) (Art 6(5)) must specify the locality in which the vehicles are to be stopped (s 4(10), Art 6(10)). All written authorisations (ie those made initially by a superintendent or those emergency ones subsequently approved by a senior officer) must specify:
(a) the name of the authorising officer;
(b) the purpose, including, where relevant, the serious arrestable offence involved (s 4(14), Art 6(14));
(c) the locality where vehicles are to be stopped (s 4(13), Art 6(13)).

3.134 The person in charge of the vehicle is entitled to apply, within 12 months, for a written statement of the reasons for the stop (s 4(15), Art 6(15)). Unlike a stop and search under s 1 (Art 3), however, the constable is under no duty to tell the citizen of that entitlement.

Duration

3.135 An emergency road check must be reported to a senior officer as soon as is practicable. It and all others may then continue for up to seven days in the first instance and can be renewed for seven-day periods (s 4(11), (12), Art 6(11), (12)). In some cases (eg an escaped prisoner) the road check will have to operate continuously but in others (eg the reconstruction of a crime in the hope of attracting witnesses), it can be confined to particular times. Section 4(11)(b) (Art 6(11(b)) provides accordingly.

Search of vehicles stopped at road checks

3.136 It will be noted that the scheme of s 4 (Art 6) is to enable the power of stopping under s 163 of the Road Traffic Act 1988 (Art 180 of the RT (NI) Order 1981) to be used for the purposes set out in s 4 (Art 6). Two consequences follow from this. First, the power is confined to constables in uniform. Second, the power is one to stop a vehicle and not to search it. As to detaining the vehicle, remarkably this power is not explicitly mentioned in either s 4 (Art 6) or s 163 (s180). It would, however, be open to the courts to imply a power to detain the vehicle for the purposes mentioned in s 4 (Art 6), viz to communicate with the occupants (see *DPP v Carey* (1970) and *Lodwick v Sanders* (1985)). In cases involving s 4(1)(a)(c) and (d) (Art 6(1)(a)(c) and (d)) the police will be seeking persons in order to arrest them. If they decide to do so, a power to enter and search the vehicle in order to arrest a person for an arrestable offence, or to recapture a person unlawfully at large, is specifically provided by s 17(1)(b) and (d) (Art 19(1)(b) and (d)) respectively (a 'vehicle' being 'premises' for the purpose of s 17 (Art 19) entry powers (see s 23, Art 25)). Once an arrest is made, s 32 (Art 34) authorises a search of the vehicle for evidence of the offence for which the person has been arrested. If the police have insufficient grounds to make an arrest, there may be reasonable suspicion that the vehicle or its occupants are carrying stolen or prohibited goods. In this case, a s 1 (Art 3) search is appropriate, subject to the duties to inform the person of the matters specified in s 2 (Art 4) and compile a record of the search. If the person stopped under s 4 (Art 6) refuses to co-operate with the police, he must be allowed to continue unless the constable has sufficient reason to arrest him, or to search him and/or the vehicle under s 1 (Art 3), or to detain the vehicle for any road traffic inspection. A sharp contrast exists between the various duties which must be observed in a s 1 (Art 3) search and the silence of s 4 (Art 6) as to the way in which the police officer should treat the motorist. This is, in the main, understandable given the usually fleeting nature of a stop under s 4 (Art 6) and the usually co-operative attitude of the motoring public. However, there are circumstances, especially under s 4(1)(c) (Art 6(1)(c)), where a sensitive approach may be crucial to police/community relations and the officers should be briefed to explain to the motorist the precise purpose of the stop.

OTHER POWERS TO STOP VEHICLES

3.137 Section 4(16) of PACE (Art 6(16)) makes it clear that the purposes of s 4 (Art 6) are without prejudice to other powers to stop vehicles. The basic power is s 163 of the

Road Traffic Act 1988 but, as has been indicated, the precise purposes for which it may be used are uncertain. Clearly it can be used for road traffic purposes, eg to examine a vehicle for roadworthiness or to warn the driver of a flooded road or accident ahead; but it has been suggested (see para 3.45) that it should not be used for non-traffic purposes. Another alternative to PACE is offered by the common law. Thus, prior to the implementation of PACE and during the miners' strike in 1984, the police successfully relied upon their common law duty to preserve the peace as the basis for stopping vehicles, checking them for travelling pickets, persuading them to turn back, and, on refusal, arresting them. The conditions for exercising this common law power are that the police (a) honestly and (b) reasonably consider that there is (c) a real risk of a breach of the peace, in the sense that it is in close proximity both in place and time (*Moss v McLachlan* (1985)). Condition (b) will depend upon a multitude of factors including, as in *Moss v McLachlan*, whether there have been recent, similar events which have resulted in disorder. But this alone is not, it is submitted, enough. For otherwise all travellers in the direction of, for example, an industrial dispute, all-night party or a fox hunt are deemed to be troublemakers. The police need instead to investigate further to determine whether the particular people stopped pose a real threat to the peace. Since most of the PACE road check powers are dependent on a serious arrestable offence ((1) to (3) in para 3.131, ante), the common law power is a useful adjunct to deal with public order problems (eg suspected hunt saboteurs, travelling hippies, and see now the powers under s 65(2) of the CJPOA 1994 and s 14C of the Public Order Act 1986 considered below para 3.68). It consists of a power to stop a vehicle, make inquiries of its passengers (if a search is required and consent refused, then PACE or other stop and search powers are needed) and arrest them if a breach of the peace is imminent and the passengers will not retreat: and being a common law power it is not trammelled by the procedural requirements of PACE. Sanctions for misuse of the power are to lodge a complaint or to sue for false imprisonment.

POWERS TO STOP PERSONS PROCEEDING

3.138   The Criminal Justice and Public Order Act 1994 creates two powers to stop persons and to direct them not to proceed in a particular direction. While not stop and search powers they are stop powers and are clearly based on the common law powers used in the miners' strike of 1984 and discussed above, para 3.137.

Raves

3.139   Sections 63 to 67 of the CJPOA 1994 (as amended by the Anti-social Behaviour Act 2003) provide powers to deal with unlicensed night-time raves which no longer just applies to open land but includes premises such as a barn, warehouse, etc. Section 63 applies to gatherings of 20 or more persons (whether or not trespassers) at which amplified music is played during the night and is such, by reason of its loudness and duration, as is likely to cause serious distress to the inhabitants of the locality. If, as respects any land in the open air, a superintendent (who does not have to be present at the scene) or above reasonably believes that:

(a)   two or more persons are making preparations for the holding there of a gathering to which this section applies,

(b)   ten or more persons are waiting for such a gathering to begin there, or

(c)   ten or more persons are attending such a gathering which is then in progress,

he may give a direction that those persons and any other persons who come to prepare or wait for or to attend the gathering are to leave the land and remove any vehicles or other property which they have with them on the land (sub-s (1) and (2)). Such a direction may not be given in respect of an exempt person, that is the occupier of the land, any member of his family and any employee or agent of his or any person whose home is situated on the land (sub-s (10)). Persons who know such a direction has been given who fail to leave, or who return within seven days of the direction being given, commit an offence for which they may be arrested (s 63(6), (7) and (8)). Section 64 deals with powers to enter the land and seize vehicles or sound equipment, while s 66 allows a court to order the forfeiture of sound equipment following a conviction for an offence under s 63.

3.140   Where such a direction has been given a constable in uniform who reasonably believes that a person, other than an exempt person as defined above, is on his way to a gathering which is the subject of such a direction, he may:

(a)   stop that person, and

(b)   direct him not to proceed in the direction of the gathering (s 65(1), (3)).

3.141   The power may only be exercised within five miles of the boundary of the gathering (s 65(2)). A person who knows that a direction not to proceed has been given to him and who fails to comply with that direction commits an offence punishable on summary conviction by a fine not exceeding level 3 on the standard scale (s 65(4)). A constable in uniform who reasonably suspects that a person is committing such an offence may arrest him without a warrant. One may note that the power under this section is to stop persons. If they are in a vehicle either s 163 of the Road Traffic Act 1988 can be relied upon to stop the vehicle, or the common law power considered in *Moss v McLachlan* (1985) (see para 3.137, ante).

Trespassory assemblies

3.142   Sections 70 and 71 of the CJPOA 1994 add three new sections, 14A, 14B and 14C, to the Public Order Act 1986. Section 14A provides that if at any time a chief officer of police reasonably believes that an assembly is intended to be held in any district at a place on land to which the public has no, or only a limited, right of access and that the assembly:

(a)   is likely to be held without the permission of the occupier of the land or to conduct itself in such a way as to exceed the limits of any permission of his or the limits of the public's right of access and

(b) may result —
  (i) in serious disruption to the life of the community, or
  (ii) where the land, or a building or a monument on it, is of historical, architectural, archaeological or scientific importance, in significant damage to the land, building or monument,

3.143 he may apply to the council of the district for an order prohibiting for a specified period, not exceeding four days and within a radius of five miles from a specified centre, the holding of all trespassory assemblies in the district or part of it, as specified. On receipt of such an application, a council in England and Wales may, with the consent of the Secretary of State, make such an order in the terms of the application or with such modifications as may be approved by the Secretary of State (s 14A(1), (2) and (6)). In the Metropolitan and City of London police areas the respective Commissioners may, with the consent of the Secretary of State, make such an order (s 14A(4) and (5)).

3.144 Section 14B(1) makes it an offence for a person who knows of the prohibition to organise such an assembly; sub-s (2) makes it an offence for a person who knows of the prohibition to take part in such an assembly; and sub-s (3) makes it an offence to incite an offence under sub-s (2). All three are summary offences: those under sub-s (1) and (3) are punishable by up to three months' imprisonment and/or a level 4 fine, while that under sub-s (2) is punishable only by a level 3 fine. A constable in uniform may arrest without a warrant anyone he reasonably suspects of committing any of these offences (sub-s (4)).

3.145 Section 14C provides that if a constable in uniform reasonably believes that a person is on his way to an assembly within the area to which an order under s 14A applies which the constable reasonably believes is likely to be an assembly which is prohibited by that order, he may, within the area to which the order applies, ie a 5-mile radius from a specified centre:
(a) stop the person, and
(b) direct him not to proceed in the direction of the assembly.

3.146 A person who knows such a direction has been given to him who fails to comply with it is guilty of a summary offence punishable by a level 3 fine (sub-s (3) and (5)). A constable in uniform may arrest without warrant any person he reasonably suspects to be committing such an offence (sub-s (4)). As under s 65 (above) the power is a power to stop persons. Vehicles may be stopped under s 163 of the Road Traffic Act 1988 or the common law power considered in *Moss v McLachlan* (1985).

3.147 In *DPP v Hancock and Tuttle* (1995) it was held that an arrest under s 5(4) of the Public Order Act 1986, using threatening etc words or behaviour, was exercisable only by the constable who warns the person to stop engaging in offensive conduct because the subsection uses the words 'which the constable warns him to stop'. The wording of s 65 and the new s 14C does not require that the arresting officer be the officer who gave the direction not to proceed.

INFORMATION IN ANNUAL REPORTS

3.148 Chief Officers of Police in the provinces and the City of London are required by s 12 of the Police Act 1964 to report annually on the policing of their area to their police committee, and in the Metropolis the Commissioner makes a report to the Home Secretary who is the police authority for the Metropolis. Section 5(1) (Art 7(1)) requires that such annual reports contain information:

(a) about searches recorded under s 3 (Art 5) and carried out in the police force area during the period to which the report relates, and

(b) about road checks set up in that area during that period.

3.149 The information about searches must include the number and category of searches and consequential arrests made in each month under s 1 (s 5(2), Arts 3, 7(2)) but not the number of charges which followed. The information about road checks must include the reasons for authorising each road check and the result of each (s 5(3), Art 7(3)) and also gives the number of vehicles stopped and the number of roads obstructed. The report should also, it is suggested, give information about the locality and duration of each road check, and any hostility provoked by the checks. These reports can form the basis of research into how the powers in PACE are being used. They are collated by the Home Office and published annually as a Statistical Bulletin.

SEARCHES BY CONSTABLES EMPLOYED BY STATUTORY UNDERTAKERS

3.150 'Statutory undertakers' are defined by s 7(3) as 'persons authorised by any enactment to carry on any railway, light railway, road transport, water transport, canal, inland navigation, dock or harbour undertaking' (Art 9(3) – 'aerodrome, dock or harbour'). Most have their own police force, the best known being the British Transport Police who police the premises of the British Railways Board, any subsidiary, or any party who employs them under a police services user agreement (see the Transport Police (Jurisdiction) Act 1994), but there are others such as the Port of Liverpool Police, the Dover Harbour Board Police and the Port of London Authority Police. Legislation already existed empowering such constables to stop, detain and search persons employed by or on the premises of those undertakings, for example, s 54(1) of the British Transport Commission Act 1949; s 157 of the Port of London Act 1964; and the Mersey Docks and Harbour (Police) Order 1975 (SI 1975 No 1224) made under s 14 of the Harbours Act 1964, which is identical to s 157 of the Port of London Act 1968. Section 6(1) of PACE (Art 8(1)) gives a constable the power to stop, detain and search vehicles before they leave a goods area on the premises of the statutory undertaker. 'Goods area' is any area used wholly or mainly for the storage or handling of goods, and which is included in the premises of the statutory undertaker (s 6(2), Art 8(2)).

British Nuclear Fuels plc – premises and goods

3.151 Section 6 of the Public Stores Act 1875 created a power to stop and search persons, vehicles or vessels reasonably suspected of conveying any of Her Majesty's stores which are stolen or unlawfully obtained. Originally applied to the Metropolitan Police, it was extended to constables of the Ministry of Defence Police by the Special Constables Act 1923 and to constables of the Atomic Energy Authority Police by Sch 3 of the Atomic Energy Authority Act 1954. Section 6(3) of PACE extended the power to constables appointed under the Special Constables Act 1923 to police premises in the possession, or under the control of, British Nuclear Fuels plc; or, in Northern Ireland, to special constables appointed to police premises controlled by military forces (s 6(4)). They are deemed to be constables deputed by a public department and any goods or chattels in the possession of BNF plc are deemed to be Her Majesty's (and therefore public) stores. It is the practice to give drivers of goods vehicles entering premises policed by the above a pass specifying the goods carried. This is then checked on exit and random searches are made. As a result constables carrying out such duties do not have to comply with the provisions of ss 1-3 of PACE. Indeed the premises are not public places within that Act, thus s 6 of PACE confers a power to stop and search such vehicles randomly and without the safeguards applicable to vehicles searched under s 1. Persons cannot be searched unless the power under s 1 is available, ie the person must be in a public place and there must be reasonable suspicion. In such a case all the requirements of the Act and Code A apply.

3.152 Provisions made under ss 13 and 13A of the Aviation Security Act 1982 and ss 22 and 23 of the Aviation and Maritime Security Act 1990 enable the Secretary of State for Transport to direct airport managers and harbour authorities to arrange for the proper searching of vessels, premises and persons in their area of operation. These powers are confined to harbours and airports and the ships and aircraft thereon and are not dealt with in detail. One may, however, note that while the powers can be exercised by private security forces and authorise the search of persons and premises on the airport or within the harbour; premises used only as a private dwelling, of which there are many in harbours containing marina developments, may only be searched under the authority of a magistrate's warrant, and by a constable who is a member of a police force maintained under the Police Act 1964 (or the Police Authority for Northern Ireland), or a constabulary, such as the British Transport Police or Port of London Police, which has made an agreement under s 96 of PACE 1984 (Art 16 of the Police (Northern Ireland) Order 1987). Under this provision they accept the same complaints procedure as police forces maintained under the Police Act 1964 and, in effect, accept the codes of practice under the 1984 Act and 1989 Order.

SPORTING EVENTS

3.153 Under the Sporting Events (Control of Alcohol etc) Act 1985 an officer can stop and search a public service vehicle (including a chartered train), or motor vehicle capable of carrying eight or more passengers (and which is carrying two or more), which is en route to or from a designated sporting event if he has reasonable suspicion that alcohol is being, or has been, carried on it (s 7(3)). Under s 7(2) he can also search a person on reasonable suspicion of having committed an offence under the Act. These include the carrying of alcohol on public transport or at a designated sports ground, or of containers which are used to hold drink and which, when empty, are normally discarded or returned to a supplier but which are capable of causing injury (eg a beer bottle), or the offence of supplying alcohol at a designated sporting event without a magistrate's order. Under s 7(1) the officer can enter any part of the designated sports ground (eg directors' hospitality lounge) to enforce the Act. These wide powers are still subject to PACE and Code A, in particular the requirement of reasonable suspicion. Thus, for example, the officer must have the requisite degree of suspicion (Code A, paras 1.6, 1.7) of a particular individual (eg a bulging jacket, clanking of bottles in a carrier bag, sound of an opened can). Routine or random searches can only be justified with the individual's consent (assuming that it is an informed and freely given consent) or as a condition of entry to premises (and that the search is sufficiently proximate to them).

4 Powers to enter and search premises

INTRODUCTION

4.1 At common law the Englishman's 'home was his castle'. In the seventeenth century justices began to grant warrants to enter premises and search for stolen goods. Increasingly statutory powers of entry were granted and there are now a range of entry and search powers available to investigators. Nowadays safeguards are provided against the abuse of power. These are largely contained in PACE and the Code of Practice for the searching of premises by police officers and the seizure of property found by police officers on persons or premises (Code B). In addition to PACE there are a number of other statutory powers many of which are regulated by Code B.

4.2 The exercise of a power of entry, search and seizure will always trigger issues under art 8 and must be justified under art 8(2). Independent judicial scrutiny is an important element in considering whether the conditions in art 8(2) are satisfied. On this see *R v Chesterfield Justices, ex p Bramley and Feldman* (2000).

4.3 It is to be noted that a breach of art 8 will not, of itself result in exclusion of evidence (Ormerod (2003) *R v Khan*.)

4.4 Recognition of human rights principles is built into Code B for the first time, at para 1.3 as follows:

> 'Powers of entry, search and seizure should be fully and clearly justified before use because they may significantly interfere with the occupier's privacy. Officers should consider if the necessary objectives can be met by less intrusive means.'

4.5 Paragraph 1.5 reminds investigators that if the Code and Act are not complied with evidence gained may be 'open to question.'

4.6 Part II of PACE 1984 (Part III of the PACE (NI) Order) deals with the powers and procedures whereby the police and civilians designated under the Police Reform Act

2002 may, first, enter and search premises and, second, seize and retain property discovered during a search of premises. The Act (Order) codifies much of the earlier statutory and common law and implements some of the recommendations of the Royal Commission on Criminal Procedure (1981) (Cmnd 8092). The passage of the Act through Parliament was dominated by discussion of the favourable treatment accorded to certain confidential information (eg medical records, journalistic material). The following preliminary points should be noted:

(a)   Part II of the Act (Part III of the Order) deals with the powers of a constable and designated civilians;

(b)   it is in part without prejudice to earlier powers (eg various statutes permitting the issue of search warrants are preserved);

(c)   as elsewhere, Part II (Part III of the Order) must be read in conjunction with the Code of Practice B, for the latter arguably includes items of sufficient importance to have merited inclusion within the former;

(d)   the broad powers of seizure in s 19 (art 21) accompany all powers of search contained in this or any other statute and consensual searches, but are dealt with separately at para 4.128, post;

(e)   Part II (Part III of the Order) deals with powers of entry and search in relation to premises and 'premises' are given an extended meaning, as follows.

THE MEANING OF 'PREMISES' (s 23, Art 25)

4.7   Throughout the Act (Order), and with particular relevance to this chapter, 'premises' are defined very widely. They include 'any place'. This can be of a private or public nature and open or enclosed, and, somewhat incongruously, vehicles, vessels, aircraft, hovercraft, tents and other movable structures are specifically mentioned as examples in s 23 (art 25). Thus, a garden, a forecourt, a public registry office, a car in a garage, a bicycle, a houseboat, a caravan and a workmen's tent are included. As to limitations, a Canadian court in *Re Laporte and R* (1972) has held that a person's body cannot fall within the word 'place', and, whilst an English court is likely to follow suit, it is difficult to imagine what else cannot be counted as premises, especially since s 23 (art 25) does not offer an exhaustive definition. The word 'place' arose for consideration in *Powell v Kempton Park Racecourse Co Ltd* (1899) in the context of the Betting Act 1853 and Lord James suggested that:

> 'There must be a defined area so marked out that it can be found and recognised as the place where the business is carried on and wherein the bettor can be found. Thus, if a person betted on Salisbury Plain, there would be no "place" within the Act. The whole of Epsom Downs, or any other racecourse, where betting takes place, would not constitute a "place": but directly a definite localisation of the business of betting is effected, be it under a tent or even a moveable umbrella, it may be well held that a "place" exists ...'

4.8   The ideas of delineation and localisation are helpful, but his Lordship's opinion was clearly tied to the narrow context of betting and, given the 1984 Act's (1989

Order's) broader context of the detection of crime, it is highly likely that a racecourse, football ground or private park open to the public will qualify as a 'place' and therefore 'premises'. Where the premises constitute a 'public place', the police do not need any special powers to enter and search (eg Salisbury Plain). However, there may be parts within a public place (eg a tent) which do count as 'premises' and therefore require the special powers of entry in Part II of the Act (Part III of the Order). Moreover, if the police wish to dig up the land itself, whether it is public or private, the consent of the landowner or one of the powers to be discussed below must be available.

LIMITATION ON THE DEFINITION OF PREMISES BY ss 17(2)(B) AND 32(7) (Arts 19(2)(B) AND 34(7))

4.9 These provisions limit the definition of premises where they consist of 'separate dwellings'. This term is well known in housing legislation and in relation to Rent Acts it has been interpreted as follows:

'There is a letting of a part of a house as a separate dwelling ... if, and only if, the accommodation which is shared with others does not comprise any of the rooms which may fairly be described as "living rooms" or "dwelling rooms" ...' (*Cole v Harris* (1945))

4.10 A kitchen or lounge is fairly described as a 'living room' and thus a person who shares such a room with others in the same building cannot regard his sleeping quarters as a separate dwelling for the purposes of ss 17 and 32 (arts 19 and 34). The following examples illustrate the meaning of 'separate dwelling', but it must be emphasised that each case will depend upon its particular facts and that the police should consequently investigate the circumstances whenever time permits. If time does not permit, and the police enter separate dwellings, the entry and search will be unlawful.

(a) D, a student, occupies a house with four other students. He has a study bedroom and shares the kitchen, bathroom and toilet facilities. If D commits an offence, the entire premises are subject to a search for D (s 17, art 19) or evidence of his offence (s 32, art 34).

(b) Students occupy self-contained flats in a block in which only the bathroom and toilet facilities are shared. Each flat is a separate dwelling and the limitations of s 17(2)(b) (art 19(2)(b)) and s 32(7) (art 34(7)) apply. If, therefore, one student commits an offence, only the dwelling in which he is, or is reasonably believed to be, or in which he was when arrested, or immediately before arrest, can be entered and searched together with the bathroom and toilet, and the communal parts.

4.11 Where the property is in multi-occupancy the warrant should specify that part to which it is directed (*R v South Western Magistrates' Court and Metropolitan Police Comr, ex p Cofie*). A failure by the Constable to specify that she wanted to search a specific part of a multi-occupancy house breached the requirements of s 15 (6) (a) (iv) in that it did not specify in explicit terms the particular premises which it was desired to search rendered the warrant unlawful.

4.12   Note, however, that if D is arrested for an arrestable offence under s 18, 'premises' are not so limited, and any premises occupied or controlled by D may be searched if there are reasonable grounds to believe that there is evidence in them. (See further for the meaning of 'separate dwelling', Hill and Redman, *Law of Landlord and Tenant* (18th edn, para C 309).)

4.13   The broad scope of s 23 (art 25) is of particular significance when it is remembered that all the powers of entry and search dealt with in this chapter concern 'premises'. Its generality can be contrasted with the three attempts which the Standing Committee made at defining 'offshore installation' in s 23 (art 25). Reliance was finally placed on the earlier version in s 1(3)(b) of the Mineral Workings (Offshore Installations) Act 1971, viz, 'any installation which is maintained, or is intended to be established, for underwater exploitation or exploration', eg an oil-drilling platform.

4.14   It is important to note that the power of entry and search, whether under a warrant or under a statutory power, is generally a power to enter and search the premises, not persons in or on those premises. There is an exception under s 23 of the Misuse of Drugs Act 1971 where magistrates can issue a warrant to enter and search premises and any person found there, but generally the search is confined to premises. Where a person is arrested on premises a power to search the person arises under s 32 (art 34) (see para 5.153, post). If the premises or place is one to which the public has access and is not a dwelling, the stop and search power under s 1 of PACE 1984 may apply to permit the search of persons.

PART A: GENERAL POWERS OF ENTRY AND SEARCH

4.15   These arise under the authority of a search warrant, or on or after an arrest, or when a breach of the peace is involved, or under specific, miscellaneous statutory powers. The renowned cases of *Leach v Money* and *Entick v Carrington* (1765) remain authorities for the proposition that any invasion of property is a trespass unless supported by a legal power. As will be seen, however, the breadth of legal powers contained in Part II of the Act provides the police with ample opportunity to avoid such civil liability. There is, in addition to the statutory and common law powers, the ability to search premises with the consent of the owner or occupier. The various powers are now dealt with together with searches carried out with consent, commencing with powers to enter and search premises with a warrant.

ENTRY AND SEARCH UNDER A SEARCH WARRANT

'There is no mystery about the word "warrant"; it simply means a document issued by a person in authority under power conferred in that behalf authorising the doing of an act which would otherwise be illegal.' (Lord Wilberforce in *IRC v Rossminster Ltd* (1980))

4.16 The common law permitted only one type of search warrant – a justice of the peace could authorise a warrant to search for stolen goods. Over the years Parliament provided specific warrant powers: indeed, s 26 of the Theft Act 1968 (Theft Act (NI) 1969, s 25) in practice superseded the solitary common law power. These statutory powers do not conform to a standard formula but ss 15 and 16 of PACE 1984 (arts 17 and 18 of the NI Order) now provide a standard form of application for, and standard execution of, all search warrants whether issued under the authority of an Act passed before or after the 1984 Act (1989 Order).

4.17 With the exception of a superintendent's power to issue an authority to search under s 26(2) of the Theft Act 1968 (which was repealed by Sch 7 of PACE 1984; s 25(2) of the Theft Act (NI) 1969 was repealed by Sch 7 of the 1989 Order), all pre-existing powers survived the 1984 Act (s 8(5)) and the 1989 Order (art 10(5)). The piecemeal development of statutory warrant powers meant that under the law as it existed before the 1984 Act and the 1989 Order, warrants could be obtained to search for items which it is an offence knowingly to possess, for example, stolen goods, drugs, firearms, explosives (hereinafter prohibited goods) and for evidence of specific offences under the authority of a particular statutory power, for example, illegal gaming under s 43(4) of the Gaming Act 1968. However, there was no general power to issue a warrant to search for evidence of an offence which was not prohibited goods or not specifically provided for. One could obtain a warrant to search for evidence of fraud under the Hop (Prevention of Fraud) Act 1866 but not for evidence of murder. The law was therefore ripe for reform. The Royal Commission on Criminal Procedure (1981) recommended the retention of these existing powers, most of which permitted a magistrate to issue a warrant to search premises, including the premises of someone not himself implicated in the offence or of someone innocently possessing prohibited goods, but recommended a general power to issue a warrant to search for evidence of crime which is reasonably believed to be on premises which are not occupied or controlled by the suspect. However, it sought to mark the seriousness of the intrusion on innocent citizens, by:
(a) confining such searches to 'grave offences'; and
(b) making the issuing authority a circuit judge.

4.18 The PACE Act (Order) follows that recommendation but draws a distinction between the type of material sought: broadly the distinction is between non-confidential and confidential material.

4.19 In respect of non-confidential evidence a magistrate may issue a warrant if, but only if, the offence is a 'serious arrestable offence' (defined by s 116 (art 87) and discussed at paras 2.99-2.107, ante).

4.20 In respect of confidential material only a circuit judge can order its production or issue a warrant to search for and seize it if the offence is a serious arrestable offence, though if the confidential material could have been the subject of a magistrate's warrant before PACE 1984, the offence need not be a serious arrestable offence (ss 9-14 and Sch 1 (arts 11-16 and Sch 1) deal with the procedure to be adopted and define confidential material, see Part B of this Chapter, post).

SUMMARY OF THE LAW

4.21   The PACE Act (PACE Order) superimposes the warrant for evidence and the special procedure for obtaining confidential material on the existing statutory and common law powers. Since s 8 (art 10) refers to 'relevant evidence' (defined by s 8(4) (art 10(4)) as 'anything that would be admissible in evidence at a trial for the offence') it could be argued that all applications for warrants to search for evidence of a serious arrestable offence, including those for seeking prohibited goods, which will often be evidence of a serious arrestable offence (eg a search warrant for the proceeds of a £1 million bullion robbery), must be made under s 8 (art 10). The effect of this interpretation would be to confine pre-existing powers to arrestable or general offences. It is submitted that this is not the intended effect of s 8 (art 10). If, for example, the material sought is £1 million in gold bullion which is the proceeds of a robbery, an application for a warrant should be sought under s 26(1) of the Theft Act 1968 (Theft Act (NI) 1969, s 25). If, however, the material sought is other relevant evidence of that offence, it is unobtainable under the 1968 Act and if it is likely to be of substantial value to the investigation (for example, the vehicle used in the robbery), application must be made under s 8 (art 10). If the material sought is documents in the possession of a bullion dealer which are likely to identify persons dealing in the bullion, they are likely to be confidential material (special procedure material under s 14(1)(a), art 16(1)(a)) and subject to the special procedure set out in Sch 1 and considered in Part B of this Chapter, post. As a further complication there will be occasions, admittedly rare, when the material is prohibited goods but is also held in confidence by a third party, for example, documents stolen from a government department and passed to a journalist who holds them in confidence. Section 9(2) (art 11(2)) provides that pre-existing statutory powers to issue a warrant for such material cease to have effect and the material must then be sought via the special procedure in the 1984 Act (1989 Order). (Note that in these rare cases the offence need not be a serious arrestable offence, though it often will be.) Sections 15 and 16 (arts 17, 18) of the Act apply criteria governing the issue of all warrants.

4.22   Before PACE 1984 search warrants were comparatively rare, accounting for some 17% of all searches. The wide-ranging post-arrest search powers under ss 18 and 32 of PACE 1984 (arts 20 and 34 of the NI Order) together with the ability of the police to continue to persuade the owner or occupier to consent to a search were thought likely to lead to even less reliance on the search warrant. This was confirmed by research Lidstone and Bevan ('Search and Seizure under the Police and Criminal Evidence Act' (Sheffield: University of Sheffield Faculty of Law, 1992, Ch 3).

4.23   It was further predicted that the new warrant under s 8 of PACE 1984 would, given that it was directed towards evidence of a serious arrestable offence which is in possession of innocent third parties and is not held under an obligation of confidence, rarely be used. The real impact of PACE 1984 is to be seen in the use of the special procedure under s 9 and Sch 1 of the Act. A survey of provincial police forces revealed that all had made use of these powers to a greater or lesser extent ranging from 2 to 150 applications between 1 January 1986, when the Act came into force, and 1 September 1989, the date of the survey. In total there were over 1,500 applications under Sch 1 in provincial forces, some of which were multiple applications, ie seeking two or more orders or warrants, with the result that 1,629 were granted, consisting of 41 warrants and 1,588 production orders. Only seven applications were refused. In addition 469 cases were recorded in which confidential material was obtained with the consent of the person in possession, but it was made clear that consent had been obtained in many more cases and accurate records of consensual obtaining of material were not kept. As one would expect, the Sch 1 procedure is used much more by the capital's police than by provincial forces. These powers will be dealt with in detail in Part B, para 4.194 et seq.

NATURE OF A WARRANT

4.24 Provided that the applicant for a warrant acts in good faith, sets out his application fully, complies with the terms of the warrant and executes it in accordance with s 16 (art 18) of the 1984 Act, he is immune from legal action by the occupier even if the warrant has been improperly issued. The occupier's remedy in such a case lies against the issuing authority, but it will be extremely difficult to substantiate the complaint. For, though the magistrate acts judicially in assessing whether there is sufficient ground for issuing a warrant (*Hope v Evered* (1886)), the application is heard ex parte and the governing test is that of reasonable grounds – a test which is readily satisfied in practice. The Act (Order) does offer some assistance here, since s 15 (art 17) and the Code of Practice provides a checklist of criteria which must be satisfied for all search warrants, and s 8 (art 10) and Sch 1 list those which a magistrate or circuit judge must additionally observe when hearing an application for a warrant or order for production under the Act in relation to a serious arrestable offence involving confidential information. Earlier statutory powers of search gave magistrates a discretion as to whether to issue a warrant even if a prima facie case is made out and s 8 (art 10) retains this principle – a magistrate 'may' issue such a warrant. The Royal Commission (1981) noted the 'comment that magistrates may exercise insufficient care in ensuring that a warrant is necessary; and that too often they merely rubber stamp police requests' (Report, para 3.37).

APPLICATIONS FOR A WARRANT – SUMMARY

4.25

(a)	Warrants for serious arrestable offences	1984 Act, s 8 (1989 Order, Art 10) and Code of Practice
(b)	Warrants for material which it is an offence to possess	1984 Act, s 15 (1989 Order, Art 17), terms of particular governing statute eg s 26 of the Theft Act 1968 Code of Practice

(c)	Any warrant involving confidential information	1984 Act, ss 9-14 Sch 1, (1989 Order arts 11-16 and Sch 1) Code of Practice
(d)	Manner of execution of all warrants	1984 Act, ss 16, 19 (1989 Order arts 18, 21) Code of Practice

4.26   The following preliminary points should be noted.:

(i)   Sections 15 and 16 (arts 17 and 18) govern the application for and execution of search warrants issued under PACE 1984 or Order, and any other enactment whether passed before or after PACE 1984 and Order. Importantly s 15(1) (art 17(1)) states that

> 'an entry on or search of premises under a warrant is unlawful unless it complies with this section and s 16' (art 18).

It is not clear from the wording of s 15 whether 'it' refers to the 'warrant' or the entry and search. The clearer formulation in art 17(1) of the PACE (NI) Order, which states 'an entry on or search of premises under a warrant is unlawful unless the warrant complies with this Article and is executed in accordance with Article 18', makes it clear that it is the entry on or search of premises which is unlawful if ss 15 and 16 (arts 17 and 18) are not complied with. (See *R v Longman* [1988] Crim LR 534 and *R v Central Criminal Court and British Railway Board, ex p AJD Holdings Ltd* (1992) – para 4.100, post.)

(ii)   One distinction between (a) and (b) (above) is that material sought under (a) need not be unlawfully possessed or involve a breach of the law, whilst material under (b) must meet that requirement and must also be governed by a statutory power to issue a warrant. For example, stolen goods, drugs, explosives and obscene publications come under (b), whereas documents indicating the source of, for example, the explosives can only be obtained under s 8 (art 10) if the offence is a serious arrestable offence (s 116 (art 87) defines 'serious arrestable offence' and is discussed at para 2.99-2.107, ante).

(iii)   Warrants under (b) are issued under other legislation and can cover offences which may or may not be serious arrestable offences.

(iv)   In all cases the occupier or owner of the premises to be searched need not be suspected of an offence. Indeed, applications for a warrant (particularly under s 8) are likely to be made more often in respect of third parties who are not themselves suspected of involvement.

(v)   The complexity of these procedures is intensified by the fact that some of the preconditions for obtaining a search warrant appear in the Act (Order) whilst others are contained in Code of Practice B.

(vi)   The issuing authority will usually either be a magistrate or a circuit judge (a county court judge in NI) (under the special procedure provisions (see para 4.194, post) or under the terms of certain pre-existing statutes – eg Incitement to Disaffection Act 1934). The 1984 Act did not endorse a recommendation of the Royal Commission (1981) (para 3.45) that senior police officers should be allowed to authorise warrants in cases of urgency. However, some statutes, which do permit such authorisation by the police, survive the 1984 Act (eg Explosives Act 1875, s 73; Official Secrets Act 1911, s 9(2); Licensing Act 1964, s 45; but not the Theft Act 1968, s 26(2), which was repealed by Sch 7 of the 1984 Act. The same provision in s 25(2) of the Theft Act (NI) Act 1969 is also repealed by Sch 7 of the NI Order). The remaining authorisations are not warrants and are not therefore governed by ss 15 and 16 of the 1984 Act (arts 17, 18). The powers of seizure under s 19 (art 21) do, however, apply.

APPLICATION FOR A WARRANT – GENERAL

4.27 An application for a search warrant can in principle be made by any police officer, but Code B 3.4 (a) requires each application to be supported by a signed written authority from an officer of at least Inspector Rank (or, if the application is urgent, by the most senior officer on duty). This is a prudent safeguard given the sometimes difficult legal questions which may arise on an application, eg whether the offence is a serious arrestable one or involves confidential information (in which case the special procedure may arise and the approval of at least a superintendent is necessary; see para 4.175, post). If the search may have a significantly adverse effect on police/community relations, the community liaison officer should be consulted (except in urgent cases) (Code B 3.5). The local police/community consultative group, where it exists, or its equivalent, should be informed as soon as practicable after a search has taken place where there is reason to believe that it might have an adverse effect on relations between the police and the community (Code B, 3.5). This is a welcome recognition of the unease which can be generated, principally amongst ethnic minorities, by insensitive or heavy-handed policing and which has attracted so much publicity in the past. If such an effect is likely, it will be good police practice for the liaison officer and/or a member of the police/community panel (see s 106) to witness the execution of the warrant.

4.28 An application is heard ex parte. It must be supported by an information in writing (s 15(3), art 17(3)) and the issuing authority may ask questions of the officer (s 15(4), art 17(4)). While circuit judges hearing an application for a warrant under Sch 1 may ask pertinent questions, magistrates rarely do so, indeed they see little scope for doing so. Section 15(2) (art 17(2)) places the applying constable under a duty to state:
(i)   the grounds for the search;
(ii) the empowering statute; and
(iii) to specify the premises to be entered and searched; and
(iv) to identify, so far as is practicable, the articles or persons to be sought.

4.29 The central requirement is (i). In addition to the requirements of s 15. Code 3.6 requires the application to contain the following additional information:
(i)   the grounds for the application, including, when the purpose of the proposed search is to find evidence of an alleged offence, an indication of how the evidence relates to the investigation (Code 3.6(d));

(ii) to specify that there are no reasonable grounds to believe the material to be sought when making application to (a) justice of the peace or a judge, consists of or includes items subject to legal privilege and (b) to a justice of the peace consists of or includes excluded material or special procedure material (Code 3.6(e)).

4.30   It is also to be noted that, if applicable, a request for the warrant to authorise a person or persons to accompany the officer who executes the warrant.

4.31   Code B Note of Guidance 3A does not require the officer to reveal the identity of an informant, though the officer concerned should be prepared to deal with the accuracy of previous information provided by the source. In a study carried out by the previous authors, in 61.0% of warrants issued under the Theft Act 1968, the grounds for the search was the formula 'as a result of information received from a previously reliable source' or a variant of it. The word 'informant' is often taken by magistrates to mean the sort of person who is himself involved in crime and who may be at risk if his identity is revealed. In this context it is used to describe any person who supplies information, eg the mother of the thief, a barmaid in whose pub the thief tried to sell property stolen from her, or a witness who saw D leave premises which had been burgled, carrying a bulky black plastic sack. In each of these cases the magistrate could be told the source of the information, though it need not, of course, be set out in the information. Questioning which might reveal this is something of a rarity largely because magistrates recognise that there may be a need to protect sources and assume that all 'information received' is from such a source.

4.32   Code B 3.1 and 3.2 require the police:
(a) to check that information received is accurate, recent and supplied in good faith, not provided maliciously and, if based on an anonymous source, that corroboration has been sought; and
(b) to make reasonable inquiries to establish what, if anything, is known about the likely occupier, the nature of the premises and whether they have been previously searched (many forces keep a register of premises previously searched for this purpose).

4.33   The Code is a useful checklist for magistrates who should at least establish that these requirements have been satisfied.

4.34   As to (iii), s 15(2)(b) (art 17(2)(b)) imposes a statutory duty on the applicant to 'specify the premises which it is desired to enter and search'. While s 15(2)(c) allows a degree of flexibility in identifying the articles or persons to be sought by the phrase 'as far as is practicable', s 15(2)(b) provides no such flexibility. It is an unqualified duty to specify correctly the premises to be searched. In the pre-PACE case of *R v Atkinson* (1976) it was held that a warrant to enter flat 45 did not authorise the search of flat 30. This was said to be 'not so much a misdescription of premises as a description of other premises'. The words of the statute are clear and the words of the Code should not be taken as permitting laxity in identifying and specifying the premises to be searched.

4.35   As to (iv) it must be accepted that a certain amount of leeway in the identification of the property sought (though perhaps not of the person) is justified, particularly in respect of stolen goods. Hence the phrase 'as far as is reasonably practicable' in s 15(2)(c) (art 17(2)(c)). However, the study carried out by the previous authors revealed that a number of warrant applications used generic descriptions such as 'electrical goods' or 'ladies' clothing' which also appeared on the warrant as a description of the goods sought. Even allowing for the difficulty in being specific this should not have been accepted as satisfying s 15(2)(c) (art 17(2)(c)). Neither should it satisfy s 15(6) which requires that a warrant specify:

(a)
  (i)   the name of the person who applies for it;
  (ii) the date of issue;
  (iii) the enactment under which it was issued; and
  (iv) the premises to be searched; and
(b) shall identify, so far as is practicable, the articles or persons sought.

4.36 In *R v Central Criminal Court and British Railway Board, ex p AJD Holdings Ltd* (1992) a warrant granted to British Rail police under s 9 and Sch 1 of PACE 1984 was held to be invalid because it failed to comply with s 15(6)(b). The information referred to 'all records of business dealings relating to the finances of [the company] namely, letters, notes ....', whereas the warrant referred to letters and notes but failed to identify them as records of financial dealings. The warrant did not therefore comply with s 15 and was invalid under s 15(1).

4.37 Similarly in *R v Reading Justices, ex p South West Meat Ltd* (1992). There a warrant to search the premises of South West Meat Ltd was issued to the Avon and Somerset Police at the instigation of the Meat Intervention Board, a government department with no express powers to enter and search premises. Documents were seized and retained by the Board. There were a number of errors and discrepancies in the information, the warrant and the execution of it. Principally it was issued under the Theft Act 1968 though the documents sought were not stolen goods (s 8 of PACE 1984 would have been appropriate if a serious arrestable offence was involved), the description of the objects sought was too general, the documents sought were not specified with precision and the persons who could accompany the police were not identified in the warrant. It followed that the warrant was invalid under s 15(1), the entry and search under it were unlawful, therefore there was no authority to seize and retain the documents which the court ordered should be returned to South West Meat Ltd.

4.38 In *R v Hunt* (1994) one of the grounds for appeal was that a warrant, issued under s 20C(1) of the Taxes Management Act 1970, was invalid because the officers entitled to enter under the warrant were not named; instead the warrant, while naming the officer in overall charge, provided for not more than 55 officers to enter the premises. The Court of Appeal held that this did not invalidate the warrant. (The court went on to say that if the warrant had been technically defective, the court could have refused to exclude the documents seized under it, either pursuant to s 78 or under its common law powers, there being no prejudice to the appellants by stating the numbers rather than the names. This is consistent with the common law approach to exclusion of evidence. It by no means follows that admitting evidence seized unlawfully would have such an adverse effect on the fairness of the trial that it ought not to be admitted, and the common law has steadfastly refused to exclude real evidence simply because it was unlawfully obtained (see *R v Wright* (1994), considered at para 4.131, post and *R v Stewart* (1995) considered at para 2.134, ante and para 8.98, post). However, if action is taken before trial, as in South West Meat Ltd above, the fact that there is no lawful authority to seize and retain means a court can order the police to return the evidence.)

4.39 In addition to the requirements of s 15 the requirements of the authorising statute must also be complied with. In *Darbo v DPP* (1992) a warrant issued under s 3 of the Obscene Publications Act 1959 was held to be invalid because it authorised a search not only for 'obscene articles' as stated in s 3, but also for 'any other material of a sexually explicit nature' (which may or may not have been obscene) thereby wrongly conferring a search power beyond that authorised by s 3. This rendered the search warrant ultra vires and meant that the police were not acting in the execution of their duty in entering and searching the premises. The occupier was not then guilty of wilfully obstructing the constables under s 51(2) of the Police Act 1964.

4.40 Code B 3.8 stipulates that, if a warrant is refused, no further application in respect of the same premises can be made unless it is supported by additional grounds. If that happens, however, there is no obligation on the police to reveal the existence of the earlier application and this is believed to have led to 'forum shopping' in those rare cases in which a magistrate has refused an application. This is very unlikely except in relation to out-of-hours applications. Procedures under which the clerk must be contacted first and he directs the police to a magistrate are designed to ensure that this does not happen. Where such procedures are not in place magistrates, or their clerks, should inquire about this so that each application can be judged in its proper context.

4.41 A renewed application without additional grounds would almost certainly render the issue of the warrant unlawful and a potentially successful application for abuse of process.

4.42 The Royal Commission (1981) suggested (para 3.42) a two-stage procedure whereby the police would apply ex parte for an order directed to the occupier to produce the evidence. If he objected, he could appeal to the court against the order. If he then lost, a warrant could be issued. The Act adopts an inter partes procedure for certain types of evidence of a confidential nature (Sch 1, para 4.86, post), but for all other types of warrants the opportunities for a disgruntled occupier to challenge the issue of a warrant are slender. The issuing authority is not obliged to state its reasons and the contents of the warrant (see para 4.47, post) do not disclose anything of the judicial reasoning.

4.43 The 1984 Act (1989 Order) does not increase the degree of specificity of a search warrant. Though a copy of the warrant must be given to the occupier, or left on the premises (s 16(5) to (7)) (art 18(5) to (7)) and the occupier has the right to inspect a copy of the warrant, endorsed with the result of the search, which must be deposited at the court of issue (in Northern Ireland the court in which the premises searched is situated) (s 16(9) to (12) (art 18(9) to (12)), this will not disclose the reason why those premises were searched. The notice of powers and rights which Code B 6.7 requires the officer conducting the search to give to the occupier is equally uninformative in this respect. In *R (Cronin) v Sheffield Magistrates* (2003) an occupier challenged the issue of a search warrant under Arts 6 and 8 of the ECHR. The challenge failed (an appeal to Strasbourg is anticipated) but the Court held that, unless public interest immunity applies, the occupier may be entitled to a copy of the information. Applications for warrants are without notice proceedings, sometimes applications are made out of court to magistrates and, even when the application is made at court, no transcript is kept. In this case the evidence was that the application took less than three minutes but still there was no record. The case decided that there is no requirement for the court to give reasons but principles of accountability suggest that more detailed records ought to be kept. In *R v Rotherham Magistrates' Court, ex p Todd* (2000) it was held that the important public interest in protecting the rights of citizens against unlawful invasion could be a consideration on an application for a stay of proceedings on the grounds of abuse of process or to exclude evidence under s 78. Although the search was unlawful there was no question of mala fides and the evidence was admitted.

4.44 Generally an attempt to discover the source of any information will be met with a claim to privilege against disclosure based on public interest and by the principle that the police are protected against tortious action provided that they apply for a warrant in good faith and act in obedience to its terms (Constables Protection Act 1750, s 6). (See *Hope v Evered* (1886). In *R v Reading Justices, ex p South West Meat Ltd* (1992) (considered above, para 4.37) the court held that the protection of the Act was not available to the police because what had occurred was not 'in obedience' to the terms of the warrant.)

4.45 But immunity may be lost if there is unreasonable delay about making a decision to prosecute (*IRC v Rossminster* (1980)).

4.46 The occupier's remedy could lie against the magistrate for exceeding his jurisdiction (Justices of the Peace Act 1979, s 45; *Horsfield v Brown* (1932)) but, unless he could prove bad faith on the part of the magistrate, the only remedy is to seek judicial review of the court's decision. To do so would require strong evidence to show that the issuing court had no reasonable grounds on which to act and, even if successful, such an action does not bring an award of damages. Section 27 of the Administration of Justice Act 1964 provides for an indemnity out of public funds to be given to magistrates against whom damages have been awarded provided that they have acted reasonably. For a review of the liability of magistrates and in particular for a discussion as to whether an action is still available at common law against magistrates who act in bad faith but within their jurisdiction, see *Re McC* (1984).

CONTENTS OF A WARRANT

4.47 All search warrants must specify the name of the applicant, the date of issue, the empowering statute, the premises to be searched and, where practicable, the articles or persons sought (s 15(6), art 17(6)); the time when the search is to take place need not be stated, but under s 16(3) (art 18(3)) all warrants must be executed within one month. The reference to the empowering statute in s 15(6)(a)(iii) (art 17(6)(a)(iii)) will mention the offence suspected and the type of material which is sought, but beyond this the occupier has no 'right to be informed of the "reasonable grounds" of which the judge was satisfied' (Lord Wilberforce in *IRC v Rossminster* (1980)). Some earlier statutes required the officer executing the warrant to be named therein (eg Firearms Act 1968, s 46; see further Appendix 5 to the Royal Commission on Criminal Procedure's Law and Procedure volume), but s 16(1) now permits any constable to execute a warrant. Section 125 of the Magistrates' Courts Act 1980 provides that certain warrants, including search warrants, may be executed anywhere in England and Wales by any person to whom it is directed or by any constable acting within his police area. All police areas in England and Wales contain a number of petty sessional areas (Northern Ireland is one police area). Section 125 therefore permits a constable in one petty sessional area to seek a search warrant for execution in another petty sessional area within the same police force. If the warrant is directed to a named police officer, that officer can execute it anywhere in England and Wales. Research shows that it is not uncommon for police officers to apply to magistrates in their area for a search warrant in respect of premises in another petty sessional area but within their force area. One warrant was issued by magistrates in a town in Wiltshire in respect of premises in a Midlands town in a different police and petty sessional area. Magistrates make much of their local knowledge in the issue of warrants. Clearly such knowledge can play no part in the issue of a warrant in respect of premises in another area. The citizen is disadvantaged in such a case because s 16(9) to (12) of PACE 1984 (art 18(9) to (12) of the Order) requires the police to return the executed warrant, duly endorsed, to the court of issue, where the occupier of the premises may inspect it provided he does so within the period of 12 months from its return to the court (s 16(12)). If issued by a magistrate in another area the occupier will have to travel to that area, assuming he has the wit to examine the copy warrant given to him, which will indicate in which petty sessional area it was issued. In Northern Ireland the duty is to return the endorsed warrant to the court for the area in which the premises searched are situated (art 18(c)). It would seem that the framers of the 1984 Act did not anticipate that magistrates would be issuing warrants in respect of premises outside their petty sessional area. Despite the fact that a magistrate's jurisdiction to issue search warrants is not limited to his petty sessional area, it would be in the interest of the public, with little if any detriment to the police, if he exercised his undoubted discretion and refrained from doing so (unless there is some pressing reason why he should deal with the application) and referred the police applicant to a justice of the peace for the petty sessional area in which the premises are situated.

4.48   Code B 8.2 restates the requirement in s 16(9) (art 18(9)) that the executed warrant be endorsed to show whether the articles sought were found and whether other articles were seized. In addition the endorsement must include the date and time of execution, the name of the officer executing it (warrant number and duty station only if a terrorism investigation) and whether a copy of the warrant, and the Notice of

Powers and Rights (see para 4.156, post) were handed to the occupier, or whether they were left on the premises, and if so where.

CONDUCT OF SEARCHES (S 16, ART 18, CODE B)

4.49 Sections 15 and 16 (arts 17 and 18) apply to the application for issue, and to the execution, of all warrants to enter and search premises and the Code of Practice supplements these provisions and makes special provision for search warrants for excluded or special procedure material. Considerable cross-reference between the Act and the Code of Practice is necessary. As to searches by consent, the safeguards in the Code are considered in para 4.78, post. The sanction against over-zealous police conduct lies in the occupier's withdrawal of consent, but this may be difficult to enforce once the police are inside the premises.

Who may enter and search?

4.50 Any constable or an investigator who has been designated under the Police Reform Act 2002 may exercise the entry and search powers (eg s 16(1) (art 18(1)) in relation to warrants). 'Constable' in this context refers to the office rather than the rank. An officer must be identified as 'the officer in charge of the search' (code B2.10). He or she is assigned specific responsibilities under the Code. Paragraph 2F of the notes for guidance suggest the officer in charge should normally be the most senior officer present, but allows for an officer of lower rank to be appointed if that officer is more conversant with the facts and it is more appropriate for that officer to be in charge of the search. Where all officers in a premises search are of the same rank one of them must be appointed the 'officer in charge'.

4.51 In the case of Sch 1 warrants and warrants issued under Sch 5 of the Terrorism Act 2000 an officer of at least the rank of Inspector must be designated 'officer in charge' of the search.

4.52 Warrants issued under s 8 (art 10) and existing or future statutes are subject to ss 15 and 16 (arts 17 and 18), and s 16(2) (art 18(2)) provides that a warrant may authorise persons to accompany any constable who is executing it. (In *R v Hunt* (1994) a warrant authorising 55 officers to enter without naming them was held to be valid but in *R v Reading Justices, ex p South West Meat Ltd* (1992), where the police obtained a warrant on behalf of the Meat Intervention Board, the failure to include officers of the Board on the warrant meant that they had no right to enter the premises.) This may be a social worker in offences involving children, or a community relations officer or community leader in searches which might have an adverse effect on police/public relations. In the previous authors' study no warrant authorised anyone else to accompany the police though on one occasion the police took a carpenter along to lift floorboards. One may note in this context s 48(9) of the Children Act 1989 under which the applicant, usually a social worker, may apply for a warrant authorising any constable to assist in the exercise of an emergency protection order (EPO), using reasonable force if necessary. The court may issue the warrant where it appears that the person attempting to exercise the powers under the EPO (that is, a power to enter specified premises and search for the child subject of the order, s 48(3)), has been, or is likely to be, prevented from doing so by being refused entry to the premises, or access to the named child (s 48(9)). The warrant must be addressed to a constable and executed by him. The applicant must be allowed to accompany him if he desires and the court does not direct otherwise (s 48(10)). The court may also direct that the constable be accompanied by a registered medical practitioner, registered nurse or registered health visitor if he so chooses (s 48(11)). The child should be named or, if not named, identified as clearly as possible (s 48(13)).

Timing of the search

4.53   All warrants must be executed within one month of issue (s 16(3), art 18(3)) and can only be used once (s 4(2) of the Protection of Children Act 1978 and s 17(1) of the Video Recording Act 1984, both of which prescribed different periods, are amended by Sch 9 of the CJPOA 1994 so that the standard period of one month prescribed by s 16(3) applies). In one city studied by the previous authors 48.0% of the warrants issued were returned unexecuted. All but one of these were warrants issued under the Misuse of Drugs Act 1971. They were obtained as part of a major drugs operation and were, effectively, renewed if not executed within a month. Searches must, if possible, be conducted at 'a reasonable hour' (s 16(4), art 18(4)) (Code B 6.2) unless this might frustrate the purpose of the search. Previous codes gave some guidance as to what is reasonable. Police are to have regard, among other considerations, to the times of day at which the occupier of the premises is likely to be present. They should not search at a time when he, or any other person on the premises, is likely to be asleep unless not doing so is likely to frustrate the purpose of the search. This permits much flexibility and a late night or early morning search may often be the best time to find the occupier at home. The 'dawn raid' did not occur very often in the previous authors' research study. Armed raids took place at this time because few people were about, thus reducing the risk of injury if shots were fired. Significantly the most recent edition of the code (2003) omits the guidance on what is a 'reasonable hour'.

Procedure for entry

4.54   For all warrants, the officer in charge of the search must identify himself to the occupier or, in his absence, to any person who 'appears to the constable to be in charge of the premises' (s 16(6)(b), art 18(6)(b)). The latter condition could include a suspect's girlfriend or a firm's employee or a student who is sharing a house (bearing in mind the broad definition of 'premises' – para 4.7, ante). It could perhaps extend to a caretaker or a workman engaged, in the occupier's absence, on repairs to property or even to a child. But if the constable is not in uniform, it would be most unwise to undertake a search of premises occupied only by children. In such circumstances a neighbour or other responsible person should be called in to take care of the child. If the constable is not in uniform, he must prove his office (s 16(5)(a), art 18(5)(a)) and production of his warrant card will be the standard method. He must in any event produce the search warrant and give a copy to the occupier or person in charge (s 16(5)(b) and (c), art 18(5)(b) and (c)). In *R v Chief Constable of Lancashire, ex p Parker* (1993) a declaration that the execution of a warrant was invalid was granted. The warrant issued under s 9 and Sch 1 of PACE 1984 included a schedule of documents which satisfied all the requirements of s 15(6) but the police detached part of the schedules and replaced them with photocopies. Therefore they failed to produce the whole of the original warrant to the applicants in breach of s 16(5)(b). The police admitted a breach of s 16(5)(c) in supplying the occupant with a copy of the warrant without the schedules which had become detached. It was argued on behalf of the police that they were entitled to retain the documents seized despite the breaches arguing that s 22(2)(a) (considered at para 4.139, post) permitted the retention of material even if unlawfully seized. The court rejected this argument holding that s 22(2)(a) did not confer a right to retain documents seized unlawfully.

4.55   Section 16(5) and (6) (art 18(5) and (6)) do not prevent the police entering the premises without identifying themselves or producing the warrant when it is necessary to maintain the element of surprise, eg lest the occupier flush drugs down the lavatory or prepare to meet the police with force. Section 16(5) refers to the time of occupation rather than the time when the duties are to be performed. Code B 6.4 and 6.5 indicate the normal procedure when there is no need for surprise and the exceptional circumstances in which there is such a need. This view was upheld in *R v Longman* (1988). There one of the officers posed as an Interflora lady in order to gain entry and only complied with the section and Code after entry but before the search. It was argued on behalf of the appellant that the entry and search were unlawful because the mandatory rules set out in ss 15, 16 and Code B had not been complied with and that s 16(5) indicated the time at which certain events should happen and certain formalities be observed. The Court of Appeal held that the words of the section mean that when search warrants are being executed certain formalities should be observed; whereas the time at which they should be carried out is determined by Code B, 6.5 makes it clear that the time when those formalities have to be observed when entry is obtained by force or subterfuge is after entry. The officer is required at the earliest opportunity, after entry and before search, to announce his identity, produce the warrant card and search warrant and, at the first reasonable opportunity, give the occupier a copy of the search warrant. Code B 6.7 requires that the officer conducting a search, whether under a warrant, under a post-arrest power or with consent, also provide the occupier with a Notice of Powers and Rights (discussed at para 4.156, post). When the search is carried out under a warrant the notice should be given together with a copy of the warrant. The failure to explain the purpose of a search in breach of Code 5.5 (now 6.5) was held to take two police officers outside the execution of their duty in *Lineham v DPP*. If the occupier, or person in charge, is not present, copies of the notice and of the warrant should be left in a prominent place on the premises or appropriate part of the premises and endorsed with the name of the officer in charge of the search, the police station to which he is attached and the date and time of the search. The warrant should be endorsed to show that this has been done. If premises have been entered by force, as they usually will be if the occupier or person in charge is not present, as well as in circumstances when the occupier is present, the officer in charge must satisfy himself that the premises are secure on leaving them either by arranging for the occupier or his agent to be present or by any other appropriate means.

Extent and method of search

4.56   Schedule 1 warrants are dealt with at para 4.92, post; as for other warrants, the search may only extend to the purpose for which the warrant was issued (s 16(8), art 18(8)). Thus, bulky items such as video recorders would not justify as minute a search as would drugs, cash or jewellery. On the other hand, where documents are being examined, the extent of the search may be considerable. For the police cannot seize every document they come across and examine it at leisure back at the police station (cf *Reynolds v Metropolitan Police Comr* (1984)). They must have a reason for believing that each document they seize is relevant to the purpose of the search. The search cannot continue by virtue of the warrant once the items are found or it becomes apparent that they are not on the premises (Code B 6.9B; eg a rapid search for television sets reveals nothing). However, the search could continue under another power, eg if evidence is discovered of another offence, the occupier is arrested and the police wish to search for evidence of that offence (s 32(2)(b), art 34(2)(b)).

4.57   Where the search goes clearly beyond the terms of the warrant the seizure is unlawful. In *R v Chief Constable of the Warwickshire Constabulary, ex p Fitzpatrick* the Divisional Court held that the lawfulness of a search requires compliance with both ss 15 and 16. The police were investigating a conspiracy to defraud and obtained six warrants under s 8 of PACE. The applicants were persons connected with the management of wire limited companies belonging to the Venture Group which was concerned with business loans. Other than describing the stated offence as conspiracy to defraud, no further details were given in the warrants. The officers executing the warrants seized containers and files which they believed might contain relevant evidence with the intention of conducting a detailed examination elsewhere.

4.58   Substantial amounts of material seized from the second applicants' home from which the tenth applicant traded concerned a housing association unconnected with the other applicants. The applicants argued that there was a breach of s 15(6)(b) of PACE 1984 in that the warrants failed to identify with sufficient particularity the articles sought and were not limited in line therefore the search went beyond the extent required for the purpose for which the warrant was issued (s 16(8)).

4.59   The court held that, because it was not possible to define each company's role in the conspiracy alleged or to have a set timetable for the extent of the fraud they were investigating, there was no need to give details of the offence in the warrant. The police made no attempt to justify the seizure of the documentation relating to the housing association was held to be unlawful.

4.60 In *R v Southwark Crown Court and HM Customs and Excise, ex p Sorsky Defries* the court had taken the some view obiter. Significantly in a third decision of the Divisional Court, *R v Chesterfield Justices, ex p Bramley* the court held that if items were seized unlawfully that did not render the search itself unlawful but the items improperly seized had to be returned immediately with the possibility of liability of damages. This decision confirmed that the police could not lawfully take away material that included items covered by legal privilege because those items are outside the scope of the warrant. The court refused the application for a declaration that the entry search and seizure was unlawful; it set out guidelines for situations where legally privileged material was likely to be found. These included the following:
1. the warrant itself may authorise an independent lawyer or a CPS lawyer to accompany the police to give advice on the status of documentation which might be subject of legal privilege;
2. where there is a lot of material to be examined it may not be taken elsewhere to be sorted unless to do so is within the scope of the warrant;
3. the police do not have to take claims of legal privilege at face value but if, following seizure, the privilege is established, the material must be returned forthwith;
4. where legally privileged material may be encountered during the search it is advisable to exclude searching officer from the enquiry to which the material may relate;
5. where agreement cannot be achieved on the spot as to what material is covered by privilege it is desirable to package separately for later examination any item which might be subject to privilege.

4.61 The court were however unwilling to interpret the power confirmed by s 8(2) and limited by s 6(8) as entitling a constable to retain control over documents for examination to establish whether they might be relevant evidence of a crime. Consequently a power to remove material for the purpose of sifting it elsewhere where it is not practicable to examine it on the spot was provided in the Criminal Justice and Police Act 2001 ('CJPA 2001')

4.62 CJPA 2001, ss 50-66 and Schs 1 and 2 give powers to remove material for the purpose if sifting it elsewhere where it is not practicable to examine it on the spot. This power addresses the practical difficulties emanating from the *Bramley* decision. Section 50 provides that where a constable or other person exercising an existing power of search is unable to determine whether something may be or may contain something for which he is authorised to search and it is not reasonably practicable to ascertain whether and to what extent it is such material, he can remove it in order for that to be determined (s 50(1)). Where it is not possible to separate the material in order to identify that which he may seize and that which he may not, he is authorised to seize it (s 50(2)); this would cover material on a computer. Subsection 3 details the only factors which are to be taken into account in determining the meaning of 'reasonably practicable', these are:

(i)   how long the process would take;
(ii) the number of people needed to do the job;
(iii) whether, if carried out then and there, it would involve damage to property;
(iv) the equipment needed;
(v)   in the case of separation of material, whether the process of separation would risk prejudicing the use of any of the material, for instance by damaging material in a computer.

4.63   Code B para 7.7 counsels officers to only exercise this power of seizure when it is necessary and warns them not to remove any more material than necessary. Officers are required to consider the implications for the owners and must consider if removing copies or images of relevant material would be a satisfactory alternative.

4.64   CJPA 2001, s 51 permits seizure from an individual where there is a power to search him and it is not reasonably practicable to determine whether what has been found can be seized. As in s 50 the officer must have reasonable grounds for believing that the items may or may contain material he is entitled to search for and, if so, that there is a power to seize them. The factors for judging whether it is reasonably practicable to determine whether the material can be seizes are the same as under s 50. Section 52 provides that the occupier of premises from which material has been seized under ss 50 or 51 must be given a written notice specifying what has been seized and the grounds on which it was seized.

Force

4.65   All powers of entry and search allow the police to use reasonable and proportionate force if necessary (s 117, art 88). This is discussed generally at para 2.111, ante and in the context of searches at para 4.153, post.

APPLICATIONS TO A MAGISTRATE FOR A WARRANT FOR EVIDENCE OF A SERIOUS ARRESTABLE OFFENCE (s 8 OF PACE 1984, Art 10)

4.66   Section 8 of PACE 1984 (art 10) applies to serious arrestable offences and fills the many gaps in the previous warrant procedure, for example, in relation to a murder weapon, tools used in a robbery, evidence of kidnapping or commercial fraud. Moreover, it relates to evidence of such offences even if the holder is not suspected of complicity in the offence, whereas many earlier statutory powers were confined to the instruments and proceeds of a particular crime held by a suspect. In addition to the requirements of s 15(2) (art 17(2)) and the Code of Practice (explained in para 4.100, ante), the magistrate must be satisfied of the matters mentioned in s 8(1) (art 10(1)). 'Satisfied' has been held to import the ordinary civil standard of proof on the balance of probabilities in the context of Sch 1 of PACE and is likely to be interpreted similarly here (*R v Norwich Crown Court, ex p Chethams* (1990)). The criteria in s 8(1) are as follows.
(i)   A serious arrestable offence is involved (for consideration of this concept, see para 2.14, ante). In the previous authors' study a s 8 warrant referred to stolen

copper cable. In order for such a theft to be a 'serious arrestable offence' the thief would have to obtain a substantial financial benefit or the loser suffer a serious financial loss. This could only be so if the amount of copper cable was so large as to fill the high rise flat in which it was said to be. Even if this were so, a warrant under s 26 of the Theft Act 1968 would be much more appropriate.

(ii) The relevant material is on the premises.

(iii) The material is likely to be of substantial value to the investigation, whether on its own or together with other evidence. The material could thus be the proceeds of a crime; or evidence of its commission, eg murder weapons, skeleton keys; or evidence confirming other material already held by the police such as fingerprints or a gun to match up with bullets found at the scene of a murder. This last example illustrates the importance of the phrase 'together with other material' – a gun without more will not prove murder.

NB: Evidence which is the proceeds of a serious arrestable offence may be sought under s 8 (art 10), but, as suggested earlier, it is more appropriate to seek it under the particular statutory authority which already permits a warrant to search for such evidence. There may be occasions when the proceeds and evidence of the commission of the serious arrestable offence or other confirmatory evidence are all to be found on the same premises. There is then no legal reason why the application for all evidence should not be made under s 8 (art 10), and it will be convenient since the same grounds apply to all three types of evidence (see *R v Reading Justices, ex p South West Meat Ltd* (1992) where a warrant under the Theft Act 1968 was issued to search for stolen objects and documents. Section 8 would have been appropriate if a serious arrestable offence was involved.) However, there is no necessity to use the s 8 (art 10) procedure if the evidence sought is the subject of an existing statutory authority to issue a warrant. An example from the previous authors' study of the use of PACE Act powers may clarify. An armed robbery of a filling station was carried out by a man described as white, 6ft 5ins tall, wearing a trilby hat. Following a press appeal an anonymous caller named one JB as the man responsible. JB, aged 19, fitted the description. Police wished to search his premises for the firearm used, the money stolen and the trilby hat worn. A warrant under the Firearms Act 1968 and the Theft Act 1968 could have been sought to search for the first two items but while the hat could be seized if found in the course of the search (s 19, art 21), a search for the hat could not continue once the items mentioned in the warrants had been found (Code B 5.9). A warrant under s 8 was granted, the robbery being a serious arrestable offence and all the other requirements being satisfied, to search for all three items.

(iv) The material is likely to be relevant in the sense of being admissible before a court (s 8(1)(c) and (4), art 10(1)(c) and (4)). The reference to likelihood is understandable given the difficulties of predicting the evidential aspects of a trial which may take place many months later. But, taken together, requirements (iii) and (iv) impose a degree of specificity on the police which ought to exclude the presentation of mere background information which is not potentially admissible at a trial.

(v) The evidence is neither excluded nor special procedure material nor subject to legal privilege (for which, see Part B para 4.194 et seq, post). This requirement, set out in s 8(1)(d) (art 10(1)(d)), raises difficult legal issues and the magistrates' clerk must play an advisory role. Indeed he should vet each application for issues such as arose in the case of *R v Guildhall Magistrates' Court, ex p Primlak Holdings Co (Panama) Inc* (1989). Warrants under s 8 had been issued to search the offices of two firms of solicitors for documents relating to the sale of vessels by the collapsed bankers Johnson Matthey. The police believed offences of false accounting had been committed and therefore that the documents did not attract legal privilege, being held with the intention of furthering a criminal purpose within s 10(2) of the 1984 Act (art 12(2)) (see para 4.175, post). An application for judicial review of the issue of the warrants succeeded, the court holding that there was no material upon which the magistrates could be satisfied that there were reasonable grounds for believing that the correspondence sought did not include items within s 8(1)(d) (art 10(1)(d)). Even if, as the police alleged, legal privilege had been lost, the material was almost certainly held in confidence and was therefore special procedure material. Magistrates should not entertain an application under s 8 (art 10) for a warrant to search for material in the possession of a solicitor in his capacity as legal adviser, and should look with suspicion upon such an application in respect of material held by any businessman in relation to that of any other business. Such material will almost certainly fall into one or other of the three categories mentioned in s 8(1)(d) (art 10(1)(d)). The correct procedure for obtaining it is to make an application under s 9 and Sch 1 of the 1984 Act (art 11 and Sch 1 of the 1989 Order).

(vi) The authority of a warrant is needed because one of the conditions in s 8(3) (art 10(3)) is satisfied – essentially because the police have already tried to gain entry, or have been refused entry, or are unlikely to obtain permission to enter, or because speed demands a warrant. These conditions emphasise that a warrant is a last resort and that the police should be prepared to answer questions from the issuing authority along these lines. The reference to a search being 'frustrated or seriously prejudiced' in s 8(3)(d) (art 10(3)(d)) refers to the dangers of concealment or destruction of the evidence through wilful design or the course of nature (eg the deterioration of perishable matter). Section 8(3)(c) (art 10(3)(c)) commonly covers cases where the police have already tried to gain access to the premises.

(vii) It is implicit in the requirements of s 8(3) (art 10(3)) that the police seek access to the material with consent unless this is impracticable or likely to frustrate the purposes of the search. However, it is not a condition precedent to the Justice's ability to grant a warrant that other powers to obtain the material have been tried without success, or have not been tried because they were bound to fail. Thus in *R v Billericay Justices, ex p Harris Ltd* (1990) the issue of a s 8 warrant to search for and seize falsified tachograph discs and other documents was upheld even though the police had the power under s 99 of the Transport Act 1968 to require the person to produce and permit the inspection of such documents. This power had been used by the police on other occasions when they suspected that not all the documents were produced and, having no power to search in such circumstances, their inquiries were frustrated. Suspecting similar non-production they quite properly used s 8.

POST-ARREST POWERS OF SEARCH

Search following arrest for an arrestable offence (s 18, art 20)

4.67   Where a person has been arrested away from his home, for example, at a police station, it will often be necessary for the police to enter and search his premises for evidence of the offence. At common law the legality of searches after arrest was, however, open to doubt but the police carried out such searches relying on consent, bluff and ignorance of the law. In *McLorie v Oxford* (1982) the Divisional Court resolved the doubts and held that, once a person has been arrested away from his premises, the police have no common law power subsequently to search the premises. Section 18 reversed this decision and restored the position to what the police in practice believed it to be. The summary power of arrest provided by s 24 (art 26) (discussed at paras 5.28-5.54, post) together with the fact that a majority of offences with which the police daily deal are arrestable offences, meant that the s 18 (art 20) search power would be relied upon most often.

4.68   The power of search under s 18 (art 20) is available where a person has been arrested for an arrestable offence and extends to premises which are 'occupied or controlled' by that person. There is no room for 'reasonable belief' here (the premises must in fact be 'occupied or controlled' by the suspect) and, lest the suspect give a false address, the police should seek to confirm the occupation or control by, for example, documentary evidence found on the premises or by asking neighbours. 'Controlled' is not defined. It clearly extends beyond normal occupation and could include a person who has a legal title over the premises such as the landlord of a boarding house or even a block of flats. It may well extend further to cover an arrested night watchman or caretaker or office manager. The degree of control which a person exercises, the location of the premises and the relationship between that person and the person under arrest will determine the degree of suspicion that the premises contain evidence; eg if D owns a flat occupied by his girlfriend, she would clearly be in a position to store articles stolen by D. In *R v Badham* (1987) (discussed at para 4.75, post) it was held that the search power under s 32(2)(b) (art 34(2)(b)) was an immediate power, that it had to be exercised at the time of arrest, and that a constable could not return to the premises in which the arrest took place some four hours later in order to search them. Section 18 (art 20) is not so limited. Indeed in most cases the search will take place some time after the arrest. It would also seem that the power may be exercised more than once in respect of the same premises. It can clearly be exercised in respect of premises occupied by D and in respect of premises controlled by D, but suppose premises occupied by D are searched with negative results? Later D makes admissions and directs the police to where the property is hidden. There appears to be no reason why another s 18 (art 20) search should not take place.

4.69   Section 18 envisages two types of search:
(a) where the person is in police detention at a police station and the police decide to search his premises;
(b) where the person is arrested away from a police station and the police wish to search the premises before taking him to the station.

4.70   In the first case, the search must be authorised in writing by an officer of at least the rank of inspector. In the second case the constable may act without prior authorisation and need only inform an inspector or more senior officer after the search has taken place (s 18(5), (6), art 20(5), (6)). This type of search preserves the ideas underlying *Dallison v Caffery* (1965), where Lord Denning permitted a constable a degree of latitude in investigating an offence before taking a person to a police station, provided only that the constable acts reasonably. This principle is preserved in ss 18 and 30 (arts 20 and 32) and is discussed at para 5.140, post.

4.71   Section 18(1) (art 20(1)) gives the constable the power to enter, s 18(3) contains the element of reasonableness with regard to the extent of the search, and s 18(5A) (art 20(5)) demands that the person's presence at the place of search be 'necessary for the effective investigation of the offence'. This last condition is likely to be satisfied in many cases. It would not normally apply to a person caught red-handed since a search of his premises would not assist the investigation of the offence for which he has been arrested. However, s 18(1) (art 20(1)) allows a search for evidence of 'some other arrestable offence which is connected with or similar to' that offence. Thus, for example, the search of premises of a thief caught red-handed could be authorised for evidence of other stolen property.

4.72   The phrase 'similar to that offence' in s 18(1) (art 20(1)) is not likely to lead to difficulty. For example, robbery, burglary, obtaining by deception and blackmail are similar to theft, the goods obtained by such offences being regarded as 'stolen' (s 24(4) of the Theft Act 1968). Criminal damage by destroying property can also be theft of that property and forgery may be similar to deception or be the means of deception. The phrase is clearly not broad enough to cover the facts of *Jeffrey v Black* (1978) where the accused was charged at a police station with theft of a sandwich from a public house and the police subsequently searched his premises for evidence of drug offences. However, it would be permissible in such circumstances to search the premises if there are reasonable grounds to believe that D has committed other offences of theft. It should be noted that, if the accused is arrested at the police station for another offence under s 31 (art 33), a fresh exercise of the s 18 (art 20) search power is permissible. Thus, if in the above case D had been arrested for theft of a sandwich and found to be in possession of drugs, he would also be arrested for the drug offence and a s 18 search could then be carried out for drugs. Furthermore, the terms of s 19 (art 21) and the general inclusionary rule of evidence mean that the police may seize and use at trial any evidence (except items subject to legal privilege) of other offences which they discover during the search even if it is dissimilar to, or unconnected with, the offence for which the person has been arrested.

Written record of authorisation

4.73   An inspector (or higher ranking officer) who authorises a search under s 18 (art 20) or to whom such a search is subsequently reported under s 18(6) (art 20(6)), must make a written record of the authorisation or that a search under s 18(5) (art 20(5)) has taken place (s 18(7), art 20(7)). (This is a record by the supervisory officer and has nothing to do with records which must be made by the officer in charge of the search in search registers (see para 4.157, post).) In *R v Badham* (1987) a Crown Court judge ruled that the authorisation should be in the form of an independent document which the constable should take with him to the premises to be searched. This ruling ignores s 18(8) (art 20(8)), which requires the record to be in the custody record when the person in occupation or control of the premises is in police detention, and s 18(5) which permits a search without such authorisation. Be that as it may, the Notice of Powers and Rights which Code B 6.7 requires officers conducting searches under the s 18 (art 20) power, or any other power, to serve on the occupier, contains a section for the signature of the person authorising the search and this should satisfy the requirement of *R v Badham*.

SEARCH OF PREMISES UPON MAKING AN ARREST (ss 18, 32(2)(B), Arts 20, 34(2)(B))

4.74   Section 32 (art 34(2)(b)) covers the situation where the police have arrested a person and wish to search those premises on which he has been arrested or in which the person was immediately before the arrest. Section 18 (art 20) deals with the situation where a person has already been arrested for an arrestable offence away from his own premises and the police now wish to enter and search premises occupied or controlled by him. Section 18 (art 20) is confined to arrest for arrestable offences while s 32(2)(b) (art 34(2)(b)) applies to an arrest for any offence. The sections can thus overlap but they each offer distinctive features. Taken together they afford the police ample opportunity to search the premises of an arrested person, and have considerably clarified and altered the common law. One may also note that s 17 (art 19) authorises entry to and search of premises for persons who are to be arrested for an arrestable offence and other offences. The s 18 or the s 32(2)(b) power (arts 20, 34(2)(b)) may follow such entry and arrest. It must be emphasised that a search of premises for evidence following an entry under s 17 (art 19) can only follow if an arrest is made. A common reason for seeking a warrant to search premises, rather than use ss 17, 18 or 32(2)(b) (arts 19, 20 and 34(2)(b)) is that the person sought may not be on the premises. If he is not, the occupiers may be alerted and remove any evidence of that or any other offence. Section 19 (art 21) permits the seizure of such evidence if the constable comes across it in the search for the person but does not authorise a search (see para 4.131, post).

Section 32

4.75   The common law allowed the police to search an arrested person and his 'immediate surroundings' (*Dillon v O'Brien* (1887), *Elias v Pasmore* (1934); cf the position in the United States where a search is confined to the 'immediate vicinity' of the arrest – *Chimel v California* (1969)). Section 32 (art 34) contains no such spatial limitation, except that imposed by s 32(7) (art 34(7)) in respect of premises consisting of two or more separate dwellings (discussed at para 4.03, ante). 'Premises', it will be recalled (see para 4.7, ante), are given a wide interpretation by s 23 (art 25). They need not be owned by the arrested person and thus the facts of *Elias v Passmore* (1934) and *McLorie v Oxford* (1982) are encompassed. In the former the plaintiff was arrested on the premises of the National Unemployed Workers Movement, its offices were searched and papers were seized. In contrast, s 18 (art 20) only covers premises which are 'occupied or controlled' by the arrested person. Consequently, when the police have arrested X on emerging from his house, they can search it under s 32 (art 34) (because he was there 'immediately before' the arrest) or under s 18 (art 20). If, however, X has just left someone else's house, they can only use s 32 to search those premises and must use s 18 (art 20) to enter and search X's house. As regards *McLorie v Oxford*, premises could have been, but were not, searched at the time of arrest and it was held that the common law did not permit the police to return later to search them. Despite the fact that s 32(2)(b) (art 34(2)(b)) contains no time limit on the exercise of the search power, in *R v Badham* (1987) a Crown Court refused to regard an attempted entry some four hours after the arrest as lawful under s 32(2)(b), thus perpetuating the common law. The court felt that s 32(2)(b) (and presumably art 34(2)(b)) was an immediate power, and that it would be wrong to have an open-ended right to go back to the premises where an arrest had taken place. That, however, ignores the availability of the s 18 (art 20) power. When the arrest is for an arrestable offence s 18 (art 20) is not an immediate power and usually is exercised some time after the arrest. If D is arrested for an arrestable offence in premises occupied or controlled by him it makes no difference which power is used. It may be convenient to search the premises at the time of the arrest (which may then be under s 18 or s 32(2)(b), arts 20, 34(2)(b)), but there is no reason why the s 18 (art 20) power may not be exercised then or later. Indeed, as suggested in para 4.22 (ante) there appears to be no reason why the s 18 power should not be exercised more than once in respect of the same premises, subject to reasonable cause and authorisation. A search under s 32(2)(b) (art 34(2)(b)) can only take place if the police have reasonable grounds to believe (s 32(6), art 34(6)) that the premises contain evidence of the crime for which the person has been arrested, whereas s 18 (art 20) permits a search if there are reasonable grounds for suspecting not only that there is evidence of the offence for which D was arrested on the premises but also evidence of 'connected or similar offences'. It is a question of fact in every case whether there were such grounds (*R v Beckford* (1991)). Section 166 of the Criminal Justice and Public Order Act 1994 makes it an offence for an unauthorised person to sell, offer or expose for sale a ticket for a designated football match in any public place or place to which the public have access or, in the course of trade or business, in any other place. Though only a summary offence sub-s (4) makes it an arrestable offence. There is then a power to search the person, under s 32, and a power to search premises occupied or controlled by the person (s 18) or in which he was immediately before being arrested (s 32(2)(b)). 'Premises' includes a car and if the person is controlling the car or he is arrested in or near the car, it can be searched under either one of these powers. If the person is one of a number of ticket touts using a car as a place to store tickets those powers may not be available to search that car. However, sub-s (5) provides that s 32 shall have effect as if the power conferred on a constable to enter and search any vehicle extended to any vehicle which the constable has reasonable grounds for believing was being used for any purpose connected with the offence.

4.76 (NB: Powers of search on arrest equivalent to those under s 32(2)(b) (art 34(2)(b)) discussed above are available to police officers executing a warrant of arrest or arresting on reasonable suspicion in Scotland or Northern Ireland (or in England, Wales or Scotland in the case of Northern Irish police).

4.77 In the study carried out by the previous authors less than 2.0% of searches were carried out under the authority of s 32(2)(b). There was some evidence of under-recording due to a misunderstanding of the recording requirements of the Code of Practice, nevertheless when both powers are available, as usually they are when an arrest takes place on or near premises in which D was, the s 18 (art 20) power will be relied upon because of the lower threshold of suspicion and the wider range of evidence which can be sought. This is so even though s 19 (art 21) permits the seizure of evidence of unrelated offences which the police come across during a lawful search under any of the search powers available to the police. If, for example, A is arrested at his house for fraud offences, and during a search the police discover evidence of drug offences, the prosecution may use the evidence in any trial for the latter offences. Only items which a constable has reasonable grounds to suspect are subject to legal privilege cannot be seized under s 18 or s 32 (arts 20, 34) (s 19(6), art 21(6)). As to the meaning of 'legal privilege', see para 4.166, post. Material which is 'excluded material' or 'special procedure material' (see para 194, post), and for which a warrant under s 8 (art 10) either cannot be issued (see para 4.166, ante) or which must be sought under the special procedure set out in Sch 1, may be seized under ss 18, 32 or 19 (arts 20, 34 and 21) thus by-passing the special procedure. Because s 32(2)(b) (art 34(2)(b)) authorises the search of premises in which the arrested person was 'immediately before he was arrested' the special procedure may also be by-passed using this power, eg if D, suspected of fraud, is arrested leaving his accountant's office, that office may be searched for evidence of the fraud.

ENTRY AND SEARCH WITH CONSENT

4.78 Research into pre-PACE Act practice indicated that more than half of all searches by the police were conducted with consent. Despite the availability of ss 18 and 32 (arts 20, 34) following arrest, almost one-third of post-arrest searches in the study carried out by the previous authors were said to have been carried out with the consent of the occupier or the person under arrest. It was anticipated that the police would continue to seek consent. Indeed the Royal Commission pointed out that, 'it is only rarely that the police do not receive consent to enter when looking for evidence, since people are often anxious to co-operate and allow the police every facility' (Report, para 3.41). Nevertheless it was not anticipated that consent would be relied upon in preference to the clear post-arrest powers provided. Code B 5 requires that:

(1) the consent must be of a person entitled to grant entry to the premises and the officer must make inquiries to satisfy himself that the person is in a position to give such consent, and the consent must, if practicable, be given in writing on the Notice of Powers and Rights before the search takes place (see para 4.156, post for the Notice of Powers and Rights);

(2) before seeking consent the officer in charge of the search shall:

    (i) state the purpose of the proposed search, and its extent. The information must be as specific as possible, particularly regarding the articles or persons being sought and the parts of the premises to be searched if at the time the person is not suspected of an offence, tell him so;

    (ii) inform the person concerned that he is not obliged to consent and that anything seized may be produced in evidence.

4.79 The use of the words 'state' and 'inform' in Code B 5.2 suggests that the person should be told orally. It is submitted that it is not sufficient to obtain a signature on a form which contains a written statement of the Code requirements without reading them to the person concerned. The Code B 5.3 makes it clear that an officer cannot enter and search premises under 5.1 if the consent has been given under duress, and he cannot continue if the consent is withdrawn before the search is complete. The above raises a number of questions which must be addressed.

WHO IS ENTITLED TO CONSENT?

4.80 The Code of Practice B 5.1 calls for the written consent 'of a person entitled to grant entry to the premises'. In law the consent to enter premises creates, in this context, a bare licence. This may be given expressly or impliedly and the Code requirement of written consent means that an express licence is given. A bare licence can be withdrawn at will. Once it is withdrawn the visitor must leave the premises, and if he does not do so within a reasonable time, he becomes a trespasser. The person who is in exclusive possession or exclusive occupation of the premises can give a licence to enter to anyone he likes. In this context the householder, be he owner, occupier or tenant, has exclusive possession and the authority to license entry. However, in the course of ordinary family life other members of the household may invite persons on to the premises. Even a squatter may invite third parties on to the squatted property as licensees (*R v Edwards* (1978)). The householder may revoke the licence so granted (*Robson v Hallett* (1967)). A constable seeking consent to enter premises cannot easily determine who has the right to exclusive possession or exclusive occupation, and the authority to give or refuse a licence, or which members of the household have the actual or ostensible authority to grant a licence to enter. The issue in law is whether the visitor, be he constable or citizen, is entitled to assume that the person granting consent has the authority to do so. In normal circumstances anyone with a right of occupation has the authority to invite others to enter for purposes reasonably related to the purposes of the occupation. In *R v Jones and Smith* (1976) it was held that Smith had entered in excess of the licence granted by his father, which did not include entry to steal, and Smith had no authority to license Jones's entry in order to steal. The householder's spouse who has a right of occupation by virtue of the Matrimonial Homes Act 1983, s 1 is entitled to invite any visitor he or she pleases into the house, and the licence granted is not subject to revocation by the householder. The same applies to a co-habitant, whether he/she has an equitable interest in the property or is a bare licensee, but the 'sub-licence' granted by such a bare licensee/co-habitant is subject to revocation by the householder (*McGowan v Chief Constable of Kingston-upon-Hull* (1967)). Children of the household, with the exception of those of tender years, will have implied authority to invite visitors into the house for ordinary social and business purposes (eg gas meter reader) including police officers carrying out their duties. Children of tender years may have the implied authority to invite friends into the house but it would not be reasonable to assume that they have the authority to invite strangers or police officers. It would in any event be foolish to rely upon the consent of a minor. The occupier, and no doubt the spouse of the occupier, can override or withdraw the consent given by a member of the household who had the authority to grant consent. However, in *R v Thornley* (1980) it was held that once the police enter premises at the invitation of the occupier (the wife in Thornley) they can remain there for as long as the invitor so requests, even though a joint occupier (the husband in Thornley) orders them to leave. Although there is no English case directly on the point, it would seem that an invitation to enter given by children of the household, be they adults or young persons, can always be overridden by the occupier. The fact that they pay rent or make a contribution to household expenses does not give them an exclusive right to occupy. In this respect they would appear to be in no better position than a lodger who, although he has exclusive occupation of rooms in the house, in the sense that nobody else is entitled to share the use of the rooms with him, is not in exclusive possession (see Blackburn J in *Allan v Liverpool Overseers* (1874), and *Street v Mountford* (1985)). A lodger or sub-tenant will, of course, have the authority to consent to a search of the room occupied by him, but the occupier may be able to override or withdraw that consent depending on the terms of the agreement. One may note at this point that the Code B, Notes for Guidance 5A, states that in situations such as lodging houses and similar places where the occupier of a room does not have an exclusive right to occupation as against the landlord, searches should not be made on the basis solely of the landlord's consent unless the tenant is unavailable and the matter is urgent. That is an eminently sensible approach.

Meaning of 'consent'

'A man cannot be said to be truly willing unless he is in a position to choose freely, and freedom of choice predicates, not only full knowledge of the circumstances on which the exercise of choice is conditional, so that he may be able to choose wisely, but the absence of any feeling of constraint so that nothing shall interfere with the freedom of his will.' (*Bowater v Rowley Regis Corpn* (1944), cited with approval by Lord Hodson, in *ICI v Shatwell* (1965))

4.81   One cannot doubt that an occupier whose consent to a search is requested after being 'cautioned' in accordance with Code B 5.2 and who then signs the form of consent, has made a free choice and has truly consented. Unfortunately that is not the reality. For example, in the study carried out by the previous authors the majority of those consenting to a search were in custody following their arrest. At no time were they told that they need not consent, instead they were presented with a printed form which complied the Code B in that it contained all the requirements of B 5.1-5.4. They were told their premises were to be searched and told to sign the form. It may be doubted whether in these circumstances the arrested person was 'in a position to choose freely'. Few will have known that they could have refused. Code B 5.3 says, 'An officer cannot enter and search premises ... if the consent has been given under duress.' Threats, violence and illegally used force would clearly exclude consent. The psychologically coercive effect of detention in a police station is well known and the fact that consent was obtained from a person in police custody places a particularly heavy burden on the prosecution to prove that such consent was full and free in the above sense. The 1991 Code B 4.1 retreated from the position adopted in the first Code which stated 'the consent must be given in writing'. The current (2003) Code says, '... the consent must, if practicable, be given in writing'. It is submitted that this does not mean that implied consent, as when the occupier remains silent in response to a request, or nods or otherwise signifies consent, will suffice. Express consent is still required but need not be in writing if it is not practicable to obtain written consent. 'Practicable' in this context cannot apply to matters relating to the search, such as the need to make a speedy entry in order to save life. Section 17(1)(e) (art 19(1)(e)) provides for such a situation (see para 4.100, post). It can only apply to circumstances in which the person giving consent is incapable of giving it in writing, eg he is unable to write or has a disability which prevents him doing so. One may further note that the person who gives consent may withdraw it at any time before the search commences, or during the search. A search may not then take place or continue unless, of course, another search power is available, eg the occupier is arrested. The consent may also be a limited consent. Statutory search powers are all limited to a search to the extent that is reasonably required for the purpose of discovering the evidence sought. The person consenting may impose a similar limit, or limit the search to particular areas, eg 'you cannot search the children's room'. A search in excess of such limitation will be unlawful. If a constable is lawfully on the premises, as he will be if there with full and free consent, he has the powers of seizure under s 19 (art 21). If the consent obtained is not a full and free consent, the entry on and search of the premises will be unlawful and the constable will be a trespasser. This may be relevant as to whether or not he is acting in the execution of his duty if he is assaulted in the course of the search (see *Robson v Hallett* (1967) and *Darbo v DPP* (1992)). It may also be relevant to the admissibility of evidence at a subsequent trial (s 78, art 76, see para 2.125, ante), to a civil action for trespass and to any disciplinary proceedings resulting from an illegal search and seizure. Failure to observe any provision of a Code of Practice is admissible and relevant in determining any issue raised in such actions (s 67(11), art 66(10)).

Consent v power

4.82 Reliance on consent rather than exercising the available s 18 (art 20) power was justified by senior police officers as follows:

'The spirit, and the intention of PACE 1984 was to cut down on the coercive use of police powers of arrest and search and to enhance the rights of suspects in our care. The police service is complying with these objectives by obtaining consents in place of s 18 authorities on suitable occasions.'

4.83 By-passing the legal controls on the exercise of powers damages the citizens they were designed to protect. There is no requirement of reasonable suspicion or belief; no limitation on the extent of the search and, though few realise it, s 19 (art 21) is available, if the consent is genuine, and anything which is reasonably believed to be evidence of a crime, or obtained in consequence of a crime may be seized. If the consent is not a genuine consent the police are operating with unwitting illegality. More damaging is what may be described as 'witting illegality' as when official policy urges reliance on consent rather than exercise powers. Constables may then feel justified in using deceptive tactics in order to obtain a signature on a consent form. An interesting comparison on the use of consent relates to stop and search powers. The 2003 Code para A1.5 prevents searches with consent when no power exists. This measure was a response to community concerns and it is considered incongruous that the search of premises is still permitted with consent while the search of a person is not. It is at least arguable that a search of premises with consent where no power exists may be a breach of Art 8 of ECHR. In *R v Sanghera* (2001). The failure of the police to obtain the consent of the occupier and have the consent form signed was considered by the Court of Appeal. The dependant, a sub-postmaster was convicted of theft. He had claimed to be the victim of a robbery and made a witness statement. Despite the lack of consent the police indicated on the premises searched. It was submitted that the evidence of the Finding of a sum of £4,390 should be excluded. The trial judge found there was a breach of the Code and admitted the evidence. The Court of Appeal found there had been a breach of para B1.3 (now 5.1) but there was no issue as to the reliability of the evidence and dismissed the appeal. There was a lack of appreciation by the police of what the Code required. The court found that the defendant would have consented but he would have requested to be present. It is submitted that consent should not be used as a substitute for the exercise of a power.

ENTRY AND SEARCH WITHOUT WARRANT (s 17, Art 19)

4.84 Section 17 (art 19) provides a wide-ranging power to enter and search premises without a warrant in order to arrest persons or to save life, limb or property. So far as the entry and search for persons is concerned, reasonable grounds for believing that the person is on the premises must exist and there is a limitation on search in respect of separate dwellings and, like all search powers, it is a search only to the extent reasonably required for the purpose for which the power was exercised.

Entry in order to execute a warrant of arrest or commitment (s 7(1)(a)(i) and (ii), art 19(1)(a)(i) and (ii))

4.85   There is a large number of statutes authorising the issue of arrest warrants. However, the wide powers of arrest without warrant under ss 24, 25, Sch 2 (arts 26, 27, Sch 2), and contained in numerous statutes, mean that arrest warrants are comparatively rare. When they are issued they are usually issued under s 125 of the Magistrates' Courts Act 1980 (art 20(3) of the Magistrates' Court (NI) Order 1981). Section 17(1)(a) of the 1984 Act (art 19(1)(a) of the NI Order) makes it clear that a constable may enter and search premises in order to execute such warrants and, if necessary, he can use reasonable force (s 117, art 88). In *Jones v Kelsey* (1986) it was held that a warrant issued under s 16(1) of the Criminal Courts Act 1973 to arrest for breach of a community order, was a warrant to arrest a person in connection with an offence within s 125(4) of the MCA 1980. It follows that such a warrant is within s 17(1)(a) (art 19(1)(a)) and the power to enter premises in order to execute it is available. In *R v Peacock* (1988) it was held that a means inquiry warrant issued under s 83(1)(b) of the MCA 1980 for non-payment of a fine was not issued 'in connection with an offence', therefore the s 17 power is not available in respect of such warrants. As to the execution of warrants of arrest, see para 5.179, post. Doubt existed under the earlier law as to whether the police could enter premises in the reasonable belief, as opposed to knowledge, that the person named in the warrant was there. A New Zealand case (*Mathews v Dwan* (1949)) had concluded that there was no such power. Section 17(2)(a) (art 19(2)(a)) resolves the doubt in the constable's favour: he can enter if he has reasonable grounds for believing that the person is on the premises. To resolve further doubts, warrants of commitment under s 76 of the Magistrates' Courts Act 1980 (art 92 of the Magistrates' Courts (NI) Order 1981) are included in s 17(1)(a)(ii) (art 19(1)(a)(ii)). These warrants are issued against those who default in paying a magistrates' court order, such as a fine following conviction or an order for maintenance.

Entry in order to make an arrest without warrant for an arrestable offence (s 17(1)(b),Art 19(1)(b))

4.86   At common law there is no general power for the police to enter premises without a warrant to make an arrest. Moreover, the courts will not construe a statutory power of arrest without a warrant as including a power of entry (*Morris v Beardmore* (1980), *Finnigan v Sandiford* (1981)). Parliament must confer the power expressly. (For the power to enter premises in order to require a breath test of the driver of a motor vehicle in an accident involving injury to a third party, or to arrest a person who fails a breath test or refuses to provide a sample of breath, see the Road Traffic Act 1988, s 6(6); Road Traffic (Amendment) (NI) Order 1991, art 145(6) considered at para 4.112, post.) The common law did, however, permit entry in order to arrest a felon, and s 2(6) of the Criminal Law Act 1967 similarly allowed it for the more serious offences. Section 17(1)(b) (art 19(1)(b)) preserves and extends this power for it applies to arrestable offences, and s 24 (art 26) (see para 5.28, post) extends that concept to include common law offences and a number of statutory offences. If therefore an offence within this concept has been committed or is reasonably suspected to have been committed, a constable who knows, or has reasonable grounds for believing (s 17(2)(a), art 19(2)(a)), that a person known to have committed or reasonably suspected of having committed such an offence is to be found on premises, may enter, by force if necessary (s 117, art 88), to arrest that person. It is essential that a constable exercising this power:

(a) has reasonable grounds for suspecting that an arrestable offence has been committed; and

(b) has reasonable grounds for believing that the person who has committed that offence is on the premises to be entered (see *Kynaston v DPP* (1987), *Chapman v DPP* (1988) and *Riley v DPP* (1989)).

4.87 In order to determine whether the police have lawfully entered under s 17(1)(b) (art 19(1)(b)) the court must be told the reason for the arrest. The power of entry under s 17(1)(b) (art 19(1)(b)) is confined to 'arrestable offences' and does not therefore apply to those lesser offences for which s 25 offers a power of arrest (eg *Bailey v Wilson* (1968) – entry to prevent assault; *R v McKenzie and Davis* (1979) – entry to arrest under the Sexual Offences Act 1956). In *Riley v DPP* (1989) police entered premises to arrest A and one of them was assaulted by R. His appeal against conviction for assaulting the police officer in the execution of his duty was allowed. The justices had not been told why A was being arrested, there was no evidence before them that the arrest was lawful and for an arrestable offence, therefore it was not possible to say that the police officer was acting in the execution of his duty when they purported to enter under s 17(1)(b).

4.88 Section 29 of the Criminal Justice and Public Order Act 1994 inserts a new s 46A into PACE 1984 which permits a constable to arrest a person released on bail subject to a duty to return to a police station who fails to attend at the appointed time. This is an arrest for an offence and the offence is that for which he was originally arrested and bailed (s 46A(2), art 47A of the NI Order inserted by art 7 of the Police (Amendment (NI) Order 1995) (see para 6.189, post). If the original offence was an arrestable offence then s 17(1)(b) (art 19(1)(b)) provides a power of entry to premises to effect the arrest.

Entry to arrest for specified offences (s 17(1)(c) art 19(1)(c))

4.89 Section 17(1)(c) (art 19(1)(c) which is differently worded) extends the power of entry to particular arrest powers mentioned in the subsection, which, though not arrestable offences, are seen as requiring a power to enter premises in order to effect the arrest. These are as follows.

(i) The offence under s 1 of the Public Order Act 1936, the prohibition on the wearing of uniforms in connection with political objects. The power of arrest for this offence under s 7(3) of the POA 1936 is preserved by s 26(2) and Sch 2 of PACE 1984. The other offences to which the section related have been repealed by the Public Order Act 1986. Schedule 2, para 7 of the POA 1986 deleted the reference to these offences in s 17(1)(c)(i) and added the offence under s 4 of the 1986 Act, causing fear or provocation of violence (s 17(1)(c)(iii)). Section 4(3) of the POA 1986 provides the power of arrest and s 17(1)(c) of the 1984 Act the power to enter premises in order to do so. Note that the POA 1986 creates two arrestable offences, riot (s 1) and violent disorder (s 2) and s 155 of the CJPOA 1994 makes the offence under s 19 (publishing etc material intended or likely to stir up racial hatred) an arrestable offence by virtue of s 24(2) of PACE 1984 (see para 5.33, post) for which there is a power of entry under s 17(1)(b). (In Northern Ireland the offences under art 9 (threatening words or behaviour) and art 21 (wearing uniform in public) of the Public Order (NI) Order 1987 are arrestable under art 24 of that Order and art 19 of the PACE Order provides the power of entry on to premises in order to effect the arrest.)

(ii) The offences of 'squatting' created by ss 6, 7, 8, and 10 of the Criminal Law Act 1977. The CLA 1977 had supplied a power of entry. It was repealed by Sch 7, Part I of PACE 1984 and is replaced by s 17(1)(c)(ii). The Criminal Justice and Public Order Act 1994 makes a number of amendments to the 1977 Act's provisions, principally by extending the scope of the exemption from the offence under s 6, the use or threat of violence to secure entry into premises, of the displaced residential occupier and extending that exemption to a newly defined 'protected intending occupier', and providing for quicker and more effective means of repossessing premises occupied by squatters. The latter involves an ex parte application to a circuit judge sitting in the county court for an interim possession order which it is expected will be granted on the day of application, and will contain a written notice requiring squatters to leave within 24 hours. A further date for hearing will be fixed at which the order will be confirmed unless the squatter applies for the interim order to be set aside. Section 75 creates an offence of knowingly or recklessly making a false statement for the purpose of obtaining, or resisting the making of, an interim possession order. It is an either way offence punishable on conviction on indictment by two years' imprisonment, a fine, or both. On summary conviction six months' imprisonment, a fine not exceeding the statutory maximum, or both. No power of arrest is provided but s 25 of PACE 1984 is available if an arrest condition is satisfied.

4.90 A squatter who fails to leave within 24 hours of the interim order, or who returns within one year of the order, commits a criminal offence. These offences are created by s 76 of the CJPOA 1994. Subsection (2) provides that anyone present on the premises as a trespasser (and sub-s (6) provides that the person in occupation at the time of the service of the order shall be treated as such) during the currency of the order commits an offence, but sub-s (3) provides that no offence is committed: if he leaves within 24 hours of the service of the order and does not return; or if a copy of the order was not fixed to the premises in accordance with the rules of court. Subsection (4) provides that a person who was in occupation of the premises at the time of the service of the order but leaves them, commits an offence if he re-enters the premises as a trespasser or attempts to do so within one year of the day on which the order was served. The offences are summary offences punishable by six months' imprisonment, a fine not exceeding level 5 or both, but sub-s (7) provides that a constable in uniform may arrest without warrant anyone who is, or whom he reasonably suspects to be, guilty of an offence under s 76. The power to enter premises in order to effect the arrest is provided by s 17(1)(c)(iv) (added by s 168(2) and Sch 10, para 53(a) of the CJPOA 1994).

4.91 The powers of entry and search provided by s 17 are only exercisable by a constable in uniform: s 17(3). This follows from the fact that the arrest powers in relation to squatters are only available to a constable in uniform, and it is believed that this will reduce the possibility of physical resistance by squatters.

4.92 Section 9 of the Criminal Law Act 1977 created an offence of trespass on diplomatic premises and the power of arrest for such offence is preserved by s 26(2) and Sch 2 of the 1984 Act but, for obvious reasons, no power of entry on to such premises is given. (There is no equivalent provision in the Northern Ireland Order.)

4.93 Section 17(1)(c) (art 19(1)(c)) places the offences mentioned therein on a par with arrestable offences as regards powers of entry to effect an arrest. However, they remain inferior in other respects. The wider investigative powers available on arrest for an arrestable offence under s 24, the powers of entry and search of premises under s 18 following an arrest for an arrestable offence, and the extended detention powers if a serious arrestable offence is involved are not available for the s 17(1)(c) offences. On the other hand, it should be noted that s 32 gives the constable power to enter and search the premises (which includes vehicles) where a person has been arrested (or where he was immediately before arrest) and this power extends to a s 17(1)(c) offence, including those under s 76 of the CJPOA 1994.

Entry for the purpose of arresting children remanded or committed to local authority care or unlawfully at large and whom a constable is pursuing (s 17(1)(c) and (cb) (added by the Prisoners (Return to Custody) Act 1995))

4.94 The power in s 17(1)(ca) authorises entry for the purpose of arresting, in pursuance of s 32 (1A) of the Children and Young Persons Act 1969, any child or young person who has been remanded or committed to local authority accommodation under s 23 of that Act.

4.95 Sub-section (cb) authorises the arrest of any person who is unlawfully at large while liable to be detained:
(i) in a prison, remand centre, young offender institution or secure training; or
(iii) in pursuance of s 92 of the Powers of Criminal Courts (Sentencing) Act 2000 (dealing with children and young persons guilty of grave crimes) in any other place.

4.96 Sub-section (d) authorises entry for the purpose of recapturing any person whatsoever who is unlawfully at large who is being pursued.

Entry in order to recapture a person who is unlawfully at large and whom a constable is pursuing (s 17(1)(d), art 10(1)(d))

4.97 This power replaces the ancient but uncertain position at common law (see *Genner v Sparkes* (1704)). The reference to 'recapture' covers an escaped prisoner, an escaped mental health patient, an escaped illegal immigrant and an arrested person who has escaped from police custody. 'Pursuing' would clearly cover 'hot pursuit', as it did under the common law (*McLorie v Oxford* (1982)). But in *D'Souza v DPP* (1992) the House of Lords took a narrow view of the term 'pursuing'. The appellant's mother had absconded from a mental hospital where she had been lawfully detained and returned to the family home. Some three hours later the police went to her home believing her to be there and unlawfully at large. The appellant refused entry to the police who then purported to enter under s 17(1)(b). The appellant resisted and was later convicted of assaulting the police in the execution of their duty. Quashing the conviction the House of Lords, while accepting that the patient was unlawfully at large, held that the police were not empowered to enter under s 17(1)(b). Although the officers were seeking her they were not 'pursuing' her. 'Pursuing' connotes an act of pursuit, a chase no matter how short in time or distance and does not cover a situation in which the police form an intention to arrest and decide to put it into practice by resorting to premises where they believe the person to be. The difficulty for the police is that no offence is involved in absconding from a mental hospital. If, however, a person who has committed an arrestable offence escapes from police custody or from a prison he remains an arrestable offender and s 17(1)(b) (art 19(1)(b)) is available to gain entry to premises. Prison breach is also a common law misdemeanour punishable by imprisonment without limit so that is also an arrestable offence.

4.98 Article 19(1)(ca) and (cb) of the 1989 Order, added by art 4 of the Police (Amendment) (NI) Order 1995 permits entry on to premises for the purpose:

'(ca) of recapturing a person who is, or is deemed for any purpose to be, unlawfully at large while liable to be detained in prison, young offenders centre, training school, remand centre or remand home or in any other place in pursuance of s 73 of the Children and Young Persons Act (NI) 1968; and

(cb) of arresting a person in pursuance of s 49(1) of the Prison Act 1952 or s 40(1) of the Prisons (Scotland) Act 1989.'

4.99 As the wording of these Articles suggests, the power is available even when the person is unlawfully at large from elsewhere in the UK.

Entry in order to save life or limb, or to prevent serious damage to property (s 17(1)(e), art 19(1)(e)), or to deal with or prevent a breach of the peace (s 17(6), art 19(6))

4.100 Section 17(1)(e) (art 19(1)(e)) seeks to reflect the common law, although the position was for long unclear. Early cases suggested a power of entry to prevent murder (*Handcock v Baker* (1800)) or to terminate an affray (*R v Walker* (1854)). In the only modern authority, the Divisional Court in *Swales v Cox* (1981) summarised, without discussion, the common law as permitting anyone to enter premises without a warrant to prevent murder, to apprehend a felon who had been followed there or to prevent an imminent felony, and as permitting a constable to enter in pursuit of an offender running away from an affray. Section 17(1)(e) (art 19(1)(e)) adopts the crisp summary of this common law used by the Royal Commission 1981 (para 3.38). The policy behind it is sensible, although it should be noted that there is no express requirement that the threat be seen by the constable as serious or urgent. It is, however, strongly arguable that the very nature of the power implies that such requirement be present. Furthermore, unlike the other entry powers in s 17 (art 19), s 17(1)(e) (art 19(1)(e)) is not subject to the procedural qualifications of s 17(2). To exempt it from s 17(2)(b) (art 19(2)(b)) (limitation on search of premises comprised of two or more separate dwellings) is understandable given the sometimes urgent circumstances which may necessitate entry, and to exempt it from s 17(2)(a) (art 19(2)(a)) (reasonable belief that the person is on the premises) is appropriate when the police are not seeking a person but, for example, a bomb on the premises. However, this latter exemption removes from the power any standard of reasonableness and highlights its potentially speculative ambit, eg the search of a football coach (being 'premises' under s 23 (art 25)) when the police suspect offensive weapons but do not suspect any particular person. Furthermore there is no requirement that the threat to life, limb or property should concern the premises in question, eg the police can enter if they believe that the premises contain material such as burglary or arson equipment which may be used against other premises or if a person who has planted a bomb elsewhere is on the premises. The following examples illustrate the scope of s 17(1)(e) (art 19(1)(e)).

(i)   entry in order to deal with or prevent child or wife-battery;
(ii) entry into a block of flats where a kidnapper is believed to be. All the flats can be searched since the limiting definition of s 17(2)(b) (art 19(2)(b)) does not apply;
(iii) entry into the offices of an extreme political organisation where the police believe offensive weapons are kept, or are being prepared, for use at a protest or at a political demonstration, though the police need not suspect that any individual culprits are present; vehicles and coaches fall within the definition of premises (s 23) and can thus be entered and searched under s 17(1)(e) (art 19(1)(e));
(iv) where X, a known kidnapper or blackmailer, works for company Y, the latter's premises could be searched for evidence of X's whereabouts or modus operandi;
(v)   entry to private premises in which a party is being held following a complaint from a guest that a drunken brawl is taking place or is threatened. (A public house, at least while open to the public, is a public place and no special entry powers are needed.);

(vi) entry to a flat in which youths are believed to be making petrol bombs. A search warrant can be obtained if there are reasonable grounds to believe this is happening but s 17(1)(e) (art 19(1)(e)) is not limited by that requirement. Ostensibly it is not novel since it aims to repeat the common law, but the position at common law was for so long obscure that the statutory elucidation could give impetus to its use. There is, however, no evidence of such use. In the research carried out by the previous authors only 5.6% of entries were made under s 17 and only one of these was justified under s 17(1)(e).

4.101   It is to be noted that the power to force entry under s 17(1)(e) does not extend to a power to enter to search for the address of the next of kin of someone who, as a result seriously injured in a road accident, was unconscious in hospital (*R v Veneroso* (2002)).

4.102   Whilst s 17(5) (art 19(4)) abolishes all common law powers to enter premises without a warrant, s 17(6) (art 19(5)) retains any such power which is designed 'to deal with or prevent a breach of the peace'. Cases in the nineteenth century (*Timothy v Simpson* (1835), *R v Walker* (1854)) established a right of entry for a constable to deal with an actual breach of the peace. *Thomas v Sawkins* (1935) went further. Three policemen had attended a public meeting on private premises, organised to protest against the Incitement to Disaffection Bill and to call for the resignation of the local chief constable. The Divisional Court held that the police have the right to enter and remain on premises where they have reasonable grounds to apprehend that a breach of the peace is imminent or is likely to occur. In *McConnell v Chief Constable of Greater Manchester Police* (1990) the Court of Appeal (Civil Division) confirmed that a breach of the peace can take place on private premises for the purpose of entitling a constable, who genuinely suspected on good grounds that a breach of the peace may occur, to make an arrest. In *Lamb v DPP* (1989) the Divisional Court held that a constable has an independent right at common law to remain on premises if he reasonably anticipates a breach of the peace on those premises. The constable, who accompanied a woman to the house in which she had lived with the occupier in order to recover her belongings, was told to leave by the occupier but remained standing in the garden by the kitchen door. The occupier attacked the woman in the kitchen. The constable entered in order to prevent a breach of the peace and was himself attacked. Magistrates, who had found the constable was a trespasser, asked the Divisional Court whether, in those circumstances, he was acting in the execution of his duty in remaining. Answering in the affirmative the Divisional Court appeared to be accepting that the constable was a trespasser, but in stating that he had an independent right to remain they seem to be saying that he was not, the common law right to remain and to enter the premises if the anticipated breach of the peace occurred making his presence on the premises lawful. In *McLeod v Metropolitan Police Comr* (1994) the police were sued for trespass following their attendance at the appellant's house to ensure no breach of the peace while her former husband removed furniture from her house under a county court order. The appellant was not at home and the ex-husband was admitted by the appellant's mother. The appellant returned when most of the furniture had been loaded into a van.

She was angry and demanded the van be unloaded. One of the police officers insisted that the van was not to be unloaded and that any disputes be sorted out between the respective solicitors. Her action for trespass against the police was dismissed, the judge holding that the officers had been carrying out their duty to prevent a breach of the peace which they reasonably apprehended and that they were entitled to enter and remain on private property without the consent of the owner or occupier in carrying out that duty. Her appeal was also dismissed. The Court of Appeal, Civil Division, held that at common law the police had a power to enter premises without a warrant to prevent a breach of the peace occurring there if they reasonably believed a breach was likely to occur on the premises, a power expressly preserved by s 17(6) of PACE 1984. The power was not restricted to entering premises where public meetings were being held. The police had therefore a lawful excuse for entering the plaintiff's property.

4.103 However, before exercising the power of entry on to private premises, the police had to have a genuine belief that there was a real and imminent risk of a breach of the peace occurring and were required to act with great care and discretion, particularly when exercising the power of entry against the wishes of the owner or occupier. This decision confirms *Thomas v Sawkins* (above), which has been doubted by many academics who sought to confine it to public meetings on premises. McLeod makes it clear that it cannot be so confined and confirms the breadth of the common law power. The retention of this power in PACE 1984 (and the NI Order) 'affords the police a desirable degree of flexibility in responding to situations requiring their urgent intervention but which are not readily susceptible to precise statutory definition' (Notes accompanying the PACE Bill). There appeared to be no common law requirement that the breach of the peace be imminent or serious. Indeed, it may arise 'whenever harm is actually done or is likely to be done to a person or in his presence to his property or a person is in fear of being so harmed through an assault, an affray, a riot, unlawful assembly or other disturbance' (*R v Howell* (1981)). The decision in McLeod, while extending *Thomas v Sawkins* to private premises, does require 'a real and imminent risk of a breach of the peace occurring', thus placing some limitation on the exercise of this extremely broad power.

4.104 The view was confirmed when the case subsequently went to the European Court of Human Rights (*McLeod v UK* (1999)) which held that on the facts the police entry was a disproportionate response to the objective of preventing a breach of the peace and that there had been a breach of Art 8 of the Convention.

4.105 The Public Order Act 1986 (the Public Order (NI) Order 1987) puts into statutory form the common law offences of riot and unlawful assembly and replaces much of the Public Order Act 1936, in particular the catch-all offence in s 5 of the 1936 Act, which is now contained in ss 4 and 5 of the 1986 Act. This Act also leaves the common law unaffected which means that there remains a broad and flexible power, the parameters of which are, unlike the statutory offences, incapable of precise definition.

4.106 The compendium of powers in s 17(1)(c), (e) and (6) (art 19(1)(c), (e) and (5)) thus arms the police with considerable ability to deal with and prevent breaches of the peace and the powers may well overlap each other. Section 17(1)(e) (art 19(1)(e)) may be seen as directed towards the most serious and urgent threats to the peace (and it is not, after all, restrained by s 17(2), art 19(2)) but as regards lesser disturbances it will overlap with the other powers, particularly in England and Wales, the power in s 4 of the POA 1986. Since this offence may be committed in public or in private (there is an exception in relation to dwellings contained in s 4(2)) it is likely that greater reliance will be placed on the statutory offence with its concomitant power of entry in order to effect an arrest under s 17(1)(c)). The common law breach of the peace is, however, wider than the s 4 offence. The s 4 offence covers conduct intended to cause a person to believe that immediate unlawful violence will be used, or whereby that person is likely to believe that such violence will be used. The common law covers 'conduct which is itself a breach of the peace and no more' (*Marsh v Arscott* (1982)). Fortunately for the police officer, neither the Act nor Code of Practice requires him to specify to the occupier of the premises which power he is using; he need only state that he 'reasonably apprehends an imminent breach of the peace' so as to justify his entry on to the premises. These three powers are particularly useful in the preventive context, especially when it is recalled that they can be used against 'premises', as widely defined by s 23 (art 25) (subject to the qualification in s 17(2) (art 19(2)). As regards the s 17(1)(e) (art 19(1)(e)) power, see para 4.100(iii), post). Examples of this preventive object would include police attendance at political meetings (wheresoever held), sporting events, night-clubs, private domestic disputes and 'blood sports' on private land where the presence of demonstrators is feared. It may be noted that s 68 of the Criminal Justice and Public Order Act 1994 creates an offence of aggravated trespass. This offence is committed by persons who trespass on land in the open air and in relation to any lawful activity which persons are engaging in, or who are about to engage in on that or any adjoining land, or who do anything which is intended by them to have the effect of:

(a) intimidating those persons or any of them so as to deter them from engaging in that activity;
(b) of obstructing that activity; or
(c) of disrupting that activity.

4.107 This is a summary offence punishable by three months' imprisonment, a fine not exceeding level 4, or both, but s 68(4) provides that a constable in uniform may arrest without warrant a person reasonably suspected to be committing the offence.

4.108 In most cases the constable will be invited on to the land to protect those engaging in the lawful activity and will need no power of entry. If a situation does arise in which the police are not invited on to land where trespassing protesters are then the common law power to enter to prevent a breach of the peace is available as may be the power under s 17(1)(e).

4.109 Sections 63 to 66 of the CJPOA 1994 provide powers to deal with unauthorised raves which are held on land in the open air. Persons attending need not be trespassers, the landowner may have given permission for the rave to take place on his land. A constable seeking to enter on the land in order to exercise the powers provided by the

1994 Act would be a trespasser but for s 64 which permits an officer of at least the rank of superintendent who reasonably believes that circumstances exist on the land which would justify the giving of a direction under s 63, to persons to leave the land and remove any vehicles, to authorise any constable to enter land:

(a) to ascertain whether such circumstances exist; and

(b) to exercise any power conferred on a constable by s 63 or s 64(4).

4.110 Such powers include the power to give a direction under s 63(2) and to arrest persons who, knowing that such a direction has been given, fail to leave the land as soon as practicable, or who having left again enter the land within seven days of the day on which the direction was given; and the power to enter in order to seize vehicles or sound equipment which has not been removed from the land after a direction to do so has been given.

PROCEDURAL REQUIREMENTS FOR POWERS UNDER s 17, Art 19

4.111 Only in relation to entry to arrest for squatting offences under the Criminal Law Act 1977 must the constable act in uniform (s 17(3), repealing s 11 of the CLA 1977). However, the use of uniformed officers may often be desirable under other entry powers as part of a policy of sensitive policing, eg entries and searches in ethnic neighbourhoods, and it is unfortunate that the Code of Practice does not mention the prudence of considering whether to use such officers. Except in relation to his powers under s 17(1)(e) (art 19(1)(e)), a constable must generally act reasonably. Note the following conditions in particular.

(i) He can only enter and search if he has reasonable grounds to believe that the person sought is on the premises (s 17(2)(a), art 19(2)(a)). As has been noted (see paras 2.90-2.92, ante), 'reasonable grounds to believe' is a high standard approaching certainty of belief that the person sought is on the premises to be entered. In practice a constable may then be tempted to rely on a lesser standard, but he should be aware of the fact that in this area he is more likely to be called upon to justify his actions than in many others, especially if force is used in order to gain entry.

(ii) He can only search to the extent that is reasonably required (s 17(4), art 19(3)). Since most of the powers in s 17 (art 19) are directed against persons, a search of, for example, drawers and small cabinets would be unreasonable and therefore unlawful, and the occupier's remedy lies in an official complaint or the launching of a civil action. Any evidence seized by an unlawful search cannot lawfully be retained (*R v Chief Constable of Lancashire, ex p Parker and McGrath* (1993), discussed at para 4.160, post, but is unlikely to be excluded if relevant (*R v Wright* (1994) discussed at para 4.131, post). Section 17(4) (art 19(3)) does not apply where entry and search are made in accordance with s 17(1)(e) (art 19(1)(e)). Accordingly, for example, a search under the latter provision for explosives would justify, as well as require, a more detailed examination of the premises.

(iii) Where the premises consist of separate dwellings, eg a boarding house or block of flats, the constable (except in relation to s 17(1)(e), art 19(1)(e); see para 4.100, ante) can only enter and search that dwelling in which he reasonably believes the person to be and any communal areas on the premises, eg a bathroom, cloakroom, garden or leisure/community centre to be shared by the occupiers of a block of flats (s 17(2)(b), art 19(2)(b)).

(iv) The constable may use reasonable force to enter and search the premises in relation to all the above-mentioned powers (s 117, art 88). For a fuller discussion of reasonable force, see para 2.111, ante, and in the context of the search of premises see para 4.153, post.

(v) Broad powers of seizure accompany the powers in s 17: see para 4.128, post.

ENTRY TO REQUIRE A BREATH TEST OR TO EFFECT AN ARREST FOR DRIVING WITH EXCESS ALCOHOL IN THE BLOOD

Motor vehicles

4.112   Under s 5(1) of the Road Traffic Act 1988 it is an offence for a person:

(a)   to drive or attempt to drive a motor vehicle on a road or other public place; or

(b)   to be in charge of a motor vehicle on a road or other public place,

4.113   after consuming so much alcohol that the proportion of it in his breath or blood or urine exceeds the prescribed limit.

4.114   Section 6 of the RTA 1988 provides a procedure for taking a preliminary breath test and under s 6D a constable may arrest without warrant if:

(a)   as a result of the preliminary test he has reasonable grounds to suspect that the proportion of alcohol in that person's breath or blood exceeds the prescribed limit; or

(b)   if that person fails (or refuses) to supply a specimen of breath for a breath test when required to do so and the constable reasonably suspects that he has alcohol in his body.

4.115   Police officers have no general power to enter premises without the consent of the occupier in order to require a screening breath test or to make an arrest under s 6 but in the circumstances provided for by s 6E there is such a power as follows:

4.116   Section 6E states:

(1) A constable may enter any place (using reasonable force if necessary) for the purpose of -

(a)   imposing a requirement by virtue of section 6(5) following an accident in a case where the constable reasonably suspects that the accident involved injury of any person, or

(b)   arresting a person under section 6D following an accident in a case where the constable reasonably suspects that the accident involved injury of any person.

4.117   This power was amended by the Railways and Road Transport Safety Act 2003 and is broader than the old s 6 in that the injury may be to any person including the driver.

4.118   There is also a power of entry provided by s 4(7) of the RTA 1988. Under this subsection a constable may enter premises (if need be by force), for the purpose of arresting a person whom he has reasonable cause to suspect is or has been committing an offence under s 4 [driving, or attempting to drive or being in charge of a motor vehicle, whilst unfit to drive through drink or drugs]. A constable may enter any place where that person is or is reasonably suspected to be. Thus if D, who has provided a positive breath test or has failed or refused to provide one, runs off and takes refuge in particular premises, a constable may enter in order to arrest him, not for the positive breath test or failure to provide one, but because he has reasonable cause to suspect an offence under sub-s (4) and reasonable cause to suspect that the person is in the premises he seeks to enter.

Railways and tramways

4.119   The Transport and Works Act 1992, Part II, Chapter I, creates similar provisions to deal with alcohol or drug abuse by persons working on the railways or tramway systems. Chapter I of Part II of the Act applies to railways, tramways and a system using any other mode of guided transport specified for the purposes of the Act by the Secretary of State. However, the Act applies only to those railways etc which are used, or intended to be used, wholly or partly for the carriage of members of the public. Section 39 excludes the operation of ss 4-11 of the Road Traffic Act 1988 from such means of transport and the Act creates a scheme which is very like that applying to motor vehicles but which applies only to railways, tramways and similarly guided forms of public transport. Thus a bus driver will be dealt with under the RTA 1988, whereas a tram driver will be dealt with under the TWA 1992.

4.120   Section 27 makes it an offence for persons working in such systems, either in a capacity in which they can control or affect the movement of the vehicle, driver, guard, conductor, signalman, etc, or in a maintenance capacity, including supervisors and look-outs, to be unfit to carry out that work through drink or drugs; or to have consumed so much alcohol that the proportion in his breath, blood or urine exceeds the prescribed limit. (If an employee commits an offence under s 27 the responsible operator or employer also commits an offence unless he shows that he exercised all due diligence to prevent such an offence: s 28.) Section 29 provides the power to require breath tests where there is reasonable cause to suspect that a person who is working in one of the above capacities has alcohol in his body, or such person has been working in one of those capacities and still has alcohol in his body; or where an accident or dangerous incident occurs and an act or omission of the person may have caused it. A person who, without reasonable excuse, fails to provide a specimen commits an offence (s 29(5)).

4.121   Section 30(1) and (2) provides that a constable may arrest without warrant:

(1)   a person whom he reasonably suspects is or has been committing an offence under s 27;

(2)

(a)   where as a result of a breath test he reasonably suspects that the proportion of alcohol in the person's breath or blood exceeds the prescribed limit;

(b)   where a person fails to provide a specimen of breath when required in pursuance of s 29.

4.122   Section 29(3) provides that in order to effect an arrest under s 30(1) a constable may enter (if need be by force) any place where that person is or where the constable with reasonable cause suspects him to be.

4.123   Section 29(4) provides the same power of entry in order:

(a)   to require a breath test of a person in the case of an accident which the constable has reasonable cause to suspect involves the death of, or injury to, another person; or

(b)

(i)   to arrest a person who as in s 29(2)(a) has given a breath test as a result of which the constable reasonably suspects that the proportion of alcohol in the breath or blood in the person's body exceeds the prescribed limit, or

(ii)   to arrest a person who as in s 29(2)(b) has failed to provide a specimen of breath having been required to do so.

ENTRY WITHOUT WARRANT FOR CERTAIN OTHER STATUTORY PURPOSES

4.124   There are some statutes which permit the police and/or other officials to enter premises without a warrant for purposes other than to make an arrest. Many of them are designed to enable the police or such officials to enter and 'keep an eye' on a particular activity and thus supervise or police the particular activity. For example, s 43(2) of the Gaming Act 1968 allows a constable to enter premises without a warrant to examine whether the terms of a gaming licence are being observed. Section 17 of PACE 1984 (art 19 of the Order) is 'without prejudice' to these other enactments and they thus escape the procedural restraints of s 17(2) and (4) (art 19(2) and (3)). Relevant statutes (some have been replaced) are listed in Appendix 4 to the Royal Commission's Law and Procedure Volume. They include powers for the Department of Environment and the Inland Revenue and various sections of the Customs and Excise Acts and, since Parliament regularly adds to the list, there are many others (eg Bees Act 1980, the Licensing (Occasional Permissions) Act 1983, Water Act 1989, Food Safety Act 1990).

ENTRY AND SEARCH BY OTHER OFFICIALS AND CITIZENS

4.125   Part II of the Act relates only to constables and authorised civilian investigating officers and therefore does not affect the many statutory powers which have been given to other officials to enter premises. Each continues to be governed by the terms of the empowering statute. Some allow the official to be accompanied by police officers (eg British Fishing Boats Act 1983), some allow entry to search for and seize evidence (Companies Act 1985, s 448, as amended by the Companies Act 1989). In *Dudley Metropolitan Borough Council v Debenhams plc* (1994) a routine inspection by a trading standards officer under s 29(1) or (2) of the Consumer Protection Act 1987 was held to be a search within Code B. Mrs Justice Smith, giving the judgment of the Divisional Court, held that a search took place when a person entered premises and looked around. No physical interference with goods was necessary. In order to avoid the application of Code B the council had to satisfy the court that a routine inquiry was not a search. Sections 27 and 28 of the Trade Descriptions Act 1968 contain entry and inspection powers which are identical to those in the Fair Trading Act 1973. These powers are also applied to the Trade Marks Act 1994 by s 93 of that Act. Section 56 of the Clean Air Act 1993 provides a power of entry to premises by environmental officers, and there is also provision for obtaining a warrant from a magistrate. There are also entry powers under the Weights and Measures Act 1985; the Consumer Credit Act 1974 and the Energy Conservation Act 1981. In the light of the above decision Code B applies to these entry powers if they amount to a search as defined above; but ss 15 and 16 of PACE 1984 apply only to the issue and execution of warrants 'to constables' (s 15(1)). Other powers are more concerned with inspection but can occasionally result in the seizure of evidence of an offence, for example, warrants reinforcing the power to inspect electricity meters or to cut off power supplies (s 2 of the Rights of Entry (Gas and Electricity Boards) Act 1954, as amended by the Gas Act 1986 and the Electricity Act 1989). Such a warrant was executed in *R v Stewart* (1995) where the accused sought exclusion of evidence of fraudulent abstraction of electricity and theft of gas under s 78 of PACE 1984 following alleged breaches of Code B and s 16 of PACE (see paras 4.53-4.56, ante). Holding that it was not necessary to determine whether PACE 1984 and Code applied, the Court of Appeal upheld the decision of the trial judge to admit the evidence, there being no unfairness in admitting real evidence of meter tampering (see further para 8.98, post).

4.126 As to the rights of entry available to members of the public, these are based on old and uncertain common law. *Handcock v Baker* (1800) recognised a right of entry to prevent murder and, obiter, a felony and *Timothy v Simpson* (1835) can be construed as permitting entry to deal with a breach of the peace. The last two rights are, however, not clearly stated in the cases. *Swales v Cox* (1981) on the other hand accepted without argument that a citizen could enter premises without a warrant:

(1) to prevent murder,

(2) to arrest a felon who has been followed to the premises, and

(3) to prevent an imminent felony.

4.127 (Police powers to enter premises to arrest and for the purposes mentioned above are dealt with in s 17 of PACE 1984 (art 19 of the 1989 Order) discussed above.) It will be seen from s 24(4) and (5) (see para 5.25, post) that the powers of a citizen to make an arrest are tied to the concept of an arrestable offence but they do not coincide precisely with his common law rights of entry.

POWERS OF SEIZURE

4.128   May the police seize evidence of offences other than that for which they are searching? The common law gives an affirmative answer provided that the evidence implicates the person in a serious offence and the police act reasonably by, for example, not detaining such evidence for longer than is necessary (*Ghani v Jones* (1970)). The Royal Commission on Criminal Procedure (1981) agreed that the police should be allowed to seize such additional evidence provided that it was evidence of a grave offence (para 3.49). If it was not or if the police failed to observe the Commission's proposed procedure for searches, the evidence could not be used at trial. Such an exclusionary rule would have been a departure for English law and was a controversial suggestion. As the Royal Commission observed:

> 'We appreciate that the obligatory exclusion of evidence at trial may appear an inflexible restriction, but the right of members of the public to be free from general searches must be respected' (para 3.49).

4.129   The Government appreciated this 'inflexible restriction' and pointed to:
(i)   the practical difficulties which a constable would face when he is searching for offence X and discovers evidence of offence Y and who must then decide if Y is a grave offence;
(ii)   the controls on police misbehaviour and unreasonable searches which are offered by ss 15, 16 (arts 17, 18) and the Code of Practice.

4.130   The Act (and Order) therefore rejects an automatic exclusionary rule, permits the police to seize evidence of any offence whilst exercising their search powers, and then gives the trial court the power to exclude evidence if its admission would have such an adverse effect on the fairness of the trial that it ought not to be admitted (s 78, art 76). However, real evidence was not excluded at common law simply because it had been unlawfully obtained, and there are indications that a similar approach will be taken under s 78 (see *R v Wright* (1994) considered at para 4.131, post, and *R v Stewart* (1995) considered at para 8.169, post).

SCOPE OF SEIZURE

4.131   Section 18(2) (art 20(2)) allows the police to seize anything for which they are entitled to search under s 18 (art 20), ie for the primary arrestable offence or some other arrestable offence which is connected with, or similar to, it. Section 8 (art 10) carries its own seizure power for evidence of the offence mentioned in the warrant (s 8(2), art 10(2)), as does a special procedure warrant (Sch 1, para 13 (para 10 of the NI Order)). For pre-1984 warrant powers the governing statute specifies what may be seized. Section 19 (art 21 of the Order) of the 1984 Act is in addition to any of these other powers of seizure (s 19(5), art 21(5)). It applies whenever a constable is lawfully on premises and when he does not already have a power of seizure. A constable need not be aware of the basis for his presence; he may barge in to arrest a person for an arrestable offence in total ignorance of the provisions of s 17(1)(b) (art 19(1)(b)), but still be lawfully on the premises: see *Foster v Attard* (1985). He may, however, lose his lawfully present status if, for example, he were there with the occupier's consent and that consent is withdrawn. It is also arguable that a failure to comply with the requirements of ss 15 and 16 (arts 17 and 18) in the application for or execution of a search warrant, renders the constable's presence on the premises unlawful. Thus if, having found the items mentioned in a search warrant, the officer continues with the search in breach of s 16(8) (art 18(8)), his presence on the premises is no longer lawful. Section 19 is primarily directed towards items which the police discover adventitiously, eg the police enter premises by virtue of a search warrant issued under the Theft Act 1968 (Theft Act (NI) 1969). They can seize stolen goods (s 26(3)). If they stumble across evidence of a different offence, eg drugs, the evidence can be seized if s 19 (art 21) is satisfied. It will be seen that s 19(2) and (3) (arts 21(2) and (3)) supplement the powers of seizure under ss 8, 18 (arts 10, 20) and other statutes. The only relevant sections of the 1984 Act (1989 Order) which do not carry their own seizure power are ss 17 and 32 (arts 19 and 34). Consequently s 19 (art 21) applies particularly thereto. The reference to 'anything' in the various seizure powers covers not only all forms of property but also an inanimate object such as fingerprints.

Power of search	*Power of seizure*
s 8 (art 10)	s 8(2); s 19 (art 21)
s 18 (art 20)	s 18(2); s 19 (art 21)
Sch 1	Sch 1, para 13; s 19 (para 10; art 21)
Other statutory warrant powers	Terms of the particular statute; s 19 (art 21)
Any other power (ss 17, 32, Arts 19, 34)	s 19 (art 21)

4.132 Whenever a constable is lawfully on premises he may, by virtue of s 19 (art 21), seize anything which on reasonable grounds he believes:
(i)   to be evidence of the offence which he is investigating (s 19(3)(a), art 21(3)(a));
(ii) to have been obtained in consequence of any offence, eg during a search for drugs, he can seize the fruits of a theft such as a television set bought out of stolen money (s 19(2)(a), art 21(2)(a));
(iii) to be evidence of any other offence, eg on searching the premises of a person arrested for theft, he can seize prohibited drugs implicating a person who shares the premises (s 19(3)(a), art 21(3)(a)). However, the words 'any other offence' relate only to domestic offences and not to offences allegedly committed outside the UK (*R v Southwark Crown Court, ex p Sorsky Defries* (1995)). Evidence relating to offences outside the UK can be obtained under s 7-9 of the Criminal Justice (International Co-operation) Act 2003.

4.133   Section 19 (art 21) applies to evidence of any offence, serious or minor. Section 8(4) (art 10(4)) defines 'relevant evidence' as anything that would be admissible at a trial for an offence. The omission of the qualifying adjective 'relevant' in s 19 (art 21) suggests that 'evidence' is used in its popular sense of 'facts in support of ' rather than its technical sense of 'admissible evidence'. There are, however, two limitations on the power of seizure. First, the police must believe that seizure is necessary lest the article be 'concealed, lost, altered or destroyed' in relation to (i) and (iii) (s 19(3)(b)). As regards (ii), 'damaged' is added to the criteria (s 19(2)(b): the NI Order includes 'damaged' in (2) and (3)(b) suggesting that it was an unintended omission in s 19(3)(b)). Thus, if a photograph or copy of the article will suffice for the investigation (and copying facilities are available on the premises), that should be done (s 21(5), art 22(5), gives the police the power to photograph or copy). Second, the constable cannot seize any articles which he has reasonable grounds to believe are subject to legal privilege (s 19(6), art 21(6)). This limitation applies to all powers of seizure. An important consequence flows from the fact that legally privileged material is the only category of material exempt from seizure, which is that excluded or special procedure material is not immune from seizure if the police are lawfully on premises, whether under search powers, or with consent to search or interview, or under a warrant which has not been obtained under the special procedure (Sch 1). The complexities of ss 9-14 (arts 11-16) and Sch 1 can thus be avoided if one of these other search powers is employed or the constable is otherwise lawfully on the premises and he comes across such material. If the occupier or holder of the information objects to the seizure, he may face a charge of obstructing a constable in the execution of his duty. For example, if the police are searching a social worker's house under the authority of the Misuse of Drugs Act 1971 and come across evidence of a crime involving a client of the social worker, they can seize it, even though it may qualify as excluded material under s 12 (art 13).

4.134   Two further points may be noted.
(i)   If the police discover evidence which is held by an innocent purchaser, the police must explain to the holder that he may face civil or criminal proceedings if he tries to part with it (Code B 7.4). Such proceedings may take the form of an action for damages or a criminal prosecution for an offence of handling, theft or obtaining by deception, depending on the circumstances of possession and disposal. However, the innocent purchaser for value may in some circumstances obtain a title to the goods which then cease to be stolen (s 24(3) of the Theft Act 1968). He thus commits no offence if he disposes of those goods. Under a Sch 1 search, contempt proceedings can only follow deliberate disobedience of a court order for production.
(ii)   Even if the police search premises unlawfully (eg without a proper consent, authorisation or in breach of ss 15 and 16 (arts 17 and 18) and thus seize articles unlawfully, the articles may still be admissible in evidence, subject to s 78 (art 76) (see para 2.125, ante). See, for example, *R v Wright* (1994). Customs and Excise officers searched a flat under s 18 and seized £16,000 in cash and a gold necklace worth £9,000 which was admitted in evidence on a charge of possession of cocaine with intent to supply. The appellant argued that this evidence should not have

been admitted because (a) it was not relevant, and (b) the search had been unlawful because it had not been authorised by an inspector and no record of the search had been made in the custody record. Dismissing the appeal it was held that the evidence was relevant and properly admitted. There had been no deliberate breach of Code B. The trial judge had found as a fact that the search had been authorised and had taken the breach of the Code into account and concluded that it would not be unfair to the appellant to admit the evidence. The Court could not review the finding of fact and the trial judge had properly exercised his discretion under s 78. More serious breaches of the statute or Code may well result in exclusion and the police may also face a disciplinary charge or a civil action for their unlawful conduct.

COMPUTERS

4.135   Special provision is made for the seizure of information contained in computers. The phrase 'contained in a computer' must be read as including information stored on disc or tape which is not stored in the computer but is only accessible through the medium of a computer. Any other interpretation would exclude so much material as to render the provision virtually useless. It follows that the constable can seize a computer disc or tape or, if he only requires specific information which is on the disc or tape, a print-out of the relevant part (ss 19(4), 20, arts 21(4), 22). However, the ease with which information can be concealed within a computer (eg by the use of trigger words before access is allowed) and the possibility that the computer on the premises is merely a local terminal for a central database held elsewhere mean that specialist officers will be needed to conduct the search, and that frequently a complete tape must be studied or taken away. Such officers will need to study the operating manual which governs the computer and to interview the computer controller and/or programmer. Section 20 (art 22) extends the s 19(4) (art 21(4)) provision to all powers of seizure contained in any statutory provision passed or made before or after the 1984 Act (1989 Order) and to the powers of seizure under ss 8 and 18 (arts 10 and 20) and to the power of seizure when executing a warrant to search for and seize excluded or special procedure material contained in para 13 of Sch 1 to the 1984 Act (para 10 of Sch 1 to the 1989 Order). Thus, whenever there is a statutory power to seize material, there is a statutory power to require a print-out of computerised information which has been obtained in consequence of an offence or, more usually, which is evidence of an offence, eg a constable executing a warrant under the Obscene Publications Act 1959 may, having seized obscene material, require a print-out of information contained in a computer about the source of the supply of such material.

4.136   The Computer Misuse Act 1990, s 1, makes unauthorised access to computer material an offence. Section 10 of that Act provides that this offence shall not apply to the exercise of law enforcement powers. Section 162 of the Criminal Justice and Public Order Act 1994 deals with the insertion into computer programs of provisions for access only by authorised persons or a particular class of persons.

4.137   After para 10(b) of the Computer Misuse Act the following words are added:

'nothing designed to indicate a withholding of consent to access to any program or data from persons as enforcement officers shall have effect to make access unauthorised for the purposes of the said section(1)(1)'.[of the Computer Misuse Act].

4.138   In this section 'enforcement officer' means a constable or other person charged with the duty of investigating offences; and withholding consent from a person 'as' an enforcement officer of any description includes the operation, by the person entitled to control access, of rules whereby enforcement officers of that description are, as such, disqualified from membership of a class of persons who are authorised to have access.

POST-SEARCH AND SEIZURE

4.139   The following provisions apply whichever statutory power of seizure is used:

(i)   List of seized articles (s 21(1), (2), art 23(1) and (2)) – After seizing any article, the constable must, within a reasonable time, supply the occupier or custodian of the article with a record of what has been seized (cf the common law position, *Arias v Metropolitan Police Comr* (1984)). The obligation only arises, however, if that person requests it. The request may be made at the time of the seizure or subsequently. In searches involving the seizure of many documents, the 'reasonable time' for compiling the record may well be considerable.

(ii)   Owner's access to seized articles – The prospect of the police being allowed to seize evidence from innocent third parties and the controversy surrounding police access to confidential information alerted MPs to the disruption which seizure could cause to that party's business. The Government responded with s 21 (art 23). This applies to all seized articles and permits the person who had custody or control of the article to apply to the police personally or through a representative (eg a lawyer) for (1) supervised access to the article, and/or (2) photographs or copies of the article. For small items the police can usually allow the owner to photograph or copy them under supervision (s 21(4)(a), art 23(4)(a)); but large numbers of documents they can do themselves 'within a reasonable time' (s 21(4)(b), (6), (7), art 23(4)(b), (6), (7)) and can presumably charge the owner for the expense of doing so. However, the obligation to allow access to, or copying of, the articles can be avoided if the officer in charge of the investigation has reasonable grounds to believe that the investigation would be prejudiced thereby (s 21(8), art 23(8)). There is no reference to 'serious' prejudice and this could tempt the police to deny access on the basis that lengthy documentary evidence is currently being examined and that the inconvenience of copying it or allowing access to it would hamper police investigations. However, Code B 6.9 requires that the grounds for refusal of access be recorded and they could thus be examined in subsequent proceedings under the Police (Property) Act 1897 (or challenged on judicial review, see *Allen v Chief Constable of Cheshire Constabulary* (1988)).

The 'investigation' in s 21(8) (art 23(8)) which may be prejudiced can include those against other people, eg an investigation into D's alleged fraudulent activities may lead to investigations of his associates.

(iii) Retention of seized articles – Articles may only be retained for as long as is necessary (s 22(2), art 24(1)). What is 'necessary' will depend on the purposes for which they are held and s 22(2) (art 24(2)) lists the most common as follows.

   (a) For use as evidence at trial for any offence. For example, if the article is subsequently of no use to the police who seized it, it may be retained for the benefit of other agencies. The 'necessity' principle in s 22(1) (art 24(1)) means that where a photograph or copy will suffice, the article should not be retained (s 22(4), art 24(4), endorsing *Ghani v Jones* (1970)). In *R v Chief Constable of Lancashire, ex p Parker and McGrath* (1993) police obtained a warrant under s 9 and Sch 1 of PACE 1984 and a schedule of the documents to be seized was appended to the warrant. Unfortunately, the police removed the original schedule and showed the occupier a photocopy in breach of s 16(5)(b). They also breached s 16(5)(c) by giving the occupier a copy of the warrant minus the schedule. This made the search and seizure unlawful. An argument by the police that s 22(2)(a) permitted the retention of unlawfully seized documents was rejected. The section can only apply to the retention of lawfully seized articles.

   (b) For forensic examination.

   (c) To establish the article's lawful owner when it is believed to have been obtained unlawfully. Other examples include retention for the purpose of an appeal, or where the return of property is against public policy, eg where D is acquitted of, or not prosecuted for, drug offences, it is clearly right for the police not to return the seized drugs. Some items seized for expedient reasons (eg weapons, articles for escape) cannot be retained once the person is released from police detention or custody of a court (s 22(3), art 24(3)).

(iv) Remedies for impropriety – The owner's remedies for impropriety by the police consist of: (i) a civil action (ii) a complaint under the police disciplinary code and procedure; and (iii) recourse to the Police (Property) Act 1897 if he believes that the police are unnecessarily retaining his property. By s 1 of that Act (and see further the Police (Disposal of Property) Regulations 1975, SI 1975/1474) he can apply to a magistrates' court for an order to return the property or to force the police to justify its retention. Code B Note of Guidance 7A instructs the police to advise the owner of this procedure 'where appropriate'. This means where the owner or claimed owner has made it clear to the police that he objects to their retention of the property.

EXAMPLES OF THE VARIOUS POWERS IN OPERATION

4.140   The following examples illustrate the operation of the powers thus far discussed and the consensual search. In all these situations the constable will be lawfully on premises for the purposes of s 19 (art 21) and the powers of seizure provided will be available to the constable. All the examples are subject to the requirement of reasonable cause to suspect or believe as appropriate.

Example 1

4.141   D, a self-employed businessman, is arrested while driving home from his office for an offence of fraud (an arrestable offence under s 24, art 26). The car (premises within s 23, art 25) may be searched for evidence of that, or a connected or similar offence (s 18, art 20), being premises under his control; or under s 32(2)(b) (premises in which he was when or immediately before being arrested). D's house (premises occupied by him) may be searched (s 18, art 20) as may his office (premises under his control). If during the search of any of these premises the police come across evidence of a totally different offence, eg child sex abuse, that may be seized under s 19 (art 21). If evidence of the fraud is held by D's accountant it will be held in confidence and will be special procedure material as defined by s 14 (art 16) (see para 4.184., post). A s 8 (art 10) warrant cannot be issued to search for and seize the material, instead application must be made under s 9(1) (art 11(1)) and Sch 1 (see para 4.194, post). However, if D was arrested in the accountant's office, or immediately on leaving that office, the office may be searched for evidence of the fraud (s 32(2)(b), art 34(2)(b)) and the material seized even though it is special procedure material.

Example 2

4.142   D is disturbed while hooking dresses from racks in a clothing store by means of a flexible pole with a hook on the end, which he inserted through the letter box. He is seen to make off with a quantity of clothes and drive off in a car, the registration number of which is noted. The car belongs to a known criminal who lives in the area and who has a caravan in an adjoining police area. A watch is kept on both premises but the car is not at either. Section 17(1)(b) (art 19(1)(b)) is available to authorise entry to either premises to arrest D if, but only if, there are reasonable grounds for believing that D is on the premises. If D is arrested on the premises, s 32(2)(b) (art 34(2)(b)) authorises the search of those premises for evidence of the offence for which he is arrested. If D is not on the premises, no search for evidence of the offence may be made except with the written consent of a person entitled to consent. If while searching for D the police come across garments which are believed to be those stolen (eg they look in a wardrobe in which a man may hide) they may be seized under s 19(3) (art 21(3)). If there is reason to believe that D may not be on the premises, s 17 (art 19) will not be available but a search warrant under s 26 of the Theft Act 1968 (s 25 of the Theft Act (Northern Ireland) 1969) may be sought if there are reasonable grounds to believe the stolen garments are on the premises. If D is seen driving the car, he may be arrested on reasonable suspicion of theft and his car (premises, s 23, art 25) may be searched under s 18 (art 20), or s 32(2)(b) (art 34(2)(b)). D's house and caravan may be searched under s 18. (As an alternative to arresting D immediately, his car may be searched under s 1 of PACE 1984 (art 3 of the PACE (NI) Order 1989).) If D's unattended car is found, the s 1 (art 3) power is the only means of lawfully searching the car prior to D's arrest (see para 3.49, ante).

Example 3

4.143 D, who is reasonably suspected of committing a number of burglaries, is arrested while leaving the premises occupied by his girlfriend. Those premises may be searched under s 32(2)(b) (art 34(2)(b)) and premises occupied by him, eg his home, may be searched under s 18 (art 20).

Example 4

4.144 D, an unemployed youth, is arrested in the bedroom of a house in which the kitchen and living room are shared with other young persons, for possession of prohibited drugs. All the rooms in the house may be searched for evidence of that offence (s 32(2)(b) and (7), art 34(2)(b) and (7)). If evidence of other offences is found in rooms occupied by D or the others, it may be seized under s 19 (art 21).

Example 5

4.145 As in (d) but D occupies a self-contained flat and shares only the bathroom and toilet. Only his rooms and the bathroom and toilet may be searched, since he occupies a 'separate dwelling' (s 32(7), art 34(7)); see further para 4.7, ante.

Example 6

4.146 A number of youths are disturbed while in the course of a burglary and make off in several directions. One youth is spotted by a mobile patrol who give chase. The youth runs into a greengrocer's shop. The police, exercising their s 17 (art 19) power, pursue him into the shop and find him hiding in a backyard toilet. No search of the premises for evidence takes place after the arrest, there being no reasonable belief that evidence of the offence would be found there. However, at the police station it emerges that the arrested youth had been carrying a radio cassette player when he left the scene of the burglary which, it was thought, he might have hidden on the greengrocer's premises. In these circumstances there is no statutory power to enter and search the premises. The s 32(2)(b) (art 34(2)(b)) power is only available immediately after the arrest (*R v Badham* (1987)) and, since D does not occupy or control the premises, the s 18 (art 20) power is not available. A search of the premises can therefore only take place with the consent of the occupier, in writing or, if such consent is not forthcoming, with the authority of a magistrates' warrant under s 26 of the Theft Act 1968 (s 25 of the Theft Act (NI) 1989).

Example 7

4.147   Police are called to a house by neighbours who heard screams and sounds of a fight. On arrival the police hear sounds of a fight. Their entry on to the premises is justified by s 17(1)(e) (art 19(1)(e)). On entry they find a man who has been severely beaten. The occupants, a prostitute and another male, are arrested. The flat is searched under s 32(2)(b) (art 34(2)(b)) and blood-stained clothing belonging to the occupants and the victim is seized. Some hours later the victim alleges that the woman had invited him to the house for sex. Having entered he was attacked by the male and female and robbed of £150. Section 32(2)(b) (art 34(2)(b)) is no longer available (*R v Badham* (1987)) but s 18 (art 20) is, robbery being an arrestable offence, and the premises occupied by the arrested persons may be searched for the stolen money.

Example 8

4.148   A police officer investigating burglaries is making house-to-house inquiries. He is invited into a house by the occupier and while there he sees a video recorder which fits the description of one stolen in the burglaries. The occupier says she bought it off a man who said he had lost his job and was forced to sell some of his belongings. She paid a reasonable price. Even if the occupier is not guilty of handling stolen goods and is not arrested, the video recorder may be seized under s 19(3) (art 21(3)). In the absence of an arrest no search can take place without written consent. If the occupier is arrested the premises may be searched for evidence related to the offence of handling eg other stolen goods.

LIMITATION ON THE EXTENT OF NON-WARRANT SEARCHES

4.149   Premises may be searched only to the extent necessary to achieve the object of the search, having regard to the size and nature of whatever is sought (ss 17(4), 18(3) and 32(3), arts 19(3), 20(3) and 34(3), Code B 6.9). A similar provision applies to all warrant searches (s 16(8), art 18(8)). All searches must therefore be commensurate with the size and nature of the material sought. 'Premises' may bear a narrower meaning in relation to ss 17 and 32 (ss 17(2), 32(7)). All searches *'must be conducted with due consideration for the property and privacy of the occupier ... and with no more disturbance than necessary'* (Code B 6.10). The extent of the 'disturbance' will depend on the nature of the material sought, eg vehicles as opposed to cash. An occupier's remedy for an excessive search is to lodge a complaint and, in extreme cases, a civil action can be contemplated. To prevent such incidents, and to avoid allegations that the police have in other respects exceeded their powers or 'planted evidence', it is good police practice to ensure the presence of a third party, especially when the suspect is not present, eg if arrested and detained elsewhere and a search is undertaken under s 18 (art 20). While there is no provision for a suspect to be present during such a search it is common practice in some police forces to take the suspect who is in custody with them on the search. This serves two purposes: (i) it prevents any allegation of 'planting' of evidence; and (ii) the suspect can save the police time by indicating where the property sought is. (Code C 10.1 requires that a person whom there are grounds to suspect of an offence must be cautioned before any questions are put to him about that offence but a caution is not required when the questions are aimed at obtaining co-operation in a search. In searches under ss 18 or 32(2)(b) (arts 20 or 34(2)(b)) the person will have been arrested and already cautioned but the danger is that questions during the search may become an interview if they are regarding his involvement or suspected involvement in a criminal offence (Code C 11.1A). A series of questions directed at establishing to whom the property found in the course of a search belongs may not be an interview (*R v Cohen* (1993)) but questioning beyond that should take place at the police station in a formal interview unless Code C 11.1 applies (*R v Cox* (1993) see paras 8.4-8.8, post).)

4.150   If the search is conducted under s 18(5) (art 20(5)) or s 32(2)(b) (art 34(2)(b)) the suspect will be present. If the occupier wishes to ask a friend, neighbour or other person, eg a solicitor, to witness the search he must be allowed to do so. Code B 6.11 goes on to suggest that the occupier may not be allowed to do so if there are reasonable grounds for believing that this would seriously hinder the investigation. If the occupier is not under arrest, the police have no power to refuse to allow a third party to witness the search. If that person does in fact seek to hinder the search he may be committing the offence of obstructing the police in the execution of their duty. This should be sufficient sanction and if the occupier does seek to exercise this right, the Code provides that a search may not be unreasonably delayed for this purpose. There is, unfortunately, no obligation on the police to inform the occupier of this right. The Notice of Powers and Rights, which Code B 6.7 requires to be given to the occupier, makes no reference to this right, therefore it will seldom be exercised.

OBTAINING ENTRY UNDER SS 17, 18 OR 32 (Arts 19, 20 or 34)

4.151   For all the forms of entry and search discussed above, other than entry and search under a warrant and with consent, the constable must attempt to communicate with the occupier or, adopting a tighter test than for warrants (see s 16(6), art 18(6)), with 'any other person entitled to grant access to the premises' (Code B 6.4). (See the discussion of this term in the context of consent at para 4.80, ante.) The officer in charge must explain the authority under which he seeks entry and ask the occupier to admit him. However, Code B 6.4 does not demand such pleasantries if:
(i)   the premises are known to be unoccupied; or
(ii)   the occupier or person entitled to grant access are known to be absent; or
(iii) there are reasonable grounds for believing that to alert the occupier would frustrate the search or endanger life, eg if the items sought are readily disposable, or the occupier or other person on the premises is believed to be dangerous.

4.152   When the premises are occupied the officer must identify himself (by warrant number in terrorism cases, otherwise by name) and if not in uniform, show his warrant card, state the purpose of the search and the grounds for undertaking it before a search begins, unless (iii) above applies.

Force

4.153 All the powers of entry and search, but not searches with consent, allow the police to use reasonable and proportionate force if necessary (s 117, art 88). For a fuller discussion of reasonable force, see para 2.111, ante. It can be noted in the present context that it must be shown that force is 'necessary'. Thus, if a constable is met by a householder, he must, even if he holds a warrant for arrest, seek permission to enter, for only if he is refused will force become 'necessary' (cf *Swales v Cox*, post). There are, however, many circumstances in which the constable is absolved from the need for such courtesies, eg where the premises are not occupied (apart from the object of the search) by anyone who could give access to them, or where an armed man is pursued on to them. As to the meaning of 'force', the hallowed law of trespass means that 'force' may amount to very little effort. Thus, if a constable

> 'meets an obstacle, then he uses force if he applies any energy to the obstacle with a view to removing it. It would follow that, where there is a door which is ajar but is insufficiently ajar for someone to go through the opening without moving the door and energy is applied to that door to make it open further, force is being used. A fortiori force is used when the door is latched and you turn the handle from the outside and then ease the door open. Similarly, if someone opens any window or increases the opening in any window, or indeed dislodges the window by the application of any energy, he is using force to enter ...' (*Swales v Cox* (1981))

4.154 As to what is 'reasonable and proportionate', this will obviously depend on all the circumstances and in particular the type and amount of resistance met. Code B 6.6 lists exhaustively the circumstances where force will be necessary:
(i)   where access has been refused;
(ii) where it is not possible to communicate with the occupier so as to obtain access;
(iii) where one of the conditions in Code B 6.4 applies (see para 4.151, ante), eg the door must be broken down lest evidence be destroyed or lest a dangerous suspect be forewarned.

4.155 If force has been used against the premises, the officer in charge must make sure that they are secure before leaving (Code B 6.13). On returning to the police station, the officer in charge of the search must make a record of any damage caused in the search register (see para 4.157, post). As to compensation, provided that the entry and use of force have been lawful, whether by warrant or otherwise, the occupier has no right to recompense for any damage caused on his premises.

NOTICE OF POWERS AND RIGHTS

4.156 The balancing of powers with safeguards is fine in principle but in practice fails because the citizen against whom the powers are exercised is all too often ignorant of both. Code B 6.7 attempts to redress the balance. An officer conducting a search to which the Code applies, that is all the entry and search powers discussed above, including warrant searches, must unless it is impracticable to do so provide the occupier with a copy of a notice, termed 'A Notice of Powers and Rights'. The notice, which is in standard form comprising an original and a duplicate, must:

(i) specify whether the search is made under a warrant or under one of PACE 1984 (Order) powers. Provision is made on the notice for the signature of the person giving consent to be appended. This suggests that the information required to be given when seeking consent (see Code B 5.2) should be given orally and the written authority, if practicable, be given on the notice;

(ii) summarise the extent of the powers of search and seizure conferred by PACE 1984 (Order);

(iii) explain the rights of the occupier, and of the owner of property seized in accordance with Code B 7.1-7.6 (see s 19, art 21), set out in the Act (Order) and Code;

(iv) explain that compensation may be payable in appropriate cases for damage caused in entering and searching the premises, and giving the address to which an application for compensation should be directed; and

(v) state that a copy of the Code of Practice is available for consultation at any police station. If the occupier is present, the notice should, if practicable, be given to the occupier before the search begins (together with the warrant if a warrant search). While the Act and Code do not require the constable to allow the occupier time to assimilate the contents of the notice (and the warrant), the purpose behind the notice will not be accomplished unless such time is given. Where force or subterfuge is used to gain entry, it may be necessary to secure the premises so as to ensure that the property sought is not disposed of before providing the information required by Code B 6.5 and the Notice of Powers and Rights (cf *R v Longman* (1988) discussed at para 4.55, ante), but whenever the occupier is present the information and notice should by analogy to the warrant be provided before the search begins. If the occupier is not present a copy of the notice (and copy warrant if appropriate) must be endorsed with the name of the officer in charge of the search (warrant number only if a terrorism investigation), the police station to which he is attached and the date and time of the search. (If a warrant search the warrant must be endorsed to show that this has been done.) The notice (and warrant if appropriate) must then be left in a prominent place on the premises. The original of the notice should be retained and appended to the premises searched register.

PREMISES SEARCHED REGISTER

4.157 Code B 8.1 stipulates that a search register be maintained at each sub-divisional police station, in which all records required by the Code are to be entered. Code B 8.1 sets out the matters to be included in the register. These include the address of the premises searched; the time and date of the search; the authority under which the search was made; a list of the articles seized; whether force was used and details of any damage caused. A copy of the warrant or consent where appropriate must be appended to the register or a note made in the register of where they are kept. As indicated in para 4.78, ante, the written consent will normally be contained in the Notice of Powers and Rights. The original of this notice should then, and in all other searches, be appended to the search register.

PART B: SPECIAL POWERS TO OBTAIN MATERIAL OR TO SEARCH PREMISES (s 9, Art 11 AND Sch 1 OF PACE 1984 AND 1989 ORDER) INTRODUCTION

4.158   Before PACE 1984 the police lacked a general power to obtain material which was likely to be relevant evidence of an offence by A but was in the possession of B who was not himself implicated in the crime. If the material happened to be prohibited articles which it was an offence to possess, such as stolen goods, drugs, firearms, etc, a search warrant could be obtained to search for and seize the material even if it was innocently possessed by B. If not within that category there was no general power to obtain access to such material. An exception is provided by the Bankers' Books Evidence Act 1879. Under this Act a High Court Judge may order the inspection of any entries in a banker's books, on application by a party to civil or criminal proceedings. This procedure is, however, of limited use as an investigative tool. First it is confined to banks, second to bankers' books (this includes computerised accounts but not bank managers' notes or diary or paid cheques and credit slips) and third, to current legal proceedings, in other words a charge must have been laid or a summons issued (see para 4.308, post). Banks could not consent to requests by the police for access to material not covered by the Act because to do so would lay them open to an action for breach of confidentiality (a banker's duty of confidentiality being firmly established in *Tournier v National Provincial and Union Bank of England* (1924)). If that duty did not extend to bank managers' notes, banks feared that they might be exposed to an action for defamation if such notes were surrendered voluntarily. Alternatively such co-operation with the police might lead to loss of custom. If legally compelled to disclose information no civil action could follow and, it was thought, customers would understand the necessity to comply with the law. The Royal Commission (1981) recognised this dilemma, which was not confined to banks, when it observed:

> 'It is only rarely that the police do not receive consent to enter when looking for evidence ... However where property or information is held on a confidential basis the holder may be unwilling to disclose it for fear of being sued for breach of duty by the person from whom he received it. Where consent is not immediately forthcoming there may be some temptation for the police to resort to bluff or trickery to obtain the evidence. At present there are few statutory provisions allowing the police to search for evidence during an investigation ... We consider that there will be rare circumstances where a compulsory power is needed, and should be available to the police before a charge. But ... we think that it should be a limited power and one subject to stringent safeguards.' (Report, para 3.41)

4.159   As for other evidence held by third parties, s 8 (art 10) now gives the police the opportunity to apply for a search warrant if any serious arrestable offence is involved. The confidential basis which might be jeopardised by such searches aroused considerable furore during passage of the 1984 Bill and forced the Government to make concessions so as to protect confidential information. Sections 9 to 14 (arts 11-16) and Sch 1 were the result of this modification. The attempted balancing of the rights of the citizen and the needs of the police service result in much complexity. In essence three new categories of material were created. The first of these, legally privileged material, is always unavailable to the police unless the client, whose privilege it is, surrenders it and permits the police access to the material. The second category, excluded material, may also be given its literal meaning. In exceptional circumstances a circuit judge (county court judge in Northern Ireland) may make an order for the production to a constable of, or issue a warrant to search for and seize, excluded material. This is rare and will be considered later (para 4.211, post). Subject to this exception excluded material cannot be the subject of a magistrate's warrant or a judicial order permitting police access to it. Access can, however, more readily be obtained to the third category of material, special procedure material. As the name implies the 1984 Act (1989 Order) created a special procedure under which application may be made to a circuit judge (county court judge) for an order requiring the person in possession of the material to produce it to a constable for him to take away, or give him access to it. (These procedures can be circumvented and excluded and special procedure material can be searched for and seized using the powers under s 32(2)(b) (art 34(2)(b)) and s 19 (art 21). See para 4.140 example 1.) The introduction of these provisions coincided with an upsurge in offences of fraud much of which resulted from the economic boom of the early 1980s. This led to a massive increase in mortgage lending in which banks plunged into a market previously the province of building societies. This provided opportunities for fraud which were seized upon. Government privatisation schemes also provided opportunities for those who saw the opportunity to make a quick profit regardless of the legality. Much of the responsibility for investigating these offences fell to the Metropolitan Police and City Company Fraud Department which pioneered the use of the power provided by s 9 (art 11) and Sch 1 of the 1984 Act (1989 Order) and it is in this area that the real impact of Part II of PACE 1984 (Part III of the PACE Order) is to be seen. Similar (but not identical) powers are also provided by the Drug Trafficking Act 1994, the Terrorism Act 2000, and the Proceeds of Crime Act 2002. The definition of the three categories of material is considered below and the procedure set out in Sch 1 of the 1984 Act (1989 Order). The similar powers mentioned above will then be considered in Part C. Figure 2 (on p 156) shows in schematic form the routes to be taken to obtain an order or warrant permitting access to, or the search for, material which is evidence of a serious arrestable offence.

4.160 General preliminary points should be borne in mind:
(i) The onus is very much on the police to check, before applying for an order or warrant, whether it will involve excluded or special procedure material, for once the police are in possession of an order or warrant, and have gained access to premises, the occupier of premises cannot prevent them from seizing material under s 19 (art 21). Only legally privileged material is totally exempt from seizure. If the order or warrant is invalid, for example it fails to comply with s 15 of PACE 1984 or it applies to excluded material which is not available under s 9 and Sch 1 of that Act, it may be declared invalid on judicial review: see for example *R v Central Criminal Court and British Railway Board, ex p AJD Holdings* (1992), and *R v*

Chief Constable of Lancashire, ex p Parker (1993) considered at paras 4.36 and 4.54 respectively, ante. The issuing circuit judge has no power to review or rescind an order or warrant issued under Sch 1 (*R v Liverpool Crown Court, ex p George Wimpey plc* (1991)).

(ii)   Where the following provisions apply, the holder of the confidential information may well be placed in an extremely uncomfortable moral position. If he refuses to disclose it, he will probably face the prospect of a hearing before a Crown Court under Sch 1. If he does disclose it, he breaks the confidence owing to his client. However, the latter course may be encouraged in the knowledge (1) even if the person holding the material is subject to a duty of confidence, the public interest may justify, or even compel its disclosure (*R v Ataou* (1988)), and (2) there is no confidence in iniquity (*Gartside v Outram* (1856) cited with approval in *R v Leeds Magistrates' Court, ex p Dumbleton* (1993)); disclosure may not therefore expose him to civil liability. It will be seen that the procedures for obtaining access to material held in confidence require that other methods of obtaining the material, which would include approaching the person in possession, but not necessarily the person subject of the investigation, to see if he will surrender it voluntarily. Only if he declines to do so need the statutory procedures be used. For example, in *R v Singleton* (1995) a dentist voluntarily gave to the police a cast of S's teeth which they subsequently matched with bite marks on the murder victim. S appealed against his conviction arguing that since he had refused to give a dental impression (an intimate sample under s 62 of PACE 1984) the only way in which the cast could be admitted in evidence was by the special procedure under s 9 and Sch 1 of PACE 1984 but since it was excluded material it was unavailable to the police by that procedure. The Court of Appeal dismissed his appeal. Taking a broad approach the Court held that the object of the Act was to protect disclosure of personal records as referred to in s 11. The person to be protected was the person who had acquired or created the record, not the suspect in a particular case. If that person voluntarily disclosed the record he did not seek or require the protection given by the Act. It was for the person identified in s 11(1) to decide whether he wished to make disclosure, bearing in mind the degree of confidence reposed in him. If he decided it was his duty to retain the record, the Act provided the procedure the police must follow to obtain access to it. The fact that the police could not have obtained what was excluded material did not affect the option to disclose voluntarily. The suspect's consent was not required, indeed it would be foolish to put the suspect on notice that the police were attempting to obtain access to this kind of material. Having looked at Hansard and parliamentary debates (following *Pepper v Hart* (1993)) the Court concluded that it could not have been the intention of Parliament that a s 9 and Sch 1 application should be the exclusive method of access to such material. In these circumstances it is doubtful if the duty of confidence, if it existed, would have survived against the public interest in the detection of serious crime.

(iii) Even if an application by the police under Sch 1 to search for excluded or special procedure material fails, the evidence (apart from legally privileged items) is not privileged at the trial stage, for the laws of criminal evidence have refused to extend privilege beyond the client and lawyer relationship. For example, a journalist who successfully opposes an application for an order under Sch 1, can still be ordered to appear at the trial for the accused by subpoena duces tecum, as can any witness. He has the option of refusing to attend and taking the consequences of the law of contempt (cf *A-G v Mulholland* (1963)).

(iv) The following paragraphs do not contradict the non-disclosure provisions of the Data Protection Act 1998, which protect the disclosure of personal data, because those provisions have no application if disclosure is required for:

(a) the prevention or detection of crime;

(b) the apprehension or prosecution of offenders;

(c) the assessment or collection of any tax or duty (s 28 of that Act).

(v) Matters are complicated by s 114(2) which permits the Treasury by order (subject to annulment by Parliament) to add a new s 114A to the 1984 Act for the purposes of investigations by officers of the Customs and Excise. This has been done by Reg 6 of PACE 1984 (Application to Customs and Excise Order (SI 1987/439)) which has the effect of removing the protection of Sch 1 from 'Material in the possession of persons who acquired or created it in the course of any trade, business, profession, or other occupation or for the purpose of any paid or unpaid office and which relate to an assigned matter.'

Thus, warrants obtained by Customs' officers under Customs' legislation to search for and seize business records would proceed in the normal way, without reference to Sch 1 of the 1984 Act, and the facts of *IRC v Rossminster* (1980), for example, would be unaffected.

(vi) If a terrorist investigation, as defined by s 32 Terrorism Act 2000, is involved, excluded material, as defined by ss 11, 12 and 13 (arts 13, 14 and 15) (discussed at paras 4.277 to 4.280, post) can be the subject of a production order or exceptionally a warrant to search for and seize the material, under Sch 5 to that Act – see paras 4.277 et seq.

(vii) The only common factor which applies to search warrants issued under the 1984 Act (1989 Order) or other statutes, is that legally privileged items cannot be obtained by a warrant. Nor can they be seized under the powers of seizure which operate during a search of premises (s 19(6), art 21(6)).

(viii) Material obtained by compulsory powers provided for the investigation and prosecution of crime is held by the police under a duty of confidence and must not be disclosed to third parties unless:

(a) a subpoena duces tecum is issued against the police requiring the production in court of documents seized; or

(b) the material is in the public domain (for example, documents have been read out in court) when the duty of confidence no longer exists.

Where a subpoena has been served the police should not disclose seized documents in advance of the attendance at court without giving the owner of the documents notice of the subpoena and a reasonable opportunity to state his objection (*Marcel v Metropolitan Police Comr* (1991)). However, in *R v Southwark Crown Court, ex p Customs and Excise Comrs* and *R v Southwark Crown Court, ex p Bank of Credit and Commerce International (SA)* (1990), the Divisional

Court held that copies, but not the originals, of material seized by Customs and Excise under similar powers, could be passed to the foreign law enforcement agency for whose investigation the production of the material is required. See now the Criminal Justice (International Co-operation) Act 2003.

4.161   In *Tate Access Floors Inc v Boswell* (1990) it was held that an Anton Piller order, compelling a defendant to disclose documents and information, could not be made when the civil proceedings involved an allegation of facts which could give rise to a criminal charge, because it would infringe the defendant's privilege against self-incrimination. In Marcel (above) it was said that the privilege against self-incrimination was not available to the respondent when the documents were in the possession of the police. If, however, the police exercise their PACE Act (Order) powers, the documents obtained may be available to a party to a civil action by the issue of a subpoena duces tecum.

4.162   It is appropriate here to remind the reader that there are five categories of material which need to be distinguished:
(i)   material covered by pre-1984 (1989) statutory warrant powers;
(ii)   material which can be obtained under s 8 of the 1984 Act (art 10 of the 1989 Order);
(iii) special procedure material defined by s 14 (art 16); obtainable only in accordance with Sch I under either set of access conditions set out in the Schedule;
(iv)   excluded material, defined by ss 11, 12 and 13 of the Act (arts 13, 14 and 15 of the Order); unobtainable unless another statutory warrant power exists and the special procedure is followed;
(v)   legally privileged material, defined by s 10 (art 12), unobtainable under any statutory power.

4.163   The following paragraphs are concerned with (iii) to (v). Schematically, the procedure is as follows:

Material	Authority	Procedure
Any material, other than legally privileged material, sought for Customs and Excise purposes	Customs and Excise legislation	Obtainable by warrant regardless of the 1984 Act's (1989 Order's) provisions in exclude and special procedure material
Excluded or special procedure material relating to a terrorist offence	Prevention of Terrorism (Temporary Provisions) Act 1989, Sch 7	Obtainable by order of a circuit (county court) judge or by warrant of such a judge
Any material, other than legally privileged or excluded material, relating to during trafficking offences	Drug Trafficking Offences Act 1994, ss 55, 56	Obtainable by order of a circuit judge or a search warrant issued by such a judge

4.164 *NB: While s 9(2) (art 11(2)) prevents the use of search warrants under statutory provisions existing before the 1984 Act (1989 Order) to search for legally privileged, excluded or special procedure material, search warrants in statutes passed after the 1984 Act (1989 Order) may not do so, eg the Cinemas Act 1985, s 13(3) does include the above prohibition while the Public Order Act 1986, s 24 does not.

Items subject to legal privilege (s 10, art 12)

4.165 Since this material is most often to be found in the possession of members of the legal profession one may expect disputes as to whether the material sought is legally privileged material. If it is not, the material is likely to be held in confidence and therefore special procedure material and subject to the procedure outlined below (paras 4.182-4.215, post). If it is, there is no lawful procedure in English law by which a person can be compelled to produce or give access to the material and it cannot be seized during a search of premises. The common law of evidence has long recognised a privilege against the compulsory disclosure of a party's legal advice in both civil and criminal proceedings. The 1984 Act (1989 Order) extends this protection to the pre-trial investigative stage and clarifies the common law which, following the decision in *Truman (Frank) Export Ltd v Metropolitan Police Comr* (1977), was unclear. As regards warrants issued by virtue of the 1984 Act (1989 Order), the exemption for legally privileged material is simply stated (s 8(1)(d), art 10(1)(d)). As regards warrants issued under statutory provisions which pre-date the 1984 Act (1989 Order), the same result is achieved by a more obscure route. Section 9(2) (art 11(2)) nullifies all such provisions as regards legally privileged, excluded and special procedure material. Schedule 1 provides a procedure under which access to special procedure material and, exceptionally, excluded material may be obtained but makes no such provision for legally privileged material. As regards statutory provisions which post-date the 1984 Act (1989 Order) they are not subject to the nullification process of s 9(2) (art 11(2)) unless the statute providing the warrant power incorporates s 9(2), eg the Cinemas Act 1985 does, the Public Order Act 1986 does not. It is, however, inconceivable that such statutes will be interpreted as permitting entry to premises to search for and seize legally privileged material. The privilege is thus secured. Furthermore, the definition which follows has a wider relevance since the privilege applies to limit the general powers of seizure set out in s 19 (art 21) (see para 4.128, ante).

DEFINITION OF LEGAL PRIVILEGE

4.166 The definition of legal privilege in s 10 (art 12) follows that of the 16th Report of the Law Reform Committee (para 17), which in turn sought to reflect the common law. Legal privilege attaches to the following items when in the possession of a person who is entitled to possession of them. First, communications between a professional legal adviser and his client, or any person representing his client, made in connection with the giving of legal advice to the client. This advice need not be related to any legal proceedings. Second, communications between a professional legal adviser and his client, or any person representing his client or between any of these three and a third person, made in connection with or in contemplation of and for the purposes of legal proceedings. Third, privilege attaches to items enclosed with or referred to in either of the above communications, and made in connection with the giving of legal advice or in connection with or in contemplation of and for the purposes of legal proceedings. It must be emphasised that the privilege is that of the client, not the legal adviser. It follows that if a document is not privileged in the hands of the client, it is not privileged in the hands of the solicitor (*R v Peterborough Justices, ex p Hicks* (1977) and see *R v Leeds Magistrates' Court, ex p Dumbleton* (1993) considered below). Like any privilege it can be waived but only by the client whose privilege it is.

4.167   The relationship of lawyer/client may be seen as creating a circle around the parties. It is only communications arising within the circle created by the relationship and which are made for the purposes of giving legal advice or which are made in connection with or in contemplation of legal proceedings and for the purposes of those proceedings that are privileged. Similarly, items enclosed with such communications are only privileged if they are made within that relationship in connection with the giving of legal advice or in connection with or in contemplation of legal proceedings and for the purposes of those proceedings. See, for example, *R v R* (1994) where a blood sample provided by the defendant to his solicitor which was then the subject of a DNA test by defence experts was held to be subject to legal privilege. The prosecution was not therefore permitted to call the expert to give evidence of his analysis of the specimen of blood.

4.168   Materials which, though made within a solicitor/client relationship but which are not concerned with the giving of legal advice or legal proceedings actual or contemplated, are not privileged. For example, in *R v Crown Court at Inner London Sessions, ex p Baines & Co Ltd; Baines* (1988) it was held that material consisting simply of documents relating to the financing and purchase of a house (conveyancing material) was not legally privileged. Thus what might be described as the commercial activities of a solicitor do not necessarily give rise to legal privilege, though such material will almost always be special procedure material. Material which was in existence before the relationship came into being does not become legally privileged by being brought into the relationship whether by the client or a third party (*Ventouris v Mountain* (1991)). In *R v Guildhall Magistrates' Court, ex p Primlak Holdings Co (Panama) Ltd* (1989) police obtained warrants under s 8 of the 1984 Act to search for and seize documents in the possession of two firms of solicitors which related to the sale of vessels by the collapsed bankers, Johnson Matthey. The magistrate was persuaded that because offences of false accounting had been committed, the documents did not attract legal privilege because of s 10(2) (see below). A judicial review of the decision to issue the warrants succeeded (see para 4.66(v), ante). Arguably s 10(2) was of no relevance in this case. Legal privilege probably did not apply to the documents either because they related to commercial rather than legal matters, or because they were original documents not made within the lawyer/client relationship for the purposes of legal advice or legal proceedings. Thus if D, who has been charged with forgery, passes documents alleged to have been forged to his legal adviser, those documents are not legally privileged. Thus a forged receipt held by a firm of solicitors is not legally privileged, not because of s 10(2) of PACE 1984, held with the intention of furthering a criminal purpose, but because it was not created within the lawyer/client relationship (see *R v Crown Court at Northampton, ex p DPP* (1991)). If they are passed to an expert for his opinion, they remain unprivileged (see *R v King* (1983), forgery not legally privileged) but the report made by the expert is privileged being made within the relationship and for the purposes of legal proceedings. The forged documents can be the subject of a search warrant under s 7 of the Forgery and Counterfeiting Act 1981, the documents not being special procedure material in the hands of the solicitor because they would not have been received in confidence, there being no confidence in iniquity (see para 4.160, post). The decision in *R v Leeds Magistrates' Court, ex p Dumbleton* (1993) confirms the argument set out above. A company, T Ltd, had a marketing agreement with the OMC Group which successfully sued it for £3 million. There were insufficient assets to satisfy the judgment and it was alleged that OMC had forged documents to show that T Ltd had a beneficial interest in a number of properties one of which was owned by P. He complained to the police about the alleged forgeries. The appellant Dumbleton, a solicitor and legal adviser to OMC, had sworn an affidavit in support of an application by them for a charging order which was supported by the allegedly forged letters. Police sought and obtained a warrant under the Forgery and Counterfeiting Act and entered the solicitor's office and seized documents. The appellant applied for an order quashing the issue of the warrant because the magistrate could not have been satisfied that the documents were not legally privileged or special procedure material. Legally privileged material cannot be the subject of a warrant and s 9(2) (art 11(2)) takes away the power of a magistrate to issue a warrant under that Act for special procedure material. Instead application must be made to a circuit judge (county court judge in Northern Ireland) under Sch 1, para 3 (the second set of access conditions discussed at para 4.211, post) for an order requiring the solicitor to produce the documents to a constable. If the conditions in Sch 1, paras 12 and 14 (paras 9 and 11 in Northern Ireland) are satisfied a warrant to enter and search the premises may be issued but in no case can legally privileged material be seized (see para 4.211, post).

4.169 Refusing the application it was held that the documents were not legally privileged within s 10 (art 12) not being articles enclosed with or referred to in a communication made in connection with legal proceedings, except in the sense that the forged letters were used to deceive the court. 'Made' as used in s 10 (art 12) meant 'lawfully made' and did not extend to a forged document. In any event they were held with the intention of furthering a criminal purpose and could not be legally privileged by virtue of s 10(2) (art 12(2)) considered below. The court went on to hold that the material sought could not have been special procedure material because it could not have been held in confidence, there being no confidence in iniquity. The warrant was therefore lawfully issued.

4.170 When the investigation involves solicitors there will usually be questions raised about the legal status of particular documents. Where an order for production of the documents is sought the hearing is inter partes and the party holding the documents can be expected to argue a claim for legal privilege but applications for a warrant are usually made ex parte, the onus is then on the police and the judge fully to explore the status of the documents sought. In *R v Crown Court at Southampton, ex p J and P* (1993) the Solicitors' Complaints Bureau and the police were investigating a firm of solicitors concerning suspected theft from an elderly client and other dishonesty. Believing that the firm's accounting records and client files would confirm this the police obtained warrants under s 9 and Sch 1, the application being made ex parte on the ground that notice of the application might seriously prejudice the investigation (see para 4.194, post). The applicants challenged the warrants on three grounds:

(i)   they were too widely drawn, extending to material which was not the proper subject of the investigation, for example all the firm's accounts were included because the police believed that other unspecified offences had been committed;

(ii) they wrongly included material subject to legal privilege; and

(iii) they should have been applied for inter partes.

4.171   The Divisional Court allowed the application and quashed the warrant on all three heads. On the issue of legal privilege it was agreed that the accounting records were unlikely to contain legally privileged material but the client files might well do so. There was the question whether there had been a waiver of the privilege by some of the clients whose privilege it is and whether any privilege might have been lost in respect of documents held with the intention of furthering a criminal purpose under s 10(2) (art 12(2)), neither of which had been canvassed before the judge. The Divisional Court offered the following guidance:

(a)   it is necessary to balance the competing interests of the investigation of crime and the confidentiality of communications between solicitor and client;

(b)   the police should draw the attention of the judge to the material which is arguably legally privileged and provide sufficient information to enable him to reach a decision as to whether or not it is privileged. Legal advice may be necessary to assist the judge in cases of doubt. It may not be possible to satisfy the judge that every document in a file, or every file in a category, is not legally privileged but if the investigation is relatively narrow it should be possible to exclude privileged material with precision.

4.172   The Court agreed that an inter partes hearing might have been more appropriate in this case because:

(1)   an inter partes order would have frozen the material in the possession of the firm;

(2)   the Law Society had already seen the accounts;

(3)   the police already had some ledger sheets;

(4)   the firm were aware of the investigations some nine months earlier; and

(5)   the solicitors were under a duty to account to their clients thus providing an alternative source of investigation.

4.173   One may note that the Trade Marks Act 1994, s 87 provides that communications between a person and his registered trade mark agent, or for the purpose of obtaining, or in response to a request for, information which a person is seeking for the purpose of instructing his registered trade mark agent, shall be privileged against disclosure like legal privilege. It follows that all that is said above, and possibly below as respects criminal purposes, applies to such communications.

4.174 The identity of a person contacting a solicitor is not information subject to legal privilege (*R v Minshull Crown Court, ex p Miller Gardner Solicitors* (2002)). The applicants acted for a client 'NH' who was charged with possession of firearms with intent. They challenged the issue of a warrant under Sch I to search their premises for personal records in the name of NS and BH on the basis that the information requested was subject to legal privilege. The police were seeking details of telephone numbers and dates in order to help trace the owner of the vehicle in which the gun had been found. It was believed that the owner has telephoned the solicitors during May 2001. The court held that there had been no breach of Art 8 because the application was necessary in the interests of public safety and the prevention of crime. There is no requirement that an application relating to a solicitor's office should be on notice although this may be preferable in some cases.

FURTHERING A CRIMINAL PURPOSE (s 10(2), Art 12(2))

4.175 Items held with the intention of furthering a criminal purpose are not items subject to legal privilege (see *R v Leeds Magistrates' Court, ex p Dumbleton* (1993) above). Copies of letters containing legal advice, given in good faith, warning a client of risky conduct which he is contemplating is not within s 10(2) (art 12(2); *Butler v Board of Trade* (1971)). In *R v Central Criminal Court, ex p Francis & Co Ltd; Francis* (1988) it was held that 'intention' in s 10(2) (art 12(2)) may include that of a client or third party, reflecting the position at common law as laid down in *R v Cox and Railton* (1884). A production order had been made against a firm of solicitors under s 27 of the Drug Trafficking Offences Act 1986 (the procedure is similar to that under Sch 1 of the 1984 Act (1989 Order) and the definition of legally privileged, excluded and special procedure material has the same meaning as in the 1984 Act (1989 Order)). The order required the solicitors to give the police access to correspondence and attendance notes in respect of property transactions entered into by a client. Police suspected that the client was being used as the innocent dupe of a relative who was using the client as a means of salting away the proceeds of drug trafficking. The Divisional Court refused an application for judicial review of the decision to issue the production order holding that the documents were held with the intention of furthering a criminal purpose within s 10(2), even though the criminal intention was not that of the solicitor or client but of a third party. The House of Lords (Lords Bridge and Oliver dissenting) upheld the Divisional Court. In doing so the majority rejected the literal interpretation of s 10(2) by the Divisional Court in *R v Crown Court at Snaresbrook, ex p DPP* (1988) when refusing an order for production of a legal aid application in the possession of the Law Society, which the police believed would support a prosecution of the applicant (who was suing the police for assault) for perverting the course of justice. Glidewell LJ held that the application for legal aid came within s 10(1) even if it contained untrue statements. The 'intention of furthering a criminal purpose', which would deprive the document of its legal privilege must, he held, be that of the person holding the material, the Law Society in that case, which clearly had no such intention. The majority of their Lordships in Francis thought that such an interpretation would frustrate the main purpose of Part II of the 1984 Act. The belief that the legislature could not have intended to restrict the effect of s 10(2), and therefore the power of the police to detect crime by confining it to cases where the solicitor had the intention to further a criminal purpose, together with the need to interpret the section so as to reflect the common law, persuaded the majority to 'improve' upon the words of the section and to reflect what was almost certainly the intention of Parliament. The fact that the privilege is that of the client, not of the solicitor, supports their Lordships' view that the client's intention (or that of a third person using the client) to further a criminal purpose should negate the privilege. The majority in rejecting the literal interpretation of the section in *R v Crown Court at Snaresbrook, ex p DPP* (1988) thought that it did not necessarily undermine that decision. Lord Goff took the view that legal privilege would not be lost under s 10(2) (art 12(2)) where a communication made by a client to his solicitor contained untrue statements which, if acted upon, could lead to a prosecution for perjury. One may accept this in so far as it refers to the position before trial but the privilege must surely be lost in relation to proceedings for perjury arising out of the evidence given at the trial. The decision in *Dubai Bank Ltd v Galadari (No 6)* (1991), that communications in furtherance of a crime or fraud were not protected from disclosure if they were relevant to an issue in the action, whether or not the plaintiff's claim was founded on that crime or fraud, strongly supports the decision in Francis and the view expressed above. One may also note that the court has jurisdiction to give a solicitor directions as to how they should continue to deal with funds and assets held or controlled on behalf of a client against whom there is prima facie evidence that he had obtained them fraudulently. Such directions could include notifying third parties who might have a claim against the client or his assets (and possibly the police investigating the fraud), notwithstanding the solicitors' professional duty of confidentiality towards their client (see *Finers v Miro* (1990)). The Law Society's view is that the decision in Francis is to be narrowly construed as being limited to the situation in which the client is being used as intermediary or an innocent tool by third parties, but the breach made in the wall of legal privilege may be much wider.

4.176   The broad definition of legal privilege in s 10 extends to all searches (including that by consent), since s 19 (art 21) excludes legally privileged material from the powers of seizure which operate during a search of premises. However, s 19 (art 21) does not prohibit the use at trial of any legally privileged material which is seized. Moreover, the common law allows evidence, including that subject to legal privilege, to be used at trial howsoever it has been obtained (*Calcraft v Guest* (1898); *Butler v Board of Trade* (1971)). Thus at common law, if the police exceed their search powers and seize legally privileged material, or even steal it, the material can be used in a subsequent prosecution. On the other hand, since the police have no power to seize such material (s 19(6), art 21(6)) and hence no power to retain it, it is possible for the owner to take prompt legal action to recover it (see the facts of *IRC v Rossminster* (1980)). The only other safeguard is the court's discretion under s 78 (art 76) to exclude improperly obtained evidence.

As indicated in para 2.134, ante, the courts have with some exceptions exercised their discretion only in respect of confessional evidence. However, if the police were to seize communications between a client and his solicitor during a search of the client's house and seek to use these at the trial for the offence in respect of which the client consulted the solicitor, it would be tantamount to denying the accused his 'fundamental right' to consult a solicitor and must have 'such an adverse effect on the fairness of the trial' as to justify its exclusion.

EXCLUDED MATERIAL (ss 11-13, Arts 13-15)

4.177   Sections 11 to 13 (arts 13 to 15) contain the definition of excluded material. The material covered may, with the exception of 'journalistic material', be described as personal and confidential material. Such material will rarely be of evidential value; but even when it is and even when a most serious crime is under investigation, the legislature decided that the proper balance between the public interest in the detection of crime and the privacy of the individual lay in excluding access to such material, except where a warrant could previously have been issued authorising the search for and seizure of such material (see the discussion of s 9(2) (art 11(2)) in para 4.211, post; such material is not protected from search and seizure by Customs and Excise: see para 4.160(v), ante).

4.178   Excluded material consists of three sub-categories:
(1)   personal records;
(2)   human tissue or tissue fluid taken for the purpose of diagnosis or medical treatment;
(3)   journalistic material (s 11, art 13).

4.179   Two preliminary points may be noted.
(i)   There is a degree of overlapping in these provisions. For example, a doctor's records of a patient can fall within s 11(1)(a) or (b); those held by a social worker could fall within any of the categories in s 12.
(ii)   A common theme in s 11 (art 13) is the element of confidentiality required before material can be regarded as 'excluded'. The law on confidence is uncertain and embryonic. Confidentiality may be express, eg an undertaking signed by a counselling agency before advice is given. More often it will arise by implication, eg a doctor's relationship with a patient imports confidentiality by custom rather than any express undertaking. 'Implication' may mean that a third party can be subject to a confidence if he knows or ought to know that the relevant information is confidential, eg a marriage counsellor or priest who is passed documents by X relating to Y (*Seager v Copydex* (1967); *Coco v Clark* (1969)). The degree to which the general law of confidence applies to s 11 (art 13) is unclear. If it does, it has been held that a confidence cannot attach to information which is already in the public domain, but it can if the information can only be discovered after considerable research (*Schering Chemicals Ltd v Falkman Ltd* (1981)). Thus, a journalist who thoroughly researches for an article on the financial operations of a company could claim that his material is held in confidence even though that

material could be discovered by any diligent research of published statistics and articles. Again, if the general law of confidence applies, a principle of that law is that there is no 'confidence in iniquity', eg a criminal pursuit, and therefore one party to such a confidence cannot sue if the other discloses it (*Gartside v Outram* (1856); *Initial Services Ltd v Putterill* (1968); *R v Leeds Magistrates' Court, ex p Dumbleton* (1993)). This would enable the police to nullify in large measure the scope of s 11 (art 13) by simply arguing that the relevant material concerns a serious arrestable offence under investigation, is not confidential in the first place, and therefore the material is not protected from search and seizure and may, with the exception of journalistic material, be the subject of a warrant under s 8 (art 10). Unlike the other material referred to, journalistic material which is not held in confidence, though not excluded material, is special procedure material and is subject to the Sch 1 procedure (see para 4.196, post).

Personal records (ss 11(1)(a), 12, arts 13(1)(a), 14)

4.180 This covers personal records which a person has acquired or created in the course of any trade, business, profession or any other occupation or for the purpose of any paid or unpaid office and which he holds in confidence. Section 12 (art 14) defines 'personal records' as documentary and other (eg computerised) records concerning an individual (whether living or dead) who can be identified from them and relating:
(a) to his physical or mental health;
(b) to spiritual counselling or assistance given or to be given to him; or
(c) to the counselling or assistance given or to be given to him, for the purposes of his personal welfare, by any voluntary organisation or by any individual who –
  (i)   by reason of his office or occupation has responsibility for his personal welfare; or
  (ii) by reason of an order of the court has responsibilities for his supervision.

4.181 This is a comprehensive definition. The 'personal records' may be 'acquired' eg by a social worker through dealings with a client; or 'created' eg by a psychiatrist or probation officer during the course of advice to a client. The following points may be noted.
(i)   The excluded material consists of 'documents and other records' (s 12, art 14). 'Document' has the same meaning as given in s 10 of the Civil Evidence Act 1968 (s 118(1)) (Part I of the Civil Evidence Act (NI) 1971 (art 2)) and therefore includes a photograph, disc, tape, film or microfilm. Given this broad non-exclusive definition, the phrase 'other records' as used here and in s 11(1)(c) (art 13(c)) appears to be superfluous.
(ii) The records need not consist solely of excluded material. For example, a social worker's records may contain much information which is neither confidential nor related to a client's personal welfare, but which is mixed up with information which is. Even if the material sought by the police consists entirely of the non-confidential

part of the mix, it remains excluded and unavailable. The wording of s 8 (art 10) and Sch 1, para 2 would not seem to permit any severance of the material or an application only for the non-confidential material.

(iii) Section 12 (art 14) significantly cuts down the apparent width of s 11 (art 13). 'Personal records' must concern an individual (living or dead) who can be identified 'from them'. One possible interpretation of this phrase is that the individual can be identified without recourse to other records; eg if the records contain only a number which refers to an individual who can only be identified by reference to a master list, the record is not a 'personal record' for the purposes of s 12 (art 14). Such an interpretation would expose many personal records to the risk of seizure where for security reasons the records do not enable the individual to be identified without recourse to another record. A preferable interpretation is that records are 'personal records' if the individual to whom they relate can be identified from the record itself or a related record.

(iv) The records must relate to one of the three matters mentioned in s 12 (art 14), as follows.

(a) Physical or mental health – This clearly covers records kept by doctors, hospitals, midwives, health visitors and certain social workers such as mental welfare officers and others concerned with the physical and mental health of individuals. The previous authors' research revealed a case in which access to hospital out-patient records in order to identify a man who had killed another and was himself injured in the struggle, was denied by a circuit judge who rejected the argument that the records were administrative rather than personal. In *R v Central Criminal Court, ex p Brown* (1992), the Divisional Court held that there was no power under s 9 and Sch 1 of PACE 1984 to make a production order in respect of a medical report (excluded material) held by a hospital administrator, there being statutory power to issue a warrant to search for and seize such material. Similarly, in *R v Crown Court at Cardiff, ex p Kellam* (1993) it was held that hospital records of a patient's admission and discharge from a mental hospital were personal records as defined by s 12 and therefore unobtainable under s 9 and Sch 1 of PACE 1984 even though they were material to a murder investigation. The only avenue open to the police in such a case is to seek disclosure with consent (see *R v Singleton* (1995) considered at para 4.160, ante).

There is no requirement that the holder of the records be professionally qualified. Thus any person who holds himself out as concerned with the physical or mental health of another can benefit, eg physicians not recognised by the British Medical Association such as osteopaths, faith healers and hypnotists.

(b) Spiritual counselling or assistance given or to be given – The key word here is 'spiritual'. It is not qualified in any way and can bear a number of meanings. It clearly covers religious advice and this can extend to unusual, if not dangerous, religious sects such as the Moonies (which sect enjoyed charitable status until 1983). The Government considered and then rejected the possibility of adding 'bona fide' to s 12(b) (art 14(b)) so as to exclude such organisations from the benefit of claiming protection under the Act. It would, however, be open to a court to use the doctrine of public policy to reject claims to confidentiality by such organisations. In the Oxford English Dictionary 'spiritual' may also mean 'of, pertaining to, affecting or concerning the spirit or higher moral qualities'. This would therefore include the Church of Scientology and other organisations which do not acknowledge a God but purport to promote the greater fulfilment of man's qualities. If this interpretation is adopted, the protection could extend, for example, to Alcoholics Anonymous, and bodies designed to assist the rehabilitation of offenders, for they by publicity or direct action aim to improve moral standards. Finally, the word 'spiritual' can literally include those who claim to communicate with spirits and s 12(c) (art 14 (c)) could apply to any records kept by a spiritualist.

(c) Counselling or assistance given or to be given for the purposes of personal welfare – Records which fall within this category include social work or similar activities, whether professional or not; marriage guidance councils; the NSPCC; the Samaritans; refuges and organisations aimed at assisting alcoholics, drug addicts, the victims of rape or wife-battery; legal advice and records held by unqualified volunteers at advice centres, which do not fall within legal privilege (para 4.67, ante); information held by a personnel officer; homosexual clubs. Again there is no qualification of 'bona fide' and the category could extend in theory to controversial organisations such as the Paedophile Information Exchange; though it would again be open to the courts to invoke public policy to strike out such claims. The Government intended school records to be covered by this category (Standing Committee E, 17 January 1984, col 534). The courts now look at Hansard for guidance (*Pepper v Hart* (1993)) and therefore such records are likely to be included within the definition.

Section 12(c)(ii) (art 14(c)(ii)) was added at a late parliamentary stage of the PACE Bill to make clear that protection could extend to agencies responsible for a person because of a court order. This covers the probation service, social services departments (responsible for a person in care, eg at a foster home, or under a supervision order), mental health institutions and even the prison service. For example, the police may wish to see records held by the Samaritans concerning an arsonist who is known to have contacted such organisations before. If records are kept, they fall within s 12. If no records are kept the excluded material provisions do not of course apply, but the agency's representative can be ordered to appear at the trial and he cannot claim privilege for the conversation. This last point deserves emphasis since it applies to all potential witnesses (save professional legal advisers), even though they may be able to resist the police application to see the documentary evidence before trial. The stark choice facing such witnesses is break their confidence or risk imprisonment for contempt of court (see *A-G v Mullholland* (1963)).

(v) Information held in confidence. Section 11(1)(a) (art 13(1)(a)) stipulates that the personal records must be held in confidence. This is defined by s 11(2) (art 13(2)) and in relation to personal records the obligation of confidence will normally be implied rather than expressly stated in the relationship.

Human tissue or tissue fluid (s 11(1)(b), art 13(1)(b))

4.182 This is the least problematical of the three categories of excluded material. The tissue will usually be held in confidence by a person connected with a hospital, clinic or laboratory who may well be a non-clinical administrator, rather than a doctor or scientist. The tissue or fluid will usually have been taken from a person who is suspected of a serious arrestable offence. It will not include objects removed from the body such as bullets or packets of drugs secreted or swallowed. These are not human tissue or tissue fluid and can be the subject of a s 8 (art 10) search warrant if not surrendered voluntarily. Swabs and smears taken from the victim of a crime for forensic comparison with the blood or semen of the suspect are probably not within s 11(1)(b) (art 13(1)(b)) not being 'taken for the purposes of diagnosis or medical treatment'. If held in confidence such material will be special procedure material but since the obligation of confidence probably relates to the police, rather than to the victim, the forensic scientist will be able to hand the items to the police without fear of a civil action by a victim who seeks to withdraw from a prosecution and prevent the police obtaining access to those samples. Rape units set up in hospitals to provide an alternative source of examination and counselling for victims of rape who are reluctant to complain to the police raise interesting questions. Staff are trained in the collection of forensic evidence which will be stored for one month so as to be available should the victim decide to complain. Material collected may well include human tissue fluid, but it is probably not 'taken for the purposes of diagnosis or medical treatment' and is not then excluded material. It will almost certainly be held in confidence and will be special procedure material, which is potentially available to the police. When a doctor is in possession of human tissue or tissue fluids which are likely to be evidence of a serious arrestable offence, there is no legal process which can oblige him to surrender them but he may do so voluntarily (see *R v Singleton* (1995) where a dentist voluntarily surrendered a dental impression of a suspect's teeth which enabled police to match bite marks on the victim to the suspect). Guidance issued by the General Medical Council leaves it to the individual's professional judgment as to whether he should break his patient's confidence. If the patient is subsequently convicted, the doctor is protected from a civil action for breach of confidence, there being 'no confidence in iniquity' (see *R v Leeds Magistrates' Court, ex p Dumbleton* (1993)). If the patient is arrested and not proceeded against or acquitted, the doctor may be at risk of such an action. Doctors can therefore be placed in an invidious position if asked to volunteer such material. The development of DNA profiling (genetic fingerprinting) made the obtaining of human tissue or tissue fluid of great importance in relation to certain categories of crimes, particularly rape. The provisions under discussion, together with the fact that an intimate sample (which includes blood, semen and other tissue fluids) can only be taken from a suspect arrested for a serious arrestable offence with his written consent (see s 62 (art 62) discussed at paras 7.106-7.115, post), means that there is no legal process under which either the doctor or the suspect can be compelled to provide the evidence which will conclusively prove whether or not the suspect was involved. However, the technological advances in DNA profiling and the redefinition of 'intimate sample' and 'non-intimate sample' by s 58 of the Criminal Justice and Public Order Act 1994 make it largely unnecessary to obtain blood, urine or semen. Saliva is no longer an intimate sample and a swab taken from the mouth but not including any other body orifice is now a non-intimate sample which can be taken without consent subject to the requirements of s 63 of PACE 1984. The restrictions imposed by s 11(1)(b) (art 13(1)(b)) are therefore no longer an obstacle to the investigation of serious crime.

Journalistic material (ss 11(1)(c), 13, arts 13 (i)(c), 15)

4.183 In 1983 the media launched a vociferous campaign to exempt journalists from the search warrant procedures of the PACE Bill. The campaign came in the wake of the House of Lords' decision in *British Steel Corpn v Granada Television Ltd* (1981) which refused to recognise a journalist's privilege to protect the confidentiality of his sources, and of s 10 of the Contempt of Court Act 1981 which permits his interests to be weighed in the balance before disclosure is ordered. The campaign was successful, although sections of the media changed their minds and sought to remove the exemption from the Bill. The exemption is found in ss 11(1)(c) and 13 (arts 13(1)(c) and 15). It is broadly drafted, covering material 'acquired or created' by a person 'for the purposes of journalism' (s 13(1), art 15(1)). This includes all branches of the media; it is not tied to professional journalists, covering eg the 'amateur' editor of a newsletter; it may arguably cover a letter sent to an editor for publication; it encompasses all the research and background material which a journalist has 'acquired' to write his article, eg information from secret sources, or has 'created' for the purpose, eg interviews with the subjects of his investigation. 'Document' includes 'a map, plan, photograph, disc, tape, film or microfilm' (s 118 (art 2) which adopts s 10(1) of the Civil Evidence Act 1968 (Part 1 of the Civil Evidence (NI) Act 1971)). The phrase 'records other than documents' in s 11(1)(c) (art 13(1)(c)) would thus appear to be redundant. To cope with unsolicited material, s 13(3) (art 15(3)) provides that if the supplier intends that it should be used for the purposes of journalism the recipient is to be taken as having received it for that purpose. This intention may be expressed, as where the material is accompanied by a covering letter to that effect, or perhaps more often implied from the fact that it is sent to a newspaper, broadcasting company or a journalist. In order to be excluded material, journalistic material must be held in confidence. There is, however, a separate definition governing such material. Section 11(3) (art 13(3)) includes the definition applied to other forms of excluded material by s 11(2) (art 13(2)) but adds a requirement that journalistic material be held continuously (by one or more persons) subject to such an undertaking, restriction or obligation since it was first acquired or created for the purposes of journalism. Thus, if a disaffected civil servant passes documents to a journalist, who passes them to another more senior journalist for evaluation, who passes them to his editor, then it is held in confidence so long as each receives it for the purposes of journalism. If this chain of purposes is broken, eg the journalist passes the documents to a non-journalist expert for evaluation, then although the continuity of confidence is maintained the continuity of purpose is not since the expert does not acquire them for the purpose of journalism. If this is correct the documents are no longer excluded material within s 11 (art 13) but will be special procedure material (s 14(1)(b), art 16(1)(b)). Similarly, if the material is passed to the newspaper's lawyers, it is unlikely that they will receive it 'for the purposes of journalism', rather it will be received, and intended by the sender to be received, for the purposes of legal advice. As indicated in the discussion of legal privilege (see para 4.166, ante) an existing document not created within the relationship of lawyer/client does not attract legal privilege. This too will be special procedure material (s 14(1)(b), art 16(1)(b) discussed at para 4.184, post). Does the material regain its excluded material status if the lawyer returns it to the journalist with his opinion? It will be received for the purposes of journalism and no doubt the lawyer intends that it be received for that purpose but it is doubtful whether the lawyer imposes an obligation of confidence on the journalist. The material may not therefore regain its excluded material status once it is lost. Where material is passed to a journalist for publication it is questionable whether there can be an obligation of confidence in relation to that material. The supplier will no doubt not wish his identity to be revealed but journalists are given protection against the disclosure of sources by the Contempt of Court Act 1981, s 10 – see *In An Inquiry Under the Company Securities (Insider Dealing) Act 1985* (1988). If therefore the material is not held in confidence it is not excluded material but, if it is journalistic material, it will be special procedure material under s 14(1)(b) (art 16(1)(b)). (For a discussion of the limited access to excluded material provided by s 9(2) and Schedule 1, para 3 (art 11(2) and Sch 1, para 3) see para 4.211, post.)

SPECIAL PROCEDURE MATERIAL (s 14, Art 16)

4.184 This category of material, as the name implies, is available to the police provided application is made under Sch 1 and in accordance with that Schedule. In England and Wales, more than 2,000 orders for production of special procedure material, or warrants to search for and seize such material, were granted in the first three years of PACE 1984. These have enabled the police to investigate crimes which they were previously unable to investigate and to obtain evidence in respect of other crimes which they were previously unable to obtain, or were able to obtain only after a charge had been laid under the Bankers' Books Evidence Act 1879.

4.185 Special procedure material falls into two sub-categories:
(i)   journalistic material which is not excluded material; and
(ii)   material to which s 14(2) (art 16(2)) applies.

Journalistic material which is not excluded material (s 14(1)(b), art 16(1)(b))

4.186   Journalistic material is only excluded material if it consists of documents or records other than documents and is continuously held in confidence. A document or record not so held, or any other form of material, whether it is held in confidence or not, which is acquired or created for the purposes of journalism, is special procedure material. Thus, if as argued in para 4.211, ante, material passed to a journalist for publication is not held in confidence, it clearly is journalistic material as defined by s 13 (art 15) but is not excluded material. It is, however, special procedure material. Photographs taken by press photographers of incidents during a riot were the subject of the first reported case in which an order was made for production of special procedure material which was 'journalistic material' (*R v Crown Court at Bristol, ex p Bristol Press and Picture Agency Ltd* (1986)). Though the photographs were 'documents or records other than documents', they were not held in confidence but clearly were 'created for the purposes of journalism' and therefore special procedure material. Videotapes showing members of the Animal Liberation Front held by the BBC have been the subject of a production order. Other film or photographs of demonstrations (eg the 'poll tax' disorder in London in 1990) and of sporting events (involving physical assaults by participants or spectators) have been handed over to the police, either in response to a production order or to the threat of one. Such material created by journalists for the purposes of journalism lacks the requirement that it be held in confidence and is not therefore excluded material but is special procedure material. Articles other than documents or records other than documents, even if held in confidence for journalistic purposes, will not be excluded material but will be special procedure material. Thus if A passes to B, a journalist, a diary belonging to an alleged rapist together with a ski-mask which he wore to hide his face whilst committing the offences, the diary, if held subject to an obligation of confidence, is excluded material and unavailable except with consent of the journalist, while the ski-mask is special procedure material and potentially available under Sch 1, para 2. If the diary is not held in confidence, being intended for publication, it too is special procedure material and similarly potentially available under Sch 1, para 2.

Special procedure material to which s 14(2) (art 16(2)) applies

4.187   Special procedure material to which s 14(2) (art 16(2)) applies is business and financial information which, though held in confidence, is of a less sensitive nature than legally privileged or excluded material. Material is special procedure material if it:
(a)   is not legally privileged or excluded material;
(b)   is in the possession of a person who acquired or created it in the course of any trade, business, profession or other occupation or for the purposes of any paid or unpaid office; and
(c)   is held in confidence, which is defined in exactly the same terms as that in s 11(2) (art 13(2)) for the purposes of excluded material.

4.188 (b) above covers every form of paid occupation but covers only unpaid activities which involve the holding of an office, eg the treasurer or secretary of a club, trades' union branch or local or national society. To prevent an employer or company creating special procedure material simply by passing it to an employee or associated company under an obligation of confidence, s 14(3), (4) and (5) (art 16(3), (4) and (5)) provide as follows.

(i)   Where material is acquired by an employee from his employer in the course of his employment, or it is acquired by a company from an associated company, it is only special procedure material if it would have been immediately before its acquisition (s 14(3)(a) and (b), art 16(3)(a) and (b)). 'Associated company' has the meaning assigned to it by the Income and Corporation Taxes Act 1988, s 416 (s 14(6), art 16(6)).

(ii)   Similarly, if the material is created by an employee in the course of his employment or is created by an associated company, it is only special procedure material if it would have been had the employer or associated company created it (s 14(4) and (5), art 16(4) and (5)).

4.189 Banks and building societies are the main holders of special procedure material which will be of evidential use to the police, followed by eg accountants, solicitors (conveyancing matter and non-legally privileged material), estate agents, financial brokers, insurance brokers, telecommunications companies and journalists in all parts of the media.

4.190 The following examples are given to illustrate the interrelationship of search warrant powers and the access provisions provided in respect of excluded or special procedure material.

Example I

4.191 Following a gold bullion robbery, a serious arrestable offence (s 116, art 87).

(i)   The Theft Act 1968, s 26 (Theft Act (NI) 1969 s 25) or s 8 of PACE 1984 (art 10 of the 1989 Order) can be used to search for and seize the stolen bullion.

(ii)   A bullion dealer has documentary material which may indicate to whom the stolen bullion has been sold. If these documents are held in confidence (and they may not be if the principle that there is no confidence in iniquity applies) they will be special procedure material and may be obtained by application to a circuit (county court) judge under Sch 1, para 2. If not held in confidence, a warrant under s 8 (art 10) may be obtained.

(iii)   An investigative journalist has documentary material which purports to identify the man who masterminded the robbery. If held in confidence it is excluded material and not available by any legal process.

(iv)   An accountant has material which is believed to implicate company X in a 'laundering operation' which converted the stolen bullion into gold coins. If held in confidence (and again the principle that there is no confidence in iniquity may mean that it is not) this is special procedure material and may be obtained by application under Sch 1. If not held in confidence a s 8 (art 10) warrant may be obtained.

(v) A number of suspects are arrested. They claim they do not know each other. All have mobile telephones which, it is believed, they used to contact each other before and during the robbery. The telephone company has computerised records of calls made to and from the telephones owned by the suspects (such automatically recorded records are admissible as real evidence rather than hearsay evidence: *R v Spiby* (1990)). These are special procedure material and may be obtained by application under Sch 1. The premises of the suspects may be searched under s 18 (art 20) or s 32(2)(b) (art 34(2)(b)).

(vi) The cars used in the robbery were stolen, resprayed and renumbered. It is believed that garages owned by friends of the suspects were used. A warrant under s 8 (art 10) may be obtained to search for evidence that the cars were altered in these garages.

(vii) Large deposits of money, thought to be the proceeds of the sale of the bullion, are believed to have been made in bank and building society accounts held by the suspects. The records of these accounts are special procedure material and may be obtained by application under Sch 1, para 2.

Example 2

4.192 A multiple rapist is sought. It is known that he has a disease which he transmitted to his victims.

(i) A special clinic which a suspect has recently attended for treatment holds blood and other tissue samples taken from the suspect for the purposes of diagnosis. This is excluded material and unobtainable by any legal process.

(ii) The suspect has visited a psychiatrist. His records are also excluded material and unobtainable.

(iii) The suspect is a lorry driver. His employer has records of delivery routes on the days on which the rapes were committed which will show that the suspect was in the area of each rape on the day in question. These are only special procedure material if they would have been so had the employer created the records (s 14(4), art 16(4)). If they are special procedure material they may be obtained by application under Sch 1, if not a warrant under s 8 (art 10).

(iv) A journalist has a tape-recording of a telephone conversation with a man who claimed to be the rapist. This is journalistic material in the form of a document but is unlikely to be held in confidence either because there is no confidence in iniquity or because it cannot be implied from the circumstances, which would appear to imply an intention that it be published. The tape is, however, special procedure material (s 14(2)(b), art 16(2)(b)) and may be obtained by application under Sch 1.

4.193 The following should be noted.

(a) The person in possession of excluded or special procedure material may surrender it voluntarily or allow the police access to it (see *R v Singleton* (1995) discussed at para 4.160, ante).

(b) It will be seen from the above that there will often be a question whether or not the material is special procedure or excluded material or indeed legally privileged material and whether a s 8 (art 10) warrant should be sought or a s 9, Sch 1 order. In such a case the s 9, Sch 1 order should be sought. The issue can be determined by the circuit judge, who can then issue an order under Sch 1 whether or not the material is special procedure provided it is not excluded or legally privileged material (see *R v Crown Court at Preston, ex p McGrath* (1992) considered at para 4.204, post).

(c) Excluded and special procedure material may be seized in the course of a search under a warrant or a post-arrest power and in any circumstance in which the police officer is lawfully on the premises (s 19, art 21). This latter power is not a power to search for the material. However, s 32(2)(b) (art 34(2)(b)) permits the search of premises in which the person was when arrested or immediately before being arrested provided there are reasonable grounds to believe that evidence of the offence for which he was arrested is to be found on those premises. Thus if the suspected rapist in 2(i) above is arrested in or on leaving the special clinic, a search of that clinic may be made for the sample of blood and tissue fluid (this may not now be necessary given the redefinition of 'intimate sample' and 'non intimate sample' by the Criminal Justice and Public Order Act 1994 – hair or saliva may now be taken without consent in such a case and may suffice for a DNA profile: see Chapter 7). Similarly if the suspect is arrested in or on leaving the psychiatrist's office. If a man suspected of fraud is arrested in or on leaving the office of his accountant, that office may be searched for evidence of the fraud.

(d) Special procedure material as defined by s 14(2) (art 16(2)) is not protected in so far as it relates to offences within the jurisdiction of Customs and Excise (assigned matters) (see para 4.160(v), ante).

(e) If a 'terrorist investigation', as defined by s 32 of the Terrorism Act 2000 is under way, Sch 5 of that Act provides a procedure, similar to the Sch 1 procedure, which permits a circuit judge (county court judge in NI) to issue an order requiring the production of excluded or special procedure material in circumstances in which the excluded material would not be available in respect of a non-terrorist investigation (see para 4.99, post).

PROCEDURES FOR OBTAINING ACCESS TO EXCLUDED OR SPECIAL PROCEDURE MATERIAL (s 9, Art 11 AND Sch 1)

Introduction

4.194 Section 9(1) (art 11(1)) provides that a constable may obtain access to excluded or special procedure material for the purposes of a criminal investigation by making application under Sch 1 and in accordance with that Schedule. Section 9(2) (art 11(1)) further provides that any statutory provisions existing before the 1984 Act (1989 Order) which authorised the issue of a search warrant to a constable shall cease to have effect so far as it relates to the authorisation of searches:

(a) for items subject to legal privilege;

(b) for excluded material; or

(c) for special procedure material consisting of documents or records other than documents.

4.195   The effect of s 9(2) (art 11(2)) is to prevent a magistrate issuing a warrant under a pre-PACE Act (Order) statute when the material sought falls into one of the above categories. Legally privileged material is never obtainable; but as regards excluded material or special procedure material in documentary form, application must be made to a circuit (county court) judge under Sch 1 either for an order requiring the person in possession of the material to produce it to the police, or for a warrant authorising a constable to enter and search premises for the material. Schedule 1 therefore provides that a circuit (county court) judge may make an order requiring production of the material if either of two sets of access conditions is fulfilled. The first set of access conditions applies when special procedure material (not legally privileged or excluded material) is sought, which would not have been available before criminal proceedings were commenced under any statutory provision existing before the 1984 Act (1989 Order), which may be evidence of a serious arrestable offence, and which is held by a person not himself suspected of involvement in that offence, eg the suspect's bank or building society accounts. The second set of access conditions applies to excluded material and special procedure material in documentary form which, but for s 9(2) (art 11(2)), could have been the subject of a search warrant under a statutory provision existing before the 1984 Act (1989 Order), eg documents stolen from a Government department and passed to a journalist. A warrant under s 26 of the Theft Act 1968 (s 25 of the Theft Act (NI) 1969) could have been obtained but for s 9(2) (art 11(2)). Application can be made to a circuit (county court) judge for a production order or, in certain circumstances, for a warrant to enter and search the premises. Note that there is no requirement in Sch 1, para 3, that the offence be a serious arrestable offence.

The procedure under Sch 1

4.196   No application for a production order or warrant under Sch 1 can be made without the authority of an officer of at least the rank of superintendent (Code B 2.4). Application for access to, or an order of production of, special procedure material is made to a circuit judge (county court judge in Northern Ireland) and the hearing of the application will take the form of an inter partes hearing at which the person in possession of the material can resist the making of the order (Sch 1, para 7). It was held in *R v Crown Court at Leicester, ex p DPP* (1987) that the only parties to an application for an order under Sch 1, para 4 are the police and the person or institution thought to be in possession of the material. The person to whom the obligation of confidence is owed by that person or institution has no right to be notified of the proceedings or to be present. As with all warrants, an application for a warrant under Sch 1 will be ex parte (but there may be circumstances in which an application under the first set of access conditions is made inter partes – see *R v Crown Court at Southampton, ex p J and P* (1993) and will be subject to s 15 of PACE 1984 (art 17 of the NI Order) (see paras 4.47-4.48, ante).

Notice of an application

4.197 A notice of application for a production order must be served upon the person believed to be in possession of the material sought. Schedule 1 says nothing about the period or form of the notice. In practice at least seven clear days' notice is given either by registered post or recorded or personal delivery. If a bank or building society is involved, and particularly if more than one account or branch is involved, the notice should be served on the headquarters with a copy to the branch(es) concerned. If the respondent is an unincorporated association, the notice should name the chairman or secretary (*R v Central Criminal Court, ex p Adegbesan* (1986)). Where a company is involved, the notice must be served on the company secretary or clerk or similar officer, and where a partnership is involved, on one of the partners (Sch 1, para 9 – the 1989 Order does not contain an equivalent provision). The proper address for service in the case of a company is the registered or principal office, and in the case of a partnership the principal office of the firm. In all other cases it will be the last known address of the person to be served (Sch 1, para 10). The notice must accurately describe the respondent and all the material sought. Since to conceal, destroy, alter or dispose of the material after service of the notice may be contempt unless any of these are done with the leave of a judge or the written permission of a constable (Sch 1, para 11, art 8), it is only fair that the respondent be made aware of exactly what material is sought. In the Adegbesan case the notice gave no clue as to the material sought and as Watkin LJ observed (at p 117):

> 'It would be impossible for a person who was a recipient of such a notice ... to know whether he was complying with the clear provisions of para 11 of Schedule 1 unless he was informed precisely of what it was he was called upon to preserve.'

4.198 The most satisfactory method of conveying this detail is in writing but there may be occasions when oral communication (by the investigating or supervisory officer) will suffice (*R v Crown Court at Manchester, ex p Taylor* (1988)). The crucial requirement is that the respondent be informed. In *R v Central Criminal Court, ex p Carr* (1987), Glidewell LJ suggested that the notice ought to indicate the general nature of the offence or offences under investigation (eg 'fraud', 'robbery') and the address of the premises where the material is alleged to be. Further details such as may be included in the information and which will be given to the judge need not be included in the notice to the holder of the material. However, any material given to the judge must be served upon the party against whom the notice is served before the application is heard (*R v Crown Court at Inner London Sessions, ex p Baines and Baines* (1988)). Note that Sch 1, para 11 (art 8) does not state that concealment etc after receipt of a notice is contempt of court. The facts that PACE 1984 and Order do not create a specific offence and that the notice of an application is not an order of a court, suggest that the only offence involved in such concealment etc is that of obstructing the police (s 89(2) of the Police Act 1996). If the police have grounds to suspect that the respondent will conceal etc the material sought, they should seek a warrant (Sch 1, paras 12 and 14 (paras 9 and 11)).

4.199   The recipient of the notice will be holding the material subject to an undertaking of confidence given to the customer or client who is the subject of the police investigation. Is he therefore under a duty to inform the customer or client of the application? In *Barclays Bank plc v Taylor* (1989) the Court of Appeal upheld the striking out of an action by Mr Taylor against the bank for breach of duty in failing to inform him of applications made under the 1984 Act and in failing to contest them. The decision makes it clear that the banks are under no duty to inform a client or to contest an application, however, the question whether the recipient of a notice was under a legal duty not to inform the client was less than satisfactorily answered. Lord Donaldson thought that the banks were 'no doubt free to ignore a request [by the police] that [the client] not be informed of the application'. However, his Lordship went on to say that 'he would have been surprised and disappointed if they had done so in the context of a criminal investigation unless they were under a legal obligation to do so'. No doubt banks and reputable organisations will not disappoint the Court of Appeal but in the absence of a legal obligation not to inform the client the less reputable may well feel that their loyalty lies with the client in this matter. Section 39 of the Terrorism Act 2000 makes it an offence to make a disclosure likely to prejudice the investigation, knowing or having reasonable cause to suspect that a warrant or order has been issued, made or applied for under Sch 5 to that Act. A similar provision in relation to orders or warrants sought under the 1984 Act (1989 Order) would be appropriate, but applicable only if such a requirement is contained in the notice. The form of notice used by the Metropolitan Police sets out para 11 of Sch 1 (which states that the recipient must not conceal etc the material sought) and specifically requests that the customer/client not be informed. This serves to put the recipient on notice that to do so may hinder the investigation. Should that request be ignored, there is the possibility of an offence under s 89(2) of the Police Act 1996, obstruction of a police officer.

Hearing the application

4.200   The notice is followed by a hearing inter partes, though increasingly banks and similar institutions are not contesting such applications. This trend was boosted by the decision in *Barclays Bank plc v Taylor* (1989) that they are under no duty to do so. It is for the police to satisfy the judge that the access conditions contained in Sch 1, paras 2 or 3 are fulfilled (see *R v Crown Court at Acton, ex p Layton* (1993) where it was said that the burden rested on the Crown to make a clear revelation to the Court of all appropriate material in their possession so that the judge could make a safe conclusion as to whether the access conditions were fulfilled). However, in an inter partes application where both parties had all the material information then, albeit that the Crown had a responsibility to see that the judge was provided with the information, a respondent could not complain if he had the material also but chose not to let the court see it. In *R v Norwich Crown Court, ex p Chethams* (1991) the Divisional Court rejected the argument that 'satisfied' as used in para 1 of Sch 1 meant 'satisfied so as to be sure' (the criminal standard of proof), holding that the ordinary standard of judicial satisfaction is satisfaction on the balance of probabilities (the civil standard of proof). In the absence of an express provision to the contrary it was this latter standard which is to be employed by the judge hearing an application under Sch 1. The practice is to prepare an information which sets out all the relevant details of the offence under investigation and in so doing seek to establish that all the access conditions are satisfied. The constable will then take the oath and either state the facts as set out in the information or, in an uncontested case where the judge has already read the information, answer any questions the judge may ask. There must be evidence that all the first or second set of access conditions have been fulfilled. Any statements which have no substance and which are to the prejudice of the party against whom the order is sought, will be excluded by the judge (*R v Crown Court at Inner London Sessions, ex p Baines and Baines* (1988)).

4.201   The judge must exercise a high degree of caution and not be personally satisfied that the statutory requirements have been met (*R v Central Criminal Court, ex p Bright* (2001)). Where the judge fails to take sufficient care, the warrant is liable to be set aside (*R v Southwark Court, ex p Sorsky Defries* (1996)). Full disclosure is essential and the judge must be told of anything to the knowledge of the applicant which may against making the order.

THE FIRST SET OF ACCESS CONDITIONS

4.202   The first set of access conditions is fulfilled if:
(a)   there are reasonable grounds for believing –
    (i)   that a serious arrestable offence has been committed;
    (ii)   that there is material which consists of or includes special procedure material and does not also include excluded material on premises specified in the application;
    (iii) that the material is likely to be of substantial value (whether by itself or together with other material) to the investigation in connection with which the application is made; and
    (iv)   that the material is likely to be relevant evidence;
(b)   other methods of obtaining the material –
    (i)   have been tried without success; or
    (ii)   have not been tried because it appeared that they were bound to fail; and
(c)   it is in the public interest, having regard –

    (i)   to the benefit likely to accrue to the investigation if the material is obtained; and

    (ii) to the circumstances under which the person in possession of the material holds it, that the material should be produced or that access to it should be given.

4.203   The conditions set out in para 2(a) and (b) are factual and are similar to those in s 8(1) (art 10(1)). If the serious arrestable offence is specified in Sch 5, Pt I or II, there will be no difficulty in satisfying the judge. If, however, the offence is a serious arrestable offence because of the consequences set out in s 116(6) (art 87(6)), an explanation will be necessary.

4.204   It will, of course, be necessary to show that the material sought consists of or includes special procedure material. In *R v Preston Crown Court at Preston, ex p McGrath* (1992) it was held that the reference in para 2(a)(ii) of Sch 1 to 'material which consists of special procedure material or includes special procedure material' was a reference to material which had the legal quality of special procedure material either as to its entirety or as to some part. The argument that an order under the first set of access conditions could only apply to material shown to be special procedure material or to material inseparable from it was rejected. Acceptance of that argument would have meant that separate and sequential application would have to be made under Sch 1 and s 8. That would be cumbersome and would endanger the integrity of the material which was the subject of the s 8 application. Thus it is possible to apply for an order (or warrant) under Sch 1 where the material is special procedure material which is mixed with other material which could be the subject of a warrant under s 8 (or any other warrant power). It should not, however, be thought that an application under the first set of access conditions can be made for material which is special procedure material but which includes excluded material or legally privileged material. These materials cannot be mixed because there is no power to issue an order or warrant in respect of legally privileged material and excluded material can only be the subject of an order or warrant if the second set of access conditions apply. It follows that it may in some cases be more important to show that the material sought does not include excluded or legally privileged material. This will seldom be the case when financial institutions such as banks and building societies are involved, but could be problematic if journalistic material is sought given that this material can be either excluded or special procedure material and possibly more problematic where solicitors' offices are involved. A possible interpretation of Sch 1, para 2(a)(ii) is that an order under para 4 cannot be made if there is excluded material (or legally privileged material) on the premises as well as special procedure material even if the material is separate and identifiable as such but a preferable interpretation is that such an order can be made if the special procedure material is separate and identifiable.

4.205   In order to satisfy the judge that the material 'is likely to be of substantial value (whether by itself or together with other material) to the investigation' it will be necessary to describe the offence under investigation, what other evidence there is and how the material sought relates to the investigation. Such material may be only a small part of a much larger pattern of evidence but still be 'of substantial value'. 'Relevant evidence' in relation to an offence means anything that would be admissible in evidence at a trial for the offence (s 8(4), art 10(4)).

4.206 The requirement in para 2(b) emphasises the need to approach either the person under investigation, or the holder of the material, in an attempt to obtain the material with their consent or attempt to use other practicable methods of obtaining the material. Only rarely will the police wish to alert the person to the fact that he is under investigation and the fact that the person holding the material may lay himself open to a civil action if he allows access without a court order means that few will do so. Nevertheless, the judge must be satisfied that the application under s 9, and Sch 1, is the last resort (*R v Crown Court at Lewes, ex p Hill* (1991)), therefore some attempt must be made to obtain the material without resort to the legal powers. It is, however, one thing for a dentist voluntarily to give the police the dental impression of a suspect in a murder case (*R v Singleton* (1995)), but quite another for a banker voluntarily to disclose details of a client's financial dealings. Even if one is aware that there will no voluntary disclosure it will often be necessary to approach the holder of the material to establish that he has it and possibly to obtain a clear description of the material which is to be subject of an application under Sch 1. For example, a bank may confirm that they hold an account in the suspect's name, or more than one account, but will require a court order before giving access to it or them. In *R v Crown Court at Lewes, ex p Hill* (1990) a police officer obtained an order under the Bankers' Books Evidence Act 1879 to inspect bank records in respect of H. He later obtained an order under s 9 and Sch 1 of PACE 1984 giving him access to the same bank records but failed to make it clear to the judge that opportunities arising from the order under the 1879 Act had not been fully exploited. On an application for judicial review of the decision to issue the order under PACE 1984, it was held that in the absence of such information the judge could not have been satisfied as to the requirements of para 2(b) and the order should not have been made. The Divisional Court further stated that the applicant for a production order was under an obligation to ensure that all relevant material, even if it was adverse to his case, was before the court (see also *R v Crown Court at Acton, ex p Layton* (1993)). This is not to say that the 1879 Act must be used before the 1984 Act procedure, but where the 1879 Act is used, it must be fully exploited and the 1984 procedure used only as a last resort when the 1879 Act proves ineffective or insufficient.

The public interest requirement

4.207 Schedule 1, para 2(c) requires that the judge be satisfied that it is in the public interest that the material be produced or access to it be given, having regard:
(i)   to the benefit likely to accrue to the investigation if the material is obtained; and
(ii) to the circumstances under which the person in possession of the material holds it.

4.208 The first of these requirements suggests that the more important the material is to the investigation the greater the public interest is in allowing the police to obtain it. In every case the offence must be a serious arrestable offence and once it is established that the material is of substantial value to the investigation there seems to be little to put into the scales which would outweigh this public interest. The circumstances in which the material is held can only refer to the fact that the holder owes a duty of confidence to a third party. A banker, for example, can point to his duty of confidentiality and the possible damage to his relationship with other clients if that duty is breached. However, the purpose of the production order under Sch 1 is to enable him to breach that duty without incurring legal liability and, since the vast majority of clients will accept that he must comply with a judicial order, the banker/ client relationship is unlikely to be damaged. In *R v Central Criminal Court, ex p Carr* (1987) Glidewell LJ appeared to disregard para 2(c)(ii) in taking the view that once it is shown that the documents are in the premises and that they are likely to be of substantial value to the investigation and relevant evidence, it followed that it was in the public interest that they be produced. This approach was confirmed by the Queen's Bench Divisional Court in *R v Crown Court at Northampton, ex p DPP* (1991). Granting judicial review of a judge's refusal to issue an order under s 9 and Sch 1 against a firm of solicitors, Taylor LJ held that once a judge had concluded under para 2(a)(i) of Sch 1 that a serious arrestable offence had been committed, it was hardly consistent to find anything other than that it was an offence for which there was a public interest in bringing the matter to justice. In *R v Crown Court at Acton, ex p Layton* (1993) the then managing director of National Car Parks was charged with conspiracy to defraud by dishonestly acquiring information about a rival's business affairs. His appeal against the issue of an order to produce special procedure material, in part based on the argument that the public interest was not served by the issue of the order, was dismissed. In relation to the public interest it was said:

> 'Having regard to the allegations of industrial espionage of the kind which was said to have gone on here, the proposition that the public interest would not be served by obtaining the documents in question was unarguable.'

4.209   The view that once a serious arrestable offence has been found to have been committed there must be a public interest in granting the order is now subject to the interpretation relation of the court in *R v Central Criminal Court, ex p Bright* (2001). The court gave examples of matters which might be subject to the public interest, as follows: the effect of the order on third parties, the antiquity of matters under investigation and any apparent disproportion between what might possibly be gained by the production of the material and the offence to which it was said to relate.

4.210   In *R v Crown Court at Bristol, ex p Bristol Press and Picture Agency Ltd* (1986) unpublished photographs taken by press photographers of a riot were sought by the police. The newspapers raised two issues under para 2(c)(ii): first, that allowing police access to the photographs would compromise the impartiality of the press; and second, that it would increase the risk of injury to photographers. On the first issue the judge took the view that the impartiality of the press would not be compromised if they were compelled to produce them under a court order. As to the second issue, he took the view that photographers were at greater risk when taking photographs for publication than in disclosing unpublished photographs. The public interest therefore lay in making the order for production. Similarly in *Re an Application under s 9 PACE* (1988) where it was held that it was in the public interest to order the production of unpublished or untransmitted journalistic material where it would be of benefit to the criminal investigation into offences arising out of the Wapping demonstrations. Such an order would not undermine the freedom or independence of the press nor increase the risk of injury to journalists.

THE SECOND SET OF ACCESS CONDITIONS

4.211 Section 9(2) (art 11(2)) provides that any Act (including a local Act) passed before PACE 1984 (or 1989 Order) under which a search of premises for the purposes of a criminal investigation could be authorised by the issue of a warrant to a constable shall cease to have effect so far as it relates to the authorisation of searches:
(a) for items subject to legal privilege; or
(b) for excluded material; or
(c) for special procedure material consisting of documents or records other than documents.

4.212 The effect of s 9(2) (art 11(2)), is to prevent a magistrate issuing a warrant under a pre-existing statutory authority if the material sought falls within the definition of legally privileged, excluded or special procedure material in documentary form. Legally privileged material is never obtainable; but as regards excluded material and special procedure material in documentary form, instead of making an application to a magistrate for a warrant under the particular statute, application must now be made to a circuit (county court) judge under para 3 of Sch 1, the second set of access conditions. These conditions are fairly easily satisfied, the rationale being that since the material would, but for s 9(2) (art 11(2)), have been obtainable under a magistrate's warrant, there is no need to adopt the more restrictive conditions which apply in relation to material which can never be the subject of such warrants. The access conditions are:
(a) there are reasonable grounds for believing that there is material which consists of or includes excluded or special procedure material on premises specified in the application;
(b) but for s 9(2) (art 11(2)) a search of the specified premises could have been authorised by the issue of a warrant to a constable under a statutory provision other than Sch 1 of the 1984 Act (1989 Order); and
(c) the issue of such a warrant would have been appropriate. If these conditions are fulfilled the judge may make an order requiring the person who appears to him to be in possession of the material to produce it to a constable or give him access to it.

4.213 The following points may be noted.
(1) Excluded material and special procedure material, if in documentary form, are obtainable under para 3 of Sch 1. For example, a Government official passes secret documents to a journalist with a view to exposing alleged malpractice by

Government ministers. Assuming they are held in confidence, they are excluded material under ss 11(1)(c) and 13 (arts 13(1)(c) and 15). But for s 9(2) (art 11(2)) the documents could be the subject of a search warrant under the Theft Act if stolen, or under the Official Secrets Act. A magistrate cannot now issue a warrant in respect of the documents under either Act, instead application must be made under Sch 1, para 3 (the second set of access conditions) for an order for production of the documents. If the order is not complied with, a warrant may be issued. If any of the conditions in para 14 of Sch 1 (para 11 of the 1989 Order) are satisfied, a warrant may be sought in the first instance rather than an order (see para 4.194, post). Note that there is no requirement that the offence be a serious arrestable offence.

(2)   Section 9(2) (art 11(2)) does not apply to statutory powers of search created after the 1984 Act (1989 Order) unless the creating statute applies it. This has been done by the Cinemas Act 1985. Section 13(3) authorises a magistrate to issue a warrant to enter premises reasonably suspected of being used as a cinema without a licence (an offence under s 10(1) of the Act) and to search for and seize apparatus or things subject to forfeiture. Section 13(8) applies s 9(2) of the 1984 Act to this search power. This may be contrasted with s 24 of the Public Order Act 1986 which authorises a magistrate to issue a warrant to search premises for racially inflammatory material, possession of which is an offence under s 23 of the Act. Section 9(2) does not apply to this search power, therefore legally privileged, excluded or special procedure material may be searched for and seized if it is racially inflammatory as defined by s 23. It is difficult to imagine legally privileged material falling within this definition but, in the absence of a definition of 'journalist' or 'journalism', one can imagine circumstances in which such material is in possession of a newspaper published by an extreme fascist group which could be either excluded or special procedure material. (In Northern Ireland, art 14 of the Public Order (NI) Order 1987, which provides a power to issue a warrant to search for material which is evidence of an offence under art 13 of that Order (stirring up racial hatred), is subject to art 11(2) of the PACE Order 1989. Such evidence in possession of a newspaper will be either excluded or special procedure material and obtainable only by application under Sch 1.)

THE ORDER

4.214   An order under Sch 1 is an order that the person who appears to the circuit (county court) judge to be in possession of the material to which the application relates shall:

(a)   produce it to a constable for him to take away; or

(b)   give him access to it, not later than the end of a period of seven days from the date of the order or the end of such longer period as the order may specify (Sch 1 para 4).

4.215   Where the material consists of information contained in a computer, it must be produced in a visible and legible form in which it can be taken away or the constable given access to it – eg a print-out (Sch 1, para 5). Most orders will require that the material be produced for a constable to take away. Such material is to be treated as material seized by a constable for the purposes of ss 21 and 22 (arts 23 and 24) (see para 4.139, ante). One may note that there is no power to question the person about the material produced, which may often need explanation. Failure to comply with an order is a contempt of court (Sch 1, para 12). There is no provision for a warrant to be issued following the failure to comply with an order based on the first set of access conditions being fulfilled, though there is when an order is made following the fulfilment of the second set of access conditions.

WARRANT TO SEARCH FOR EXCLUDED AND SPECIAL PROCEDURE MATERIAL

4.216   The 1984 Act (1989 Order) envisages that an application for the production of or access to documents at an inter partes hearing will be the normal procedure. It should be noted that s 15 (art 17) of PACE 1984 and Order applies to an application for a warrant under Sch 1, in particular the judge is empowered to question the constable on oath (see para 4.100, ante). Applications for a warrant under Sch 1, paras 12-14 (paras 9-11 of the Order) are very much the exception accounting for only 2.5% of applications granted in the first 33 months of the 1984 Act's operation. Applications for warrants should never become a matter of routine (*R v Crown Court at Maidstone, ex p Waitt* (1988)).

4.217   The Schedule envisages two situations in which a warrant may be issued.
(i)   In the first situation in which a warrant may be issued, the judge must be satisfied that either the first (para 2) or the second (para 3) set of access conditions are fulfilled and, in addition, any of the further conditions set out in Sch 1, para 14 (para 11 of the Order) (para 12(a)(i) and (ii); para 9(a)(i) and (ii) of the Order). The additional conditions relate to the practicability of communicating with the person entitled to grant access to the premises or the material sought; to the likely disclosure of official secrets contained in the material sought if a warrant is not issued; and, perhaps most commonly in this first situation, the likelihood that service of a notice of application for an order of production may seriously prejudice the investigation for the purposes of which the application is sought, or another investigation (para 14(a) to (d); para 10(a) to (d) of the Order). In relation to this last condition Code B 3.7 requires that an application for a warrant under para 12 (para 9) shall, where appropriate, indicate why it is believed that service of notice of an application for a production order may seriously prejudice the investigation. If the reason is that the person in possession is implicated in the serious arrestable offence under investigation, it may be more appropriate to arrest him and search the premises for the material (excluded or special procedure) under post-arrest powers of search, ss 18 or 32(2)(b) (arts 20 or 34(2)(b)). The usual procedure is to make the application ex parte but in *R v Crown Court at Southampton, ex p J and P* (1993) it was said that there may be circumstances (in relation to a warrant issued when the first set of access conditions are satisfied) in which the application

may be made inter partes. There two solicitors were under investigation and five factors militated against proceeding on an ex parte basis:

(1) an inter partes order would have frozen the material in their possession;
(2) the accounts had already been seen by the Law Society so it would be pointless to tamper with them;
(3) the police already had copies of some of the ledger sheets;
(4) the applicants had already had nine months to cover their tracks since the matter had been referred to the DPP; and
(5) as solicitors the applicants were under a duty to account to their clients.

(ii) The second situation envisages a warrant being issued when the second set of access conditions has been fulfilled and an order has been made under Sch 1, para 4, but it has not been complied with. This applies only in those cases in which the material sought (which, unlike the first set of access conditions, may be excluded or special procedure material) could, but for s 9(2) (art 11(2)), have been the subject of a magistrate's warrant but, in compliance with the Act (Order) has been the subject of an order for production under para 4 of Sch 1. If the person in possession of the material fails to comply with the order a circuit (county court) judge may issue a warrant to enter premises and search for and seize the material. Failure to comply with an order is contempt of court; but the person in possession may decide to defy the court and refuse to deliver up the material, hence the warrant procedure. Strangely, there is no jurisdiction to issue a warrant to search for and seize material which was the subject of an order issued under the first set of access conditions when the order has not been complied with. The application for a warrant under Sch 1 must comply with s 15 of PACE 1984 (art 17 of the PACE Order) (para 4.14, ante). Once a circuit (county court) judge has made an ex parte order issuing a warrant under para 12 of Sch 1, he has no power to entertain an inter partes application to review his order. If it is believed that the warrant was erroneously issued, application should be made to the Queen's Bench Divisional Court for judicial review of the decision (*R v Liverpool Crown Court, ex p Wimpey plc* (1991)).

REASONS FOR MAKING AN ORDER

4.218   The PACE Act 1984 does not require a judge to give reasons for issuing an order or warrant under Sch 1 but in *R v Crown Court at Southampton, ex p J and P* (1993) the Court identified a need for this to be done. The need doubtless stems from the increase in applications to the High Court to quash orders or warrants issued under Sch 1.

EXECUTING A WARRANT ISSUED UNDER Sch 1

4.219   In addition to the requirements of s 16 (art 18) (considered at paras 4.49 to 4.65) which apply to the execution of all warrants, Code B 6.14 stipulates that an officer of the rank of inspector or above take charge of and be present at a search made under a warrant issued under Sch 1. He is responsible for ensuring that the search is carried out with discretion and with as little disruption as possible to business or other activities carried on in the premises. After securing the premises to ensure that no material leaves the premises without his knowledge, he should ask for the documents or other records to be produced. He may also, if necessary, ask to see the index (if there is one) to files held on the premises; an inspection may be made of any files which, according to the index, contain any of the material sought. A more extensive search of the premises may only be made if the person refuses to produce the material or to allow access to an index, or if it appears that the index is incomplete, or if the officer in charge has reasonable grounds to believe that such a search is necessary in order to find the material sought. Since constables executing such a warrant are lawfully on premises, the general power of seizure contained in s 19 (art 21) and the access provisions in s 21 (art 23) apply (see paras 4.128, ante). It should be emphasised that material seized is held by the police under a duty of confidence (*Marcel v Metropolitan Police Comr* (1991) – see para 4.160(viii), ante). In *R v Crown Court at Leeds, ex p Switalski* (1991), on an application for judicial review of a decision to grant search warrants under s 9 and Sch 1 in respect of a solicitor's office, Leonard J pointed out that the circuit judge has to balance two conflicting public interests – the interest in the prevention of crime and the interest in maintaining the confidentiality of communications between clients and their legal advisers. He continued:

> 'I regard this second interest … as of the greatest importance and indeed vital for the maintenance of confidence in the legal system. Therefore, the police who have obtained warrants, such as the present, have a very special responsibility to ensure that any information obtained, however inadvertently, is not misused. I would anticipate that in some cases it may well be thought right that the police would be required to give an express undertaking as to the way in which the information will be used so as to emphasise the gravity of the matter.'

4.220   Legally privileged material cannot, of course, be lawfully seized under a warrant or under s 19 (art 21) seizure powers. If such material is inadvertently seized it should be returned to the original holder. It cannot be retained under s 22(2)(a) of the PACE (art 24(1)): see *R v Chief Constable of Lancashire, ex p Parker and McGrath* (1993) discussed at para 4.139, ante. Any attempt to use it in evidence is likely to be met with its exclusion under s 78 (art 76) of PACE Act (Order) (see para 2.125 ante).

4.221   The following examples illustrate the operation of s 9 (art 11) and Sch 1 and its relationship to the s 8 (art 10) warrant. Councillors and local government officials are the subject of an investigation into allegations of fraud and corruption involving local and national companies, which are serious arrestable offences (s 116 (art 87)).

(a)   Councillors and officials are believed to have received large sums of money from a national building contractor. Their bank and building society accounts can be the subject of an application for a production order under Sch 1, para 2 (the first set of access conditions).

(b)   A former councillor is believed to have acted as the 'go-between' and to have received moneys from local and national companies for his consultancy services.

His bank and building society accounts can be the subject of an application for a production order under Sch 1, para 2 (the first set of access conditions). His home and office may be searched under a s 8 (art 10) warrant for evidence of his involvement and of the companies' involvement with him. (Alternatively he may be arrested and both premises searched under ss 18 and 32(2)(b) (arts 20 and 34(2)(b)).)

(c) Documents belonging to the former councillor are held by his accountant. These are special procedure material and may be the subject of an application for a production order under Sch 1, para 2 (the first set of access conditions).

(d) The national building contractor has been approached by the police but their officers refuse to co-operate on the advice of their solicitor. There are grounds to believe that service of a notice of an application for an order under para 4 of Sch 1 would lead to shredding of the material sought. An application may be made for a warrant to search for and seize the material (special procedure material) under paras 12 and 14 of Sch 1 (paras 9 and 11 of the Order).

(e) A national newspaper has been conducting its own investigation into the allegations of corruption. They have a great deal of evidence including taped interviews with colleagues of the former councillor in which they detail their involvement in various frauds and implicate the former councillor. These are excluded material if held in confidence and cannot be the subject of an application under Sch 1, para 2 (the first set of access conditions), nor can they be the subject of an application under para 3 (the second set of access conditions). Reliance must be placed on the co-operation of the newspaper.

(f) A local newspaper has received a file of invoices and receipts stolen from a local building firm which prove fraud and corruption by a number of local councillors. This is excluded material if held in confidence, special procedure material if not. In either event the material could have been the subject of a warrant under the Theft Act 1968, s 26 (Theft Act (NI) 1969, s 25). Such a warrant cannot now be issued (s 9(2), art 11(2)) but an application can be made for a production order under Sch 1, para 3 (the second set of access conditions) or a warrant, if the conditions discussed in para 4.211, ante, apply.

(g) A local councillor, reasonably suspected of fraud and corruption, is arrested on leaving the registered office of a building company which it is believed has been paying him to enable them to obtain building contracts. The office can be searched for material which may be evidence of the offence (s 32(2)(b), art 34(2)(b)) and such material may be seized even if it is special procedure material. The home of the councillor may be searched under s 18 (art 20).

(h) A firm of solicitors acted for the building company in negotiating contracts and in the purchase of land from the local authority. The documents relating to the sale of land are not legally privileged (*R v Crown Court at Inner London Sessions, ex p Baines and Baines* (1987)) and, applying the same principle, nor are the documents relating to negotiation of contracts. They are, however, special procedure material and may be the subject of an application under Sch 1, para 2 (the first set of access conditions). In no circumstances can they be the subject of a s 8 (art 10) warrant.

PART C: PARTICULAR POWERS TO ISSUE A SEARCH WARRANT OR TO OBTAIN ACCESS TO MATERIAL

4.222   The powers to obtain material considered in this section are powers which are available only in respect of particular offences, or in order to trace the proceeds of crime which are subject to confiscation, and powers to search for or obtain materials which are relevant to an investigation carried out by police forces in other jurisdictions. The powers are contained in:

(a)   the Proceeds of Crime Act 2002;
(b)   Drug Trafficking Act 1994;
(c)   the Terrorism Act 2000;
(d)   the Criminal Justice (Confiscation) (Northern Ireland) Orders 1990 and 1993;
(e)   the Security Service Act 1989;
(f)   the Intelligence Services Act 1994;
(g)   the Official Secrets Acts 1989 and 1911;
(h)   the Criminal Justice Act 1987;
(i)   the Bankers' Books Evidence Act 1879.

The Proceeds of Crime Act 2002

4.223   It has long been recognised that criminals were making substantial sums of money from crime which they retained even after conviction. Powers of forfeiture were initially introduced by the Powers of Criminal Courts Act 1973. The Hodgson Report (1984) led to the Drug Trafficking Offences Act 1986 which put into place for the first time a system for the confiscation of assets when a defendant was convicted of a drug trafficking offence. There followed a series of legislative provisions to deal with forfeiture of assets. The Criminal Justice Act 1988 ('CJA 1988') introduced confiscation proceedings for all non-drug indictable offences. This was followed by the Criminal Justice (International Co-operation Act) 1990 which introduced assistance provisions, further money laundering offences and gave power to seize cash over £10,000 if it was being imported or exported. Consolidation of the provisions relating to confiscation in drug cases was made in the Drug Trafficking Act 1994 ('DTA 1994'). The Proceeds of Crime Act 1995, came into force on 1 November 1995, and further amended the CJA 1988.

4.224   Two government reports provided the background to the Proceeds of Crime Act 2002. Firstly, the Third Report of the Home Office Organised and International Crime Directorate Working Group on Confiscation, entitled 'Criminal Assets', recommended both a national confiscation agency and rationalisation of the confiscation legislation. Secondly a report by the Performance and Innovation Unit of the Cabinet Office, entitled 'Recovering the Proceeds of Crime', concluded that a new Act was necessary because of 'anomalies in the legal regime' and because of 'significant deficiencies' in its use. The conclusions of the PIV Report provides the basis of the Act.

4.225   The Proceeds of Crime Act 2002 ('PCA 2002') consolidates, updates and strengthens existing legislation and enacts a range of new powers. Its main provisions are:
(i)   the consolidation of existing legislation
(ii)   the extension of criminal court powers to make confiscation orders
(iii)   the rationalisation of powers to the Crown Court
(iv)   enhanced post-conviction confiscation powers
(v)   the establishment of the national Assets Recovery Agency (ARA)
(vi)   the broadening of liability for money laundering offences
(vii) the introduction of civil proceedings in the High Court for the forfeiture of assets without conviction if it can be established that there are reasonable grounds to suspect that assets are the proceeds of, or to be used in, criminal activities.

4.226   Part 8 of PCA 2002 creates a range of investigatory powers, some of which are similar to PACE and Terrorism Act powers. But all recognise the importance of investigative measures which facilitate enquiries with banks and other financial institutions.

4.227   The following orders are available on application by an 'appropriate officer' (the distinction as to who is an appropriate officer depends on the type of investigation being conducted):
(i)   production orders
(ii)   search and seizure warrants
(iii)   disclosure orders
(iv)   customer information orders
(v)   account monitoring orders.

4.228   These powers may be used in investigations, defined by PCA 2002, s 341, into the following:
(i)   'Confiscation': an investigation into whether a person has benefited from his criminal conduct or as to the extent or whereabouts of the benefits from his criminal conduct. (An appropriate officer is the Director of ARA, an accredited financial investigator, a constable, a customs officer.)
(ii)   'Civil recovery': to examine whether property is recoverable property or associated property, who holds the property, its extent and whereabouts. (An appropriate officer is the Director of ARA.)
(iii)   'Money laundering': whether a person has committed a money laundering offence. (An appropriate officer is an accredited financial investigator, a constable, a customs officer.

4.229   A person benefits from criminal conduct if 'he obtains property as a result of or in connection with criminal conduct which is defined as conduct which constitutes an offence in England or Wales or which would constitute an offence if it occurred there (s 76).

4.230   Recoverable property is the property equal to the benefit the person has received from his criminal conduct and associated property is defined by PCA 2002, s 245 and includes any interest in the recoverable property.

4.231   A person commits a money laundering offence if he commits

(i)   an offence of concealing, disguising, converting or transferring or removing criminal property (s 327),

(ii)   an offence of entering into or being concerned in an arrangement knowing or suspecting that it facilitates the acquisition, retention, use or control of criminal property by or on behalf of another (s 328);

(iii)   an offence of acquiring, using or possessing criminal property (s 329).

4.232   Unless in each case he makes or intends to make an authorised disclosure ie he notifies the police or the National Criminal Intelligence Service.

Production orders (s 345)

4.233   An appropriate officer may apply for a production order requiring a specified person to produce specified material relating to an investigation. The order will usually require the material to be produced within seven days unless the judge considers that period to be inappropriate. It will specify whether the officer has power to take the material away or just to have access to it.

4.234   Before the order is granted, the requirements in PCA 2002, s 346 are that the judge must be satisfied that there are reasonable grounds to believe the following:

(i)   that the specified person is in possession or control of the material and that the material is likely to be of substantial value (whether by itself or with other material) to the investigation; and

(ii)   that

    (a)   in the case of a confiscation investigation, the person has benefited from his criminal conduct; or

    (b)   in the case of a civil recovery investigation, the specified property is recoverable property or associated property; or

    (c)   in the case of a money laundering investigation, the specified person has committed a money laundering offence.

4.235   PCA 2002, s 346(5) contains a public interest test whereby there must be reasonable grounds for believing that that it is in the public interest for the material to be produced or for access to it to be given, having regard to the following:

(i)   the benefit likely to accrue to the investigation if the material is obtained;

(ii)   the circumstances under which the person specified in the application as appearing to be in possession or control of the material holds it.

4.236   PCA 2002, s 347 give the judge a further power where he has made a production order to make an order requiring any person who appears to an appropriate officer to be a person entitled to grant entry to premises to enable the officer to gain access to the material.

4.237   A production order overrides any restrictions on the disclosure of information except that it cannot require disclosure of material covered by legal professional privilege or which is excluded material as defined by PACE. Material may be retained for 'so long as it is necessary' to keep it rather than a copy and it may be held until the proceedings are completed.

Search and seizure warrants (ss 352 and 353)

4.238   A search and seizure warrant may be issued when either a production order has not been complied with (PCA 2002, s 352) or in situations where there can be no production order (PCA 2002, s 353).

4.239   An appropriate officer may apply for a search and seizure warrant to a judge. The judge must be satisfied that a production order made in relation to the material sought has not been complied with and there are reasonable grounds for believing that the material is on the specified premises or that s 353 is satisfied in relation to the warrant. The application must state the following:
(i)   a person specified in the application is subject to a confiscation investigation or a money laundering investigation; or
(ii)   property specified in the application is subject to a civil recovery investigation;
(iii)   the warrant is sought for the purposes of the investigation;
(iv)   the warrant is sought in relation to the premises specified in the application;
(v)   the warrant is sought in relation to material specified in the application, or that there are reasonable grounds for believing that there is material falling within s 353 (6), (7) or (8) on the premises.

Requirements where production order not available

4.240   The requirements where a production order is not available are contained in PCA 2002, s 353 and have similarities to PACE Pt II orders. But they go further in that the do not exclude special procedure material.

4.241   Firstly there must be reasonable grounds for suspecting that:
(a)   in the case of a confiscation investigation, the person has benefited from his criminal conduct; or
(b)   in the case of a civil recovery investigation, the specified property is recoverable property or associated property; or
(c)   in the case of a money laundering investigation, the specified person has committed a money laundering offence.

4.242   Secondly, either the first or second set of conditions in sub-ss (3)-(10) must apply.

4.243

Subsection (3): The first set of conditions is that there are reasonable grounds for believing that:
(a)   any material on the premises specified in the application for the warrant is likely to be of substantial value (whether or not by itself) to the investigation for the purposes of which the warrant is sought;

(b) it is in the public interest for the material to be obtained, having regard to the benefit likely to accrue to the investigation if the material is obtained, and

(c) it would not be appropriate to make a production order for any of the reasons mentioned in sub-s (4).

4.244 Subsection (4): The reasons are that:

(a) it is not practicable to communicate with any person against whom the production order could be made;

(b) it is not practicable to communicate with any person who would be required to comply with an order to grant entry to the premises;

(c) the investigation might be seriously prejudiced unless an appropriate person is able to secure immediate access to the material.

4.245 Subsection (5): The second set of conditions is that:

(a) there is reasonable grounds for believing that there is material on the premises specified in the application for the warrant and that the material falls within sub-s (6), (7) or (8),

(b) it is in the public interest for the material to be obtained, having regard to the benefit likely to accrue to the investigation if the material is obtained, and

(c) any one or more of the requirements in sub-s (9) is met.

4.246 Subsection (6): In the case of a confiscation investigation, material falls within the subsection if it cannot be identified at the time of the application but it:

(a) relates to the person specified in the application, the question whether he has benefited from his criminal conduct or any question as to the extent or whereabouts of his benefit from his criminal conduct, and

(b) it is likely to be of substantial value (whether or not by itself) to the investigation for the purpose of which the warrant is sought.

4.247 Subsection (7): In the case of a civil recovery investigation, material falls within the subsection if it cannot be identified at the time of the application but it:

(a) relates to the property specified in the application, the question whether it is recoverable property or associated property, the question as to who holds any such property, any question as to whether the person who appears to hold any such property holds other property which is recoverable property, or any question as to the extent and whereabouts of any property mentioned in this paragraph, and

(b) is likely to be of substantial value (whether or not by itself) to the investigation for the purposes of which the warrant is sought.

4.248 Subsection (8): In the case of a money laundering investigation, material falls within the subsection if it cannot be identified at the time of the application but it:

(a) relates to the person specified in the application or the question whether he has committed a money laundering offence, and

(b) is likely to be of substantial value (whether or not by itself) to the investigation for the purposes of which the warrant is sought.

4.249 Subsection (9): The requirements are that:

(a) it is not practicable to communicate with any person against whom the production order could be made;
(b) it is not practicable to communicate with any person who would be required to comply with an order to grant entry to the premises;
(c) the investigation might be seriously prejudiced unless an appropriate person is able to secure immediate access to the material.

Disclosure orders

4.250   The Director of the Asset Recovery Agency may make an application to a judge for a disclosure order (PCA 2002, s 357) in relation to confiscation and civil recovery investigations but not money laundering investigations. The order authorises the director to send a notice to anyone who they believe has information relevant to the investigation requiring them to:

- answer questions either at a time specified in the notice or at once, at a specified place;
- provide specified information by a time and in a specified manner;
- produce documents, or documents of a description specified in the notice, either at or by a time specified or at once, and in a manner specified.

4.251   The judge must be satisfied that there are reasonable grounds to believe that information which may be provided under the order is likely to be of substantial value (whether or not by itself) to the investigation and that there are reasonable grounds to believe that it is in the public interest for the information to be provided having regard to the benefit likely to accrue to the investigation if the information is obtained.

4.252   It is an offence if without reasonable excuse a person fails to comply with, or makes a false or misleading statement, or recklessly makes a false or misleading statement (s 359). The penalty for this offence is imprisonment for up to six months and a fine not exceeding level 5 on the standard scale, a relatively low penalty when viewed against the possible implications of providing the information – one of which is the evidential admissibility of the statement made in response to a production order. A statement will be admissible if there are proceedings under Part 2 or 4 (confiscation provisions), under s 359, on a prosecution for perjury, on a prosecution for some other offence, where, in giving evidence, the person makes a statement inconsistent with the production order statement provided evidence relating to the order is adduced or a question relating to it is asked.

4.253   The production order is a useful investigative power but it does not confer the right to require a person to answer questions of a privileged nature or to produce excluded material. A lawyer must provide the name and address of his client if required to do so. It is to be noted that the provision of information is required notwithstanding any other restriction on the disclosure of information. Material may be retained for 'so long as it is necessary' to keep it rather than a copy and it may be held until the proceedings are completed.

Customer information orders; Account monitoring orders

4.254 Customer information orders (PCA 2002, s 363) and account monitoring orders (PCA 2002, s 370) are made on application to a judge. There must be reasonable grounds to believe that the person against whom the order is made is subject to a confiscation or money laundering or civil recovery investigation. Orders are made against named financial institutions who must supply information which would otherwise be unavailable in respect of the customer and any account specified. Customer information orders require the disclosure of details such as addresses, account details, registered offices etc while an account monitoring order enables real time monitoring of financial transactions. It is an offence to fail to comply with a customer information order, a failure to comply with an account monitoring order is a contempt of court. The evidence obtained from these orders is admissible under the same criteria as for disclosure orders.

The Drug Trafficking Act 1994

4.255 The Drug Trafficking Act 1994 ('DTA 1994') is a consolidation of the Drug Trafficking Offences Act 1986 and certain provisions of the Criminal Justice (International Co-operation) Act 1990 which relate to drug trafficking. The whole of the DTOA 1986 is repealed with the exception of ss 24(6), 32, 34 and 40(1), (3) to (5). The DTA 1994 enables courts in the UK to recover the proceeds of drug trafficking. This phrase is very broadly defined by s 1 as is the phrase `drug-trafficking offence'. Both definitions extend to acts and offences committed outside the normal jurisdiction of the UK. The powers of confiscation apply to all drug trafficking offences for which an offender is to be sentenced in the Crown Court. Many drug trafficking offences will be serious arrestable offences. In such cases the power to obtain a search warrant to search for evidence under s 8 of PACE 1984 (art 10 of the 1989 Order) and the power to apply for an access or production order (and in some circumstances a search warrant) in respect of excluded or special procedure material under Sch 1 of PACE 1984 and Order, will be available. However, because an offence can only be a serious arrestable offence if it is committed within the jurisdiction of the UK courts, and the drug trade is international, the DTA 1994 provides powers to obtain access to or the production of materials (and in certain circumstances a search warrant). Given the extraordinarily wide provisions (`intentionally draconian', per Lord Lane CJ in *R v Dickens* (1990) and cf *R v Robson* (1991)) available under the DTA 1994 to trace a person's assets, these powers are an indispensable means of enforcing them. They are modelled on PACE 1984, Sch 1, but are not confined to serious arrestable offences and contain other significant differences. The Act also contains incentives to encourage co-operation in drug trafficking investigations, and to discourage hindrance of such investigations. The DTA 1994 similarly has an incentive to encourage co-operation.

The powers under the Drug Trafficking Act

4.256   DTA 1994, ss 55 to 59 provide powers to obtain access to or the production of material which is likely to be of substantial value to investigations into drug trafficking, and, in limited circumstances, a warrant to enter premises to search for such material. These powers are similar to powers contained in Sch 1 of PACE 1984. The definitions of legally privileged, excluded and special procedure material are the same but there are significant procedural differences. These are as follows.

(i)   An order under DTA 1994, s 55 can only be sought for the purposes of an investigation into drug trafficking. 'Drug trafficking' is defined by s 1 of the DTA 1994. It means doing or being concerned in any of the following in England, Wales or elsewhere: producing, supplying, transporting, importing or exporting a controlled drug in contravention of the Misuse of Drugs Act 1971 or a corresponding law, or manufacturing or supplying a scheduled substance within the meaning of Sch 12 of the Criminal Justice (International Co-operation) Act 1990, where to do so is an offence if done in England or Wales, using any ship for illicit traffic in controlled drugs in circumstances amounting to an offence under s 19 of that Act, conduct which is an offence under s 49 of the DTA 1994 (concealing or transferring the proceeds of drug trafficking) if it took place in England or Wales, and acquiring, having possession of or using property in circumstances amounting to an offence under s 51 of the DTA 1994 (acquisition, possession or use of proceeds of drug trafficking) if it took place in England and Wales (s 1(1)(a) to (g)). Also included is what may be described as the 'handling' of the proceeds of drug trafficking in England, Wales or elsewhere, that is entering into or being otherwise concerned in an arrangement whereby:

    (a)   the retention or control by or on behalf of another person of the other's proceeds of drug trafficking is facilitated; or

    (b)   the proceeds of drug trafficking by another person are used to secure that funds are placed at the other person's disposal or used for the other person's benefit to acquire property by way of investment (s 1(2)).

(ii)   Unlike applications under Sch 1 of PACE 1984 and Order, there is no provision for the person in possession of the material sought to contest the issue of the order. The application is to a circuit judge and may be made ex parte to a judge in chambers (DTA 1994, s 55(6)) and, as with production orders under the PTA 1989, provision is made (by Crown Court Rules) for the person subject of the order to seek its discharge or variation (s 55(7)) (Crown Court Rules 1982, r 26B).

(iii)   The conditions of which a judge must be satisfied are fulfilled, and which are less restrictive than those under PACE 1984, are set out in sub-s (4). They are that:

    (a)   there are reasonable grounds for suspecting that a person specified in the application has carried on or has benefited from drug trafficking;

    (b)   there are reasonable grounds for suspecting that the material to which the application relates:

        (i)   is likely to be of substantial value (whether by itself or together with other material) to the investigation for the purpose of which the application is made, and

      (ii)   does not consist of or include items subject to legal privilege or excluded material; and

  (c) there are reasonable grounds for believing that it is in the public interest, having regard:

      (i)   to the benefit likely to accrue to the investigation if the material is obtained, and

      (ii)   to the circumstances under which the person in possession of the material holds it (s 55(4)(a) to (c)).

It will be noted that conditions (a) and (b) require only the lower threshold of reasonable suspicion, while condition (c) requires reasonable grounds for believing (for a discussion of these concepts see paras 2.81 to 2.92, ante). All the other production orders require reasonable belief in respect of all the conditions. The application must specify with some particularity what material is sought. This is important not only because the person in possession is not present to contest the application, but also to enable the judge to determine that the material does not consist of or include legally privileged or excluded material (defined in exactly the same terms as Sch 1 of PACE 1984 discussed at paras 4.65 and 4.70, ante). One may note that sub-s (6) states that an application 'may' be made ex parte to a judge in chambers. This connotes a discretion and there may, as was indicated in *R v Crown Court at Southampton, ex p J and P* (1993), be circumstances in which an inter partes application would be appropriate (see para 4.92, ante).

(iv) The material which can be obtained under a s 55 order is anything except legally privileged or excluded material (DTA 1994, s 55(4)(b)(ii) and (10)(a)). There is no reference to special procedure material. Such material is, however, obtainable under a s 55 order and such an order is not confined to material within that definition (it was thought that an order under PACE 1984, Sch 1 could not be issued in respect of mixed material, that is special procedure and other material not being excluded or legally privileged material; however, this argument was rejected in *R v Crown Court at Preston, ex p McGrath* (1992) discussed at para 4.284, ante). This is more clearly the case under s 55 where a judge can issue a s 55 order in respect of any material provided it is not legally privileged or excluded material. In addition s 55 overrides any obligation of secrecy or confidentiality imposed on the holder of any material whether statutory or not, and may apply to material in the possession of a Government department (s 55(10)(b) and (c) and see further s 59). 'Material' is not defined. It clearly includes documents as defined by s 10 of the Civil Evidence Act 1968 but would also include anything in tangible form even if not a document within that definition. Information contained in a computer is included. It must be produced in a visible and legible form so that it can be taken away or read (s 55(9)).

(v) When a judge makes an order for access to material under DTA 1994, s 55(2)(b) he may also, on the application of a constable, make an order requiring the person entitled to grant entry to the premises to allow a constable to enter the premises to obtain access to the material (s 55(5)). This is not a power to enter and search but merely facilitates entry to premises in those cases in which the person named in the access order is not the person entitled to grant access to the premises. Such an order is not required when a production order is issued because the material can be brought out of the premises. The entry order should name the person to whom it is directed. On one interpretation of s 55(5) the application for the entry order should accompany the application for an access order. However, a more likely interpretation is that it can be made at the same time or afterwards. If, for example, a constable is refused entry to premises after an access order has been served, it is simpler to permit him to apply for an entry order rather than seek a warrant because the access order has not been complied with.

(vi) Despite the similarity to PACE 1984 (and Order) and the Terrorism Act 2000 order for production of or access to material, Code of Practice B does not apply to applications for orders under the DTA 1994.

(vii) Section 57 of the DTA 1994 provides that for the purposes of ss 21 and 22 of PACE 1984 an investigation into drug trafficking shall be treated as if it were an investigation of or in connection with an offence; and material seized in pursuance of an order under s 55 shall be treated as if it were material seized by a constable – see paras 4.128-4.47, ante.

Search warrants

4.257   Section 56 of the DTA 1994 authorises the issue of a search warrant by a circuit judge in respect of drug trafficking offences as defined by s 1 of that Act (see para 4.120(i), ante). The breadth of that definition means that no offence need have been committed within the jurisdiction. A constable or an officer of Customs and Excise may apply. The application for a search warrant under this Act is governed by s 15 of PACE 1984 and its execution by s 16 of that Act and Code of Practice B. A warrant may be issued if the judge is satisfied that any of three sets of conditions set out in sub-s (2)(a), (b) and (c) are fulfilled.

- Section 56(2)(a): The first is the most obvious, that a s 55 order for access to or production of the material has not been complied with.
- Section 56(2)(b): The second is that the conditions set out in sub-s (3) are fulfilled.

4.258   The first of these is that there is reasonable cause to suspect that a specified person has carried on or benefited from drug trafficking.

4.259   The second is that the conditions in s 55(4)(b) and (c) are satisfied (reasonable cause to suspect that the material sought is likely to be of substantial value to the investigation and reasonable grounds for believing that it is in the public interest, having regard to the benefit to the investigation and to the circumstances under which the person holds the material).

4.260   The third is that it would not be appropriate to make an order under s 55 because:

(i)   it is not practicable to communicate with any person entitled to produce the material;

(ii) it is not practicable to communicate with any person entitled to grant access to the material or to the premises on which the material is situated;

(iii) the investigation might be seriously prejudiced unless a constable can secure immediate access to the material.

4.261   Section 56(2)(c): The third is that:

(a) there are reasonable grounds for suspecting that a specified person has carried on or has benefited from drug trafficking;

(b) there are reasonable grounds for suspecting that there is on the premises material relating to the specified person or to drug trafficking which is likely to be of substantial value (whether by itself or together with other material) to the investigation, but that the material cannot at the time of the application be particularised; and

(c)

(i)   it is not practicable to communicate with any person entitled to grant entry to the premises;

(ii) entry to the premises will not be granted unless a warrant is produced; or

(iii) the investigation might be seriously prejudiced unless a constable can secure immediate access to the material.

4.262   Code B 3.7 requires that as respects applications for warrants under Sch 1 of PACE 1984 and the Terrorism Act 2000 the reasons why the investigation may be prejudiced must be stated. Though not applicable to applications under s 56, circuit judges will undoubtedly require that the reasons be stated. One may note here that it is for the police to satisfy the judge that all the access conditions are satisfied and the burden rests on them to make a clear revelation to the court of all appropriate material in their possession so that the judge may make a safe conclusion as to whether they are fulfilled (see *R v Crown Court at Acton, ex p Layton* (1993)). Since the application can be made ex parte and in chambers, there is no reason why there should not be such clear revelation. The issue of a warrant under the conditions set out in s 56(2)(a), (b) and (3) is understandable. Surprise is sometimes essential when there is reason to believe that the material sought might be removed or destroyed if the s 55 procedure were adopted. The s 56(2)(c) and (4) warrant is less easy to justify. The requirement that it is not possible to particularise the material sought comes close to authorising a fishing expedition. There is a contradiction between this provision and the requirements of ss 15 and 16 of PACE 1984 which apply to s 56 warrants. Section 15(2)(c) states that it is a constable's duty to identify, so far as is practicable, the articles to be sought, while s 15(2)(b) requires that the warrant similarly identify the articles sought. The absence of any particularity in the s 56(2)(c) and (4) conditions of issue suggests that neither of these requirements can be satisfied. Section 16(8) limits the search to the extent required for the purpose for which the warrant was issued. If the purpose is to search for unspecified material such a limitation is of no consequence.

Powers of seizure and retention

4.263   Section 56(5) provides for a power of seizure and the retention of material sought in the warrant. A warrant under s 56 does not authorise the search for legally privileged or excluded material, therefore such material cannot be seized under the warrant. However, excluded material and any other material not specified in the warrant except legally privileged material, may be seized under the provision of s 19 of PACE 1984 provided the conditions set out in that section are fulfilled (see paras 4.128-4.131, ante). Section 57 provides that a drug trafficking investigation shall be treated as an investigation of or in connection with an offence for the purposes of ss 21 and 22 of PACE 1984 and that material seized be treated as if seized by a constable. It follows that the provisions of those sections apply to material seized under s 56 or produced under a s 55(2)(a) order.

Offences of prejudicing an investigation

4.264   Section 58 of the DTA 1994 provides that where an order under s 55 has been made or applied for and not refused, or a s 56 warrant issued, it is an offence for any person, knowing or suspecting that the investigation is taking place, to make any disclosure which is likely to prejudice the investigation. It is a defence for a person charged with such an offence to prove (on the balance of probabilities): that he did not know or suspect that the disclosure was likely to prejudice the investigation; or that he had lawful authority or reasonable excuse for making the disclosure. Section 58(3) recognises that legal advisers could be put in a difficult position if they were subject to this provision and provides that it is not an offence for a professional legal adviser to disclose any information or other matter:

(a)   to, or to a representative of, a client of his in connection with the giving by the adviser of legal advice to the client; or

(b)   to any person –

    (i)   in contemplation of, or in connection with, legal proceedings; and

    (ii)   for the purpose of those proceedings.

4.265   However, sub-s (3) does not apply in relation to any information or other matter which is disclosed with a view to furthering a criminal purpose.

4.266   The offence, like the offence under the POT Act 1989, s 17, is punishable by five years' imprisonment or a fine or both on conviction on indictment, and by six months' imprisonment, a fine or both on summary conviction.

Disclosure of information held by a Government department

4.267   Section 59 of the DTA 1994 provides a procedure under which a Government department (defined by sub-s 13 as an authorised department for the purposes of the Crown Proceedings Act 1947) can be required to disclose material held by them which:

(a)   has been submitted to an officer of an authorised Government department by the defendant or by a person who has at any time held property which was realisable property;

(b)   has been made by an officer of an authorised Government department in relation to the defendant or such person; or
(c)   is correspondence which passed between an officer of an authorised department and the defendant or such person.

4.268   An order for production to the High Court may be made without allowing an officer of the material-holding department to appear. When the material has been produced to the High Court, the court may make a further order for the disclosure of the material to a receiver, police officer, member of the Crown Prosecution Service or an officer of Customs and Excise. However, this order cannot be made unless an officer of the material-holding department is permitted to make representations and, except in relation to a receiver, only if it appears to the court that the material is likely to be of substantial value in exercising functions in relation to drug trafficking. Material disclosed to a police officer, Crown prosecutor or Customs and Excise officer may be further disclosed for purposes relating to drug trafficking and material may be produced or disclosed notwithstanding any obligation of secrecy or other restriction on disclosure whether statutory or otherwise (s 59(5)-(10)).

Terrorism investigations

4.269   The Terrorism Act 2000 and the Anti-terrorism Crime and Security Act 2001 contain the statutory provisions to combat the increasing threat from terrorism, and the growth in powers is an indication of the Government's concern. While the former Act was seen as an attempt to address many of the deficiencies of previous legislation, the later Act was passed in the wake of the threat from Al Qa'ida after the 11 September 2001 atrocities. A derogation in connection with the ATCSA 2001 was issued under the Human Rights (Designated Derogation) Order 2001 (SI 2001 No 3644)

4.270   The Terrorism Act 2000 gives the police wide-ranging powers to obtain materials which are relevant to a terrorist investigation. It is this concept, rather than 'a serious arrestable offence', which governs the issue of warrants or orders. A 'terrorism investigation' is defined by TA 2000, s 32 and means an investigation of:
(a)   the commission, preparation or instigation of acts of terrorism;
(b)   an act which appears to have been done for the purposes of terrorism
(c)   the resources of a prescribed organisation
(d)   the possibility of making an order under section 3 (3), (which relates to the prescription of an organisation by the Secretary of State) or
(e)   the commission, preparation or instigation of an offence under the Terrorism Act

Legally privileged, excluded and special procedure material

4.271   Search warrants under the Explosives Act 1875, s 73, the Offences Against the Person Act 1861, s 65 or the Firearms Act 1968, s 46 are obviously available to police investigating terrorism offences but these are subject to s 9(2) of PACE 1984 (art 11(2) of the 1989 Order) which removes the jurisdiction of magistrates to issue such warrants when legally privileged, excluded or special procedure material is involved. Schedule 5 of the Terrorism Act 2000 makes provision:

(i)   for magistrates to issue a search warrant authorising the entry to and search of premises for evidence relevant to a terrorism investigation which does not include legally privileged, excluded or special procedure material, all of which are defined as in PACE 1984 (PACE Order 1989) (Sch 5, para 1);

(ii)   for a circuit (county court) judge to issue an order for the production of or access to excluded or special procedure material (but not legally privileged material), required for the purposes of a terrorism investigation (CJPOA 1994, Sch 5, para 5) to include a person who appears to the judge 'to have in his possession, custody or power any of the material to which the application relates');

(iii) for a circuit (county court) judge to issue a warrant to enter and search premises and to seize excluded or special procedure material (but not legally privileged material) which is required for the purposes of a terrorism investigation Sch 5 para 11;

(iv)   in a case of great emergency a superintendent or above may, by written order, give a constable the power to search which a magistrate could give under (i) above, or which a judge could give under (iii) above Sch 5 para 15.

4.272   The above provisions will now be considered in more detail.

The warrant to search for material other than legally privileged, excluded or special procedure material

4.273   Schedule 5, para 1, provides that a magistrate may issue a warrant, which is similar to the s 8 (art 10) warrant in PACE 1984 and Order. The magistrate must be satisfied that a terrorism investigation is being carried out and that there are reasonable grounds for believing:

(a)   that there is material on the specified premises which is likely to be of substantial value (whether by itself or together with other material) to the investigation;

(b)   that the material does not consist of or include items subject to legal privilege, excluded material or special procedure material; and

(c)   that the issue of a warrant is likely to be necessary in all the circumstances of the case.

4.274   A warrant issued under para 1 authorises the constable to enter the premises, to search them and any person found there, and to seize and retain anything found there or on any person, other than legally privileged material, if there are reasonable grounds for believing:

(a)   that it is likely to be of substantial value (whether by itself or together with other material) to the investigation; and

(b)   that it is necessary to seize it in order to prevent it being concealed, lost, damaged, altered or destroyed (Terrorism Act 2000, Sch 5, paras 1 (3), 5).

4.275   This warrant is subject to ss 15 and 16 of PACE 1984 (arts 17 and 18 of the 1989 Order). Section 15(2)(c) (art 17(2)(c)) requires that the warrant identify (so far as is practicable) the articles (material) to be sought while s 16(8) (art 18(8)) confines the search to the extent required for the purpose for which the warrant was issued. It follows that para 1 (3) rather clumsily incorporates s 19(3) of PACE 1984 (art 21(3) of the 1989 Order) which permits the seizure of anything found in premises which is evidence of an offence, and similarly permits the seizure and retention of anything found on the premises (and persons), including excluded or special procedure material, but does not authorise the search of the premises for such material.

Order for production of excluded or special procedure material

4.276–4.277 Schedule 5, para 5 provide a procedure under which a constable can make application to a circuit judge (county court judge in Northern Ireland) for an order requiring the production to a constable of material consisting of excluded or special procedure material (but not legally privileged material) for him to take away, or to give a constable access to it. The procedure is based on Sch 1 of PACE 1984 (PACE Order 1989) but there are significant differences. They are as follows.

(i) The material must be sought for the purposes of a terrorist investigation not a serious arrestable offence, though such an offence may often have been committed by terrorists (para 5(1)).

(ii) An order may apply to excluded or special procedure material, but not to legally privileged material (para 8). It may also apply to material in the possession, custody or power of government departments (para the CJPOA 19949).

(iii) An order may apply to material which is not yet in existence or in the possession of the person concerned, but is expected to come into existence or become available to the person within 28 days of the date of the order. Such an order will require the person concerned to inform the police as soon as possible after it comes into existence or becomes available to him (para 7(2)(a).

(iv) The conditions of which a judge must be satisfied are simply (a) that a terrorist investigation is being carried out and that there are reasonable grounds for believing that the material is likely to be of substantial value (whether by itself or together with other material) to that investigation; and (b) that it is in the public interest that the material be produced or that access be given to it, having regard–
   (1) to the benefit likely to accrue to the investigation; and that it is in the public interest to produce or have access
   (2) to it having regard to the circumstances under which the person in possession holds it (para 6(3)).

(v) Unlike the Sch 1 procedure there is no provision for the person in possession of the material to contest the application, which is made ex parte. Instead provision is made (by Crown Court Rules) for the person subject to the order to seek the discharge or variation of the order (para 10).

This puts a heavy burden on the circuit (county court) judge who, in the absence of any evidence from the person in possession of the material, must take the police evidence largely, if not entirely, on trust; and the recipient's application for discharge or variation is dependent upon the amount of information which accompanies the order. In *R v Crown Court at Middlesex Guildhall, ex p Salinger* (1993) the Divisional Court, refusing an application for judicial review of a judge's decision to issue an order for the production of a video of interviews with two men charged with terrorist offences (the Lockerbie air crash), and his refusal to discharge the order, regretted the absence of any guidelines on the procedure to be adopted under Sch 7 and gave the following guidance, emphasising that they are not hard and fast rules, since the judge has a discretion as to how information should be disclosed and at what stage.

Guidance of the Divisional Court

(1) The application had to be accompanied by a written statement of the material evidence on which the constable wished to rely, although the statement did not have to disclose the nature and source of sensitive information. The constable had to appear before the judge and be ready to supplement his statement by oral evidence.

(2) If the judge decided to make the order, he had to give directions as to what, if any, information ought to be served with the order. It was desirable that such information be given in writing and be as full as possible without compromising security.

(3) If the judge decided that it was inappropriate to serve any information other than that contained in the order itself, he has to consider whether the information ought to be served in the event of an application to discharge or vary being made. It was desirable, if it could be done without compromising security, that the information be available to the applicant before the hearing of an application to obviate the possible need for an adjournment.

(4) An application to vary or discharge had, if possible, to be made before the judge who made the ex parte order, and it was desirable for the same officer who gave evidence at the ex parte hearing to attend. If the nature of the information itself was sensitive, the judge had to prohibit questions and advise the applicant, if it was the case, that he had been given information which satisfied him that the conditions for making the order had been met; but that the information could not be disclosed.

On an application for discharge or variation the judge can re-examine the order on its merits and not simply consider whether it was unclear, imprecise or technically defective.

(vi) The period within which the material must be produced or access given to it shall be seven days or such longer or shorter period as the judge thinks appropriate in the particular circumstances (para 5(4)(b)).

(vii) The order may, on the application of a constable, include an order that the person who appears to be entitled to grant entry to the premises allow a constable to enter to obtain access to the material (para 5(5)).

As with a Sch 1 order, material held in a computer must be produced in a visible and legible form in which it can be taken away or read (para 8). A para 3 order is to be treated as an order of the Crown Court (para 10) and failure to comply with an order will be contempt of court.

Warrant to search for excluded or special procedure material

4.278 On application by a constable a circuit (county court) judge may issue a warrant if satisfied:

(a) that an order made under para 5 has not been complied with; or

(b) that there are reasonable grounds for believing that there is on the premises material consisting of or including excluded or special procedure material, that it does not include items subject to legal privilege and that the conditions in para 12 (3) and (4) are fulfilled and a condition in para 12(2) is fulfilled in respect of that material.

APPLICATION OF PACE 1984, SS 15 AND 16 (PACE ORDER 1989, ARTS 17 AND 18) AND THE CODE OF PRACTICE

4.279 Sections 15 and 16 of PACE 1984 (arts 17 and 18 of the PACE Order 1989) apply to the issue and execution of search warrants issued under Sch 5 of the Terrorism Act 2000 (see paras 4.14 et seq, ante). Code of Practice B also applies to Sch 5 searches (Code B 1.3(c)). Of particular relevance to such searches is Code B 3.4, which states that no application for a production order or warrant under Sch 5 may be made without the authority of an officer of at least the rank of superintendent, and Code B 3.7 which requires that an application for a warrant under Sch 5 must indicate why the issue of a production order may seriously prejudice the investigation. Code B 2.9 states that in a terrorism investigation search there is no need for the officer conducting the search to identify himself by name, the warrant number is sufficient. Similarly Code B 4.3 states that a Notice of Rights and a copy warrant may be endorsed only with the officer's warrant number. Code B 6.14 requires that an officer of at least the rank of inspector take charge of a search under Sch 5. This also applies to searches under Sch 1 of PACE 1984 and Order and is discussed at para 4.219, ante.

EXPLANATION OF SEIZED OR PRODUCED MATERIAL

4.280 A circuit (county court) judge may, on application by a constable, order any person specified in the order to provide an explanation of any material seized under a warrant issued under paras 1 or 11 or produced under a production order issued under para 5 (para 13(1)). Such an order will not require the disclosure of legally privileged information but a lawyer may be required to disclose the name and address of his client (para 13(3)). Statements made in response to an order may not be used in evidence against the person except for an offence of knowingly or recklessly making a false or misleading statement (para 13(4) and 14). Failure to comply with such an order will be contempt of court.

Written orders to search in urgent cases

4.281 TA 2000, Sch 5, para 15 provides that a police officer of at least the rank of superintendent who has reasonable cause to believe that the case is one of great emergency and that in the interests of the state immediate action is necessary, may by written order signed by him give any constable the authority which may be given by a warrant under paras 1 or 11 of Sch 5. The written order may be accompanied by a notice requiring the person to provide an explanation of any material seized in the same terms and subject to the same conditions as the para 13 requirement considered in para 4.280. Failure to comply with such a notice without reasonable excuse is a summary offence (para 16(5)).

Secretary of State for Northern Ireland's powers in relation to certain terrorist offences.

ORDER TO SEARCH

4.282   The power to order a search applies in Northern Ireland only. Under Sch 5 para 19 the Secretary of State may by a written order which relates to specified premises give to any constable in Northern Ireland an equivalent authority to a search warrant under para I or II. The order shall not be made unless:

(a)   it appears to the Secretary of State that the information which it would be necessary to provide to the court in support of an application for a warrant would if disclosed, be likely to place any person in danger or prejudice the capability of the police to investigate an offence under s 15 (fund raising for terrorist purposes), s 16 (use or possession of money for terrorist purposes), s 17 (making arrangements to enable money to be used for terrorist purposes), s 18 money laundering and s 56 (directing terrorist organisations)

PRODUCTION ORDER

4.283   Under Sch 5 para 20 the Secretary of State may make an order under para 5 provided the conditions at (a) and (b) above apply.

4.284   Under Sch 5 para 21 the Secretary of State may issue a written order to require any person in Northern Ireland who is specified in the order to provide an explanation of any material seized in pursuance of an order under para 19 or produced or made available to a constable in pursuance of an order made by virtue of para 20. Again conditions in 1(a) and (b) above must apply.

POWERS OF SEIZURE

4.285   The powers of seizure contained in s 19 of PACE 1984 (art 21 of the 1989 Order) are available whenever a constable is on premises executing a warrant under paras 1 or 11 or a written order under paras 15 or 16 which give the same authority to enter and search premises. A terrorist investigation is to be treated as an investigation of or in connection with an offence, therefore ss 21 and 22 of PACE 1984 (access to and copying of material seized and retention of such material) apply in respect of material seized or obtained under any of the Sch 5 powers (para 17). This position is the same in Northern Ireland where arts 23 and 24 are expressed to apply to any statutory provision, including any passed or made after the making of the 1989 Order. These are discussed at para 4.47, ante. It will be noted that the warrant powers authorise the search of persons. Such a search must be by a person of the same sex (para 10(2)).

The Security Service Act 1989

4.286 Before the passing of this Act, the security service (MI5) had no statutory basis for its activities. Section 1 of the SSA 1989 remedies this and puts MI5 under the authority of the Home Secretary. Its function is the protection of national security, and in particular its protection against threats from espionage, terrorism and sabotage, from the activities of agents of foreign powers and from actions intended to overthrow or undermine parliamentary democracy by political, industrial or violent means and to safeguard the economic well-being of the UK against threats posed by the actions or intentions of persons outside the British Islands (s 1(2) and (3)). (The Security Service Act 1996 extended the jurisdiction to include acting in support of the prevention and detection of serious crime.) Examples of threats to the economic well-being were given by the Home Secretary as 'a threat from abroad in respect of a commodity' such as oil or the use by foreign powers of 'covert intelligence methods to obtain scientific and technical secrets' (Hansard, HC, vol 145, col 221). Section 2(1) provides for the appointment of a Director General to control the Security Service. He is responsible for the efficiency of the Service and is under a duty to ensure that there are arrangements for securing that no information is obtained by the Service except so far as is necessary for its functions and that such information is not disclosed except for that purpose or the prevention or detection of crime (s 2(2)(a)).

4.287 He must also ensure that the Service takes no action to further the interest of any political party (SSA 1989, s 2(2)(b)). The arrangements under s 2(2)(a) must also ensure that such information is not used for prospective or actual employees except in accordance with provisions approved by the Secretary of State (s 2(3)). Section 2(4) requires an annual report from the Director General.

Grounds for issue

4.288 SSA 1989, s 3(2) gives the Secretary of State the authority to issue a warrant authorising the taking of actions specified in it if he:
(a) thinks it necessary to obtain information which –
  (i) is likely to be of substantial value in assisting the Service to discharge any of its functions; and
  (ii) cannot be reasonably obtained by other means; and
(b) is satisfied that satisfactory arrangements are in force under s 2(2)(a) with respect to the disclosure of the information obtained. The subjective nature of the grounds for issue is only marginally qualified by the requirements of (a)(i) and (ii) and (b).

Procedures for the issue of warrants

4.289   Warrants must be issued personally by the Secretary of State or, in urgent cases, by a senior departmental official of Grade 3 or above. In the latter case the Secretary of State must have authorised the issue of the warrant, by telephone or similar means to the official, and a statement of this fact must be endorsed on the warrant (SSA 1989, s 3(3)). Warrants issued by the Secretary of State last for six months but may be renewed by him at any time before they expire for a further six months from the date of renewal. An urgent warrant issued by a senior official lasts no more than two working days. It can, of course, be replaced by a warrant issued by the Secretary of State but it seems that, assuming the matter is still urgent and the Secretary of State is not available in person, further warrants may be issued by that official (s 3(4) and (5)). The Secretary of State is legally bound to cancel any warrant if satisfied that the action authorised by it is no longer necessary (s 3(6)). Unlike search warrants which may be executed only once, a s 3 warrant stays in force for six months (or two working days if an urgent warrant) and authorises actions throughout that period.

4.290   Section 4 provides for the appointment of a Security Service Commissioner by the Prime Minister. The Commissioner must be, or have been, a judge of the High Court or above, whose functions include the keeping under review of the exercise of the Secretary of State's power to issue warrants under s 3. The present incumbent, Lord Justice Stuart-Smith, in his first annual report under the 1989 Act, declined 'in the public interest' to disclose the number of warrants issued under s 3 in 1990. The 'comparatively small number' of warrants issued were all found to have been properly issued under the 1989 Act.

The Criminal Justice (Confiscation) (Northern Ireland) Orders 1990 and 1993

4.291   The principal Order is the 1990 Order. The 1993 Order amends and adds to the 1990 Order by creating new offences and extending existing offences to correspond with provisions in the Criminal Justice Act 1993, which itself amended the DTOA 1986 and which are now incorporated into the DTA 1994, and repeals arts 30(3) and (5) and 36 of the principal Order.

4.292   The principal Order provides:
(a)   for courts to order the confiscation of assets of offenders convicted of highly profitable crime;
(b)   for courts to order the confiscation of proceeds of drug trafficking;
(c)   for certain enhancement of court enforcement powers in order to secure payment of confiscation orders; and
(d)   further provision in connection with drug trafficking.

4.293   In this respect the Order does for Northern Ireland what the Drug Trafficking Act 1994 and the Criminal Justice Act 1988 does for the rest of the UK. So far as investigative powers are concerned, art 31 of the Order provides for a county court judge to make an order requiring the production of, or access to, material in connection with a drug trafficking investigation in exactly the same terms as s 55 of the DTA 1994 (see para 4.256, ante). Article 32 authorises the issue of a warrant to search for and seize such material in exactly the same terms as s 56 of the DTA 1994 (see para 4.121, ante). Article 33 provides that access and retention requirements imposed in respect of seized material by arts 23 and 24 of the PACE (NI) Order 1989, apply to material seized under arts 31 and 32 of the 1990 Order. The powers of seizure when a constable is lawfully on premises provided by art 21 of the 1989 Order are available when a constable is lawfully on premises enforcing an order or executing a warrant under the 1990 Order. 'Items subject to legal privilege', 'excluded material' and 'premises' are defined as in the 1989 Order. As in the DTA 1994 'items subject to legal privilege' and 'excluded material' cannot be the subject of an order or warrant under the 1990 Order. Article 35 creates offences of prejudicing an investigation into drug trafficking by disclosing information about orders or warrants applied for or issued, which equate with those under s 58 of the DTA 1994 (see para 4.264, ante). Article 36 provides the incentive to assist drug trafficking investigations by providing immunity from civil or criminal liability to persons who disclose such information, in the same terms as s 50(3) of the DTA 1994 (see para 4.124, ante). Article 34 of the 1990 Order provides a procedure under which Government departments may be required to disclose material held by them, which equates to that provided by s 59 of the DTA 1994 (see para 4.267, ante).

The Intelligence Services Act 1994

4.294   As we have seen, the Security Service Act 1989 placed MI5 on a statutory footing. The Intelligence Services Act does the same for MI6 and its communications arm the Government Communications Headquarters (GCHQ), and in much the same way. The 1994 Act seeks to define the activities of MI6 and GCHQ and places them under the control of the Secretary of State. A tribunal and Commissioner will scrutinise their operational activities and a parliamentary committee will oversee the non-operation activities. The functions of the Intelligence Service are broadly stated in s 1(1):
(a)   to obtain and provide information relating to the actions or intentions of persons outside the British Islands; and
(b)   to perform other tasks relating to the actions and intentions of such persons.

4.295   Those functions are stated to be exercisable only:
(a)   in the interests of national security, with particular reference to the defence and foreign policies of Her Majesty's Government in the UK; or
(b)   in the interests of the economic well-being of the UK; or
(c)   in support of the prevention or detection of serious crime (s 1(2)).

4.296   GCHQ's functions are set out in s 3. The central function is to monitor or interfere with electromagnetic, acoustic and other emissions and to obtain and provide information derived from or related to such emissions or equipment and from encrypted material. Its functions are also only exercisable as in (a) to (c) above (s 3(2)). The operation of the Intelligence Service is under the control of a Chief of that Service (s 2), and the operation of GCHQ under a Director (s 4), both appointed by the Secretary of State.

4.297   Sections 5 and 6 provide for the authorisation of actions by the issue of a warrant by the Secretary of State in terms similar to that in the 1989 Act. Section 5(1) provides that no entry on or interference with property (trespass to land or property) shall be unlawful if authorised by a warrant issued by the Secretary of State. Such a warrant may be issued on the application of the Security Service, the Intelligence Service or GCHQ and can authorise the taking of such action as is specified in the warrant in respect of specified property or in respect of wireless telegraphy so specified if the Secretary of State:
(a)   thinks it is necessary for the action to be taken on the ground that it is likely to be of substantial value in assisting the applicants in carrying out their functions; and
(b)   is satisfied that what the action seeks to achieve cannot reasonably be achieved by other means; and
(c)   is satisfied that satisfactory arrangements are in force under s 2(2)(a) of the Security Services Act 1989 (arrangements for disclosure of information obtained under a warrant) and that any information obtained under the warrant will be subject to those arrangements.

4.298   This is very similar to the warrant provisions of the 1989 Act but significantly sub-s (3) of the 1994 Act provides that a warrant authorising the taking of action in support of the prevention or detection of serious crime may not relate to property in the British Islands. This appears to recognise that PACE 1984, together with the other statutory provisions discussed in this chapter, provides ample powers to deal with serious crime within the UK.

4.299   Subsection (4) permits the Security Services to make an application for a warrant under sub-s 5(2) of the 1994 Act authorising the Service (or a person acting on its behalf) to take such action as is specified on behalf of the Intelligence Service or GCHQ and where such a warrant is issued the functions of the Security Service shall include the carrying out of that function whether or not it would otherwise be within its function. However, such an application can only be made if: (a) the action is one in respect of which the Intelligence Service or GCHQ could make such an application; and (b) it is not taken in support of the prevention or detection of serious crime (sub-s (5)). The procedure for the issue and the duration of such warrants is governed by s 6 of the 1994 Act, which is the same as the provisions in s 3 of the 1989 Act.

The Official Secrets Act 1989

4.300   The Official Secrets Act 1989 reforms the law by repealing the controversial 'catch-all' provisions of s 2 of the Official Secrets Act 1911. The law now concentrates on the nature of the information disclosed and the damage done by such disclosure. It replaces the broad terms of s 2 with six defined categories of official information and makes the unauthorised disclosure of them an offence. These are:

(1) security and intelligence;
(2) defence;
(3) international relations;
(4) information obtained in confidence from other states or from international organisations;
(5) information likely to result in an offence or other related consequences;
(6) special investigations under statutory warrant issued under the Security Service Act 1989, s 3, or under s 5 of the Intelligence Services Act 1994 or by an authorisation given under s 7 of that Act, or the Interception of Communications Act 1985, s 2.

4.301 In categories (1) to (5) it must be established that specific damage has been caused by the unauthorised disclosure. Where the accused is not a Crown servant or government contractor, it is a defence for him to prove that he did not know, or had no reasonable cause to believe, that the specific damage was likely to be caused. As far as present or former Crown servants or a Government contractor are concerned, any unauthorised disclosure of information relating to security or intelligence will be treated as harmful. In category (6) the prosecution must prove unauthorised disclosure of information about, or obtained by, action under a warrant under the 1985 or 1989 Acts. Section 11(1) and (2) of the Official Secrets Act 1989 makes the offences under the Act arrestable offences by inserting into s 24(2) of PACE 1984 a reference to offences under the 1989 Act (other than offences under s 8(1), (4) or (5)) (see para 5.13, post). Section 11(3) extends the power to issue search warrants under the Official Secrets Act 1911, s 9(1), to these arrestable offences and applies the restriction on the issue of such warrants in respect of legally privileged, excluded or special procedure material, imposed by s 9(2) of PACE 1984 (art 11(2) of the 1989 Order), to s 9(1) of the 1911 Act. The effect is to require an application under Sch 1 of PACE 1984 (or Order) whenever the material sought could have been obtained under a s 9(1) warrant, had the material not been legally privileged, excluded or special procedure material.

The Criminal Justice Act 1987

4.302 Section 1 of this Act establishes a Serious Fraud Office, presided over by a Director under the superintendence of the Attorney-General, to investigate and prosecute serious or complex frauds. The SFO is unique in that it comprises lawyers and police officers operating as an investigative team assisted by accountants. Section 2 provides the investigatory powers. They are based on the powers given to inspectors of the Department of Trade and Industry by the Companies Act 1985 and the Financial Services Act 1986. Cases referred to the SFO will only be investigated by them if it appears to the Director on reasonable grounds to involve serious or complex fraud. He must be satisfied that either the fact and/or the law are complex, or there is great public interest or concern. Account is also taken of the need to use the SFO's s 2 powers, and normally whether the value of the alleged fraud exceeds £1 million. However, the s 2 powers are exercisable not only in relation to a person suspected of such fraud, but also to 'the affairs, or aspects of the affairs of any person'.

Procedure

4.303   The Director may by notice in writing to the person whose affairs are to be investigated ('the person under investigation'), or any other person whom he believes has relevant information:

(1)   require him to attend at a specified time and place, and answer questions or otherwise furnish information with respect to any matter relevant to the investigation (s 2(2)). There is no right to refuse to answer such questions on the grounds that to do so may incriminate the person and there is no right to obtain particulars of the investigation (*R v Serious Fraud Office, ex p Nadir* (1990)). However, any statement made in response to such questioning cannot be used as evidence in relation to the offence under investigation except as a prior inconsistent statement (s 2(8)). It is an offence knowingly or recklessly to make a false or misleading statement (s 2(14)) and any statement obtained under s 2(2) can be used as evidence of that offence. A person cannot be required to disclose legally privileged information but a lawyer can be required to disclose the name and address of a client (s 2(9)). This overrides the duty not to do so except on the order of a court (see the *Professional Conduct of Solicitors* (1993), para 16.04 and *Pascall v Galinski* (1969)). There is no protection for information which is otherwise confidential except that a banker can only be required to breach an obligation of confidence if the person to whom it is owed consents or the requirement is made by the Director (or his delegate) personally;

(2)   require him to produce at a specified time and place any specified documents which appear to the Director to relate to any matter relevant to the investigation or any other document of a specified class which appear to him so to relate (s 2(3)). The Director can require an explanation of any document produced and may take copies or extracts from them. If they are not produced the person required to produce them may be required to state, to the best of his knowledge, where they are (s 2(3)(a) and (b)). 'Documents' includes information recorded in any form (s 2(18)), and, so, for example, requirement to produce a computer print-out or a transcript of recorded conversation can be made. The power to require an explanation of documents under s 2(3)(a) means that documents which are not comprehensible to the investigator can be required to be translated into a comprehensible form. As with information, legally privileged documents cannot be the subject of a requirement under s 2(3) (s 2(9)) and bankers cannot be required to produce documents in breach of their obligation of confidence except with the consent of the person to whom it is owed or if the Director (or his delegate) personally makes the requirement. Otherwise there is no protection for excluded

or special procedure material as defined by PACE 1984 (PACE Order 1989). It should be noted that the requirement under s 2(2) and (3) (and the search warrant under s 2(4)) is not confined to evidence likely to be of substantial value to an investigation (as is the case with PACE Act and Order production orders and warrants and other orders and warrants considered in this section). Relevance to the investigation is the only criterion.

4.304 The 1987 Act provided that the s 2 powers could be used on a request made by the Attorney General of the Isle of Man, Jersey and Guernsey. Section 164(2) of the Criminal Justice and Public Order Act 1994 amends s 2 to permit the exercise of the s 2 powers on the request of the Secretary of State, acting under s 49(2) of the Criminal Justice (International Co-operation) Act 1990, in response to a request from an overseas court, tribunal or authority. However, the s 2 powers cannot be exercised for an overseas authority unless the Director is satisfied on reasonable grounds that the offence in respect of which the request is made involves serious or complex fraud (s 2(1A) and (1B) as inserted by s 164 of the CJPOA 1994). Provision is made for the transmission of any evidence obtained in similar terms to those in the Criminal Justice (International Co-operation) Act 1990

Search warrant

4.305 Section 2(4) authorises a magistrate to issue a warrant to enter and search premises for documents relevant to an investigation if the magistrate is satisfied that there are reasonable grounds for believing:
(a)
    (i)   that a person has failed to comply with an obligation to produce them under s 2(3); or
    (ii)   it is not practicable to serve a notice under s 2(3); or
    (iii) that the service of a notice might seriously prejudice the investigation; and
(b) that the documents are on the premises specified in the information (s 2(4)).

4.306 The warrant authorises a constable to enter (using such force as is reasonably necessary) and search the premises and to take possession of the documents specified and to take such steps as are necessary to preserve them and prevent interference with them (s 2(5)). This power must be read in conjunction with the powers of seizure, access and retention contained in ss 19-22 of PACE 1984 (arts 21-24 of the 1989 Order), which apply to this warrant power. It would therefore seem that the power to take possession and steps to preserve them is intended to deal with the situation in which there is a large number of documents which cannot immediately be removed from the premises. Thus a files storage room may be secured and only supervised access, or no access, allowed to it during the course of the search. Sections 15 and 16 of PACE 1984 (arts 17 and 18 of the PACE Order 1989) (para 4.14, ante) apply to this warrant as does Code of Practice B (see Code B 1.3(a)). It follows that the application must be by written information (complaint in Northern Ireland) on oath (see also s 15(4) of the 1984

Act) which must specify the premises to be entered and to identify, so far as is practicable, the documents sought. Similarly the warrant, which authorises entry on one occasion only (s 15(5), art 17(5)), must specify the premises and documents sought. Though Code B 3.7 does not specifically apply to applications for this warrant, the application should indicate why it is believed that service of a notice requiring production of the documents might seriously prejudice the investigation. In addition to the requirements of s 16 (art 18), s 2(6) and (7) of the 1987 Act require that unless it is not practicable in the circumstances, a constable executing a warrant under s 2(4) must be accompanied by a member of the SFO or a person, though not a member of the SFO, who has been designated by the Director to accompany him. The former will usually be the lawyer supervising the investigation; the latter may well be an accountant who is assisting and advising the investigation. As with the requirement to produce documents, a warrant cannot authorise the seizure of legally privileged documents but there is no protection for excluded or special procedure material. Section 2(10), which gives limited protection to bankers, appears to apply only to a requirement under s 2(3).

Offences

4.307   It is an offence knowingly or recklessly to make a false or misleading statement in response to a requirement under s 2 (s 2(14) and (15)). It is also an offence for a person who knows or suspects that an investigation by the police or the SFO into serious or complex fraud is being or is likely to be carried out to falsify, dispose of, or to cause or permit the falsification, concealment, destruction or disposal of, documents which he knows or suspects are or would be relevant to an investigation. It is a defence for the person accused to prove that he had no intention of concealing the facts disclosed by the documents (s 2(16) and (17)).

The Bankers' Books Evidence Act 1879, s 7

4.308   The procedure under s 9(2) and Sch 1 of PACE 1984 (art 11(2) and Sch 1 of the NI Order), under which a judge may issue an order for access to or the production of special procedure material, has considerably reduced the reliance on s 7 of the Bankers' Books Evidence Act 1879 but this Act remains in force and may be used in those cases in which a serious arrestable offence is not involved. Section 7 provides that: on the application of any party to legal proceedings a judge may order that such a party be at liberty to inspect and make copies of any entry in a banker's books for any of the purposes of such proceedings. That order may be made without summoning the bank or other party, and must be served on the bank three clear days before the order is to be obeyed, unless the judge otherwise orders. The following may be noted.
(1)   The Act is confined to banks. This is a severe limitation given the increased role of building societies and other financial institutions.
(2)   The Act is confined to bankers' books. While this includes the computerised accounts, it does not include such things as the bank manager's notes and diary, paid cheques and credit slips, for which a witness summons will be required.

(3) Legal proceedings (criminal or civil) must have been instituted by charge or summons in criminal cases.

(4) Before making the order the judge should satisfy himself that the application is not a 'fishing expedition' to find material on which to hang a charge, but should consider whether the prosecution, who normally make such an application, have in their possession other evidence against the defendant (*Williams v Summerfield* (1972)).

(5) The order ought to be limited to a certain specific period and ought not to be oppressive (*R v Marlborough Street Magistrates' Court, ex p Simpson* (1980)).

(6) The fact that the defendant has given notice that he intends to plead guilty is not a reason for refusing the order (*Owen v Sambrook* (1981)).

(7) Section 7 gives the court power to authorise the inspection of the bank account of a person who is not a party to the proceedings, but this power should only be exercised within narrow limits (see the twofold test set out by Lord Esher MR in *South Staffordshire Tramways Co v Ebbsmith* (1895)).

(8) An order may be made after the conclusion of a trial as well as before trial. This might be useful in criminal confiscation proceedings where the Drug Trafficking Act 1994 or PACE 1984 procedures are not available (see *D B Deniz Nakliyati TAS v Yugopetrol* (1991)).

CROSS-BORDER ENFORCEMENT

Criminal Justice and Public Order Act 1994, ss 136-141

Warrants of arrest

4.309 CJPOA 1994, s 136 permits a warrant of arrest of a person charged with an offence issued in England, Wales or Northern Ireland, to be executed in Scotland (without endorsement) by any constable or police force in the country of issue or the country of execution as well as by any other person within the directions in the warrant (s 136(1)). Similarly, such a warrant issued in Scotland or Northern Ireland may be executed (without endorsement) in England or Wales (s 136(2)) and such warrants issued in England or Wales or Scotland may be executed (without endorsement) in Northern Ireland (s 136(3)). The section applies equally to warrants of commitment and warrants to arrest witnesses issued by a judicial authority in England and Wales or Northern Ireland; and warrants for committal or imprisonment of witnesses issued by such authority in Scotland (s 136(7)). A person arrested under a warrant shall be taken, as soon as reasonably practicable, to any place to which he is committed by, or may be conveyed under, the warrant. Section 136(5) provides that a constable executing a warrant may use reasonable force and shall have the powers of search conferred by s 139. That section provides powers to search the person on arrest which are identical to those provided by s 32 of PACE (Art 34 of the 1989 Order) (see para 4.75, post) and powers to search premises which are identical to those in s 32(2)(b) of PACE (Art 34(2)(b)). In each case the powers are subject to the same requirements and limitations as in the PACE Act and NI Order and the definition of premises is the same. Non-Scottish constables executing a warrant of arrest in Scotland have the same powers and duties as they would have if the execution had been by a constable of a Scottish police force and the person arrested has the same rights as if arrested by such a constable. An English or Welsh police officer executing a warrant in Northern Ireland is governed by PACE and vice versa.

Powers of arrest

4.310   CJPOA 1994, s 137 provides that subject to the conditions specified in sub-s (4) being satisfied, any constable of a police force in England or Wales who has reasonable grounds for suspecting that an offence has been committed or attempted in England or Wales and that the suspected offender is in Scotland or Northern Ireland, may arrest without warrant the suspected person wherever he is in Scotland or Northern Ireland (s 137(1)). Similarly, any constable in Scotland may arrest a suspected offender anywhere in England, Wales or Northern Ireland (s137(2)) as may a constable in Northern Ireland arrest a suspected offender in England, Wales or Scotland (s 137(3)). The conditions applicable to sub-ss (1) and (3) above are that:

(a)   the suspected offence is an arrestable offence (see PACE, s 24 (Art 26) discussed at paras 5.28-5.54, post); or

(b)   in the case of any other offence, it appears to the constable that the service of a summons is impracticable or inappropriate for any of the reasons specified in s 138(3). (These are the arrest conditions to be found in PACE, s 25 (Art 27) discussed at paras 5.55-5.74) (s 137(4).)

The condition in respect of sub-s (2) is that it appears to the constable that it would have been lawful to arrest had the suspected person been in Scotland (s 137(5)).

An English or Welsh or Northern Irish police officer arresting in Scotland must take the arrested person to the nearest convenient designated police station in England or Northern Ireland, or to a designated police station in the police area in England, Wales or Northern Ireland in which the offence is being investigated, as soon as reasonably practicable. If the person is arrested in Northern Ireland by English or Welsh police the duty is to take the person to the nearest convenient DPS in England or Wales or to a DPS in the police area in which the offence is being investigated. Similarly if a Northern Ireland police officer arrests in England or Wales (s 137(7)). English or Welsh police officers arresting in Scotland or Northern Ireland, or Northern Irish police arresting in England, Wales or Scotland, may use reasonable force and have the powers of arrest and search conferred by s 139. As indicated above these are the powers to search persons or premises on arrest conferred by s 32 (Art 34) of PACE (Order).

The Codes of Practice do not directly apply to English, Welsh or Northern Irish constables exercising powers in Scotland, but they will do so indirectly for, as indicated in para 2.37, ante, the Codes enshrine certain principles of fairness which are applicable whether or not the officers are statutorily bound by them.

The protection of s 89(2) of the Police Act 1996 (assaults on and obstruction of a constable in the execution of his duty) is extended to Scottish or Northern Irish constables executing a warrant or otherwise acting in England or Wales under the above provisions by adding a new sub-s (4) to s 51. Similarly, the English and Northern Irish constable is given the protection of the Scottish equivalent of s 51 contained in s 41 of the Police (Scotland) Act 1967 when acting under the above provisions in Scotland, and the English or Scottish constable executing a warrant or otherwise acting under the above provisions in Northern Ireland is given the protection of the Northern Irish equivalent of s 51 contained in s 7 of the Criminal Justice (Miscellaneous Provisions) Act Northern Ireland 1968 (CJPOA 1994, Sch 10, paras 14, 18 and 25).

The Crime (International Co-operation) Act 2003

4.311   Increasing freedom of movement of persons and globalisation of markets have combined to bring about a situation in which the location of witnesses and other evidence is often outside the jurisdiction. A number of measures were implemented by the Criminal Justice (International Co-operation) Act 1990 which have been replaced and extended by the C(IC)A 2003.

Service of overseas process in the UK

4.312   C(IC)A 2003, s 1 provides that where the Secretary of State receives any process or other document, together with a request for the process or document to be served on a person in the UK, the Secretary of State will make arrangements to serve the process or document or forward it to the appropriate police officer to enable service. C(IC)A 2003, s 2 contains the requirement that the process must be accompanied by a notice which sets out the following:
(i)   there is no obligation under the law of the UK imposed by the service
(ii)   the person may wish to seek advice as to the possible consequences of failing to comply with the process under the law of the country where it was issues
(iii)   under the law of that country he may not be accorded the same rights and privileges as a party or a witness as would be accorded to him in proceedings in the UK.
This does not mean that the Secretary of State will receive a request for process in every case in which a foreign authority wishes to serve process in the UK. Article 5 of the Mutual Legal Assistance Convention (MLAT) provides the process will normally be posted direct to the person unless there are reasons for considering that despatch by post will be ineffective.

Requests for assistance in obtaining evidence abroad

4.313   C(IC)A 2003, s 7 deals with the making of requests for the obtaining of evidence overseas for use in the UK. There will be circumstances where informal arrangements will be made between investigating authorities; s 7 sets out the formal arrangements. An application must be made by the prosecuting authority to a judge in circumstances where assistance is required to obtain any evidence where there are reasonable grounds to suspect that an offence has been committed and that proceedings have been instituted or the offence is being investigated. A *designated* prosecuting authority may itself request assistance without the assistance of the court (s 7(5)). Designated authorities include the Crown Prosecution Service and the Serious Fraud Office. The request for assistance under s 7 may be sent to a court or to any authority recognised by the government of the country in the jurisdiction in question (C(IC)A 2003, s 8). Where evidence is obtained pursuant to a request for assistance under s 7 the evidence may be not, without the consent of the appropriate overseas authority, be used for any other purpose other than that specified in the request.

Foreign surveillance operations

4.314   C(IC)A 2003, s 83 inserts s 76A to the Regulation of Investigatory Powers Act 2000 to permit foreign police or customs officers, who are carrying out lawful surveillance, to continue the operation in the UK. The Schengen Convention provided that officers keeping a person under surveillance in their own country could require neighbouring Schengen countries to provide assistance if the surveillance crossed their borders.

C(IC)A 2003, s 76A provides authority for foreign officers to continue surveillance for a period up to five hours from the time of entry into the UK. This is to enable arrangements to be made for UK officers to continue the surveillance. The section does not come into force until an order under sub-s (9) has been laid before Parliament and approved by a resolution of each House.

Further provisions

4.315   The C(IC)A 2003 contains other provision in relation to the following:
- freezing orders – ss 11 and 12
- nominating a court to receive evidence – s 15
- extension of statutory search powers – s 16
- search warrants in relation to offences committed outside the UK – s 17
- provisions relating to evidence seized which is required for proceedings outside the UK – s 19
- overseas freezing orders – s 20.

5 Arrest

INTRODUCTION AND HUMAN RIGHTS

5.1   An arrest is a detention the purpose of which is to bring the detainee into the custody of the law (Williams, 1954). Every year just under two million people are arrested by the police. A study conducted in 1993-4 (Home Office Research Study 185) found that in three-quarters of cases, arrests were made as a result of a reaction to information – eg from the public or through the police control room. 24% of arrests were the result of 'proactive' policing – either as a result of surveillance or enquiries, or stop and search procedures. Around 1,313,000 persons were arrested for notifiable offences in 2002/03 (Ayres, Murray and Fiti (2003)).

5.2   The exercise of a power of arrest has serious implications and must be carried out lawfully, in a non-discriminatory way and only when there are reasonable grounds to suspect that the person arrested has committed, is committing or is about to commit an offence. Detention or arrest in order to bring a person to court is an exception to the right to liberty provided for in Article 5 of the ECHR.

5.3   Article 5 provides:

(1) Everyone has the right to liberty and security of the person. No one shall be deprived of his liberty save in the following cases and in accordance with a procedure prescribed by law:

(a)   the lawful detention of a person after conviction by a competent court;

(b)   the lawful arrest or detention of a person for non-compliance with the lawful order of a court or in order to secure the fulfilment of any obligation prescribed by law;

(c)   the lawful arrest or detention of a person effected for the purpose of bringing him before the competent legal authority on reasonable suspicion of having committed an offence or when it is reasonably considered necessary to prevent his committing an offence or fleeing after having done so;

(d)   the detention of a minor by lawful order for the purpose of educational supervision or his lawful detention for the purpose of bringing him before the competent legal authority;

(e) the lawful detention of persons for the prevention of the spreading of infectious diseases, of persons of unsound mind, alcoholics or drug addicts or vagrants;

(f) the lawful arrest or detention of a person to prevent his effecting an unauthorised entry into the country or of a person against whom action is being taken with a view to deportation or extradition.

(2) Everyone who is arrested shall be informed promptly, in a language which he understands, of the reasons for his arrest and of any charge against him.

(3) Everyone arrested or detained in accordance with the provisions of paragraph (1)(c) of this Article shall be brought promptly before a judge or other officer authorised by law to exercise judicial power and shall be entitled to trial within a reasonable time or to release pending trial. Release may be conditioned by guarantees to appear for trial.

(4) Everyone who is deprived of his liberty by arrest or detention shall be entitled to take proceedings by which the lawfulness of his detention shall be decided speedily by a court and his release ordered if the detention is not lawful.

(5) Everyone who has been the victim of arrest or detention in contravention of the provisions of this Article shall have an enforceable right to compensation.

5.4   Article 5 (1)(c) sets out the grounds for arrest they are: the existence of reasonable suspicion that the person has committed an offence, when it is reasonably considered necessary to prevent a person committing an offence; and when it is reasonably considered necessary to prevent the person fleeing after having committed an offence. These requirements are contained in domestic law through PACE provisions. In every case the purpose must be to bring the person arrested before a competent judicial authority but the existence of such a purpose is to be considered independently of its achievement (*Brogan v United Kingdom* (1988)). This means that release without charge will not necessarily breach Article 5. Nor does the absence of proceedings mean that the arrest is unlawful. There may however be circumstances where unlawful arrest could result in a stay of proceedings for abuse of process (Corker and Young, 2003) and in rare circumstances evidence could be exclude under s 78 of PACE. The more likely remedy would lie in an action for damages (Clayton and Tomlinson, 2004).

5.5   Article 5 (2) sets out the requirement that a person arrested must be promptly informed in a language which he understand of the reasons for his arrest and of any charges made against him. These requirements again are broadly contained in the PACE regime.

The development of the law of arrest

5.6   This chapter is concerned in the main with the power to arrest a person without a magistrates' warrant. According to Blackstone, arrest is 'the apprehending or restraining of one's person in order to be forthcoming to answer an alleged or suspected crime' (Commentaries (1830) p 289). Faced with the changes wrought by PACE 1984 a modern-day Blackstone might amend the definition to read:

> 'Arrest is the apprehending or restraining of one's person in order to detain him at a police station while the alleged or suspected crime is investigated and in order that he be forthcoming to answer an alleged or suspected crime.'

5.7 This is because the law of arrest is no longer simply machinery for ensuring the appearance of an alleged offender at court to answer the charges laid. The power to arrest without warrant has developed over the years as an investigative tool for getting a suspected person into a police station where he can be questioned about the offence of which he is suspected. Arrest can also be preventive, as where a person is arrested to prevent a breach of the peace; and protective, as where mentally ill or inebriated persons are arrested for their own protection. The commission of an offence is not a prerequisite of such arrests but the vast majority of arrests without a warrant are for offences and justify the above definition. Arrest without warrant on reasonable suspicion, as indicated in paras 2.02-2.08, ante, requires no more than a limited degree of suspicion but was, in the early part of this century, subject to the principle that arrest at such an early stage in the investigation was the exception, the general rule being that arrest should take place at the end of the investigation. There were then restrictions on the questioning of suspects in custody following an arrest and there was therefore no advantage to the police in arresting at an early stage in the investigation. To avoid this constraint on custodial questioning the practice of inviting a person to attend at a police station to assist the police in their inquiries developed. Those who accepted the invitation seldom did so voluntarily, believing that they were under the coercion of a legal authority. Hence the media phrase 'assisting with inquiries', which is apt to cover a lawful arrest, a genuine voluntary attendance or an unlawful detention.

5.8 In 1964 the Judges' Rules, which had been developed by the Judges and the Home Office to control custodial questioning of suspects, were amended to permit custodial questioning following a lawful arrest, provided the person had not been charged with or informed that he would be prosecuted for the alleged offence (Home Office Circular 89/1978 Rule 1). In 1967 s 2 of the Criminal Law Act abolished the distinction between felonies and misdemeanours and created the concept of the arrestable offence, an offence for which the sentence was fixed by law or was under any statute punishable by five or more years' imprisonment. This included all former felonies and many misdemeanours and, as the law was brought up to date in later years, almost all offences of theft, criminal damage or violence, which account for the great majority of serious offences dealt with by the police, were arrestable on reasonable suspicion. These changes led to arrest on reasonable suspicion becoming the rule rather than the exception, and to arrest for questioning becoming accepted practice. Even so the practice of inviting persons to a police station to 'help with inquiries' continued to be used to avoid the constraints which followed a lawful arrest.

5.9   The Royal Commission on Criminal Procedure (1981) acknowledged the fact that the primary purpose of arrest in modern times is to get the suspect into a police station where detention, questioning and other forms of investigation will follow (as will be seen in Chapter 6, post, the legal controls on police detention proved ineffective and further facilitated this change of purpose). The police station has long been recognised as a psychologically coercive venue in which the pressure to make admissions or confessions can be more effectively applied. Despite or because of this, changes in the law since the beginning of this century combined to make the police station the focal point of the investigation of crime.

5.10   The changed role of the law of arrest was given the stamp of judicial approval by the House of Lords in *Holgate-Mohammed v Duke* (1984) before PACE 1984 came into force. A constable arrested a person whom he reasonably suspected of burglary, solely because he believed the offence could not be proved without a confession and that such a confession was more likely to be forthcoming if she were questioned in, what is accepted to be, the coercive atmosphere of a police station. The House of Lords held that in exercising his discretion to arrest (under powers similar to those in s 24(5), (6) and (7) of PACE 1984 (Art 26(5), (6) and (7)), the constable was entitled to take that fact into consideration. Thus arrest for questioning was lawful at common law. PACE 1984 set the seal on that development by providing a form of summary arrest for all serious crime and by authorising the detention of the arrestee without charge in order to secure or preserve evidence of the offence for which he was arrested or to obtain such evidence by questioning him.

Proposals for reform

5.11   The proposals of the Royal Commission on Criminal Procedure had:

'... two main and interrelated objectives: to restrict the circumstances in which the police can exercise the power to deprive a person of his liberty to those in which it is genuinely necessary to enable them to execute their duty to prevent the commission of offences, to investigate crime, and to bring suspected offenders before the courts; and to simplify, clarify and rationalise the existing statutory powers of arrest, confirming the present rationale for the use of those powers.' (Report, para 3.75)

5.12   The Royal Commission, while accepting the 'necessity principle' which would have restricted the exercise of powers of arrest to those occasions when it was necessary according to stated criteria, declined to apply it at the point of arrest. Instead they proposed that it apply when the question of detention following arrest is being considered in the police station. PACE 1984, which is the source of most powers of arrest without warrant, also declined to apply a necessity principle at the point of arrest in respect of serious offences but does so at the point of arrest for minor offences. The principle is also applied when the detention of a person following an arrest without warrant for any offence is being considered.

The present law of arrest

5.13 The simplification of the law intended by PACE 1984 has not been achieved. The foundation for simplification was laid down by the repeal of all the statutory powers of arrest, including those in local Acts, which authorised the arrest of a person without warrant for an offence, or to arrest a person otherwise than for an offence without a warrant or an order of the court, which existed before PACE 1984 came into force (s 26(1), (Art 28(1)). The majority of the police powers to arrest without warrant are contained in PACE 1984 which broke new ground in providing a potential power of arrest for every criminal offence (ss 24, 25, 26 and Sch 2, arts 26, 27, 28 and Sch 2). However, matters are complicated by the creation of two categories of offences and four categories of powers of arrest.

(1) The first category of offence and first category of arrest power is the 'arrestable offence'. It carries with it a power of summary arrest; that is, a person reasonably suspected of having committed an arrestable offence may be arrested without more. There are also a number of investigative powers attached to an arrest for an arrestable offence and, if it is a serious arrestable offence, further investigative powers are available. This category includes all the serious criminal offences which were previously arrestable offences, the serious common law offences which were not previously within that definition, and a number of other offences which, while not necessarily serious, are included in order to attract to them the additional investigative powers which are available on an arrest for an arrestable offence.

(2) The second category of offence and second category of arrest power may be termed the 'general offence'. This includes all offences which are not arrestable offences or the subject of a power of arrest preserved by Sch 2, and offences against local byelaws. A person reasonably suspected of having committed a general offence may only be arrested if it appears to the constable that a summons cannot be served or is inappropriate in the circumstances. Conditions, known as 'general arrest conditions', one of which must be satisfied before a constable can arrest for a general offence, are set out in s 25(3) (Art 27(3)) and import the 'necessity principle' in respect of this category of offence. Within this category are all the summary offences, including motoring offences, from depositing litter to driving without lights, and summary offences created after PACE 1984 was passed, eg s 14 of the Cinemas Act 1985.

(3) The third category of powers of arrest may be termed 'preserved powers of arrest'. These are a number of statutory powers of arrest created before PACE 1984 (PACE Order 1989) in respect of offences which, though not serious enough to be categorised as arrestable offences, require a power of summary arrest and such powers are preserved by s 26(2) and Sch 2 (Art 28(2) and Sch 2). As statutes are updated this category will be subject to deletion.

(4) The fourth category of powers of arrest may be termed 'post-PACE Act powers of arrest'. These are powers of arrest provided by statute passed since PACE 1984 (PACE Order 1989) when new offences are created, or old offences updated. The offences are not serious enough to be arrestable offences but the general arrest

conditions in s 25 of the PACE (Art 27) are considered to be inappropriate. The Public Order Act 1986 and the Criminal Justice and Public Order Act 1994 are examples of post-PACE Acts creating offences and providing a summary power of arrest. This category will be added to over the years by the inclusion of new arrest powers in the offence-creating statute.

5.14 The criterion of 'reasonable grounds for suspecting' which applies to the powers of arrest provided by ss 24 and 25 (Arts 26 and 27) and to the other categories of arrest powers, is discussed generally in paras 2.81-2.91, ante, but is now considered more particularly in the context of the law of arrest.

REASONABLE GROUNDS FOR SUSPECTING

5.15 The threshold requirement for a valid arrest at common law was 'reasonable cause to suspect that the person was guilty of a felony'. This requirement was given statutory force by the Criminal Law Act 1967 which abolished the distinction between felonies and misdemeanours and created the concept of an arrestable offence. This concept was perpetuated by s 24 of PACE 1984 (Art 26 of the PACE (NI) Order) which also lays down the requirement of reasonable cause to suspect as the threshold requirement for arrest under ss 24(4)(b), 24(5)(b), 24(6) and 24(7)(b). There is no such requirement in respect of an arrest under s 24(4)(a) or s 24(7)(a), the fact that the person is in the act of committing an arrestable offence or is about to do so is sufficient. Under s 24(5)(a) the fact that the person is guilty of an arrestable offence is sufficient justification for the arrest. However, arrests under these provisions are comparatively few and greatest reliance is placed on s 24(6) which provides that a constable may arrest without warrant where he has reasonable grounds for suspecting that an arrestable offence has been committed and reasonable grounds for suspecting the person to be guilty of that offence. Even if no arrestable offence has in fact been committed and the person arrested is not therefore guilty of it, the arrest is still lawful provided that the constable had the dual reasonable cause to suspect required by the subsection. Arrest under s 25, which is subject to the requirement that the service of a summons is impracticable or inappropriate because any of the general arrest conditions set out in s 25(3), is also subject to the over-arching requirement that the constable has reasonable grounds to suspect the person of having committed or attempted to commit the offence or of being in the course of committing or attempting to commit it. It is therefore understandable that reasonable suspicion has been described as 'the source from which all a police constable's powers of summary arrest flow' (per Bingham LJ, *Chapman v DPP* (1988)). Section 2 of the Criminal Law Act 1967 used the words, 'may arrest without warrant anyone whom he, with reasonable cause suspects ...', importing an express requirement that the constable actually suspects. The different formulation in PACE 1984 provisions, 'may arrest anyone whom he has reasonable grounds for suspecting', suggested a change in the law so that actual suspicion was not required. However, in *Siddiqui v Swain* (1979) the Divisional Court held that the same wording in s 8(5) of the Road Traffic Act 1972 (now s 6(5) of the RTA 1988) 'import the further requirement that the constable in fact suspects'. In *Chapman v DPP* (1988) this was assumed without argument to be the true construction of the similar words used in s 24 (and s 25). Actual suspicion is crucial not only because it justifies the deprivation of a person's liberty but also because the constable is required by s 28, which codifies, with modifications, the common law principles set out by the House of Lords in *Christie v Leachinsky* (1947), to inform the person of the reasons for the arrest. He must therefore reasonably suspect the existence of facts amounting to an arrestable offence of the kind which he has in mind. The officer must not only actually suspect the existence of fact providing reasonable grounds to arrest, those facts must also exist. Thus in *Plange v Chief Constable of South Humberside Police* (1992), officers received a complaint giving them reasonable grounds to arrest but proceeded to arrest after the complaint had been withdrawn. The arrest was therefore unlawful.

WHAT ARE 'REASONABLE GROUNDS FOR SUSPECTING'?

5.16 There is no statutory definition of the phrase 'reasonable grounds for suspecting'; its meaning must be deduced from the decided cases, but since each case has to be determined on its own facts it remains an elusive concept. Two actions for false arrest and imprisonment provide an indication of the low standard which the courts have set.

5.17 In *Ward v Chief Constable of Avon and Somerset Constabulary* (1986) shops had been looted after riots in the Bristol area. A detective sergeant received information, from what he described as a reliable source, that a looted television set had been carried into premises occupied by the person with whom W was cohabiting. W admitted him to the premises and consented to a search. Thirteen Easter eggs were found. A confectionery shop had been among those looted. W claimed to have bought them from a local supermarket for 37p each. The officer was suspicious. The price was too low and there were no price labels on the eggs nor any sign that they had been removed. He then arrested W for theft of the eggs. In an action for false arrest the trial judge found against W and the Court of Appeal dismissed her appeal. It had been argued on her behalf that the detective sergeant should have made further inquiries before arresting her and in the absence of such inquiries there was no reasonable cause to suspect theft. The Court of Appeal held that there was reasonable cause, it was thin but the question was, was it sufficient? Holding that it was, the Court said:

> 'Looking objectively, as one should, DS Edwards did have reasonable cause for making the arrest. He found the eggs in circumstances which aroused his suspicion and called for explanation. He was given an explanation that was apparently untrue. He disbelieved it, and on good grounds. It could not be said that no reasonable constable should have exercised his discretion so as to make the arrest. He might have decided not to arrest, but he was entitled to do what he did.'

5.18 It will be recalled that in *Holgate-Mohammed v Duke* (1984) the House of Lords held that once a constable has reasonable cause to suspect a person to be guilty of an arrestable offence he has a discretion to arrest and it is a proper exercise of that discretion to arrest in order to question the person in the police station where a confession was more likely to be forthcoming. This decision encourages the arrest first and ask questions later approach. In the above circumstances the opposite approach seems preferable. Under the present law the DS, being lawfully on premises, could seize the eggs under s 19 of PACE 1984 (Art 21 of the PACE Order) and make inquires of the supermarket and/or the looted shop in order to establish whether they were stolen goods. An arrest could then be made if it was established that they were.

5.19 In *Castorina v Chief Constable of Surrey* (1988) police believed a burglary at the plaintiff's former workplace to be an 'inside job'. They were told that the plaintiff had recently been sacked. Having ascertained that she was of previous good character and without further inquiry, the police went to her home and arrested her. She was held for almost four hours before being released without charge. In an action for false arrest and imprisonment the trial judge awarded her damages on the ground that there was no reasonable cause to suspect her. He took the view that 'reasonable cause' meant an 'honest belief founded on a reasonable suspicion leading an ordinary cautious man to the conclusion that the person arrested was guilty of the offence'. Such a man would have made further inquiries before arresting. In allowing the Chief Constable's appeal the Court of Appeal held that the judge had applied too severe a test in asking whether the officers had an honest belief. 'Reasonable cause' was an objective issue and had nothing to do with the officer's subjective state of mind. The judge had therefore misdirected himself. Woolf LJ suggested that, when it is alleged that an arrest was unlawful, three questions must be asked:

(1) Did the arresting officer suspect that the person arrested was guilty of the offence? The answer to this depends on the findings of fact as to the officer's state of mind and is in that sense subjective.

(2) Assuming that the officer had the necessary suspicion, was there reasonable cause for that suspicion? This is an objective requirement to be determined by the trial judge (therefore a matter of law) though it may fall to be determined on the basis of facts found by the jury.

(3) If the answer to these questions is in the affirmative, then the officer has a discretion to arrest (ss 24, 25 (Arts 26, 27) use the words 'may arrest' not 'must') and this discretion must be exercised in accordance with the principles set down in *Associated Provincial Picture Houses Ltd v Wednesbury Corpn* (1948) (the Wednesbury principles of reasonableness).

5.20 The central question in this case was (2), but the question was not whether the facts would lead an ordinary cautious man to the conclusion that the person was guilty of the offence. It was enough that those facts could lead a reasonable man to suspect that he was guilty.

5.21 In allowing the appeal Purchas LJ said:

'In the circumstances of this case, and I emphasise that every case has to be determined upon its particular facts, I am satisfied that the arresting officers had reasonable cause to suspect that the plaintiff was guilty of this unusual burglary.'

5.22 It is difficult to see what facts in this case could have led a reasonable man to suspect that C was guilty of the burglary and there is a danger that the threshold requirement for an arrest has been set too low. The Court's rejection of the need to make further inquiries is particularly worrying. On this issue Purchas LJ said:

> 'There is ample authority for the proposition that courses of inquiry which may or may not be taken by the investigating officer before arrest are not relevant to the consideration whether on the information available to him at the time of the arrest he had reasonable cause for suspicion. Of course, failure to follow an obvious course in exceptional circumstances may well be grounds for attacking the executive exercise of that power under the Wednesbury principle.'

5.23 This approach was supported by Woolf LJ and Sir Frederick Lawton but if this means, and it is by no means certain that it does, that there is no duty to make further inquiries in order to provide the facts founding reasonable cause for suspicion, then despite the judicial unanimity, this cannot be accepted as a correct statement of law. It is one thing to say that once there is sufficient information to found reasonable cause for suspicion there is no need to make further inquiries before arresting. It is quite another to say that there is no need to make such inquiries in order to provide that information. The authorities cited (*Holgate-Mohammed v Duke* (1984) and *Ward v Chief Constable of Avon and Somerset Constabulary* (1986)) are authorities for saying that once the officer has reasonable cause for suspicion, there is no legal requirement to make further inquiries before exercising the power to arrest. Thus in Ward it was said that:

> 'It was unnecessary for the police to probe every explanation ... Complete proof need not be obtained if the grounds for suspicion were themselves reasonably sufficient' (emphasis added).

5.24 They do not support the proposition that there is no legal requirement to make further inquiries in order to establish reasonable cause for suspicion. A judge must be satisfied that the officer actually held the requisite suspicion. That can only be determined by reference to the particular facts, but there must be some facts which would lead a reasonable person to that suspicion. A constable may in fact suspect but, unless there are reasonable grounds upon which that suspicion can be founded, there is no reasonable cause for suspicion. Consequently a police officer who has a suspicion which is not based on reasonable grounds must make further inquiries in order to provide that basis. (See further Clayton and Tomlinson 'Arrest and reasonable grounds for suspicion' LS Gaz, 7 September 1988, p 22.)

5.25 The question of whether the officer making the arrest was required to have reasonable grounds or whether it was acceptable for other officers to have the necessary grounds was considered in *O'Hara v Chief Constable of the Royal Ulster Constabulary* (1996). Lord Steyn approved the following passage from Feldman, *Civil Liberties and Human Rights in England and Wales* (1993):

'Where reasonable grounds for suspicion are required in order to justify the arrest of someone who turns out to be innocent, the Act requires that the Constable personally had reasonable grounds for the suspicion and it would seem to follow that he is not protected if, knowing of the case, he acts on orders from another officer, who, perhaps does have such grounds. On the other hand under statutes which require only the objective existence of reasonable grounds for suspicion, it is possible that the officer need neither have the reasonable grounds for himself nor suspect anything: he can simply follow orders.'

5.26   O'Hara was arrested in connection with a murder under s 12(1)(b) of the Prevention of Terrorism (Temporary Provisions) Act 1984 on suspicion that he was a terrorist. Subsequently released without charge, O'Hara brought an action for, inter alia, wrongful arrest. The arresting officer had received information at a briefing from a more senior officer and although the evidence was scant the House of Lords held that he had, and it was necessary to have, grounds. In part the grounds were subjective in that it was necessary for the officer to have formed a genuine suspicion in his own mind that the person to be arrested had been concerned in acts of terrorism, it was also partly objective because there must be reasonable grounds for the suspicion that he had formed. The mere fact that he had been instructed to effect the arrest by a more senior officer was not capable of amounting to reasonable grounds for the necessary suspicion within the meaning of s 12(1). The court also held that it was not necessary to prove that the facts were in fact true.

5.27   In *Hough v Chief Constable of Staffordshire* (2001) the issue of whether an officer's suspicion is formed on the basis of an entry on the Police National Computer arose. The police made a routine check on a vehicle driven by the claimant and found that there was an entry suggesting that the occupants of the car were thought to be armed with a firearm. The Court of Appeal held that where the arresting officer's suspicion is formed on the basis of an entry on the PNC, that entry is *likely* to provide the necessary objective justification. In this case there was an urgent need and the arrest was considered lawful. Where no such urgency exists further enquiry ought to be conducted, not least because of the possibility of inaccurate entries.

ARRESTABLE OFFENCES (PACE ACT 1984, s 24, PACE ORDER 1989, Art 26)

5.28   Section 24(1) provides for a power of summary arrest in respect of arrestable offences as defined in that section. 'Summary' in this context means done with despatch and without formalities. A number of advantages accrue from defining an offence as an arrestable offence, attracting to it a power of arrest unfettered by the formalities which attend an arrest under s 25 (Art 27). There is discretion to arrest as indicated by the words 'may arrest' in s 24(4) (Art 26(4)). The constable may be guided by criteria such as those which govern the power to arrest under s 25 (Art 27) contained in the general arrest conditions and may, in an appropriate case, decide to proceed by way of a summons. He may, however, arrest where there is reasonable cause to suspect an arrestable offence has been committed, even if none of the criteria mentioned in s 25(3)

(Art 27(3)) applies. As will be seen in Chapter 6, post, criteria for detention without charge after arrest permit such detention, initially for a maximum of 24 hours (s 41(1)), in order to secure or preserve evidence or to obtain it by questioning. Section 18 permits the search of premises without a warrant following arrest for an arrestable offence and it is this power which will enable the police to 'secure or preserve' evidence while the person is being detained without charge. As the decision in *Holgate-Mohammed v Duke* (1984) indicates (a decision on an almost identically worded discretionary power to arrest as is provided by s 24 (Art 26), it is perfectly proper to take into account the need to question the person in the police station in exercising that discretion, and by analogy it will be equally proper to take into account the need to search premises for evidence of the offence. The availability of these investigative powers explains the need for a power of summary arrest and will be a strong inducement to exercise the powers provided by s 24 (Art 26). If the offence is, or proves to be, a serious arrestable offence, additional investigative powers become available. Those relevant to the decision to arrest are as follows.

(a) Continued detention without charge beyond the normal maximum of 24 hours in order to secure or preserve evidence or to obtain it by questioning may be authorised by a superintendent for up to 12 hours beyond the initial 24 hours. A magistrates' court may authorise further detention either from the initial 24 hours or from the period of detention authorised by a superintendent, for up to 36 hours, also in order to secure, preserve or obtain evidence, and that period may be extended for up to a further period of 36 hours but not to exceed 96 hours' detention without charge in total (ss 42, 43 and 44) (Arts 43, 44 and 45).

(b) The right of an arrested person to see a solicitor (s 58, art 59) and to have someone informed that he has been arrested (s 56, art 57) may be delayed for up to 36 hours.

5.29 The availability of these additional investigative powers also explains the need for a power of summary arrest, quite apart from the seriousness of the offence, and it will be perfectly proper for a constable to take into account the need to invoke these provisions in deciding whether to exercise his discretion to arrest.

5.30 (One may note that this power of arrest may be exercised by English, Welsh and Northern Irish police in Scotland, by English and Welsh police in Northern Ireland and by Scottish or Northern Irish police in England and Wales: see s 137 of the Criminal Justice and Public Order Act 1994.)

Scope of arrestable offences

5.31 For the purposes of the Act (Order) the following categories of offence are arrestable offences:

(a) offences for which the sentence is fixed by law (s 24(1)(a), art 26(1)(a)) – the only such offences are murder and treason,

(b) offences punishable by five years' imprisonment (s 24(1)(b), art 26(1)(b)). By omitting the phrase 'under or by virtue of any enactment' from the previous definition in the Criminal Law Act 1967, s 24(1)(b) (Art 26(1)(b)) extended the definition of an arrestable offence to include common law offences, such as kidnapping, conspiracy to defraud or corrupt public morals, attempting to pervert the course of justice and false imprisonment. This category must, however, be considered against the background of the following restrictions on sentencing.

(i) Persons not previously sentenced to imprisonment. Section 1 of the Criminal Justice Act 1991 restricts the power of a court to impose a custodial sentence on a convicted person unless:

(a) the sentence for the offence is fixed by law (see (a) above); or
(b) the offence is triable only on indictment and a sentence of imprisonment has previously been passed on the offender by a UK court.

These restrictions do not mean that an offence committed by such a person is not an arrestable offence in respect of him. Section 24(1)(b) refers to offences for which a person over 21 (not previously convicted) may be sentenced to five or more years' imprisonment. Therefore such an offence is an arrestable offence whoever commits it and despite any restrictions on sentencing applicable to that person.

(ii) The Magistrates' Courts Act 1980 (s 33) (Art 46(4) of the Magistrates' Courts (Northern Ireland) Order 1981). This provision restricts the sentencing power of a magistrates' court in respect of certain offences triable either on indictment or summarily which, if the value involved is £5,000 or less, must be tried summarily (s 22 of the 1980 Act as amended by s 46 of the CJPOA 1994 (Art 4(8) of the Fines and Penalties (NI) Order 1984 as amended by the Criminal Justice (NI) Order 1994)) and can be punished by no more than three months' imprisonment. This restriction is to be ignored for the purposes of s 24(1)(b) (Art 26(1)(b)). Thus an offence of criminal damage, normally punishable by up to ten years' imprisonment, and therefore an arrestable offence, remains one even if the value of the damage is £5,000 or less.

Arrestable offences under s 24(2) (Art 26(2))

5.32 These CJPOA 1994 offences represent the growing number of arrestable offences which have been increased by the Police Reform Act 2002, Sch 6 which inserted a new Sch 1A into PACE and subsequent amendments in the Criminal Justice Act 2003.

5.33 The following is the Schedule inserted in PACE 1984 after Sch 1.

[SCHEDULE 1A
Specific Offences which are Arrestable Offences]

[1   Customs and Excise Acts

An offence for which a person may be arrested under the customs and excise Acts (within the meaning of the Customs and Excise Management Act 1979 (c 2)).

2 Official Secrets Act 1920

An offence under the Official Secrets Act 1920 (c 75) which is not an arrestable offence by virtue of the term of imprisonment for which a person may be sentenced in respect of them.

[2A Wireless Telegraphy Act 1949

An offence mentioned in section 14(1) of the Wireless Telegraphy Act 1949 (offences under that Act which are triable either way).]

3 Prevention of Crime Act 1953

An offence under section 1(1) of the Prevention of Crime Act 1953 (c 14) (prohibition of carrying offensive weapons without lawful authority or excuse).

4 *Sexual Offences Act 1956*

An offence under—
(a) section 22 of the Sexual Offences Act 1956 (c 69) (causing prostitution of women; or
(b) section 23 of that Act (procuration of girl under 21).

5 Obscene Publications Act 1959

An offence under section 2 of the Obscene Publications Act 1959 (c 66) (publication of obscene matter).

[5A Firearms Act 1968

An offence under section 19 of the Firearms Act 1968 (carrying firearm or imitation firearm in public place) in respect of an air weapon or imitation firearm.]

6 Theft Act 1968

An offence under—
(a) section 12(1) of the Theft Act 1968 (c 60) (taking motor vehicle or other conveyance without authority etc); or
(b) section 25(1) of that Act (going equipped for stealing etc).

7 Theft Act 1978

An offence under section 3 of the Theft Act 1978 (c 31) (making off without payment).

8 Protection of Children Act 1978

An offence under section 1 of the Protection of Children Act 1978 (c 37) (indecent photographs and pseudo-photographs of children).

9   Wildlife and Countryside Act 1981

An offence under section 1(1) or (2) or 6 of the Wildlife and Countryside Act 1981 (c 69) (taking, possessing, selling etc of wild birds) in respect of a bird included in Schedule 1 to that Act or any part of, or anything derived from, such a bird.

10

An offence under—
(a)   section 1(5) of the Wildlife and Countryside Act 1981 (disturbance of wild birds);
(b)   section 9 or 13(1)(a) or (2) of that Act (taking, possessing, selling etc of wild animals or plants); or
(c)   section 14 of that Act (introduction of new species etc).

11   Civil Aviation Act 1982

An offence under section 39(1) of the Civil Aviation Act 1982 (c 16) (trespass on aerodrome).

[11A

An offence of contravening a provision of an Order in Council under section 60 of that Act (air navigation order) where the offence relates to—
(a)   a provision which prohibits specified behaviour by a person in an aircraft towards or in relation to a member of the crew, or
(b)   a provision which prohibits a person from being drunk in an aircraft, in so far as it applies to passengers.]

12   Aviation Security Act 1982

An offence under section 21C(1) or 21D(1) of the Aviation Security Act 1982 (c 36) (unauthorised presence in a restricted zone or on an aircraft).

13   Sexual Offences Act 1985

An offence under section 1 of the Sexual Offences Act 1985 (c 44) (kerb-crawling).

14   Public Order Act 1986

An offence under section 19 of the Public Order Act 1986 (c 64) (publishing etc material likely to stir up racial or religious hatred).

15   Criminal Justice Act 1988

An offence under—
(a)   section 139(1) of the Criminal Justice Act 1988 (c 33) (offence of having article with a blade or point in public place); or

(b) section 139A(1) or (2) of that Act (offence of having article with a blade or point or offensive weapon on school premises).

16 Road Traffic Act 1988

An offence under section 103(1)(b) of the Road Traffic Act 1988 (c 52) (driving while disqualified).

17

An offence under subsection (4) of section 170 of the Road Traffic Act 1988 (failure to stop and report an accident) in respect of an accident to which that section applies by virtue of subsection (1)(a) of that section (accidents causing personal injury).

18 Official Secrets Act 1989

An offence under any provision of the Official Secrets Act 1989 (c 6) other than subsection (1), (4) or (5) of section 8 of that Act.

19 Football Spectators Act 1989

An offence under section 14J or 21C of the Football Spectators Act 1989 (c 37) (failing to comply with requirements imposed by or under a banning order or a notice under section 21B).

20 Football (Offences) Act 1991

An offence under any provision of the Football (Offences) Act 1991 (c 19).

21 Criminal Justice and Public Order Act 1994

An offence under—
(a) section 60AA(7) of the Criminal Justice and Public Order Act 1994 (c 33) (failing to comply with requirement to remove disguise);
(b) section 166 of that Act (sale of tickets by unauthorised persons); or
(c) section 167 of that Act (touting for car hire services).

22 Police Act 1996

An offence under section 89(1) of the Police Act 1996 (c 16) (assaulting a police officer in the execution of his duty or a person assisting such an officer).

23 Protection from Harassment Act 1997

An offence under section 2 of the Protection from Harassment Act 1997 (c 40) (harassment).

24   Crime and Disorder Act 1998

An offence falling within section 32(1)(a) of the Crime and Disorder Act 1998 (c 37) (racially or religiously aggravated harassment).

25   Criminal Justice and Police Act 2001

An offence under—
(a)   section 12(4) of the Criminal Justice and Police Act 2001 (c 16) (failure to comply with requirements imposed by constable in relation to consumption of alcohol in public place); or
(b)   section 46 of that Act (placing of advertisements in relation to prostitution).

[26   Licensing Act 2003

An offence under section 143(1) of the Licensing Act 2003 (failure to leave licensed premises, etc).]

[27   Sexual Offences Act 2003

An offence under—
(a)   section 66 of the Sexual Offences Act 2003 (exposure);
(b)   section 67 of that Act (voyeurism);
(c)   section 69 of that Act (intercourse with an animal);
(d)   section 70 of that Act (sexual penetration of a corpse); or
(e)   section 71 of that Act (sexual activity in public lavatory).

5.34   The Criminal Justice Act 2003 inserted the following offences into the schedule:
1.   an offence under s 36 of the Criminal Justice Act 1925 (making an untrue statement in order to obtain a passport)
2.   an offence under s 5(2) of the Misuse of Drugs Act 1971 (possession of cannabis or cannabis resin)
3.   an offence under s 174 of the Road Traffic Act 1988 (making false statements and withholding information in order to obtain a driving licence).

CONSPIRACY, ATTEMPTING, INCITING, ETC (s 24(3))

Arrestable offences under s 24(1)(a) and (b)

5.35   It has already been noted that s 24(1)(b) makes common law conspiracy and other common law offences, such as incitement, arrestable offences provided that the conspiracy or offence incited is punishable by five or more years' imprisonment. Most conspiracies and attempts are now statutory offences. Section 3 of the Criminal Law

Act 1977 and s 4 of the Criminal Attempts Act 1981 (Art 4 of Criminal Attempts and Conspiracy (NI) Order 1983) provide that penalties for respectively a conspiracy or attempt to commit what are now arrestable offences by virtue of s 24(1)(a) and (b), are punishable to the same extent as the full offence. Incitement is still a common law misdemeanour and when tried on indictment it is punishable by imprisonment at the discretion of the court. Incitement to commit an offence which is triable either way or on indictment only is therefore within s 24(1)(b) as an offence for which a person may be sentenced to imprisonment for five years. Aiding, abetting, counselling or procuring is, by the Accessories and Abettors Act 1861, s 8 (as amended by the Criminal Law Act 1977), punishable to the same extent as commission by the principal offender. It follows therefore that such offences are arrestable if the principal offence is arrestable.

Arrestable offences by virtue of s 24(1)(c) and (2) (Art 26(1)(c) and (2)) (s 24(3), art 26(3))

5.36 Since the offences to which s 24(2) applies are not punishable by five years' imprisonment, it follows that conspiring or attempting to commit or inciting, aiding, abetting, counselling or procuring the commission of them are not automatically arrestable offences. Special provision needs to be made for them and s 24(3) does so. Schedule 15, para 98, of the Criminal Justice Act 1988 amends s 24(3)(b) of PACE to exclude the offence of attempting to commit an offence under s 12(1) of the Theft Act 1968 (taking and driving away a motor vehicle etc). Conduct which may be preparatory to such an offence is covered by s 9 of the Criminal Attempts Act 1981 (interference with motor vehicles). (NB: Section 2(1) and (2)(e) of the Criminal Attempts Act 1981 provide that any provision in any enactment (whenever passed) conferring a power of arrest in respect of the offence shall have effect with respect to the offence of attempting to commit that offence. This is apt to provide a power of arrest in respect of attempts to commit an arrestable offence. Section 24(3), which is without prejudice to s 2 of the 1981 Act, applies to conspiracy, aiding, abetting, counselling or procuring and is therefore much wider than s 2 of the CAA 1981 but so far as attempts are concerned it is co-extensive.)

5.37 The combined effect of s 24(1)(a), (b), (c) and (2) (Art 26(1), (a), (b), (c) and (2)) is to make all the more serious offences and many of the most commonly committed offences, which may be comparatively trivial in the commission, arrestable offences. Thus they cover, for example, murder, manslaughter, offences involving explosives, offences under Part I of the Forgery and Counterfeiting Act 1981, the major offences against the person, all the offences under the Criminal Damage Act 1971, almost all the Theft Act offences, offences of corruption and related inchoate and secondary offences. Many of these were arrestable under the 1967 Act and, while the actual number of offences added by PACE 1984 (1989 Order) is small, the frequency with which they are likely to be committed adds significantly to the list of arrestable offences. The list of offences punishable by five or more years' imprisonment is regularly added to.

THE POWERS OF ARREST FOR ARRESTABLE OFFENCES (s 24(4)-(7), Art 26(4)-(7))

5.38   Though drafted differently these provisions re-enact the powers of arrest previously contained in s 2(2)-(5) of the Criminal Law Act 1967 (the power of a constable to enter premises without a warrant to arrest a person under these powers was previously contained in s 2(6) of that Act and is now to be found in s 17(1)(b) of PACE 1984 (Art 19(1)(b)) (see para 4.33, ante). Section 24(4) and (5) (Art 26(4) and (5)) contain powers of arrest which are available to anyone while those under s 24(6) and (7) (Art 26(6) and (7)) are available only to a constable, which term refers to the ancient office of constable requiring attestation before a justice of the peace (see para 2.41, ante).

POWERS OF ARREST – ARREST BY A PRIVATE CITIZEN (s 24(4) AND (5), Art 26(4) AND (5))

5.39   Section 24(4) and (5) (Art 26(4) and (5)) provide what are often described as 'citizen's arrest powers' but they are available to constables as well. Since constables have wider powers provided by s 24(6) and (7) (Art 26(6) and (7)) they will rarely need to rely on these powers except possibly in the exceptional circumstances considered below.

Section 24(4) (Art 26(4))

5.40   Under s 24(4)(a) (Art 26(4)(a)) any person may arrest without a warrant any person who is in the act of committing an arrestable offence. There is no question of reasonable cause to suspect that the person is committing such an offence. Either he is or he is not. If he is in the act of committing an arrestable offence, the arrest is lawful; if he is not, it is unlawful. Conversely, s 24(4)(b) (Art 26(4)(b)) authorises the arrest without warrant by anyone, private citizen or constable, of anyone whom he has reasonable grounds for suspecting to be committing an arrestable offence. It matters not whether the person is in fact committing an arrestable offence so long as the arrestor has reasonable grounds for suspecting that he was doing so. Thus, when the manager of a store saw D in the toilets in a dazed condition and in possession of a syringe, questioned D about drugs and, when D tried to leave, took hold of him and said, 'You are not going anywhere', he had lawfully arrested D under s 24(4)(b) (*R v Brosch* (1988)). In that case D was clearly in the act of committing the arrestable offence of being in possession of prohibited drugs. In other cases it may not be so easy to determine when the person is in the act of committing an arrestable offence. Store detectives will often rely on this power to arrest persons in the act of shoplifting. Theft will be complete when a person takes goods from the shelf and conceals them about his person (*R v McPherson* (1973)), when he switches labels with the intention of offering a lower price for the goods than was on the original label (*R v Morris* (1983)) or assumes any of the rights of an owner with the dishonest intent to permanently deprive (*DPP v Gomez* (1993)). Such persons will clearly be in the act of committing an arrestable offence (theft) while in the store. If they are permitted to leave the store they are likely to be in the act of committing the offence for some short time after leaving but it is not clear how long after the appropriation they will continue to be in the act of committing theft. In *R v Self* (1992) a suspected shoplifter was chased from the store and arrested after a short chase by a passer-by. The arrest under s 24(5) was unlawful because no offence had been committed (see discussion below). Arguably an arrest under s 24(4)(b) would have been valid if, as is likely, the theft continues while D is fleeing the scene but is still in the immediate vicinity of the store (see commentary at [1992] Crim LR 573). D is likely to be in the act of committing theft when stopped outside the store or some way down the street and if he runs off during the time he is being pursued, though it is not clear how far or how long the pursuit may continue. If D is not pursued, or is pursued but lost, and is seen in a cafe some 15 minutes after the theft, he is unlikely to be 'in the act of committing an arrestable offence'. The citizen/ store detective must then rely on s 24(5) (Art 26(5)) if an arrestable offence has been committed.

Where an arrestable offence has been committed (s 24(5), art 26(5))

5.41   It is clear from the opening words of s 24(5) (Art 26(5)) that it is an essential precondition for arrest under this subsection that an arrestable offence has been committed. This provides a trap for the unwary citizen by preserving the rule laid down in respect of arrests for felony in *Walters v W H Smith & Son Ltd* (1914). P reasonably suspected that D had stolen a particular book from his stall and arrested him under the common law power which is now s 24(5) (Art 26(5)). Other books had been stolen but not the particular book, therefore no felony (arrestable offence) had been committed in respect of it. P was held liable in damages. Little consideration has been given to this aspect of the law of arrest. The Criminal Law Revision Committee (1965 Cmnd 2695) was prepared to protect the citizen who arrests a person who is reasonably suspected of being in the act of committing an arrestable offence but who is not in fact doing so (s 24(4)(b), art 26(4)(b)) or the citizen who arrests a person without any reasonable suspicion who is in fact guilty of having committed an arrestable offence (s 24(5)(a), art 24(5)(a)). The committee was not, however, prepared to offer protection to the citizen who reasonably suspects that an arrestable offence has been committed when it has not, and arrests a person whom he reasonably believes has committed it. That PACE 1984 continues this refusal to offer protection to a citizen who reasonably, but wrongly, suspects the commission of an offence, is demonstrated by the decision in *R v Self* (1992). The prosecution alleged that a store detective and an assistant saw D take a bar of chocolate and leave without paying for it. They followed him and saw him place the bar of chocolate under a car. The store detective picked it up and asked D to return to the store with her. The assistant said, 'You have been shoplifting'. There was a scuffle and D ran off followed by a man who had seen what had happened. He arrested D. In his defence to the charge of theft D said he had forgotten about the chocolate bar and had no intention of stealing it. He was acquitted of theft but convicted of two charges of assault with intent to resist arrest.

5.42   On appeal it was argued that since D had been acquitted of theft no arrestable offence had been committed; therefore D's arrest under s 24(5) was not lawful and the convictions for assault with intent to resist a lawful arrest could not stand. The Court of Appeal, accepting this argument, held that the words of s 24(5) did not admit of argument. Subsection (5) made it abundantly clear that the power of arrest without a warrant where an arrestable offence had been committed required, as a condition precedent, that an offence be committed. If subsequently there was an acquittal of the alleged offence, no offence had been committed. It followed that the two offences of assault contrary to s 38 of the Offences Against the Person Act 1861, could not be committed because there was no power to arrest. As will be seen later (para 5.164, post) one may use reasonable force to resist an unlawful arrest which, despite the good faith of the arrestor, this was. Implicit in this decision is the acceptance that the offence, had there been one, was committed inside the store and was no longer being committed when the arrestor arrested outside the store. An arrest at an earlier point when the defendant was reasonably suspected of committing an offence could have been justified under s 24(4)(b) which is not subject to the condition precedent that an arrestable offence must have been committed.

5.43   Section 24(5)(a) (Art 26(5)(a)) provides that where an arrestable offence has been committed any person may arrest without warrant any person who is guilty of the offence. The subsection makes the arrest lawful not because of facts and circumstances existing and known to the arrestor at the time of the arrest but because the arrested person is subsequently proved to be guilty of the offence. It is difficult to imagine a person who was convicted of the offence for which he was arrested subsequently suing the arrestor for false arrest because the arrestor had no reasonable grounds for suspecting that he had committed the offence. The Criminal Law Revision Committee thought the provision 'unimportant, as even without it we do not believe a person would be held liable' (para 13); but the Committee included it to put the point beyond argument. Children under ten years of age (eight in Northern Ireland) present store detectives and other private individuals with a particular problem. They are conclusively presumed to be incapable of committing a crime. This means that not only can they not be convicted, but also that no crime at all is committed by an infant. It follows that if an eight-year-old is seen stealing from a shop, no arrestable offence, indeed no offence, is committed and therefore there is no power of arrest. In the absence of such a power the child cannot lawfully be detained even though it is in the child's interest that he be detained and his parents, and/or the Social Services, be informed. The most that can be done is to inform the police and local authority, assuming the child can be identified. The police may be able to take the child into police protection (see s 46 of the Children Act 1989, discussed at para 6.25, post) and the local authority has a duty under s 47 of that Act to investigate where there is reasonable cause to suspect that a child is suffering, or is likely to suffer, significant harm. If so they may take care proceedings under s 31 of that Act.

5.44   (NB: The House of Lords restored the common law presumption that a child aged between 10 and 14 is doli incapax and can only be convicted of an offence if that presumption is rebutted by clear positive evidence that the child knew that his act was seriously wrong, such evidence not consisting merely in the evidence of the acts amounting to the offence itself. (*C (a minor) v DPP* (1995) overruling the decision of the Divisional Court in *C v DPP* (1994). Neither case affects the power to arrest.)

5.45 Section 24(5)(b) (Art 26(5)(b)), on the other hand, requires reasonable grounds for suspecting the person to be guilty of the offence. The legality of the arrest is not affected by the fact that the person arrested did not commit the arrestable offence if there were such reasonable grounds, provided that the offence was committed by someone. For example, security officers arrested three men reasonably suspected of theft from their employer. Two were subsequently acquitted, the third was convicted. The conviction made it clear that an arrestable offence had been committed therefore the arrest of those acquitted was lawful under s 24(5)(b) (Art 26(5)(b)). The acquittal of all three would not render the arrest unlawful. The position would be different if the acquittals were based on the fact that an arrestable offence was not committed (see *R v Self* (1992) considered in para 5.40, ante).

ARREST AS A STEP IN THE CRIMINAL PROCESS

5.46 Arrest is a step in the criminal process and an arrest by a private person (or a constable) is lawful only if he intends to take the alleged offender to a constable or magistrate as soon as possible, thereby commencing the criminal process. In *R v Brewin* (1976), B purported to arrest a child in order to take him to his father to be dealt with. It was held that the arrest was unlawful and B was liable for false imprisonment. However, provided the arrest is made with the intention of taking the arrested person to the police, it is not invalidated if the arrestor changes his mind en route. In *John Lewis & Co Ltd v Tims* (1952) the House of Lords held that it was lawful for a store detective to take a suspected shoplifter to his employer for a decision whether to prosecute. Since it is the employer who takes the decision and the employee is merely his agent, taking the arrested person to the employer is a necessary first step in the criminal process and doubtless the arrest is intended as such. The rule applies to all arrests but as will be seen a constable is permitted greater scope for action prior to taking the arrested person to a police station (s 30(10), art 32(13) discussed in para 5.147, post).

Arrest by a constable (s 24(6) and (7), art 26(6) and (7))

Section 24(6) (Art 26(6))

5.47 Section 24(6) (Art 26(6)) contains the power which will be relied upon by police constables for the majority of arrests for an arrestable offence. This power, like that in sub-s (7), is only available to a constable and authorises an arrest without warrant when the constable has reasonable grounds for suspecting that an arrestable offence has been committed, and he has reasonable grounds for suspecting the person to be guilty of the offence. It follows that an arrest is lawful even if:

(a) no arrestable offence has been committed, and

(b) such an offence has been committed but not by the arrested person,

5.48   provided that in each case there were reasonable grounds for suspicion.

5.49   Had a constable arrested in the case of *Walters v W H Smith and Son Ltd*, ante, the arrest would have been lawful. Thus in *Davidson v Chief Constable of North Wales* (1994) a store detective gained the impression that D and H had taken a tape cassette without paying for it. She was wrong. H had in fact paid for it. D and H left the store and went to a nearby cafe. The police were called and D and H were pointed out to the police as suspected thieves. Police arrested both but released them after two hours when the truth had been established. D sued the store detective and the police. The Court of Appeal (Civil Division) upheld the decision of the trial judge to withdraw the case from the jury on the basis that the police had lawfully arrested under s 24(6) – they had reasonable grounds to suspect that an arrestable offence had been committed and had no case to answer. There was similarly no case against the store detective. The police were not her agent and had acted independently on the information received. Had the store detective arrested D and H there is no doubt that the arrest would have been unlawful. (One may note here the decision of the House of Lords in *Martin v Watson* (1995) that where a complainant had falsely and maliciously given a police officer information indicating that a person was guilty of an offence and the facts were solely within the complainant's knowledge, in this case an allegation of indecent exposure, so that the officer could not have exercised any independent discretion and the false information had been a determining factor in the decision to prosecute, the complainant, although not technically the prosecutor, could be said to be in substance the person responsible for the prosecution and liable in damages for malicious prosecution.)

5.50   The arrest of a child under ten years of age (eight in Northern Ireland) may also be lawful, even though no crime is committed in law, though a crime is committed in fact. The question will be, did the constable reasonably suspect that an arrestable offence had been committed? If the child is not obviously under ten years of age, the constable could reasonably suspect this. However, if the child is obviously under ten years of age he could not so suspect and an arrest would then be unlawful. If the constable is in doubt as to the age of the child, he may consider taking the child into police protection under s 46 of the Children Act 1989 (see the discussion at paras 5.28, ante and 6.12, post). It is arguable that a child under the age of criminal responsibility who is committing what would be an arrestable offence if he was older, is 'likely to suffer significant harm', the threshold requirement for the exercise of the 'police protection' power.

Section 24(7) (Art 26(7))

5.51   Section 24(7)(a) (Art 26(7)(a)) provides a constable with a power to arrest without warrant anyone who is about to commit an arrestable offence. There is no question of reasonable suspicion. Either the person is about to commit such an offence or he is not. If he is, the arrest is lawful; if he is not, it is unlawful. On the other hand, s 24(7)(b) (Art 26(7)(b)) provides the same power subject to reasonable grounds for suspecting the person to be about to commit an arrestable offence. One may note at this point that while s 28 (Art 30) requires persons arresting under ss 24, 25 (Arts 26, 27) or any other power to inform the person arrested of the fact that he has been arrested and the reasons for the arrest, there is no requirement that the arrestor specify the particular arrest power he is relying on. He can, therefore, rely on whichever power authorises the arrest in the particular circumstances with the benefit of hindsight. The difficulty with the sub-s (7) power is to determine what the purpose of it is. In creating its predecessor (s 2(5) of the Criminal Law Act 1967), the Criminal Law Revision Committee (1965 Cmnd 2695) relied on common law authority which empowered any person to arrest without warrant anyone who was about to commit a felony. If the person was arrested before he had committed or attempted to commit the arrestable offence, the Committee suggested that the constable could 'bring him before a magistrates' court with a view to his being bound over to keep the peace ...'. Alternatively the constable could release him, when the danger of the arrestable offence being committed or attempted has passed, on the analogy of the power of a constable to detain a person temporarily in order to prevent the commission of a felony or breach of the peace (para 16) (see now *Albert v Lavin* (1982) for a modern statement of the common law power, discussed in para 5.84, post). If the person has committed or attempted to commit an arrestable offence, the constable has a power of arrest under s 24(6) (Art 26(6)). The law of attempts has been changed since the Criminal Law Act 1967 and a person will now be guilty of a criminal attempt when he does an 'act which is more than merely preparatory to the commission of the offence' (Criminal Attempts Act 1981, s 1, Criminal Attempts and Conspiracy (NI) Order 1983). What is 'a more than merely preparatory act' is a question of fact for the jury and may be an earlier stage than under the common law (see *R v Jones (KH)* (1990)). However, it is a question of fact in each case and the police, who in many cases cannot allow the crime to be committed, may have to wait until what may be a dangerous last moment before arresting if they are to be sure that an attempted crime has been committed. For example, in *R v Campbell* (1991) police had information that a sub-post office was to be robbed. On an October day C was seen riding a motor cycle in the vicinity. He wore a helmet and gloves and sunglasses. He put his hand into a pocket which contained something heavy. He stopped some 30 yards from the post office and took off his sunglasses. He looked around before turning away. Half an hour later he walked back towards the post office. He was arrested in front of the post office and when searched an imitation firearm was found together with a threatening note. He maintained that he had decided not to rob the post office but was arrested before he could return to his motor cycle and leave. His conviction for attempted robbery was quashed on appeal. In the Court of Appeal, while accepting that the question whether C had done a more than merely preparatory act was for the jury, it was open to the judge to rule that there was no evidence that he had, and in these circumstances, where C had not even entered the post office, it is extremely unlikely that it could have been said that he had performed an act which could properly be called an attempt.

5.52   Fortunately there is the offence under s 18 of the Firearms Act 1968, carrying an imitation firearm with intent to commit an indictable offence, of which C was convicted.

5.53   It follows that in practice the s 24(7) (Art 26(7)) power will only be used when a person threatens to commit an offence of violence to persons or property but does not take any steps to put the threat into effect. The power is then exactly the same as the power to arrest for an actual or threatened breach of the peace. In both cases the person can be taken before a court with a view to having the person bound over to keep the peace. At common law a person may be detained short of arrest if he threatens a breach of the peace and released once the threat ceases to exist. Section 30(7) (Art 32(10)) requires the release of a person arrested at a place other than a police station if, before arriving at the police station, the grounds for arrest cease to exist (see para 5.138, post). Applied to an arrest under s 24(7) (Art 26(7)) this makes the power identical with the common law power though it is an arrest rather than detention (see example (5) in para 5.33, post). There are also a number of substantive offences which may be committed by the person who is 'about to commit an arrestable offence'. The most common is that of going equipped for stealing, contrary to the Theft Act 1968, s 25 (Theft Act (NI) Act 1969, s 24(1)), which is an arrestable offence by virtue of s 24(1)(c) of PACE 1984 (Art 26(1)(c)). Possessing a firearm with intent to injure, contrary to the Firearms Act 1968, s 16, and possession of explosives, contrary to the Explosive Substances Act 1883, s 4, are substantive offences punishable by more than five years' imprisonment and therefore arrestable offences by virtue of s 24(1)(b) (Art 26(1)(b)).

5.54   The following examples illustrate the operation of the various arrest powers.
(1)   D is seen by a store detective putting a packet of bacon, which he has not paid for, into an inside pocket of his coat. D may be arrested under s 24(4)(a) or (b) (Art 26(4)(a) or (b)). If a constable sees D in the act of stealing, he may also arrest D under the same powers.
(2)   D is seen acting furtively in a store by a store detective. He hides behind a display counter and is seen to put his hand inside his coat. He does this twice more and leaves the store having made no purchases. He is arrested outside the store. The arrest is justified under s 24(4)(b) (Art 26(4)(b)) if, as is likely, the observed conduct is accepted as reasonable grounds for suspecting that D is in the act of committing an arrestable offence even if D was not in fact committing an arrestable offence. A constable may also arrest under that subsection but can also rely on s 4(6) (Art 26(6)). Here too the lawfulness of the arrest depends upon the existence of reasonable suspicion that an arrestable offence has been committed and that D committed it.
(3)   A valuable ring is stolen from a jeweller. Only two persons were in the shop at the time of the theft, D and X. X left the shop. D remained. P arrested D though he had no reasonable grounds to suspect that he was responsible. It transpires that D and X work as a team and both are convicted of the theft. The arrest is lawful by virtue of that conviction (s 24(5)(a), art 26(5)(a)). P could be the jeweller or a constable for both could rely on s 24(5)(a) (Art 26(5)(a)). However, if P was a

constable he could not rely on s 24(6) (Art 26(6)) which requires reasonable grounds for suspecting that D had committed the arrestable offence.

(4) D is in a jeweller's shop examining a tray of rings. As he starts to leave the jeweller notices a ring is missing from the tray. D refuses to submit to a search and runs away. The jeweller gives chase and eventually arrests D. The ring is not stolen. It had dropped behind the counter. D ran off because he had previous convictions for theft and was afraid he would be implicated. The arrest is unlawful. Section 24(5) (Art 26(5)) gives a power to arrest only where an arrestable offence has been committed, no matter how reasonable the grounds for suspecting D may be. If a constable made the arrest in these circumstances it would be lawful under s 24(6) (Art 26(6)) since the jeweller's story plus D's conduct would provide reasonable grounds to suspect the commission of an arrestable offence and that D had committed it.

(5) D is in the High Street threatening violence to a travel agent who has ceased to trade and deprived D of a holiday he had booked and paid for. He clearly intends to carry out his threat but has taken no steps to do so. A constable may arrest D under s 24(7) (Art 26(7)), and take him before a magistrates' court with a view to having him bound over to keep the peace. Alternatively, he may release D once the threat of an arrestable offence being committed has passed, as it is likely to once D has been arrested. Section 30(7) (Art 32(10)) requires the release of a person arrested at a place other than a police station if the constable is satisfied that there are no grounds for keeping him under arrest. This section would appear to require the release of D if he is arrested for being about to commit an arrestable offence and the danger of its commission has passed. The constable (or a citizen) may also rely on the common law power to arrest or detain a person who is likely to cause a breach of the peace. If arrested, a magistrates' court may similarly bind him over to keep the peace and, if detained, he may be released once the danger of a breach of the peace has passed.

THE GENERAL ARREST POWER (s 25, Art 27)

5.55 Where a constable reasonably suspects that any offence which is not an arrestable offence or an offence in respect of which there is a summary power of arrest, has been committed or attempted, or is being committed or attempted, he may arrest the person he suspects of having committed etc the offence (the relevant person (s 25(2), art 27(2)), only if it appears to him that the service of a summons is impracticable or inappropriate because any of the general arrest conditions are satisfied (s 25(1), art 27(1)). (This power may be exercised in Scotland and Northern Ireland by any police officer in England and Wales, and by a Scottish or Northern Irish police officer in England or Wales – see s 137 of the Criminal Justice and Public Order Act 1994)

5.56 It is crucial to distinguish here between the arrestable offence (s 24, art 26), the preserved arrest power offence (Sch 2) and the general offence (s 25, art 27). Under s 24 (Art 26) and the various powers preserved by Sch 2 (discussed in para 5.138, post) the discretion to arrest is unfettered, whilst in the case of a general offence the discretion is fettered and an arrest is lawful only if the service of a summons is impracticable or inappropriate because any general arrest condition in s 25(3) (Art 27(3)) is satisfied. In theory the constable should apply criteria similar to these general arrest conditions in deciding whether to exercise his discretion to arrest for an arrestable offence or any other offence carrying a summary power of arrest. In practice, however, he will be more concerned with other factors such as the need to question the suspect or to exercise powers of search. These are not matters which can be considered in relation to an arrest under s 25 (Art 27), nor, given the nature of the general offences, will the constable need to do so very often. (In those rare cases in which a search of premises is required it can only be carried out under s 32(2)(b) (Art 34(2)(b)) (considered at para 4.74) or with consent.) In relation to offences to which the preserved powers of arrest apply they are offences which require a power of summary arrest not because they are serious but because the nature of the offence makes service of a summons impracticable or inappropriate (eg persons unlawfully at large, illegal entrants to the UK). Since the passing of PACE 1984 various laws have been enacted which provide summary powers of arrest for the same reasons as the preserved powers of arrest. A constable must then know which offences are arrestable offences, which offences carry a preserved power of arrest or a power of summary arrest, all three categories being arrestable summarily, and which offences are general offences. Since this latter category will only be arrestable if a general arrest condition is satisfied, it follows that a constable must also know the general arrest conditions. These conditions are designed to confine the arrest for general offences only to those occasions when it is necessary. The general arrest conditions, as set out in s 25(3) (Art 27(3)), are:

(a) that the name of the relevant person is unknown to, and cannot be readily ascertained by, the constable;

(b) that the constable has reasonable grounds for doubting whether a name furnished by the relevant person as his name is his real name;

(c) that –
   (i) the relevant person has failed to furnish a satisfactory address for service; or
   (ii) the constable has reasonable grounds for doubting whether an address furnished by the relevant person is a satisfactory address for service;

(d) that the constable has reasonable grounds for believing that arrest is necessary to prevent the relevant person –
   (i) causing physical injury to himself or any other person;
   (ii) suffering physical injury;
   (iii) causing loss of or damage to property;
   (iv) committing an offence against public decency; or
   (v) causing an unlawful obstruction of the highway;

(e) that the constable has reasonable grounds for believing that arrest is necessary to protect a child or other vulnerable person from the relevant person.

5.57 Arrest is possible 'if it appears to him [the constable] that service of a summons is impracticable or inappropriate' because any of these conditions is satisfied. This suggests a subjective test, ie the constable need only act honestly and need not show any reasonable grounds for his decision. However, the requirements in conditions (b), (c)(ii), (d) and (e) all specify reasonable grounds whilst the remaining conditions (a) and (c)(i) are matters of fact. The test is therefore objective.

5.58 A constable cannot be said reasonably to doubt that the relevant person has given his correct name and address simply because in his experience people who commit offences do not give correct details (*G v DPP* (1989)). Such cynicism has no reasonable basis. It must be emphasised that the arrest is for an offence; the constable must, therefore, first tell the suspect what offence he is suspected of. Having done so he should then request the suspect's name and address. In doing so he need not inform a suspect why he wants it, for example, to facilitate service of a summons (*Nicholas v Parsonage* (1987)).

SERVICE OF A SUMMONS IMPRACTICABLE OR INAPPROPRIATE (s 25(3)(A), (B) AND (C)(I) AND (II), Art 27(3)(A), (B) AND (C)(I) AND (II))

5.59 General arrest conditions (a), (b) and (c) are concerned with the likely effectiveness of the summons procedure; (a) and (b) are self-explanatory. The question raised by conditions (c)(i) and (ii) is, 'What is a satisfactory address for service?' and it is partially answered by s 25(4) (Art 27(4)):

' … an address is a satisfactory address for service if it appears to the constable–
- (a) that the relevant person will be at it for a sufficiently long period for it to be possible to serve him with a summons; or
- (b) that some other person specified by the relevant person will accept service of a summons for the relevant person at it.'

5.60 The commission of offences in the UK by foreign nationals created problems for the police. Because process could not be served in the offender's country, s 25 (Art 27) was relied upon to justify the arrest of the foreign national who was then subjected to 'instant' justice. For example, a French lorry driver drives dangerously in the UK and causes an accident. The Crime (International Co-operation) Act 2003 enables the police to serve process in a foreign state (ss 1 and 2). This means that an arrest under s 25(3) (Art 27(3)) may not be justified simply on the basis that service of process is impracticable or inappropriate because the alleged offender is not a UK resident.

SHORT-TERM RESIDENCY

5.61 Section 25(4)(a) (Art 27(4)(a)) envisages the situation in which a person is temporarily residing at a particular address but is likely to have moved on before a summons can be served, eg the itinerant vagrant staying at a charitable hostel, the traveller or gypsy, or simply the holidaymaker staying at a guest house. The average time for the service of a summons was 88 days (Royal Commission Research Study No 9 (1981)) and may be longer in areas in which a seasonal variation in the prosecution workload is experienced. The address of such persons will seldom be a satisfactory address for service. If therefore such a person is unable to offer an alternative address which is a satisfactory address, or to specify someone, who must by implication reside at a satisfactory address, who will accept service of a summons on his behalf, he will be arrested. In the case of the person with no fixed abode, specifying someone willing to accept service of a summons is the only way to avoid arrest.

VERIFICATION OF NAME, ADDRESS OR SPECIFIED PERSON

5.62   A power to detain while the name, address or other details were verified was removed from the PACE Bill at an early stage following protest, but a process of verification must take place and in many cases where it appears to the constable that verification can be obtained in a reasonably short time, he should explain to the relevant person that verification is necessary and should invite him to remain with him, while the verification takes place. He should also explain that non-co-operation will result in immediate arrest. If the person refuses to remain, then he must be arrested. Indeed, such a refusal will give the constable further reasonable grounds for doubting that the name or address is correct or that the address is satisfactory. Where the verification process appears likely to take some time the person may be arrested. The guiding principle should be that of protecting the dignity of the individual and subjecting him to the least inconvenience or embarrassment. For example, if it will take an hour to convey a person to a police station and a shorter time to verify the details, it may be more convenient for him to remain with the constable while the verification takes place. On the other hand, it may be less embarrassing to arrest him and take him to a police station for verification than invite him to wait in a busy street for 15 minutes or more. Section 25(1) (Art 27(1)) gives a discretion to arrest when a general arrest condition is satisfied. The constable need not do so if the objective of ensuring that a summons can be served may be achieved without arrest. If an arrest is made and the verification process is completed in the relevant person's favour before he arrives at a police station, the constable is under a legal duty to release the person (see s 30(7) (Art 32(10)) discussed in para 5.138, post). At the police station the duty to release, once the grounds for detention (which in the case of an arrest under s 25 are also the grounds for arrest) cease to exist, rests with the custody officer (see s 34(2) discussed in para 6.32, post).

PROTECTIVE AND PREVENTIVE ARREST (s 25(3)(D)(I)-(V) AND (E), Art 25(3)(D)(I)-(V) AND (E))

5.63   These general arrest conditions are concerned with the necessity to arrest in order to protect persons or property or in order to put an end to the offence or prevent further offences.

PHYSICAL INJURY TO RELEVANT PERSON OR ANOTHER (s 25(3)(D)(I), Art 27(3)(D)(I))

5.64   As to general arrest condition (d)(i), the most obvious situation is that in which the relevant person has committed, or is committing or attempting to commit, a minor assault (ie not a serious assault amounting to an arrestable offence) upon the person of another and is still threatening violence when the police arrive. Service of a summons may well be practicable but totally inappropriate if there are reasonable grounds for believing that he will continue to be violent and to cause injury to others. The other obvious case is where the relevant person threatens to harm himself. Both examples may overlap with other powers of arrest. The first coincides with arrest for a breach of the peace and in the second the relevant person may be mentally disordered and the power to arrest under s 136 of the Mental Health Act 1983 (Mental Health (NI) Order 1986) (preserved by Sch 2 of PACE 1984 and the 1989 Order) may be invoked. In neither of these cases, however, need the person have committed an offence, whereas an offence is an essential prerequisite in the case of an arrest under s 25 (Art 27).

INTERFERENCE WITH WITNESSES

5.65 The general arrest conditions do not, unlike the detention conditions after charge in s 38(1)(a)(v) (Art 39(1)(a)(v)) (discussed in para 6.74, post), refer to arrest in order to prevent interference with the administration of justice or with the investigation of an offence. However, if such interference takes the form of threats of violence to persons against whom the original offence was committed or who are witnesses to it, then condition (d)(i) is appropriate to deal with the situation. If there are reasonable grounds to believe that the relevant person will interfere with the course of justice or the investigation of the offence by destroying evidence, then condition (d)(iii) would be appropriate.

ARREST TO PREVENT THE RELEVANT PERSON SUFFERING PHYSICAL INJURY (s 25(3)(D)(II), Art 27(3)(D)(II))

5.66 General arrest condition (d)(ii) is concerned with the situation where the suspected offender is likely to be physically attacked by others, for example by relatives of the victim. This is particularly likely in cases involving sexual offences against children. It must be appreciated that threats of violence towards a suspected offender may justify the arrest of those uttering those threats and a constable should be slow to arrest D because P threatens to commit an offence against D. However, the arrest of D is often the only practical solution, particularly if a number of persons utter such threats. Arresting them and leaving D at large is likely to exacerbate the situation.

CAUSING LOSS OF OR DAMAGE TO PROPERTY (s 25(3)(D)(III), Art 27(3)(D)(III))

5.67 'Property' is not defined but in this context it is likely to be interpreted as meaning property of a tangible nature, real or personal. There is no need to extend it to include animals as do other statutory definitions, since s 12(1) of the Protection of Animals Act 1911, which permits the arrest of a person in order to prevent harm to animals which are the subject of an offence under that Act, is preserved by s 26(2) and

Sch 2 to this Act. Where there are reasonable grounds to believe that it is necessary to arrest in order to prevent damage to, or the destruction of, property belonging to another, there will be a power to arrest under s 24(6) (Art 25(6)), since causing criminal damage is an arrestable offence. However, general arrest condition (d)(iii) applies to the loss of or damage to any property, including property owned by the relevant person. If then D, P's estranged husband, finds P in the domestic home with her boyfriend, attacks the boyfriend and proceeds to break up the home, the property being damaged may well belong to D and such damage is not an offence of criminal damage and the assault may not amount to an arrestable offence. However, D may be arrested for the general offence of assault on the boyfriend because condition (d)(iii) is satisfied. The arrest may have a salutary effect on D and if, before arriving at the police station, the constable is satisfied that there is no longer a threat to property D must be released (s 30(7), art 32(10)). An alternative method of dealing with such a situation is to use the common law power to detain a person committing or about to commit a breach of the peace. If D calms down and the threat to the peace disappears, D may be released (see *Albert v Lavin* (1982) and the discussion in para 5.84, post).

5.68   Note that s 25(3)(d)(iii) (Art 27(3)(d)(iii)) is not qualified and refers to any damage to property. Together with the summary power of arrest under s 24 (Art 26) for the offence of criminal damage the police have ample powers to arrest in order to prevent damage to property.

EVIDENCE RELATING TO THE OFFENCE

5.69   The property which may be lost or damaged may well be evidence of the offence which D is alleged to have committed. Most property offences are arrestable under s 24 (Art 26) but there may be occasions when the relevant person is in possession of, or will have access to, property which is evidence of the general offence of which he is suspected and it may be reasonable to believe that it will be destroyed if D remains at large. In such a case general arrest condition (d)(iii) will be satisfied. For example, A approached a constable in the street and complained that D had just shown him indecent photographs of children. Possession of such photographs is an offence under s 160 of the Criminal Justice Act 1988 (as amended by s 84 of the CJPOA 1994) which is triable only summarily though it is now punishable by imprisonment for up to six months (s 86(1)of the CJPOA 1994). D may well give his correct name and address so that a summons may be served but is likely to destroy the photographs if left at large. D may then be arrested. When D is arrested there is a power to search him or the premises in which he was arrested or in which he was immediately before he was arrested for evidence of the offence (s 32(2)(a)(ii) and (b), art 34(a)(ii) and (b)).

COMMITTING AN OFFENCE AGAINST PUBLIC DECENCY (s 25(3)(D)(IV),Art 27(3)(D)(IV))

5.70   This general arrest condition is qualified by s 25(5) (Art 27(5)) so as to impose the further condition that an arrest for an offence against public decency can only be made if the conduct takes place in circumstances where members of the public going about their normal business cannot reasonably be expected to avoid the person to be arrested. Since the purpose of this general arrest condition is to enable the constable to remove by arrest the offending person in the circumstances mentioned, it is clear that 'offence against public decency' must refer to offences involving public nudity by such a person, rather than those involving indecent advertisements or displays. The most common offences against public decency are those of indecent exposure – wilful etc exposure of the person (penis) with intent to insult a female, contrary to s 4 of the Vagrancy Act 1824 and similarly s 28 of the Town Police Clauses Act 1847. There is also a rarely used common law offence of outraging public decency, usually committed by exposing the body in public or doing lewd acts. The statutory offences can only be committed by a male against a female while the common law offence may also be committed by a female, eg a Lady Godiva. In addition the Indecency with Children Act 1960 created the offence of indecency towards a child (under 14) which, in so far as it requires merely incitement to do an act of gross indecency, is very similar to the offence of indecent exposure. Persons reasonably suspected of committing any of these offences can only be arrested if the offence is committed in the circumstances stated in s 25(5), eg a man indecently exposing himself in a busy shopping precinct can expect to be arrested as may the person sunbathing nude on a busy seaside promenade or bathing nude on a busy public beach not set aside for that purpose (note that s 25 (Art 27) permits arrest for offences against local byelaws if a general arrest condition is satisfied whereas previously local byelaws did not normally carry a power of arrest). Female nudity, apart from nude bathing, is not specifically made an offence by statute, though it can be an offence at common law. Thus a woman running bare-breasted across a football pitch commits the common law offence of indecent exposure and may be arrested under s 25(3)(d)(iv) (Art 27(3)(d)(iv)). The power to arrest a woman soliciting in a public place for the purposes of prostitution under s 1(3) of the Street Offences Act 1959 is preserved by s 26(2) and Sch 2 of PACE 1984. Therefore the question whether soliciting is an offence against public decency does not arise.

MALE IMPORTUNING AND INDECENCY BETWEEN MEN

5.71   It is an offence under s 32 of the Sexual Offences Act 1956 for a man persistently (ie more than one invitation or a series of invitations) to solicit or importune in a public place for an immoral purpose. 'Immoral purpose' may include a man soliciting a woman of any age to have intercourse with him even if the sexual intercourse would not be criminal, eg with a consenting female over 16 (*R v Goddard* (1990)) (see also the Sexual Offences Act 1985, s 1), and importuning men of any age for homosexual purposes. It is doubtful whether the offence can be described as an offence against public decency for the purposes of s 25(3)(d)(iv), in which case arrest for the offence will depend upon another general arrest condition being satisfied. Section 41 of the Sexual Offences Act 1956 permits anyone to arrest without warrant anyone found committing an offence under s 32 (and ss 30 and 31). Clearly, so far as the citizen is concerned, this power is unaffected by the repeal of constables' statutory powers of arrest by s 26 of PACE 1984. It is clear that 'anyone' in s 41 of the 1956 Act includes a constable, but Sch 6, para 9 of PACE 1984 amended s 41, adding at the end of the section the words, 'but a constable may only do so in accordance with s 25 of the Police and Criminal Evidence Act 1984'. The result is that the citizen has a greater power of arrest than a constable, albeit only in respect of the offences to which s 41 applies (see further the discussion at para 5.82, post). Most offences of buggery or of gross indecency are arrestable offences being punishable by five or more years' imprisonment, but some forms of both offences are general offences being punishable by only two years' imprisonment (see s 3 of the Sexual Offences Act 1967). Few of these offences will be committed in public though gross indecency in the form of, for example, mutual masturbation may take place in public toilets and in such a situation s 25(3)(d)(iv) may permit an arrest.

OBSTRUCTION OF THE HIGHWAY (s 25(3)(D)(V), Art 27(3)(D)(V))

5.72   General arrest condition (d)(v) deals with those situations in which an offence of unlawfully obstructing the highway is committed and the person committing the offence refuses to move, for example, the protester who sits down in the highway. If he refuses to move on request the only way to prevent the offence continuing is to arrest him. The condition would be satisfied if the facts of *Gelberg v Miller* (1961) were repeated. A motorist refused three requests to move his car parked in a restricted street. When the police threatened to move it, he removed the distributor arm. While s 25 does enable a constable to arrest for parking on a double yellow line, it is only in circumstances of non-co-operation that an arrest would be necessary or permissible for such a trivial offence.

PROTECTION OF CHILDREN AND OTHER VULNERABLE PERSONS (s 25(3)(E), Art 27(3)(E))

5.73   General arrest condition (e) may overlap with condition (d)(i) in that a child or other vulnerable person may be threatened with physical injury. However, condition (e) is wider and would include the reasonable belief that a child or other vulnerable person might suffer psychological damage if the relevant person is left at large. This would require circumstances in which the child or vulnerable person lives in close proximity to the relevant person and will usually involve a close relationship between them. Since most sexual offences against a child are arrestable offences, condition (e) must be directed at lesser offences such as that contained in s 1 of the Indecency with Children Act 1960 which is punishable, on summary conviction, by up to six months' imprisonment or a fine of £2,000 or both. If, for example, a stepfather were to commit an act of gross indecency towards his stepdaughter, or incite her to such an act with him, the offence under s 1 is committed. In such circumstances it may be wrong to leave the child in a position of moral danger and possibly at risk of being the victim of a more serious offence. Section 25(3)(e) (Art 27(3)(e)) would enable a constable to arrest the stepfather and s 38(1)(a)(ii) (Art 39(1)(a)(ii)) would permit his detention after charge if the circumstances give rise to a reasonable belief that it is necessary to protect the child from physical harm. The reasonable belief that D may commit more serious sexual offences if released would satisfy the latter subsection. While D is detained steps may be taken to protect the child, by alerting social services who may take proceedings under the Children Act 1989 in respect of the child. Alternatively, if D is charged with an offence the police may now impose a condition of D's release on bail that he live elsewhere until the case is tried (Bail Act 1976, s 3(6) as amended by s 27 of the Criminal Justice and Public Order Act 1994).

5.74 Also within condition (3)(e) is the offence of being drunk while in charge of a child under s 2 of the Licensing Act 1902. The domestic situation in which a violent man is threatening his wife or cohabitee would satisfy condition (e) but overlaps with condition (d)(i) if the threat is of physical injury, or (d)(iii) if it is of damage to property. The relevant person must have committed an offence and the conditions do not provide a means of removing a person from the domestic home in the absence of an offence. Where an injunction has been granted under the Domestic Violence and Matrimonial Proceedings Act 1976 to which a power of arrest is attached under s 2(3) of that Act, or an order of a magistrates' court has been made under s 16 of the Domestic Proceedings and Magistrates' Courts Act 1978 prohibiting the person from entering the matrimonial home and a power of arrest is added under s 18 of that Act, a person who enters in breach of the injunction or order, or who threatens or uses violence towards the spouse or cohabitee, may be arrested by virtue of the above powers. These powers of arrest were not repealed by s 26(1) (Art 28(1)) since they are orders of a court, not a power of arrest provided by an Act. Where no injunction or order has been granted but an offence, which is not an arrestable offence within s 24, has been committed in such a domestic situation, then arrest may be justified because general arrest condition (d)(i) or (e) is satisfied. Where a breach of the peace takes place or is apprehended, common law powers to arrest or detain may be invoked (see para 5.84, post).

PRESERVED POWERS OF ARREST WITHOUT WARRANT (s 26(2), Art 28(2) AND Sch 2)

5.75 (NB: Schedule 2 of the PACE (NI) Order 1989 contains a different list of preserved powers of arrest but the categories are not dissimilar.) Schedule 2 lists 21 statutes which contain powers authorising a constable to arrest without a warrant or court order. Each is preserved because there is, or is thought to be, a need for powers of arrest, unfettered by the general arrest conditions, in respect of offences which are not sufficiently serious to be categorised as arrestable offences, or in order to preserve existing powers of arrest of persons who have not committed criminal offences but must be detained either for their own safety or because they are illegally at large. The powers will be considered according to eight broad categories into which they fall.

(1) Category I – Persons unlawfully at large including persons absent from places where they were lawfully detained, deserters or absentees from HM Forces and illegal immigrants. The following powers fall into this category:

Repatriation of Prisoners Act 1984, s 5(5)

Mental Health Act 1983, ss 18, 35(10), 36(8), 38(7) and 138

Reserve Forces Act 1980, Sch 5

Bail Act 1976, s 7 (person in breach of bail condition or likely to breach bail)

Immigration Act 1971, s 24(2) and paras 17, 24 and 33 of Sch 2 and para 7 of Sch 3

Children and Young Persons Act 1969, ss 32 and 32(1)(1A) as substituted by Sch 12, para 27, of the Children Act 1989 (child absent without consent from a place of safety or local authority accommo-dation in which he is required to live)

Naval Discipline Act 1957, ss 104 and 105

Army Act 1955, ss 186 and 190B

Air Force Act 1955, ss 186 and 190B

Visiting Forces Act 1952, s 13

Prison Act 1952, s 49

(2) Category II – Terrorism and related offences

Emergency Powers Act 1920, s 2 (a power of arrest may be attached to regulations made under the Act)

Military Lands Act 1892, s 17(2) (power to make byelaws in respect of military lands and to arrest persons in breach of those byelaws, cf Greenham Common)

Schedule 2 also preserved some arrest provisions under the Prevention of Terrorism (Temporary Provisions) Act 1984. That Act was repealed and replaced by the Prevention of Terrorism (Temporary Provisions) Act 1989. Section 14 of the 1989 Act provides a power of arrest without warrant for offences under ss 2, 8, 9, 10 and 11 of the Act (s 14(1)(a)). Persons concerned in the commission etc of acts of terrorism may also be arrested without warrant (s 14(1)(b)) as may a person subject to an exclusion order provided that if the arrest is made in Great Britain the exclusion order was made under s 5 of the 1989 Act; if in Northern Ireland, under s 6 of the Act (s 14(1)(c) and (3)).

(3) Category III – Protection of animals

Animal Health Act 1981, ss 60(5) and 61(1)

Protection of Animals Act 1911, s 12(1)

(The general arrest conditions in s 25(3) do not permit arrest to prevent continuing harm to animals or the spread of disease by obstructing or impeding a constable enforcing the provisions of the 1981 Act. The power of arrest under s 61(1) of the 1981 Act is preserved to prevent the spread of rabies.)

(4) Category IV – Road traffic offences   PACE 1984 preserved the powers of arrest under the Road Traffic Act 1972. That Act has been overtaken by the Road Traffic Act 1988, ss 4(5), 6(5) and 103(3) which provide an unfettered power to arrest persons driving etc under the influence of drink or drugs, or with excess alcohol in the blood, or driving while disqualified. An unfettered power of arrest is required to prevent the person continuing to drive. For the power to enter premises to arrest see para 4.112, ante.

(One may note that the Transport and Works Act 1992, Part II, Chapter I, creates similar offences in relation to railway, tramway or other modes of guided transport as is specified by the Secretary of State which are used or intended to be used for the carriage of members of the public.)

Section 39 expressly excludes the operation of ss 4-11 of the Road Traffic Act 1988 in relation to such forms of transport and creates a very similar scheme which is applicable to persons working on such transport systems in a capacity which controls the movement of the vehicle or in a maintenance capacity. Section 27(1) creates the offences of being unfit to control the movement of the vehicle or to do the job of maintenance, while s 27(2) creates the offence of working in one of those capacities with excess alcohol in the blood. Section 29 provides a power to require a breath test when there is reasonable cause to suspect that a person who is, or has been working in one of the above capacities, or where there has been an accident or serious incident and there is reasonable cause to suspect that the person was working in one of the above capacities and his act or omission may have been a cause. Section 30(1)-(2) provides a power of arrest without warrant if he reasonably suspects that the person has committed an offence under s 27(1) or if as a result of a breath test he has reasonable cause to suspect that the proportion of alcohol in the breath or blood exceeds the prescribed limit, or if the person fails (which includes refuses) to provide a specimen.

Section 30(3) provides a power to enter premises in order to arrest under sub-s(1)-(2) and in order to require a breath test in the case of an accident involving death or injury to another (see para 4.41, ante).

(5) Category V – Soliciting for the purpose of prostitution

> Street Offences Act 1959, s 1(3) (the section gives a constable a power to arrest without warrant for the offence of soliciting in a public place for the purpose of prostitution. This area of law is currently under review and the power of arrest is preserved pending the final recommendation of the Criminal Law Revision Committee.)

(6) Category VI – Arrest for protection

> Mental Health Act 1983, s 136 (power to arrest a mentally disordered person to take him to a place of safety).

(7) Category VII – Election offences

> Section 36, Sch 1 of the Representation of the People Act 1983 (persons suspected of personation).

(8) Category VIII – Squatting and public order offences

(a)   Squatting offences

Criminal Law Act 1977, ss 6(6), 7(11), 8(4), 9(7) and 10(5). The Criminal Law Act 1977 created a number of offences in connection with the adverse occupation of premises, known colloquially as 'squatting', and gives a uniformed constable a power of arrest in respect of those offences with the exception of the offence created by s 6. That exception (using or threatening violence for the purpose of gaining entry to premises known to be occupied by someone opposed to such entry) is covered by general arrest conditions: PACE Act 1984, s 25(3)(d)(i) and (iii).

The general arrest conditions are inappropriate to the other offences under the 1977 Act given the need to arrest in order to put an immediate end to the offence and/or to enable the offenders to be physically removed from the premises. The powers of arrest provided by the sections mentioned above were therefore preserved. Section 17(1)(c) of PACE 1984 restates the power previously contained in s 11 of the 1977 Act to enter premises in order to arrest a person for these offences. This power is discussed at para 4.34, ante. A new civil procedure for an interim possession order seeks to enable the person entitled to possession to regain it more quickly. Sections 72 to 76 of the Criminal Justice and Public Order Act 1994 amend the squatting provisions and create a number of offences related to the interim possession order. Section 76 of the 1994 Act makes it an offence for a person to remain on the premises as a trespasser during the currency of the order, or, having left the premises, to re-enter or attempt to re-enter the premises as a trespasser after the expiry of the order within one year beginning with the day on which it was served. Sub-s (7) provides that a constable in uniform may arrest such an offender without warrant.

(b)   Public order offences

Public Order Act 1936, s 7(3). Section 7(3) gives a constable a power to arrest without warrant any person reasonably suspected of committing an offence under s 1 (wearing a uniform signifying association with any political organisation in a public place or at a public meeting). Sections 4 and 5 of the 1936 Act were repealed by the Public Order Act 1986. The offence under s 4, which prohibited a person having with him an offensive weapon at a public meeting or procession, overlapped with the offence under s 1 of the Prevention of Crime Act 1953. The repeal of s 4 means that the 1953 Act must be relied upon where a person has with him at a public meeting or procession any offensive weapon. The common law offences of riot, rout, unlawful assembly and affray were replaced by the 1986 Act. Subsection 1 and 2 create the offences of riot and violent disorder respectively. On conviction on indictment riot is punishable by ten years' imprisonment and violent disorder by five years' imprisonment. Therefore both are arrestable offences as defined by s 24(1)(b) of PACE.

The Act also created a number of offences to which are attached summary powers of arrest. The following sections permit a constable to arrest anyone he reasonably suspects is:

s 3(6) – committing an affray;

s 4(3) – causing fear or provocation of violence;

s 12(7) – knowingly failing to comply with conditions imposed on a public procession;

s 14(7) – knowingly failing to comply with conditions on a public assembly;

s 18(4) – using threatening etc words or behaviour;

s 32(4) – entering football premises in breach of an exclusion order.

Four sections provide a power to arrest a person reasonably suspected of committing an offence but only if the constable is in uniform:

s 13(10) – taking part in a prohibited procession;

s 14B(4) – organising, taking part in or inciting a person to take part in the holding of an assembly prohibited by an order made under s 14A;

s 14C(4) – failing to comply with a direction not to proceed in the direction of an assembly prohibited by an order made under s 14A (ss 14A, 14B and 14C added to the 1986 Act by s 70 of the Criminal Justice and Public Order Act 1994);

s 39(3) – two or more persons trespassing on land.

There is also a power of arrest for the offence under s 5(4) of causing harassment, alarm or distress but only if the person:

(a) engages in offensive conduct which the constable warns him to stop, and

(b) engages in further offensive conduct immediately or shortly after the warning.

(NB: In *DPP v Hancock and Tuttle* (1995) it was held that the words 'the constable' in (a) meant that only the constable who warns the person to stop may arrest under s 5(4).)

5.76   The Criminal Justice and Public Order Act 1994 provides the police with powers to remove trespassers from land, to prevent unauthorised raves, to remove disruptive trespassers and amends the Public Order Act 1986 to create a new offence of trespassory assembly. Each of these offences carries a power to arrest without warrant. The offences are as follows.

(1)   Section 61 – Trespassing on land with the common purpose of residing there.

If the senior officer present reasonably believes the terms of subsection (1) are satisfied he may direct the persons to leave the land and to remove their vehicles and property.

A person who knows that such a direction has been given which applies to him who fails to leave, or who having left enters the land again within three months of the day on which the direction was given, commits an offence. Though a summary offence punishable by up to three months' imprisonment, a level 4 fine, or both, sub-s (4) permits a constable in uniform who reasonably suspects that a person is committing the offence to arrest without warrant (s 61(1), (2) and (4)). Subsection (3) provides that the direction to leave, if not communicated by the senior officer present, may be communicated by any constable at the scene. The arresting officer need not therefore have given the direction thus avoiding the difficulty caused by the drafting of s 5(4) of the 1986 Act – see *DPP v Hancock and Tuttle* (1995) above.

(2)   Section 63 – A superintendent or above who reasonably believes that two or more persons are making preparations for an unauthorised rave to be held in the open air which ten or more persons are waiting to attend or are attending, may give a direction that they leave the land and remove any vehicles or property from the land.

If that direction is not communicated by the superintendent it may be communicated by any constable at the scene. It is an offence for a person who knows that a direction has been given which applies to him to fail to leave or, having left, to return within a period of seven days beginning with the day on which the direction was given. This offence is punishable to exactly the same extent as that under s 62 and sub-s (8) gives a constable in uniform the power to arrest without warrant a person reasonably suspected of committing this offence (s 63(1)-(8)).

(3) Section 65 – A constable in uniform who reasonably believes that a person is on his way to an unauthorised rave which has been the subject of a direction under s 63(2) has the power to stop the person and direct him not to proceed in the direction of that rave.

A person who knows that such a direction has been given to him and fails to comply commits an offence and a constable in uniform who reasonably suspects that a person is committing this offence may arrest him without warrant. (NB: 'Exempt persons' includes the occupier, any member of his family, employees, agent or any person whose home is on the land in question, all of whom cannot be the subject of a direction under ss 63 or 65.)

Section 68

5.77   A person commits the offence of aggravated trespass if he trespasses on land in the open air and, in relation to any lawful activity which persons are engaging in or are about to engage in on that or adjoining land in the open air, does there anything which is intended by him to have the effect:

(a)   of intimidating those persons or of any of them so as to deter them or any of them from engaging in that activity; or

(b)   of obstructing that activity; or

(c)   of disrupting that activity.

5.78   ('Lawful activity' means an activity which does not involve an offence or trespass on the land.) This offence is punishable by three months' imprisonment, a level 4 fine, or both but sub-s (4) provides that a constable in uniform who reasonably suspects that a person is committing an offence under this section may arrest him without warrant (s 68(1)-(4)).

5.79   (It should be noted that s 17(1)(c) of PACE 1984 provides a power to enter premises in order to effect the arrest of a person for an offence under s 1 of the 1936 Act and s 4 of the 1986 Act. This is discussed at para 4.34, ante. In relation to s 63 of the CJPOA 1994 (power to stop unauthorised raves), s 64 allows a superintendent who reasonably believes that circum-stances exist which would justify the giving of a direction under s 63 to authorise any constable to enter the land: (a) to ascertain whether such circumstances exist; and (b) to exercise the powers conferred on a constable by s 63, eg the power of arrest under s 63(8), or the powers of seizure provided by s 64(4).)

5.80   The Sporting Events (Control of Alcohol etc) Act 1985 created a number of summary (or general) offences involving the possession of intoxicating liquor and drink containers capable of causing injury, eg cans and bottles, in connection with a designated sporting event in a designated sports ground or on a specified vehicle. Section 7 provides that a constable may arrest a person whom he has reasonable grounds to suspect is committing or has committed an offence under the Act. Section 7 makes no reference to attempting to commit, as does s 25 of PACE 1984. The nature of the offences under the 1985 Act leaves little scope for an attempted offence but, if the conduct falls short of the commission of an offence under the 1985 Act, the power to arrest for an attempt to commit an offence under s 25 of PACE 1984 may be used subject to an arrest condition being satisfied. The Football Spectators Act 1989, s 2 created the offence of not being an authorised spectator entering or remaining on premises as a spectator during a period relevant to a designated football match. Section 2(4) provides a power to arrest without warrant a person reasonably suspected of committing such an offence.

5.81 Section 29 of the Criminal Justice and Public Order Act 1994 inserts a new s 46A into PACE 1984 which permits a constable to arrest a person released on bail subject to a duty to return to a police station who fails to attend at the appointed time. This is an arrest for an offence and the offence is that for which he was originally arrested and bailed (s 46A(2) and s 34(7)). The equivalent power in Northern Ireland is provided by art 47A of the 1989 Order, inserted by art 7 of the Police (Amendment) (NI) Order 1995 (see further para 6.189, post).

POWERS OF ARREST OF PERSONS WHO ARE NOT CONSTABLES (s 26(1), Art 28(1))

5.82 Section 26(1) (Art 28(1)) repeals only those statutory powers which enable a constable to arrest without warrant for an offence or for conduct which is not an offence (eg a mentally disordered person in a public place). 'Constable' refers to the ancient office of constable (see para 2.41, ante). Consequently, statutory powers of arrest given to 'any person' (see eg Theft Act 1978, s 3(4); Sexual Offences Act 1967, s 5(3); Criminal Justice Act 1967, s 91; Sexual Offences Act 1956, s 41 (and see s 32 discussed at para 5.71, ante); Licensing Act 1902, s 1; Prevention of Offences Act 1851, s 11; Vagrancy Act 1824, s 6 (as amended by the Criminal Justice Act 1948, s 68) and others (eg Customs and Excise officers and immigration officers) who are not constables, are unaffected by the repeal. Moreover since a constable comes within the term 'any person', the powers of arrest directed to any person may be exercised by a constable. In *DPP v Kitching* (1990) the Queen's Bench Divisional Court held that s 91 of the Criminal Justice Act 1967, which provides that, 'Any person who in a public place is guilty, while drunk, of disorderly behaviour, may be arrested without warrant' had not been repealed by s 26 of PACE 1984. Section 26 and Sch 2 purport to abolish the power of arrest whereas para 21 of Sch 6 implies that s 91 remains in force. This latter provision made it clear that a constable's power to arrest under s 91 survived by directing that a constable arresting under s 91 take the person to a treatment centre. The Divisional Court held that the power to arrest was unaffected by s 25 by reason of the express provision in s 25(6) that the section shall not prejudice any power of arrest conferred apart from s 25. It follows that other powers which permit 'any person' to arrest without warrant are similarly unaffected by s 25. Therefore a constable exercising such a power of arrest is not under a legal duty to comply with s 25 – except in relation to an arrest under s 41 of the Sexual Offences Act 1956 (power to arrest in cases of soliciting by men), since para 9 of Sch 6 of PACE 1984 amends that section by adding the words, 'but a constable may only do so in accordance with s 25 of the Police and Criminal Evidence Act 1984'. A Home Office Circular on PACE 1984 suggests that it may be prudent to use these powers only when a s 25 condition is met. Unlike the preserved powers of arrest set out in Sch 2, there will seldom be a need for summary arrest in respect of the offences dealt with by the statutes referred to and compliance with s 25 will not therefore be detrimental to the police.

COMMON LAW POWERS OF ARREST

5.83   Section 25(6) (Art 27(6)) and s 26 (Art 28) repealed only statutory powers of arrest. Consequently the one power of arrest which the common law confers, namely arrest for breach of the peace, was not affected by the Act (*DPP v Orum* (1989)). A breach of the peace was at one time thought to be any breach of the Queen's peace, but in *R v Howell* (1982) the Court of Appeal said:

'We are emboldened to say that there is a breach of the peace whenever harm is actually done or is likely to be done to a person or in his presence to his property or a person is in fear of being harmed through an assault, an affray, a riot, unlawful assembly or other disturbance.'

5.84   The decision emphasises that violence, actual or apprehended, is an essential ingredient of a breach of the peace. It follows that loud noise and boisterous behaviour is not, without more, a breach. Any person may arrest for a breach of the peace committed in his presence, or where he has reasonable cause to believe a breach of the peace will be committed by a person in the immediate future unless he is arrested, or where a breach of the peace has been committed and he has reasonable grounds to believe it will be renewed if he is not arrested (Howell). Where a breach is reasonably apprehended a brief detention and restraint may be sufficient to enable the culprit to calm down, and no further action will be necessary. The common law permits such detention. Lord Diplock in *Albert v Lavin* (1982) put it thus:

'Any person in whose presence a breach of the peace is being or reasonably appears to be about to be, committed has the right to take reasonable steps to make the person who is breaking or threatening to break the peace refrain from doing so; and those reasonable steps in appropriate cases will include detaining him against his will. At common law it is not only the right of every citizen, it is also his duty, although, except in the case of a citizen who is a constable, it is a duty of imperfect obligation.'

5.85   It is then lawful temporarily to detain and restrain a person breaking or threatening to break the peace without arresting him. If he desists or ceases to threaten a breach of the peace, he may be released. If he persists he may be arrested. Resistance to such restraint is unlawful. A breach of the peace is not a substantive offence but a magistrates' court may deal with it by binding over the person to keep the peace. For powers of entry to effect an arrest for, or to prevent or stop, a breach of the peace see para 4.100, ante. (One may note the overlap between this common law power and the statutory power under s 24(7) (Art 26(7)) which authorises a constable to arrest a person who is committing, or who is reasonably suspected to be about to commit an arrestable offence, discussed in para 5.51, ante.)

Arrest for fingerprinting and to obtain non-intimate samples

Arrest to obtain fingerprints (s 27, art 29)

5.86   (NB: PACE 1984, s 61 and the NI Order, art 61 are the same, therefore only s 61 will be referred to.)

5.87   A person arrested for a recordable offence (an offence which is listed in the National Police Records (Recordable Offences) Regulations 1985, SI 1985/1941, as amended by SI 1989/694 and SI 1997/566, made under s 27(4)), who is detained at a police station, charged with or been informed that he will be reported for such an offence, will have his fingerprints taken without his consent if the circumstances set out in s 61(3) and (4) apply (see paras 7.189-7.198, post). He may also have them taken if he is arrested, detained and charged with, or reported for, any offence if he consents in writing (s 61(2)). If the person is convicted of a recordable offence his fingerprints may also be taken without his consent (s 61(6)), and if given a custodial sentence they will be taken while in prison service custody. The purpose of taking fingerprints post charge and conviction is not so that they may be used in evidence, rather it is to enable the police to build up a data bank of fingerprints for purposes of comparison. Section 27 (Art 29) is concerned with the comparatively rare situation in which a person has been convicted of a recordable offence, has not been in police detention for that offence, did not have his fingerprints taken in the course of the investigation by the police, or since the conviction, ie he was not given a custodial sentence in respect of that offence. In these circumstances he may at any time not later than one month after the date of the conviction, be required by any constable to attend a police station so that his fingerprints may be taken (s 27(1), art 29(1)). Such a requirement must give the person a period of at least seven days within which he must attend at the police station, and may direct that he attend at a specified time or between specified times of the day (s 27(2), art 29(2)). If the person fails to comply with a requirement any constable may arrest him without warrant (s 27(3), art 29(3)). 'Month' means a calendar month (Interpretation Act 1978, Sch 1) and in computing the period the date of the conviction will normally be excluded and the date of the requirement included (*Radcliffe v Bartholomew* (1892)). For example, if D is convicted on 30 May, a constable has until 30 June (effectively 23 June since the requirement must give seven days within which to attend a police station) to make the requirement. The power to arrest arises at the end of the seven-day period whenever it is made, eg D is convicted on 30 May. P makes the requirement on 4 June specifying that D attend between 5pm and 6pm during the next seven days. Assuming the requirement is made in time to enable D to attend between those times, the power of arrest is available from 11 June. If made after 7pm on 4 June, that day cannot be counted in the seven days. One may note that the power of arrest is not limited to within one month of the conviction – if a requirement is made within that period and is not complied with, D may be arrested at any time thereafter.

Arrest to obtain samples (ss 61, 62 and 63 of PACE 1984 and Order as amended by the CJPOA 1994, the Criminal Justice Act 2003 and the Police (Amendment) (NI) Order 1995))

5.88   The taking of intimate and non-intimate samples is regulated by ss 62 and 63 of PACE 1984 (Arts 62 and 63 of the NI Order), discussed more fully in paras 7.200–7.214, post. The development of DNA profiling since 1984 has brought about changes in the law to meet the needs of this new technology. Originally the above samples could only be taken in respect of an arrestable offence. Sections 54 and 55 of the Criminal Justice and Public Order Act 1994 amend ss 62 and 63 respectively, to permit samples to be taken in respect of recordable offences, as defined above in relation to fingerprints.

5.89   Section 54 (Art 10 of the 1995 Order) inserts a new sub-s (1A) into s 62 to permit an intimate sample to be taken from a person who is not in police detention but from whom, in the course of the investigation of an offence, two or more non-intimate samples suitable for the same means of analysis have been taken which have proved insufficient, if (a) an officer of at least the rank of Inspector authorises it; and (b) the person consents in writing. The purpose is to take the pressure off the police to seek intimate samples of the person in police detention when a non-intimate sample will do. The person may be on remand in prison or on bail but provision is made to take samples in prisons or the person can attend a police station to have a sample taken. However, an intimate sample cannot be taken without the suspect's written consent and there is no power to require a person to attend a police station for a sample to be taken and no power to arrest for such a purpose as there is in relation to non-intimate samples.

5.90   The Criminal Justice Act 2003 inserted sub-ss (2A)-(2C) which permit the police to take a non-intimate sample without the appropriate consent if two conditions are satisfied.

(1)   under sub-s (2B) if the person is in police detention in consequence of his arrest for a recordable offence.

(2)   if:
  (a)   he has not had a non-intimate sample of the same type and from the same part of the body taken in the course of the investigation of the offence by the police, or
  (b)   he has had such a sample taken but it proved insufficient.

5.91 The purpose of this provision and the amendment to s 61 in respect of the taking of fingerprints is to enable checks to be made on the National DNA/Fingerprint databases for a speculative search to be carried out and to confirm (within a few minutes) the identity of a suspect when his fingerprints are on record.

5.92 Section 55 (Art 11) adds new sub-ss (3A) and (3B) to s 63. Subsection (3A) permits a non-intimate sample to be taken whether or not the person is in police detention and without the appropriate consent if:

(a) he has been charged with or informed that he may be prosecuted for a recordable offence; and

(b) either he has not had an intimate sample taken from him in the course of the investigation of the offence by the police or he has had one taken but either it was not suitable for the same means of analysis or, though so suitable, the sample proved insufficient.

5.93 Subsection (3B) provides that a non-intimate sample may be taken without the appropriate consent if a person is convicted of a recordable offence. The fact that the person will have been charged or reported or convicted means that the sample is not required for evidential purposes in relation to that offence but is required to build up a data bank of samples or data resulting from the analysis of the sample.

5.94 Section 58 of the 1994 Act (Art 8) redefines the terms 'intimate and non-intimate samples' to facilitate the use of more non-intimate samples for DNA analysis.

5.95 Section 56 of the 1994 Act (Art 12) adds a new s 63A which authorises the use of fingerprints, samples or the information derived from samples in 'speculative searches', that is the checking of fingerprints, samples or the information derived against records held by or on behalf of the police or held in connection with or as a result of an investigation of an offence (s 58(4)). Subsection (3) provides that where any power to take samples is exercisable in relation to a person the sample may be taken in a prison or other institution to which the Prison Act 1952 applies. Subsection (4) provides a power to require a person who is neither in police detention nor police custody on the authority of a court to attend a police station to have a [non-intimate] sample taken when such a sample can be taken as provided by:

(a) s 63(3A) (a person charged with or reported for a recordable offence); or

(b) s 63(3B) (a person convicted of a recordable offence);

5.96 but in respect of (b) only if either he has not had a sample taken from him since the conviction or he has had a sample taken from him (before or after the conviction) but either it was not suitable for the same analysis or, though so suitable, the sample proved insufficient (s 63A(4)). The period allowed for requiring a person to attend a police station is, in respect of (a), one month beginning with the date on which the appropriate officer (defined by sub-s (8)) was informed that the sample was not suitable or proved to be insufficient; and, in respect of (b), one month beginning with the date of conviction or one month beginning with the date the appropriate officer is informed that the sample was not suitable or insufficient (sub-s (5)). 'Month' has the same meaning as above in relation to fingerprints. A requirement under sub-s(4) must give the person at least seven days within which he must attend, and may direct him to attend at a specified time of day or between specified times of day (sub-s (6)).

5.97   A constable may arrest without warrant a person who has failed to comply with a requirement under sub-s (4).

5.98   (NB: It is clear from the above that the power to require a person to attend to have a sample taken, and the power to arrest for failure to comply, only applies to non-intimate samples. The power under s 62(1A) to take an intimate sample from a person not in police detention depends upon the consent of the person. It would be inappropriate to require such a person to attend a police station, or to arrest if he fails to do so, if he chooses not to consent. If he consents there is no need for such powers.)

REQUIREMENTS OF A VALID ARREST (s 28, A^RT 30)

5.99   Arrest is the assertion of a legal authority. That authority will stem, in the main, from the statutory powers provided by ss 24 and 25 (Arts 26 and 27), the preserved statutory powers, statutory powers of arrest created since PACE 1984 (1989 Order), and the common law powers. The requirements of the powers, principally the existence of reasonable grounds for suspecting that an arrestable or general offence has been committed, and in respect of general offences, that a general arrest condition is satisfied, must be complied with if the arrest is to be lawful. But there were other requirements laid down by the common law which applied to all persons exercising a power of arrest. These were that the arrest be made in a particular way and that particular information be supplied to the arrested person. If either of these requirements were not complied with the arrest was unlawful. Section 28 (Art 30) put these requirements into statutory form for arrest and modified them slightly in respect of arrest by a constable. Since the common law remains the basis of the law, the common law rules will be considered together with s 28 (Art 30) and the modifications that section makes to those rules.

THE MECHANICS OF ARREST

5.100   Arrest consists in the seizure or touching of a person's body with a view to his restraint and with the intention to subject the person to the criminal process. The intention must be made known to the person arrested. Words alone may amount to an arrest if they:

> 'In the circumstances of the case, were calculated to bring to the accused's notice, and did bring to the accused's notice, that he was under compulsion and thereafter he submitted to that compulsion.' (Lord Parker CJ, *Alderson v Booth* (1969))

5.101   In *R v Inwood* (1973) it was made clear that, 'There is no magic formula; only the obligation to make it plain to the suspect by what is said and done that he is no longer a free man.'

5.102   Words which brook no misunderstanding are the simple words 'I arrest you' though it was held in *R v Brosch* (1988) that these words are not a prerequisite of a valid arrest – physical seizure may suffice. If the suspect submits to the words of arrest it is a valid arrest, subject to the duty to inform him of the grounds for arrest, though in the case of a citizen's arrest, but not an arrest by a constable; where the reasons are obvious there is no duty to inform. If the suspect does not submit there is no arrest until there has been a touching or seizure of the person (*Genner v Sparks* (1704)). In *Hart v Chief Constable of Kent* (1983) this ancient case was applied to an arrest under the breathalyser law. D supplied a specimen of breath while standing on his doorstep. The test proved positive and the constable told D of this and that he was under arrest. The constable took hold of D's arm before he pulled back into his house. It was held that D had been arrested outside his house and the constable was then entitled to enter in pursuit of D by virtue of his common law power (see now s 17(1)(d) (Art 19(1)(d)) discussed in para 4.97, ante. For powers to enter to require a breath test or to arrest for driving with excess alcohol in the blood, see para 4.112, ante. Where the person arrested is known or believed to be deaf, or cannot understand English or is otherwise incapable of understanding, eg is drunk, the arrestor need only do what is reasonable when he discovers the inability (*Tims v John Lewis Ltd* (1951) reversed on another point by the House of Lords (1952), and *Wheatley v Lodge* (1971)).

5.103   Where the arrest is made by physical seizure of the person, words indicating that the person is under arrest should accompany the seizure in order to make it a valid arrest at common law. There are, of course, circumstances which make it impossible or even unnecessary to tell the person he is under arrest and in the former case the person should be informed as soon as practicable after the arrest. Section 28(1) (Art 30(1)) confirms the common law rule that where the arrest is made by physical seizure the arrest is not lawful unless the person is told of the fact of arrest, and states that where an arrest is made without the person being informed that he is under arrest, the arrest is not lawful unless he is informed as soon as practicable after the arrest. Section 28(2) (Art 30(2)) modifies the common law rule in respect of an arrest by a constable by requiring the constable to inform the person in such a case even when it is obvious that he has been arrested.

REASONS FOR ARREST

5.104   The common law requires not only that it must be made clear to the arrested person that he is under legal compulsion, but also that he must be told the reasons for the arrest. A failure to give the reasons, or the giving of the wrong reasons, renders the arrest unlawful (*Christie v Leachinsky* (1947)). The rule is subject to limited exceptions. There is no duty to inform the arrested person where:

(i)   the circumstances are such that he must know the general nature of the offence for which he is arrested; and

(ii)   he makes it impossible to inform him by, for example, running off or attacking the arrestor (see *R v Brosch* (1988) considered at para 5.40, post, where both these reasons applied),

5.105   or where the person is a possibly violent criminal who cannot be approached in the normal way, and see s 14 of the Northern Ireland (Emergency Provisions) Act 1978, considered in *Murray v Ministry of Defence* (1988). Technical or precise language need not be used, still less a precise charge formulated at the stage of arrest. However, it has been held that the statement 'I am arresting you on suspicion of burglary' was not sufficient information to enable the person to know what was the burglary of which he was suspected (*R v Telfer* (1976)). The fact that the officer could easily have obtained sufficient detail to make it clear by use of his radio was important in that decision. The need for fuller information is made clear by the purpose of the requirement which, in the words of Viscount Simon in *Christie v Leachinsky* (1947):

'... turns on the elementary proposition that in this country a person is, prima facie, entitled to his freedom and is only required to submit to restraints upon him if he knows in substance the reason why it is claimed that this restraint is imposed'.

5.106   As Lord Simonds, in the same case, said: 'Blind, unquestioning obedience is the law of tyrants and of slaves: it does not yet flourish on English soil.' That this legal requirement is supported by common sense is demonstrated by research which shows that people acquiesce more readily in the exercise of coercive powers accompanied by an explanation for their use, but are likely to respond aggressively to the unreasoned use of such powers (Police and People in London, Policy Studies Institute (1983)).

AMBIGUOUS STATEMENTS AND WRONG REASONS

5.107   In *Gelberg v Miller* (1961) the court took the view that a motorist, who had been told that he was being arrested for obstructing the police (for which no power of arrest existed), had been lawfully arrested for obstruction of the highway (for which a power of arrest did exist). The word 'obstruction' was sufficient to communicate to him 'in substance' why he was being arrested. However, the decision may be explained on the ground that the purpose of the arrest was obvious to the motorist and the exception to the rule in *Christie v Leachinsky* (1947) applied.

5.108   A similar result could have been achieved in *R v Redman* (1994). A PC saw an officer struggling with one youth and another, R, was trying to secure the release of the youth. She took hold of his arm, told him the other youth was under arrest and told him to go home. R swore and, claiming the youth had done nothing, continued to try to free him. The PC pulled R away and told him he was under arrest for obstruction. He pushed her and kicked her. She and another officer restrained him and during the struggle the PC was kicked in the stomach and thigh. He later escaped from the police van but was recaptured. He was convicted of escape and common assault. On appeal against conviction it was contended that the real issue was whether he had been lawfully arrested; if not he should have been acquitted. The Crown conceded that if the arrest was unlawful the force used by R was not unreasonable. Allowing the appeal the Court of Appeal held that there was a power of arrest at common law for obstruction of the police in the execution of their duty where its nature was such that it caused, or was likely to cause a breach of the peace, or was calculated to prevent the lawful arrest or detention of another. The prosecution and defence had addressed the jury on the basis of obstruction, but the trial judge directed them in terms of a power of arrest under s 5 of the Public Order Act 1986. In these circumstances the Crown did not seek to maintain the conviction, however, it is likely that if the trial judge had not introduced a different ground the arrest could have been upheld on the basis that the word 'obstruction' was, in the circumstances, sufficient to inform R that he was under arrest for obstruction of a police officer in the execution of his duty which was calculated to prevent the lawful arrest of another (the arrest being under s 25). This may be contrasted with *Edwards v DPP* (1993). There police purported to arrest a man for obstruction under the Misuse of Drugs Act 1971, having seen him put a substance in his mouth. Another man intervened to prevent the arrest and the appellant intervened to release the other person. It was conceded that there was no power to arrest for obstruction under the MDA 1971, it being repealed by s 26 of PACE, but magistrates held the arrest was lawful under s 25 of PACE. E's appeal was allowed. It was clear that the reason for E's arrest was obstruction and it was impossible to infer any other reason. The police gave no reason for the arrest which was therefore not lawful under s 25. The constitutional importance of giving the correct reason was stressed and, in the context of s 25, this means not only stating the offence for which the person is being arrested, but also the arrest condition which justifies the arrest, if practicable.

5.109 In *R v Kulynycz* (1970) the wrong reason for the arrest was given originally and the true reason given at the police station later. It was held that the arrest was unlawful in its inception but was made lawful from the moment the true reason was given, there being no need to release and to re-arrest in order to make continued detention lawful. In *Lewis v Chief Constable of the South Wales Constabulary* (1991) the Court of Appeal approved the decision in Kulynycz in dismissing an appeal against the award of damages for false imprisonment. This followed the arrest of two women on reasonable suspicion of burglary, who were not told the reasons for the arrest until ten minutes afterwards in respect of one woman and 23 minutes in respect of the other. The women were then detained for five hours. Upholding the trial judge's ruling that the unlawfulness of the arrest ceased once reasons had been given, the court said that there was nothing in s 28 about the effect of subsequently giving reasons, but while it could not make an earlier period of arrest lawful, it could make the arrest lawful thereafter.

5.110 These decisions should not be relied upon in order to justify the giving of inadequate, ambiguous or wrong reasons for the arrest. As was said in *Edwards v DPP* (1993), 'Giving the correct reason for an arrest is of the utmost constitutional importance.'

5.111 However, there is, it is submitted, no legal requirement to state the legal authority upon which the arrest is based. If, for example, an arrest is made for an arrestable offence, there is no need to specify the precise statutory authority for the arrest, provided that correct and adequate reasons are given for it. The fact that the officer states that he is acting under a particular statutory power which does not in fact authorise arrest in the particular circumstances, but the arrest is authorised by another statutory or common law power, should not affect the validity of the arrest. This view is supported by the decision of the Supreme Court of South Australia in *Warke v Daire* (1983) where it was held that an arrest was not vitiated by the fact that the arresting officer thought he was acting under a power which did not authorise the arrest when he had other powers upon which he could rely. The officer did not tell the person which power he was acting under but had he done so it is submitted that it would not have vitiated the arrest. The purpose of the rule in *Christie v Leachinsky* (1947) is to enable the arrested person to challenge the arrester's reasonable suspicion and to inform him in broad terms what it is that he is accused of. It is not intended to enable a legal argument to take place about the authority for the arrest. With the exception of an arrest under s 24(5)(a) (Art 26(5)(a)), the legality of the arrest is judged on the circumstances existing at the time of the arrest.

5.112   The fact that the arrested person is not charged with the offence for which he was arrested does not vitiate it if he was in fact committing or about to commit an arrestable offence or there were reasonable grounds to suspect that he was committing or was about to commit or had committed such an offence or any other offence. On the other hand, the fact that the arrested person pleads guilty to the offence for which he was arrested does not of itself render his arrest and detention lawful if he had not been told that he was being arrested and the reasons for it (*Hill v Chief Constable of South Yorkshire* (1990)). Section 28(3) (Art 30(3)) confirms the common law rule that no arrest is lawful unless the person arrested is informed of the ground for the arrest at the time of, or as soon as practicable after, the arrest. Of the phrase 'at the time of … arrest' Glidewell LJ said:

> '[It] does not in my view mean simply the precise moment at which the constable lays his hands on the defendant and says "I am arresting you"; it comprehends a short but reasonable period of time around the moment of arrest, both before and, as the statute itself specifically says, after.' (*Nicholas v Parsonage* (1987))

5.113   Section 28(4) (Art 30(4)) modifies the common law rule in respect of arrest by a constable by requiring that the person be so informed even when the ground for arrest is obvious. As under the former law, however, there is no requirement to inform a person that he is under arrest or of the ground for arrest, if it was not reasonably practicable to do so because the person escaped from arrest before he could be informed (s 28(5), art 30(5)).

5.114   If the arrest is unlawful because the reasons for it have not been given, or incorrect reasons have been given, a third party seeking to prevent the arrest is not himself open to arrest for obstruction of or assault upon a constable in the execution of his duty (*Edwards v DPP* (1993)).

5.115   'Practicable' as used in s 28 (Art 30) is not defined. Its meaning will depend on the circumstances. If the reason why he was not informed at the time of arrest is because he was violent, it will be practicable to inform him once he ceases to be so; or if he was drunk, when he is sober. Normally it will be the arresting person who imparts the information but the section simply requires that the person arrested be informed and in those situations in which it is impracticable to inform him at the time of arrest the section will be complied with if he is informed by, for example, the custody officer, once he has sobered up or calmed down at the police station. If it is not practicable to inform the accused of the ground for the arrest at the time of the arrest, the arrest is not invalidated because of a failure to inform when it became practicable to do so (*DPP v Hawkins* (1988)). The limitations of this decision should be noted. The issue was whether the constable was acting in the execution of his duty when he was assaulted by the person he had arrested. Because the person was violent it was not practicable to inform him of the reasons for the arrest. When it became practicable at the police station he was not told, or was given the wrong reason. The decision that the arrest was lawful between these two periods meant the constable was acting in the execution of his duty. However, a civil court hearing an action for false imprisonment, while doubtless agreeing with the Divisional Court that the arrest was lawful from the point when it was not practicable to inform the person up to the point when it became practicable to do so, would be likely to find the arrest unlawful from then on and the resultant detention a false imprisonment.

5.116   In *Dawes v DPP* (1995) modern technology combined with the common law and statutory requirements to produce a novel legal issue. It was argued that D was unlawfully arrested because, having been trapped in a car the door locks of which were automatically locked when he entered in order to take it without the owner's consent, he had not been informed of the reason for his arrest as soon as practicable as required by s 28. The vehicle had been set up to trap those seeking to take it without consent. The ignition key was left in but the ignition switched off after the vehicle had travelled about 30 metres and was alarmed to alert the police to the taking of the vehicle. They responded fairly quickly and then told D that he was under arrest and why. The Divisional Court dismissed his appeal holding, inter alia, that there was no question that D was arrested when the doors closed on him. That brought into play s 28. On the facts the court was entitled to find, as the magistrates' and Crown Court did, that the arrest was not unlawful because he was told as soon as practicable that he was under arrest and the reasons for it. It was emphasised that had the facts been different, for example, the police had been slow to respond or had left him locked in the car for any length of time, the finding might have been different. The Court also suggested, per curiam, that it might be prudent for police forces who wish to use this type of device to consider whether it would be practicable to put in the car something which would advise the person detained that he was under arrest and the reasons for it. This would pave the way for an entirely mechanical arrest which would, nevertheless, be lawful.

5.117   The interpretation of the common law rules applying to arrest is still of relevance in interpreting s 28 (Art 30). Technical or precise language was not required under the rule in *Christie v Leachinsky* and will not be required under s 28. In *Abbassy v Metropolitan Police Comr* (1990), a civil action arising out of an arrest under the pre-PACE Act law, the Court of Appeal took the view that an arrest for 'unlawful possession of a motor car' was apt to describe the offence under s 12 of the Theft Act 1968, taking a motor vehicle without consent. While suggesting that the constable would have been well advised to use more precise language, the Court of Appeal thought it would be wrong to lay down a higher standard than that indicated by the House of Lords in *Christie v Leachinsky*. Sedley LJ in *Clarke v Chief Constable of North Wales* (2000) recognised something of the reality of practical policing in confirming that technical language is not necessary, he went on to state:

> 'I have no difficulty with the proposition that technical or formal words are unnecessary. Although no constable ever admits to saying "you're nicked for handling this gear" or "I'm having you for twocking this motor", either will do and, I have no doubt, frequently does'

5.118   The advice to use 'more precise language' should be heeded. A constable exercising such an important coercive power should be sure that he has a power of arrest and of the grounds upon which he is exercising that power. It is, as suggested earlier, reasonable that an arrest for which true and adequate grounds were given should not be vitiated by the constable's mistaken reliance on a particular power which does not authorise that arrest, when another power does, but, it is submitted, it is not reasonable to excuse the giving of wrong or inadequate reasons for the exercise of such a power. It is no doubt reasonable not to expect the constable, still less a citizen, to be specific. Dishonestly taking or obtaining property belonging to another may be one of a number of Theft Act offences and determining which it is may be a task for a lawyer. *In Wilson v Chief Constable of Lancashire* (2000) an arrest was made for theft of cheques. The defendant was not told when and where the alleged offences had been committed, nor was it made clear the type of theft of cheques he was suspected of. The arrest was unlawful because the claimant had not been given sufficient information to allow him a sufficient opportunity to respond. The statement 'I am arresting you for stealing' together with information identifying the property alleged to be stolen, when and from whom, should be sufficient even if the actual charge proves to be robbery, obtaining by deception or handling stolen goods.

GROUNDS FOR ARREST UNDER s 25 (Art 27)

5.119   In *Nicholas v Parsonage* (1987) the Divisional Court rejected a submission that, when asking for a name and address under s 25, the constable is required to indicate why the name and address is required, ie so that a summons might be served. Glidewell LJ said:

> 'As a general principle, I would hold that at the time of arrest the arresting constable must indicate in some words ... the offence for which the defendant is being arrested. If he goes on and says: "I am arresting you because you have not given your name and address", so much the better. He has then given all the detail that could possibly be required.' (At p 204.)

5.120 It should be noted that in that case the constable did tell the defendant what the offence was that he had committed and asked him for his name and address. When it was refused he told the defendant that he had the power to arrest him if he did not give his name and address. Only on this being refused did he arrest the defendant. This approach appears to be correct in principle. It is suggested that while the general principle enunciated by Glidewell LJ must be accepted as the maximum required by law, a constable would be well advised to go further. Before arresting under s 25 (Art 27) when general arrest conditions (3)(a) and (b) are satisfied, a constable might adopt the following procedure:

(a) inform the relevant person of the offence he is alleged to have committed, using non-technical language;
(b) request the relevant person's name and address;
(c) if refused, warn the relevant person that he will be arrested unless his name and address is given;
(d) if still refused, arrest and, if practicable, tell the relevant person that he is being arrested for the offence he is alleged to have committed.

5.121 In respect of other arrest conditions it may be necessary to explain the legal significance of a failure to satisfy the conditions.

5.122 For example, if a holidaymaker living at a temporary address in a holiday resort gives the constable his name and the temporary address, which the constable with his local knowledge believes to be a temporary address, eg a guest house, it would be reasonable and within the spirit of the Act, to explain that the address given is not a satisfactory address for the service of a summons and that unless such an address is forthcoming he will be arrested. Only if no such address is forthcoming should he be arrested. The simple principle underlying conditions 25(3)(a) to (c) (Art 27(3)(a) to (c)) is the avoidance of arrest if a summons will suffice. The relevant person should then be given a reasonable opportunity to avoid arrest by supplying the information which would enable him to do so. So far as the other arrest conditions are concerned it may be impractical to lay down any hard and fast rules but the general principle should also be the avoidance of arrest where possible. Thus a person obstructing the highway should be warned that he will be arrested if he does not move and arrested only when that warning is ignored. If a constable has reasonable grounds for believing that arrest is necessary to prevent the relevant person causing harm to other persons (s 25(3)(d)(i), art 27(3)(d)(i)), and the circumstances permit, the relevant person should be informed of this so that he may seek to persuade the constable that his suspicions are unfounded.

DUTY TO GIVE REASONS FOR THE EXERCISE OF OTHER COERCIVE POWERS

5.123 In *Pedro v Diss* (1981) the power to stop and search under s 66 of the Metropolitan Police Act 1839 was equated with arrest and a duty imposed to give reasons for the stop, detention and search. In *Brazil v Chief Constable of Surrey*

(1983) the duty to give reasons was extended to the search of persons following arrest. The former duty is now a statutory one under s 2(2) and (3) of PACE 1984 (Art 4(2) and (3) of the PACE Order) but there would appear to be a common law duty to give reasons for the exercise of any coercive power if the exercise is to be lawful. In any event, it is common sense to do so and thereby reduce the risk of resistance.

VOLUNTARY ATTENDANCE AT A POLICE STATION OR ELSEWHERE

5.124   Section 29 (Art 31) states:

'Where for the purpose of assisting with an investigation a person attends voluntarily at a police station or at any other place where a constable is present or accompanies a constable to a police station or any such other place without having been arrested –
(a) he shall be entitled to leave at will unless he is placed under arrest;
(b) he shall be informed at once that he is under arrest if a decision is taken by a constable to prevent him from leaving at will.'

5.125   The police did not always tell the media whether a person was under arrest for an offence or whether he was voluntarily assisting them with their inquiries. The media, therefore, used the phrase 'assisting with inquiries' to cover both possibilities and to avoid defaming a person who had not been arrested. However, the phrase disguised a third possibility, that the person was detained short of arrest against his will. As was seen in para 5.6, ante, the police regularly used what was in fact unlawful detention in order to avoid the legal constraints in questioning a suspect who had been arrested, or simply because there was no ground for arrest. Once in the coercive atmosphere of a police station he could be interrogated. In this way the constable's suspicion could be turned into reasonable suspicion and then into a prima facie case, or occasionally the suspicion or reasonable suspicion dispelled. If this practice was permitted to continue, the elaborate procedure under Part IV of the Act to control police detention of suspects and to safeguard them against possible abuse would be useless, since a person is not in police detention for the purpose of that Part of the Act unless he has been arrested for an offence and taken to a police station and detained there, or detained elsewhere in the charge of a constable (s 118(2, art 2(3)) (discussed in para 6.6, post). It follows that a person who is voluntarily in a police station assisting with police inquiries is not in police detention, nor is a person taken to a police station against his will without being arrested and who is detained there.

Attends voluntarily or accompanies a constable

5.126   By referring to a person who attends voluntarily and one who accompanies a constable to a police station or other place, s 29 (Art 31) distinguishes between the true volunteer and the person who believes he is under legal compulsion but who is not (for a discussion of consent and voluntariness in this context see para 2.93, ante).

A constable may say 'I require you to accompany me to the police station' or couch it in the form of a request. The intention may be to arrest or simply to get the person to a police station where inquiries can more conveniently be carried out, but in neither case is the person lawfully arrested, and if he believes he is under compulsion he clearly is not a volunteer either. If the intention was to arrest, this will become clear on arrival at a police station and the suspect should then be informed that he is under arrest and of the reasons for the arrest. If the intention was not to arrest, or if the person is a genuine volunteer, it may emerge during the questioning and investigation that there are reasonable grounds for arrest for an offence, not necessarily the offence under investigation. If the constable then decides that the person is not free to leave, he must be informed at once that he is under arrest. Section 29(b) (Art 31(b)) must be read as referring to a decision by the constable to prevent him from leaving at will because there are reasonable grounds for arrest for an offence, and, if it is a general offence, that a general arrest condition is satisfied, for only then will a constable be empowered to arrest for a general offence.

Attends voluntarily at or accompanies a constable to, a police station or any other such place where a constable is present (s 29, art 31)

5.127 In a majority of cases it will be a police station to which the person goes voluntarily or accompanies a constable, but there will be other places. The key words are 'any such other place' and will cover cases where, for example, a constable asks a suspected shoplifter to accompany him to the manager's office while inquiries are made into the allegation, or employees are asked to attend at an office within the workplace where a constable is in order to assist in an investigation of theft from the workplace. Such persons are free to leave at will unless arrested and s 29 (Art 31) seeks to ensure that, if the constable determines that they are no longer free to leave, they will immediately be arrested and told that they are under arrest and of the ground for it, thus making it perfectly clear that their status has changed.

Rights of a volunteer

5.128 The volunteer or person who accompanies a constable to a police station or other place, may be a witness or a suspect against whom there is, as yet, insufficient evidence to arrest. Since both are free men they not only have the right to leave at will, they can also demand that a solicitor or friend be present at any interview. Code C 3.21 now requires that the person be told that he has the right to free and independent legal advice in person or on the telephone. Since the person is not under arrest the request cannot lawfully be delayed. Code C 3.21 emphasises that the person is free to leave unless arrested and, if it is decided that he is no longer free to leave, he must be informed at once that he is under arrest and brought before the custody officer. He is then treated as any other detained person and should be told of his right to have someone informed of his arrest (s 56 discussed at para 7.48, post) and to consult a solicitor (s 58 discussed at para 7.56, post). If he is not placed under arrest but is suspected of an offence, para 10.1 of Code C requires that he be cautioned in the terms set out in para 10.4 before being questioned in order to obtain evidence of the offence under investigation. The caution is required whenever a person is suspected of an offence, as opposed to reasonably suspected which is the trigger for when he may be arrested. A volunteer or person who accompanies a constable and who is a suspect should therefore be cautioned before being questioned and informed that he is not under arrest, is not obliged to remain and may obtain free legal advice (Code C 3.15). It should be noted that Code C 3.15 applies to volunteers in a police station. Code C 10.1 on the other hand applies to persons anywhere, and C 10.2 requires that a person who is not under arrest but who is cautioned before or during an interview be told that he is not under arrest and is not obliged to remain with the officer. This clearly applies to the person who attends voluntarily or accompanies a constable to 'any other place where a constable is present'. The 'fundamental right' to leave (Lord Elton, House of Lords, Hansard, 5 July 1984, col 502) is ever present until the person is arrested. It would appear that much use is still being made of the facility for voluntary attendance by some forces (McKenzie, Morgan and Reiner, 'Helping the Police with their Inquiries: the Necessity Principle and Voluntary Attendance at the Police Station', [1990] Crim LR 23). The authors cite a detective sergeant's explanation of the utility of this practice:

> 'First, suppose there is a crime report showing "not detected", so why not interview him as a witness to see if he becomes a suspect. Second, most of the cases and the suspects are suitable for summons. Therefore there's no pressure to complete the paperwork [as there is with a charge]. Third, it's convenient because you set the time, and last it avoids the time clock consideration. If arrest is necessary later, it doesn't count.'

5.129   The first reason may be given some credence but if the Code of Practice is followed little is in fact gained. The second reason is specious. The arrested suspect can be reported for summons and bailed thus relieving the pressure of paperwork. The third reason is more convincing and is probably the main reason why so much reliance is put on voluntary attendance.

The relevant time for arrest of a volunteer or person who accompanied a constable to a police station

5.130   Detention without charge is limited by s 41 (Art 42), and the time from which the period of detention is to be calculated, 'the relevant time', is determined by reference to that section, which provides for a number of eventualities. Section 41 (Art 42) provides that in the case of a person who attends voluntarily at a police station, or accompanies a constable to a police station without having been arrested, the relevant time is the time of his arrest. The possible disadvantage to the arrested person of this provision is discussed at para 6.35, example 4, post. It is clear that voluntary attendance can be used to avoid the constraints on detention imposed by PACE 1984.

Custody officers and volunteers

5.131 Since a volunteer or person who accompanies a constable is not in police detention, the custody officer has no statutory duties in respect of him and the period of his attendance is not subject to supervision or review. However, the custody officer, or person in charge at a non-designated station, would be well advised to ensure:

(i)   that constables, in whose charge volunteers are, are aware of their responsibilities under Code C, discussed above; and

(ii) that supervisory officers are also aware of the presence of volunteers or persons who accompanied a constable to the police station (see Code C, Notes for Guidance 1A).

PERSONS ARRESTED ELSEWHERE THAN AT A POLICE STATION (s 30(1) AND (2), Art 32(1) AND (2))

5.132   Section 30(1) and (2) (Art 32(1) and (2)) require that where a constable, otherwise than at a police station, arrests a person for an offence, or takes a person into custody after his arrest by some person other than a constable, the person shall be taken to a designated police station or, in the special circumstances set out in s 30(3)-(5) (Art 32(3)-(5)), to a non-designated police station, as soon as practicable after his arrest unless s 30(7) or 30(10) apply see para 5.138-5.150. A 'designated police station' is a police station designated by the chief officer of police for the area as one to be used for detaining persons arrested and for which one or more custody officers will be appointed (s 35) (Art 37). As will be seen (para 6.19, post), a custody officer at a designated police station must be independent of the investigation, and one of his duties is to supervise detention (ss 36-39) (Arts 37-40). A non-designated police station will not be staffed by appointed custody officers and, being small stations, may have no police officer independent of the investigation to act as custody officer, the independence being a key element in the scheme for safeguarding the detainee (see 36(7) (Art 37(7)) discussed in para 6.21, post).

PERSONS ARRESTED IN POLICE AREA A FOR AN OFFENCE IN POLICE AREA B

5.133   In *R v Khan* (1990) officers from the West Midlands Serious Crime Squad arrested Khan in Caernarfon for an offence committed in Birmingham. They appear to have driven him from Caernarfon directly to Birmingham rather than, as s 30 seems to require, taking him to a police station in the area in which he was arrested. The Court of Appeal, in quashing Khan's conviction, doubted the authenticity of a confession allegedly obtained from Khan during the car journey. Section 30 was not considered but, it is submitted, the requirement that an arrested person be taken to a police station 'as soon as practicable' cannot be interpreted as permitting a delay of what might be several hours in taking the person to a police station in the area in which his arrest was sought, rather than a police station in the area in which he was arrested. During such a journey the arrested person is not in police detention and has none of the protections which the Act and Code of Practice provide to detained persons. (It should be noted that Code C 11.1 states that following a decision to arrest a suspect he must not be interviewed except at a police station unless the delay would lead to one of the consequences set out in Code C 11(a)-(c). For a definition of 'interview' see Code C 11.1A. It would seem that the 'casual conversation between suspect and police officer en route from Walsall to Bristol' in *R v Younis and Ahmed* (1990), in which admissions were made, would still not be an interview, while that in Khan clearly would be; see further para 8.7(3), post.) If no questioning of the arrested person in order to obtain evidence in relation to the offence for which he was arrested takes place in the police station in the area in which he was arrested, the 'detention clock' does not start until the arrested person arrives at the first police station to which he is taken in the area in which his arrest was sought, see s 41(3) discussed in para 6.35, post. There is then no detriment to the police in complying with s 30 and the arrested person is in the same position as he would be had he been arrested in the area in which his arrest was sought. (NB: Northern Ireland is one police area. The duty to take a person to a police station should there be interpreted as the nearest designated police station, or non-designated police station, if appropriate.)

ARREST BY CONSTABLES WORKING IN THE AREA COVERED BY NON-DESIGNATED STATIONS (s 30(3), Art 32(3))

5.134 Section 30(3)-(5) (Art 32(3)-(5)) lays down the conditions which must be satisfied before a person arrested for an offence or taken into custody can be taken to a non-designated police station. The former provides that where an arresting officer is working in an area covered by a non-designated police station the person may be taken to any police station unless it appears to the constable that it may be necessary to keep the arrested person in police detention for more than six hours. This will be the case in respect of some 75% of arrests (see Royal Commission, para 3.96), which will either be arrests under s 25 (Art 27) for comparatively minor offences where the purpose of the arrest will be to identify the arrested person or check that the address given is a satisfactory address; or arrests of more serious offences which require little, if any, investigation.

5.135 Conditions under which any constable may take arrested persons to non-designated stations (s 30(5), art 32(5))

5.136 Section 30(5) (Art 32(5)) permits any constable to take an arrested person to a non-designated police station if either of two conditions in s 30(5)(a) (Art 32(5)(a)) are satisfied and the condition in s 30(5)(b) (Art 32(5)(b)) is also satisfied. The conditions are:

(a)

    (i)   the constable has arrested him without the assistance of any other constable and no other constable is available to assist him;

(ii) the constable has taken him into custody from a person other than a constable without the assistance of any other constable and no other constable is available to assist him; and

(b) it appears to the constable that he will be unable to take the arrested person to a designated police station without the arrested person injuring himself, the constable or some other person.

5.137 Section 30(3) and (5) (Art 32(3) and (5)) are independent of each other, the former applying only to a constable working in the area of a non-designated police station, the latter to any constable whether or not he is working in such an area (as to the use of reasonable force in such circumstances see para 5.86, post). The Northern Ireland Order contains an additional reason for taking an arrested person to a non-designated station. That is that it appears to the constable that he will be unable to take him to a designated station without exposing the arrested person or himself to unjustifiable injury. In the circumstance in which policing takes place in Northern Ireland this is understandable. As to constables at non-designated police stations assuming the functions of a custody officer, see s 36(7)-(8) (Art 37(7)-(8)) discussed in para 6.21, post). Section 30(6) (Art 32(7)) requires that where the first police station to which an arrested person is taken is not a designated police station, he shall be taken to such a station not more than six hours after his arrival there unless he is released previously.

DUTY TO RELEASE OR RELEASE ON BAIL WHEN THE GROUNDS FOR ARREST NO LONGER EXIST (s 30(7), Art 32(10))

5.138 Section 30(7) (Art 32(10)) reaffirms the common law duty to release a person who has been arrested otherwise than at a police station if, before arriving at a police station, the constable becomes aware that the grounds upon which the arrest was made no longer exist (s 30 presupposes that there was a lawful arrest for which grounds existed; if there were no grounds the detention of the person is unlawful from the start and is not in law an arrest). A central purpose of the requirement that a person arrested be informed of the grounds for the arrest, laid down by *Christie v Leachinsky* (1947) and now by s 28(3) (Art 30(3)), is to enable a person to show that there are no grounds for his arrest. If he can do so or show that the reasonable grounds relied upon for the arrest are not in fact reasonable, the arrestor is then bound to release him and any detention beyond that point is unlawful (*Wiltshire v Barrett* (1966)). The police rarely, if ever, complied with this duty, believing that such a release would expose them to an action for false imprisonment. However, the reverse is true. The creation by s 25 (Art 27) of a category of arrest based on the requirement therein that a general arrest condition be satisfied before an arrest is permitted, adds a new dimension to the statutory duty to release when the constable is satisfied that there are no grounds for keeping the person under arrest. Where, for example, a person is arrested under s 25 (Art 27) because general arrest condition (3)(b) (belief that the name given is not his real name) is satisfied, but before reaching a police station the constable is satisfied that the name given is his real name, the person must be released. The requirement that the constable must be 'satisfied' that there are no grounds for keeping the person under arrest is clearly subjective and will result in the cautious constable continuing with the arrest in borderline cases while the bolder constable releases. That is permissible, but in a clear case it will not be permissible to use the subjective nature of the test in order to continue with an arrest which should be ended. Where a person is released under s 30(7) (Art 32(10)), the releasing constable must record the fact that he has done so as soon as practicable after the release (s 30(8) and (9)) (Art 32(11) and (12)), presumably in his pocket book unless his own force instructions direct otherwise (the duty to release in the circumstances of s 30(7) (Art 32(10)) after the person arrives at the police station falls on the custody officer; see s 37 (Art 38), discussed in para 6.32, post).

5.139   Section 30 has been amended by the Criminal Justice Act 2003 to permit 'street bail'.

Delay in taking arrested person to police station and street bail

5.140   Section 30 has been amended by the Criminal Justice Act 2003 so that an arrested person does not have to be taken to a police station if either s 30(7A) or (10A) apply.

5.141   The Act amended s 30 (7) to read,

'A person arrested by a constable at any place other than a police station must be released without bail if the condition in subsection (7A) is satisfied.'

5.142   The condition is that, at any time before the person arrested reaches a police station, a constable is satisfied that there are no grounds for keeping him under arrest or releasing him on bail under s 30A.

5.143   The new s 30A makes provision for a person to be bailed without attending a police station. He must be given a notice which sets out the following :
(a)   the offence for which he was arrested
(b)   the ground on which he was arrested
(c)   the fact that he is required to attend a police station, and
(d)   the time when he must attend.

5.144   A power of arrest is given under s 30D for   failure to attend the specified police station unless he has been notified under s 30C that he is no longer required to attend.

5.145   Section 30(10A) has been inserted to permit a person who has been arrested to be taken to a place other than a police station if his presence at that place is necessary in order to carry out such investigations as it is reasonable to carry out immediately.

5.146   These provisions represent a pragmatic resolution to the circumstances where it may be necessary to carry out investigations promptly and to avoid the delay associated with taking the arrested person to the police station. They will be interpreted strictly to ensure that they are not used to circumvent legal advice procedures and the requirement to be taken elsewhere must be to carry out necessary enquiries which, it is submitted, will in the majority of cases be where it may be possible to establish innocence and avoid unnecessary detention and bureaucracy.

DELAY IN TAKING A PERSON TO A POLICE STATION (s 30(10), Art 32(13))

5.147   Section 30(10) (Art 32(13) provides that nothing in s 30(1) (Art 32(1)) shall prevent a constable delaying taking a person who has been arrested to a police station if the presence of that person elsewhere is required for such investigations as it is reasonable to carry out immediately. An earlier contradiction in the common law (see Lord Porter in *John Lewis & Co Ltd v Tims* (1952) and Lord Denning in *Dallison v Caffery* (1965)) is resolved. Section 30(10) thus links up with:

(a)   the duty to release under s 30(7) (Art 32(10)), in that it permits the reasonable investigation of matters which might confirm or deny the reasonable suspicion upon which the arrest was made; and

(b)   the duty under s 28(3) (Art 30(3)) to inform the person of the grounds for arrest.

5.148   If, for example, D is arrested on reasonable suspicion of burglary on a particular date and time but claims on being arrested that X can prove conclusively that he was elsewhere at that time, it may be reasonable to investigate that alibi immediately, particularly if X is to be found reasonably close to the point of arrest, and consequently necessary that D accompany the constable. Similarly, it may be reasonable to take D to his home to search for the proceeds of the burglary, for example, if the arrest is made in public and it is possible that word of his arrest may reach relatives or friends who may then dispose of the evidence before the constable can return to search his premises (see s 18(5) of PACE 1984 (Art 20(5) of the 1989 Order) discussed at para 4.22, ante). What is 'reasonable' is a question of fact. In *Dallison v Caffery* it was held that a constable had acted reasonably in taking D to a house where he claimed to have been working at the time of the offence. In *McCarrick v Oxford* (1982), a constable who had arrested D reasonably suspecting that he was driving whilst disqualified, was also held to have acted reasonably in refusing to take D to his house where he had a letter from the Crown Court stating that the disqualification was suspended pending an appeal. The constable tried to confirm the suspension by radio but failed to do so, there being no record of it at any criminal records office. It was, therefore, reasonable for the constable to assume that police records were correct.

5.149   In *R v Keane* (1992) D was arrested and his flat was searched. During the search he was interviewed and admitted possession of a firearm and cannabis. En route to the police station they stopped to search D's car which had been left in a pub car park. The time between arrest and arrival at the police station was 29 minutes.

Dismissing his appeal against conviction based in part on a breach of s 30(1), the Court of Appeal inclined to the view that there had been a breach but held that since D was experienced in police procedure admitting the evidence had no adverse effect on the fairness of the trial. Had D been an inexperienced young man the court might have taken a different view. In *R v Khan* (1993) s 30(10) was relied upon to search D's flat for drugs. During the search he was interviewed intermittently for about one hour. Drugs were found and a further 45-minute interview took place. The trial judge excluded part of the first interview and all of the second. D's appeal, based in part on the contention that there had been a breach of s 30(10), was dismissed but the Court of Appeal warned against using s 30(10) to circumvent the safeguards imposed by PACE 1984 and Codes – see further para 8.7(3), post. A relevant consideration is whether the period of detention of D is likely to be reduced by taking the action which was in fact taken or requested. In *Dallison v Caffery* the detention would have been shorter if D's alibi was verified. In *McCarrick v Oxford* it would not have been, given the constable's belief in the accuracy of police records. Section 30(11) (Art 32(14)) provides that where there is delay in taking the arrested person to a police station, the reasons for it shall be recorded when he first arrives at a police station. (Persons detained under para 16 of Sch 2 of the Immigration Act 1971 may under para 18 of that Schedule be taken to and from their place of detention in order to ascertain their nationality or citizenship, or for making arrangements for their admission to another country. Section 30(13) (Art 32(16)) provides that nothing in s 30(10) (Art 32(13)) shall be taken to affect this power.)

Exemptions

5.150   Section 30(12) (Art 32(15)) exempts from the provisions of s 30(1) (Art 32(1)) a number of powers of arrest in respect of which the duty to take a person to a police station is inappropriate. These are as follows.

(a) Arrest and detention of a would-be immigrant who is refused leave to enter and who may be detained on board the ship or aircraft or elsewhere (paras 16(3) and 18(1) of Sch 2, of the Immigration Act 1971) (s 30(12)(a), art 32(15)(a)).

(b) Persons arrested for being drunk and disorderly or drunk and incapable who may under s 34(1) of the Criminal Justice Act 1972 be taken to a detoxification centre (a treatment centre for alcoholics approved by the Secretary of State), where they exist (s 30(12)(b), art 32(15)(b)).

(c) Persons arrested and detained under s 15(6) or (9) of the Prevention of Terrorism (Temporary Provisions) Act 1989 who may be detained on board the ship or aircraft which brought them, if they are excluded persons, or at such place as the Secretary of State may direct (s 30(12)(c), art 32(15)(c)).

ARREST FOR A FURTHER OFFENCE (s 31, Art 33)

5.151   Part IV of the Act (Part V of the Order) limits the period of detention without charge following an arrest and s 41(2) (Art 42(2)) provides a formula for determining the time from which the period of detention is to be calculated (the relevant time). In the usual case this will be the time at which the arrested person arrives at the first police station to which he is taken. Where a person has committed more than one offence it would be possible to obtain extended periods of detention by the simple expedient of arresting on offence A, obtaining the maximum period of detention for that offence, then on the release of the person, arresting him for offence B thus commencing a new period of detention. This process could be repeated through as many offences as can be discovered. Section 31 (Art 33), in conjunction with s 41(4) (Art 42(3)), excludes this possibility by requiring that where a person has been arrested for offence A and is at a police station in consequence of that offence, and it appears to a constable that, if he were released from that arrest he would be liable to arrest for some other offence B, he shall be arrested for that offence. Section 41(4) then provides that the time from which the period of detention in respect of that other offence B is to be calculated, shall be the time from which detention in respect of the 'original' offence A was calculated.

5.152 For example: D is arrested for taking and driving away a motor vehicle. He arrives at the first police station to which he is taken at 10am, that is the time from which the period of detention in respect of that offence is to be calculated (the relevant time). If during questioning the arrested person admits to a number of burglaries which the constable is satisfied he did commit, he must be arrested for those other offences. The 'relevant time' in respect of those offences is also 10am (ss 31 and 41(4)) (Arts 33 and 42(3)). The phrase 'and it appears to a constable that ... he would be liable to arrest ...' would seem to mean that there are reasonable grounds for suspecting that the person has committed the other offences (and if it is a general offence that a general arrest condition is satisfied), for only then would it appear to a constable that the person is liable to arrest. The former practice in some police forces of arresting on a minor (holding) charge in order to question the suspect on a more serious charge is not entirely precluded by this section. However, when combined with the custody officer's duty to charge or release a person without charge when there is sufficient evidence to do so in respect of the offence for which he was arrested (s 37(7)(a) and (b), art 38(7)(a) and (b)), and the review of detention of persons detained without charge or after charge under s 40 (Art 41), the provisions of s 31 (Art 33) are likely to end the practice.

SEARCH OF PERSON ON ARREST (s 32, Art 34)

5.153 Where an arrest is made at a place other than a police station, s 32 (Art 34) authorises the search of the person arrested and of the premises in which he was when arrested or immediately before arrest (as for search of premises under this section see para 4.75, ante). It should be stressed that:
(a) this power is available to a constable whenever he arrests outside a police station whether under s 24, s 25 (Art 26 or 27), a preserved statutory power of arrest, a statutory power of arrest created since the passing of PACE 1984 (1989 Order) or

under a common law power of arrest (but not detention under the common law power); and

(b) this power is complementary to the power under s 18 (Art 20) (which permits search of premises occupied or controlled by a person arrested for an arrestable offence). Search of persons arrested other than at a police station is the concern of this section. Search of persons arrested at a police station and of persons detained following arrest is governed by ss 54 and 55 (Arts 54 and 55) and is discussed in para 7.20, post;

(c) the search may now include a search of the mouth – see para 5.159, post.

DANGEROUS PERSONS

5.154   Section 32(1) (Art 34(1)) provides that a constable may search a person arrested other than at a police station if he has reasonable grounds for believing that he may present a danger to himself or others. The search (which may now include the mouth – see para 5.159, post) will be for articles which he might use to cause physical injury to himself or others, but there is no requirement that the constable has reasonable grounds for believing that any such article is in his possession, merely that he has reasonable grounds for believing the arrested person may present a danger to himself or others. Such a belief will be present when a person is arrested for an arrestable offence involving violence or threats of violence or for an offence where general arrest condition s 25(3)(d)(i) (Art 27(3)(d)(i) and possibly (d)(iii) and (e)) apply. In such cases the violent nature of the offence alleged to have been committed or the reasonable belief that it is necessary to arrest to prevent physical injury to the arrested person or others, will provide the reasonable belief that he may present a danger to himself or others. Where the arrest is necessary to prevent damage to property or to protect a child or other vulnerable person, the circumstances of the likely damage and the nature of the threat to the child or other vulnerable person may similarly give grounds for the reasonable belief that he may present such a danger. Where the arrested person appears to be mentally deranged or suicidal he may present a danger to himself or to others and in such a case drugs or pills which might be taken by the arrested person may be the articles to be searched for as well as any weapon of offence.

SEARCH FOR ARTICLES OF ESCAPE OR EVIDENCE

5.155   Section 32(2)(a) (Art 34(2)(a)) provides a power to search the arrested person (which now includes the mouth – see para 5.159, post) for anything:

(i)   which he might use to assist him to escape from lawful custody; or

(ii) which might be evidence relating to an offence.

5.156   However, the power may not be exercised unless the constable has reasonable grounds for believing that the arrested person may have something concealed on him for which such search is permitted (s 32(5), art 34(5)). The police argued strongly for the removal of this requirement on the basis that a person in respect of whom there was not the slightest suspicion has, nevertheless, been known to become violent, produce a weapon and attack the policeman conveying him to a police station. The more obviously dangerous person will have been searched under s 32(1) (Art 34 (1)) since he 'may present a danger' to the constable. Where articles are found in consequence of such a search, they may also be evidence of an offence; for example, D is arrested for robbery in which a knife was used to threaten the victim. Those circumstances give rise to the reasonable belief justifying a search under s 32(1) (Art 34(1)) and s 32(2)(a)(i) and (ii) (Art 34(2)(a)(i) and (ii)) and the knife may be seized under s 32(8) or (9) (Art 34(8) or (9)). Where there are reasonable grounds for believing evidential articles are concealed on the person, which there will be in many more cases than there will be in respect of articles of escape, a search may reveal both kinds of articles. The position is, then, that the risk of harm to an arresting constable or the risk of escape is not as great as may be suggested by the police, since there will usually be a lawful justification for a search. Nevertheless, there will be arrests in which there are no reasonable grounds for search under s 32(1) (Art 34(1)) or (2)(a)(i) and (ii). In some of these cases search will be with, and in others without, consent. In the latter circumstances the constable runs the risk of a civil action and/or disciplinary proceedings, but the risk of complaint by the arrested person is probably less than the risk of harm to the constable. In such circumstances a constable will proceed to search.

Limitation on the extent of search of the person

5.157 Section 32(3) (Art 34(3)) states that the power to search conferred by s 32(2) (Art 34(2)) is only a power to search to the extent that is reasonably required for the purpose of discovering any such thing or any such evidence. That can be an important limitation in the context of a search of premises under s 32(2)(b) (Art 34(2)(b)), but is of limited value in the context of the search of persons under s 32(2)(a) (Art 34(2)(a)). More so since s 32(3) (Art 34(3)) does not apply to searches under s 32(1) (Art 34(1)) (the search of a dangerous person). The article sought in a search of the person under either subsection may be quite small and only discoverable by a strip or intimate search. Neither form of search is feasible in most arrest situations and this is recognised by s 32(4) (Art 34(4)) which limits the clothing which a constable may require to be removed in public to an outer coat, jacket or gloves (but note that the search may extend to the search of the person's mouth (s 32(4) as amended by s 59(2) of the CJPOA 1994)). (The NI Order includes 'headgear'.) If such clothing is removed the search in public will be limited to a 'pat down' of the body over remaining clothing and a search of pockets, waist bands or stocking tops where articles may be concealed. More thorough searching of clothing by, for example, opening seams, is not appropriate in an arrest situation. Since s 32(4) (Art 34(4)) refers to removal of clothing in public there will be a temptation to construe the provision as permitting the removal of other garments in private, for example, in the back of a police van, particularly in an arrest for possession of drugs which might easily be disposed of. However, it is clear from the provisions for search of persons in police detention that strip searching is an exceptional procedure to be carried out only at a police station which may, even more exceptionally, be followed by an intimate search (see ss 54 and 55 and Code C 4.1 and Annex A discussed in paras 7.15-7.19 and paras 7.34-7.47, post). A search of the person can, of course, take place with the consent of the person to be searched. It must, however, be a genuine consent and not obtained by duress. In the context of an arrest it may be difficult to persuade a court that the arrestee consented to a strip search and, if the court is not so persuaded, the constable's actions will be seen as unlawful resulting in the possible exclusion of any evidence found; a finding that the constable was not 'acting in the execution of his duty' if the arrestee is prosecuted for assaulting the constable, or in a civil case, a finding that the constable assaulted the arrestee (see the discussion at para 2.28, ante). If there is a reasonable belief that anything may be concealed which requires a more thorough search than is permitted by s 32 and that it may be used to escape from custody, then resort may be had to the use of handcuffs (see para 5.173, post).

5.158 Search of the person extends to bags etc carried by the person. However, in an arrest situation it may not be possible to do so. If this is the case the arresting constable should ensure that the arrested person is not permitted access to it and it can then be searched at the police station.

Search of a person's mouth

5.159 The former definition of 'intimate search' in s 118 of PACE 1984 as 'a search which consists of the physical examination of a person's body orifices' caused problems for the police, particularly following an arrest for possession of prohibited drugs. The mouth is a 'body orifice' therefore a search of the person's mouth could only be carried out within the terms of s 55 of PACE. In *R v Hughes* (1994) the Court of Appeal held that there was no intimate search when the appellant was forced to spit out the drug contained in his mouth when held by the nose, there being no physical intrusion into a body orifice. That decision was of considerable help to the police but s 59 of the Criminal Justice and Public Order Act 1994 renders reliance on that decision unnecessary by redefining 'intimate search', by adding the words 'other than the mouth' to the existing definition, which is also moved from s 118 of PACE and added to s 65 of that Act. Thus a search of a person's mouth following an arrest is now permitted, using reasonable force if necessary (s 117 of PACE), if the terms of s 32(1) or (2) and (5) apply. Article 5 of the Police (Amendment) (NI) Order 1995 amends art 19(1) of the 1989 Order to the same effect.

Seizure and retention of articles found

5.160 Section 32(8) (Art 34(8)) provides that a constable searching a person under s 32(1) (Art 34(1)) may seize and retain anything he finds, if he has reasonable grounds for believing that the person searched might use it to cause physical injury to himself or to any other person, eg D is arrested for an offence of violence and is found to be in possession of a knife. It may be seized under s 32(8) (Art 34(8)). Section 32(9) (Art

34(9)) provides that where a constable searches a person under s 32(2)(a) (Art 34(2)(a)) he may seize and retain anything he finds, other than an item subject to legal privilege, if he has reasonable grounds for believing:

(a) that he might use it to assist him to escape from lawful custody; or
(b) that it is evidence of an offence or has been obtained in consequence of the commission of an offence.

5.161 What are reasonable grounds for a particular belief is a question of fact in each case. The mere fact that a person carries a penknife is not enough, but if the person is violent and has resisted arrest that may be grounds for the reasonable belief that he may use the penknife to escape. Whether there are reasonable grounds to believe the item is evidence of an offence (not necessarily the offence for which the person was arrested) will depend upon the nature of the item and the offence. If the offence is theft of money then any moneys found on the person may be evidence of the offence and any goods carried may have been obtained in consequence of that offence, ie purchased with the stolen money. However, one cannot reasonably believe this to be so unless there are objective facts pointing to such a purchase. Since s 32(9)(b) (Art 34(9)(b)) permits the seizure of evidence of an offence or things obtained in consequence of the commission of an offence, this creates the same wide power to seize evidence etc in respect of the search of persons as is provided by s 19 (Art 21) in respect of the search of premises. Sections 19-22 (Arts 21-24) govern the process of seizure, the retention by the police of items seized and access to those items while they are in the possession of the police (see further paras 4.44-4.56, ante).

5.162 Section 32(10) (Art 34(10)) does not affect the power provided by s 43 of Terrorism Act 2000 which authorises the stop and search of a person liable to arrest under s 41 of that Act to establish if he has in his possession any thing which may constitute evidence that he is a terrorist. Subsection (3) requires that such searches of persons be carried out by persons of the same sex.

Search to preserve property

5.163 The decision in *R v Churchill* (1989) exposed a further limitation on the power conferred by s 32(2) (Art 34(2)). C was arrested on reasonable suspicion of burglary. The police requested the keys of his car, which was unlocked, in order to take the car to the police station to be searched and where it would be safe rather than left unlocked in a public place. C refused to hand them over and, during a struggle, he struck a police officer. At his trial for assault occasioning bodily harm, it was submitted on C's behalf that the keys were not 'evidence relating to an offence' within s 32(2)(a)(ii) (Art 34 (2)(ii)), therefore the police had no power to search C and the force used to do so was unlawful. The trial judge rejected this submission and held that the car might have contained evidence and the keys could be equated with the car. C's appeal against conviction was allowed, the trial judge being wrong in equating the keys with the car; accordingly the prosecution had failed to establish that the police were acting lawfully in requiring the keys. The Court of Appeal suggested that the case could have been argued on the basis of the duty of the police to preserve property, citing *Rice v Connolly* (1966). Arguably the constable's conduct in searching for the keys to lock the car fell within the general duty to preserve the property of an arrested person and to prevent crime against that property. The search for the keys would not, it is submitted, involve an unjustifiable use of powers associated with that duty. As such the police would be acting lawfully. (If after explanation of why they were required D refused to hand over the keys and police were unable to secure the car it may be argued that D had assumed the risk of harm or loss, thus excluding the police from civil liability for any harm or loss.) Had the car been locked and the police had reasonable cause to suspect (s 18, art 20) or believe (s 32(2)(b), art 34(2)(b)) that evidence of the crime was to be found in it, the police would have had the power to search it for evidence of the burglary. A car is 'premises' within s 23 (Art 25) and s 18 or s 32(2)(b) (Art 20 or art 34(2)(b)) authorises a search of the car. Section 117 (Art 88) permits the use of reasonable force in the exercise of these powers. Searching for and seizing the keys could be described as 'a necessary ancillary action' (see commentary, 1989 Crim LR 228) to that search. Alternatively one could point out to the owner that 'reasonable force' includes breaking a window to gain entry. That may produce the keys more quickly than a resisted search of the person.

THE USE OF FORCE TO EFFECT AN ARREST

5.164   The use of reasonable force to effect an arrest or in the prevention of crime is permitted by s 3 of the Criminal Law Act 1967 (Criminal Law Act (NI) 1967). There is, in s 117 of PACE 1984 (Art 88 of the 1989 Order), a general power permitting a police officer to use reasonable force, if necessary, in the exercise of powers conferred by the Act and which do not depend for their exercise on the consent of some person. There is, then, an overlap between the two provisions, but the intention would appear to be to provide the police with a power to use reasonable force in the exercise of all other powers without affecting the power under s 3 of the 1967 Acts. Section 3 states:

> 'A person may use such force as is reasonable in the circumstances in the prevention of crime, or in effecting or assisting in the lawful arrest of offenders or suspected offenders or of persons unlawfully at large.'

5.165   The use of reasonable force is not confined to arrests for serious crimes which are arrestable offences but is available in all arrests, even an arrest for a minor offence. However, the important words are 'such force as is reasonable in the circumstances'. The circumstances of an arrest for a minor offence, eg violent resistance, may justify the use of considerable force which would not be justified where the arrest is for a serious arrestable offence in which no resistance is offered (see *Reed v Wastie* (1972)). In *Sturley v Police Comr* (1984) a policewoman lawfully arrested a middle-aged lady for assaulting her. Another constable was present, but the policewoman sought to restrain the lady by putting her left arm behind her back and twisting the wrist. In doing so the wrist was broken. Mars-Jones J, in awarding damages against the police, held that it was not a proper form of restraint in the circumstances. Two police officers should have been able to restrain her by holding both her hands by her sides. One officer on her own could use a hammerlock and bar. The arresting officer must, then, take account of the kind of person he is arresting. Obviously, what may be reasonable force in respect of a muscular man may not be reasonable when applied to a woman of small stature. One constable alone may use greater force than two or more, but when assistance is readily available which will reduce the amount of force necessary to restrain the arrested person it must be called for and used. That much is common sense, but there is no clear answer to the question, 'how much force can be used in particular circumstances?', simply because circumstances vary so greatly. The arrestor is expected to employ balancing criteria when no such criteria have been clearly articulated and in circumstances which do not permit of mature reflection but often demand an immediate response to what could be, or appear to be, a dangerous situation. The law's answer to the question would appear to be, as much force as is believed to be reasonably necessary in order to effect the arrest in the circumstances reasonably believed to exist. This is drawn from the decision of the House of Lords in *A-G for Northern Ireland's Reference (No 1 of 1975) (1977)* where their Lordships considered the Northern Ireland equivalent of s 3 in a case in which a soldier shot and killed a fleeing suspect whom he mistakenly believed to be a terrorist. Lord Diplock made it clear that the test of reasonableness should be applied realistically:

'The jury should remind themselves that the postulated balancing of risk against risk, harm against harm, by the reasonable man is not undertaken in the calm analytical atmosphere of the court room ...' (Ibid, p 138)

5.166 In evaluating the arrestor's conduct the question for the jury is:

'Are we satisfied that no reasonable man (a) with the knowledge of such facts as were known to the accused or **reasonably** believed by him to exist, (b) in the circumstances and time available to him for reflection, (c) could be of opinion that the prevention of the risk of harm to which others might be exposed if the suspect were allowed to escape justified exposing the suspect to the risk of harm to him that might result from the kind of force that the accused contemplated using.' (Per Lord Diplock, ibid, p 137)

5.167 One must agree with the learned authors of Smith and Hogan *Criminal Law* (7th edn, 1992) at p 254, fn 17, that in the light of *R v Williams* (1987) and *Beckford v R* (1988) this should be read as if the highlighted 'reasonably' were omitted.

5.168 In *Simpson v Chief Constable of South Yorkshire Police* (1991) S, who had been arrested, charged with and convicted of malicious wounding and threatening behaviour, sought to sue the police for false imprisonment, alleging that the use of excessive force in effecting the arrest made the arrest unlawful. Holding that the conviction was not a bar to an action for assault, the Court of Appeal rejected this argument. Fox LJ said:

'The circumstances of many arrests were such that errors of judgment might be made. If the arrest was itself justified in law, such errors in the mode of conducting it, although they might be the basis for other remedies, did not seem to be a good basis for invalidating the arrest itself which was necessary in the public interest.'

5.169   While therefore excessive force does not render unlawful an arrest which was lawfully justified, the use of excessive force can result in a civil action or criminal prosecution for assault and, where death results from excessive force, a charge of manslaughter, see the prosecution, and subsequent acquittal (*The Times* 15 June 1995), of the officers who sought to arrest Joy Gardner, an illegal immigrant. It should be emphasised that reasonable force is only permitted in order to effect an arrest (or in self-defence or the prevention of crime). Shooting a fleeing burglar or joy-rider is not force used in self-defence, neither would it be reasonable (*R v Clegg* (1995)). Neither can it be justified as reasonable force to effect an arrest.

Mistaken belief that the use of force is justified

5.170   As is clear from the above question for the jury, where a person mistakenly believes the use of force is necessary and the force used would have been reasonable and justified if the facts had been as he believed them to be, then the arrestor will be acquitted of any offence if evidence is adduced of reasonable grounds for the belief and that evidence is not disproved. This is in line with the decision of the Divisional Court in *Albert v Lavin* (1982) which, reluctantly, followed earlier dicta in holding that a mistake of fact cannot found a defence of self-defence unless it is based on reasonable grounds. However, the Court of Appeal (Criminal Division) in *R v Williams (Gladstone)* (1987) stated that the reasonableness of the defendant's belief was relevant only to the question whether the belief was in fact held. If it was held, its unreasonableness is irrelevant on the question of guilt or innocence. The jury should be directed first that the prosecution has the burden of proving the unlawfulness of the appellant's actions; second, that if he might have been labouring under a mistake as to the facts he must be judged according to that mistaken view; third, this was so whether, on an objective view, the mistake was reasonable or not. This decision was approved by the Privy Council in *Beckford v R* (1988). There D's defence to a charge of occasioning actual bodily harm was that he thought he was preventing P, who may have been lawfully arresting V, from assaulting V. The jury was directed that, if P was acting unlawfully, D had a defence only if he believed on reasonable grounds that P was acting unlawfully. This was held to be a misdirection. This clarifies the law in relation to a mistake of fact in the use of reasonable force in self-defence and the law is now as the Criminal Law Revision Committee (14th Report, Cmnd 7844 (1980) para 283) recommended that it should be, and as the Draft Criminal Code proposes that it should be (see Law Commission 177 (1989) – A Draft Criminal Code for England and Wales, Vol 1 clause 44). This view of the criminal law was applied by the Court of Appeal (Civil Division) in *Blackburn v Bowering* (1995). D1 was the subject of a judgment debt and was seen by court bailiffs near his home. A fracas ensued in which D2 became involved. Both were charged with assault on officers of the court in the execution of their duty under s 14(1)(b) of the County Courts Act 1984. The county court judge ruled that it was no defence that they did not know the bailiffs were acting in the execution of their duty and held that the offence was absolute following *R v Forbes and Webb* (1865). Allowing the appeal it was held that in a prosecution under s 51 of the Police Act 1964 or a complaint under s 14 of the County Courts Act 1984 it was not incumbent on the prosecution or complainant to prove that the defendant knew or believed that the victim was a police or court officer. However, to be criminal an assault had to be unlawful. Reasonable force applied in self-defence is not unlawful (*R v Williams* (1987)). If a defendant applies force to a police or court officer which would be reasonable if the person was not a police or court officer, then if he believes that the person is not a police or court officer, even if the belief is unreasonable, he has a good plea of self-defence (*Beckford v R* (1988)). The mistake must be a mistake of fact (particularly as to the victim's capacity) and not a mistake of law as to the authority of the person acting in that capacity. A mistake of law will not operate to exonerate a person who resists what is in law a valid arrest, nor will it assist a constable who acts in the mistaken belief that a person has already been lawfully arrested. This is made clear by the decision in *Kerr v DPP* (1995). The appellant appealed against her conviction for assaulting a police officer in the execution of his duty. The police officer took hold of the appellant in order to detain her mistakenly believing she had been arrested by a colleague. As he was cautioning her she punched him. The appellant's argument that he was not acting in the execution of his duty because he was unlawfully detaining her when she had not in fact been arrested, was described by the Divisional Court in quashing the conviction, as a point of law unanswerable in favour of the appellant. Arrest is a matter of law and the constable's mistaken belief that the appellant had been arrested did not give him the legal authority to detain her. The court suggested that an alternative charge of common assault might succeed in such a case, but in this case there was no such alternative. However, had there been the appellant might still have succeeded. She would have been entitled to use reasonable force to resist the unlawful act of the constable, the only question being whether the force used was reasonable in the circumstances.

The use of force after arrest

5.171   The Code of Practice C 8.9 states:

'Reasonable force may be used if necessary for the following purposes:
(i)   to secure compliance with reasonable instructions, including instructions given in pursuance of the provisions of a code of practice; or
(ii) to prevent escape, injury, damage to property or the destruction of evidence.'

5.172   Once the arrest has been effected and the suspect, if he was violent or resisted arrest, has been subdued or has ceased to be violent, he is in police custody and thereafter the use of force, which must always be reasonable force, is only justified for the purposes mentioned in the Code C 8.9. The use of force for other purposes, or the use of excessive force for the Code's purposes, invites the sanctions of the criminal law, the civil law and the Discipline Code, and any constable using gratuitous or excessive force against a person in custody can expect to be subjected to all three..

The use of handcuffs

5.173   The use of handcuffs in order to restrain an arrested person is not covered by the Act but may be considered under the head of the use of reasonable force, and to some extent links up with the criteria justifying an arrest or search on arrest. For example, if the arrest is justified because the suspected offender is violent and may cause harm to himself or others, a search for articles which might be used to cause physical injury or assist an escape may be justified and also the use of handcuffs. Their use would not, however, be justified when the offence is not one of violence and there are no reasonable grounds for believing the person will become violent or attempt to escape. Home Office guidance to chief officers of police makes it clear that their use is the exception rather than the rule. Thus para 4.65 of the Consolidated Circular to the Police on Crime and Kindred Matters (1977) states:

> 'Whether a prisoner should be handcuffed must depend on the particular circumstances, as for instance the nature of the charge and the conduct of the person in custody. Handcuffing should not be resorted to unless there is fair ground for supposing that violence may be used or an escape attempted. Handcuffing cannot be justified unless there are special reasons for resorting to it.'

Use of force to resist lawful arrest

5.174   The use of force to resist lawful arrest or detention is not permitted, and may result in a charge of assault with intent to resist lawful arrest by anyone under s 18 or s 38 of the Offences Against the Person Act 1861, or a charge of assaulting or obstructing a constable in the execution of his duty under s 51 of the Police Act 1964. It is no defence that the arrest was honestly and reasonably believed to be unlawful, ie a mistake of law, not a mistake of fact (*R v Fennell* (1970); *Albert v Lavin* (1982) but see *Blackburn v Bowering* (1995) and *Kerr v DPP* (1995) above, para 5.170). Nor is it a defence to a charge of assault on a constable that he was not known to be a constable (*R v Forbes and Webb* (1865); *Kenlin v Gardiner* (1967)). The same principle applies where force is used to prevent the arrest of another person or to assist in his escape (*Albert v Lavin* (1982)). In *Hills v Ellis* (1983) D intervened in the arrest of a person believing that the constable had the wrong man. The arrest was, nevertheless, lawful and D was convicted of obstructing the constable in the execution of his duty despite his good motive. In *R v Mark* (1961) D said he thought a constable was a robber and intervened in order to protect the supposed victim. The jury was directed that, if D acted under an honest and reasonable belief that the constable was a robber, they should acquit. That decision has now been overtaken by *R v Williams (Gladstone)* (1987) discussed earlier, so that D will now be judged on the facts as he believed them to be, the reasonableness, or otherwise, of that belief going only to the question of whether he actually held it. However, the mistake in Mark was one of fact and not a mistake as to the legal basis of the arrest, a mistake of law as in *R v Fennell* (1970). In *Kerr v DPP* (1995), considered at para 5.170, ante, it was the police officer who mistakenly believed that the person was under arrest and sought to detain her by taking hold of her. His mistake did not make the unlawful act lawful and he was not therefore acting in the execution of his duty.

Use of force to resist an unlawful arrest

5.175　An unlawful arrest is a crime and reasonable force may be used in self-defence or in the prevention of crime (see the facts of *Kerr v DPP* (1995) considered at para 5.170, ante). In Fennell the Court of Appeal, per Widgery LJ, said:

> 'It was accepted in the court below that if the arrest had been, in fact, unlawful the appellant would have been justified in using reasonable force to secure the release of his son. This proposition has not been argued before us and we will assume, without deciding it, that it is correct ... Where a person honestly [and reasonably] believes that he or his child is in imminent danger of injury it would be unjust if he were deprived of the right to use reasonable force by way of defence merely because he had made some genuine mistake of fact. On the other hand if the child is in police custody and not in imminent danger of injury there is no urgency of the kind which requires an immediate decision and a father who forcibly releases the child does so at his peril.'

5.176　Here too the decision of the Court of Appeal in *R v Williams (Gladstone)* (1987) (see para 5.170, ante) now applies so that the bracketed words should be deleted. A person is to be judged on the facts as he believed them to be and the reasonableness of the belief is relevant only to the question whether such a belief was in fact held. If the arrest is, or is believed to be, unlawful, the force used to resist it must be reasonable and not excessive. If the force used is excessive, the person using such force can be arrested and charged with assault. See, for example, *R v Ball* (1989) where B resisted the arrest of his brother in the belief that it was unlawful. At his trial for assault occasioning actual bodily harm, it was assumed the arrest was unlawful and the sole issue for the jury was whether B had used too much force. The jury decided he had and convicted him, the conviction being upheld by the Court of Appeal (Criminal Division). The citizen would be well advised not to interfere with or resist an arrest, but to make a complaint after the event, unless there is the danger of injury or urgency referred to by Widgery LJ, above.

ARREST WITH A WARRANT

5.177　Section 1(1) of the Magistrates' Courts Act 1980 (hereinafter MCA 1980) provides that:

'upon an information being laid before a justice of the peace ... that any person has, or is suspected of having, committed an offence the justices may ...

(a) issue a summons directed to that person requiring him to appear before a magistrates' court for the area to answer the information, or

(b) issue a warrant to arrest that person and bring him before a magistrates' court for the area ...'

5.178 Section 1(4) limits the issue of an arrest warrant in respect of persons aged 17 and over to indictable offences punishable by imprisonment, or where the defendant's address is not sufficiently established for a summons to be served on him. Even before PACE 1984 came into force the police seldom sought warrants to arrest for an offence in the first instance. Since the police have a power of summary arrest for arrestable offences (s 24 of PACE 1984, art 26 of the PACE Order 1989) and for all other offences when the service of a summons is impractical or inappropriate (s 25, s 26(2) and Sch 2 of PACE 1984 (Arts 27, 28(2) and Sch 2 of the PACE Order 1989) and other statutory powers), there is likely to be even less reliance on the arrest warrant. Prior to PACE 1984 an arrest warrant might have been sought when a person's address was not sufficiently established for a summons to be served on him, a circumstance anticipated by s 1(4) of the MCA 1980. Section 25(3)(c) of PACE 1984 provides a power to arrest without a warrant in such circumstances and that power of arrest is not confined to the time at which the offence was committed. Section 25(1) (Art 27(1)) refers to the past and the present: 'has been committed or attempted, or is being committed'. Suppose, for example, D who is reasonably suspected of committing an offence is stopped by a constable and required to give his name and address. He persuades the constable that the address given is a satisfactory address for service of a summons when it is not. D is permitted to go on his way having been told he will be reported for the question of a prosecution to be considered. Some days later the constable sees D in the street. He is then aware that the address given is not a satisfactory address. D is still reasonably suspected of having committed an offence and may be arrested under s 25 (Art 27) if a general arrest condition is satisfied, as it is unless D can persuade the constable otherwise. It should be noted that if a summons is served and the accused fails to appear the court may be able to proceed in his absence (ss 11 and 12 of the MCA 1980) and if this is not possible the court may issue a warrant for his arrest, sometimes referred to as a 'bench warrant' (s 13 of the MCA 1980). There are two possible reasons, the practicability of a summons apart, why a warrant of arrest under s 1 of the MCA 1980 should be sought post PACE 1984. The first, and most likely, is for the protection of the constable. Suppose D, who is reasonably suspected of having committed an arrestable offence, is known to be in certain premises. He, and his family, are known to the police and likely to resist violently entry in order to arrest. Though s 17(1)(b) of PACE 1984 (Art 19 of the 1989 Order) authorises the entry into premises in order to arrest a person for an arrestable offence, and s 117 of that Act (Art 88 of the Order) authorises the use of force, a warrant of arrest under s 1 of the MCA 1980 may be sought in order to obtain the protection of the Constables Protection Act 1750, under which a constable has a complete defence to a civil action if, in good faith, he executes a warrant strictly according to its terms. Section 17(1)(a) of PACE 1984 gives a power to enter premises in order to execute such a warrant. The warrant authorises the use of force but s 117 of PACE 1984 (Art 88 of the 1989 Order) is also available where the s 17 (Art 19) power is exercised. The second possible reason for reliance on an arrest warrant rather than PACE 1984 powers to arrest without warrant is that an arrest warrant can be issued when the information alleges that a person 'has, or is suspected of having committed an offence' (s 1 of the MCA 1980). This would appear to permit the issue of a warrant on suspicion alone, unsupported by objectively reasonable grounds. However, the criterion of reasonable suspicion as the threshold for arrest without warrant is pitched so low that the difference, if there is one, is hardly perceptible (see paras 2.81-2.92, ante).

Execution of a warrant of arrest etc – s 33

5.179   Section 125 of the Magistrates' Courts Act 1980 provides that a warrant of arrest issued by a justice of the peace shall remain in force until it is executed or withdrawn; and that such a warrant, together with warrants of commitment or distress (other than for non-payment of rates) or a search warrant, may be executed anywhere in England and Wales by any person to whom it is directed or by any constable acting within his police area. Formerly a warrant to arrest a person 'charged with an offence' could be executed by a constable notwithstanding that he did not have it in his possession at the time, provided it was shown to the person arrested, if he demanded to see it, as soon as practicable. Since this only applied to warrants to arrest a person 'charged with an offence' it meant that it was unlawful to arrest a person for whom a warrant of committal or distress, and in particular a warrant to arrest for non-payment of a fine, had been issued, unless the constable had the warrant in his possession at the time (*De Costa Small v Kirkpatrick* (1979)). Section 33 of PACE 1984 removed this fetter and amended s 125(3) of the Magistrates' Courts Act 1980 to read:

'(3) A warrant to which this subsection applies may be executed by a constable notwithstanding that it is not in his possession at the time; but the warrant shall, on the demand of the person arrested, be shown to him as soon as practicable.'

5.180   (The law in Northern Ireland was amended by art 156 of the Magistrates' Courts (Northern Ireland) Order 1981.)

5.181   The warrants to which this rule applies include a warrant to arrest a person in connection with an offence, warrants to arrest for desertion from HM Forces, warrants of committal or distress and warrants issued under the Domestic Proceedings and Magistrates' Courts Act 1978 (Magistrates' Courts Act 1980, s 125(4) as amended by PACE 1984, s 33). In *Jones v Kelsey* (1987) it was held that a warrant issued under s 16(1) of the Powers of Criminal Courts Act 1973 to arrest for breach of a community service order was 'a warrant to arrest a person in connection with an offence' within the meaning of s 125(4), the offence either being an offence under s 16 of the 1973 Act or the original offence for which the order was made. See also *R v Peacock* (1988).

CROSS-BORDER ENFORCEMENT

5.182   Sections 136 to 140 of the Criminal Justice and Public Order Act 1994 provide for cross-border enforcement of warrants to commit or arrest whether in respect of persons alleged to have committed an offence or of witnesses. Thus a warrant of arrest can be executed in Scotland or Northern Ireland by English or Welsh police officers and vice versa, without endorsement. English and Welsh police officers may also arrest without warrant a person reasonably suspected of an arrestable offence or any other offence if an arrest condition is satisfied, if the person is in Scotland or Northern Ireland and Scottish and Northern Irish police may similarly arrest persons in England or Wales. Powers of search of the person arrested and premises are also available as they are for an arrest in England, Wales or Northern Ireland.

6 Detention

INTRODUCTION AND HUMAN RIGHTS

6.1 As was indicated in Chapter 5, there was a time when arrest without warrant was generally not possible unless the police were in a position to charge the person with the offence for which he was to be arrested. The arrest then came at the end of the investigation and there was no problem of detention without charge in a police station for long periods before the person was charged and appeared before a court. In Scotland, subject to certain exceptions, the general rule is still that an arrest without warrant must be accompanied by a charge (*Chalmers v HM Advocate* (1954)), but south of the border the law has moved on to permit arrest at an early stage in the investigation, often long before there is sufficient evidence to charge the suspect. As a result of these changes the investigation of crime now tends to start with an arrest on reasonable suspicion, which is often arrest for questioning (cf *Holgate-Mohammed v Duke* (1984)), and the suspect is detained in a police station while the investigation proceeds.

6.2 Article 5 (3) of the European Convention guarantees a prompt appearance before a judge or other judicial officer. In *Brogan v United Kingdom* the ECHR stated that the length of time that a person could be detained before such appearance without infringing the requirement had to be judged in the light of the object of the Article, which is to protect an individual's right to liberty against arbitrary state interference

The present law – summary

6.3 PACE 1984 recognises that the police station is the venue for the investigation of most serious offences by providing that detention without charge may only be authorised if it is necessary to secure or preserve evidence or to obtain it by questioning. This is identical to the criteria for such detention recommended by the Royal Commission on Criminal Procedure (1981). The Act also follows the Commission's recommendation that 24 hours from the time the arrested person arrives at the police station should be the maximum period of ordinary detention without charge. However, while the Commission recommended that detention beyond 24 hours should be permissible only in respect of 'grave offences' and with the authority of a magistrates' court, the Act departs from that recommendation in a significant way. Detention beyond 24 hours is only possible in respect of ' arrestable offences' (the Criminal Justice Act 2003 amended s 42(1)(b) in order to extend detention beyond 24 hours for arrestable offences – previously it had been for serious arrestable offences as defined in s 116) rather than 'grave offences'. A superintendent or more senior police officer may authorise continued detention for up to 12 hours beyond the initial 24 hours, if there are reasonable grounds for believing such detention to be necessary to secure or preserve evidence, or to obtain it by questioning and if certain other conditions are satisfied. Thus the police may authorise up to 36 hours of detention without charge. A magistrates' court may issue a warrant of further detention authorising detention without charge for up to 36 hours relying on the basic criteria of the necessity to secure, preserve or obtain evidence and other conditions to be discussed. That warrant can again be extended by a magistrates' court for up to 36 hours but in no case can the overall detention period exceed 96 hours. An application for a warrant of further detention can be made at any time during the 36 hours of detention authorised by the police and can therefore be applied for during the initial period of 24 hours' detention when it is clear from the outset that more than 36 hours will be required. In such a case there will be no need to seek authority from a superintendent for continued detention, for the period authorised by the warrant will commence on the expiry of the initial 24 hours of detention without charge. There are two reasons for this departure from the recommendation of the Royal Commission on Criminal Procedure, one administrative, one practical. The administrative reason is that applications to a magistrates' court for warrants of detention after 24 hours would create a significant workload. By permitting the police to authorise detention up to 36 hours that workload is significantly reduced. The practical reason is that there will be cases in which the police will consider it necessary to delay the detainee's right of access to a solicitor. As we shall see in Chapter 7, such delay is possible for up to 36 hours, though in practice such delay has been severely limited by the decision in *R v Samuel* (1988) and the impact of European Human Rights decisions. The Act requires the attendance of a detainee before a court on an application for a warrant of further detention and permits the detainee to be legally represented. Permitting the police to authorise detention for up to 36 hours thus postpones the possibility of legal representation of the detainee.

6.4   Reviews of detention, before and after charge, must be carried out six hours after detention is authorised and thereafter at intervals of nine hours. If the grounds for detention cease to exist, or if continued or further detention is not authorised, the person must be:

(a)   released, conditionally or unconditionally, or

(b)   charged and released on bail to appear before a court, where necessary subject to conditions, or

(c)   charged and taken before the next available court.

6.5 Grounds for detention after charge are clearly stated and there is a Code of Practice for the Detention, Treatment and Questioning of Persons by the Police (in this Chapter referred to as 'Code C'), breach of which is a disciplinary offence and which governs the treatment of persons detained. (The table on p 319 summarises the detention provisions in schematic form.) The detention procedures are supervised by an officer who is given the title of 'custody officer'. This officer authorises the initial detention without charge and detention after charge and the release of persons from detention can only be authorised by a custody officer. Certain police stations are designated as stations which are to be used for the purpose of detaining arrested persons and it is at these stations that custody officers perform their duties. 'The institution of the custody officer is a major development in the ethos of policing' (junior Home Office minister, House of Lords, Debates, 9 July 1984, col 571) and provides an element of direct personal account-ability for ensuring that persons detained are properly treated and their rights safeguarded. The importance of this relatively junior police officer (he will normally be a sergeant) cannot be over-emphasised. The discussion of Part IV of PACE 1984, as amended by subsequent legislation, will consider first some definitions; then the institution of the custody officer; detention without charge and the various duties of the custody officer and others in relation to such detention; detention after charge and the duties relating thereto; and bail and remands in police custody. These provisions apply to adults and arrested juveniles but there are a number of additional provisions for juveniles.

DEFINITIONS

Police detention (s 118(2), art 2(3) and (4))

6.6 The entire thrust of Part IV of the Act is concerned with detention at a police station following arrest for an offence. 'Police detention' is defined by s 118(2) as follows:

> 'A person is in police detention for the purposes of this Act if –
> (a) he has been taken to a police station after being arrested for an offence or after being arrested under s 41 of the Prevention of Terrorism (Temporary Provisions) Act 2000 or Sch 5 para 6 of that Act by an examining officer who is a constable);
> (b) he is arrested at a police station after attending voluntarily at the station or accompanying a constable to it, and is detained there; or is detained elsewhere in the charge of a constable,
> except that a person who is at a court after being charged is not in police detention for those purposes.'

6.7 Section 118(2A) is inserted by the Police Reform Act 2002 to include where a person is in the lawful custody of an investigating officer or an escort officer so defined under the Act (see para 2.122–2.124).

6.8 Article 2(3) of the 1989 Order also includes:

'(c) he is arrested at a police station after being taken to the station in pursuance of a direction under s 16 of the Prison Act (Northern Ireland) 1953' (added by art 3 of the Police (Amendment) (Northern Ireland) Order 1995).

6.9 This covers the situation in which a person detained in a prison in Northern Ireland is brought to the police station by prison officers and is arrested there by police officers investigating offences other than that for which the person was imprisoned. The person would not have been taken to a police station under arrest, he would not be a volunteer nor would he have accompanied a police officer to the police station.

6.10 It is clear from this definition that:
(i) a person arrested for an offence otherwise than at a police station is not in police detention during the period following his arrest and before he actually arrives at a police station and is not therefore in police detention during any period of post-arrest investigation such as is permitted by s 30(10) (Art 32(13)) (see para 5.147, ante); and
(ii) in the case of a person who voluntarily attends at or accompanies a constable to a police station without being arrested (see s 29 (Art 31) discussed at paras 5.127-5.128, ante), he is not in police detention during the period before he is arrested at the police station.

6.11 Section 41 (Art 42) (see para 6.108(c) example 5) links up with this definition by providing that the time from which the period of detention is to be calculated ('the relevant time') will, with minor exceptions, be in the case of (i) the time of arrival at the police station and, in the case of (ii), the time of arrest. The phrase 'is detained elsewhere in the charge of a constable' covers those situations in which an arrested person having been taken to, or arrested at, a police station, is taken from there prior to being charged to some other place; for example, where he is taken to premises which are to be searched, or to a field where property is hidden, or is taken in detention to a court while application is made for a warrant of further detention or for an extension of such a warrant. A person at a court after being charged is not in police detention and s 58 of PACE 1984 (right of access to a solicitor and police power to delay such access) under s 58 of PACE does not apply but there is a common law right to see a solicitor on request – see *R v Chief Constable of South Wales, ex p Merrick* (1994). He will be in police detention while being conveyed from a police station to a court, or from a court to a police station where he is to be further detained after charge if remanded to a police station under s 128 of the Magistrates' Courts Act 1980 (see para 6.195, post) but not if, following charge or conviction, he is remanded to police cells in the absence of prison accommodation.

6.12 In *R v Kerawalla* (1991) K was arrested by Customs officers in a hotel room where he had gone to meet J, who had previously been arrested at Heathrow following the discovery of a large quantity of drugs. A senior officer authorised delay in allowing him access to a solicitor under s 58(8) which applies when a person is 'arrested and held in custody in a police station or other premises' (s 58(1)). Customs delayed taking him to a police station arguing that s 30(10) of PACE 1984 applied (see para 5.147, ante). The Court of Appeal disagreed but even if the subsection applied K was not in police detention as defined by s 118. Section 58 does not therefore apply but there is the common law right of access – see *Ex p Merrick* above. (Both cases are discussed further in Chapter 7, post.)

6.13 For hospitalisation during a period of detention at a police station, see s 41(6) (Art 42(4)) discussed at para 6.127, post. For hospitalisation following arrest before being taken to a police station, see para 6.104, post. For hospitalisation after charge, see s 46(9) (Art 47(5)) discussed at para 6.104, post.

6.14 Persons who are not arrested for an offence, eg a person arrested under s 136 of the Mental Health Act 1983, persons in custody awaiting extradition proceedings or persons in custody awaiting deportation, are not in police detention for the purposes of PACE 1984. However, Code C (para 1.10) directs that its provisions apply to persons in custody at a police station whether or not they have been arrested for an offence, except Code C, section 15 (reviews and extension of detention) which applies solely to persons in police detention. For conditions of detention, see the Code C, sections 1 to 9, and Chapter 7, post. Code C. para 1.12 specifies those who are not covered by the Code. They are people arrested on warrants issued in Scotland under CJPOA 1994, s 136(2) or without warrant under s 137(2) (cross-border power of arrest); people arrested under s 142(3) of the Immigration and Asylum Act 1999 for the purpose of having their fingerprints taken; people who have been served notice of detention under the Immigration Act 1971; convicted or remanded prisoners detained in police cells under the Imprisonment (Temporary Provisions) Act 1980; persons detained for examination under the Terrorism Act 2000 (covered by the Code issued under the Terrorism Act 2000); persons detained under stop and search powers except as required by Code A.

Designated police stations (s 35, art 36)

6.15 The separation of the custodial and the investigative powers of the police is an important safeguard for the detained person. Someone who is independent of the investigation is much more likely to take an objective view, hence the introduction of the custody officer. Ideally every police station would have officers appointed to carry out such duties but that is impracticable given first, the large number of police stations, ranging from the two-man rural station to the city centre station staffed by large numbers of police, and second, the small number of personnel able to carry out the duties of custody officer. It would be equally impracticable to require policemen in rural areas to take every arrested person to the city centre station which has a custody officer when it might involve travelling a considerable distance. The chief officer of police for each area must therefore designate a number of police stations which are, subject to s 30(3) to (5) (Art 32(3) and (4)) (see paras 5.134-5.137), to be used for the purpose of detaining arrested persons (s 35(1)). The duty is to designate sufficient stations to provide enough accommodation for that purpose (s 35(2), art 36(2)). But within that duty a chief officer may designate a station which has not previously been designated, and may direct that a designation of a station previously made shall cease to operate (s 35(3), art 36(3)). This provides the necessary flexibility to enable a chief officer to take account of seasonal or other factors which affect the arrest rate and create a temporary need for more accommodation. For example, the opening up of a seaside resort for its summer season or large-scale picketing during an industrial dispute may call for police stations in the area to be designated or mobile police stations and cell blocks to be designated for the period of the season or the dispute. 'Designated police station' therefore means a police station for the time being designated under this section (s 35(4), art 36(4)).

Times to be treated as approximate only (s 45(2), art 46)

6.16   Whereas previously there were no firm time limits within which arrested persons could be detained, under this part of the Act there are. Section 45(2) (Art 46) provides that a period of time or a time of day is to be treated as approximate only. This is not intended to undermine the safeguards which the Act provides. Perhaps the best explanation of the section's purpose is provided by the Australian Law Reform Commission, who said of a similar scheme:

> 'Perhaps it will not be taken amiss if we say that we trust that common sense will prevail in the application of these provisions in the courts, and that justices, magistrates and judges will not require police officers to go about like rally drivers armed with stop-watches and minute-by-minute log books. The time limit we recommend is merely a statutory guide to reasonable conduct. It should be viewed in that perspective.' (Para 97)

6.17   Section 45(2) (Art 46) must be subject to an overriding requirement of reasonableness and good faith. For example, if a review of D's detention is due at 10.15pm and the inspector or custody officer goes off duty at 10pm, it would be permissible, and make good sense, to review the detention at 9.45pm rather than leave it for the relief inspector or custody officer who might find it difficult to review the detention with so little time to acquaint himself with the case. Alternatively the review may be delayed for 30 minutes to allow such time. On the other hand, to delay a review for an hour because the interviewing officer believes the suspect 'is about to crack' would be an abuse of s 45(2) (Art 46) (cf para 6.157, post).

Custody officers at police station (s 36, art 37)

6.18   Section 36(1) provides that one or more custody officers shall be appointed for each designated station. In *Vince v Chief Constable of Dorset Police* (1992) it was held that s 36(1) placed upon the chief constable a duty to appoint sufficient custody officers to ensure that at least one of their number was normally available at each designated police station to perform the functions of that office, but, subject to the

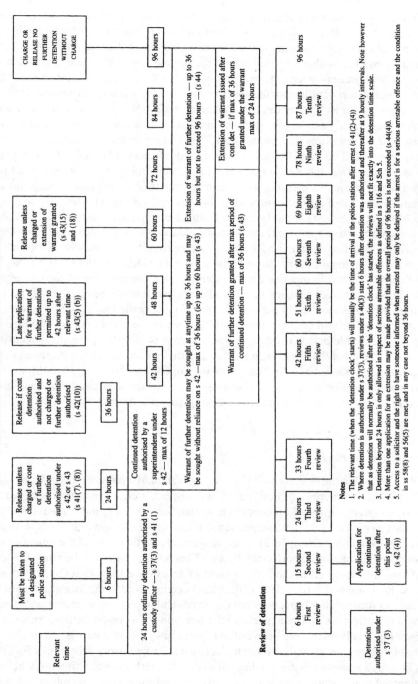

fulfilment of that statutory requirement questions as to whether it might be necessary to require other officers to carry out the functions of custody officer, or whether custody officers ought to be appointed to more than one police station, were matters within the chief constable's discretion as to the deployment of his officers. The custody officer, who must be of at least the rank of sergeant (s 36(3), art 37(3)), must be appointed by the chief officer of police for the area in which the designated police station is, or by such other officer as he may direct (s 36(2), art 37(2)). Where an appointed custody officer is not readily available to perform the functions of a custody officer, an officer of any rank may perform them (s 36(4), art 37(4)). This provision is intended for a 'real emergency' (Lord Edmund Davies, House of Lords Debates, 18 October 1984, col 112) but that is not what sub-s (4) says. Even in such an emergency it is suggested that only a senior constable, preferably one who has qualified for the rank of sergeant and is therefore aware of the duties involved, should be permitted to perform those duties. The Minister of State told the House of Lords that 'the Association of Chief Police Officers agrees that, apart from exceptional circumstances, a probationary constable should not be called upon to act as custody officer but, like us, they feel it prudent to allow for exceptional circumstances' (House of Lords Debates, 19 October 1984, col 1113). It is difficult to imagine a probationary constable performing the duties of a custody officer except perhaps in a non-designated station – see para 6.09, post. A custody officer is required to perform the functions specified in Code C as soon as is practicable but he will not be in breach of this code in the event of delay provided the delay is justifiable and that every reasonable step is taken to prevent unnecessary delay. The fact that there has been a delay and the reason for it must be stated in the custody record (Code C 1.1A). This provision, together with s 45(2) (Art 46), follows the recommendation of the Royal Commission on Criminal Justice (1993) and gives custody officers justifiable latitude in carrying out their duties.

An independent officer

6.19   Given that the custody officer is the equivalent of a judicial officer with a duty to look after the interests of both police and suspect, a clear separation between the investigative and custodial functions is essential. Section 36(5) and (6) (Art 37(5) and (6)) seek to provide for such independence whenever possible within the operational limits which apply. Section 36(5) states the general rule that none of the functions of a custody officer should be performed by an officer who, at the time when they fall to be performed, is involved in the investigation of an offence for which the person is in police detention at that time. If an officer has been involved in the investigation of the offence at some earlier time, he is not debarred. Unless that involvement was deep it should not affect his ability to perform the functions of a custody officer impartially. Where the involvement was deep but not immediate, it would be wise (though not a statutory requirement) for the officer to declare it to a supervisory officer (cf s 36(7), art 37(7) which requires that arresting officers who perform such functions at non-designated police stations do so). Such involvement may prove an embarrassment if at trial the defence seeks to raise his involvement and conduct. Section 36(5) is subject to s 39(2) (Art 40(2)) which relieves the custody officer of his duties in relation to an arrested person when the person is transferred to the custody of an officer investigating the offence, eg if the person is taken from the police station to the scene of the crime. That officer is then under a duty to ensure that the person is treated in accordance with the Act and Code of Practice and is therefore temporarily in the position of a custody officer. He is not then independent, but, since he makes no decisions concerning detention, he does not breach the principle of separation between the two functions.

6.20 The Police Reform Act 2002 permits police authorities to designate civilian custody and escort officers – their powers are detailed in Chapter 2 paras 2.122–2.124.

Arrested persons at non-designated stations

6.21 Section 30(3) and (4) (Art 32(3) and (4)) permit an arrested person to be taken to a non-designated police station. Where those circumstances apply the functions of a custody officer are performed by an officer who is not involved in the investigation of the offence for which the person is in detention, if such an officer is readily available (s 36(7)(a), art 37(7)(a)). If he is not, the officer who took him to the police station, usually, but not invariably, the arresting officer, or any other officer, may perform these functions (s 36(7)(b), art 37(7)(b)). References to 'custody officer' therefore include these officers (s 36(8), art 37(8)). However, whenever the officer who took the person to a police station is to perform the functions of a custody officer, he shall, as soon as practicable (s 36(10)), inform an officer of at least the rank of inspector who is attached to a designated police station, that he is to do so (s 36(9)). That supervisory officer should then ensure that the detention at a non-designated police station is permitted in the circumstances and that the officer complies with the Act and Code of Practice in dealing with the person detained. It is important that supervision is provided for the following reasons. Pre-PACE research suggested that 75% of suspects are dealt with within six hours and, while Home Office figures do not specifically refer to this period, what figures there are suggest that post-PACE a majority are released within this period. Section 30(3) (Art 32(3)) permits that majority of suspects to be taken to a non-designated police station when the arresting officer is working in the area covered by that station, while s 30(4) (Art 32(4)) permits potentially violent persons who have been arrested single-handedly by any constable, to be taken to such a police station. Taken together those provisions could permit a very large number of persons to be taken to non-designated police stations. Though most will be minor offenders and the purpose of detention will often be identification of the person or verification of an address following arrest under s 25 (Art 27), some will be more serious offenders. It is the latter who require the protection offered by the institution of the custody officer and it is possible that s 30(3) and (4) (Art 32(3) and (4)) and s 36(7) (Art 37(7)) provide a means of undermining that protection and also of depriving the suspect of other forms of protection provided by designated police stations. For it is at such police stations that duty solicitors attend and the lay visitor scheme operates. It is therefore incumbent upon super-visory officers who wish to comply with the spirit of the Act, rather than simply the letter, to ensure that non-designated police stations are used only in an emergency or for minor cases which involve identification or verification of names and addresses.

Other duties performed by a custody officer (s 36(6), art 37(6))

6.22   Interpreted strictly, s 36(5) (Art 37(5)) would prevent a custody officer performing routine administrative or procedural duties which may have an investigative function as well; for example, searching the person, taking fingerprints or identifying the arrested person. In order to clarify the position s 36(6) (Art 37(6)) states that nothing in s 36(5) (Art 37(5)) is to be taken to prevent a custody officer from:

(a)   performing any function assigned to custody officers by this Act or a code of practice issued under it;

(b)   carrying out the duties imposed on custody officers under s 39 of this Act (Art 40) (duty to ensure that detainees are treated in accordance with the Act and Codes of Practice);

(c)   doing anything in connection with the identification of a suspect (this does not include identity parades which, under the Code of Practice governing parades, must be supervised by a uniformed inspector); or

(d)   doing anything under ss 7 and 8 of the Road Traffic Act 1988 (taking samples of breath etc) (Arts 144, 146 and 147 of the Road Traffic (Northern Ireland) Order 1981).

Detention under the Terrorism Act 2000

6.23   The treatment of persons detained under the Terrorism Act 2000, s 41 and Sch 7 is governed by Sch 8 of that Act and, although there is a familiar thread in the language, the regime differs from that of PACE. The purpose is to allow the police wider powers of investigation than for other offences and detention is permitted for up to seven days from the time of arrest or examination at a port. Section 41 is the successor to s 14 (1)(b) of the Prevention of Terrorism (Temporary Provisions) Act 1989 which was the subject of a derogation under Art 15 of the European Convention of Human Rights. The ECHR had held that each of the applicants in *Brogan v United Kingdom*, all of whom had been detained under the PT(TP)A 1989, were detained in violation of Art 5(3). Even the shortest of the four periods of detention considered, that of four days and six hours, was outside the requirements of Art 5. There was no judicial oversight in the PT(TP)A 1989 but this is built into s 41 of the new Act through the requirement to obtain judicial authorisation after 48 hours.

6.24   Paragraph 1 of Sch 8 requires that any person arrested under s 41 or Sch 7 must be taken as soon as is reasonably practicable to a police station designated by the Secretary of State. Formerly police stations at Castlereagh, Armagh and Londonderry were designated in Northern Ireland and Paddington Green police station in London was regarded as suitably equipped to hold terrorist suspects. The initial period of detention is 48 hours which is subject to the PACE regime and the suspect must be released unless detention is necessary. The first review of detention must be carried out as soon 'as is reasonably practicable after the time of the person's arrest'; thereafter reviews must be carried out not less than every 12 hours. Postponement of reviews are subject to the same criteria as in s 40(9) of PACE 1984. Inspectors carry out reviews during the 24-hour period and thereafter an officer of at least the rank of superintendent is responsible. In order to authorise continued detention the review officer must be satisfied that the investigation is being carried out diligently and expeditiously.

Detention of juveniles and children

6.25   Section 52 of PACE 1984, which stated that the detention provisions did not apply to a child under ten years of age who is arrested without a warrant for an offence other than homicide, was repealed by Sch 15 of the Children Act 1989. The same provision deleted the reference to s 52 in the definition of 'arrested juvenile' in s 37(15) of PACE 1984. An 'arrested juvenile' for the purposes of the detention provisions now means: 'a person arrested with or without a warrant who appears to be under the age of 17'. The result is that the detention provisions apply to children over ten years of age but who appear to be under the age of 17 (see Code C 1.5), who are arrested for an offence with or without a warrant. Children under ten are conclusively presumed to be incapable of committing a crime (doli incapax) and are therefore exempt from criminal responsibility in all circumstances. They cannot therefore be the subject of police detention which only follows arrest for an offence. (See the discussion of powers of arrest in para 5.43, ante and the discussion of non-criminal detention of children at para 6.28, post.)

6.26   The equivalent sub-articles in art 38 of the NI PACE Order impose a duty on the custody officer to inform the arrested juvenile, parent or guardian and supervisor if subject to a supervision order, of the fact of the arrest and the grounds for detention, similar to the requirement in s 34(2) of the Children and Young Persons Act 1933 as amended by s 57 of PACE 1984, discussed in paras 6.28 and 6.28 below. Section 57 of the 1984 Act substituted subsections for s 34(2) of the Children and Young Persons Act 1933. They require that:
(a)   the parent or guardian of the child or young person be informed of the fact that he has been arrested, the reason for the detention and the place of the detention;
(b)   if at the time of arrest he is the subject of a supervision order, the supervisor be informed as in (a).

6.27   'Parent or Guardian' in s 34(2) includes a local authority if the child is in its care. (The term 'in care' is used in Code C to cover all cases in which a juvenile is 'looked after' by a local authority under the terms of the Children Act 1989 (Code C 1.7(a)(i)).) Section 118 of the 1984 Act similarly defines 'parent or guardian' for the purposes of the 1984 Act. (See also Code C, para 1.7 and Notes of Guidance 1C and 1D, and paras

3.7, 3.8 and 3.9 and Notes of Guidance 3C.) Section 57 and the Code of Practice ensure that the adult responsible for the care of the arrested child is informed of the arrest, why he has been arrested and where he is being detained. If the arrested juvenile is in local authority care but is living with his parents, they, as well as the local authority, should normally be contacted unless they are suspected of involvement in the offence (Code C, Notes of Guidance 3C).If the arrested juvenile is know to be subject to a court order under which a person or organisation is given any degree of statutory responsibility to supervise or otherwise monitor him reasonable steps must be taken to notify that person or the responsible officer in the organisation. An arrested juvenile should not be placed in a police cell except in the circumstances mentioned in Code C 8.8 (it is not practicable to supervise him if not placed in a cell or the cell is more comfortable than other secure accommodation in the police station), and may not in any circumstances be placed in a cell with a detained adult (Code C 8.8). (See also s 31 of the Children and Young Persons Act 1933 which further requires that a girl be detained in the care of a woman.) For discussion of the treatment of juveniles, see para 7.254, post.

Non-criminal detention of children (Children Act 1989, s 46 (Children (Northern Ireland) Order 1994, Art 65)

6.28   The power of a constable to take a child to a place of safety, previously contained in the Children and Young Persons Act 1969, s 28, is replaced by the power to take a child into 'police protection'. Where a constable has reasonable cause to believe that a child (defined as a person under the age of 18) would otherwise be likely to suffer significant harm, he may:

(a)   remove the child to suitable accommodation and keep him there; or

(b)   take such steps as are reasonable to ensure that the child's removal from any hospital or other place in which he is then being accommodated is prevented (s 46 of the Children Act 1989, art 65 of the Children (NI) Order 1994).

6.29   ('Harm' includes impairment of development and 'development' means physical, intellectual, emotional, social or behavioural development (s 31(9) of the Children Act 1989, art 2 of the Children (NI) Order 1994).)

6.30   When a constable has exercised this power the child is referred to as having been taken into 'police protection' rather than police custody or detention. No child may be kept for more than 72 hours (under the previous law the maximum was eight days). As soon as practicable after taking the child into police protection, the constable must ensure that the case is inquired into by the officer designated by the chief officer of the police area concerned. Having completed the inquiry, that officer must release the child from police protection unless there is still reasonable cause to believe that he would still be likely to suffer significant harm. In addition he must as soon as possible:

(a)   inform the local authority in the area in which the child was found, of the steps taken or to be taken;

(b) tell the local authority (the appropriate authority) within whose area the child is ordinarily resident, where the child is being accommodated;
(c) inform the child, if capable of understanding, of the steps taken with respect to him and the reasons for taking them and any further steps which may be taken;
(d) take such steps as are reasonably practicable to discover the wishes and feelings of the child;
(e) where the child was taken into police protection by being removed to accommodation which is not provided by a local authority or as a refuge, secure that he is moved to accommodation which is so provided;
(f) he must also take such steps as are reasonably practicable to inform –
 (i) the child's parents;
 (ii) a person who is not a parent but who has parental responsibility for him; and
 (iii) any other person with whom he was living immediately before being taken into police protection,
 of the steps taken with respect to the child and the reasons for taking them (s 46(3) and (4), art 65(3)-(6)).

6.31 While the child is in police protection, the designated officer may apply on behalf of the appropriate authority for an emergency protection order to be made under s 44 of the Children Act 1989 (Art 64 of the Children (NI) Order 1994). If he does so, the period of the order (maximum of eight days) runs from the time when the child was taken into police protection under s 46 (Art 65) (s 45(3), art 64(2)). The police do not assume parental responsibility for Children Act purposes whilst the child is in their protection. Instead there is a general duty to safeguard the child's welfare. In particular parents, those with parental responsibility, any person with whom he was living before being taken into police protection or a person in whose favour a contact order has been made (or a person acting on their behalf) should be permitted such contact as the designated officer considers is both reasonable and in the child's best interest.

General limitation on police detention (s 34, art 35)

6.32 Section 34 introduced the scheme for ensuring that a person is detained after arrest only when necessary. Section 34(1) lays down the important principle that a person arrested for an offence (not a person arrested under s 27 (Art 29) (fingerprinting), s 63 of the CJPOA 1994 (samples), or under other powers to arrest other than for an offence, eg under the Mental Health Act 1983) shall not be kept in police detention except in accordance with the provisions of Part IV of the Act. This general principle is followed by a general duty imposed upon the custody officer (subject to an exception to be mentioned), to order the immediate release of a person in police detention if at any time:

(a) he becomes aware that the grounds for detention of that person have ceased to apply; and
(b) he is not aware of any other grounds on which the continued detention of that person could be justified under the provisions of this Part of the Act (s 34(2), art 35(2)).

6.33   A failure to release in accordance with s 34(2) (Art 35(2)) may be taken into account by a trial judge in determining whether a confession is admissible under PACE 1984, s 76 (Art 74) or s 78 (Art 76): see *R v Davison* (1988) considered at para 8.112, post.

6.34   The grounds for detention without charge are set out in s 37(2) (Art 38(2)) and those for detention after charge in s 38(1) (Art 39(1)) and it is these grounds to which s 34(2) (Art 35(2)) refers. Section 40 (Art 41) provides for periodic reviews of a person's detention which will assist in making the custody officer aware of whether the grounds for detention have ceased to exist. It will be seen later that there are a number of provisions which require the release of a person in police detention upon the expiry of a time limit (s 41(7), art 42(5) – expiry of 24 hours' detention s 42(10), art 43(9) – release following continued detention; s 43(15) and (18), art 44(14) and (17) – release upon refusal of an application for, or upon the expiry of, a warrant for further detention s 44(7) (Art 45(7)) – release on refusal of an extension of a warrant of further detention). The duty to release under s 34(2) (Art 35(2)) is thus confined to:

(a)   release of a person on his arrival at a police station because the grounds for his arrest have ceased to exist and there is no other ground to detain him;

(b)   release of a person who has been previously detained at a police station under s 37(3) (Art 38(3)) (ie to secure or preserve evidence or to obtain it by questioning), but in respect of whom the grounds for detention no longer exist;

(c)   release of a person charged and detained under s 38(2) (Art 39(2)) (for example, to ascertain his name and address), when the reasons for that detention no longer exist;

(d)   release of a person who was arrested for an offence, who was released on bail subject to a duty to attend at a police station (s 47), and who so attends but there is insufficient evidence to charge him and no reasonable grounds to detain him under s 47(5).

6.35   The following examples illustrate the operation of the duty to release under s 34(2) (Art 35(2)).

(1)   D is brought to a police station under arrest for an offence. The custody officer determines that there is insufficient evidence to charge him with that offence and that there are no grounds for detention without charge under s 37(2) (Art 38(2)). He must order the immediate release of D.

(2)   As in (1) above but the custody officer reasonably believes that there are grounds for detention without charge under s 37(2) (Art 38(2)), it being necessary to question D. He authorises the detention under s 37(3) (Art 38(3)). A review officer conducting a review of that detention (whether at a first or subsequent review, or on a review following the authorisation of continued detention under s 42 (Art 43) or under a warrant of further detention under s 43 (Art 44), or an extension of that warrant under s 44 (Art 45)) determines that the grounds for such detention have ceased to exist and so informs the custody officer. The latter is now aware that the grounds for the person's detention no longer exist and, unless there are other grounds, he must order the immediate release of D. Similarly if the investigating officer reports that, following an interview with D, there is not enough evidence to detain him further.

(3)   D has been detained in custody as in (2) above and is charged after six hours of detention. The custody officer decides that his release is not required by s 38(1) (Art 39(1)) and authorises his detention on one of the grounds set out in s 38(1) (Art 39(1)). The custody officer himself reviews this case and this makes him aware that the grounds for detention no longer apply. He must order the immediate release of D.

(4)   D is arrested for a general offence because his name and address are not known (general arrest conditions (a) and (c) of s 25(3)) (Art 27(3)). He is charged with the offence, detained in custody after charge under s 38(3) (Art 39(3)) and two hours later his name and address are determined and verified. The custody officer must order the immediate release of D.

6.36   The operation of s 34(2)(b) is illustrated by the following examples.

(5)   D is arrested in police area A for a minor offence but the grounds for detention cease to exist. D is wanted in police area B for murder. If there are grounds for D's arrest on that charge, he should then be arrested, the reasonable grounds for suspicion coming from police in area B. The custody officer is not then under a duty to release D but may authorise his detention under s 37(3) (Art 38(3)). (As to the relevant time in such a case see s 41(4) discussed at para 6.108 (example 7, post).) Note that Northern Ireland is one police area for the purposes of art 42.

(6)   D is arrested on suspicion of fraud, interviewed and then bailed to attend a police station. When he returns to answer his bail the police investigation has still not produced sufficient evidence to charge him. He may be released on bail or without bail if it is felt that such evidence will not be forthcoming.

6.37   If D in the above example is merely wanted for questioning by the other police force, there being no grounds for arrest, he cannot be kept in police detention but can only be requested to assist by remaining at a police station voluntarily.

6.38   (NB: In *R v McKenzie* (1971) it was doubted whether an arrest under what is now s 6(5) of the Road Traffic Act 1988 (Art 146(3)(b) of the Road Traffic (NI) Order 1981) (driving with excess alcohol in the blood) was an arrest for an offence. Section 34(6) (Art 35(7)) resolved any doubt by stating that it is. A custody officer may therefore release a motorist arrested for such an offence on bail to return to a police station after a forensic examination of blood or urine, or to a court after he is charged.)

6.39   The exception to the duty to release under s 34(2) is provided by s 34(4) (Art 35(4)). There is no duty to release if it appears to the custody officer that the person arrested for an offence was unlawfully at large when arrested, eg where he was an absconder from a remand home or had escaped from prison or, in the case of Northern Ireland, if he has been brought to the police station from a prison or similar establishment in pursuance of a direction under s 16 of the Prison Act (NI) 1953 and arrested at the police station for another offence. Article 4A of the 1989 Order (added by art 3(3) of the Police (Amendment) (NI) Order 1995), requires that references to release, with or without bail, be treated as a reference to the person being returned to the custody of the governor of the custodial establishment from which he was taken to the police station.

6.40 Section 34(3) (Art 35(3)) provides that no person in police detention may be released except on the authority of a custody officer at the police station where his detention was authorised, or, if authorised at more than one station, a custody officer at the station where it was last authorised.

Release on bail or without bail

6.41 If D is to be released, the question of whether he should be released unconditionally or subject to bail arises. Section 34(5) (Art 35(6)) requires that a person released under s 34(2) (Art 35(2)) shall be released without bail unless it appears to the custody officer that:

(a) there is need for further investigation of any matter in connection with which he was detained at any time during the period of his detention; or

(b) that, in respect of any such matter, proceedings may be taken against him, or he may be reprimanded or warned under s 65 of the Crime and Disorder Act 1998, and if it so appears, he shall be released on bail.

6.42 If (a) or (b) apply he shall be released on bail. Section 34(5) (Art 35(6)) represents the previous practice of releasing a person to return to a police station when there is a need for further inquiries into the offence or matters connected with it, eg the investigation of an alibi or forensic examination of some material. When a person is released under s 34(2) (Art 35(2)) and there is such a need, there is a duty to release on bail to return to a police station. The duty to release on bail when proceedings may be taken against the person (s 34(5)(b), art 35(6)(b)) was an innovation. Previously the person had to be released unconditionally and informed that he might be prosecuted and would receive a summons in due course if a decision to prosecute was taken. (Section 43(3) of the Magistrates' Courts Act 1980 only permitted bail to a police station when there was a need for further inquiries.) Under s 47(3) of the 1984 Act (Art 48(1)) bail is duly defined as a duty to appear at a magistrates' court or to attend at a police station. So it is possible for the custody officer to bail a person to return to a police station in the circumstances envisaged by s 34(5)(b) (Art 35(6)(b)). (Art 35(6) is drafted differently to s 34(5) but the effect is the same.) (See further the discussion at paras 6.174-6.183, post.) It should be noted that the duty to release on bail under s 34(5) is applicable only to a release under s 34(2), ie when grounds for detention cease to apply. Release on the expiry of time limits or authorised periods of detention is a release under the various provisions imposing those limits or authorising the period of detention and all those provisions give the custody officer a discretion to release on bail or without bail.

Final warning scheme (Crime and Disorder Act 1998, s 37)

6.43 Section 37 of the Crime and Disorder Act 1998 established the youth justice system. Its principal aim is to prevent offending by children and young persons. It set up Youth Offending Teams (Yot) and, among other provisions, introduced a 'final warning scheme' to divert children and young people from their offending behaviour disposing of offences by reprimand or final warning before they enter the court system. Bail may be granted for a number of reasons which can include:

(a) prior to decision to reprimand/finally warn/charge:
    (i) further investigation into the offence
    (ii) referral to the Yot to check local records of offending history, where there is no conviction recorded on the Police National Computer
    (iii) referral to the Yot for an assessment of the young person.
(b) following a decision to reprimand/finally warn:
    (i) to enable the reprimand or final warning to be delivered by a trained police officer, possibly at a final warning clinic;
    (ii) to enable the reprimand or final warning to be delivered by a trained police officer as part of a restorative process, possibly with the victim present.

6.44 (Detailed guidance on the operation of the final warning scheme is available on the following websites: www.homeoffice.gov.uk and www.youth-justice-board.gov.uk.)

Re-arrest following release under s 34(2)

6.45 The release provisions on the expiry of a time limit on police detention, or of an authorised period of detention, prohibit re-arrest for the same offence for which the person was arrested and detained unless new evidence comes to light justifying such a re-arrest. However, there is no similar provision in respect of release under s 34(2). Given that the release must be on bail to return to a police station if there is a need for further investigation and that in many cases the grounds for detention which cease to apply will be the grounds justifying the original arrest under s 25, there is no need for such a provision. If the release is on the basis that there is not sufficient evidence to charge, that there are no grounds for further detention and no need for further investigation, any re-arrest of that person must be based on new evidence which has come to light since the release.

6.46 Section 46A (added by s 29(2) of the Criminal Justice and Public Order Act 1994) provides a power to arrest without warrant a person who has been released on bail subject to a duty to return to a police station, who fails to do so at the appointed time. Section 34(7) (added by s 29(3) of the CJPOA 1994) provides that such an arrest be treated as an arrest for an offence and the offence in connection with which he was granted bail shall be deemed to be that offence. It is arguable that such a person could always be re-arrested for the offence in connection with which he was bailed if he is still reasonably suspected of committing it and the original power of arrest is still available. Be that as it may s 46A clearly provides a power of arrest. (For consideration of whether the detention clock continues from the point of release on bail or starts afresh, see para 6.189, post.)

Duties of a custody officer before charge (s 37, art 38)

6.47 Where a person is arrested for an offence without warrant (which now includes the arrest of a person bailed to return to a police station who fails to do so – s 46A of

PACE 1984 added by s 29(2) of the CJPOA 1994), or under a warrant not endorsed for bail (see s 117(2) of the Magistrates' Courts Act 1980), the custody officer at each police station where he is detained shall, as soon as practicable after the person arrives at the police station, or if arrested at the police station, as soon as practicable after that arrest (s 37(10), art 38(10), Code C 1.1) determine whether he has before him sufficient evidence to charge that person with the offence for which he was arrested. He may detain the person at the police station for such period as is necessary to enable him to do so (s 37(1)(a) (note that s 37(1)(b) is repealed by the CJPOA 1994), art 38(1)). A person may be arrested for more than one offence and under s 31 (Art 33) for further offences which come to light after the person's arrival at the police station under arrest for the initial offence. Clearly the duty under s 37(1) (Art 38(1)) must be carried out in respect of each offence and, as Code C 1.1 emphasises, as expeditiously as possible. The Royal Commission on Criminal Justice 1993 pointed out that it is not always feasible to comply with the Code requirements immediately and surmised that custody officers may have falsified the custody record in the mistaken belief that there was no latitude for delay. Code C 1.1A meets the Commission's call for amendment by providing that the custody officer is required to perform the functions specified in the Code as soon as is practicable. He is not in breach of the Code in the event of delay if that delay is justifiable and every reasonable step is taken to prevent unnecessary delay. Any delay must be recorded in the custody record with the reason for it. Note for Guidance 1H explains that this provision is intended to cover the kind of delays which may occur in the processing of detained persons because, for example, a large number of suspects are brought into the police station simultaneously, or all interview rooms are in use, or where there are difficulties in contacting an appropriate adult, solicitor or interpreter.

6.48   It will be seen (paras 6.108-6.131, post) that police detention starts, in a majority of cases, on the arrival of the arrested person at the police station (s 41(2), art 42(2)(c)). The 'detention clock' will then have started in all cases, and in the case of arrests under s 31 (Art 33), will be well advanced, before a decision to authorise detention without charge is made, particularly if there are a number of persons arrested and awaiting processing. It follows that review of detention under s 40 (Art 41), which starts six hours after detention is authorised (s 40(3)(a), art 41(3)(a)), may well commence some time after the 'detention clock' has started. Research by McKenzie et al, Helping Police with their Inquiries (1990) Crim LR 22, showed a range of 'waiting time' of between 0 minutes to 2 hours 6 minutes in a sample of observed receptions and 0 minutes to 1 hour 57 minutes in a sample of custody records (p 26 fn 15). Section 34(7) (added by s 29(3) of the CJPOA 1994) provides that an arrest under s 46A (failure to attend a police station having been bailed to return) is an arrest for the original offence in respect of which the person was bailed. The custody officer must carry out his duties following the arrest but if he authorises detention without charge he must be aware that the detention clock continues from the point at which the person was bailed.

6.49   The exchange between the custody officer, the arresting officer and the person arrested could easily become an interview if questions are asked about the person's involvement in the offence (see paras 8.13-8.24, post). The custody officer's task is to determine whether there are grounds to charge the person with the offence, and if not whether there are grounds to detain without charge. Whilst he may ask questions of the arresting officer in order to make his decision, it is inappropriate, and in conflict with his independent status, to question the arrested suspect about his involvement in the offence. Code C 3.4 now emphasises this by requiring the custody officer to note any comment the person might make in relation to the arresting officer's account but not to invite comment. If he authorises the detention of the person he must inform that person as soon as practicable and in any case before he is questioned about any offence. Again a note must be made of any comment made in respect of that decision but no comment shall be invited. No specific questions regarding his involvement in the offence, nor in respect of any comment made in response to the arresting officer's account or the decision to detain, shall be put to the person by the custody officer.

Insufficient evidence to charge

6.50 If the custody officer determines that there is not sufficient evidence to charge the arrested person, and where possession of drugs is concerned he is entitled to take the view that there is insufficient evidence until he has the forensic analysis (*R v Mehmet* (1989)), he must release him either on bail (to return to a police station) or without bail, unless the custody officer has reasonable grounds for believing that his detention without charge is necessary to secure or preserve evidence relating to the offence for which he is under arrest or to obtain such evidence by questioning him (s 37(2), art 38(2)). These are the only grounds for detention, continued detention under s 42 (Art 43), further detention under s 43 (Art 44), or detention on attendance at a police station following release on bail subject to a duty to attend there (s 47(5)) (although in relation to continued or further detention other conditions must also be satisfied (see paras 6.133 and 6.144, post). There is no prohibition on re-arrest for the same offence following release under s 37(2) (Art 38(2)) as there is in respect of re-arrest following release from detention under s 41(7) (Art 42(5)), s 42(10) (Art 43(9)) and s 43(18) (Art 44(17)) (ss 41(9), 42(11) and 43(19), arts 42(7), 43(10) and 44(18)) (as to re-arrest after release from detention see para 6.132, post).

Where there is sufficient evidence to charge

6.51
(a) If the custody officer determines that there is sufficient evidence to charge the person with the offence for which he was arrested, the person shall either:
(a) be charged (s 37(7)(a), art 38(7)(a)). In this case the question whether the person is released on bail or detained in custody is governed by s 38 (Art 39) (see para 6.64, post) and, if he is detained, his detention in custody is subject to review under s 40 (Art 41) (see paras 6.157–6.173, post) and the duty to bring him before a magistrates' court is governed by s 46 (Art 47) (see para 6.104, post); or

(b)   be released without charge either on bail or without bail (s 37(7)(b), art 38(7)(b)). This will   arise because the police may decide, not to prosecute, or simply to caution the person. Section 37(8) (Art 38(8)) provides that where a decision on prosecution has not yet been taken, the custody officer has a duty to inform the person of this. Thus, if a person is to be prosecuted, he will not have his hopes raised by a release without charge.

6.52   Section 37(8) (Art 38(8)) also presents the custody officer with another option, that is at the time to inform the person in an appropriate case that he is not to be prosecuted or that he will be cautioned. The custody officer may find that he is in a position to exercise this option more often. The decision not to prosecute, or to caution, often has to be made or ratified by higher ranks than custody officers and sometimes requires consultation with other agencies. However, the provision of uniform prosecution and cautioning criteria (see HOC 18/1994 – revised National Standards for Cautioning) means that some decisions can be made by lower ranks. A number of police forces have already adopted 'instant' cautioning schemes which enable decisions to be made by these ranks and permit the caution to be given within a matter of hours of the offender being arrested. Not only does this save time by reducing the administrative procedure, it also reduces considerably the anxiety associated with waiting for a decision.

6.53   (There are provisions in s 28 of the Criminal Justice Act 2003 to amend s 37(2)–(7) to allow the custody officer to release without charge and on bail in order for consultation to take place with the Director of Public Prosecutions (Crown Prosecution Service) to enable a decision to be taken whether to prosecute or caution. This follows on from the Auld Report, and the DPP is to issue guidance on the operation of this section.)

6.54   The fact that the suspect is charged by a custody officer does not necessarily mean that the proceedings are instituted by the police for the purposes of the Prosecution of Offences Act 1985, s 3(2) (*R v Stafford Justices, ex p Customs and Excise Comrs* (1991)). Thus the fact that Customs and Excise officers arrest and take a person to a police station does not mean that they cease to be responsible for the prosecution.

Bail of a person released without charge

6.55   Under the previous law, bail to return to a police station was only possible when inquiries had to be made before sufficient evidence to charge was available. Under the 1984 Act (s 47(3), art 48(1)), references to 'bail' in this part of the Act are references to bail subject to a duty to appear before a magistrates' court, or to attend at a police station. If, therefore, there is sufficient evidence to charge but there is some doubt as to the appropriate charge, or it is a case in which the person may not be charged or in which he may be cautioned, the person may be released on bail subject to a duty to attend at such police station at such time as the custody officer may appoint. The person must then attend and may be charged or cautioned, the recognisance entered into being enforceable as if it were a recognisance to attend a magistrates' court (s 43(2) of the Magistrates' Courts Act 1980 as amended by s 47(8)) (Arts 48 and 49 of the Magistrates' Courts (NI) Order 1981 (Art 48(5))). Should the person's attendance not be required, the custody officer may notify the person in writing of that decision (s 47(4), art 48(7)) (see further, para 6.187, post).

Person unfit to be charged (s 37(9), art 38(9))

6.56 If a person under arrest is unfit to be charged or to be released without charge, he may be kept in police detention until he is. The commonest cause of such unfitness will be intoxication due to alcohol or drugs. Custody officers should be aware that 'Many infirmities are known to mimic alcohol and/or drug intoxication' (Home Affairs Committee, Deaths in Police Custody, p 93) and the concern expressed by the Police Complaints Authority at the increase in deaths in custody has highlighted the need for constant vigilance.

6.57 Code C 9.5 places a duty on the custody officer to ensure a detainee receives appropriate clinical attention, or, in urgent cases, send the person to a hospital, or call another medical practitioner, if it appears that a person brought to a police station is suffering from physical illness or a mental disorder, or is injured or otherwise appears to need clinical attention. This applies whether or not the person complains and whether or not he has had medical treatment elsewhere.

Arrest for more than one offence

6.58 Where the arrest is for more than one offence, or where there is an arrest for a further offence, there may be different determinations in respect of each offence; eg there may be sufficient evidence to charge on offence A but insufficient evidence in respect of offence B. Code C 16.1 provides that in such a case it is permissible to delay bringing the person before a custody officer for charging on offence A until there is sufficient evidence on offence B (see para 6.25, post). However, if the person is brought before a custody officer on offence A the person must be charged with offence A but will not be released if the custody officer authorises detention without charge in respect of offence B.

Detention without charge

6.59 The custody officer may authorise detention without charge, if having determined there is not sufficient evidence to charge the person, he has reasonable grounds for believing such detention is necessary on the grounds stated in s 37(2) (s 37(3), art 38(2) and (3)). The purpose of detention is clearly to enable the police to obtain the evidence necessary to sustain a charge. To 'secure' means to obtain or get, usually by search of the suspect's premises or other premises.

6.60   To 'preserve' means to keep safe from harm, which requires a belief that the suspect will, if released, remove, destroy or tamper with the evidence which the police have not yet been able to secure. This clearly does not cover the situation where the suspect is reasonably believed to be likely to interfere with witnesses or otherwise obstruct the course of justice. In such a case the evidence will be available, the suspect must then be charged and his detention after charge will be permissible under s 38(1)(a)(v) (Art 39(1)(a)(v)). 'Obtain such evidence by questioning him' clearly refers to interrogation of the suspect. Arrest for questioning then becomes detention for questioning.

Written records and informing the detained person

6.61   Where a custody officer authorises a person who has not been charged to be kept in police detention, he shall, as soon as is practicable, make a written record, in the presence of the person arrested, and at that time inform the person orally of the grounds for his detention (s 37(4) and (5), art 38(4) and (5)). Section 34(2) of the Children and Young Persons Act 1933, as amended by s 57 of PACE 1984, requires that the parent or guardian of an arrested juvenile be informed of the fact that the juvenile has been arrested and detained and the place of detention. If at the time of the arrest the juvenile is subject to a supervision order, the supervisor must be informed (see para 6.30, ante). (Article 38(1) to (3) of the PACE (NI) Order requires the custody officer to inform a juvenile arrested without warrant and detained without charge under art 38(2):

(a)   that he has reasonable grounds for believing that his detention is necessary in connection with an offence, and to state the offence;

(b)   to take such steps as are practicable to identify the person responsible for the juvenile's welfare; and

(c)   if the person is identified and it is practicable to do so, to inform the person of the arrest and the offence alleged to have been committed by the juvenile.

6.62   The persons who may be responsible for the juvenile's welfare are the parent or guardian. (This includes a local authority if the child is in care (s 118 of PACE 1984), or any other person who for the time being has assumed such responsibility. If a supervision order under the CYP Act (NI) 1968, or a probation order under s 1 of the Probation Act (Northern Ireland) 1950, is in force the supervisor or probation officer is also to be informed, in every case, 'as soon as it is practicable'.) The duty to inform the detainee shall not apply where the person is, at the time the written record is made,

(a)   incapable of understanding what is said to him;

(b)   violent or likely to become violent; or

(c)   in urgent need of medical attention (s 37(6), art 38(6)).

6.63   (b) and (c) are self-explanatory. (a) would include incapacity by reason of not understanding the language or deafness as well as the more usual incapacity by reason of drink or drugs. Code C 1.8 provides that where the information is not given for any of these reasons, he must be given it as soon as is practicable. If the incapacity is due to an inability to understand English or deafness, Code C 3.12 requires that the custody officer call an interpreter as soon as is practicable, and ask him to provide the information. (See Chapter 7, Code C, section 13 on interpreters and detained persons generally.) Code C (para 3.1) repeats the duty under s 37(5) to inform the detainee of the grounds for detention. It is a summary of the statutory duties and should not be taken to detract from them. The Code (para 3.1) also requires the custody officer at the same time to inform the detainee of his statutory rights under s 56 to have someone informed of his detention, and under s 58 to consult with a solicitor and to consult the Code of Practice governing detention or any other Code of Practice. In addition to the oral information, Code C 3.2, post, requires a written statement of these three rights and a signed acknowledgment of receipt on the custody record. Interpreters may also be required to impart this information (Code C 3.6). (If the detainee waives his right to consult with a solicitor he should also be asked to sign a waiver on the custody sheet at this time.) For further discussion of these procedures, see Chapter 7.

Charging – Code C 16

6.64 Code C 16.1 requires that when the officer in charge of the investigation reasonably believes that there is sufficient evidence to provide a realistic prospect of the detainee's conviction, he should without delay bring him before the custody officer who shall be responsible for considering whether or not he should be charged. If, however, the detained person is suspected of more than one offence, it is permissible to delay bringing him before the custody officer until the above condition is satisfied in respect of all the offences. The restriction on continued questioning applies when the investigating officer is satisfied that all the questions considered relevant to obtaining accurate and reliable information about the offence have been put to the suspect. This includes allowing the suspect an opportunity to give an innocent explanation and asking questions to test if the explanation is accurate and reliable, for example to clear up ambiguities or clarify what the suspect said, and has taken account of any other available evidence (Code 11.6 discussed in Chapter 8 post).

6.65 This applies to inquiries made of a person who is detained under s 37(2) and (3) (Art 38(2) and (3)) in order to obtain evidence by questioning the person, and also to inquiries made of persons not yet in police detention, being either those who are not yet arrested or those who are arrested and taken somewhere for investigation before being taken to a police station as permitted by s 30(10) (Art 32(13)) (discussed at para 5.147, ante). One may further note that when other offences are revealed during the period when a person is in police detention, he must be arrested for those offences (s 31) and the relevant time for the purposes of calculating the period of detention is the time of arrival at the police station on his arrest for the original offence (s 41(4), art 42(2)(c)). Thus whilst it is permissible to delay charging until there is sufficient evidence to prosecute all offences successfully, regard must be had to the detention clock, which may not permit much delay. If no extension is possible, the person should be charged with the offences for which there is sufficient evidence and a remand in police custody sought to continue the investigation into the remaining offences (see s 128(7)

of the Magistrates' Courts Act 1980 as amended by s 48 of PACE 1984, discussed at
para 6.195, post).

6.66   If the custody officer determines that there is sufficient evidence to charge the
person, he must either do so or release the person without charge (see s 37(7)(b), art
38(7) discussed in para 6.51, ante). When a detained person is charged with or informed
that he may be prosecuted for an offence he must be cautioned in the following terms:

> 'You do not have to say anything. But it may harm your defence if you do not
> mention now something which you later rely on in court. Anything you do say
> may be given in evidence.'

6.67   This amended caution takes account of the provisions of s 34, 36 and 37 of the
Criminal Justice and Public Order Act 1994 (as amended by s 58 of the Youth Justice
and Criminal Evidence Act, 1999, discussed at paras 8.42-8.45, post) but given that the
person will have been cautioned in the same terms on a number of occasions before
charge, this caution must be seen as a final reminder of the effect of non-disclosure of
any fact to be relied upon at trial. Where the restriction on drawing inferences from
silence applies, the caution shall be:

> 'You do not have to say anything, but anything you do say may be given in
> evidence.'

6.68   At the same time he must be given a written notice showing particulars of the
offence with which he is charged and including the name of the officer in the case,
unless a terrorist offence in which case only the officer's warrant or identification
number need be given, together with his police station and the reference number for
the case. So far as is possible the charge should be stated in simple terms whilst
showing the precise offence with which he is charged. The notice must begin with the
words 'you are charged with the offence(s) shown below' followed by the caution as
stated above and the details of the offence(s). If the person is a juvenile or mentally
disordered or mentally handicapped the notice shall be given to the appropriate adult.

6.69   There are restrictions on questioning a person once the officer in charge of the
investigation or the custody officer believes there is a realistic prospect of conviction
(Code C 11.6). These clearly apply after charge but a limited form of questioning after
charge is permitted and an officer may bring to the notice of the person charged a
written statement made by another person, or the content of an interview with that
person, provided that Code C 16.4 is complied with.

6.70   As to showing another person's statements or the contents of an interview
with him, a true copy of the statement must be handed to him or the content of the
interview record brought to his attention (playing back the tape of the interview), but
nothing must be said or done to invite any reply or comment save to caution him that
anything he does say may be given in evidence and to remind him of his right to legal
advice. If the person cannot read the officer may read the statement to him. If a juvenile
or mentally disordered or mentally handicapped, a copy of the statement must be
given to, or the content of the interview record brought to the attention of, the
appropriate adult.

6.71 As to questioning after charge, questions may only be asked if they are necessary for the purpose of:

(a) preventing or minimising harm or loss to some other person or to the public; or
(b) for clearing up an ambiguity in a previous answer or statement; or
(c) where it is in the interests of justice that the person should have put to him, and have an opportunity to comment on, information concerning the offence which has come to light since he was charged or informed that he may be prosecuted.

6.72 Before putting such questions the person must be cautioned that he does not have to say anything but that anything he does say may be given in evidence and reminded of his right to legal advice.

6.73 (NB: The caution is limited to the fact that anything he says may be given in evidence because s 34 of the Criminal Justice and Public Order Act 1994 permits proper inferences to be drawn from the failure to mention a fact which is later relied upon at trial when being questioned 'at any time before he was charged with the offence'. It does not therefore apply to anything said, or not said, in the above circumstances.)

Grounds for detention after charge – s 38(1) as amended by the CJPOA 1994, ss 28, 168(2) and Sch 10, para 54

6.74 Where the person is charged, s 38(1) (Art 39(1)) imposes a duty on the custody officer to release, either on bail or without bail, unless, in the case of an adult offender, one or more of the six conditions discussed below is satisfied, in which event he may authorise that person's detention after charge. As to bail after charge see s 47 discussed at para 6.176, post. In *R v Samuel* (1988) it was held that a suspect could not continue to be denied access to a solicitor under Annex B of Code C once he was charged with an offence, even though questioning was to continue in respect of other offences. If the suspect is charged with one offence and a remand in custody is to be sought under s 128(7) of the Magistrates' Courts Act 1980, he must be allowed access to a solicitor for a reasonable time before the hearing (Code C, Annex B, A(a) 5). The amendments made by the CJPOA 1994 are comparatively minor. Section 38(1), as originally drafted, required the custody officer to order the release of a person arrested and charged unless one of three specified grounds existed. Section 28(2) of the CJPOA 1994 replaces the sub-paragraphs (i), (ii) and (iii) with five new sub-paragraphs which bring the criteria for refusing police bail more closely into line with the criteria for refusing bail by a court as set out in para 2 of Part I of Sch 1 to the Bail Act 1976.

6.75 It should be noted that all the criteria set out in s 38(1)(a) and (b) require the more exacting standard of reasonable cause to believe on the part of the custody officer (see further on this concept para 2.04, ante). Section 38(2A), added by s 28(3) of the CJPOA 1994, further requires that the custody officer in taking decisions under s 38(1)(a)(i) to (v), but not (vi), shall have regard to the same considerations as those which a court is required to have regard to in taking the corresponding decisions under para 2 of Part I of Sch I to the Bail Act 1976. A court must be satisfied that there are 'substantial grounds' for believing that releasing the defendant on bail would result in one or other of the undesirable consequences set out below. A subjective belief that one or more may result is not enough, such a belief must be based on reasonable grounds, but that does not mean that they must be satisfied beyond reasonable doubt. The court is being asked to speculate and such speculation is not amenable to proof according to the rules of evidence which apply on a trial of the issue. The prosecution express their opinion, police officers tell the court what they have been told by prospective witnesses, none of which is admissible evidence at trial. Indeed, it was accepted by the court in *R v Mansfield Justices, ex p Sharkey* (1985) that the strict rules of evidence do not apply. The deliberate use of the words 'reasonable cause to believe' in relation to the custody officer's application of the criteria, rather than 'substantial grounds for believing' suggest a lower standard in the police station where even more clearly the rules of evidence do not apply. However, a custody officer, no less than a magistrate, cannot rely on a subjective belief based on flimsy, insubstantial or irrational grounds. There must be a belief based on reasonable grounds, that is facts and circumstances which would lead an impartial third party to believe that one or more of the undesirable consequences set out in s 38(1) would result from the release of the person.

6.76   The considerations which a court must take into account are set out in para 9 of Part I of Sch 1 to the Bail Act 1976.

(i)   The nature and seriousness of the charge and the probable method of dealing with the defendant for it. The more serious the charge the greater the likelihood of a prison sentence and the greater the likelihood that D may abscond rather than face that prospect.

(ii)   The character, antecedents, associations and community ties of the defendant. A married man with children and a job living in his own house is much less likely to abscond than an unmarried man with no ties. This does not mean that a person living in a hostel should not be granted bail. The lack of roots is merely one factor which increases the risk that he might jump bail. Linked to a bad character/past record the lack of roots may justify refusal of bail. Depending on the offence the bad character may increase the likelihood of a custodial sentence and thus increase the likelihood that he may abscond. On the other hand a good character may tend to balance the risk created by the lack of roots.

(iii)   The defendant's previous record of answering to bail. Clearly the fact that he has failed to answer to his bail and/or he has committed offences whilst on bail will go against him, while the fact that he has previously answered to his bail suggests that he can be trusted to do so on this occasion. The removal of the right to bail when a person is charged with an indictable or either way offence which appears to have been committed while the defendant was on bail must be borne in mind. It is added to the reasons for refusing bail in paras 2 to 6 of Part I of Sch I to the Bail Act 1976 by s 26 of the CJPOA 1994.

(iv)   The strength of the prosecution case. The weaker the prosecution case the stronger the argument for bail. The stronger the case the greater the likelihood of conviction and a possible custodial sentence depending on the offence and character of the accused.

6.77 This list is not exhaustive. The reasons for refusing bail set out in s 38(1)(a)(i)-(v) are similar to those which apply to a court, hence the need to apply the same considerations as a court. The custody officer will have the added difficulty that he is more closely involved than is a court and remaining impartial is that much more difficult. Nevertheless that is what he must do.

(a) Section 38(1)(a)(i) (Art 39(1)(a)(i)) – The name or address of the person arrested cannot be ascertained or the custody officer has reasonable grounds for doubting whether a name or address furnished by him is his real name or address.

    This embodies the general arrest conditions in s 25(3)(a), (b) and (c) (Art 27(3)(a), (b) and (c)), (see para 5.34, ante). It will permit detention after the person has been charged if the arrest condition still applies but it is, of course, applicable to all offences, whether arrestable or general.

(b) Section 38(1)(a)(ii) (Art 39(1)(a)(ii)) – The custody officer has reasonable grounds for believing that the person arrested will fail to appear in court to answer to bail.

    This is the most obvious ground for refusing bail and is to be found in Part I of Sch 1 to the Bail Act 1976 as para 2(a)(i). It will apply at one extreme to the minor offender of no fixed abode; and, at the other extreme, to the serious offender who is of a fixed abode and well known but who, because of the seriousness of the offence and perhaps also because of his previous record, is likely to get a custodial sentence if convicted. If released he may then abscond and flee the jurisdiction.

(c) Section 38(1)(a)(iii) (Art 39(1)(ia)) – In the case of a person arrested for an imprisonable offence, the custody officer has reasonable grounds for believing that the detention of the person arrested is necessary to prevent him from committing an offence. This criterion appears as para 2(a)(ii) in Part I of Sch 1 to the Bail Act. One may note that s 26 of the CJPOA 1994 removes the normal presumption in favour of bail where it appears to the court that a person charged with any offence which is not a purely summary offence, committed the offence while on bail. While that does not apply to police bail the fact that the person has committed the offence while on bail may provide the reasonable grounds for believing that if he was bailed he would commit further offences. See also the facts of *R v Mansfield Justices, ex p Sharkey* (1985) and *R v Bournemouth Justices, ex p Cross* (1988), considered at para 6.176, post.

(d) Section 38(1)(a)(iii) – In the case of a person who has attained the age of 18, the custody officer has reasonable grounds for believing that the detention of the person is necessary to enable a sample to be taken from him under s 63B PACE 1984. The Criminal Justice Act 2003 amends s 63B to provide for the age to be lowered to 14 on condition that in the case of someone under 17, testing is done in the presence of an appropriate adult.

(e) Section 38(1)(a)(iv) (Art 39(1)(a)(iv)) – In the case of a person arrested for an offence which is not an imprisonable offence, the custody officer has reasonable grounds for believing that the detention of the person arrested is necessary to prevent him from causing physical injury to any other person or from causing loss of or damage to property. There is an obvious overlap between this condition and that in (iii) since physical injury to another will be an offence as may loss of or damage to property, unless it is the person's own property, but this applies to persons arrested for non-imprisonable offences, whereas (iii) applies to imprisonable offences.

(f) Section 38(1)(a)(v) (Art 39(1)(a)(v)) – The custody officer has reasonable grounds for believing that the detention of the person arrested is necessary to prevent him from interfering with the investigation of offences or of a particular offence. This criterion appears as para 2(a)(iii) in Part I of Sch 1 of the Bail Act 1976. Such interference may well be an offence so that there could be an overlap with (ii) above. Threatening witnesses could be seen as such interference so that there may also be an overlap with (iii) above as well.

(g) Section 38(1)(a)(vi) (Art 39(i)(a)(vi)) – The custody officer has reasonable grounds for believing that the detention of the person is necessary for his own protection. This could involve the disturbed offender who threatens to harm himself or the offender who is threatened with harm by family or friends of the victim. There are many offences, particularly offences of violence and sexual offences against children, which provoke violent reaction in the community. Whilst it is wrong in principle that a person should be detained in custody because others threaten to break the law, realistically it may be the only way to protect him.

Driving with excess alcohol in the body and arrest for failure to surrender to bail to a police station

6.78   Because s 6(5) of the Road Traffic Act 1988 does not use the word 'offence', there was some doubt as to whether an arrest under that section was an arrest for an offence. Section 34(6) clears up any doubt by providing that it is. Thus a person arrested for such an offence can be bailed to a court following a charge or, if a blood or urine sample requires forensic analysis, be released without charge and bailed to return to a police station. However, if in either case the person is still unfit to drive, s 10 of the Road Traffic Act 1988 permits his detention until he is fit to drive. There is therefore no need to rely on s 38(1)(b) in such a case. (In Northern Ireland the Road Traffic (Northern Ireland) Order 1981 contains the equivalent provision.) Section 29(5) of the Transport and Works Act 1992, which provides the equivalent power of arrest in respect of persons driving etc railed vehicles, states that failure or refusal to provide a specimen of breath is an offence.

6.79   Section 46A of PACE 1984, added by s 29 of the CJPOA 1994, provides a power of arrest for failing to surrender to police bail to return to a police station. Section 34(7) of PACE 1984, also added by s 29 of the CJPOA 1994, states that a person arrested under s 46A shall be treated as arrested for an offence and that offence shall be deemed to be the offence in connection with which he was granted bail. It follows that a person arrested under s 46A falls to be considered under s 38(1) when charged but the fact that he failed to surrender to the bail granted earlier may provide reasonable grounds for believing he will not surrender to custody and justify refusal of bail under s 38(1)(a)(i).

ARRESTED JUVENILE – ADDITIONAL GROUND FOR DETENTION
(s 38(I)(B)(II), Art 39(I)(B)(II))

6.80   If the person charged with an offence is an arrested juvenile, all the grounds for detention after charge under s 38(1)(a) (Art 39(1)(a)) apply, but in addition he may be detained if the custody officer has reasonable grounds for believing that he ought to be detained in his own interests. Section 38(1)(b)(ii) (Art 39(1)(b)(ii)) offers no guidance as to when this will arise. Section 38(1)(a)(vi) (Art 38(1)(a)(ii)) permits detention 'for his own protection', a phrase which could overlap with 'in his own interests' but which the Minister of State at the Home Office thought implied a threat of specific harm (Standing Committee E, 14 February 1984, col 1127). An example given in Committee was of the truant who boards a train at Carlisle without paying his fare and is arrested in London. His parents cannot come to collect him until the next day. Though he has been charged it would not be in his interests to release him to wander the streets of London. It should be noted that such detention is only permissible after a juvenile has been arrested and charged with an offence.

6.81   If the custody officer authorises an arrested juvenile to be kept in police detention under s 38(1) (Art 39(1)), he shall, unless:
(a)   he certifies that, by reason of such circumstances as are specified in the certificate, it is impracticable for him to do so; or
(b)   in the case of an arrested juvenile who has attained the age of 12 years, that no secure accommodation is available and that keeping him in other local authority accommodation would not be adequate to protect the public from serious harm,

6.82   secure that the arrested juvenile is moved to local authority accommodation (s 38(6)). A certificate made under this section must be produced to the court to which the juvenile is first brought after being detained.

6.83   Section 23 of the CYPA 1969, as amended by ss 60 and 62 of the CJPOA 1994, provides that if a court remands a juvenile who is charged with, or convicted of, one or more offences, and commits that juvenile for trial or sentence, and bail has been refused, then the remand must be to local authority accommodation. Exceptionally the court may remand the juvenile to secure accommodation if the person:
(a)   is charged with or convicted of a violent offence or sexual offence (as defined below) or an offence punishable in the case of an adult by 14 or more years' imprisonment; or
(b)   has a recent history of absconding while remanded to local authority accommodation and is charged with or has been convicted of an imprisonable offence alleged or found to have been committed while he was so remanded,

6.84   and the court is of the opinion that only a requirement to keep the person in secure accommodation would be adequate to protect the public from serious harm from him (s 23(5) of the CYPA 1969). (See *R v Croydon Youth Court, ex p G (a minor)* (1995) below.) At present the courts may impose a 'security requirement' only when remanding children aged 15 and 16 (the powers introduced by the CJ Act 1991 are not yet in force but are subject to transitional arrangements). Section 20 of the CJPOA

1994, extended these powers to include persons aged from 12 to 14. The change to s 38(6) and the addition of s 38(6A) reflect the changes to the power of the courts.

6.85 'Impracticable' in s 38(6)(a) refers to circumstances such as inclement weather or other difficulties in transporting the juvenile. Code C, Notes for Guidance 16B makes it clear that neither the juvenile's behaviour nor the nature of the offence make it impracticable. The lack of secure accommodation similarly does not make it impracticable to transfer the juvenile, that is a factor to be considered only in relation to a juvenile over 12 years of age when s 38(6)(b) applies.

6.86 'Sexual offence' means any of the following:
(a) an offence under the Sexual Offences Act 1956, other than an offence under s 30, 31 or 33 to 36 of that Act;
(b) an offence under s 128 of the Mental Health Act 1959;
(c) an offence under the Indecency with Children Act 1960;
(d) an offence under s 9 of the Theft Act 1968 of burglary with intent to rape;
(e) an offence under s 54 of the Criminal Law Act 1977;
(f) an offence under the Protection of Children Act 1978;
(g) an offence under s 1 of the Criminal Law Act 1977 of conspiracy to commit any of the offences in paras (a) to (f) above;
(h) an offence under s 1 of the Criminal Attempts Act 1981 of attempting to commit any of these offences;
(i) an offence of inciting another to commit any of those offences.

6.87 (Section 38(6A) and s 31 of the Criminal Justice Act 1991 as substituted by Sch 9, para 45 of the CJPOA 1994.)

6.88 'Violent offence' means any offence which leads to, or is intended or likely to lead to, a person's death or to physical injury to a person, and includes an offence which is required to be charged as arson (whether or not it would otherwise fall within this definition).

6.89 The phrase 'serious harm' in s 6(b) is not defined but s 38(6A) of PACE provides that in s 38 any reference, in relation to an arrested juvenile charged with a violent or sexual offence, to protecting the public from serious harm from him shall be construed as a reference to protecting members of the public from death or serious personal injury, whether physical or psychological, occasioned by further such offences committed by him (s 38(6A)).

6.90 This subsection applies only to juveniles charged with violent or sexual offences, as defined above. In supporting s 38(6)(b) during debates on the Criminal Justice Act 1991, Earl Ferrers clearly thought that a juvenile alleged to have frequently committed a series of domestic burglaries would come within the subsection (Hansard, HL, Vol 529, col 169). However, it was made clear by the Divisional Court in *R v Croydon Youth Court, ex p G (a minor)* (1995) that mere repetition of an offence is not sufficient. The Court considered the meaning of 'serious harm' in s 23(5) of the Children and Young

Persons Act 1969, as substituted by s 60(1) of the Criminal Justice Act 1991, which allows the remand of a young person to a remand centre or prison, rather than local authority care, if the conditions of the subsection are satisfied (see above) and the court is 'of the opinion that only such a requirement would protect the public from serious harm from him'. Leggatt LJ said:

'…section 23 does not produce the result that where a young person was charged with or had been convicted of an offence punishable in the case of an adult with imprisonment for a term of 14 years or more the court could, after the requisite consultation, be of the opinion without more that remanding him to a remand centre would be adequate to protect the public from serious harm. The offence of handling stolen goods was punishable by a 14-year prison sentence but the commission of the offence did not necessarily cause any direct harm to the public. Even a dwelling-house burglary was not necessarily calculated to cause serious harm if, for example, the burglar was careful only to enter unoccupied houses in daylight and steal television sets. A series of such offences, if apprehended, could not be aggregated so as to render serious such harm as might be caused by them. In any particular case, it might be proper to infer from the record of the young person that the public was liable to incur serious harm at his hands having regard to the nature of the offences with which he has been charged or of which he has been convicted or the manner in which he had carried them out. Although it would not be necessary to conclude that there was a risk of death or serious personal injury being caused, the court would have to be satisfied that the young person whom they were minded to remand was liable to cause harm that could be sensibly described as serious on account of the nature of the offence or offences that might be committed and not merely the risk of repetition.'

6.91 (See s 21 of the Children Act 1989 for the categories of children for whom local authorities must provide accommodation. These include juveniles they are requested to receive under s 38(6) of PACE 1984.)

6.92 In s 38 'Local authority accommodation' means accommodation provided by or on behalf of a local authority within the meaning of the Children Act 1989, s 22(2) (s 38(6A) and art 25(2) of the Children (NI) Order 1994, and 'local authority' has the same meaning as in that Act (Order) (s 38(8)).

6.93 'Secure accommodation' means accommodation provided for the purpose of restricting liberty (s 38(6A) and art 44(1) of the Children (NI) Order 1994). (Section 38(6B) provides the local authority, or anyone acting on their behalf, with the power to detain juveniles transferred to their accommodation.)

6.94 (In the Northern Ireland PACE Order the duty is to take the juvenile to a place of safety as defined in s 180(1) of the CYPA (Northern Ireland) 1968 which does not include a police station (Art 39(6), (7) and (8)).)

6.95   The amended s 38(6)(b) overtakes the decision in *R v Chief Constable of Cambridgeshire, ex p Michel* (1991) where the Divisional Court held, in a reserved judgment, that a custody officer was not required by s 38 to transfer an arrested juvenile into the care of a local authority where he was dissatisfied with the proposed arrangements for the secure detention of the juvenile but confines it to juveniles aged 12 and over where the custody officer certifies that the accommodation would not be adequate to protect the public from serious harm from that juvenile. Code C 16.6 restates the duty of the custody officer under s 38(6) to try to make arrangements for the juvenile to be taken into the care of a local authority to be detained pending appearance in court unless he certifies that it is impracticable to do so, or, in the case of a juvenile of at least 12 years of age, no secure accommodation is available and there is a risk of serious harm to the public as defined in s 38(6A). Notes of Guidance 16B states that except as provided for in Code C 16.6, neither the juvenile's behaviour nor the nature of the offence with which he is charged provides grounds for the custody officer to decide that it is impracticable to seek to arrange for his transfer to the care of the local authority. Similarly, the lack of secure local authority accommodation shall not make it impracticable for the custody officer to transfer him. The availability of secure accommodation is only a factor in relation to a juvenile aged 12 or over when the local authority accommodation would not be adequate to protect the public from serious harm from the juvenile. The obligation to transfer a juvenile to local authority accommodation applies as much to a juvenile charged during the daytime as it does to a juvenile held overnight subject to a requirement to bring the juvenile before a court under s 46 of PACE 1984. This, together with s 38(6)(b), makes it clear that a juvenile under 12, no matter how dangerous to the public he might be, must be transferred to local authority accommodation unless it is impracticable within s 38(6A). Once the arrested juvenile is transferred to local authority accommodation the duties of the custody officer in relation to him cease (s 39(4), art 40(4)).

6.96   Section 38(6B) of PACE 1984 gives the local authority, or anyone acting on their behalf, a statutory authority to detain juveniles transferred to them under s 38(6).

6.97   Paragraph 27 of Sch 12 to the Children Act 1989 substitutes a new s 32(1A) of the Children and Young Persons Act 1969, and permits a constable anywhere in the UK or Channel Islands, to arrest without warrant any juvenile who is:
(a)   absent without permission from a place of safety to which he had been taken under s 16(3); or
(b)   absent without permission from local authority accommodation having been required to live there by a residence requirement under s 12AA or to which he has been remanded under s 23 of the 1969 Act.

6.98   On arrest the person must be conducted to the place of safety or local authority accommodation from which he is absent, or to a place specified by the responsible person (the person who made the arrangements under s 16(3) or the authority designated under s 12AA or s 23) at that person's expense (s 32(1B) and (1C)).

6.99   Section 23 of the CJPOA 1994 adds a new s 23A to the CYPA 1969 which permits a constable to arrest without warrant a person who has been remanded or committed to local authority accommodation under s 23 of the 1969 Act subject to conditions which the constable has reasonable grounds to suspect have been broken. Unless arrested less than 24 hours before the time at which he was remanded to appear before a court, in which case he must be brought before that court at the due time, the person must be taken as soon as practicable, and in any event within 24 hours after his arrest, before a justice of the peace for the petty sessional area in which he was arrested. In calculating the 24-hour period no account shall be taken of Christmas Day, Good Friday or any Sunday.

Authorised detention – informing the detained person

6.100   If the release of the person arrested and charged is not required by s 38(1) (Art 39(1)), the custody officer may authorise him to be kept in police detention (s 38(2), art 39(2)). Where he does so, the custody officer is under a duty to record the grounds for detention and to inform the arrested person in precisely the same terms, and subject to the same exceptions, as when he authorises police detention without charge (s 38(3), (4), (5) and (6)) (Art 39(3) to (6)) (see para 6.61, ante).

Duty to release or take a charged person before a court (s 46, art 47)

6.101   If the custody officer becomes aware that the detention of a person, who has been charged with an offence and who has been detained under s 38(1) (Art 39(1)), is no longer justified under that subsection, he must release him under s 34(2) (Art 35(2)). However, if the detention after charge continues to be justified and the person remains in police detention, s 46 (Art 47) makes provision for him to be brought before a magistrates' court in the shortest possible time in the four circumstances foreseen by the section, as follows. (Note that art 47 of the NI PACE Order is drafted so as to take account of the fact that there is no first sitting of magistrates' courts in Northern Ireland, therefore there is no need to specify a period in which magistrates' courts will be held.)

(a) The usual circumstances – These will arise when the police station at which he is charged and the magistrates' court before which he is to be brought are both in the same petty sessions area and the court sits daily or will be sitting on the day the man is charged (the relevant day for the purpose of the section in this circumstance) or the next day. The duty is to take the charged and detained person before that court as soon as is practicable and in any event not later than the first sitting after he is charged with the offence. In essence this means that the person will appear before a magistrates' court in the usual circumstances on the day he is charged or the next day (s 46(2) and (7)(a), art 47(2)). One may note that in this and the other circumstances discussed below, the custody officer discharges his duty under s 46 by informing the appropriate clerk to the justices (*R v Avon Magistrates' Court, ex p Broome* (1988)).

(b) The less usual circumstances – These will arise when the police station and court are in the same petty sessions area but the court is not due to sit on the day the person is charged (the relevant day) or on the next day. In these circumstances the duty under s 46(2) still applies but the custody officer at the police station at which he is charged is under a further duty to inform the clerk to the justices that there is in the area a person who has been charged and to whom s 46(2) applies (s 46(3)). The duty of the clerk is then to arrange for a magistrates' court to sit not later than the day after the 'relevant day'. Since the clerk will be informed of this on the relevant day (the day the person is charged) a court sitting will then be arranged for that day or the following day, for example where the clerk is informed on a Wednesday he must arrange a sitting for that day if practicable or at the latest for the Thursday (s 46(6)).

(c) The unusual circumstances – These will arise when the police station and magistrates' court are in different petty sessions areas and the person charged and detained is to be brought before the court in that area which will be sitting on the day on which he arrives in that area (the relevant day in this circumstance) or the next day. The duty of the custody officer is to have the person removed to that area as soon as practicable and brought before that court as soon as practicable and in any event not later than the first sitting of the court after his arrival in the area. This too will normally mean that the person appears before a court on the day he is charged or the next day (s 46(4) and (7)(b), art 47(3)).

(d) The most unusual circumstances – These will arise when, as in (c) above, the police station and court are in different areas but the court is not due to sit on the day the detainee arrives in the area or the next day. The custody officer at the receiving station must then inform the clerk to the justices for his area that he has a person in custody to whom s 46(4) applies and the clerk is then under a duty to arrange a sitting of the court on that day or the next day (s 46(5), (6) and (7)(b)).

Sundays and Holy Days

6.102   Where the day after that on which the person is charged, or arrives in the other area (the relevant day), is Christmas Day, Good Friday or a Sunday, the duty of the clerk to the justices is to arrange for a court to sit on the first day after the relevant day which is not one of those days. That is the day after Christmas which is not a Sunday, the Saturday after Good Friday or a Monday (s 46(8), art 47(4)). Section 153 of the Magistrates' Courts Act 1980 permits a court to sit on any day of the year and (if the court thinks fit) on these holy days. The court could therefore override the clerk's duty by sitting on one of those days but it is unlikely that any would wish to do so, unless exceptionally, major public disorder has arisen involving multiple arrests on or before these holy days.

Saturdays

6.103 Outside cities and large towns few magistrates' courts sit on a Saturday, even where they sit daily from Monday to Friday. If then a person is charged on a Friday, and he cannot be taken before a court on that day and no court is sitting on the Saturday, then the custody officer must (under s 46(3)) inform the clerk to the justices that he has a person in custody to whom s 46(2) (Art 47(2)) applies and the clerk must arrange a Saturday court. The same result is achieved if the court and police station are in different areas (s 46(6)). If, however, the person is charged on a Friday and does not reach the other area until the Saturday and no court is due to sit on that day, the duty of the clerk is to arrange a court sitting not later than the following Monday (Saturday being the relevant day and s 46(8) (Art 47(4)) applies to exclude the Sunday). Depending on the time of arrival in that area the spirit, if not the letter, of the law may require a Saturday court, for example where the person arrives in the early hours of Saturday morning and there is adequate time to arrange a Saturday court. Although the words 'not later than the day next following the relevant day' could be interpreted as justifying delaying a person's appearance before a court until the Monday, nevertheless it is submitted that, since the purpose of the appearance is to enable a court to decide whether the person should be released or detained in custody, the interests of the detainee, rather than the court's convenience, should be uppermost in the mind of the clerk. Since a magistrate has jurisdiction over the whole of the county in which he sits, it is quite permissible for one petty sessional court to sit on a Saturday and deal with offences committed in other sessional areas in the same county (*R v Avon Magistrates' Courts Committee, ex p Bath Law Society* (1988)). In organising a central Saturday sitting the justices' clerk should have regard to the wishes of the justices, the interests of the defendants and the administrative convenience of the police, prosecution and defence (*R v Avon Magistrates' Courts Committee, ex p Broome* (1988)).

Arrested person hospitalised

6.104 Finally, s 46(9) (Art 47(5)) makes it clear that nothing in s 46 requires a person who is in hospital to be brought before a court if he is not well enough. This may sound otiose, but the person may still be in 'police detention' in a hospital. It will be rare that the person who has been charged falls ill and has to be taken to hospital, particularly since s 37(9) (Art 38(9)) permits a person who is not fit to be charged to be kept in police detention until he is. The time spent in hospital, other than any periods of questioning there or on the way to or from, is not to be included when calculating the time spent in police detention (s 41(6)). (See para 6.127 for hospitalisation before charge.)

RESPONSIBILITIES IN RELATION TO PERSONS DETAINED (s 39, Art 40)

6.105 Section 39(1)(a) (Art 40(1)(a)) provides that, subject to sub-ss (2) and (4), it shall be the duty of the custody officer at a police station to ensure that all persons in police detention at that station are treated in accordance with the Act and the Code of Practice relating to the treatment of persons in police detention. Section 39(2)(b) (Art 40(2)) places the same duty on police officers investigating offences when the person is transferred to their custody. This dual duty is important since the person in police detention will be in the charge of each officer at some stage during his detention and each is relieved of his statutory duty towards the person while he is in the charge of the other. Thus, s 39(2)(b)(i) (Art 40(2)) relieves the custody officer of his duty under s 39(1) (Art 40(1)) if he transfers, or permits the transfer of, a person in police detention to the custody of a police officer investigating an offence, or to an officer who is to take charge of the person outside a police station; for example, an officer who is to take the person to a court or transfer him to another police station. The officer into whose custody the person is transferred assumes the statutory duty under s 39(1) (Art 40(1)) (s 39(2)(a) and (b), art 40(2)). If the person is returned to the charge of the custody officer, the investigating officer is under a further duty to report to the custody officer as to the manner in which that duty has been discharged while the detainee has been in his custody (s 39(3), art 40(3)).

ARRESTS BY RANKS SENIOR TO THE CUSTODY OFFICER

6.106   The fact that the custody officer will generally be of the rank of sergeant, or in some cases constable, means that he may sometimes be faced with the difficult situation in which an arrest is made or authorised by an officer senior to him, or the problem of a senior officer from another station trying to pull rank on him. The senior officer may then give directions which are at variance with any decision made or action already taken by the custody officer or which he would have made or taken but for the senior officer's direction. The custody officer should stand firm. It is highly likely that he will know more about daily PACE procedures, and what are the correct procedures in a particular case, than the senior officer. If the senior officer insists on his directions being followed the custody officer must refer the matter at once to an officer of the rank of superintendent or above who is responsible for the police station at which the custody officer acts (s 39(6), art 40(6)). This provision gives to the custody officer the necessary authority to ensure that he is able to carry out his important duties without having rank pulled on him. That would undermine his authority and detract from the performance of his duties. It is, of course, possible that the superintendent or more senior officer in charge of the police station will support the other senior officer rather than the custody officer, or that he is the arresting or authorising officer who makes the initial conflicting decision. In such cases the custody officer discharges his duty by pointing out that there is a conflict between them. The responsibility thereafter is that of the senior officer in charge of the police station. It should, of course, be pointed out to such officers that under PACE 1984 certain actions can only be authorised by a custody officer, eg the authorisation of detention under s 37(3) (Art 38(3)), the release of a person in police detention (s 34(3), art 35(3)) and no one, not even the Chief Constable, unless he appoints himself custody officer, can take those actions. The custody officer would, however, be well advised to record the fact that there was a conflict and what the decision was. (See Code C 2.2, which requires that for action requiring the authority of an officer of a specified rank, his name and rank must be noted in the custody record.)

Limits on period of detention without charge (s 41, art 42)

6.107   Section 41(1) (Art 42(1)) lays down the basic rule that a person shall not be kept in police detention without charge for more than 24 hours. Sections 42 and 43 then provide for authorised detention beyond that time, up to a further 12 hours on the authority of a superintendent or above, and further periods for up to an overall maximum of 96 hours on application to a magistrates' court. However, any extension beyond 36 hours can only be in respect of serious arrestable offences (as to which see paras 2.99-2.104, ante) and subject to other conditions set out in those sections. The time from which the period of detention is to be calculated (the relevant time) is determined by reference to s 41(2) (Art 42(2)).

Calculating the relevant time

6.108   In the usual case of an arrest made in a police area for an offence committed in that area, the relevant time will be the time that the person arrested arrives at the first police station to which he is taken after arrest (s 41(2)(d), art 42(1)), whether it is or is not a designated police station. Five less usual circumstances are then dealt with (Northern Ireland is one police area, therefore only (b), (c) and (d) apply):
(a)   an arrest in England and Wales in police area A for an offence committed in police area B;
(b)   an arrest outside England and Wales for an offence committed in England or Wales (or an arrest outside Northern Ireland for an offence committed in Northern Ireland);
(c)   the arrest while at a police station of a person who voluntarily attends at, or accompanies a constable to, that police station without having been arrested;
(d)   the arrest for further offences committed in police area A of a person who is already in police detention for an offence committed in that police area;
(e)   the arrest of a person for further offences committed in police area B who is already in police detention in police area A for an offence committed in that area.

6.109   As to (a), where the arrest of a person is sought in one police area in England and Wales, he is arrested in another police area, and he is not questioned in the area in which he is arrested in order to obtain evidence in relation to an offence for which he is arrested (s 41(3)(a), (b) and (c)), the relevant time is:
(i)   the time at which that person arrives at the first police station to which he is taken in the police area in which his arrest was sought; or
(ii)   the time 24 hours after the person's arrest,
whichever is the earlier (s 41(2)(a) and (3)(a), (b) and (c)).

Example I

6.110 D's arrest is sought by South Yorkshire Police for burglary in Sheffield. D is arrested for that offence in London at 6pm on a Tuesday by the Metropolitan Police. He is not questioned in order to obtain evidence of that offence and is transported to Sheffield arriving at a police station there at 10am on the Wednesday, 10am is the relevant time. (Note the special restriction on questioning imposed by Code C 14.1.)

Example 2

6.111 As in Example 1 but D was arrested at 6am on the Tuesday. The relevant time is 6am on the Wednesday and by the time D arrives in Sheffield at 10am the detention clock will already show four hours.

(Note, first, that D may be questioned in order to establish whether he is in fact the person wanted in the other area or about offences he may have committed in London, but he must not be questioned in order to obtain evidence of the offence for which he was arrested. If he is, the relevant time is that of his arrival at the police station in London. Second, the period of detention in the London police station while awaiting an escort does not count towards the overall detention period, but D is in 'police detention' and must be treated in accordance with the Act and Codes of Practice. Note particularly C 14.1.)

6.112 The assumption underlying s 41(3) is that the person whose arrest is sought in one police area but who is arrested in another police area, will either be arrested by officers from the area in which he is arrested, or by officers from the area in which his arrest is sought, but in either case that he will be taken to a police station in the area in which he is arrested, as impliedly required by s 30(10) (discussed at para 5.147, ante) and conveyed from there to the area in which his arrest is sought. In *R v Khan* (1990) officers from the West Midland Serious Crime Squad arrested Khan in Caernarfon and drove him directly back to Birmingham, allegedly obtaining a confession en route. The proper procedure in that case would have been to take the arrested person to a police station in the area in which he was arrested. Examples 1 and 2 above then apply, particularly the special restriction on questioning about the offence while he is in transit imposed by Code C 14.1.

6.113 As to (b), where a person is arrested outside England and Wales (or outside Northern Ireland), the relevant time is:
(i)   the time at which he arrives at the first police station to which he is taken in the police area in England and Wales (or Northern Ireland) in which the offence for which he is arrested is being investigated; or
(ii) the time 24 hours after that person's entry into England or Wales (or Northern Ireland) (s 41(2)(b), art 42(2)(a)),
whichever is the earlier.

(NB: This subsection will apply to persons arrested without a warrant under s 137 of the Criminal Justice and Public Order Act which permits cross-border arrest without warrant (see para 2.42, ante). Section 137(7) provides, for example, that a person arrested in Scotland or Northern Ireland by a constable from an English or Welsh force shall be taken, as soon as reasonably practicable, to the nearest designated police station in England or Wales or a designated police station in the police area in which the offence is being investigated. The relevant time will be the time at which the arrested person arrives at the police station in which the offence is being investigated or 24 hours after that person's entry into England or Wales.)

Example 3

6.114   D is arrested in France for an offence committed in Sheffield. Police officers sent to bring him to Sheffield take a channel ferry and arrive back in Dover at 10pm, Monday. They put up for the night at Dover police station and travel to Sheffield next morning, arriving at a Sheffield police station at 3pm Tuesday. That is the relevant time.

Example 4

6.115   As in Example 3, but they arrive at Sheffield at 11pm on Tuesday. The relevant time is 10pm on the Tuesday night and the 'detention clock' already shows one hour when D arrives at the Sheffield police station.

(Note there is no direct prohibition on questioning in this case but in most cases the escorting officers, even if they are investigating the offence, are well advised to refrain from questioning the person about his involvement in the offence during the journey in case objection is subsequently taken to any admission or confession obtained. (See Code C 11.1A and 11.1; see further paras 8.13–8.24, post.)

6.116   As to (c), s 41(2)(c) (Art 42(2)(b)(i) and (ii)) provides that in the case of a person who:
(i)   attends voluntarily at a police station; or
(ii)   accompanies a constable to a police station without having been arrested and is arrested at the police station,

6.117   The relevant time is the time of his arrest. He gets no credit for the period spent at a police station prior to his arrest (cf s 41(4) below). As was indicated in paras 5.127-5.128, ante, s 29 seeks to exclude the possibility that this 'voluntary attendance' may be used to undermine the safeguards applicable to a person in police detention. Yet s 41(2)(c) (Art 40(2)(b)), may operate to defeat that intention. For whilst Code C (para 3.21) requires the police to remind the person that he is free to leave the police station at any time, in practice the person, particularly a person who accompanies the constable in the mistaken belief that he is under compulsion, may well feel constrained to remain. From the police point of view the prospect of obtaining periods of detention which are in addition to those provided by the Act, and possibly in circumstances in which 'police detention' would not be permitted under the Act, may be too strong a temptation.

If s 41(2)(c) (Art 42(2)(b)) had made the relevant time in such a case the time of arrival at a police station, the temptation would not arise. (Note that Code C 12.2 provides for a continuous period of eight hours' rest in any period of 24 hours. In the case of a volunteer or person who accompanies a constable to a police station, this provision runs from the time of his arrest at the police station and not the time of his arrival.)

6.118   The detention in hospital is subject to the limits on detention imposed by this Part of the Act (see para 6.127, post).

Example 5

6.119   D accompanies a constable to a police station without being arrested. He arrives there at 3pm on Tuesday and remains there until 10am on Thursday when he is arrested. That is the relevant time.

6.120   As to (d), s 31 (Art 33) (see para 5.78, ante) provides that where a person has been arrested for an offence, is at a police station in consequence of that arrest and the constable becomes aware that he is liable to be arrested for another offence, he must be arrested for the latter as well. Section 41(4) provides that the relevant time in this case is that at which the person arrived at the police station under arrest for the original offence.

Example 6

6.121   D is arrested for possession of drugs. He arrives at the first police station to which he is taken at 2pm on Monday. He is detained without charge for questioning in relation to that offence. During that questioning he admits committing several burglaries in that police area. He must be arrested for those offences. The relevant time in respect of those latter offences is also 2pm on the Monday even though the arrest takes place on the Tuesday morning.

6.122   As to (e), s 31 and s 41(4) work well enough when the further offences for which D is arrested are committed in the police area in which he committed the original offence for which he has been arrested. However, if the further offences have been committed in another police area and s 41(4) applied, the maximum permitted period of detention may well have expired before D can be transferred to the other police area. This would leave no time for the investigation of those offences in that police area. Section 41(5) therefore provides that if:

(a)   a person is in police detention in police area A for an offence committed in that area, and

(b)   his arrest is sought for an offence committed in police area B in England or Wales, and

(c)   he is taken to area B for the purpose of investigating that offence without being questioned in police area A to obtain evidence of that offence,

6.123   The relevant time in such a case is:

(i)   the time 24 hours after he leaves the place where he is detained in police area A; or

(ii)   the time of his arrival at the first police station to which he is taken in police area B,

whichever is the earlier.

Example 7

6.124   D is arrested in London for possession of drugs. He is detained without charge for questioning about the offence. During questioning it is discovered that D's arrest is sought in Sheffield for burglary. Section 31 requires that he be arrested for that offence but D is not questioned in order to obtain evidence relating to it. D is charged with the drug offence. There are no grounds for detaining him after charge but he may be detained in respect of the burglary (s 34(2) and s 37(2)) pending his transfer to Sheffield. D leaves the London police station at 10am having been detained there for 20 hours. He arrives at Sheffield police station at 3pm the same day. That is the relevant time in respect of the burglary offence. A fresh period of detention starts from 3pm and the 25 hours D has already spent in police detention do not count towards the Sheffield offence.

6.125   Section 41(5)(i) is unlikely to apply since there are no police areas in England and Wales which are more than 24 hours' travelling time apart. It could only apply in circumstances where delay is caused by inclement weather or mechanical breakdown. If, as in Example 2 above, D is questioned in order to obtain evidence of the offence in the other police area B, then the relevant time is the time of arrival at the station in police area B under arrest for the local offence, ie s 41(4) applies, not s 41(5).

6.126   If the offence is a serious arrestable offence, extension of detention beyond the basic 24 hours may be possible. Both s 42 and s 43 permit a superintendent or magistrates' court, respectively, to take account of the distance and time involved in transferring a person to another police area when deciding how long a period of continued or further detention should be granted (see paras 6.133–6.140, post).

HOSPITALISATION OF PERSONS IN POLICE DETENTION

6.127   Where an arrested person is taken to a police station, detained there and later, before the investigation is complete, is removed to a hospital for medical attention, the crucial question is whether the person is then 'in the charge of a constable' (see s 118(2) and art 2(3) and (4) discussed at para 6.6, ante). Doubtless the hospital authorities would say that he is in their charge and nothing can be done to or in respect of the person without the consent of the doctor in charge of the person's treatment. However, if the person is questioned while in hospital by police officers seeking evidence of D's involvement in an offence, there is little difference between detention there and in a police station. The problem is neatly resolved by s 41(6) (Art 42(4)) which provides that only the time during which he is being questioned at the hospital, or on the way to or from the hospital, for the purpose of obtaining evidence relating to an offence, shall be included in the calculation of the period of detention.

Example 1

6.128   D is in police detention following arrest for burglary. After five hours' detention he is taken to hospital and remains there for five days before being declared fit to leave. He is still under arrest. The detention clock stops at five hours on the day he was hospitalised and resumes on his return to a police station.

Example 2

6.129   As in Example 1, but D is questioned for two hours while at the hospital by officers seeking the whereabouts of property stolen in the burglary. On D's release from hospital the detention clock reads seven hours.

EVIDENCE OF AN OFFENCE

6.130   Section 41(6) (and art 42(4)) refer to questioning by a police officer for the purpose of obtaining evidence of an offence, not the offence. Therefore, if D is questioned about other burglaries committed in the area but not about the burglary for which he is under arrest and in police detention, that period of questioning counts as police detention. Difficulties may arise about the purpose of questioning in some cases. For instance, D is under arrest for kidnapping and is hospitalised after arrest and after being taken to a police station. The police question him while in hospital in an attempt to discover where the victim is. The purpose of such questioning is to save life and prevent harm to the victim but should it be successful it will also provide evidence of D's involvement in the offence. Any such period of questioning will count towards the detention period. It is an interview for the purposes of Code C 11.1A and is permitted by Code C 11.1.

ARRESTED PERSON TAKEN DIRECTLY TO HOSPITAL

6.131   Section 41(6) (and art 42(4)) refer to 'a person who is in police detention' and who is removed to hospital. As indicated in the discussion of the meaning of 'police detention' (see para 6.6, ante), a person is only in police detention if he has been arrested and taken to, or arrested at, a police station, for an offence. A person who is arrested and taken directly to a hospital is not in police detention within the meaning of that phrase as defined in s 118(2) (Art 2(3)). It follows that s 41(6) does not apply to such a person. In such a case any periods of questioning while he is in hospital do not count since the detention clock has yet to start. Code C 14.2 states that if a person in police detention is in hospital he may not be questioned without the agreement of a responsible doctor and Note of Guidance 14A states that such periods of questioning count towards the total period, but the Code is silent as to questioning in the situation suggested above. Clearly the agreement of a responsible doctor would be required and even if the period of questioning does not count, the interview must be conducted in accordance with Code C.

RELEASE OF DETAINEES ON EXPIRY OF DETENTION PERIOD

6.132   Section 41(7) and (8) (Art 42(5)) provide that a person who, at the expiry of 24 hours after the relevant time, is in police detention and has not been charged, shall be released either on bail or without bail, unless continued or further detention has been authorised under s 42 or 43 (Arts 43 and 44). A person released under s 41(7) (Art 42(5)) shall not be re-arrested without warrant for the same offence for which he was previously arrested unless new evidence justifying a further arrest has come to light since his release but this does not prevent an arrest under s 46A (arrest of a person bailed to a police station who fails to attend) (s 41(9) as amended by s 29(4) of the CJPOA 1994, art 42(7)). This important provision is repeated in s 42(11) (Art 43(10)) and s 43(19) (Art 44(18)) in respect of release from continued or further detention. It covers not only re-arrest on the same evidence but also a re-arrest based on evidence which was known of and available at the time of the first arrest or which became available during the person's detention following the arrest. The evidence must be new and be discovered after the person's release. However, there is no prohibition on arrest for another offence for which he was not initially arrested (but see s 31 (Art 33), arrest for further offences) even if it is based on evidence which was available earlier than the person's release. The word 'evidence' must be given its ordinary rather than its legal meaning since arrests are often based on material which is not evidence in the legal sense. The restriction on re-arrest without a warrant leaves open the possibility that the person could be re-arrested for the same offence under a warrant issued by a magistrate and based on the same evidence as justified the initial arrest. Section 1 of the Magistrates' Courts Act 1980 does not preclude the issue of a warrant to arrest in such circumstances but it is submitted that a magistrate should not issue one if he is aware that the application is in respect of a person who has already been arrested and detained for a period for that offence and to whom s 41(9) (Art 42(7)) (or s 42(11), art 43(10) or s 43(19), art 44(18)) applies. Since a warrant of arrest is seldom sought in respect of an offence for which the police normally have a power of arrest without warrant, magistrates and their clerks should inquire whether there is a statutory restriction on the exercise of that power of arrest without warrant and refuse to issue a warrant of arrest if there is.

AUTHORISATION OF CONTINUED DETENTION (s 42, Art 43)

6.133   Section 42 (Art 43) provides for the authorisation by a superintendent, or higher rank, of detention beyond 24 hours after the relevant time, up to a maximum period of 36 hours after the relevant time. Such an officer must have reasonable grounds for believing that the three conditions set out in s 42(1) (Art 43(1)) are satisfied. Those conditions are:

(a) the detention of that person without charge is necessary to secure or preserve evidence relating to an offence for which he is under arrest or to obtain such evidence by questioning him (these are the basic grounds for detention without charge);

(b) an offence for which he is under arrest is an arrestable offence; and

(c) the investigation is being conducted diligently and expeditiously.

6.134   It should be noted that s 42(1)(a) (Art 43(1)(a)) refers to 'evidence relating to an offence' and s 42(1)(b) (Art 43(1)(b)) requires that 'an offence for which he is under arrest is a serious arrestable offence' while s 42(1)(c) (Art 43(1)(c)) refers to 'the investigation'. There is no specific requirement that the evidence sought in (a) should be evidence of the serious arrestable offence mentioned in (b), nor that the investigation referred to in s 42(1)(c) (Art 43(1)(c)) should be into that offence. It is therefore open to a superintendent, in what would be the exceptional case, to authorise continued detention in respect of the investigation of an arrestable offence where D is also under arrest for a serious arrestable offence. For example, D is arrested for an offence of rape (a serious arrestable offence) and is detained without charge under s 37(2) (Art 38(2)). After 20 hours of detention D admits committing several burglaries (arrestable offences). D must be arrested for these offences (s 31, art 33) and the relevant time is the time at which D arrived at the police station under arrest for the offence of rape. The custody officer determines that it is necessary to detain D without charge in respect of the burglaries in order to secure evidence or to obtain it by questioning D. The rape investigation is nearly complete; only the victim's statement is required but she is under sedation and cannot give a statement for some hours. D cannot be charged without that statement. If a superintendent agrees that it is necessary to detain D in order to secure or obtain evidence of the burglaries (arrestable offences), then s 42(1)(a) (Art 43(1)(a)) is satisfied. Section 42(1)(b) (Art 43(1)(b)) is also satisfied since D is under arrest for a serious arrestable offence, and, if the investigation of the burglaries is being conducted diligently and expeditiously, so is s 42(1)(c) (Art 43(1)(c)). It is clear from the parliamentary debates that this was not Parliament's intention and it would be open to a court to interpret 'offence' in s 42(1) (Art 43(1)) as referring to the original serious arrestable one. The correct procedure would then follow. In other words if D can be charged with the offence of rape, he should be taken before a court and an application made under s 128 of the Magistrates' Courts Act 1980 (as amended by s 48 of PACE 1984) for a remand to police detention for inquiries to be made into the other offences (see para 6.195, post).

6.135   If these conditions apply, the authorising officer may decide that the maximum of 12 hours' continued detention is necessary or that some lesser period may be sufficient. If a lesser period is authorised a further period up to the maximum of 12 hours (36 hours after the relevant time) may be authorised provided that the application is made before the expiry of the first period authorised and that the conditions in s 42(1)(a) to (c) (Art 43(1)(a) to (c)) are still satisfied (s 42(2), art 43(2)) (*R v Taylor* (1991)).

If the transfer of the person in police detention to another police area is proposed, the authorising officer must have regard to the distance and time the journey would take (s 42(3)).

TIME OF AUTHORISATION

6.136 No authorisation under s 42(1) (Art 43(1)) above may be given more than 24 hours after the relevant time or before the second review of the person's detention under s 40 (Art 41) has been carried out, though if a period of less than 12 hours is authorised an application to extend continued detention for a further period up to the maximum of 12 hours can be made before the expiry of the first period authorised (*R v Taylor* (1991)). The purpose of the review of detention is to determine whether the grounds for detention still apply. The second review will take place at the latest after 15 hours, and only if the review officer determines that the condition for further detention under s 37(2) (Art 38(2)) still applies (which is the same condition as in s 42(1)(a) (Art 43(1)(a)) will detention beyond 15 hours continue. The application for continued detention will be refused if any of the conditions in s 42(1)(a) to (c) (Art 43(1)(a) to (c)) do not apply but such refusal will not prevent the detention of the person up to the maximum period of 24 hours, unless the reason for the refusal is that there is no need for detention in order to secure or preserve evidence or to obtain it by questioning, eg there is sufficient evidence to charge the person or that such evidence is unlikely to be forthcoming. In such a case the person must be charged as required by s 37(7) (Art 38(7)) or released as required by s 34(2) (Art 35(2)). However, the refusal may be on the ground that sufficient evidence to charge will be obtained within the 24-hour period of detention permitted by s 41(1) (Art 42(1)), in which case detention may continue as authorised after the second review up to that time.

DUTIES OF THE AUTHORISING OFFICER

Representations

6.137 When the appropriate officer has to determine whether to authorise continued detention under s 42 (Art 43), he must give the person whose detention is being considered, or any solicitor representing him who is available at that time, an opportunity to make representations to him about the detention (s 42(6), art 43(5)). The requirement under s 42(6) (Art 43(5)) is mandatory and a purported authorisation of further detention without hearing representations on behalf of the detainee is invalid (*Re an Application for a warrant of Further Detention* (1988)). Such representations may be made orally or in writing (s 42(7), art 43(6)) but the authorising officer may refuse to hear an oral representation from the person in detention if he considers he is unfit to make them by reason of his condition or behaviour (s 42(8), art 43(7)). 'Behaviour' in this context would seem to mean violent behaviour. 'Condition' is more problematic. Clearly it would include intoxication through drink or drugs rendering the person incoherent.

Where the person is asleep he should be woken –   Code C, Note of Guidance 15C, suggests bringing the review of detention or an authorisation of continued detention forward if the person is likely to be asleep at the time when it should take place so that representations can be made without having to wake him.

Availability of a solicitor

6.138   The wording of s 42(6)(b) (Art 43(5)(b)) suggests that the solicitor need not be available at the police station to make representations. A representation by telephone is within the subsection and written representations could be delivered. The right to consult with a solicitor under s 58(1) (Art 59) is a right to do so at any time and a request to do so can only be denied in the special circumstances set out in s 58 (Art 59). Code C 6.1 provides that all people in police detention must be informed that they may at any time consult and communicate privately, whether in person, in writing or by telephone with a solicitor, and that independent legal advice is available free of charge from the duty solicitor unless his right of consultation has been delayed under s 58. A detainee who wishes his solicitor, or a solicitor, to make representations under s 42(6) (Art 43(5)) on his behalf may then telephone his solicitor or ask to see a duty solicitor. (Code C 15.3A permits other persons having an interest in the person's welfare to make representations at the discretion of the authorising officer.)

Duty to inform detainee of his rights (s 42(9), art 43(8))

6.139   Where an officer authorises the keeping of a person in police detention under s 42(1) (Art 43(1)) and at the time of such authorisation the detainee has not exercised his right under s 56 (Art 57) (to have someone informed of his arrest) or under s 58 (Art 59) (to consult a solicitor), the officer shall inform him of those rights and shall decide whether to permit him to exercise them, applying the criteria in those sections which permit delay in the exercise of the rights (s 42(9), art 43(8)). This presupposes that, on being told of these rights, the detainee requests them since both rights are available at his request but not otherwise. The decision of the officer must then be recorded in the custody record and, if the rights are refused, the reasons for the refusal shall also be recorded (s 42(9), art 43(8)).

Duty to inform and record (s 42(5), art 43(4))

6.140   Where an officer authorises continued detention of a person under s 42(1) (Art 43(1)), he has a duty to inform him of the grounds for his continued detention and to record that decision in the person's custody record. The ruling in *Re an Application for a warrant of Further Detention* (1988) requires that the authorising officer do more than merely recite the terms of s 42(1) (Art 43(1)) in the custody record. This is an important caveat – to have to state and record one's reasons for making a decision concentrates the mind significantly.

Duty to release on expiry of continued detention (s 42(10), art 43(9))

6.141 When the continued detention of a person has been authorised, the person must be released from police detention, with or without bail, not later than 36 hours after the relevant time unless (a) he has been charged with an offence (when s 38 (Art 39) applies) or, (b) his continued detention is authorised or otherwise permitted by a magistrates' court under s 43 (Art 44) (s 42(10), art 43(9)). If a person is released under this subsection, he shall not be re-arrested without a warrant for the same offence unless new evidence comes to light after his release which justifies a further arrest (s 42(11), art 43(10)) (see para 6.132, ante).

By-passing s 42 (Art 43)

6.142 In some cases it will be clear from the outset that detention will be necessary for more than the 36 hours permitted by s 41 and s 42 (Arts 42 and 43); for example, in the case of rape, forensic examination of clothing may not be completed within that period. In such a case an application to a magistrates' court for a warrant of further detention may be sought at any time within the initial 24 hours' detention. A magistrates' court may authorise detention for up to 36 hours and extend that by up to a further 36 hours provided that the overall maximum of 96 hours is not exceeded. The full 96 hours' detention can therefore be obtained without seeking an authorisation for continued detention from a superintendent under s 42. The application to a magistrates' court for detention beyond 24 hours is what the Royal Commission recommended but there are two reasons why the police have been given the power to authorise continued detention beyond the initial 24 hours up to a maximum of 36 hours and each reason indicates when s 42 will be relied upon. The first is that on an application for a warrant of further detention the detainee has a right to appear before the court and to be legally represented. Sections 56 and 58 (Arts 57 and 59) which, respectively, give the detainee the right to have someone informed of his arrest and the right to consult a solicitor, permit the police to delay those rights for up to 36 hours, the maximum period of police authorised detention. It follows that when the police wish to exercise that power of delay they will seek continued detention under s 42 (Art 43). The detainee may make representations under s 42 (Art 43) but, access to a solicitor having been delayed, there will be no solicitor representing him and a duty solicitor will not be made available to make such representations on his behalf. The second reason is administrative. It would have been possible to require a magistrates' court to hear all applications for detention beyond 24 hours and to make arrangements to deny legal representation in appropriate cases but, while over 95% of detainees are released within 24 hours, the remaining percentage, though small, represents thousands of persons and a heavy workload for magistrates' courts. Permitting the police to authorise detention beyond 24 hours and up to 36 hours reduces the workload. Magistrates and their clerks will then hope that whenever it is likely that an investigation can be completed within 36 hours, application will be made to a superintendent for continued detention, rather than to a court for a warrant of further detention. Statistics issued by the Home Office

(Arrests for Notifiable Offences and the Operation of Certain Police Powers under PACE, England and Wales, 2001/02) tell us that in 2001/02 325 warrants of further detention were applied for, of which 8 were refused and 264 (83%) of the detainees were charged.

Warrants of further detention (s 43, art 44)

6.143   Section 43(1) (Art 44(1)) provides that a magistrates' court may issue a warrant of further detention if there are reasonable grounds for believing that the detention of the person is justified. 'magistrates' court' in relation to s 43 and s 44 (extension of warrants of further detention) means a court consisting of two or more justices sitting otherwise than in open court (s 45(1)). This does not appear to preclude an application being heard by a stipendiary magistrate. Section 16(3) of the Justices of the Peace Act 1979 provides that a stipendiary magistrate can do alone any act which can be done by two justices under any law unless it contains an express provision to the contrary. (In Northern Ireland 'magistrates' court' is not defined as in s 45 of the 1984 Act but art 44(19) states that an application (complaint) under art 44 shall not be heard in open court.) A warrant will authorise the keeping of the person in police detention for such period as the court thinks fit but not exceeding 36 hours (s 43(11) and (12), art 44(11) and (12)). As with continued detention under s 42, if the person is to be transferred to another police area the court must have regard to the distance and time the journey would take in deciding the period of detention (s 43(13)). (This does not apply in Northern Ireland which is one police area.)

Grounds for further detention

6.144   A person's further detention, for the purposes of s 43 and s 44 (Arts 44 and 45) (extension of a warrant), is only justified if:
(a)   his detention without charge is necessary to secure or preserve evidence relating to an offence for which he is under arrest or to obtain such evidence by questioning him;
(b)   an offence for which he is under arrest is a serious arrestable offence; and
(c)   the investigation is being conducted diligently and expeditiously (s 43(4)).

6.145   These are identical grounds to those in s 42(1) (Art 43(1)). As was suggested at para 6.133, ante, in relation to s 42(1) (Art 43(1)), these conditions do not necessarily confine detention without charge to serious arrestable offences. They could permit a magistrates' court to grant a warrant of further detention when the evidence sought under (a) and the investigation in (c) is in respect of an arrestable offence provided that one of the offences for which the person is under arrest is a serious arrestable offence. It has been suggested (para 6.133, ante) that these conditions were not intended to permit the issue of a warrant in the circumstances mentioned and, it is submitted, a magistrates' court faced with such an application should exercise the discretion which s 43(1) (Art 44(1)) gives to it, to refuse the application even if the conditions in s 43(4) (Art 44(4)) are all satisfied. In cases where there is sufficient evidence to charge the person with the serious arrestable offence but further inquiries are necessary in respect of an arrestable offence, the person should be charged and application made under s 128 of the Magistrates' Courts Act 1980, as amended by s 47 of PACE 1984, for detention for further inquiries into that other offence (see para 6.195, post). (There is no equivalent power in Northern Ireland; the RUC considered it unnecessary.)

Time of application

6.146 The application for a warrant of further detention may be made at any time before the expiry of 36 hours after the relevant time (s 43(5)(a), art 44(5)(a)) and will depend upon a number of factors, not least the availability of a magistrates' court. If continued detention under s 42 (Art 43) has been granted, application to a magistrates' court for a warrant of further detention will be made between the twenty-fourth and the thirty-sixth hours. Where an application to a superintendent under s 42 (Art 43) is refused, an application to a court under s 43 (Art 44) is not precluded but is unlikely to be sanctioned and, if sanctioned, to succeed. If a warrant of further detention is sought without reliance on s 42 (Art 43), the application can be at any time during the initial 24 hours of police detention. In all cases governing factors will be the time at which the lawful detention ends and the time of the next sitting of a magistrates' court. Some flexibility is provided by s 43(5)(b) (Art 44(5)(b)). Thus, where it is not practicable for the magistrates' court to sit at the expiry of 36 hours after the relevant time, but the court will sit during the six hours following the end of that period, application may be made before the expiry of those six hours. Thus, if the 36-hour period expires at 7am on a Monday and a court is due to sit at 10am on that day, application may be made to that court 40 hours after the relevant time, at 11am. However, if an application is made after the expiry of 36 hours from the relevant time and it appears to the magistrates' court that it would have been reasonable for the police to have made it before the expiry of that period 'the court shall dismiss the application' (s 43(7), art 44(7)). This provision was considered in *R v Slough Magistrates' Court, ex p Stirling* (1987). There the police approached the clerk to the justices with an application for a warrant of further detention at 12.45pm, only a few minutes before the expiry of the 36-hour period of police detention. The justices were asked to hear the application but decided not to do so until after lunch. The application was finally made two hours after the expiration of the 36-hour period. The Divisional Court allowed an application for judicial review on the ground that the application could have been made between 10.30am and 11.30am and therefore the police had not acted reasonably in making the application after the expiry of the 36-hour period. Section 43(7) (Art 44(7)) is mandatory and the justices were then bound to dismiss the application. The justices could be criticised for not hearing the application before lunch but the police should have foreseen the situation and applied earlier. In *R v Sedgefield Justices, ex p Milne* (1987) the Divisional Court took the view that the police had acted reasonably in contacting the court at 9.00am when the 36-hour period was due to expire at 10.48am. The court did not sit until noon and the application, which the Divisional Court held is made when the constable gives evidence on oath as required by s 43(1) (Art 44(1)), was heard at 12.54pm. The magistrates were criticised for not hearing the application sooner given the precise time scale laid down by PACE 1984. It is clear that both the police and the courts must act reasonably, the police in making the court aware of the application as soon as they become aware of the need for further detention, and the courts in responding to the police by arranging a hearing within the time limit. Code C, Notes for Guidance 15B, recommends that applications for a warrant and its extension be made between 10am and 9pm, and if possible during normal court hours. It further suggests that it will not be practicable to arrange for a court to sit outside these hours. Section 43(6)(a) (Art 44(6)(a)) permits the detention of the person to whom the late application under s 43(5)(b) (Art 44(5)(b)) applies for the period in excess of 36 hours until the application is heard, but the custody officer must make a note in the person's custody record of the fact that he was kept in police detention beyond that period, and the reasons for it (s 43(6)(b), art 44(6)(b)) (see para 6.56, post, detention during an adjournment).

The information (complaint)

6.147　An application for a warrant of further detention must be supported by an information in writing which must state:
(a)　the nature of the offence for which the person to whom the application relates has been arrested;
(b)　the general nature of the evidence on which that person was arrested;
(c)　what inquiries relating to the offence have been made by the police and what further inquiries are proposed by them;
(d)　the reasons for believing the continued detention of that person to be necessary for the purpose of such inquiries (s 43(14), art 44(13)).

6.148　The fact that s 43(14) (Art 44(13)) does not specifically refer to a 'serious arrestable' offence supports the argument advanced earlier in para 6.144 (and para 6.133), that the wording of s 43(4) (Art 44(4)) would permit a warrant of further detention to be issued in respect of an arrestable offence when the arrest is for that offence and a serious arrestable offence. It is submitted that s 43(14)(a) (Art 44(13)(a)) should be read as if it said, 'the nature of the offence alleged to be a serious arrestable offence' etc for the purpose of stating its nature would seem to be to enable the court to determine that it is a serious arrestable offence. Category (b) above would appear to require a resume of all the matters which collectively led the arresting officer to believe that the person was guilty of the offence or which gave him reasonable grounds for suspecting that he was guilty of it, and would include hearsay, an informant's tip-off, etc. This suggests that 'evidence' in s 43(14)(b) (Art 44(13)(b)) should be given its wider, rather than its legal, meaning. As regards category (c), where the ground for the detention up to the application was the need to obtain evidence by questioning, magistrates ought to be aware of the total period of questioning undergone by the suspect during the previous 36 (or 42 hours). Where future inquiries are to be of a similar kind, magistrates may be reluctant to grant a warrant or, if they do, may do so for only a short time, since questioning during the warranted period of detention will almost always be in the presence of a solicitor (36 hours being the maximum period of denial of access) and such questioning is unlikely to be more successful than previous periods when the detainee was denied such access or when the solicitor was also present. What evidence there is suggests that those cases which, before the Act, were said to justify periods of detention of up to or in excess of 96 hours, were cases involving, for example, large conspiracies, or robberies involving several persons which required extensive inquiries of numbers of persons, sometimes some distance away. Magistrates may well feel constrained to limit authorised detention to such cases and not grant periods of detention simply to permit the police to 'crack' the suspect by long periods of questioning. Section 43(14)(d) (Art 44(13)(d)) requires the reasons to be stated for believing that the continued detention of the person is necessary for the purposes of such further inquiries. This, together with the other material, will enable the court to decide whether the detention is necessary as required by s 43(4)(a) (Art 44(4)(a)). 'Necessary' is an ordinary English word which means that the court must be satisfied that such detention is indispensable to the securing, preserving, or the obtaining of evidence by questioning, and the information provided must be directed to this end.

The standard of proof

6.149   Both s 43(1) and s 44(1) (Arts 44(1) and 45(1)) require that the magistrates' court be satisfied that there are reasonable grounds for believing that further detention is justified. Section 43(4) (Art 44(4)) then lists three specific conditions which must be met by the police in their application (see para 6.144, ante). 'Satisfied' as used in Sch 1 of PACE 1984 has been held to import the civil standard of proof on the balance of probabilities (*R v Norwich Crown Court, ex p Chethams* (1990)). Given the different context and the fact that the liberty of the individual is concerned there is a strong argument for saying that 'satisfied' as used here should import the criminal standard of proof beyond reasonable doubt.

The application

6.150   The application for a warrant of further detention must be on oath (s 43(1), art 44(1)) and the magistrates' court may not hear such an application unless the person to whom it relates:
(a) has been furnished with a copy of the information (submitted in support of the application); and
(b) has been brought before the court for the hearing (s 43(2), art 44(2)).

6.151   The person shall be entitled to be represented at the hearing and, if he is not represented when he is brought before the court, but wishes to be represented, the court shall adjourn the hearing to enable him to obtain representation (s 43(3)(a), art 44(3)(a)). This must be taken to mean 'adequate representation'. If therefore the solicitor has not had sufficient time to take full instructions the court should consider an adjournment even if the detainee's solicitor is present. Code C 2.4 states that, when a person leaves police detention or is taken before a court, he or his legal representative shall be supplied on request with a copy of the custody record as soon as practicable. Solicitors should therefore request a copy of the custody record before a hearing of the application. The person may be kept in police detention during the adjournment (s 43(3)(b), art 44(3)(b)). Such detention (and detention under s 43(6)(a), on a late application) will count towards the overall period of detention and can, it seems, be used by the police for their further inquiries. Where the application is made during an authorised period of detention this may not result in any unfairness to the detainee. For example the application is made after 30 hours of detention, there is a six hours' adjournment and the application is refused. D is released or charged more or less on time. If, however, the application is made in the thirty-fifth hour, there is a six hours' adjournment and the application is refused, D will have been in detention for five hours more than was originally authorised. If then the police use this period for further questioning of D, he may feel justifiably aggrieved. On the other hand, if questioning is not permitted during an adjournment and the application is granted, the police investigation may be hampered by such a delay. Where the application is made close to the end of a period of detention the solicitor representing his client will serve his client's interests best by ensuring that any adjournment is as short as possible.

Period of warrant

6.152   If a magistrates' court issues a warrant of further detention it must state the time at which it was issued and it will authorise the keeping in police detention of the person to whom it relates for the period stated in it (s 43(10), art 44(10)). That period may be any period the court thinks fit, having regard to the evidence before it (s 43(11), art 44(11)) but shall not exceed 36 hours (s 43(12), art 44(12)). If it is proposed to transfer the person to another police area the court shall have regard to the distance and the time the journey will take (s 43(13)). In the first edition of this book it was assumed that a warrant of further detention, granted before the expiry of the maximum period of continued detention permitted by s 42 (Art 43), would begin to operate only at the end of that period, that is after 36 hours of police authorised detention. However, it now appears to be accepted that such a warrant begins to operate from the time of issue (see the Home Office Statistical Bulletin 16/89). This does not affect the total period of detention which may be authorised. For example, D has been detained for 24 hours and the maximum period of continued detention under s 42 (Art 43) has been granted. A warrant of further detention is applied for and granted after 30 hours of detention for the maximum period of 36 hours. The warrant takes effect immediately, therefore at its expiry D will have been in police detention for 66 hours. If an extension is sought under s 44 (Art 45) the magistrates' court may extend the warrant up to the maximum permitted period of 96 hours by authorising a further 30 hours. On the expiry of the warrant the person to whom it relates must be charged or released from police detention, either on bail or without bail (s 43(18), art 44(17)), unless an extension of the warrant is granted. A person released under s 43(18) (Art 44(17)) shall not be re-arrested without warrant for the offence for which he was previously arrested unless new evidence justifying a further arrest has come to light since his release (s 43(19), art 44(18)) (see also s 41(9) (Art 42(7)) and s 42(11) (Art 43(10)) discussed in para 6.132, ante).

Extension of a warrant of further detention (s 44, art 45)

6.153   A warrant of further detention will always expire less than 96 hours after the relevant time (at 60 hours or less if the maximum period is granted to follow the initial 24 hours given that a warrant of further detention takes effect from the time of issue). It will expire after 72 hours, or less, if the maximum period is granted after continued detention under s 42 (Art 43). A magistrates' court may extend the warrant on application made by a constable. The application must be made in exactly the same way as that under s 43 (Art 44). Thus s 44(6) (Art 45(6)) extends s 43(2), (3) and (14) (Arts 44(2), (3), (13) and (19)) to an application under s 44 (Art 45)). It will be granted if the court is satisfied that there are reasonable grounds for believing that further detention of the person is justified (s 44(1), art 45(1)). Section 43(4) (Art 44(4)) (conditions which must be satisfied before a person's further detention is justified) applies to an application under s 44 (Art 45). An application for an extension can be made to any magistrates' court, as defined in s 45(1), in whose area the person is detained under a warrant of further detention. If, for example, a person so detained is transferred to another police area, a court in that area may hear the application.

Period of extension

6.154   As with the period of a warrant, the period of the extension of a warrant is at the discretion of the court, having regard to the evidence before it (s 44(2), art 45(2)), but it cannot exceed 36 hours or end later than 96 hours after the relevant time (s 44(3), art 45(3)). Where a warrant of further detention has been extended for a period ending before 96 hours after the relevant time, a magistrates' court may extend it again if satisfied that an extension is justified and the conditions in s 43(4) (Art 44(4)) are still satisfied (s 44(4), art 45(4)). Thus, a number of applications for an extension can be made and the court may extend the time so long as it does not exceed 96 hours from the relevant time. For example, 36 hours is granted under the warrant, and on an application for an extension the court grants a further 24 hours. If another application for an extension is made, the court may grant a further period of 12 hours, assuming that no application was made for continued detention under s 42 (ie 24 + 36 + 24 + 12 = 96 hours). No extension of detention without charge is permitted beyond 96 hours from the relevant time. A warrant must be endorsed with a note of the period of any extension (s 44(5), art 45(5)).

REFUSAL OF WARRANTS

Warrant of further detention refused

6.155   If an application for a warrant of further detention is refused (only 4 of the 250 applications in 1994 were) the person to whom the application refers shall forthwith be charged or released, either on bail or without bail (s 43(15), art 44(14)). However, if not charged the person need not be released before the expiry of 24 hours after the relevant time; or before the expiry of any longer period for which his continued detention is or has been authorised under s 42 (s 43(16), art 44(15)) if such detention can be justified by the need to secure, or preserve evidence, or to obtain it by questioning him. The release of the person is then either under s 41(7) (Art 42(5)) (release on the expiry of 24 hours of police detention) and the prohibition on re-arrest for the same offence under s 41(9) (Art 42(7)) applies; or it is under s 42(10) (Art 43(9)) (release on expiry of authorised continued detention) and the prohibition on re-arrest for the same offence under s 42(11) (Art 43(10)) applies. If an application for a warrant of further detention is refused, no further application can be made, unless supported by new evidence which has come to light since the refusal (s 43(17), art 44(16)). The prohibition is clear and specific. A magistrates' court has no discretion to consider a re-application based on evidence which was available before the refusal of the earlier application but which was overlooked. 'Evidence' in this context may also be accorded its wider, ordinary meaning given the nature of the application, which can clearly include matters which may not be admissible as evidence at a trial of the issues.

Extension of a warrant refused

6.156   Section 44(7) (Art 45(7)) requires that where an application for an extension is refused, the person to whom it relates must be charged forthwith or released on bail or without bail. However, as when a warrant of further detention is refused, the person's release is not required before the expiry of any period, or any extension of that period, authorised by a warrant of further detention or an earlier application for an extension, which is applicable to him if such detention is still considered necessary to secure, preserve or obtain evidence by questioning (s 44(8), art 45(8)).

REVIEW OF POLICE DETENTION (s 40, Art 41)

6.157   Periodic reviews of the detention of persons in police detention are provided for by s 40 (Art 41) by an officer known as a 'review officer'. (The review officer is also responsible for reviews of detention of suspected terrorists detained under s 41 of the

Terrorism Act 2000. See para 158 below.) Two types of detention are subject to review, detention before charge and detention after charge. The purpose of the review in both cases is to determine whether the grounds for detention still exist at the time of the review but in each case the grounds for detention are different. To mark the importance of a review of detention without charge, which in some cases may be as long as 96 hours (compared to at most 48 hours in the case of detention after charge), the review officer is an inspector or higher rank not directly involved in the investigation (s 40(1)(b), art 41(1)(b)), and in the case of detention after charge it is the custody officer (s 40(1)(a), art 41(1)(a)). Before conducting a review the review officer must ensure that the detained person is reminded of his right to free legal advice and that all such reminders are noted in the custody record (Code C 15.4 and 15.12).

Time of reviews

6.158 The first review takes place six hours after the detention was first authorised (s 40(3)(a), art 41(3)(a)) in the case of detention without charge, under s 37(3) (Art 38(3)), and in the case of detention after charge, under s 38(2) (Art 39(3)). The second review takes place not later than nine hours after the first (s 40(3)(b), art 41(3)(b)) and subsequent reviews at intervals of not more than nine hours (s 40(3)(c), art 41(3)(c)). In the case of detention before charge, the time from which the period of detention is to be calculated, the relevant time, will be earlier than the time from which the period of six hours for the first review is to be calculated. The former is usually the time of arrival at the first police station to which the arrestee is taken, the latter the time the decision to detain is taken after the evidence has been reviewed. The result is that the first review in the case of a person detained without charge will take place after the person has been in police detention for longer than six hours. For example D arrives at the station at 6pm (the relevant time). The evidence is reviewed and his detention is authorised at 7.15pm. The first review is then due at 1.15am after seven-and-a-quarter hours of police detention. Schedule 8 requires that reviews under s 41 of the Terrorism Act be carried out as soon as reasonably practicable and then at intervals of not more than 12 hours. (The range of 'waiting time' between arrival at a police station and the decision to detain has been shown to be from 0 minutes to 2 hours 06 minutes in a sample of observed receptions, and from 0 to 57 minutes in a sample of custody records. See McKenzie et al, 'Helping the Police with their Inquiries' [1990] Crim LR 22 at p 26 fn 15.)

Postponement of reviews

6.159 A review may be postponed:
(a) if, having regard to all the circumstances prevailing at the latest time (when the review should take place in accordance with s 40(3) (Art 41(3))) it is not practicable to carry out the review at that time (s 40(4)(a), art 41(4)(a)); or
(b) without prejudice to the generality of (a), if at that time the person is being questioned by a police officer and the review officer is satisfied that an interruption

for the purpose of carrying out the review would prejudice the investigation (s 40(4)(b)(i), art 41(4)(b)(i)); or
(c) if at that time no review officer is readily available (s 40(4)(b)(ii), art 41(4)(b)(ii)).

6.160 The grounds for and the extent of any delay in conducting a review, together with its outcome, must be recorded, presumably in the custody record though the Code does not say so (Code C 15.4 and 6).

6.161 Section 40(4)(b) (Art 41(4)(b)) gives two specific reasons why it will not be practicable to carry out the review at the stipulated time. The postponement while questioning is going on will not usually be longer than two hours given the Code's provisions requiring breaks normally after two hours or at recognised meal times (Code C 12.7). Since a ground for detention without charge is the need to obtain evidence by questioning, a review in the middle of an ongoing interrogation is unlikely to be particularly beneficial to the detainee since the interrogation implies that the ground still exists. Thus from the police viewpoint a review could ruin a period of interrogation by destroying a carefully nurtured psychological atmosphere in which the detainee's belief in his continued detention is an important factor. The provisions of s 76 (Art 74) (admissibility of confessions) and s 78 (Art 76) (exclusion of unfair evidence) must be borne in mind. If a court subsequently decides that the postponement (either alone or with other facts) was unjustified and perhaps used in order to increase the psychological pressure, any confession obtained may be excluded (see further Chapter 8, post). The duty to record the reasons for postponement (below) could supply evidence for such exclusion.

6.162 (One may note at this point that, while there will normally be little questioning of a person charged and detained, such a person may still be detained under s 128 of the Magistrates' Courts Act 1980, as amended by s 48, for inquiries into other offences and the review requirements under this section apply to such detention (s 128(8)(d)) (there is no equivalent power in Northern Ireland).) Postponement because there is no review officer available at the time takes account of the possibility that at one extreme the custody officer is at lunch when the review becomes due, to, at the other extreme, an emergency which takes all ranks above inspector out of the police station for a time. Section 30(3) (Art 32(3)) ensures that persons detained for six or more hours will be detained at a designated police station where custody officers must be appointed and which are likely to have a number of senior officers available, thus reducing the likelihood that a review officer will not be available. Numerous examples of more general impracticabilities can arise in a busy police station and in addition the provision in s 45(2) (Art 46) (see para 6.06, ante) that all times are approximate gives a degree of flexibility by, for example, enabling a review to be brought forward before a review officer goes off duty, or to avoid waking a sleeping prisoner (see Code C, Note of Guidance 15C).

6.163 In *Roberts v Chief Constable of the Cheshire Constabulary* (1999) an award of damages was made where the review of detention was carried two hours and twenty minutes later than it should have been. It should have been held at 5.25 am but was carried out at 7.45 am. The implications of this decision are that the detention failure to carry to carry out reviews due to neglect will render the detention unlawful and that the flexibility afforded by s 45(2) will have to be justified by sound operational reasons.

6.164 If a review is postponed it must be carried out as soon as practicable after the time when it should have been carried out (s 40(5), art 41(5)) and the review officer must record the reason for the postponement in the custody record (s 40(7), art 41(7)). The next review after the postponed review must take place nine hours after the postponed review should have taken place (s 40(6), art 41(6)). Given the range of reviews and entitlement to meals etc busy police stations may need to use wall charts to monitor each prisoner and delegate one officer whose main task will be to keep an eye on each chart and tell the custody officer or review inspector when action is needed in respect of a particular prisoner.

Purpose of the review

Detention of a person not charged

6.165 The duties of a review officer in respect of a person detained without charge are set out in s 37(1) to (6) (Art 38(1) to (6)) (duties of a custody officer before charge) with the substitution of 'review officer' for 'custody officer' and other necessary amendments. The duties are in all respects the same as those of a custody officer under s 37(1) to (6) (Art 38(1) to (6)) when a person first arrives at a police station under arrest (s 40(8), art 41(8)) (see paras 6.54-6.61, ante). If the review officer determines that there is sufficient evidence to charge the person with the offence for which he is under arrest the custody officer's duty under s 37(7) (Art 38(7)), to charge or release without charge, then arises. Only two reviews will be possible within the first 24 hours and the second review, which must take place before continued detention can be authorised (s 42(4), art 43(3)), will often take place closer to the 24-hour deadline than the 15th hour of police detention. If the review officer determines that detention must continue after the second review, the custody officer will then have to consider whether an application for continued detention under s 42 (Art 43), or for a warrant of further detention under s 43 (Art 44), should be made. If either application is made and granted, the reviews immediately following such a grant will be somewhat academic but must, nevertheless, take place. The review officer must, of course, be aware of the period of detention authorised and the grounds upon which it was granted.

Detention of person not fit to be charged

6.166 The detention of such a person is permitted by s 37(9) (Art 38(9)), and the duty of the review officer (an inspector or above) is to determine whether he is yet in a fit state to be charged (s 40(9), art 41(9)). If the decision is that he is, the custody officer's duty to charge under s 37(7) (Art 38(7)) then arises.

Detention of person after charge

6.167   The duties of the review officer (in this case the custody officer) are set out in s 38(1) to (6) (Art 39(1) to (6)) (duties of custody officer after charge) with the substitution of references to the person whose detention is under review for references to 'person arrested' (s 40(10), art 41(10)). Those duties are discussed in paras 6.64-6.73 ante. If as a result of his review the custody officer determines that the grounds for detention after charge no longer exist, he is then under a duty to order that person's immediate release from custody as required by s 34(2) (Art 35(2)), without bail unless s 34(5)(a) or (b) (Art 35(5)(a) or (b)) apply.

Arresting officer senior to the review officer

6.168   Section 40(11) (Art 41(11)) provides for the situation in which the arresting officer is senior to the review officer and he gives instructions which are, or would be, at variance with those of the review officer. The provision is identical with that contained in s 39(6) (Art 40(6)) in respect of custody officers and reference should be made to the discussion in para 6.35, ante where 'review officer' should be substituted for 'custody officer'.

Representations

6.169   The review officer is under the same duty to permit representations to be made to him as is a superintendent who authorises continued detention under s 42 (Art 43). Section 40(12), (13) and (14) (Art 41(12), (13) and (14)) are identical to the duties in s 42(6), (7) and (8) (Art (5), (6) and (7)), discussed in paras 6.137–6.142, ante, except that there is no duty to give the person such an opportunity if he is asleep. Code C, Notes of Guidance 15C, states that if the detainee is likely to be asleep when a review or authorisation of continued detention may take place, it should be brought forward so that he may make representations without being woken up. For example, D arrives at a police station at 8.45am having been arrested for armed robbery (an arrestable offence). His detention without charge is authorised at 9am. The first review takes place at 3pm, the next is due at 12 midnight. Code C 12.1 requires that he has eight hours' rest, preferably at night, therefore at 12 midnight he is likely to be asleep. The review may be brought forward to 10pm to permit an uninterrupted eight hours' sleep. If it is obvious at that time that continued detention beyond the 24 hours permitted by s 41(1) (Art 42(1)) will be required, the authorisation may take place immediately after the second review (assuming it is found that detention without charge is still necessary) (see s 42(4)(b), art 43(3)(b)). The 24-hour period of detention expires at 8.45am on the day following D's arrest and the 12 hours (or lesser period) of continued detention commences at that time. A third review is required at the end of the 24-hour period but, in the circumstances, it is something of a PACE 1984 formality.

Review by telephone or video link

6.170   The Divisional Court decided in *R v Chief Constable of Kent, ex p Kent Police Federation* that it was not permissible to conduct s 40 reviews by video link. The Lord Chief Justice held that s 40 of PACE 1984 did not permit review by video link and that the practice of s 40 telephone reviews approved by Code C: note 15 of the old code was of dubious legality. The Lord Chief Justice held that it was implicit in s 40 and explicit in s 37(5), read in accordance with s 40(8), that the detainee should be in the physical presence of the review officer. The Criminal Justice and Police Act 2001, s 73 inserted into PACE 1984 new ss 40A and 45A which allows for the use, in certain circumstances, of telephone reviews of detention and video links for other custody decisions where the review officer is at a different station from the person detained. The Act allows for pre-charge reviews under s 40(1)(b) which must be carried out by an officer of at least inspector rank to be carried out by video link, where the review officer is at a different police station to the detained person, and by telephone, but only where it is impracticable to carry out the review in person or by video link within the time scale. Video link is to be preferred to telephone, which may only be used when it is 'not reasonably practicable'. Code C, Note 15 F states that this may be 'where there are severe weather conditions or an unforeseen operational emergency prevents the review officer from attending'. This suggests that the general rule is that the review officer should be present with the detainee unless it is absolutely unavoidable. The Government are to pilot the use of video conferencing facilities for reviews and other custody decisions and the Act provides for regulations to be drawn up specifying which stations are to be piloted and, if so required, which functions should be piloted. However, before the ink was dry on these provisions the Government included a clause in the Criminal Justice Act 2003 which removed the restrictions on telephone reviews under s 40A. Clause 4 substitutes a new s 40A(1), which states that a review 'may be carried out by means of a discussion, conducted by telephone, with one or more persons at the police station where the arrested person is held' and s 40A(2), which states that sub-s (1) did not apply of the review was of the kind authorised by regulations under s 45A for using video-conferencing facilities and it was reasonably practicable to carry it out in that way.

6.171   Section 45A authorises the Home Secretary to promulgate the regulations referred to above and allows the use of video conferencing in relation to a person taken to a non-designated police station. It is the responsibility of the officer at the police station where the arrested person is held to make a record at the instance of the officer at the other end of the video link (s 45A(5)). Where representations are allowed by the arrested person or legal advisor under any of the relevant sections these may be made by video link or by fax or email (s 45A(7)).

6.172   However, a review to decide whether to authorise a person's continued detention under s 42 of PACE 1984 must be done in person. The review officer's function is to receive representations from the person detained or his solicitor as to why detention should not continue. Code C 15.2A requires him to note any comment made if the decision is to keep the person in detention but not, it seems, if the decision is that he should be released. Written representations must be retained whatever the outcome (Code C 15.5). Code C 15.2A further states that the review officer should not put specific questions to the suspect regarding his involvement (or suspected involvement) in the offence, nor in respect of any comments he may make in response to the decision to keep him in detention. Such an exchange is likely to constitute an interview as defined by Code C 11.1A and require the safeguards associated with a formal interview (see paras 8.13-8.24, post).

Legality of detention

6.173 Challenges to decisions made by custody, review and authorising officers in respect of detention are rare. Unless the detention is justified it will be unlawful. In *R (on the application of Wiles) v Chief Constable of Hertfordshire* (2002) the decision of a superintendent to authorise further detention under s 42(1) PACE 1984 was subject to judicial review. The applicant was arrested for burglary at 13.18 on 6 February 2002 and subsequently for aggravated burglary when it was established that the victims were injured during the offence. The victims of the burglary were unable to speak English and the interpreter took their statements home during the evening intending to translate them and return the following day. It was suggested that the delay occasioned by the interpreter demonstrated the investigation was not being conducted diligently and expeditiously and therefore the authorisation of continued detention was unlawful. The court held that the police were entitled to ensure they had statements in English, the applicant was detained for a serious arrestable offence and the authorisation of continued detention was lawful. Where a defendant is charged with an offence outside the permitted period of police detention he can apply to have the proceedings stayed as an abuse of process (*DPP v Park* (2002)). For circumstances which might afford the basis for an action for false imprisonment see Clayton and Tomlinson, (2004) at p 233.

BAIL BY THE POLICE (s 47, Art 48)

6.174 Where a person is released on bail under this Part of the Act it is to be bail granted in accordance with ss 3, 3A, 5 and 5A of the Bail Act 1976 as they apply to bail granted by a constable, except that nothing in that Act shall prevent the re-arrest without warrant of a person, released on bail subject to a duty to attend at a police station, if new evidence justifying a further arrest has come to light since his release (s 47(1), (2)). This exception is necessary since the arrest powers under s 7 of the Bail Act 1976 (preserved by s 26(2) and Sch 2) would not permit re-arrest in such circumstances. (Note that art 48 is redrafted to incorporate provisions of art 130 of the Magistrates' Courts (Northern Ireland) Order 1981, which deals with bail (see s 27(1)(a) of the CJPOA 1994). The law is therefore similar on both sides of the water.) Section 47(1A), added by s 27 of the CJPOA 1994, provides that the normal powers to impose conditions of bail, which has the same meaning as in s 3(6) of the Bail Act 1976, shall be available to him where a custody officer releases a person on bail under s 38(1) (including that subsection as applied by s 40(10)) but not in any other case.

Definition of 'bail'

6.175 'Bail' is defined by s 47(3) as a reference to bail subject to a duty:
(a) to appear before a magistrates' court at such time and such place; or
(b) to attend at such police station at such time,
as the custody officer may appoint.

Bail after charge – ss 38(1), 40(10) and 47

6.176 Bail to a court will follow a charge. Section 38(1) places a mandatory duty on the custody officer to release a person arrested for an offence otherwise than under a warrant from police detention, either on bail or without bail, unless one of the conditions set out in that section applies to justify his detention after charge (see para 6.64, ante). This duty also arises when a person whose detention has been under review is charged (s 40(10)). It should be noted that there is no statutory presumption in favour of bail from a police station as there is in relation to bail from a magistrates' court, but s 38(1) comes close to providing a 'right to bail'. Prior to the CJPOA 1994 the custody officer's power to grant bail was not as flexible as those available to a court, who can impose a range of conditions. Apart from the usual condition that the person attend a court at the specified date and time, the most the police could do was require a surety or sureties. This meant that many applications for bail were made to a magistrates' court in circumstances in which the police would have granted bail if they could have imposed conditions. This meant unnecessary work for magistrates and an unnecessary court appearance for the accused. The Royal Commission on Criminal Justice, in its Report (Cm 2263, 1993), recognised this and recommended that the police be given the power to impose conditions on bail after charge. Section 27 of the CJPOA 1994 gives effect to this recommendation by amending s 47 of PACE 1984 and the Bail Act 1976.

6.177 Section 27(1) amends s 47(1) to provide that a release on bail under this Part of PACE 1984 shall be a release subject to ss 3, 3A (added by s 27 of the CJPOA 1994), 5 and 5A of the Bail Act 1976. This extends the provisions of the Bail Act, including the imposition of conditions, to police bail under s 47. A new sub-s (1A) is then added to s 47 which provides that:

> 'The normal powers to impose conditions of bail (which has the same meaning as in s 3(6) of the Bail Act 1976) shall be available to him where a custody officer releases a person on bail under s 38(1) (or s 40(1)) but not in any other case.'

6.178 Section 3A is added to the Bail Act. Section 3A(1) links up with the new s 47(1A) by stating that s 3 of the 1976 Act applies to bail granted by a custody officer under Part IV of PACE 1984 in cases where the normal powers to impose conditions are available to him. However, s 3A(5) requires that 'no conditions shall be imposed under s 3 of the Bail Act 1976 unless it appears to the custody officer that it is necessary to do so for the purposes of preventing the person from:

(a)   failing to surrender to custody; or

(b)   committing an offence while on bail; or

(c)   interfering with witnesses or otherwise obstructing the course of justice, whether in relation to himself or any other person'.

6.179   The law now is that a custody officer in releasing a person on police bail, in addition to imposing the standard condition that the person surrender to custody on the specified date and time, and requiring that person to provide a surety or sureties, may require him to comply, before release or at some point afterwards, with such requirements as appear to him to be necessary to secure the objectives (a) to (c) above.

6.180   The conditions which a custody officer may impose are similar to those which a court can impose except that he cannot:

(i)   impose a requirement that the person reside in a bail hostel; and

(ii)   order reports to be compiled on the person granted bail.

6.181   The conditions most frequently imposed by the courts are:

(a)   a condition of residence (that the person lives and sleeps at a specified address);

(b)   a condition that he notify any change of address to the police;

(c)   a condition that he report to a local police station at specified intervals;

(d)   a condition that he stays indoors during specified hours;

(e)   a condition that the person does not enter specified areas or places or that he does not go within a specified distance of a particular address;

(f)   a condition that the person is not to speak to the victim of the alleged offence or any possible witnesses, directly or indirectly;

(g)   a condition that he surrender his passport.

6.182   In *R v Mansfield Justices, ex p Sharkey* (1985) miners involved in the 1984-85 strike as flying pickets were remanded on bail to await trial on a charge of threatening behaviour resulting from mass picketing of pits in the East Midlands area. They were required as a condition of bail not to picket otherwise than at their own pit. The Divisional Court upheld the imposition of that condition because otherwise the defendants would have returned to the picket lines and, given that the picketing involved intimidation and threats, further offences might have been committed. The then Lord Chief Justice suggested that there must be a real, as opposed to a fanciful, risk of further offences being committed if unconditional bail was granted, but the belief need not be based on the substantial grounds necessary to refuse bail. Ex p Sharkey involved an imprisonable offence. In *R v Bournemouth Magistrates' Court, ex p Cross* (1988) D was arrested for an offence under s 5 of the Public Order Act 1986, a non-imprisonable offence, following a protest against a local hunt. He was bailed on condition that he did not attend another hunt meeting before his next appearance in court. He was arrested for breaching that condition. On an application for judicial review the Divisional Court held that the condition had been validly imposed. The justices had believed it was necessary to prevent the commission of further offences, and they were therefore entitled to impose the condition. Since there is effectively an appeal to a magistrates' court against the imposition of conditions (see below, para 6.176) custody officers may consider imposing similar conditions in appropriate cases. In both the above cases the need to act judicially was stressed. This applies to custody officers as much as to the magistrates; it would not therefore be appropriate to adopt policies of applying the same conditions in all similar cases. Each case must be considered on its merits.

6.183 It should be noted that s 25 of the Criminal Justice and Public Order Act 1994 provides that persons awaiting trial on a charge of murder, attempted murder, manslaughter, rape or attempted rape who have a previous conviction before a UK court for one of these offences for which they were sentenced to imprisonment (or if a juvenile, long-term detention) shall not be granted bail unless there are special circumstances. (Conviction includes a verdict of not guilty by reason of insanity, a finding of unfitness to plead, discharge or a probation order.) The offence together with the previous conviction will almost always provide grounds under s 38(1) for not bailing after charge, but in any event it follows that if a court cannot grant bail a custody officer cannot.

VARIATION OF CONDITIONS IMPOSED BY A CUSTODY OFFICER

6.184 Section 3(8) of the Bail Act 1976, as substituted by s 27(4) of the CJPOA 1994, provides that where a custody officer has granted bail in criminal proceedings he or another custody officer serving at the same police station may, at the request of the person to whom it was granted, vary the conditions of bail; and in doing so he may impose new conditions or, possibly with a view to deterring such requests, more onerous conditions. The custody officer can only impose new or more onerous conditions which appear to him to be necessary for the purpose of achieving the three objectives (a) to (c) set out above (s 3A(6)). The person granted bail subject to conditions, or whose conditions have been varied under s 3(8), may make application to a magistrates' court to vary the conditions (for the procedure see Rule 84A, Magistrates' Courts (Amendment) Rules 1995 (SI 1995/585 (L3)). The court may grant bail or vary the conditions and, also it seems with a view to deterring applicants, if it varies them it may impose more onerous conditions. On determining the application the court may remand the person, in custody or on bail and, where the court withholds bail or grants bail the grant of bail by the custody officer lapses (s 43B of the Magistrates' Courts Act 1980 as inserted by Sch 3, para 3 of the CJPOA 1994).

6.185 Section 5A of the Bail Act 1976 (inserted by Sch 3, para 2 of the CJPOA 1994) requires that a custody officer who imposes conditions in granting bail, or who varies any condition of bail or imposes conditions, shall with a view to enabling the person to request him or another custody officer, or making an application to a magistrates' court, give reasons for imposing the condition or varying it. A note of the reasons shall be made in the custody record and a copy of that note given to the person subject of the bail conditions (s 5A(4)).

6.186   Section 43(1) of the Magistrates' Courts Act 1980 (as substituted by s 47(8) of PACE 1984) provides that where a person is granted bail under PACE 1984 to appear before a magistrates' court, that court may appoint a later date for his appearance and enlarge the recognisances of any sureties for him. Section 43(2) of the 1980 Act, as substituted, provides that a recognisance of a surety in respect of such bail may be enforced as if it were a recognisance in respect of bail to a magistrates' court (see the Bail Act 1976).

Bail to return to a police station

6.187   Bail to return to a police station was, under s 43(2) of the Magistrates' Courts Act 1980, only possible when inquiries into the case could not be completed. Under the 1984 Act it continues to be possible to bail a person to return to a police station in such circumstances but it is also possible to bail a person to return to a police station when inquiries have been completed and there is sufficient evidence to charge but when there is some doubt either about the particular charge or whether to charge at all (see para 6.32, ante, for a mandatory duty to release on such bail). As suggested in para 6.51, ante, there will be cases which, applying national guidelines, may not be the subject of a prosecution, or which may be dealt with by a caution. Where the decision cannot be made at the time of the person's release, release on bail to return to a police station may be considered appropriate. Where bail has been granted and the decision is not to prosecute, the custody officer may then give notice in writing to the person that his attendance at the police station is not required (s 47(4)).

Renewed detention of person bailed to return to a police station

6.188   Where there is still insufficient evidence to charge the person on his return to the police station in answer to his bail but such evidence may be secured or preserved by his detention, or obtained by questioning during such detention, there is no need to re-arrest the person on his attendance. Section 37(1)(b) requires the custody officer to determine whether there is sufficient evidence to charge a person who returns to a police station to answer to bail. If there is not, the custody officer must release him, or, if there are reasonable grounds for believing that his detention without charge is necessary to secure or preserve evidence relating to the offence or to obtain it by questioning him, the custody officer may authorise his detention without charge (s 37(2) and (3)). Section 47(6) states that where a person who has been granted bail and either has attended at the police station in accordance with the grant of bail, or has been arrested under s 46A having failed to attend, is detained at a police station any previous period of police detention is to be included in calculating the period of police detention (see below, para 6.189).

**Arrest of a person who fails to attend having been bailed to return to a police station –
s 46A added by s 29(2) of the Criminal Justice and Public Order Act 1994**

6.189   Prior to the CJPOA 1994 it seemed that a person who had been arrested and
bailed to return to a police station but who failed to do so could only be arrested:
(a) if there was fresh evidence of his involvement in that offence; or
(b) if there continued to be reasonable cause to suspect that he was involved in the
offence and the original power of arrest continued in being.

6.190   Some doubt existed as to whether a person could, in effect, be arrested twice
for the same offence as (b) suggests but s 46A, which is added to PACE 1984 by the
CJPOA 1994, makes any discussion of the issue irrelevant by providing a clear power
to arrest without warrant a person who, having been released on bail subject to a duty
to attend at a police station, fails to attend at that police station (sub-s (1)). A person
arrested under this section shall be taken to the police station appointed as the place
at which he is to surrender as soon as practicable after the arrest. What is 'practicable'
in this context depends on where the person is arrested. By providing that the arrest
under sub-s (1) is an arrest for an offence (subject to the obligation in sub-s (2)) s
46A(3) makes it clear that the provision in sub-s (2) is separate from the obligation to
take a person to a police station as soon as practicable after the arrest as required by
s 30. If the person is arrested in the vicinity of the police station to which he was bailed
to return he can be taken directly there. The provisions of s 46A(2) and s 30 then
coincide. However, if he is arrested in Hull and the police station to which he was
bailed to return is in Sheffield, there are two separate obligations. The obligation under
s 30 is to take the person to a police station, usually the one from which the arresting
officer operates, as soon as practicable. It is not practicable for the arresting officer to
take him directly to Sheffield unless he has travelled from Sheffield to effect the arrest.
There is then the obligation under s 46A(2) to take him to the Sheffield police station
as soon as practicable. The person may have to spend some time in a police station in
Hull before being collected by police officers from Sheffield and yet still be taken to
Sheffield 'as soon as practicable'. There remains the question of the detention clock
as it applies to the person arrested for failure to answer police bail. He will have spent
some time in police detention following his arrest and before being bailed. Does the
detention clock start afresh or continue from the time he was bailed? The answer is
found in a combination of ss 34(7), 47(6) and (7) of PACE 1984, which are inserted or
amended by s 29 of the CJPOA 1994. Section 34(7) provides that an arrest under s 46A
shall be treated as an arrest for an offence, and the offence shall be the offence in
connection with which he was granted bail (it is not therefore a new offence and not an
arrest for the original offence because there is fresh evidence). Section 46(6) provides
that where a person who has been granted bail and either has attended at a police
station in accordance with the grant of bail or has been arrested under s 46A for failing
to do so, is detained at a police station (under s 37(2)), any time during which he was
in police detention prior to his being granted bail shall be included as part of any
period which falls to be calculated under this Part of this Act. In other words the clock
continues from the time at which D was bailed. Section 47(7) makes the opposite
provision where the person on bail is re-arrested because there is fresh evidence,

applying the provisions of this Part of this Act as they apply to a person arrested for the first time, but excluding an arrest under s 46A.

6.191   Article 7 of the Police (Amendment) (NI) Order 1995 adds a new art 47A to the 1989 Order to produce the same effect in Northern Ireland.

RE-ARREST OF PERSONS ON BAIL TO ATTEND A POLICE STATION

6.192   Sections 41(9), 42(11) and 43(19) (Arts 42(7), 43(10) and 44(18)) prohibit re-arrest for the offence for which the person was arrested and subsequently released under ss 41(7), 42(10) or 43(18) (Arts 42(5), 43(9) or 44(17)) unless there is new evidence which has come to light since that release. Section 47(2) (Art 48(10)) makes it clear that nothing in the Bail Act 1976 prevents re-arrests. Section 47(7) (Art 48(11)) states that when the re-arrest is of a person who was released on bail subject to a duty to attend at a police station, the provisions of this Part of this Act shall apply to him as they apply to a person arrested for the first time. Thus, if there is new evidence justifying a re-arrest and the person is re-arrested before the date he is to attend the police station, the custody officer must comply with all the duties and requirements relating to detention already considered. He must treat the arrest as any other arrest and determine whether there is sufficient evidence to charge; or, if there is, to charge the person, or release him on bail or without bail, unless there are grounds for detention without charge as set out in s 37(2) (Art 38(2)). If they exist he may authorise detention without charge under s 37(3) (Art 38(3)). All the duties in respect of persons detained then apply. However, unlike a person who attends a police station to answer to bail whose detention is renewed, or a person arrested under s 46A having failed to attend a police station to answer his bail, any previous detention on the first arrest does not count towards the period of detention on re-arrest. Since the re-arrest is to be treated as a fresh arrest, the person may be bailed to return to a police station once more if there is still insufficient evidence to charge and no grounds for detention without charge but further inquiries are necessary. On the other hand, there is no provision for further bailing a person who has been bailed to attend a police station and who complies with that duty unless his detention is renewed and he is to be released without charge after that detention.

RE-ARREST OF A PERSON RELEASED WITHOUT BAIL

6.193   The provisions for releasing a person arrested or arrested and detained, against whom there is insufficient, or no evidence, to charge, all provide for release on bail (which will be bail to a police station) or without bail. As we have seen, s 47(7) (Art 48(11)) (para 6.78) provides that re-arrest of a person on bail to a police station for the offence for which he is bailed, is to be treated as a fresh arrest. However, there is no similar provision in respect of a person who is released without bail, for example, when questioning exonerates him. If new evidence then comes to light which shows that the person was in fact involved in, or responsible for, the offence for which he has been arrested and released, he may be re-arrested. It is not clear whether this is to be considered as a fresh arrest, in which case previous detention does not count, or as a continuation of detention, in which case it does. In principle such previous detention ought to be counted, otherwise it gives the police two bites at the cherry. On the other hand, the same argument applies to the re-arrest of a person on bail and it would therefore appear that such an arrest will be treated as a fresh arrest. This may be justifiable where there is a considerable time gap between arrests but it could result in a person who is detained for, say, 36 hours, being released for lack of evidence or because he is exonerated, and within another 36 hours being re-arrested for the same offence on the discovery of new evidence. On this occasion, the full 96 hours' detention might be authorised, resulting in 132 hours of police detention in respect of that offence. The unfairness suggested must, however, be balanced by the alternative possibility that a person is arrested for a serious arrestable offence, detained for the full 96 hours and released for lack of evidence. If then new evidence justifying his re-arrest is discovered and the Act provided that previous detention for that offence had to be included in calculating the period of detention, there would be no point in arresting unless there was sufficient evidence to charge. Such a provision could seriously hamper investigations. That alone is sufficient to justify treating such a re-arrest as a fresh arrest. It is submitted that a senior officer who is asked to authorise continued detention, and a magistrates' court to whom an application for a warrant of further detention is made, should be made aware of any period of police detention in respect of the offence for which the person has been re-arrested and in respect of which authorised detention is sought.

WARRANTS ENDORSED FOR BAIL

6.194   Section 117 of the Magistrates' Courts Act 1980 provides that when magistrates issue a warrant of arrest they may grant the person bail by endorsing the warrant. In criminal proceedings the endorsement will state that the person is to be released on bail subject to a duty to appear before a magistrates' court at the specified time, and in non-criminal cases, that he is to be released on entering into a recognisance (with or without sureties) conditioned for his appearance before a magistrates' court at the specified time. Where a warrant is endorsed for bail on the person entering into a recognisance without sureties, it is not necessary to take him to a police station if he agrees to a recognisance. It could be effected literally on the doorstep but the previous law did not permit this sensible approach. Section 47(8) of PACE 1984 amended s 117(3) of the 1980 Act to permit 'doorstep bail' by providing that in such a case a person need not be taken to a police station, but, if he is, he shall be released on his entering into the recognisance (s 117(3)(a)). Section 117(3)(b) covers the situation in which the endorsement provides for bail with sureties which requires that the person be taken to a police station. (Article 48(12) amended art 129 of the Magistrates' Courts (NI) Order 1981 to produce the same effect in the province.)

DETENTION FOR INQUIRIES INTO OTHER OFFENCES

6.195   Section 128(7) of the Magistrates' Courts Act 1980 permitted a magistrates' court which had decided to remand a person in custody, to commit him to the custody of a constable for a period not exceeding three clear days. Though it was legally possible to remand a person arrested but not charged with an offence, the practice was to charge the person with one offence, a 'holding charge', and seek a remand in police custody to enable him to be questioned about more substantive offences. In some areas the remand to police custody was used to permit local solicitors to see their client before he went off to a remand prison many miles away. Both were permissible since no purpose was specified in the section. Section 48 amended s 128(7) to permit a magistrates' court which has decided to remand a person in custody after applying criteria laid down in the Bail Act 1976, to commit him to detention in a police station for a period not exceeding three clear days (ie three days must intervene between the day of the remand and the day the person is due to appear in court again). Section 128(8) then stipulates that:

(a) he shall be detained under sub-s (7) only if there is a need for such detention for the purpose of inquiries into other offences;

(b) he be brought back to the court which committed him as soon as that need ceases;

(c) he is to be treated as in police detention and s 39 of the 1984 Act applies to him; and

(d) his detention is subject to periodic review under s 40 of the 1984 Act.

6.196   Since this is a newly authorised period of detention, not a continuation of authorised detention, the first review will take place six hours after the court authorises detention and the second nine hours after that and thereafter at nine-hourly intervals. The review officer in this case should be the custody officer given that the suspect has been arrested and charged, s 40(1)(a) therefore applies. However, if one ignores this fact and looks only to the offences in regard to which he has been detained for further inquiries, he has not been charged with them, therefore s 40(1)(b) could apply and an inspector is the review officer. Every person remanded under s 128 of the MCA 1980 must have been charged with the offence for which he was arrested, though not, of course, with the other offences for which he is remanded in police custody. The review officer in these circumstances should hold the rank of Inspector or above and must determine whether the need to detain for further inquiries still exists. If it does not the detainee must be taken back before the magistrates' court which committed him (s 128(8)(b)). The practical effect of this section is that, to take the most extreme case, a person may be detained for 96 hours without charge, charged and detained in custody after charge under s 38(1) and (2) for 48 hours awaiting appearance before a magistrates' court. He is then committed by that court to police detention for inquiries into other offences and detained for the three clear days, giving an overall total of 216 hours' detention. The requirement under s 31 that the person in police detention be arrested for further offences which come to light during such detention will mean that this provision will be used to clear up offences which the person may have committed in the police area in which he is detained or elsewhere. There is no equivalent provision in Northern Ireland.

POLICE DETENTION TO COUNT TOWARDS ANY CUSTODIAL SENTENCE

6.197 The actual time spent in prison following a sentence of imprisonment is determined by the Home Secretary's power to release prisoners. For these purposes, in computing the length of a sentence, any time spent in custody before trial or sentence is included (s 67(1) of the Criminal Justice Act 1967; s 26 of the Treatment of Offenders Act (NI) 1968). Section 49 of the 1984 Act (Art 49) amended 67(1) (s 26) and extends it to include periods spent in police detention under the 1984 Act (1989 Order) and any detention under s 41 of the Terrorism Act 2000. (For the correct application of s 67 of the 1967 Act see *R v Governor of Styal Prison, ex p Mooney* (1995).)

RECORDS OF DETENTION (S 50, ART 50)

6.198 Section 50(1) (Art 50(1)) requires that each police force (the Chief Constable of the PSNI) keep written records of detention for more than 24 hours resulting in release without charge, and of warrants of further detention applied for, the result, the period spent in detention under each warrant, and the subsequent disposition of the person. Since on past evidence 95% of persons will be released before 24 hours have elapsed, records under s 50(1) (Art 50(1)) will relate to only a small percentage of detainees. Section 50(2) (Art 50(2)) requires that this minimal information be included in the annual report of the chief officer under s 12 of the Police Act 1964 (s 15(1) of the Police Act (NI) 1970) and in the annual report of the Commissioner of Police of the Metropolis. The information is also published in Home Office Statistical Bulletins quarterly and annually.

SAVINGS

6.199 Section 51 (Art 51) provides that the provisions in Part IV of PACE 1984 do not affect detention under the statutory authorities listed in that section. These relate to detention of illegal immigrants, persons excluded under terrorism provisions, absentees, deserters and the like (s 51(a), (b) and (c), art 51(a), (b) and (c)). Section 51(d) (Art 51(d)) emphasises that nothing in Part IV of the Act affects the right of a person to apply for a writ of habeas corpus or other prerogative remedy. However, the provisions in Part IV have meant that detention is lawfully permitted for longer periods than previously and those remedies are therefore less effective in securing the release of persons detained.

7 Treatment and questioning of persons in police detention

7.1 As Part IV of PACE recognises, the questioning of suspects by the police at police stations plays an important part in the detection of crime. It may produce a confession which then forms the kernel of the prosecution case (Research Study No 5 for the Royal Commission (1981) found that 50 per cent of defendants made a written or oral confession and that in about 20 per cent of cases a confession was regarded as critical to the success of the prosecution); it may lead to the discovery of evidence; it may produce confessions to other crimes and thus improve the detection rate of the police force; and in any event it is likely to save police time. Lest police powers of questioning be misused, the procedure for the treatment of those in detention assumes great importance. Part V of PACE and Order and three Codes of Practice are relevant to the procedures to be followed at police stations. Code C relating to the Detention, Treatment and Questioning of Persons by Police Officers is the most important and, unless otherwise indicated, references to 'Code' in this chapter are to that one. Code D deals with the Identification of Persons by Police Officers (see paras 7.89-7.184) and Code E with Tape Recording (see paras 8.80-8.91). In addition, there are several Home Office Circulars issued to all police forces as and when the need for guidance arises and each force has its own Standing Orders which supplement the foregoing. This and Chapter 8 trace the law and procedures to be applied to a person from the time of his arrival at a police station to the time of his departure or of him being charged. The 'normal' case is considered first before turning to some special categories (eg juveniles and the mentally ill). This chapter deals predominantly with the treatment of a suspect and Chapter 8 with his questioning, although inevitably there are overlaps.

7.2 The following preliminary points should be noted. First, Part V of PACE and the Code of Practice for the Detention, Treatment and Questioning of Persons by Police Officers (Code C), must be read together. Indeed, there are matters contained in the latter which are arguably of sufficient importance to have merited inclusion in the former (eg the duty to tell the detainee of his rights). Second, both documents must be read with ss 76 and 78 in mind (Arts 74 and 76). The former directs the trial court to exclude a confession which has been obtained by oppression or which is unreliable (see further Chapter 8). The latter empowers the court to exclude evidence if the court believes that its reception would have such an adverse effect on the fairness of the trial that it ought not to be admitted (see further paras 8.101–8.140 and 8.145–8.165). Case law reveals that the courts pay close attention to the Code when considering the sections. Third, the Code in part paraphrases the provisions of the Act, but in part also supplements them. It is thus important for copies of the Code to be readily available to those in detention and for police officers to be fully acquainted with its provisions. Fourth, the 'Annexes' are to be treated as part of the Code, whereas the 'Notes for Guidance' in the Code mean just that (Code C 1.3). Fifth, while the Code does not have the same force as a statute and courts need not follow it, the Code enshrines certain principles of fairness which the courts will apply even to those involved in the investigation of crime who are not bound by it. Sixth, the Act and the Code require that certain information be conveyed to the suspect (eg the grounds for detention, s 37(5), Art 38(5)). This duty does not arise if it is impossible to perform, eg where the suspect is violent or is in urgent need of medical attention. There are two general safeguards designed to protect the citizen's rights and to guarantee good police conduct, viz documentation and the supervisory role of the custody officer.

DOCUMENTATION

7.3   PACE and the Codes of Practice accepted the opinion of the Royal Commission that strict recording of what takes place between the police officer and citizen is a critical safeguard for both parties. Consequently, frequent provision is made for recording in writing the length and terms of a person's detention. Two records are used: a custody record which deals with the general conditions of detention; and a record which relates solely to the officer's interview of a suspect.

Custody records

7.4   As soon as practicable after being detained at a police station (by being arrested there or taken there under arrest), a person must be allotted a custody record and the grounds for his detention must be recorded in it. The custody officer assumes responsibility for completing the record fully, accurately and as soon as practicable (s 39 and Code C 2.1 and 2.3). If a senior officer's permission is required for any action (eg for the taking of a non-intimate sample under s 63), his name and rank should be recorded. If the suspect is moved to another police station, the custody record (or preferably a copy) goes with him and the time of and reason for the transfer must be recorded in it. This may be very important for calculating the 'relevant time' in relation to the permissible periods of detention, when D is arrested by police force A and held for some time before being transferred to force B (see para 6.108, ante). The time of the suspect's release must be recorded and this may also be crucial in determining whether the detention time limits have been observed. Indeed all entries into the custody record must be timed and signed. There are two exceptions to the requirement:

(a) in the case of enquiries linked to the investigation of terrorism, if the officer reasonably believes that recording their name might put them in danger (Code C 2.2, 2.6, 2.6A). This safeguard is to protect officers who are involved in investigations or arrests in serious organised crime cases when there is reliable information that they may come to harm;

(b) in the case of computerised records the entry must be timed and need not be signed but must contain the operator's identification (Code C 2.6).

7.5 If the suspect is required to sign the record but refuses, the fact and time of refusal must be recorded (Code C 2.7). Hence the custody record will be a critical document at trial if a dispute develops over D's treatment (especially if D was unrepresented at the station). A properly completed record will be strong evidence in any dispute about the admissibility of confessional evidence. Code C 2.4 A provides that a solicitor or appropriate adult must be permitted to consult the custody record of a person detained as soon as practicable after their arrival at a police station. At the end of detention, when the person is released or taken before a court, he or his lawyer should be given a copy of the custody record 'as soon as practicable', if he so requests (Code C 2.4). Although a custody record must contain a number of items, none is difficult to state and can be completed promptly. Consequently, if a person is taken before a court, there can be no excuse for not supplying a copy before the appearance. Many of those released from detention, on bail or otherwise, will not demand a copy (through ignorance or lack of interest). However, like stop and search records (s 3(7), (9), Art 5(8), (9)), a copy of a custody record is available for 12 months after the person has left police detention. The detained person, his legal representative or the appropriate adult must be allowed to inspect the original custody record after giving reasonable notice and a note of any such inspection must be made on the record (Code C 2.5). The shape and design of custody records vary between police forces but the required content is uniform.

Interview records

7.6 Most interviews at police stations with suspects are now tape-recorded and there are elaborate procedures governing the security of tapes so that an accurate record is available (see further paras 8.80-8.91). In addition the interviewing officer must note the formal details of the interview (time, date, etc) in his notebook (Code E 5.1). The notebook and tapes then represent the interview record. Interviews which are not taped must be written down in an interview record. This covers all non-taped interviews with suspects, for example, those conducted at a hospital or in a police car. The record must state the place, time and length of the interview, any breaks in it, the names of those present and, if different, the time when the record was made. For interviews outside a police station, an officer's pocketbook can be used; for those at a station, special record forms are used. Any 'significant statement' made by the suspect outside the formal police station interview must be put to him at the start of the formal interview so that it may be confirmed or denied (Code C 11.4). (As to what is a 'significant statement' see para 8.54, post.)

7.7 The record must be made simultaneously unless:

(a) it is impracticable to do so, eg through violence on the part of the suspect; or

(b) it 'would interfere with the conduct of the interview' (Code C 11.7(c)), eg the suspect is unlikely to be forthcoming if the officer produces a record form and begins formalities. This may be reasonable for the occasional, urgent interviews in the street but cannot, it is suggested, be a justifiable excuse for interviews in the already formal atmosphere of a police station.

7.8 The matters to be recorded are straightforward and officers should get into the habit of compiling an interview record simultaneously in all cases, especially since the interview may be challenged subsequently and a trial court asked to exclude a confession obtained during it (see further on interviews at paras 8.13–8.40).

CUSTODY OFFICER – CIVILIANS

7.9 The custody officer has already been described (see para 6.18); suffice it to say here that he is responsible for much of the documentation and is in overall charge of the reception, treatment and welfare of a suspect. He must carry out his duties under Code C without delay, but will not be in breach of the Code if any delay which does occur is justifiable and it can be shown that all reasonable steps had been taken to avoid such a delay. Where a delay does occur, the reasons for it must be recorded on the custody record (Code C 1.1A). At a busy station he or a junior officer will spend most of his time with an eye on the 'detention clock' to ensure that statutory procedures are followed in relation to each detainee. Moreover, the categories of persons who may be at the station add to the complexity facing him, viz:

(1) 'volunteers' (those helping the police but free to leave, see further paras 5.128– 5.131),

(2) those who have been arrested, detained but not charged,

(3) those charged but not bailed, and

(4) those in custody but not necessarily arrested for an offence (eg detained under Mental Health Act or Immigration Act powers).

7.10 Research (Maguire, 1988) suggests that the custody officer can process (eg prepare a custody record, search a person and record his property, arrange for legal advice) between three and four suspects per hour but that beyond that extra custody officers are needed or a queue will develop. But even this apparently modest suggestion presupposes that the cases are straightforward (eg there are no requirements for interpreters, a strip search, or medical help) and run smoothly (eg a solicitor can be contacted immediately) and that the custody officer is not also the operations sergeant and is called away to deal with those matters. On the other hand, the type of arrests (eg regular vagrants or drunks) can greatly quicken the number of suspects dealt with. In contrast, at non-designated stations the problem is to find a suitable officer to act as a custody officer. Given his position of responsibility, the custody officer must receive the suspect in strict accordance with PACE, and 'play it by the book'. This does not, however, necessitate heavy-handed formality. Indeed such an attitude will be inappropriate for most suspects. For the vulnerable suspect (eg an elderly shoplifter) the answer is for the custody officer to do his job humanely (eg allowing the suspect to sit, explaining why he has to fill in the forms, relying on a brief search of the suspect or no search at all).

INITIAL ACTION

7.11   Those who are detained at a designated police station (either by being taken there under arrest or by being arrested there) will appear before an appointed custody officer. The first decision for him to make is whether the person should be charged or released or detained with or without charge (see s 37 (Art 38) and para 6.17, ante). A custody record should be opened at once. The custody officer is required at this stage to complete an assessment as to whether the detainee is likely to present specific risks to custody staff or themselves (Code 3.5 and 3.6). If the person is charged, release on bail has to be considered. If he is detained, the custody officer must tell him the grounds for detention as soon as is practicable (see below). The custody officer's decision at this stage will be determined by the information given to him by the arresting/ investigating officer. Practice varies as to the extent of this exchange, some police forces strictly limiting conversation, others allowing a full account of the circumstances to be relayed to the custody officer. For him to reach a reasoned decision it is suggested that at least an outline of the circumstances of, and reasons for, the arrest be given him. There is an understandable temptation for the custody officer to ask the suspect questions such as 'did you do it?' or 'what have you got to say for yourself?', and in such ways begin a conversation with him which quickly becomes an improper interview. This not only compromises his independence but may also prejudice the investigation by leading to the exclusion of any evidence thus obtained. Previous codes were silent on the subject, but now see Code C 3.4 and Code C 11.1A 11.13 where such an exchange could constitute an interview. The custody officer shall note any comment made by the person in relation to the arresting officer's account, but shall not invite comment. Having authorised detention and informed the person of the grounds, the custody officer must note any reply but, again, shall not invite comment. No specific questions should be put to the suspect regarding his involvement in the offence, nor in response to any comment made in response to the arresting officer's account or the decision to detain him lest it develop into an improper interview. (See *R v Absolam* (1988) and *R v Oransaye* (1993) and the discussion at para 8.28, post.) If D volunteers information or makes a relevant unsolicited remark to the custody officer, it should be noted in the custody record and D asked to read and sign it (Code 11.13). A similar prohibition on asking specific questions regarding involvement in the offence applies to the custody officer as a review officer, and to an inspector acting as review officer (Code C 15.2A).

7.12   Either from what another officer tells him or from his own observation, the custody officer will have at this stage to consider whether the person falls into one of the categories for which separate provision is made, ie whether an interpreter has to be called because of the person's language difficulties or deafness, or whether an 'appropriate adult' has to be called to witness the interviewing of a juvenile or the mentally ill or handicapped or whether medical assistance has to be summoned (see paras 7.247–7.267 for discussion of these groups). The investigating officer may decide instead to question such a person at once and in the absence of the third party. In that case, the permission of a more senior officer (superintendent or above) must be obtained (Code C and 11.5, Annex C; see para 8.08, ante). Given the serious evidential consequences (see paras 8.131, 8.141 and 8.153) which can flow from a person in one of these special categories being improperly treated, the vigilance of the custody officer in spotting them cannot be overstated.

7.13   The 2003 Code includes a number of additional requirements to ensure the welfare of the detainee and to assess risks to themselves or custody staff. Code 3.5 requires the custody officer to determine whether the detainee 'is or might be in need of medical treatment or attention' and to record the determination in the custody record. At this stage the custody officer must initiate a structured risk assessment process. The Code (3.6) makes it clear that this is primarily the custody officers' responsibility although it may be necessary to consult and involve others such as the arresting officer or health care professionals. It is also suggested that important information can be garnered from relatives of the detainee and from police records. There is also a requirement to check the Police National Computer as soon as practicable in order to highlight any risks. Risk assessment is an ongoing process which must be reviewed, it must be fully recorded in the custody record and the custody officer must ensure that all those who come into contact with the detainee are informed about specific risks. Home office circular 23/2000 provides more detailed guidance on risk assessment and identifies specific risk areas which should always be considered.

7.14   If the custody officer authorised the detention of the person, he must tell him (or the 'appropriate adult' where relevant, see paras 7.248–7.250, post) of the following matters (Code C 3.1-4):
(i)   his right to inform a third party of his detention (see para 7.48);
(ii)   his right to private legal advice (see para 7.56);
(iii)   his right to consult the Codes of Practice;
(iv)   his right, if a foreigner, to inform his diplomatic representatives (see paras 7.277);
(v)   if the suspect is to be detained, the grounds for the detention.

7.15   The custody officer will not be in a position to authorise detention until he has heard from the investigating officer. Once he is ready, however, he must inform the suspect as soon as practicable and note the grounds in the custody record (s 37(4), (5), Art 38(4), (5)). So, if, for example, D is arrested and taken in a drunk or violent state to a police station and the custody officer decides to authorise detention, D must be told of the grounds for detention after he comes to his senses and before questioning begins. In any event the grounds must be communicated before a suspect is questioned.

7.16   Items (i) to (iii) (and by implication (iv) and (v)) must be conveyed 'clearly' to the suspect (Code C 3.1). This is aimed at avoiding the mumbled or rapid reading of rights which can mean little to the individual. It also assists the custody officer in gauging whether the suspect falls within one of the special groups (eg a foreign citizen, the deaf). In addition the person must be given a written notice setting out the rights (i), (ii) and (iii) above, the right to a copy of the custody record on leaving police detention or being taken before a court, and an explanation of the arrangements for obtaining legal advice. An additional written notice must be given explaining the suspect's Code entitlements while in custody (see Note 3A for an outline of the content) translated into Welsh, the main ethnic minority languages and principal European languages whenever they are likely to be helpful (Note 3B).

7.17   If the suspect is not in a position to comprehend the rights (eg he is drunk, ill or violent), they must be repeated when he is (Code C 1.8). Code 3.1 further requires the officer to tell him that 'they are continuing rights which may be exercised at any stage during the period in custody'.

7.18   As will be seen, items (i) and (ii) can be delayed by a senior officer in certain circumstances for up to 36 hours (see paras 7.35 and 7.65), but this does not absolve the custody officer from the duty of telling D of his rights at the outset. The suspect is asked to acknowledge receipt of the above notices by signing the custody record and, if he refuses, the custody officer must note the refusal on the record (Code C 3.2). If an interpreter is needed, he will be used to convey the foregoing information. If D is blind or unable to read (eg illiterate, dyslexic), the written notices are useless (there is no requirement that copies in Braille are available) and the custody officer must instead ensure that a third party is 'available to help in checking any documentation' (Code C 3.12). Liberally interpreted this should require a third party's early presence so as to read the notices to D. The most appropriate person is a solicitor. Indeed, a further and crucial matter at this initial stage is for the custody officer to ask D to sign on the custody record whether he wants legal advice (Code 3.5). As will be seen, the way in which this question is put can significantly affect D's answer (see further on legal advice, para 7.58).

7.19   The reading of rights and the provision of written notices, if properly done (and this includes allowing D sufficient time to digest the information), offer considerable protection to the suspect. On the other hand, research has frequently shown (eg Sanders et al, 1989, in relation to legal advice, see para 7.60) that the fact that a person is told of his rights by no means indicates that he will exercise them.

SEARCH OF THE PERSON AT A POLICE STATION (ss 53-55 OF PACE, Arts 54-56, CODE C 4, ANNEX A)

7.20   Powers to search a person who has been arrested and who is in detention at a police station are provided by s 54 of PACE (Art 55). Intimate search powers are provided by s 55 (Art 56) and these sections contain all the powers to search persons in police detention, all previous powers of a constable to conduct such searches being abolished by s 53 (Art 54). Very occasionally a person who has been stopped under s 1 (Art 3) will be taken to a police station 'nearby' (s 2(8), Art 4(9)) in order to be searched. Since he is not under arrest a search cannot be undertaken under s 54 (Art 55) (below) and, it is submitted, in the absence of a specific power to carry out a search beyond that permitted by s 1, as limited by s 2(9), any more extensive search is unlawful (see para 3.47, ante). Clearly an intimate search cannot be carried out in such circumstances; such a search can only be carried out on persons in police detention and must be authorised by a superintendent (s 55, Art 56 and Code C, Annex A(A)). The vast majority of searches of those arrested at, or brought to a police station under arrest will be carried out under s 54 (Art 55). One may note that this section is not limited to those in police detention as defined by s 118 of PACE (Art 2(3)) which only applies to persons arrested for an offence. Thus a person arrested under s 136 of the Mental Health Act 1983 may be searched under s 54 (Art 55). A distinction is drawn between intimate and non-intimate searches. The former is defined as a search consisting of 'the physical examination of a person's body orifices other than the mouth' (s 65, Art 2(2)), and is governed by s 55 (Art 56) and Code C, Annex A(A). A 'body orifice' covers the ears, nose, rectum and vagina. A non-intimate search covers all other types of search from a 'pat down' to a strip search, including a search of the mouth, and is governed by s 54 (Art 55) and Code C, Annex A(B).

Non-intimate searches (s 54, Art 55, Code C, Annex A(B))

7.21   The section applies to persons:
(a)   brought to a police station under arrest;
(b)   arrested at a police station;
(c)   detained at a police station having been arrested and bailed to return to the police station and, having done so, who is by virtue of s 34(7) to be treated as having been arrested for the offence in connection with which he was bailed;
(d)   committed to custody in a police station by an order or sentence of the court.
(Section 54 as amended by the CJPOA 1994, s 168(2), Sch 10, para 55, Art 55.)

7.22   Three purposes may lie behind the search of such persons:
(a)   to discover evidence of the offence for which the person was arrested or of other offences;
(b)   to compile a written record of the person's possessions so as to avoid any subsequent allegations of planting of evidence by the police or of misappropriation of property;
(c)   to remove articles with which the person may cause injury to others or to himself or with which he may effect an escape. (This is a particularly important precaution, given the possibility that a person in detention may seek to take his own life, and the concern and adverse publicity which such deaths can cause.)

Search examination to ascertain identity: s 54A (Art 55A)

7.23   Section 90(1) of the Anti-Terrorism, Crime and Security Act 2001 adds s 54A (Art 55A) which creates a power to search or examine the arrested person in order to identify him. An officer of at least the rank of inspector may give an authorisation orally or in writing if an arrested person has refused to identify himself or the officer has reasonable grounds for suspecting that the person is not who he claims to be. Where authorisation is given orally it must be confirmed in writing as soon as is practicable. The purpose of the examination is to determine whether he has 'any mark' (this would include a tattoo, birthmark, injury etc) that would either help to identify him as a person involved in the commission of an offence or would establish his true identity (s 54A(1), Art 55A(1)). The search or examination may be conducted without consent if the person refuses to give it or it is not practicable to get consent (ie if the person is under the influence of drink or drugs) (sub-s (2)). A photograph or visual representation of any mark may be taken for the purposes of carrying out the search or examination. Reasonable force (s 17) may be used if it is necessary, but the representation may only be retained for the purpose for which it was taken. The person conducting the search or examination and taking the photograph must be of the same sex as the arrested person.

7.24 It should be noted that a search may, and often will, take place before the decision to release or detain the person under s 37 (Art 38) is taken.

Power to search

7.25 Searches of arrested persons at police stations are undertaken in order to discover what the suspect has with him both on arrival at the station and during the period of his detention (for search of the person after arrest and before arrival at a police station, see s 32 (Art 34) and para 5.79, ante). Articles discovered may then be seized and retained in certain circumstances. Thus, the custody officer is under a duty to ascertain everything which persons listed in (a) to (d) above have in their possession. Since s 54(1)(a) and (b) (Art 55) is not confined to persons arrested for an offence, a person arrested under s 135 or s 136 of the Mental Health Act 1983 may be searched. The power of search is available at any time during D's detention (eg after he has been visited, after he has been in a public area of the station) but he can only be searched a second time for articles with which he can cause harm or his escape (s 54(6A), added by the Criminal Justice Act 1988, Art 55(7) of the NI Order). The tasks of seizing and recording articles can be delegated (s 54(1), (3), Art 55(1)(3)), but the section requires the custody officer personally to 'ascertain' the articles. It may seem unrealistic to expect such an officer, who will have many other duties, to ascertain the possessions of each arrested person (eg where a large number of arrested football supporters reach the police station). On the other hand, the custody officer does bring a measure of independence to the investigation and occupies a close supervisory role. Consequently, he decides whether the suspect should be searched (s 54(6), Art 55(6)); if so, the extent of the search (s 54(6), Art 55(6)); and what articles may be seized and retained (s 54(3), (4), Art 55(3), (4)); and he is responsible for the safe-keeping of any seized articles (Code C 4.1).

7.26 In the majority of cases the arrested person will voluntarily turn out his pockets. For those who refuse, reasonable force can be used at the instruction of the custody officer (s 117, Art 88). The custody officer must then decide whether the person should be searched more thoroughly. Since he may know little about the suspect and since it is difficult to predict accurately a person's reaction to custody, for example, the danger he may pose to himself or others unless searched, s 54(6) (Art 55(6)) errs on the side of caution by leaving it to the judgment of the custody officer as to:

(a) whether the person should be searched – thus, any of the purposes behind a search, mentioned in para 7.22, ante, can be fulfilled;

(b) the extent of a search – this is left to his discretion and can vary from the emptying of pockets to a frisking or to a strip search (but not an intimate search for which s 55 (Art 56) applies and the authorisation of a more senior officer is needed, see para 7.35, post).

7.27   This lack of specificity in the statute allows considerable scope for police force standing orders to spell out when the custody officer should act, eg that 'all suspects shall be searched' as a matter of routine. But it has been decided that the rationale behind *Brazil v Chief Constable of Surrey* (1983) still applies, ie the officer cannot search automatically but has to consider each case on its merits (*Sheehan v Metropolitan Police Comr* (1990)). Code C suggests that where D will only be detained for a short time and not placed in a cell, a search may be unnecessary as opposed to the case where it is clear that 'the custody officer will have continuing duties in relation to that person or where that person's behaviour or offence makes an inventory appropriate' (Code C Note 4A). Whether he searches or not, it is still the statutory duty (s 54(1), Art 55(1)) of the custody officer to ascertain the detainee's possessions, and it is clearly the custody officer's decision in the final analysis as to whether a search is necessary in the particular circumstances. This may arise from the nature of the offence involved and hence the ease of concealment of evidence (eg drugs); the reaction and demeanour of the detained person when asked to empty his pockets (eg a fearful elderly woman arrested for shoplifting should not be searched); the custody officer's knowledge of the detained person (eg a well-known thief specialising in credit cards).

Strip searches

7.28   There is a danger that this discretion to search could be used to order a strip search (ie the removal of more than outer clothing, Code C, Annex A(B) 9) so as to humiliate and oppress the detained person. Three safeguards operate. First, Code C, Annex A(B) 10, makes it clear that a strip search is only allowed if the custody officer considers it to be necessary in order to seize an article which a person is not allowed to keep (eg weapons, evidence of an offence; see the grounds for seizure in s 54(4) (Art 55(5)), discussed below) and he reasonably considers that the person might have concealed such an article. Second, and more important, the custody officer is independent of the investigating officers. Much rests upon his integrity and good sense. Third, his decision, though subjective, must still be taken in good faith. Thus, a strip search undertaken mala fides, for example, 'for the fun of it' or to frighten the suspect, would be unlawful and a trespass to the person. Quite apart from risking a complaint or civil action, such misbehaviour might well persuade a trial judge to exclude evidence under s 76 and/or s 78 (Arts 74, 76). Crucially, the reasons for ordering a strip search and the result of it must be recorded in writing (Code C, Annex A(B)12).

7.29 A strip search must be carried out in accordance with Annex A(B). This requires that it must be carried out by a person of the same sex and out of sight of any persons who do not need to be present, particularly persons of the opposite sex unless an appropriate adult specifically requested by the person being searched. Except in an emergency where there is a risk of serious harm to the person detained or others, and the strip search involves the exposure of intimate parts of the body, at least two persons must be present other than the person being searched. If a juvenile or mentally disordered person, one of those must be the appropriate adult. A search of a juvenile, except in urgent cases mentioned above, must always take place in the presence of an appropriate adult unless the juvenile prefers the search to be done in his/her absence and the appropriate adult agrees. A record must be made of that decision and signed by the appropriate adult. The presence of more than two people, other than the appropriate adult, shall be permitted only in the most exceptional circumstances (eg violent resistance by the person to be searched). The search must be carried out with proper regard for the sensitivity and vulnerability of the person and though this is a power which may be carried out using reasonable force (s 117, Art 88) every effort should be made to obtain co-operation and thus minimise embarrassment. The person should not be required to remove all their clothes at the same time, thus upper garments should be replaced before lower garments are removed. The search should be conducted as quickly as possible and the person allowed to dress as soon as it is over. Where necessary the person may be required to raise their arms or stand with legs astride and to bend forward to enable a visual examination of the genital areas but no physical contact should be made with body orifices other than the mouth. If any articles are found within a body orifice other than the mouth the person should be asked to hand them over. If he/she refuses no attempt should be made to remove them but permission should be sought to conduct an intimate search under s 55 (Art 56).

The ordinary non-intimate search

7.30 An ordinary non-intimate search under s 54 must be carried out by a constable (s 54(8), Art 55(11)) of the same sex as the person to be searched (s 54(9), Art 55(12)). Reasonable force may be used if necessary (s 117, Art 88), but the custody officer should be alert to the dangers of excessive force being used. Circumstances will vary considerably as to the extent of the search. For a person arrested for theft of radios, a 'pat down' and examination of pockets and wallets should suffice. Indeed, the suspect will often co-operate by producing articles and obviating the need for a search. For a suspected drug-pusher, on the other hand, a strip search is likely to be required and the possibility of an intimate search (see para 7.34, post) should be considered.

Seizure

7.31   Any articles produced by the suspect or discovered during a search may be seized and retained by the custody officer or at his direction (s 54(3), Art 55(3)). The only potential limitation concerns clothing and personal effects. These can only be seized if the custody officer believes that any of the criteria in s 54(4) (Art 55(4)) are satisfied. Thus, they cannot be seized for an ulterior purpose such as to punish the person (for example, by seizure of his glasses). The reasons for any seizure must be explained to D and should be noted in the custody record (Code C 4.2, 4.5). 'Personal effects' are not defined but may well be delimited by force standing orders. They can include a handkerchief, comb, watch, spectacles, keys and cosmetics. It will be noted that all such items may readily be seized under s 54, eg bootlaces, belts (sub-s (4)(e)(a)); heavy boots, a cigarette lighter (sub-s (4)(a)(ii)); clothing which may be of forensic value (sub-s 4(a)(iii)); keys, sharpened comb (sub-s (4)(e)(a)(iv)); a handkerchief for traces of drugs (sub-s (4)(b)). Although injury may be self-inflicted by the glass component, it is submitted that watches and spectacles ought not in principle to be seized (unless the custody officer has grounds to suspect their misuse). The former are especially important for the detained person in view of the time limits imposed on his detention by Part IV of PACE and the periodic reviews of detention which the police must conduct (see paras 6.157–6.165), whilst the latter enable him to read the notices of rights which he has been given. Code C 4.3 excludes 'cash and other items of value' (eg jewellery) from personal effects, on the basis of self-protection for the police against allegations that such property has been misappropriated. This does not mean that a wedding or other ring or small earrings have to be seized. Their existence can simply be noted in the custody record. On the other hand, the volume of suspects may mean that the accurate recording of jewellery is impracticable.

7.32   Two clear qualifications apply to the power of seizure. First, items which the constable has reasonable grounds to believe are subject to legal privilege cannot be seized (s 19(6), Art 21(6)). Second, one aspect of the common law (*Brazil v Chief Constable of Surrey* (1983)) is retained by s 54(5) (Art 55(5)), viz a detained person shall be told the reason for the seizure unless this is impracticable because he is violent or unable to understand it. The ratio of *Christie v Leachinsky* (1947), in relation to arrest, is thus relevant for the seizure of property.

Post-search

7.33   A custody record must be kept of what the person had with him when he arrived at the police station under arrest or when he was arrested there. This includes the recording of property which has been seized (under s 32, Art 34) by the arresting officer away from the police station (Code C 4.4). The purpose and extent of the search need not be recorded unless a strip search is undertaken. Then, the custody officer must record the reason for it and its results (Code C, Annex A(B) 8). The detained person 'shall be allowed' to check and sign the record of what has been seized (Code C 4.4). This implies that he will do so only if he asks to see the record, but it is wise practice for the custody officer always to request the detained person to sign the record. If he refuses, a note of that refusal should be made. Items seized under s 54 (Art 55) can be retained for 'so long as is necessary' (s 22(1), Art 24(1)) eg as evidence, for forensic purposes, or to prevent injury (see the illustrations in s 22(2) and (3), Art 24(2), (3)). Details of the property seized must be given to the magistrates' court when the case comes before it (s 48 of the Magistrates' Courts Act 1980). The court may order the return of all or part of the property to the accused if this is in the interests of justice and his safe custody. Ideally the custody record should also note what property was retained by the suspect, what property was kept by the police, and whether property was subsequently taken from, or given to, the suspect during his detention. In other words it should be a complete history of what has happened to the suspect's property during his stay at the station. If another officer has searched him, then the custody record should bear three signatures – the suspect, the searching officer and the custody officer.

Intimate search (s 55, Art 56, Code C, Annex A(A))

7.34 An intimate search, as opposed to a strip search, means 'a search which consists of a physical examination of a person's body orifices other than the mouth', ie the ears, nose, rectum and vagina (s 65 of PACE as amended by s 59(1) of the CJPOA 1994). The pre-conditions are understandably stricter than those adopted in s 54 (Art 55) for non-intimate searches and the criterion of reasonableness is specifically adopted.

The power

7.35 Unlike the search power under s 54 (Art 55) an intimate search can only be made of a person who has been arrested and is in police detention. If, and only if, the detention of the arrested person is authorised by the custody officer, an officer of at least Inspector rank can authorise an intimate search if he has reasonable grounds to believe that:
(a) the detained person may have concealed articles which could be used to injure himself or others; or
(b) the detained person may have concealed Class A drugs with the intention of supplying those drugs to others or of exporting them.

7.36 The previous authority level was superintendent, but this was reduced to inspector by s 79 of the Criminal Justice and Police Act 2001. Code C Annex A note A5 states that where an authorising officer has doubts about authorising an intimate search by a constable he should seek advice from a superintendent or above.

7.37 The powers of Customs and Excise to undertake an intimate search for evidential purposes (s 164 of the Customs and Excise Management Act 1979) are not affected by s 55, but a statutory order (1985) has conferred on Customs and Excise the protective power of s 55(1)(a), ie allowed Customs to search additionally for weapons. Intimate searches are not regular occurrences (eg only 172 were recorded in England and Wales in 2002-03). Of these 91% were for drugs. In 61 cases Class A drugs were found and in two cases a harmful article was found.(Ayres, Murray and Fiti (2003)).

7.38   The articles in s 55(1)(a) (Art 56(1)(a)) range from a penknife to poison. As to s 55(1)(b) (Art 56(1)(b)), Class A drugs are listed in Sch 2 to the Misuse of Drugs Act 1971. Although heroin is the primary target, the list includes 85 different drugs. Less dangerous drugs in Classes B and C of the 1971 Act cannot therefore be the object of an intimate search. They include amphetamine, cannabis and Codeine. A further limitation to s 55(1)(b) is that the officer must believe that the person is carrying the drugs with the intention of supplying them to others and not merely for his own use (s 55(17), Art 56(17)). The target is the drug-dealer. At first sight this imposes a stiff burden on the officer, but in reality, if he has sufficient belief that the person is carrying drugs, he should readily and often reasonably be able to infer the necessary intent, even if the person protests that he has drugs but that they are only for his personal use. It follows from s 55 (Art 56) that an intimate search for other evidence (eg jewels or money) cannot be authorised. The Government's view was that the repugnant nature of these searches outweighed the evidential value of seized items. However, if the senior officer can find reasonable grounds to believe the presence of weapons or drugs and then authorises a search, any articles which are evidence of a crime and which are discovered by the search can be seized (s 55(12), Art 56(12)).

7.39   The objective standard prior to an intimate search requires material from which an impartial third party would be satisfied that the person has drugs or weapons concealed. There will rarely be any external evidence giving rise to such a belief, though a person's speech may be affected by articles in the mouth or his manner of walking by articles hidden in the rectum. The fact that the person who is arrested for possession of drugs has used such form of concealment previously, together with good information that he is in possession of drugs which have not been found by a normal search, would ground a reasonable belief that an intimate search is necessary. Information from a credible source might also provide the basis for such a belief. For example, D's girlfriend states that she assisted D by inserting drugs into his rectum. A further possibility is that during a strip search body orifices can be visually examined. If an object is seen, that may provide the reasonable grounds to believe that an intimate search is necessary. It must, of course, be borne in mind that during the menstruation period a woman may use tampons, but that these may also be used to conceal drugs or weapons. In such cases, the woman should be asked to remove them and replacements made available to her. An intrusive search would then be necessary only if she refused to do so and if there are reasonable grounds to believe that drugs or weapons are concealed. Such a case will be exceptional and the figures above suggest that the power is being used sparingly.

7.40   Further qualifications to the use of intimate searches are that the senior officer must reasonably believe that the article cannot be found without an intimate search (s 55(2), Annex A para 2, Art 56(2)). In some cases the detained person will produce the article voluntarily. In all cases, the person should be asked to do so, for only on refusal does the coercive power become necessary. Furthermore, the person must be told the reason for the intimate search.

Procedure

7.41 Given the intrusive nature of an intimate search, it is suggested that D be reminded of his right to legal advice. If he requests it and a lawyer is readily available, the search should be delayed until he arrives for otherwise the purpose of the reminder is defeated. If the lawyer is delayed the search can proceed but only, it is suggested, where speed is essential. The reminder need not be given in those rare cases where legal advice can be lawfully delayed under s 58(6) (Art 59(8), see para 7.65, post). The authorisation for an intimate search under s 55 (Art 56) may be given orally (eg by telephone) but it must be confirmed in writing (s 55(3), Art 56(3)). Drug offence searches must not take place at a police station (s 55(9), Art 56(9)) but at medical premises and can only be performed by a registered medical practitioner or a registered nurse (some midwives will qualify) (s 55(17), Art 56(17)). Protective searches (ie to search for weapons) can take place at a police station and a constable can be authorised by an officer of at least superintendent rank to act if it is impracticable to obtain someone else (s 55(5), (6), Art 56(5), (6)), for example, where no doctor is available and speed is imperative, or the medical practitioner who is called refuses to carry out the search. The reason for such authorisation must be recorded (Code C, Annex A(A) 8).

7.42 Section 55 (Art 56) allows medical practitioners and nurses to make an intimate search but does not compel them to do so. The British Medical Association has issued guidelines advising the profession that searches can be ethically undertaken for protective purposes and to discover heroin (but other Class A drugs are not mentioned). The Royal College of Midwives, on the other hand, has expressed reservations. Many midwives are also registered nurses and can in principle act. One of the 1,500-2,000 police surgeons is likely to be the first choice when an intimate search is authorised but a number of them consider intimate searches to be unethical and an assault and will not carry them out. If this is so, the police will then try a medical practitioner or nurse whom they know to be willing to conduct these searches. Given the availability of these 'suitably qualified persons' (s 55(17), Art 56(17)), it should be rare for a constable to be used (in 1991 and 1992 all searches were conducted by suitably qualified persons). Code 3A of C, Annex A is inserted into the 2003 Code and states that an intimate search carried out by anyone other than a registered medical practitioner or registered nurse must only be carried out as a last resort and when the authorising officer is satisfied the risks associated with obtaining the item to remain within the detainee outweigh the risks associated with removing it. The authorising officer must make every reasonable effort to persuade the detainee to hand the article over without a search and if he does authorise the search must make every reasonable effort to persuade the detainee to allow the medical professional to conduct the search. Speed in the context of protective searches is the most likely exceptional case. Where it does arise, it would be good police practice for each designated police station to select a number of police officers, of both sexes, to perform these searches and to ensure that they are trained to perform them without causing physical injury to the detained person. This is most important for, whilst reasonable force may be used by a constable (s 117, Art 88), injury can easily be caused during an intimate search and a civil action based on the use of unreasonable force could well follow. It can also be noted that s 117 (Art 88) only applies to a constable who is exercising a coercive power. It can therefore be argued that when, in the majority of cases, 'a suitably qualified person' is conducting the intimate search, s 117 (Art 88) does not authorise the use of reasonable force to enable him or her to carry it out. Since the constable is not exercising the coercive power, s 117 (Art 88) is equally inapplicable to him. An alternative argument is that the 'suitably qualified person' is acting as the agent of the constable in carrying out the intimate search, therefore s 117 (Art 88) is applicable. However, in the absence of a judicial decision supporting the latter argument the 'suitably qualified person' is exposed to the risk of civil action if he/she uses force, albeit reasonable force, to carry out the intimate search and would be well advised not to carry out the search if it can only be done with the use of force. A possible alternative to the threat of force is the decision in *R v Smith* (1985), which decided that refusal to supply a sample of hair could in the circumstances be capable of amounting to corroborative evidence (see s 62(10), Art 63(10) for a statutory provision where an intimate sample is refused). A refusal to agree to an intimate search could be regarded as analogous.

7.43 The person to be searched must be told beforehand the reason for it (Code C, Annex A(A) 2). The constable and any other person in attendance (eg lawyer or interpreter) should be of the same sex as the detained person and no unnecessary person should be present (Code C, Annex A(A) 6). The person qualified to carry out the search (except a constable searching for an article which could cause physical injury (Code C, Annex A(A) 6) need not be of the same sex, but the senior officer should be alert to religious and cultural objections which a detained person may have to a search by a doctor of the opposite sex. In the case of juveniles and the mentally disordered, the search may take place only in the presence of an appropriate adult of the same sex, unless D specifically requests the presence of an adult of the opposite sex, who is readily available. As regards a juvenile, a search can take place in the absence of an appropriate adult but only if the juvenile signifies in the presence of an appropriate adult and the adult agrees. A record shall be made of the decision and signed by the appropriate adult (Code C, Annex A(A) 5). No special provision is made for those with physical disabilities, but the special difficulties which they can create for the detained person and officer argue strongly for the sole use of a medical practitioner.

Seizure

7.44 The types of weapon which may be concealed in a body orifice include a penknife in the mouth, a wrapped razor blade concealed in the vagina, a detonator or radio transmitter designed to detonate explosives elsewhere concealed in the rectum (the objects of physical injury envisaged by s 55, Art 56 need not be to persons in the police station), and a phial of poison concealed in the nose. Whilst the purpose of s 55(1)(a), Art 56(1)(a) is to prevent physical harm, other articles discovered during an intimate search may be seized and retained for other purposes (s 55(12), Art 56(12)), eg as evidence of an offence or to prevent interference with evidence. For example, D threatens violence. He spits out a penknife, and says 'I'll still cut my throat'. It is decided to carry out an intimate search. A razor blade wrapped in foil is discovered and it may be seized. Intimate searches for drugs naturally fall under s 55(1)(b) (Art 56(1)(b)), but can also fall within s 55(1)(a) (Art 56(1)(a)) – a packet of heroin concealed in the vagina may come apart and if ingested give the carrier a fatal overdose. As with s 55(1)(a) (Art 55(1)(a)), if Class B or C drugs are discovered during a search for Class A, they can be seized and used at trial.

7.45 If a person is known, or suspected, to have swallowed articles (eg a ring), the police have no power to order an X-ray of the person. Although technically the radiographic examination is not an assault, force, in the absence of consent, would be needed to conduct it and that cannot be justified by PACE. In this situation the only solution for the police is to find a basis for detaining the person and to let 'nature take its course'. The need to secure this evidence would justify detention under PACE (ss 37(2), 42(1) or 43(4), Arts 38(2), 43(1), 44(4)).

7.46 The detained person must be told the reason for the seizure of any articles unless he is violent, likely to become so or incapable of understanding (s 55(13), Art 56(13)). The phrase 'likely to become violent' appears in other parts of PACE (eg ss 37(6), 38(5), Arts 38(6), 39(5)). It clearly applies when the person has already reacted violently to the police, but in the context of s 55 (Art 56) it may also cover the situation where the person is evidently indignant over the proposed search and further details of it are likely to provoke him to lose his temper.

Records

7.47 The custody officer must promptly record the reasons for the search, what parts of the body were searched and why, who conducted the search, who was present, and its results (s 55(10), Art 56(10), the Code C, Annex A(A) 7). Moreover, the annual reports of each police force must contain details of intimate searches in accordance with s 55(14)-(16) (Art 56(14)-(16)). These are collated by the Home Office and form a valuable basis for monitoring the use of the power.

THE RIGHT TO NOTIFY THE FACT OF ARREST (s 56, Art 57)

7.48 It is natural for a detained person to want to notify his predicament to his family or close friends. Their worries as to his whereabouts will be allayed and he may be comforted by communicating with them and the psychological pressure of police station detention is relieved. It is of course possible that he will take the opportunity of alerting his partners in crime. Section 56 of PACE (Art 57) seeks to resolve this dilemma by providing a general right for detained persons to notify third parties of their arrest, subject to the power of the police to delay the exercise of the right in certain circumstances. Brown, 1992, found that requests for notification occurred in about one-fifth of cases.

The right

7.49   The right to notify applies to a person who is arrested and held in 'custody'. In *R v Kerawalla* (1991) the Court of Appeal took the view that this only covers a person whose detention has been authorised at a police station or elsewhere, thus equating 'custody' with 'police detention'. It is respectfully submitted that this interpretation is an unnecessary gloss on the statute and is contrary to the spirit of PACE, opening up the possibility of unnecessary and even lengthy denial of the right. It is suggested that the phrase 'held in custody' is used so as to include a person who is arrested and detained (whether authorised by a custody officer or not) at premises other than a police station (for example, a person arrested for shoplifting and held at the store whilst the owner considers whether to prosecute, a Post Office worker arrested by the Post Office Investigation Department in connection with alleged offences at work or, as in *Kerawalla*, a person held in a hotel room after being arrested). Had Parliament intended this right, and the right to legal advice under s 58, to be confined to a person whose detention had been authorised, the words 'police detention' would have been used. Assuming, contrary to *Kerawalla*, that a person arrested and detained at 'other premises' has the right to notify, it arises only if the person requests it. For those detained at a police station having been brought there under arrest or arrested having attended voluntarily, Code C 3.1 supplements s 56(1) by requiring the custody officer to inform the detained person of his right to request notification, and to give him written notice of the right (Code C 3.2). The right also applies whenever the detained person is moved to another place, for example, from a police station in police force A to one in B. A request and the action taken by the custody officer must be noted in the custody record (Code C 5.8). If the request is granted, notification will normally be by telephone since this is the best way of communicating 'as soon as practicable' (s 56(1), Code C 5.1). However, the argument of police convenience should not exclude the possibility of using an officer to visit the appropriate party. This will be necessary of course if there is no telephone and there may be other circumstances which make the telephone an inappropriate method of communication (eg a shared line or publicly situated telephone, the abruptness and coldness of the telephone when news of the arrest is likely to cause distress and shock to a relative). Moreover, the police may be suspicious of the named recipient, not enough to warrant delay of the notification (below) but enough to merit a personal visit by a constable rather than the use of a telephone. Since this will involve some delay in the exercise of s 56, it is important for the visit to be arranged forthwith and advisable for a senior officer (inspector) to approve it. The object of the notification can be a relative, friend or other person who is known to the detained person or who is likely to take an interest in his welfare (s 56(1)). The 'other person' could include a Member of Parliament, clergyman, a community leader or youth club organiser. In some cases D will have no one to contact (eg he is a vagrant), whilst in many others he will not want to (see below). However, there may be cases where the custody officer should consider suggesting to D an appropriate person or representative of a social or voluntary organisation (eg if D is an overseas visitor, or he is adamant that he does not want his family informed). Only one such person is to be informed. Code C 5.1 states that, if the person cannot be contacted, up to two alternatives may be tried and that further calls are at the discretion of the custody or investigating officer. This is an unnecessary gloss on the clear wording of s 56(1) and of doubtful legality. For the only reasons for denying the notification are set out in s 56(5) and Annex B to Code C. Unless they apply, repeated calls to other persons must be made until successful.

7.50 The initial communication is made at public expense. It consists solely of notifying a third party that D has been arrested and that he is being held at place X. A simple way of doing this was suggested by the Home Office Circular issued when the right was first created (74/1978, (v)): where D is arrested at home or otherwise in the company of his family or friends, they can be told immediately of the arrest and where D is being taken. When the arrested person is informed of his right of notification, on arrival at the station, the police can reply that the notification has already taken place and the statute has already been obeyed. A similar interpretation of s 56 is possible unless as in *R v Kerawalla* (1991) (para 7.49, ante) the phrase 'held in custody at a police station or other premises' means authorised detention. If D is arrested at home he clearly is in custody at 'other premises' and if his wife is told of the arrest, the purpose of s 56 is clearly satisfied. It would be nonsensical to require the police to repeat the exercise when D has been formally detained at the police station and is in police detention if on being told of the right he nominates his wife, but if *R v Kerawalla* is followed this is what must be done. If, when detention is authorised, D nominates someone other than his wife s 56 has not been complied with and attempts must be made to contact the nominated person, subject, of course, to any permitted delay. If D is arrested at the premises of friends or in a pub in front of friends and neighbours s 56 is not satisfied by informing someone there unless the person informed is the person nominated by D when told of his right, again subject to *R v Kerawalla*.

Delaying the right

7.51 After 36 hours of detention, the right of notification cannot be withheld. This period coincides with the time when the police must seek a warrant of further detention from a magistrates' court (s 43, Art 44; see para 6.143, ante). However, until 36 hours have expired, the exercise of the right may be delayed if the following conditions apply.
(a) The person is in police detention in connection with a serious arrestable offence (s 56(2)).
(b) The delay has been authorised by at least an inspector – he can do so orally, but it must be confirmed in writing as soon as is practicable (s 56(2), (4)).

(c)   The authorising officer has reasonable grounds to believe that the proposed communication will have one or more of the following consequences.

(i)   It will interfere with evidence of a serious arrestable offence or will interfere with, or harm, other persons. So, for example, it may be essential for the safety of a hostage that, when a kidnapper is arrested, other members of the gang are not alerted. Similarly, the identity and safety of an informer might be jeopardised unless D's right of notification is delayed. Another example is where D has been arrested prematurely and the police wish to catch the rest of the gang when they attempt the robbery or meet to purchase a supply of prohibited drugs. The offence need not be the same as that for which the person was detained. For example, D is arrested for drug offences. His premises are searched and stolen goods are found. X is suspected of complicity in that and other thefts and the police hope to confront X before he is alerted that D is under arrest and before he disposes of the property.

(ii)   The communication will alert and therefore impede the arrest of others for a serious arrestable offence which has been committed; for example, a robber may be forewarned and avoid a rendezvous if he knows that the driver of the getaway car has been arrested.

(iii)   The recovery of property obtained as a result of the offence will be hindered; for example, communication with the suspect's spouse will lead her to destroy or dispose of stolen property or prohibited drugs.

(iv)   The recovery of drug-trafficking profits will be hindered by notifying a named person. This was inserted into s 56 of PACE by s 32 of the Drug Trafficking Offences Act 1986 (for Art 57, see similarly the Criminal Justice (Confiscation) (NI) Order 1990). D must have been detained for such an offence (as defined in s 1 of the DT Act 1994; and such offences are deemed to be 'serious arrestable' ones for the purposes of PACE, see s 116(2)(aa) of PACE as inserted by the 1986 Act) and the officer must believe that D has benefited from drug-trafficking (ie 'received payment or other reward in connection with drug-trafficking carried on by him or another person', s 1 of the 1994 Act). This new provision refers to the 'officer' but must, it is suggested, be interpreted subject to s 56(2) of PACE, ie to mean a senior officer of at least superintendent rank.

(v)   The recovery of other proceeds by a confiscation order will be hindered. This was added by s 99 of the Criminal Justice Act 1988 (for Art 57, see to identical effect the Order of 1990, above). Under Part VI of that Act the Crown Court (and to a lesser extent the magistrates' court) can make an order confiscating the benefits which a person has derived from committing an indictable offence. If the police fear that unlawfully obtained property will be disposed of if D notifies someone of his arrest, then (iii) above is available to delay notification, so (v) additionally permits delay where the property has been exchanged into some other form and that other form may be lost unless D's notification is delayed (eg shares bought with stolen money will be sold by an accomplice if he is told of D's arrest).

7.52 The inspector must find sufficient evidence to trigger delay of the notification in respect of each person identified by D (he may be able to do so for one but not another; thus, a blanket ban is not allowed. It must be directed against a named person, *R v Quayson* (1989)). He must after all satisfy the more demanding test of 'reasonable grounds to believe', s 56(5) (see further para 2.04). D wishing to notify a known criminal associate is clear enough but such blatant examples are unusual. Much will depend on the police suspicions about the person to be contacted, the nature of the offence and of D's arrest, and the ease with which (i) to (v) above can be accomplished (eg the ready disposal of drugs). On a league table of importance the right of notification is below the right to legal advice and the grounds for delaying it are inevitably more speculative than the narrower basis for denying legal advice (see para 7.65). Indeed delay of notification in a particular case may be justifiable when denial of legal advice is not (*R v Quayson* (1989); *R v Parris* (1989)). Consequently, it is suggested that a court is less likely to punish the delay of notification with the exclusion of evidence under ss 76 or 78 (Arts 74, 76; unless in the circumstances it amounts to 'oppression', s 76(2)(a), Art 74(2)(a)), and even less likely if D has been allowed access to legal advice. Research indicates the right is rarely delayed, with a figure of approximately 1 per cent in 1988 dropping to just under 0.2 per cent in 1991 (Brown, 1992).

7.53 The detained person must be promptly told the reason for refusing his request and the reason must be included in his custody record. That record can be inspected within 12 months from the person's release. Suspension of the right will in any event cease after 36 hours from the 'relevant time' (usually the time of arrival at the police station, s 41, Art 42; see para 6.108, ante), but it will do so earlier if either the person is charged or the reason for refusing the right ends (Code C, Annex B). In the latter event, the custody officer must remind D of the right in clear terms, ask him what he wants to do about it (*R v Cochrane* (1988); *R v Quayson* (1989)) and note the custody record accordingly (but see *R v Chahal* (1992) where D was not informed that the embargo on notification had been lifted). The review officer who conducts the early reviews of a person's detention is not legally bound to consider the operation of s 56, but, it is suggested, a conscientious officer should do so. Certainly by the time that a senior officer has to consider whether to authorise continued detention (s 42, Art 43; see para 6.133, ante), he must remind the detained person of his right under s 56 and must review any earlier decision to suspend the right (s 42(9), Art 43(8)). If a juvenile is detained, the person responsible for his welfare and, if different, the 'appropriate adult' (see para 7.131, post) must be informed of the arrest as soon as is practicable (s 57, Art 58 and Code C 3.13-3.15). The juvenile's right to notify a third party under s 56 is quite independent of the requirement in s 34(2) of the Children and Young Persons Act 1933 as amended by s 57 of PACE (Art 38 of the NI Order) which requires that the parent or guardian of a young person (and supervisor if subject to a supervision order) be informed of the fact that he has been arrested, the reason for it and the place of detention (see para 6.11, ante). So in theory an older child, for example, may prefer to use s 56 to contact another adult (eg a youth leader, an uncle), in which case the s 56 right can then be suspended just as in the case of adults. However, Brown, 1992, reported that few juveniles were given the choice to notify someone other than the person informed under s 57 of their detention. For persons who are mentally ill or handicapped, the 'appropriate adult' must be similarly and unconditionally notified of the arrest (Code C 3.15). As for foreign citizens, Code C gives them various rights to consult their diplomatic representatives (see paras 7.277, post). It also states (C Note 7A) that these rights cannot be denied or delayed under the criteria of s 56(5). This is a gloss on the statute. Commendable though it is, it should be remembered that the Code Notes for Guidance are simply that and cannot amend or displace a statutory provision.

Right to communicate

7.54   Section 56 is limited to a right of notification, ie the right of a detained person to tell a third party of the arrest and of his whereabouts. Normally the police will do so on his behalf. The right to communicate should be distinguished. Under the Code C 5.6, unless the qualifications in s 56(5) apply, a detained person is allowed to communicate with others by telephone or written message. Unlike the right to notification, telephone calls may be charged to him (for example, if a long-distance call is involved). Insufficient cash to pay for the communication should not in principle be a reason for denying it. Financial arrangements will usually be feasible. Letters can be read by the police and telephone calls listened to (Code C 5.7) and used in evidence (see *R v Ahmed* (1995) where a suspect's call from a pay phone inside the police station was routed through the internal switchboard and there intercepted, recorded and subsequently used in evidence against him). Consequently, the suspect must be warned of this and warned that his communication may be used in evidence (Code C 5.7). If a telephone call is being abused (either by its content or duration), it can be terminated by the supervisory officer. Also, an officer of at least inspector rank may delay or deny communication if he considers that a letter or telephone call will have one of the consequences set out in Code C, Annex B (listed at para 7.51, ante with the reference to serious arrestable offence being read to include an arrestable offence (Code C 5.6). A written note on the custody record should be made of any message or call (Code C 5.8). If an interpreter is used, as Note C 5A permits, it is suggested that he should be made aware of the above provisions and asked to provide an English translation of a letter or call other than to a solicitor. No communication with the suspect's lawyer may be read or listened to (Code C 5.7) and in any event is likely to be protected by legal privilege and inadmissible in evidence.

VISITS

7.55   Remarkably little attention is paid to the possibility of visits to the detained person by, for example, his family. If friends or relatives inquire at a police station about D, his whereabouts may be divulged if D agrees and if the reasons for non-communication in s 56(5) do not apply. If D refuses to allow the information to be given, that refusal should be noted and D asked to sign the custody record (Code C 5.8). If the inquiry about D is received by telephone, the custody officer must be wary of identifying and verifying the caller before responding. As to visits to see D, the custody officer's discretion governs. The availability of officers to supervise the visit and the possible hindrance to the investigation (eg a pending interview of D) caused by a visit are obvious reasons for refusing or delaying a visit (Code C Note 5B). Once D has been charged, the latter ceases to apply and the former should be overcome whenever possible. Once D has appeared in court and has been remanded in custody by judicial order, he passes into the jurisdiction of the Prison Service and limited access from outsiders is allowed in accordance with the Prison Rules. A note on the custody record should be made of any visit (Code C 5.8).

RIGHT TO LEGAL ADVICE (S 58, ART 59)

7.56 It can be argued that the right of a detained person to secure legal advice is his most important protection and Article 6 of the ECHR recognises the importance of the right. His motives for wanting it may stem from, inter alia, confusion as to his predicament, a desire for bail or the presence of a friendly face, or a fear of police malpractice. More objectively, he may need advice as to, for example, the substance of the charges against him, or the conditions and length of his detention. The pressures of police interrogation and the technicality of the criminal law mean that the interests of a suspect can only be properly secured after he has received legal advice. Apart from offering legal advice, a lawyer's presence enables him to attend and record the police interview of his client and the various procedures which may be used, to make representations to the custody and review officers over the client's proposed detention and to the custody officer on the issue of bail, to check on the physical treatment of the client, and to offer him comfort and support. Section 58 of PACE provides a general right to legal advice for those arrested and held in custody, either in a police station or other premises. Section 59 of PACE (now repealed) sought to make a reality of legal representation by amending the Legal Aid Act 1982 and extending the duty solicitor scheme at magistrates' courts to include legal advice for persons held in police stations. Subsequently under the Legal Aid Act 1988 they were taken over by the New Legal Aid Board. Subsequently the Access to Justice Act 1999 set up the Legal Services Commission (LSC) to run the Legal Aid Scheme. The Criminal Defence Service (CDS) is operated by the LSC. It provides legal aid through contracts with private firms and through services provided by employed lawyers, and operates the Duty Solicitor Scheme.

The right in outline

7.57 A distinction must be drawn between those persons detained for serious arrestable offences and those held for lesser offences. The latter have an unqualified right, on request, to consult a solicitor privately at any time (s 58(1)). The former have a qualified right since it may be delayed in certain circumstances (s 58(8)). The statutory right for both groups is one of consultation only. This must take place in private (save in relation to terrorism provisions, when the advice may have to be given in the sight and hearing of a uniformed officer, s 58(1); see para 7.162, post). The communication may be in person, by writing or by telephone. The Code of Practice extends the right so that the solicitor may usually remain with his client during the latter's interview (Code C 6.6). The Act covers persons who have been 'arrested' (s 58(1)) and this applies whether or not an offence has been committed. Thus, it covers a mentally disordered person who is found in a public place, is detained under s 136 of the Mental Health Act 1983 and is taken temporarily to a police station. The provision arises if the person is 'held in custody' at a police station 'or other premises' (s 58(1)). The latter can cover persons detained on board a ship or aircraft (or other specified place under the Terrorism Act 2000. The phrase 'held in custody' has been interpreted to mean authorised detention (*R v Kerawalla* (1991)). It is submitted that the contrary view advanced at para 7.49, ante, is preferable and even more so in the context of legal advice (ie s 58 should apply if the person is detained, or held in custody, whether or not a custody officer has authorised it). The Code of Practice again extends the right of access, subject to Annex B, to 'all people in police detention' (Code C 6.1), although the right to legal advice under s 58 does not extend to a person who is detained in police custody having been remanded there by a magistrates' court, unless there are special circumstances (eg continuing investigations about other offences), although a common law right to consult a solicitor does exist (*R v Chief Constable of South Wales, ex p Merrick* (1994)). This would seem to apply to the Kerawalla situation, when D is not in police detention. Persons 'voluntarily' in attendance at a police station have an unrestricted right to contact a solicitor since they are not in police detention and are free unless and until arrested. However, there is no obligation on the police to remind or inform them of that right unless the person is cautioned (Code C 3.15, see paras 5.128). Where a right to legal advice arises under s 58 or through a provision in the Codes, the costs of providing the advice will be met by the Legal Aid Board. The situation is different where the suspect is 'voluntarily' being questioned by non-police investigators, eg Post Office investigators, or trading standards officers, and no police officer is present. Here, whilst the investigator may have to comply with s 67(9) of PACE and have regard to relevant provisions in the Codes, there is no entitlement to free legal advice under the Legal Advice and Assistance at Police Stations (Remuneration) Regulations 1989. Thus a Post Office worker who is being investigated at his place of work by Post Office investigators, but who has not been arrested, will be entitled to legal advice but will have to pay for it.

Notification of the right

7.58 The Code of Practice contains several provisions designed to ensure that a detainee is made aware of his right to legal advice. Thus, when a person is arrested at a police station or brought there under arrest, he will appear before a custody officer who must tell him of his right to free legal advice (Code C 3.1). Provided that the delay provisions contained in Annex B do not apply, notification includes informing the person that the legal advice will be independent and free of charge and that any communication – in person, on the telephone or by writing – will be in private (Code C 6.1). Somewhat curiously, the Code refers here to a 'duty solicitor', but Code C 3.1 and Notes for Guidance 6B and 6D make it clear that notification applies to all solicitors. It is submitted that Code C 6.1 should be applied accordingly. Notification must be carried out before any questioning begins and even if it is then decided to delay access to a solicitor (see para 7.65, post). D is asked whether he wants to exercise his right and to sign the custody record confirming his decision. He is also asked to sign as to whether he has been told of his rights. It is important that the right be explained clearly and unambiguously and nothing should be said or done with the intention of dissuading the detained person from exercising the right (Code C 6.4). The custody officer must hand D a written notice repeating the right and explaining how he can obtain it (Code C 3.2). The difficulties here are that the right may be read to him discouragingly so that he signs the custody record declining legal advice without really understanding; and that he is handed the notice and told to read it in the cell when his emotions, thoughts and even literacy are unreceptive to its message. Each station must prominently display a poster in the charging area advertising the right to legal advice (Code C 6.3). Whether, in the hurly burly of a charge room, a suspect is able to spot and assimilate the poster is another matter. Moreover, illiteracy or a foreign tongue may defeat it. As regards the latter, posters in Welsh and the main ethnic and European languages should be used 'wherever they are likely to be helpful and it is practicable to do so' (Code C Note 6H). The nature of the local population, the locality of the station or its proximity to a port of entry or tourist resort, and the availability of wall space in the charge room will influence this. D must, most importantly, be reminded of his right to free legal advice before an interview starts or restarts (Code C 11.2), but a reminder should also be given in the following circumstances: before an officer reviews his detention (Code C 15.4) or a senior officer authorises his continued detention up to 36 hours under s 42 (Art 43, see para 6.133, ante); if charged, or having been informed that he may be prosecuted, a police officer wishes to draw his attention to a written statement or the contents of an interview with another person, or to question him further in relation to the offence for which he has already been charged (Code C 16.4 and 16.5) and before any identification procedure takes place (Code D 3.17) and being asked to provide an intimate sample (Code D 5.2). If at any stage a suspect requests legal advice, this must be timed and noted in the custody record, along with the steps taken by the police to secure it (Code C 6.16). The suspect must be asked to sign the record confirming his decision (Code C 3.5).

7.59 Simply telling D of his rights, particularly if it is said in an offhand fashion, does not mean that he will try to exercise them. Indeed research prior to PACE indicated that, even when informed, a large majority of suspects did not do so (see Royal Commission on Criminal Procedure 1981, paras 4.83-4.85, and Baldwin and McConville, 1979). A similar picture has emerged since PACE. Thus, Sanders et al, 1989, found that only 24.8 per cent of their sample requested legal advice, and that the reasons for not doing so included the use of at least 21 identifiable ploys or tactics by the police to discourage the right (eg reading the right to D too quickly, suggesting that he will not be detained for long, that he will have to wait for a solicitor to attend or that he can have a solicitor later, or that it is normal to interview without a solicitor – see *R v Beycan* (1990) where the custody officer wrongfully asked 'are you happy to be interviewed in the normal way we conduct these interviews, without a solicitor, friend or representative?') and a variety of reasons attributable to the suspect (eg a desire to get out of the station as soon as possible, an acceptance of the inevitable, a confidence to survive without a lawyer, the triviality of the offence meant that legal advice was not worth it, dislike of solicitors, the attitude and behaviour of the police). Due, in part, to concerns regarding the low take-up rate of legal advice raised in this research and that of Brown, 1989, the Codes of Practice were revised in April 1991, and changes made to the information given to detained persons about the right to advice. The changes included greater prominence being given to the fact that legal advice was private, independent and free and the right was a continuing one which could be exercised throughout the period spent in custody. Further research by Brown, 1992, in which he compared the take-up of legal advice before and after the revised Codes were implemented, found that 24 per cent of suspects requested legal advice before the revision, which increased to 32 per cent afterwards. This increase occurred in spite of the fact that all of the required additional information was not always given, although in nearly three-quarters of cases, the suspects were told that legal advice was free. The 1991 Codes also contained a requirement prohibiting any attempt to dissuade the suspect from obtaining legal advice, which was further amended and now reads, 'No police officer shall at any time do or say anything with the intention of dissuading a person in detention from obtaining legal advice' (Code C 6.4). If properly observed, this instruction should increase the use of legal advice. If a failure to inform suspects of any or all of the required information amounts to anything done or said, where observance does not occur, it is certainly a most useful provision for defence lawyers to deploy in seeking to exclude confessional evidence obtained in their absence under ss 76 and 78 (Arts 74, 76).

7.60   It should be noted that the various procedures to alert D of his right to legal advice only apply if he is in custody in the police station. On arrest outside or en route to the station, there is no duty to tell him of the right. Instead there is a general prohibition on questioning an arrested suspect outside the police station (Code C 11.1; for the exceptional cases where questioning is allowed, see para 8.34, post).

Waiver of the right

7.61   When the custody officer authorises a person's detention, he must tell him clearly of his rights, including the effect of s 58, and that the rights are continuing ones which may be exercised at any time (Code C 3.1). He is asked whether he wants legal advice at this time and to sign the custody record accordingly (Code C 3.5; a refusal to sign must also be noted by the custody officer in the record, Code C 2.7). Whether on being first informed, or later reminded of his right to legal advice, the suspect declines to speak to a solicitor in person, he must be informed that he may talk with one on the telephone and be asked if he wishes to do so. If he continues to waive his right under s 58 the custody officer must ask for his reasons, and any given must be recorded on the custody record (Code C 6.5). However, there is no obligation to provide reasons, and the Notes for Guidance suggest that a suspect should not be pressed to do so against his wishes (Code C Note 6K). Nevertheless, being asked to provide reasons may encourage suspects to reflect further on the need for legal advice and help to ensure that pressure is not brought to bear on suspects to waive their right, although the manner in which they are asked may either encourage or discourage them from responding (see para 7.59, ante). It may be that some reasons given will alert the custody officer to the fact the suspect has not fully grasped the scope of the right (eg 'I can't afford one'). The risk of this will be reduced where the suspect is both advised of his rights and asked for his reasons in ordinary language. In such a case, although he is under no obligation to do so, the officer will no doubt reiterate the fact that legal advice is free, for a realistic sanction against an inappropriate waiver is the readiness of the courts to invoke ss 76 and 78 (Arts 74, 76) when a solicitor is not present at an interview (see further Chapter 8, post). There will always be a gap between the reading of D's rights and an interview (for the custody officer must complete other procedures) and, when an interview begins (or restarts), the interviewing officer must remind D of his right to free legal advice and that, unless one of the exceptions in Code C 6.6 or Annex C applies (see para 7.65, post), the interview may be delayed for him to obtain it (Code C 11.2; the reminder must be noted in the record of interview by the interviewing officer). The reminder must also be given where a suspect returns to the station to answer his bail (s 47(3)), and the police propose to question him further. If legal representation has not been arranged in advance, the investigating officer may be impatient or hostile at the idea of waiting for it, or may be intent on deterring it, or the legal advice may be difficult to organise, and the suspect may be easily dissuaded from seeking it. Since the tape-recording of interviews carried out in police stations is now routine (see para 8.24, post), the quality of the reminder and the genuineness of D's consent to be interviewed without legal advice may be more readily assessed, provided of course that the tape is listened to (see paras 8.91, post). In those cases where a suspect changes his mind about seeking legal advice and agrees to an interview, the procedure below must be followed.

QUESTIONING WITHOUT LEGAL ADVICE

7.62 The general rule is that a person who asks for legal advice cannot be interviewed until he has obtained it. However, there are four crucial qualifications (Code C 6.6). If they apply the action taken should be recorded on the custody record (Code C 6.16 and Annex B A6).

(a) Legal advice may be properly delayed by a senior officer under s 58(8) of PACE (see para 7.65, post).

(b) A police officer of the rank of at least superintendent can authorise questioning of the suspect if he has reasonable grounds to believe that:

    (i)   delay whilst waiting for legal advice will involve an immediate risk of harm to persons or serious loss of, or damage to, property (once this risk has passed, legal advice should proceed unless (a) above, or (ii) and (c) below, apply); or

    (ii)   unreasonable delay to the investigation would be caused by having to wait for a lawyer to arrive.

Examples are where a solicitor may have a long way to travel and, by the time he arrives, the permissible period of detention without judicial warrant may be coming to an end. Similarly, the time for D's rest period under the Code may be fast approaching and there is an urgent need to interview him before the rest period intrudes. Again, the needs of other investigations (eg to discover the whereabouts of accomplices or of a kidnap victim) may demand immediate questioning. Another pertinent example is where the chosen solicitor is already advising another client. Wherever possible the superintendent should discover how long it will take for the solicitor to attend and take this into account when determining whether or not to authorise the interview to commence, for example he may be able to stall the questioning if the solicitor says he is about to set off. (Brown, in his 1989 study, found that 51per cent of suspects requesting legal advice saw a solicitor within an hour, and 65 per cent in 90 minutes. In his 1992 comparative study, whilst there was a minority of very lengthy delays, in just over half of the cases, contact was made within 30 minutes.) Conversely the solicitor should seek an assurance (preferably to be noted in the custody record) that questioning will not begin until he arrives (Advising a Suspect in the Police Station, Law Society, 1991, para 2.5.6(c)). If questioning cannot wait, the solicitor should be told so that he can try to organise an agent to appear on his behalf (Code C, Note 6A). He can also seek to make representations to the custody officer and, if they are written down, they may be useful later when the court considers the admissibility of evidence. To prevent abuse of (b)(ii) it should be noted that under Code C 6.8 a solicitor who, at the time of the interview, is present at the station, or who is on his way, or who is easily contactable by telephone, is deemed to be 'available', therefore the interview should be conducted in his presence and the suspect should not be asked to agree to one without him. If the solicitor arrives after the interview has started, the suspect must be told, at that point, the solicitor has arrived and asked if he would like to see him. The arrival of the solicitor and the suspect's decision must be noted on the custody record, whilst a note of the solicitor's attendance must also be made on the interview record (Code C 6.15, 6.17 and see further para 7.50). Where the solicitor is informed that the suspect would like to see him, it is imperative that he insists on a private consultation with his client (see Code C 6.1 which gives this right 'at any time'). He should also ask to see or hear the record of the interview. If legal advice is to be satisfactory and possible exclusion of evidence avoided, it is in the police's interests to accommodate such a request.

(c)   If a solicitor cannot be obtained (ie the nominated solicitor, or another from his firm, cannot be contacted or refuses to attend, and/or the duty solicitor cannot attend or the suspect refuses to use the duty solicitor scheme), an officer of at least inspector rank may permit an interview to proceed. Given the importance of legal advice and the court's tendency to exclude a confession if it is improperly denied, it is important for the inspector to verify that all reasonable attempts have been made to secure a lawyer's presence. This will include providing the suspect with a choice of up to two solicitors from a list who have indicated a willingness to attend. The custody officer has a discretion to allow for more than two choices until legal advice is secured (Code C Note 6B).

(d) If the suspect has changed his mind and no longer wants a lawyer (eg he wants to leave police custody and will not wait for a lawyer to attend), he must either give his agreement to an interview in writing or on tape, and an officer of at least inspector rank, having sought the suspect's reasons for the change, must approve the interview. The agreement to be interviewed, the change of mind and the reasons for it, together with the name of the authorising officer, must be recorded at the start of any subsequent interview (Code C 6.6). The danger of improper pressure being brought to bear on the suspect to change his mind is self-evident.

7.63 Whilst (d) above provides limited confirmation, it is suggested that all the authorisations in (a) to (d) should be put in writing and attached to the record of interview and read out on the tape. Moreover, the authorising and interviewing officers should be alert to the real possibility that a court will exclude evidence obtained in breach of these provisions.

7.64 It has been decided (*DPP v Billington* (1988); *DPP v Cornell* (1990); *DPP v Skinner* (1990)) that obtaining legal advice cannot delay the breathalyser procedure in road traffic cases. As Lloyd LJ remarked in Billington, 'the right to consult a solicitor ... does not furnish a defendant with a reasonable excuse for not providing a specimen when requested'. This does not mean that a solicitor should not be called – the suspect has after all a right to consult one in private at any time, s 58(1) (Art 59(1)). The police should therefore call one without delay (Code C 6.5) and, if he arrives very quickly or is readily available (eg he or another available solicitor may be at the station), it is suggested that he be allowed access, albeit brief, to the detainee. The detainee can also ask for a copy of the Codes of Practice (Code C 3.1(iii) and 1.2). Whilst this does not entitle him to a leisurely read from cover to cover, it is suggested that it is open for the Court of Appeal to permit him a limited time to read the relevant provisions (Code C Note 3D) (but cf the facts of Skinner, above, where ten minutes was held to be too long). Where the Notice to Detained Persons is either confusing or misleading (and research indicates that suspects do have difficulties in understanding it (Gudjonsson (1992), a mistaken belief that procedures may be delayed for the purpose of consulting the Code will not amount to a reasonable excuse (*DPP v Whalley* (1991)). On the other hand in *Hudson v DPP* (1991) the defendant was kept at the station for an hour before the breath test procedure was commenced – ample time for a solicitor to be contacted. Hodgson J in Hudson wisely suggested that the notice of rights given to D should make it clear that s 58 cannot delay the breath test, for otherwise he may be left, understandably, with the impression that he can delay the process and contact a solicitor at any time.

DELAYING LEGAL ADVICE

7.65   At the outset it should be noted first, that delaying notification of arrest (s 56, para 7.51, ante) is a quite separate matter from the postponement of legal advice (*R v Parris* (1989)), and second, that this is only possible if the suspect has been detained on suspicion of a serious arrestable offence and, in the light of *R v Samuel* (below), will rarely be justifiable. In theory, the delay may last for up to 36 hours (the police must obtain the approval of a magistrates' court if they wish the detention to continue thereafter, see para 6.143, ante), but since the suspect must be permitted to consult his lawyer for a reasonable time before the court hearing (Code C, Annex B 5) the full period of delay will not run. For example, D is due to appear in court after 34 hours of detention. His lawyer should be allowed to see him beforehand, perhaps after 33 hours. The circumstances in which legal advice may be withheld for up to 36 hours are the same as those which prevent a third party being notified of the suspect's arrest under s 56 (Art 57), viz:

(a)   the person is detained for a serious arrestable offence;
(b)   an officer of at least superintendent rank authorises the delay;
(c)   he must have a reasonable belief that one of the following facts applies -
    (i)   interference with evidence, or harm to other persons will ensue,
    (ii)   other suspects will be alerted,
    (iii)   recovery of property will be hindered,
    (iv)   the recovery of drug-trafficking proceeds will be hindered,
    (v)   a confiscation order under the Criminal Justice Act 1988 will be frustrated (s 58(8), (8A), Art 59(8), (8A)).

7.66   If one of these grounds applies, the delay in access to legal advice must cease as soon as the ground ceases. More importantly the suspect must be told (in understandable language, *R v Cochrane* (1988)) that the objection to legal advice no longer applies, asked whether he wants it, and his reply noted on the custody record (Code C, Annex B 4; cf the facts of *R v Quayson* (1989) where D was not told). Annex B 3 emphasises that the grounds set out in s 58(8) are the only grounds for delaying access to legal advice. Thus, access to legal advice cannot be delayed because the lawyer may advise his client not to answer any questions (see the facts of *R v Alladice* (1988)). It follows that:

> 'the only reason under the [Act] for delaying access to a legal adviser relates to the risk that he would either intentionally or inadvertently, convey information to confederates still at large that would undercut the investigation in progress' (Home Officer Minister, Standing Committee E, 28 February 1984, col 1417).

7.67   For example, the suspect may ask the solicitor to pass a message to his wife which sounds innocuous but which is in fact a coded instruction to alert accomplices. This reasoning is an implicit slur on the professional integrity of solicitors. However, in the light of Annex B 3 and *R v Samuel* (1988) delaying legal advice under s 58 is extremely difficult for the police to justify. First, the offence must be of a sort for which immediate access to legal advice may have one of the (i) to (v) consequences above (eg the ready disposal of drugs, speedy removal of proceeds of crime from the country).

Second, the senior officer must have grounds to believe that the suspect will try to pass a message out through his lawyer (thus, he must actually have addressed s 58(8), cf *R v Parris* (1989)). Third, the suspect must have requested a named solicitor. If the police do not know his identity, s 58(8) cannot be triggered since suspicion of solicitors per se will not suffice (see the facts of *R v Davison* (1988)). Fourth, reliance on s 58(8) must be supported by facts. Thus, in *R v Guest* (1988) the only other accomplice was dead, so there was no danger of (c)(ii) above; and alternatively the superintendent's fear that the solicitor would alert others was contradicted by the fact that the solicitor already knew of D's arrest before he was denied access. (See also *R v Cochrane* (1988).) Fifth, the emphasis of s 58(8) clearly lies on the character and record of the solicitor. The senior officer must satisfy the relatively high standard (para 2.89, ante) of 'reasonable belief' that the particular solicitor will deliberately or accidentally 'spill the beans'. Evidence of 'deliberate' complicity must be strong for this belief. The officer

> 'must believe that a solicitor will, if allowed to consult with a detained person, thereafter commit a criminal offence. Solicitors are officers of the court. We think that the number of times that a police officer could genuinely be in that state of belief will be rare' (per Hodgson J in *R v Samuel*).

7.68 The most obvious offences would be the common law one of perverting the course of justice or impeding the arrest or prosecution of an offender contrary to s 4 of the Criminal Law Act 1967. It is arguable that, if such a belief surrounds a particular solicitor, a complaint to the Law Society will have already been made.

7.69 The possibility of solicitors acting as 'innocent postboxes' is slight. Moreover,

> 'persons detained by the police are frequently not very clever and the expectation that one of [(i) to (v)] will be brought about in this way seems to contemplate a degree of intelligence and sophistication in persons detained, and perhaps a naivete and lack of common sense in solicitors, which we doubt often occurs. When and if it does, we think it would have to have reference to the specific person detained. The archetype would, we imagine, be the sophisticated criminal who is known or suspected of being a member of a gang of criminals' (per Hodgson J in *R v Samuel*).

7.70 In many cases it will be the duty solicitor who is called. He will probably be known to the police and there will be no reason to deny access. Moreover, if a particular solicitor is distrusted, the simple solution, it is suggested, is for the police to offer D another one (Annex B, Note 4). If that is accepted, then the only reason for the absence of a solicitor will be where the alternative solicitor cannot, or refuses to, attend. Another solution, where it is feared that the solicitor will unwittingly pass coded messages, is to warn the solicitor of the possibility. This is more likely to be feared where one solicitor is representing two suspects, and coded messages can be more easily passed. Even so, a considerable degree of sophisticated foresight by the suspects would be needed (it is suggested that *Re Walters* (1987), where vague fears of messages being unwittingly conveyed were upheld, cannot stand in the light of *R v Samuel* (1988)).

7.71 Code C rejects one other basis for delaying access. It follows the case of *R v Jones (Sally)* (1984). Often a solicitor is approached by the family or friends of the detained person, is retained on his behalf and attends the police station. Police have sometimes taken the view that since the detained person has not requested a solicitor there was no obligation to inform the detainee of the solicitor's presence (*R v Franklin* (1994)). In this case the police were found to be in breach of Code C, Annex B3 which required that the person be told that a solicitor had come to the station at another's request and that he sign the custody record to signify whether he wished to see him or not. The 1995 Code now includes a new C 6.15 which states that where a solicitor attends a police station to see a particular person, that person must (unless access has been delayed under s 58(8)), be informed of the solicitor's arrival, whether or not he is being interviewed, and asked whether he wants to see him. This applies whether the person has already declined legal advice, or having requested it, subsequently agreed to be interviewed without having received advice. The solicitor's attendance and the detained person's decision must be noted in the custody record. Code C, Annex B3 has not been amended in the light of C 6.15. It should now be read simply as emphasising that s 58(8) contains the only reasons for delaying access and as requiring the signature of the detained person on the custody record to signify whether or not he wishes to see the solicitor. However, the provision does not enable the solicitor to see the detained person so that they may discuss in private whether or not he wishes to have legal advice. The obligation on the police is simply to convey the information that a solicitor has arrived and ask the person if they would like to see him. Where the solicitor has been contacted by a third party, to avoid a wasted journey it is good sense for him first to contact the police station by telephone and ask to speak with the suspect before he sets off, in case the suspect has already instructed another solicitor. A difficulty may arise if the police do not notify the detained person that the solicitor is on the telephone (see *R v Franklin* (1994) commenting on *R v Chahal* (1992)). It is submitted that, whilst the Code only requires that D be notified of a solicitor's attendance at the police station, the spirit of the provision requires notification of any telephone contact so that instructions to act may be confirmed or rejected at that stage by D. If telephone contact with the person is denied, the solicitor would nevertheless be well advised to make the journey and to make a careful note of the time of both the telephone call and his arrival at the police station.

7.72 There will be some situations where (i) to (v) do not apply and legal advice has been permitted, but the police do not want certain information passed to the suspect (eg that an accomplice has also been arrested, or what an accomplice has said about the suspect's arrest). The decision to comply rests firmly with the solicitor in the light of what he thinks is best for his client.

LEGAL ADVISERS

7.73 The relative unpopularity of criminal work in the legal profession ('Many solicitors will not contemplate it ... there is an economic necessity to employ persons who have no professional qualifications to attend at the interview of suspects' (per Mann LJ in *R v Chief Constable of Avon and Somerset Constabulary, ex p Robinson* (1989))) has led to the despatch of trainee solicitors, legal executives and other clerks to advise suspects in police stations. A number of research studies on the provision of legal advice which were either conducted for the Royal Commission on Criminal Justice (Baldwin, 1992; McConville and Hodgson, 1993) or carried out by the Home Office (Brown, 1992), together with recommendations made by the Commission itself (RCCJ (1993)), raised serious concern about the delivery and quality of advice given by and the practices of legal representatives in police stations, most of whom are unqualified (see para 7.61, post). These concerns were taken up and acted upon by the Law Society and the Legal Aid Board who, in February 1995, introduced new regulations which established a scheme for registering representatives who may give advice on behalf of solicitors for which payment may be claimed (Legal Aid Board Legal Advice and Assistance at Police Stations Register Arrangements 1994). Solicitors with practising certificates are not subject to the Arrangements. Existing duty solicitor representatives (approved by the local Duty Solicitor Committee, see Duty Solicitor Arrangements 1994 para 45), must register by various dates, depending upon when they were selected as a representative and, from February 1996, must be fully accredited before applying to the Scheme. Trainee solicitors are exempt from registration until 1 February 1997. Those who have been a duty solicitor representative in the past five years, but who are no longer such, need to register from 1 February 1996. The register is kept and maintained by the Legal Aid Board. Applications for entry on the register must be accompanied by a certificate of fitness, signed by the solicitor who will supervise the representative, indicating that the person is suitable to give advice and should be regarded as so by the police (see Code C 6.13). Two types of representative may be entered on the register: 'probationary representatives', who cannot advise on 'indictable-only' offences, will be required to undertake a number of supervised and unsupervised attendances at police stations, in a six-month period during which they must produce a satisfactory portfolio of cases; and 'accredited representatives' who having submitted a satisfactory portfolio of cases must, in addition, have passed 'the relevant tests' (written and oral examinations in law, practice and procedure), unless they are exempt (Legal Aid Board Legal Advice and Assistance at Police Stations Register Arrangements 1994). The new regulations are reflected in the revised 1995 Codes which define the word 'solicitor' to be 'a solicitor who holds a current practising certificate, a trainee solicitor, a duty solicitor representative or an accredited representative included on the register of representatives maintained by the Legal Aid Board' (Code C 6.12, although note that in the draft Codes of Practice for Northern Ireland, the definition is restricted to a qualified solicitor).

EXCLUSION OF SOLICITORS DURING INTERVIEW

7.74 A solicitor may only be required to leave an interview in two situations. In both cases, the fact shall be recorded on the interview record (Code C 6.17). First, the client may ask him to withdraw. The only precaution for the solicitor here is to make sure that the client understands the implications of his request. It is suggested that he should ask the client whether he wants another solicitor and, if so, should explain how to obtain one. Second, a solicitor (as defined above) can be asked to leave if his conduct prevents an investigating officer from properly putting his questions to the suspect (Code C 6.9). Note 6D of the Notes for Guidance recognises that the solicitor's role is to 'protect and advance the legal rights of his client' and that, in so doing, the solicitor may advise his client to take a course of action which avoids providing information which would strengthen the prosecution case. Therefore, interventions to clarify the content of questions, to object to improper questions or improper methods of questioning, to advise a client not to answer particular questions or requesting he be allowed to give legal advice in private will not amount to misconduct for this purpose. Note 6D suggests that 'answering questions on the client's behalf, or providing written replies for the client to quote' might suffice. But there is a fine line between the former example and a solicitor properly assisting an inarticulate suspect. Such a suspect may reasonably require frequent interjections from the solicitor, based on the instructions given to him by the client. Another example which might give rise to exclusion could be where the solicitor constantly interrupts the interview by raising legal arguments more suited to the trial and in effect refuses to allow the officer to continue with the questioning. The initial decision to exclude a lawyer is taken by the investigating officer if he 'considers' that questioning is being improperly hindered. However, this subjective element is more than balanced by the following factors:

(1) the interviewing officer must consult an officer of at least a superintendent rank (or, if unavailable, at least an inspector who is not involved in the investigation, but in that case the inspector must subsequently report the facts to the senior officer);

(2) the officer consulted must talk to the solicitor;

(3) the officer consulted will make the final decision and he in turn is well advised to consult the contemporaneous interview record (tape or written record) in reaching it;

(4) the authorising officer should only act on the clearest evidence of improper conduct by the solicitor since removal of a solicitor is a 'serious step' (Code C 6.11) and the courts (eg *R v Samuel* (1988)) will readily condemn the wrongful denial of legal advice; and

(5) if the solicitor is excluded, the suspect must be allowed a replacement and the new solicitor will have the chance to witness the resumed interview (C 6.10).

7.75   Where a solicitor is excluded, the officer of at least a superintendent rank who took the decision (or to whom it was reported) will consider whether or not to report it to the Law Society, and Legal Aid Board if a duty solicitor is involved (Code C 6.11).

EXCLUSION OF OTHER LEGAL REPRESENTATIVES

7.76   Probationary and non-accredited representatives may be admitted to a police station to provide advice, but it is good practice for the instructed solicitor to arm his representative with a clear letter of authority to act on his behalf. The point is important, for an officer of at least inspector rank may exclude a representative if he considers that the representative 'will hinder the investigation of crime' (Code C 6.12). The chief constable can issue a force order restricting access to certain types of representatives provided that it is not a blanket ban and that each case is still decided on its merits by the inspector (*R v Chief Constable of Avon and Somerset Constabulary, ex p Robinson* (1989)). The recent changes requiring registration of legal representatives as a condition of payment by the Legal Aid Board mean these provisions will apply principally to probationary representatives, since payment will not be made for advice given by non-accredited (and non-exempt) representatives, who will therefore rarely be used. Providing proper legal advice in accordance with Note 6D will not amount to a hindrance, but the officer is specifically instructed (Code C 6.13) to check on the representative's identity and status and may take into account, for example, the existence of any previous convictions, unless they are long-standing and of a minor nature, and any information which may be contained in an authorising letter from the solicitor on whose behalf he is acting. Clearly, a carefully drafted letter explaining the representative's background and experience is very useful. If a representative is barred, the detainee and solicitor must be informed and the custody record noted (Code C 6.14), though the reasons given to the solicitor should be carefully drafted in a letter rather than given over the telephone lest defamation be inadvertently risked. If the solicitor in turn cannot attend, the Code is unclear. It is suggested that, to avoid problems of exclusion of evidence at trial, it is prudent, and certainly within the spirit of the Code, for the custody officer to see if D wishes another solicitor to be contacted, or failing this, for the duty solicitor scheme to be contacted.

7.77 If it is decided that a firm of solicitors is persistently sending unsuitable representatives, an officer of at least superintendent rank should be informed with a view to him contacting the local Law Society (Code C Note 6F).

SECURING LEGAL ADVICE

7.78 Once legal advice has been requested, provided Annex B does not apply, the custody officer must act without delay to secure it (Code C 6.5). The custody record should help here since it will indicate the time when the right to legal advice was administered and the time when the solicitor was informed. Many suspects will request a named solicitor or firm. If the suspect's solicitor cannot be contacted by the custody officer or if the suspect does not know a solicitor, he must be told of the duty solicitor scheme or be given a list of solicitors in the Regional Directory to choose from. If he opts for the latter, the solicitor becomes the suspect's own solicitor and he must claim for legal aid in the normal way. If the suspect cannot obtain a solicitor from the list, he should be allowed to try up to two alternatives and thereafter the custody officer has a discretion to permit further contacts (a discretion which he is well advised to exercise liberally in favour of the detainee). The frequency with which named as opposed to duty solicitors are requested by suspects is difficult to gauge (see Brown, 1989; Sanders, 1989). It can vary between regions, depending in part on the quality of the local duty solicitor scheme, and between the times of the day, with for example named solicitors being more available in the daytime (Sanders, 1989, estimated that one-third of legal advice sought comprised the duty scheme but acknowledged the imprecision of this estimate). Brown, 1992, in his observational study, found the number of requests for duty solicitors rose to 41 per cent after the Codes were revised in 1991 although concluded that the number of consultations with duty solicitors, which might include those where own solicitors could not be contacted, could be over 50 per cent.

7.79   Three issues arise: whether a solicitor can be contacted; whether he will give advice; and what sort of advice is given. The failure rate in making initial contact with a solicitor is unclear. Sanders, 1989, suggests that in over 25 per cent of cases where legal advice was requested, contact was not made. Brown, 1992 found this figure had decreased to 13 per cent following revision of the Codes in 1991. In both cases, one reason for the lack of contact might be because the suspect changed his mind before contact had been made. Another might be accessibility of the solicitor. If the suspect's own solicitor is to be contacted outside business hours, there is obviously a greater chance of failure, although some firms do operate a 24-hour call-out service. The ability to make contact will depend, to a large extent, on the effectiveness of the local duty solicitor scheme. Whether a solicitor will attend the station to give advice is another matter. The new Codes make it clear that the right to legal advice includes the right to speak with a solicitor on the telephone, and that where practicable this should be in private (Code C 6.5 and Note 6J), although Brown, 1992, noted that very few police stations have dedicated telephones enabling calls to be taken in private. Initial advice which is given over the telephone may suffice, for example, where the police indicate they will not be interviewing the suspect, or assure the solicitor that they will not deal with the suspect until he has slept or sobered up, but on the whole, personal attendance must be preferred. Even trivial offences (eg kerb-crawling) can have serious consequences for an individual and, if he admits to an offence, a legal presence may be needed at least to advise on bail and to explain police procedures. The requirement to attend depends, to a certain extent, on whether the solicitor is the client's own, or a duty solicitor. Attendance may be summarised as follows:

- named solicitor – solicitor's decision whether to attend;
- duty solicitor:
    - (i)   telephone advice mandatory in first instance,
    - (ii) attendance mandatory thereafter in certain circumstances,
    - (iii) attendance discretionary if the circumstances in (ii) do not apply.

7.80   As regards a solicitor named by the suspect ('own solicitor' scheme), the decision to attend belongs to the solicitor (he is not covered by the arrangements for duty solicitors – see below). Clearly, if the solicitor no longer practises in the criminal process field, that is the end of the matter (though he can pass him on to a colleague in the same firm and ethically he should surely acquaint or remind the suspect of the duty solicitor scheme). If he does still practise in the area, a serious reason should be required of him before he refuses in principle to attend (eg he is already acting for another suspect in the case and there is a likely conflict of interest, or he has experienced insuperable difficulties in representing the particular suspect). There may well be practical reasons why he does not attend (eg he is otherwise engaged, he considers that confidential advice over the telephone is possible and will suffice, the suspect is intoxicated or due for sleep and the police have expressed no intention to question him, the suspect has already been charged and the police have expressed no intention to interview him further). Such reasons do not, however, exclude the option of sending a representative to the station or appointing an agent to act. Moreover, the solicitor may be able to arrange with the custody or investigating officer a future time when he can attend (eg the following day when it is proposed to commence an interview). The overriding consideration should be whether the solicitor's presence is needed for the protection of the suspect's interests. At the end of the day, however, if a named solicitor refuses to attend, the suspect has no realistic redress, but the unrealistic option (for his current plight) is subsequently to complain to the Law Society.

7.81 As for the attendance of duty solicitors, earlier research indicated a heavy reliance upon telephone advice (see Sanders, 1989). When the Legal Aid Board took over responsibility for the duty solicitor scheme from the Law Society in 1989, it reviewed the procedures. Under the Duty Solicitor Arrangements 1994, solicitors are now required to attend a police interview or identity parade, but they are first obliged to respond to a call for advice by speaking to the suspect over the telephone, unless he 'is at or adjacent to the police station and can immediately advise the suspect in person'. In this case, the duty solicitor must notify the scheme's telephone service that he is attending on the suspect. If the suspect is 'incapable by reason of drunkenness or violent behaviour of speaking to the duty solicitor, initial advice may be postponed' (para 53(2) of the Arrangements). Here, the duty solicitor should ask the custody officer to make a note on the custody record that he should be called again when the suspect sobers up and certainly before an interview with him takes place. Where telephone advice is given, the solicitor must tell the suspect that he will attend at the police station for any interview or identification process which might take place later on, unless there is an exceptional reason which prevents him (eg the solicitor's sudden illness or where a suspect who is not yet sober demands the attendance of the solicitor who is of the opinion that, given the suspect's state of mind, it would be inappropriate to attend). If this occurs, the reason must be recorded on the legal aid costs claim form (para 54(2)). Thus, the solicitor cannot leave a duty solicitor representative employed at his firm to field and deal with requests from the AA (eg by giving the bleeper to him for the evening). Indeed, the representative can only be sent to advise the suspect if the duty solicitor has already given telephone advice and the suspect must be informed of the status of the representative before any advice is given. This requirement of telephone advice says nothing of the quality or extent of the advice and does not, for example, prevent him from giving minimal advice and then sending the representative. Good selection and training of duty solicitors (and their representatives) are the keys to sound advice.

7.82 Once telephone advice has been given, the duty solicitor (or his representative) must attend the station only if the suspect so requests and if:

(a)   he has been arrested for an arrestable offence and the police intend to interview him; or

(b)   the police intend to organise an identification procedure; or

(c)   the suspect complains to the solicitor of serious maltreatment by the police (para 54(1) of the Arrangements).

7.83   If the identification procedure or interview with the suspect will not take place until the duty solicitor has finished his period of duty, the duty solicitor should ask the police to arrange for the solicitor who is next on the duty rota to take over the case. Where the duty solicitor has given advice to the suspect at the police station, he must tell the suspect that he is entitled to ask any solicitor to continue acting for him. The duty solicitor may continue to act if the suspect requests him to do so, but he would do so in the capacity of 'own' solicitor. If the suspect names another solicitor, or prefers his own solicitor, who was previously uncontactable, to represent him, the duty solicitor must withdraw unless the suspect asks him to continue to act, in which case the request to continue must be in writing. As for (c), these Arrangements should be viewed as the minimal requirements and arguably any complaint of maltreatment should warrant the solicitor's attendance.

7.84   For those cases outside (a) to (c), the duty solicitor has a discretion over whether or not to attend. His guiding light is the interests of the suspect. Two factors are picked out in the Duty Solicitor Arrangements (para 55(1), (2)) as generally requiring his attendance, viz whether he can give satisfactory and confidential advice to the suspect over the telephone, and whether a juvenile or other person at risk is involved. There are many others: for example, whether the suspect is seriously agitated about his detention and needs calming advice; whether he needs advice as to bail; or whether he wants the solicitor to contact other people or make investigations. However, the pressures on the duty solicitor scheme are such that, in some areas of the country, cases outside (a) to (c) are likely to mean frequent non-attendance of solicitors or a heavy reliance upon representatives.

7.85   The success of the Duty Solicitor Arrangements 1994 depends upon:

(1)   the effectiveness of the more rigorous selection and reselection procedures for duty solicitors and their representatives;

(2)   the increased level of training for participants in the scheme;

(3)   the overseeing of the National Duty Solicitor Co-ordinator and his five Group Duty Solicitor Managers;

(4)   the achievement of various performance targets by each local scheme (eg availability of a solicitor in 95 per cent of cases; 80 per cent of referrals to a rota (75 per cent to a panel) within 30 minutes);

(5)   the willingness of the central Government to fund this branch of legal aid realistically; and

(6)   the eagerness of young lawyers entering the profession to undertake this type of work.

ASSISTING THE SUSPECT

7.86   As already noted (para 7.73, ante), recent research indicates that the delivery of legal advice, particularly under the 'own solicitor' schemes, which is given in police stations varies considerably (Brown, 1992). Earlier research found that solicitors commonly employed unqualified clerks to carry out police station advice work (Sanders, 1989), and this practice appeared to have changed little in subsequent years. McConville and Hodgson, 1993, suggest that as many as three-quarters of those providing advice at police stations are representatives, rather than admitted solicitors. In the absence of any training (which few in the study had received) it is not surprising that the researchers found many advisers lacked adequate legal knowledge and confidence, both in their advisory role and when dealing with the police. This, coupled with the limited information advisers obtained from the police about the case, either because they failed to ask, or because information was not forthcoming, meant they were often ill-equipped to offer considered advice in any event. The same study found that most legal advisors (nearly 78 per cent) did not intervene during the police interview, even if the questioning was obscure or overbearing, whilst Baldwin, 1992, recorded that, in 66 per cent of cases, the legal adviser said nothing at all. Where interventions did occur, they were more likely to assist the police than their client. The consequences of failing to intervene may be significant, for both suspect and police, as the case of *R v Paris, Abdullahi and Miller* (1992) illustrates, the interview in that case being subsequently ruled inadmissible on appeal under s 76 on the grounds of oppression. Concerns about the quality of legal advice and the lack of regulation by the Legal Aid Board concerning own solicitors and their representatives (as compared to the regulation of duty solicitors and their representatives) led the Royal Commission on Criminal Justice, 1993, to make recommendations that the role of advisers, which is satisfactorily represented in the Law Society booklet 'Advising the Client at the Police Station' (3rd edn, 1991), be more widely known and acted upon, that the standards which apply to duty solicitors and their representatives should apply to all who give advice at police stations, that advisers should be provided with more information about the suspect and case on arrival at the police station and that, in the long term, a review of the training, education, supervision and monitoring of police station advisers be undertaken.

7.87   In response, the Law Society and Legal Aid Board established a scheme for registering representatives who give legal advice at police stations on behalf of solicitors (see para 7.73, ante) and a training package (Becoming Skilled) which forms the basis of the training requirements which must be undertaken by representatives in order to obtain accreditation under the scheme. The quality of legal advice and the regulation of those who provide it should improve as a result (although see Bridges and Hodgson, 1995). The police have also undergone changes in their interrogation techniques, following the introduction of the 'PEACE' model of interviewing (Investigative Interviewing: A Guide to Interviewing and its companion The Interviewer's Rule Book, 1992), which encourages an ethical approach to interviewing, based on investigation rather than assumptions (see para 8.70, post). In line with the RCCJ recommendation that police apprise legal advisers of the general nature of the case and the prima facie evidence against their client, interviewing officers are encouraged to disclose sufficient information to advisers about the evidence so far obtained to enable them to give proper advice. This is particularly important in the light of the provisions on the right to silence (see paras 8.40-8.68, post), since a failure to disclose, in advance, evidence which is raised in interview may provide the suspect with reasonable grounds not to answer questions, the result being that inferences on the silence may not be drawn at trial.

7.88   When visiting a client at a police station the solicitor (or representative) should be armed with a copy of PACE, the Codes, the Law Society's Guide to Advising a Suspect, and any other suitable guide. The new Codes entitle a solicitor or representative to inspect the custody record on arrival, or as soon as possible (Code C 2.4), and this will be a valuable source of information, particularly for personal details of the suspect (if he is not already known to the adviser), his condition and in respect of any action that has already taken place since the detention period commenced. Further information about the suspect and details of the case should be requested from the custody officer, the interviewing officer and, if present, the arresting officer. It is not only the police who are tied to record-keeping. The solicitor too must keep notes of when things are done and of what is said. Notes of the former will be crucial if the accuracy of the custody record is questioned. The solicitor's own tape-recorder can easily be used for the latter, though an additional written record/summary is advisable. This function of note-taking will be demanding if the solicitor agrees to represent several suspects. Code C Note 6G makes it clear that it is the solicitor who determines, in accordance with his professional code of conduct, whether or not any conflict may arise in advising more than one client.

IDENTIFICATION

7.89   The police will often wish to conduct various identification procedures in respect of the detained person. A witness may come forward to give visual identification of the offender. Fingerprints and photographs may have to be taken to assist detection or to identify the person with official records. Samples from the person's body may need to be taken for forensic purposes. The following section deals with these procedures. Three general, opening observations should be made. First, this area is governed largely by the Code of Practice for the Identification of Persons by Police Officers (referred to as Code D in the following paragraphs) rather than by PACE 1984, and, since the whole area of identification is sensitive and controversial, breach of this Code's provisions is likely to have important evidential consequences at trial. The courts have shown themselves willing to use s 78 (Art 76) of PACE to exclude improperly obtained identification evidence (eg *R v Ladlow* (1989); *R v Gall* (1989); *R v Conway* (1990) and *R v Nagah* (1990); *R v Penny* (1992); *R v Graham* (1994)), though disputes over the admissibility of identification evidence should not generally warrant the judge holding a trial within a trial (*R v Beveridge* (1987); *R v Flemming* (1987) and *R v Martin and Nicholls* (1994)). Second, the procedures governing identification apply, with one small exception (see Code D, Note of Guidance 2A), to police officers who themselves act as identifying witnesses, as well as to witnesses from the general public (see *R v Samms, Elliot and Bartley* (1991)). Third, the following formal identification procedures should be distinguished from an accidental meeting between witness and suspect (eg an off-duty police officer recognises a person, who has come to the station on another matter, as a suspect in a crime) – see *R v Quinn* (1990); *R v Long* (1991).

7.90   Identification can involve both discovering the identity of the offender per se and testing a suspect's identification in respect of an offence. As regards the former, it is not a criminal offence to refuse to give one's name and personal details (though it is a reason to arrest for a non-arrestable offence, s 25 (Art 27), see para 5.56, ante). In theory this means that D's identity can remain unknown up to and including the trial, though fingerprints and other non-intimate samples (below) can be taken without D's consent and may reveal his identity. If they do not, D must be labelled with a number. A suspect is under no duty to disclose his address. For vagrant adults it is unlikely to raise a problem; but for vagrant juveniles, other police forces and social services should be consulted. When identifying a suspect in order to link him with an offence, detailed provisions (below) exist. However, they do not encompass every process. Thus identification of the suspect as the offender may also be made by viewing the recording of a surveillance camera or closed-circuit television system. Though this is not within PACE the courts suggest that appropriate PACE procedures be adapted (*R v Blenkinsop* (1995)). Similarly, the comparison of handwriting or of the voice and the simple tasks of taking physical measurements, weighing the person, fall outside PACE and may depend upon the suspect's consent; though the observance of ordinary procedures will often suffice to obtain these (eg D writing his own statement or completing the custody record will provide a handwriting sample or the taped interview will supply a sample of his voice (see s 76(4)(b), Art 74(6)(b), which provides that parts of an inadmissible confession may be admissible to prove that he writes or expresses himself in a particular way – discussed at para 8.140, post). The revised 2003 Code for the Identification of Persons by Police Officers has a number of new features. These include the introduction, which sets out its purpose and the purpose of identification procedures. It concerns the principal methods used by police to identify people in connection with the investigation of offences and keeping of accurate and reliable criminal records. The procedures are designed to:
*   test the witnesses ability to identify the person they saw on a previous occasion
*   provide safeguards against mistaken identification.

VISUAL IDENTIFICATION

7.91   In 1972 the Criminal Law Revision Committee in its 11th Report (Cmnd 4991) observed that 'mistaken identification [is] by far the greatest cause of actual or possible wrong convictions' (para 196). A sufficient number of cases are reported to show that the problem remains, but considerable steps have been taken in recent years to alert the courts and the police to the dangers of identification evidence. Thus, a Report by Lord Devlin (1976) HC 338 prompted the Court of Appeal in *R v Turnbull* (1977) to issue guidelines. These stressed the need for the jury to treat identification evidence with special caution and to examine it carefully. The Devlin Report also prompted the Attorney-General to issue guidelines as to how the Director of Public Prosecutions would take special precautions in preparing and prosecuting cases where identification evidence would play a part. The strictures of Turnbull are regularly repeated by the courts and, according to the Privy Council, apply to identification evidence by police witnesses as well (*Reid v R* (1989)). Turnbull makes it clear that:

(a) there is a special need for caution when the prosecution case depends on visual identification;

(b) the summing up should contain a warning of the need for caution and an explanation as to why a caution is needed;

(c) the summing up should deal with the circumstances of the identification in the particular case; and

(d) the judge should point out that even a convincing witness may be mistaken, though there is no set formula. It is sufficient that it be made clear to the jury that credibility is not enough, and the fact that they are told that a perfectly honest witness can be mistaken is sufficient (*Mills v R* (1995)). In *Scott v R* (1989) the fact that an honest witness may be convinced of the correctness of the identification and yet be mistaken was described as the fundamental danger of identification evidence.

7.92 Failure to follow the guidelines is likely to result in the quashing of a conviction. The central concern of the Turnbull guidelines is with the quality of the identification evidence. If it is poor and based solely on a fleeting glance or a longer period of observation in difficult circumstances, then the trial judge should withdraw it from the jury and direct an acquittal unless there is other evidence which supports the correctness of the identification. If the quality is good the case can be left to the jury even if there is no supporting evidence; for example, the defendant is recognised by someone who knows him well or is identified by police officers who have kept observations on the premises which were regularly visited by the defendant. Supporting evidence need not be corroboration in the technical sense. Thus in *R v Long* (1973) D was identified by three witnesses to a robbery, each of whom had only a limited opportunity to observe him. When arrested some time later he offered to help the police claiming to know those responsible for the robbery. The 'odd coincidence' that the man identified as the robber should know those involved was sufficient to support the correctness of the identification. The evidence of other identification witnesses can be supportive of other witnesses (*R v Weeder* (1980) and *R v Tyler* (1993)). In the latter case the court approved the earlier decision in *R v Ramsden* (1991) that police officers, because of their training, are potentially better identifiers than the ordinary citizen and therefore more likely correctly to identify.

7.93 The fact that other offences have been committed in a strikingly similar way may also support the identification of D as the perpetrator of the present offence or a series of offences. In *R v McGranaghan (Note)* (1995) the Court of Appeal made it clear that an identification about which the jury was not sure could not support another identification of which they were also not sure. However, the identification of the defendant by several victims can be used cumulatively once the jury was satisfied that other evidence showed all the offences to have been committed by the same man. Thus if a number of women were attacked and raped in similar circumstances and each victim provides a similar description of the attacker, the similarity between the incidents will permit them to be admitted to show that all the offences were committed by the same man. If then the jury is satisfied that all the offences were committed by the same man, whosoever that man might be, and if they are satisfied that was the case, then they are entitled to take account of the evidence relating to the other offences when reaching their decision in respect of each (*R v Downey* (1995); *R v Black* (1995); *R v Barnes (Anthony)* (1995)).

7.94 The concern of the courts to ensure, as far as is possible, the reliability of evidence of visual identification is reflected in the various procedures for obtaining evidence of pre-trial visual identification of a known suspect. There is nothing in the Act about identification procedures; these are contained in Code D and case law.

CONDUCT OF IDENTIFICATION PROCEDURES

7.95 An officer not below the rank of inspector who is not involved in the investigation will normally be responsible for the conduct of identification procedures (the 'identification officer' (para 3.11)), except where it is proposed to hold the procedure later and the identification officer is not available. In these circumstance the custody or some other officer will be responsible. The identification officer may delegate an officer or civilian support staff, not involved in the investigation, to make arrangements for and to conduct any of the procedures in paras 3.5 to 3.10. The Code permits the identification officer to consult the officer in charge of the investigation to determine which procedure to use.

7.96 Before considering the procedures in detail mention must be made of the importance of Code D para 3.1 which provides that where identification is likely to be an issue a record shall always be made of the first description given by a witness. In *Vaughan* (1997) the Court of Appeal quashed the conviction because a note of the witness' first description had not been made. Where it is not practicable to make such a note the requirement may be waived (*El Hannachi,Cooney, Ward and Tanswell* (1998)), but with technology the prudent police officer would be advised to communicate the first description by radio where it will usually be recorded or transcribed by communications staff.

7.97   The Code sets out the procedures to be followed. This depends on whether the suspect's identity is:
(a)   not known to the police
(b)   known to the police and available
(c)   known to the police and not available.

Cases where the suspect's identity is not known

7.98   If the suspect's identity is not known to the police, the following procedures may be used:
- the witness is taken to an area to search for the suspect
- the witness is shown photographs, e-fits, etc.

7.99   In the case of the former, there may have been an allegation of an offence, the scene of which will be promptly attended by the police in order to take the alleged victim to search for the offender who may still be in the vicinity or where an investigating officer decides to take the victim to the crime scene or to a place where the suspect may be found. The requirements of para 3.1 are fundamentally important in terms of securing the integrity of the identification and even though time will be of the essence the victim's first description of the offender must be recorded promptly. When a witness is taken to a particular neighbourhood or place to see whether they can identify the person they saw, it will not be possible to control the way in which the identification is made or the number, age, sex, race, general description and style of dress in other people present at the location. Regardless of whether the offence is recent, the principles set down in Code D para 3.2-3.5 must always be followed so far as it is practicable to do so. These are:
1.   Where it is practicable to do so, a record must be made of the witnesses description of the suspect before asking the witness to make an identification.
2.   Care must be taken not to direct the witnesses attention to any individual unless this cannot be avoided. However a witness can be asked to look carefully towards a group in a particular direction if it appears necessary to make sure the witness does not overlook a suspect because the witness is looking in the opposite direction and also to enable the witness to make comparisons between any suspect and others who may be in the area.
3.   Every effort should be made to keep witnesses apart and to ensure that identifications are made independently. (It is inadvisable for witnesses to travel in the same car for fear of being together when an identification is made (see *R v Miah* [2001].)
4.   Once a witness makes an identification and if there is sufficient evidence to make an arrest, any other witnesses should participate in the more formal procedures laid down in paras 3.4 onwards.
5.   A record must be kept by the investigator accompanying the witness which must include the action taken as soon as, and in as much detail as, possible. The record

should include ; the date, time and place of the relevant occasion the witness claims to have previously seen the suspect, where any identification was made, how it was made and the conditions at the time (eg weather, light, distance etc), if the witness had his attention drawn to the suspect and anything said by the witness or the suspect about the identification or the conduct of the procedure.

7.100   Para 3.3 provides that a witness may also be shown photographs, computerised or artist's composite likeness or pictures (including 'e-fit' images) in order to identify a suspect who is not known to the police and not available. The showing must be done in accordance with Annex E.

Cases when the suspect is known and available

7.101   If the suspect's identity is known to the police and they are available, the following identification procedures may be used:
- video identification
- identification parade
- group identification.

The procedures are set out in paras 3.4–3.20.

IDENTIFICATION PROCEDURES

7.102   Code D has been continually revised with new elements being added in 1991, 1995 and 2003. The most recent (2003) version of the Code together with a considerable number of confusing and often conflicting cases sets down the procedures to be followed. A very high rate of cancellation for live identification parades (52 per cent) together with the availability of technology has resulted in the current arrangements.

7.103   'Known' means there is sufficient evidence known to the police to justify the arrest of a particular person for suspected involvement in the offence; thus in *R v Rogers* (1993) D was observed by two witnesses damaging parked cars on an industrial estate. Both noticed that he was wearing a pullover. Police found D in one of the nearby units and the two witnesses arrived and identified him. A pullover was found in his car. His appeal, based on a submission that the identification evidence should be excluded as in breach of Code D, was dismissed. There was insufficient evidence to arrest D until the identification and in the context of Code D the suspect was not known to the police. (See also *R v Oscar* (1991) where D, whose clothing fitted the description of the witness exactly, was arrested near the scene of an attempted burglary within minutes of the offence and was immediately identified and no identification parade was held. The Court of Appeal agreed that a formal identification parade would have been valueless.) 'Available' means that he is immediately available to take part in the procedure or he will become available within a reasonably short time and willing to take part in any procedure which it is practicable to arrange (para 3.4).

CIRCUMSTANCES IN WHICH AN IDENTIFICATION PROCEDURE MUST BE HELD

7.104   Code D 3.12 sets out the circumstances when a procedure must be held. These are as follows:

1.   a witness has identified a suspect or purported to have identified them prior to any identification set out in paras 3.5. to 3.10 (ie a video identification, identification parade or group identification) having been held; or
2.   there is a witness available who expresses an ability to identify the suspect, or where there is a reasonable chance of the witness being able to do so, and they have not been given an opportunity to identify the suspect in any of the procedures set out in paras 3.5 to 3.10,

and the suspect disputes being the person the witness claims to have seen. In these circumstances, an identification procedure shall be held unless it is not practicable or it would serve no useful purpose in proving or disproving whether the suspect was involved in committing the offence – for example, when it is not disputed that the suspect is already well known to the witness who claims to have seen them commit the crime.

7.105   An identification procedure may also be held if the officer in charge of the investigation considers it would be useful.

7.106   The House of Lords unanimously held in *R v Forbes* that where a suspect had already been positively identified in a street identification it was still necessary to hold an identification parade. Lord Bingham, who gave the judgement, made clear that Code D was a practical document which gave police officers clear instructions – the Code was intended to be read literally. Although the decision was in relation to para 2.3 of the 1995 Code, it is of current relevance in considering Code 3.12 above. It will be noted that it provides that an identification procedure need not be held if 'it is not practicable or it would serve no useful purpose in proving or disproving whether the suspect was involved in committing the offence'. Examples given are when there is no reasonable possibility that a witness would be able to make an identification or where it is not in dispute that the suspect is already well known to the witness. We will have to wait the interpretation of where it would serve no useful purpose but the issue of whether or not it is practicable has been considered in relation to identification parades.

The practicability of holding an identification procedure

7.107   Video identification is the first choice of identification procedure and the circumstances when it will not be practicable to hold such a procedure are likely to be rare. Suspects will initially be offered a video identification unless: (a) video identification is not practicable; or (b) an identification parade is both practicable and more suitable than a video identification; or (c) group identification applies.

7.108   The identification officer and the officer in charge of the investigation will decide which option is to be offered. Paragraph 3.14 gives examples of when an identification parade may not be practicable and indicates that a video identification would normally be more suitable if it could be arranged and completed sooner than an identification parade. A suspect who refuses the procedure first offered shall be asked their reason for refusing (with advice from a solicitor/appropriate adult, if required). Reasons for refusal and representations made must be recorded. The identification officer may, after considering the reasons and any representations, arrange for the suspect to be offered an alternative which the officer considers suitable and practicable. Once again the procedures emphasise that the identification officer must keep full records in this case, including the reasons if the request is not granted.

VIDEO IDENTIFICATION (CODE D AND ANNEX A)

7.109 The 2003 version of Code D gives effect to the view that video libraries are more effective than other identification techniques.

7.110 Video identification is now to be regarded as the first alternative when visual identification is in dispute (Code 3.4). A 'video identification' is when the witness is shown moving images of a known suspect together with similar images of others who resemble the suspect (Code D3.5). Suspects are photographed in front of a neutral background and the photograph is then transferred into a computerised photographic database consisting of similar photographs. There are obvious advantages to this procedure in terms of speedy investigation and in reducing the burden on police manpower required in conducting identification parades. Video identification must be carried out in accordance with Annex A.

General (Annex A 1-9)

7.111 Broadly these are the same as for an ordinary parade. Arranging, supervising and directing the making of the video film and the showing of it must be the responsibility of an identification officer or officers who have no direct involvement with the relevant case. The film must include the suspect and at least eight other people who so far as is possible resemble the suspect in age, height, general appearance and position in life. Only one suspect shall appear on any film unless there are two suspects of roughly similar appearance, in which case they can both be shown with at least 12 other people. The suspect and the other participants must, as far as is possible, be filmed in the same positions or carrying out the same activity and in identical circumstances. If identical conditions are not practicable the reasons must be recorded or the forms provided for the purpose. Each person filmed must be identified by a number. If police officers are used any numerals or identifying badges must be concealed (and presumably all or none in police uniform). If a prison inmate is filmed, whether as suspect or not, then either all or none shall be in prison uniform.

7.112 The suspect and his solicitor, friend or appropriate adult, must be given a reasonable opportunity to see the complete film before it is shown to witnesses (this appears to be so whether he has consented or not, for unlike a covert group identification there is no reason why he and they should not see the completed film). If the suspect has a reasonable objection to the video film or any of its participants, steps shall, if practicable, be taken to remove the grounds for objection. If this is not practicable the identification officer must explain to the suspect and/or his representative why and note the objection and the reason why it was not practicable to remove it on the forms provided.

7.113   No unauthorised person may be present at the video identification. The suspect's solicitor, or if he is not represented the suspect himself, should, where practicable, be given reasonable notification of the time and place that it is intended to conduct the video identification so that a representative may attend on behalf of the suspect. Annex A, para 9 states that the suspect himself 'may not be present' when the film is shown to the witness(es) (which appears to be a prohibition on him being present), but in the absence of a person representing the suspect the viewing itself should be recorded on video.

7.114   As with all identification procedures, before the video identification takes place the suspect or his solicitor should be provided with details of the first description of the suspect by any witnesses who are to attend the parade. The suspect or his solicitor should also be allowed to view any material released to the media by the police for the purpose of recognising or tracing the suspect, provided it is practicable and will not unreasonably delay the investigation.

Conducting the video identification (Annex A, paras 10-14)

7.115   The identification officer is responsible for ensuring that witnesses are unable to communicate with each other about the case or overhear other witnesses who have seen the film before they themselves see it. There must be no discussion between him and witnesses about the composition of the film nor shall he disclose whether or not other witnesses made an identification. Only one witness at a time may view the film. As with an ordinary parade the witness must be told that the person he saw may or may not be on the video film. He should be told that he may at any point ask to see a particular part of the film again or have a particular picture frozen for him to study and that there is no limit on the number of times he can view the whole tape or any part of it. However, he should be asked to refrain from making a positive identification or saying that he cannot make one until he has seen the entire film at least twice.

7.116   Once the witness has seen the film twice and indicated that he does not want to view it or any part of it again, the identification officer should ask the witness whether the person he saw on a previous relevant occasion has been shown on the film and, if so, to identify him by number. He will then show the film of the person identified again to confirm the identification. As with a witness who identifies a suspect but cannot remember the number identified at trial, the identification officer may give evidence of the identification – see the discussion at para 7.147(ii), ante.

7.117 The identification officer must take care not to direct the witness's attention to any one individual on the video film, or give any other indication of the suspect's identity. Where the witness has made an identification by photograph, or a photo-fit, identikit or similar picture has been made, the witness must not be reminded of such photograph or picture once a suspect is available for identification by any means in accordance with Code D. Nor must he be reminded of any description of the suspect.

7.118 Where video films or photographs have been released to the media by the police for the purpose of recognising or tracing the suspect, the investigating officer must ask each witness after the parade whether he has seen any broadcast or published film or photograph relating to the offence and shall record his reply (see the discussion of the same requirement in respect of ordinary parades at para 7.147(ii), ante).

Tape security and destruction

7.119 The identification officer is responsible for ensuring that all relevant tapes are kept secure and their movements accounted for. In particular he must ensure that no officer involved in the investigation of the case against the suspect is permitted to view the video film before it is shown to any witness. All copies of a video film made in accordance with Code D and Annex A, and any copies, must be destroyed unless the suspect is charged, prosecuted or cautioned for a recordable offence. The suspect must be given the opportunity to witness the destruction or to have a certificate confirming destruction if he requests one within five days of being informed that destruction is required. Destruction in this context would not seem to include the wiping of the tape(s). The absence of a reference to wiping clean in Annex A would seem to require actual destruction of the tape. Where the suspect is prosecuted the video identification tapes may be used in evidence and will be retained with other evidence in respect of that case in accordance with force instructions.

7.220 Where video films or photographs have been released to the media the investigating officer must ask each witness after the parade whether he saw any broadcast or published films or photographs relating to the offence and shall record his reply (see para 7.147(ii), ante).

SHOWING OF FILMS AND PHOTOGRAPHS OF INCIDENTS FOR RECOGNITION OR TRACING OF SUSPECTS (CODE D 3.28)

7.121 Code D 3.28 provides that nothing in Code D inhibits an investigating officer from showing a video film or photograph of an incident to the public at large through the national or local media, or to police officers, for the purpose of recognition and tracing of suspects. Where such a broadcast or publication is made a copy of the material released by the police to the media must be kept and the suspect or his solicitor must be allowed to view it before any of the above identification procedures are carried out, provided that it is practicable to do so and would not unreasonably delay the investigation. Each witness involved in one of the above procedures must be asked whether they have seen any of the broadcast or published films or photographs relating to the offence and their replies noted (see para 7.147(ii), ante).

7.122   However, when such material is shown to potential witnesses, including police officers, for the purpose of obtaining identification evidence, it shall be shown on an individual basis so as to avoid collusion, and the showing shall, as far as possible, follow the principles for video identification (paras 7.107-7.120, ante) or identification by photographs (para 7.121, post).

7.123   The video identification procedure has significant advantages over identification procedures in that digital images will always be available whereas volunteers to participate in parades may not be, especially in circumstances where the suspect may be of unusual appearance. Issues of practicability will continue to arise in the context of identification procedures.

The practicability of holding a parade

7.124   The 1995 Code D 2.4 gave two reasons why it may be impracticable to hold a parade:
(a) the unusual appearance of the suspect;
(b) any other reason.
These were not included in the new code but Code D 3.12 has extended the provision to where it would not be practicable or 'serve no useful purpose in proving or disproving whether the suspect was involved in committing the offence. For example , when it is not disputed that the suspect is already known to the witness who claims to have seen them commit the crime.' It remains useful to analyse the cases under the 1995 Code to establish circumstances which might be interpreted to make the holding of an identification parade impracticable.

7.125   (a) speaks for itself. If D has a large birthmark covering half of his face it will be virtually impossible to find at least eight people with a similar mark. Similarly, the suspect may be unusually tall or unusually small. In such circumstances the other forms of identification are equally impracticable. If D is so unusual the witness is virtually certain to pick him out, nevertheless the alternative procedures must be considered and followed. This situation is, however, covered by the inclusion of a new para 10 which states that where a suspect has unusual physical features – a facial scar, tattoo, unusual hair colour – which cannot be replicated on other members of the parade, providing the suspect and his solicitor/appropriate adult agree, steps can be taken to hide that feature by wearing a hat or the use of a plaster etc.

7.126   (b), any other reason, appears rather open-ended but in practice is much narrower. The defence will usually challenge the decision that a parade was impracticable, in which event the officer making that decision will be called to give evidence and the onus is clearly on the police to satisfy the judge that it was impracticable in the circumstances (*R v Penny* (1992)). In *R v Britton and Richards* (1989) it was said that an inspector's decision 'must be taken on reasonable grounds and he must take all reasonably practicable steps to investigate the possibility of holding an identification parade or group identification before holding a confrontation'. This means that the possibility of seeking the assistance of the defence must be considered. The defence may be in a better position to persuade persons to volunteer than the police. The difficulty in finding volunteers will rarely be sufficient grounds for not holding a parade unless the suspect's appearance is a factor (*R v Gaynor* (1988)). It may be impracticable at the particular time but may well be practicable at a later date, possibly with the assistance of the defence in whose interest it may be that a fair identification parade take place. An extreme example of impracticability is offered by *R v Ladlow* (1989) where there were not only 11 witnesses and 21 defendants, which would have required 221 identification parades, but it was also a Bank Holiday and finding sufficient volunteers was impossible. Similarly in *R v Jamel* (1993) where the difficulty in finding volunteers of mixed white/Afro-Caribbean race and the potential delay involved in organising a parade in Brixton, where such volunteers might be found, persuaded an inspector to hold a group identification in a busy street in Kingston, Surrey. The Court of Appeal found no breach of the 1991 Code D 2.1 as it was not practicable to hold a parade ('practicable' involving the question when it was practicable). The onus then passes to D and his solicitor to put forward a realistic proposal (*R v Britton and Richards*). The fact that the witness identifies the suspect by name does not make the holding of an identification parade impracticable (*R v Conway* (1990) – the witness may have the name wrong). In *R v Campbell and Marshall* (1993) the suspect was a Rastafarian and the difficulty in obtaining members of the Rastafarian community to take part in a parade made it impracticable. In *R v Thompson* (1992) the suspect was a white Rastafarian and his refusal to wear a hat to cover up his dreadlocks, or to comb them out, made it impracticable to hold a parade there being few white Rastafarians in the community. In *R v Barclay* (1987) the suspect was mixed race and the lack of co-operation between the police and the community in Bristol following recent riots meant that only eight volunteers could be found, none of whom was sufficiently similar to the accused to make an identification parade fair. The inspector's decision that it was impracticable to hold a parade was upheld by the Court of Appeal. However, in *R v Knowles* (1994), where the suspect had bright ginger hair, a tattoo under his eye and a growth on his ear, the Court of Appeal, without indicating why, thought the difficulties of holding an identification parade had been overstated.

7.127 The suspect has a right to object to particular volunteers but excessive use of this right, as in *R v Birch, Bryant and Crowley* (1992), where 30 were objected to, may make it impracticable to hold an identification parade.

7.128 An identification parade may also be impracticable where the police know that the suspect has changed his appearance since the offence. A fair parade includes fairness to the witnesses and the police, as well as fairness to the suspect. It may therefore be impracticable to hold an identification parade when the suspect was, for example, sporting a full beard and long dark hair at the time of the offence, but appears, for an identification parade clean-shaven and having changed the colour of his hair. (In such a case the fact that the witness has recognised the suspect from an earlier police photograph can be mentioned to the jury, *R v Byrne and Trump* (1987).) Minor changes in appearance, such as having a haircut before the parade, are unlikely to render it impracticable to hold one. The fact that the victim is in hospital and likely to be there for some time may make a parade impracticable – see *R v Clifford and Parkinson* (1987).

7.129 *R v Ladlow* (1989) decided that there is an order of preference ((a), (b), (c), (d)) and that the police cannot jump from (a) to (d) without considering the intermediate positions. The order of preference now is video identification, identification parade, group identification and confrontation. (See also *R v Woolls* (1990). Identification parades are expensive and time-consuming but the police should not release a suspect in the hope of getting an identification by confrontation rather than hold an identification parade: *R v Nagah* (1990).) Likewise the order of preference applies to police officers who are to be identification witnesses (*R v Samms, Elliot and Bartley* (1991)). If the police breach these procedures the reliability of the identification evidence is likely to be undermined and there is a very real possibility that s 78 (Art 76) will be used to exclude the evidence.

7.130 It follows that the holding of an identification parade is mandatory if D disputes, or is likely to dispute, the identification evidence and he either requests a procedure or consents to one unless Code D 3.12 applies. In *Powell v DPP* (1992) police tried to stop D's car. D crashed the car and made off. He was later arrested and brought to the police station where a police officer identified him in a confrontation. The trial judge held that no identification parade was necessary because D had confessed. The Divisional Court held that even if D had confessed (which he had not) the police were not absolved from holding an identity parade, Code D applying as soon as D was brought to the police station under arrest. Contrast this case with *R v Long* (1991) where the police officer returned to the police station having failed to catch a reckless driver, only to bump into him at the police station reporting the 'theft' of his car. L did not become a suspect until after he had been identified. The Court of Appeal said that if police had gone to L's address and there identified him, there would have been no need for an identity parade. It would seem to follow that had the identifying police officer in *Powell* gone to P's home and identified him and then arrested him there would have been no need for an identity parade. However, it must be emphasised that the holding of an identity parade affords the defence a chance to show any weakness in contested identification evidence. It is therefore wrong to refuse a parade because there is already sufficient evidence to charge (*R v Allen* (1995)).

7.131 If an investigating officer considers that a parade would be useful one may only be held if D consents. If he does not consent in either case one can then consider the alternatives of a group identification, a video film or a confrontation. 'Consent' in relation to the mentally ill or handicapped must be given in the presence of the 'appropriate adult'; in relation to juveniles between 14 and 17, the consent of a parent or guardian (which includes the local authority or voluntary organisation if he is in care – Note of Guidance 1E) is needed as well as the consent of the juvenile unless under 14 where the consent of the parent or guardian will suffice (Code D 1.11; for the meaning of 'appropriate adult' see paras 7.248-7.250, post). Again, the suspect may take legal advice before the parade takes place. He may, for example, need to be told that the trial judge can comment on the accused's failure to agree to an identification parade. 'Considers' gives ample discretion to the investigating officer. He should be aware of the procedural preconditions for a parade (below), since some (eg as to the showing of photographs to a witness beforehand) may frustrate the holding of a parade and risk the subsequent exclusion of evidence.

Prior identification

7.132 The fact that the witness made a street identification shortly after the offence does not necessarily amount to impracticability. Thus in *R v Brown* (1991) the victim was attacked and robbed by a man who dragged her into an alley. Though the lighting was poor she had a good view of her attacker, who spoke with a Scottish accent. Immediately after reporting the robbery the victim toured the area in a police car and identified B as her assailant. The crime scene was very muddy and when arrested B had fresh mud on his shoes similar to that at the crime scene (note now s 36 of the CJPOA 1994 considered at para 8.60, post – inferences may be drawn from his failure to account for the mud and if the mud was proved to have come from the crime scene it would support the identification as would the fact that B spoke with a Scottish accent). B asked for an identification parade and one was held but the victim was not called upon to identify him, the view being taken that the identification in the street some 15 minutes after the robbery made an identification parade impracticable. The trial judge agreed but in dismissing B's appeal the Court of Appeal disagreed. It was not necessarily otiose to hold an identification parade after a street identification. There was a clear breach of Code D 2.1 but the cumulative effect of all the evidence left the court with no lurking doubts about the correctness of the conviction. Contrast *R v Rogers* (1993) and *R v Oscar* (1991) discussed at para 7.103, above, which suggests no breach of Code D 2.1 in similar circumstances, an identification parade being useless.

Recognition of the suspect

7.133 Code D 3.12 appears to be unambiguous but there remains a need for clarification when a witness claims to know or be acquainted with the suspect. Whether an identification parade is impracticable or it would serve no useful purpose will depend upon how well the witness knows the suspect and whether the suspect accepts that he is known to the witness. In *R v Conway* (1990) two witnesses claimed a slight acquaintance with the suspect they claimed to identify. The suspect denied being at the scene of the crime and denied knowing the two witnesses. His request for an identification parade was refused by the police because the witnesses claimed they recognised the suspect. The Court of Appeal held that they were wrong to do so. The

Court pointed out that even if the witnesses' claim to know the suspect had been a reason for refusing to hold a parade, which it was not, there was clearly an issue as to whether they were known to the suspect. While not purporting to lay down any hard and fast rule that whenever there was a dispute between a witness and a suspect as to whether they were acquainted there had to be an identification parade.

7.134   In *Conway* there was a double dispute:
(a) he denied being at the scene, and
(b) he denied that the witnesses knew him.

7.135   In such circumstances an identification parade would have helped to resolve these issues one way or another. In *R v Ryan* (1990) the Court of Appeal upheld a conviction where a witness purported to identify the defendant as an acquaintance. This case was considered in *R v Conway* but was said not to lay down any principle, being decided on its own facts. However, *R v Conway* was distinguished in *R v McClay* (1992) where the owner of a stolen bicycle saw the defendant riding the bicycle soon after the theft, recognised him and gave his name to the police. The defendant asked for an identification parade but the inspector considered that it would not be in the defendant's interests to hold one. It was argued, unsuccessfully, that the evidence of recognition should not be admitted because Code D 2.1 (now 3.4) had been breached. The Court of Appeal dismissed the appeal against conviction stating that the court wholly agreed with the comment in *R v Ryan* that 'it was rare for the court to feel concern about the rightness of a conviction based on evidence of recognition as opposed to that of identification of a stranger'.

7.136   The important point is not so much whether or how well the witness knows the suspect, but whether the suspect disputes the identification. As was pointed out in *R v Turnbull* (1977) recognition of a suspect by someone who knows him well may be good-quality identification but there remains the question of whether the identification is correct. If the suspect accepts that he is known to the suspect but denies being at the scene of the crime the identification is disputed and based on the decision in *Forbes* is mandatory.

7.137   Given the vital importance of accurate identification evidence, a court will not be fobbed off with unsupported claims of impracticability and will not readily accept alternative forms of identification such as confrontation below (see *R v Gaynor* (1988)). Similarly, a court will take a tough stance against any police malpractice or underhand method of obtaining identification in place of the parade provisions (see *R v Nagah* (1990) where D was willing to appear at an identification parade but was released so that identification by confrontation in the street could be made instead of proceeding to a parade). Similarly, they will not countenance deceit used to prevent a parade taking place. Thus in *R v Graham* (1994) D's conviction was quashed, there being 'a clear breach of Code D' where D did not request a parade because the police told him that one would be held. No parade was held and the trial proceeded without any of the identification procedures being carried out. The suspect will clearly consider requesting a parade if he protests his innocence and wishes to discredit the witness. However, research suggests that identification parades are expensive and time-consuming and 'do not provide evidence of a tangible nature and cannot be relied upon to give consistent results' (Slater, 1994 and see McKenzie, 1995). The possibility of mistaken identification arising out of a parade is still a real one, especially if the witness is not used to it and is afraid or uncertain, as over half the witnesses were in the research by Slater, above. Fear may be reduced or overcome by procedures which now permit a witness to view a parade from behind a one-way screen so that they can see without being seen. Uncertainty cannot be so easily overcome. It is important for the suspect to take legal advice before deciding whether to ask for or to refuse a parade. The Code D, Annex A 1, allows a solicitor or friend to be present at a parade and allows the suspect to take legal advice before the parade continues but here, as in the giving of legal advice generally, research (Slater, 1994, above) suggests that advice is often given by non-qualified persons who were not fully conversant with the procedures. As such they serve more to confirm the validity of the parade, often by saying nothing, than to protect the interests of their client.

Details of the first description

7.138   The Turnbull guidelines include a requirement that the trial judge point out to the jury the lapse of time between the original observation of the witness and the subsequent identification given to the police and any discrepancies in the description given to the police and the defendant's actual appearance. (See for example *R v Knowles* (1994) where the first description by a witness did not mention that his attacker had bright ginger hair, a tattoo under his eye and a growth on his ear. Not surprisingly the Court of Appeal found the identification evidence unsafe and unsatisfactory.) Prosecutors are required to supply the accused or his legal advisers with particulars of that first description whenever there is reason to believe there is a material discrepancy. It has long been the practice to disclose to the defence the notes of the identification parade, made by the identification inspector and usual for the first description of the identifying witness and photographs of the suspect taken on arrest to be disclosed. In *R v Ivan Fergus* (1993) such description and photograph was not disclosed and it was held that they are disclosable under the common law of disclosure (see *R v Ward* (1993) for an explanation of this duty). Code D 3.1 acknowledges the importance of this requirement and requires that the police make a record of the description of the suspect as first given by a potential witness before that witness takes part in any of the forms of identification mentioned above. The form of the record is not important provided that the details of the description as first given by the witness can accurately be produced from it in a written form which can be supplied to the suspect or his solicitor in accordance with Code D. However, if the witness reads and signs the record when it is made it can be used to refresh his memory if he gives evidence.

The identification parade (Code D 3.17. and Annex A)

Explanation before the parade or other identification procedure other than a confrontation (Code D 3.17)

7.139   Before a video identification, identification parade or a group identification takes place the identification officer must explain to the suspect:

(i)   the purposes of the video identification, identification parade or group identification;

(ii)   their entitlement to free legal advice; (see Code C, para 6.5)

(iii)   the procedures for holding it, including their right to have a solicitor or friend present;

(iv)   that they do not have to consent to or co-operate in a video identification, identification parade or group identification;

(v)   that if they do not consent to, and co-operate in, a video identification, identification parade or group identification, their refusal may be given in evidence in any subsequent trial and police may proceed covertly without their consent or make other arrangements to test whether a witness can identify the suspect (see para 3.21)

(vi)   whether, for the purposes of the video identification procedure, images of them have previously been obtained (see para 3.20) and, if so, that they may co-operate in providing further, suitable images to be used instead;

(vii)   if appropriate, the special arrangements for juveniles;

(viii) if appropriate, the special arrangements for mentally disordered or otherwise mentally vulnerable people;

(ix)   that if they significantly alter their appearance between being offered an identification procedure and any attempt to hold an identification procedure, this may be given in evidence if the case comes to trial, and the identification officer may then consider other forms of identification; (see para 3.21 and *Note 3C*)

(x)   that a moving image or photograph may be taken of them when they attend for any identification procedure;

(xi)   whether before their identity became known, the witness was shown photographs, a computerised or artist's composite likeness or similar likeness or image by the police; (see *Note 3B*)

(xii)   that if they change their appearance before an identification parade, it may not be practicable to arrange one on the day or subsequently and, because of the appearance change, the identification officer may consider alternative methods of identification; (see *Note 3C*)

(xiii) that they or their solicitor will be provided with details of the description of the suspect as first given by any witnesses who are to attend the video identification, identification parade, group identification or confrontation. (see para 3.1)

7.140   The above information must also be supplied in the form of a written notice and handed to the suspect. After having been given a reasonable time to read the notice he must then be asked to sign a second copy to indicate whether or not he is willing to take part in the parade or group identification or co-operate in the making of a video film (Code D 3.18).

7.141 If the identification officer and officer in charge of the investigation suspect, on reasonable grounds, that if the suspect was given the information and notice as in 3.18. above they would then take steps to avoid being seen by a witness in any identification procedure, the identification officer may arrange for images of the suspect suitable for use in a video identification procedure to be obtained before giving the information and notice.

7.142 Annex A 1 stipulates that the suspect must be given a reasonable opportunity to have a solicitor or friend present and the identification officer must ask the suspect to indicate on the second copy of the notice whether or not he so wishes, the copy then being retained by the identification inspector.

Before the identification parade

7.143 A parade may take place in an ordinary room or in one equipped with a screen permitting the witness to see the members of the parade but not be seen by them. Modern identification suites are equipped with such screens which are of considerable help to nervous or frightened witnesses. The procedures are the same whether or not a screen is used, but a screen can only be used when the suspect's solicitor, friend or appropriate adult is present or the parade is recorded on video.

7.144 Code D 3.8 stipulates that any parade must be carried out in accordance with Annex B which requires that a video recording or colour photographs be taken of the parade. This now applies in all cases, and not, as under the previous Code, only when the suspect's legal representative or a friend is absent. The video record or colour photographs will be available to the court and jury who will be able to assess the validity of the parade for themselves. It will assist in resolving disputes about such validity but may also add weight to the identifying witness's testimony.

7.145 Before the parade starts the suspect or his solicitor must be provided with details of the first description of the suspect by witnesses who are to attend the parade (Annex B 3 and Code D). If any material has been released to the media by the police for the purpose of recognising or tracing the suspect, the suspect or solicitor should be allowed to view it if practicable without unreasonable delay to the investigation.

7.146 It is the duty of the investigating officer to inform the identification officer if a witness attending an identification parade has previously been shown photographs, identikit, photo-fit or similar pictures (Annex E Note 9).

The conduct of the parade (Annex B (c) paras 3-18) (Prior to 2003 – Annex A)

7.147   It should be emphasised that no person involved in the investigation of the offence can take part in the arrangements for or conduct of any of the identification procedures, which are exclusively the responsibility of an inspector or above who is independent of the investigation (the identification officer). In *R v Jones (Terence)* (1992) it was held that the act of the investigating officer in driving D to the premises in which the parade was to take place did not form part of the conduct of a parade; but in *R v Gall* (1989) the investigating officer's conduct in driving an identifying witness to the parade, knocking on the door of the parade room, looking in and speaking to the identification officer, did amount to taking part in the conduct of the parade and rendered the identification evidence inadmissible. The provisions for the conduct of a parade are set out in Annex B (c) to Code D and 'are there to be observed and not varied at will' (*R v Quinn* (1995)). However, a failure to comply with these provisions will not necessarily result in the exclusion of identification evidence; the test is whether the admission of the evidence will have an adverse effect on the fairness of the trial, and not all breaches of Code D and Annex B will have that effect. The crucial question is whether the breach affected the integrity of the identification parade and/or the accuracy of the identification (*R v Grannell* (1989)). *R v Finley* (1993) is an example of several serious breaches of Code D and Annex A, which totally destroyed the integrity of the parade and the accuracy of the identifications. Witnesses to a robbery were shown photographs of the appellant, were not kept apart while waiting for the parade, and were not warned against discussing the case. The parade contained nobody who resembled the first description of the robber, save the defendant himself. It was held that this travesty of an identification parade rendered the conviction unsafe and unsatisfactory, and that the trial judge should have stopped the case at the end of the prosecution case.

SETTING UP THE PARADE

7.148   At the outset the suspect must be reminded of the procedure and he must be cautioned using the caution set out in Code C 10.5 or 10.6 as appropriate. All unauthorised persons must be excluded from the place where the parade is held. Once the parade has been formed everything thereafter must take place in the presence and hearing of the suspect, his solicitor or friend or any interpreter or appropriate adult. If the parade involves the use of a one-way screen anything said or done will not be in the presence and hearing of the suspect but must be in the presence and hearing of the solicitor, friend, or appropriate adult or recorded on video. The parade must consist of at least eight people, in addition to the suspect, who resemble the suspect in age, height, general appearance and position in life. Where the suspect has some facial or other feature which other participants do not have it may be possible to cover the feature or add it to the other participants. Thus in *R v Wright* (1994) D had a moustache at the time of the parade but most of the volunteers did not. With the agreement of D and his solicitor, D and each member of the parade put tape over their upper lip. An unusual hairstyle may be covered by a hat. If the feature is so unusual and the suspect does not consent to some form of cover-up, it may become impracticable to hold a parade (see *R v Thompson* (1992) para 7.67, ante). In *R v Smith (Hugh Alan)* (1991) it was held not to be unfair where the witness was shown a video of a previous parade showing the defendant with a full beard after the witness had failed to identify the defendant at a parade when he had considerably reduced his beard.

7.149   Only one suspect may be included in the parade unless there are two suspects of roughly similar appearance. In that event they may be paraded together with at least twelve other people. In no circumstances may more than two suspects be included in the same parade. Where separate parades are held they must be made up of different people. This creates problems where volunteers are difficult to find but even more difficulties are created when all the members of a particular group (eg a gang of skinheads) are possible suspects. Separate parades must be held for each member of the group unless there are two of similar appearance, in which case the rules above apply. Where police officers in uniform form an identification parade, any numerals or other identifying badges must be removed.

7.150   When the suspect is brought in, the identification officer must ask him if he has any objection to the arrangements for the parade or of the other participants in it. At this point the suspect may take advice from his solicitor or friend, if present. Where practicable, steps must be taken to remove the objection. If not, the officer must explain to the suspect why this is so. Excessive use of the right to object to those taking part in the parade may make a parade impracticable, see for example *R v Birch, Bryant and Crowley* (1992) where D objected to 30 volunteers.

7.151   The suspect may choose his own position in the line, each of which must be clearly numbered. This number will be used by the witness to indicate the person identified. He may change his position after each witness where there is more than one witness, and he must be told this after each witness has left the room (where a screen is used, after each witness has left the screen room).

THE WITNESSES

7.152   The identification officer is responsible for ensuring that, before they attend the parade, witnesses are not able to:
(i)   communicate with each other about the case or overhear a witness who has already seen the parade;
(ii)   see any member of the parade;
(iii)   on that occasion see or be reminded of any photograph or description of the suspect or be given any indication of his identity; or
(iv)   on that occasion, see the suspect either before or after the parade.

7.153   Witnesses should be brought in one at a time. The officer conducting the witness to a parade must not discuss the composition of the parade with the witness and in particular must not disclose whether previous witnesses made an identification. Immediately before the witness inspects the parade, the identification officer must tell him that the person he saw may or may not be on the parade and if he cannot make a positive identification he should say so but should not make any decision until he has looked at each member of the parade at least twice. The witness should then be asked to look at each member of the parade at least twice (under the previous Code D the witness was required to walk up and down the parade, which did not fit with the use of one-way screens – see *R v Quinn* (1995)), taking as much care and time as he wishes. When the officer is satisfied that the witness has properly looked at each member of the parade, he must ask him whether the person he saw on an earlier relevant occasion is on the parade. The witness should make an identification by indicating the number of the person concerned. If the witness makes an identification after the parade has ended the suspect and, if present, his solicitor, interpreter, friend (and/or appropriate adult) should be informed. Consideration should then be given to allowing the witness a second opportunity to identify the suspect. Where the witness makes an identification but is unable at trial to remember the number of the suspect on the parade, the identification officer may give evidence of what the witness said, even if it is out of the hearing of the defendant (*R v McCay* (1990) where the witness viewed the parade through a one-way screen). The Court of Appeal in that case said it was either an exception to the hearsay rule based on the principle of res gestae or on the statutory authority of ss 66 and 67(11) of PACE 1984. In *R v Osbourne and Virtue* (1973) the Court of Appeal held that another witness could give evidence that the identifying witness picked out the defendant on a parade where the witness was not able to do so. Both decisions have been criticised as insupportable in law but the Law Commission in their Consultation Paper No 138, 'Evidence in Criminal Proceedings: Hearsay and Related Topics', 1995, provisionally propose that such previous statements of witnesses be admissible as evidence of the truth of their contents. In the meantime it would be good practice to get the identifying witness contemporaneously to make a written and signed record of his identification, including the number used, or the identification officer could make such a record and allow the witness to read and sign it as correct. This can then be used by the witness to refresh his memory or, if he should die, fall ill or otherwise be unable to give evidence as provided for by s 23(2) and (3) of the Criminal Justice Act 1988 his statement in a document may then be admissible.

7.154   If the witness wishes to hear any parade member speak, adopt any specified posture, ie side view or back view, the identification officer should first ask the witness if he can make an identification on the basis of appearance only. When the request is to hear members of the parade speak, the witness must be reminded that the participants were chosen for their physical appearance only. Members of the parade may then be asked to comply with the witness's request to hear them speak, to see them move or adopt a particular posture. (See *R v Brown* (1991), considered at para 7.132, above, where the victim said her assailant spoke with a Scottish accent. If she had been able to identify him without hearing him speak, and it was then discovered that he had a Scottish accent, that would be good supporting evidence of the identification. Alternatively hearing him speak may help the identification and be some support for the correctness of the identification.) If the witness requests that the person they have indicated remove anything, used for the purposes of para 10 to conceal the location of an unusual physical feature, that person may be asked to remove it. When the last witness has left the identification officer must ask the suspect whether he wishes to make any comment on the conduct of the parade. Whilst the Code does not require it, a note should be taken of any comment made.

7.155   Where video films or photographs have been released to the media by the police for the purpose of recognising or tracing the suspect, the investigating officer must ask each witness after the parade whether he has seen any broadcast or published film or photographs relating to the offence and shall record his reply. This is the duty of the investigating officer not the identification officer. It follows that the reply will not form part of the notes relating to the conduct of the parade, which are automatically disclosed to the defence. There is an issue of fairness if the witness has seen a video film or photograph and there is a general duty to disclose this to the defence, possibly by attaching a copy of the record to the note relating to the parade (see Annex D, discussed at para 7.95, post, for identification by photograph).

PARADES INVOLVING PRISON INMATES

7.156   If the identification involves a prison inmate and there are no security problems about him leaving the prison or other establishment, he may be asked to participate in a identification parade or video identification in the usual way. A parade is to be held in the prison or other establishment but must be conducted, as far as is practicable, under normal parade rules. Members of the public shall make up the parade unless there are security or control objections to their admission to the establishment. In such a case other inmates may participate. The inmate suspect shall not be required to wear prison uniform unless all the others participating are inmates in uniform or members of the public prepared to wear prison uniform for the occasion.

DOCUMENTATION (ANNEX B, PARAS 23-28)

7.157   A colour photograph or video of the parade must be taken and a copy supplied on request to the suspect or his solicitor within a reasonable time. The photograph or video film must be destroyed or wiped clean at the conclusion of the relevant criminal proceedings unless the person concerned is prosecuted for a recordable offence or admits the offence and is cautioned for a recordable offence. A record of the conduct of a parade must be recorded on the forms provided, this must include any thing said by the witness or the suspect about any identifications or the conduct of the procedure and any reasons where it was not practicable to comply with any of the Code's provisions. If the identification officer asks any person to leave the parade because he is interfering in its conduct the circumstances shall be recorded as must the names of all those who are present on the parade where these are known to the police. There is, of course, no power to require volunteers to give their names. If prison inmates make up the parade this too must be recorded.

GROUP IDENTIFICATION (CODE D 3.10 AND ANNEX C)

General

7.158   A group identification takes place where the suspect is viewed by the witness among a group of people in an informal setting, though an identification carried out in accordance with Code D and Annex C remains a group identification notwithstanding that when seen by the witness the suspect was on his own rather than in a group (eg he emerges from and stands apart from the group when seen by the witness). It may be held if:

(i)   the suspect refuses to participate in an identification parade; or

(ii)   having agreed, he fails to attend an identification parade; or

(iii)   a parade is impracticable.

7.159   The suspect should first be asked to agree and the procedure explained to him in the same terms as for an identity parade, orally and in writing as set out in Code D 3.17, see para 7.139, above. Code D 3.17 envisages a group identification proceeding with D's consent and co-operation. In *R v Tiplady* (1995) trading standards officers arranged a group identification without:

(1)   attempting to hold an ID parade;

(2)   getting D's consent to the group ID; and

(3)   keeping a record of the group ID.

7.160   They were not aware that they were subject to Code D and acted in good faith. Dismissing D's appeal based on these failures, the Court of Appeal emphasised the lack of awareness and good faith while making it clear that police officers could not ignore Code D, even in good faith. If consent is not forthcoming the identification officer has a discretion to proceed without consent if it is practicable (eg by D being unwittingly surrounded by other persons and secretly observed by the witness). If a group identification is to be tried, an identification officer assumes responsibility. It must be carried out in accordance with Annex C which requires, that where practicable a video recording or colour photograph be taken immediately after the group identification has taken place (with or without the suspect's consent) so as to give a general impression of the scene and the number of people involved. The better alternative, again subject to practicability, is to video the whole process from start to finish. If neither of these alternatives is practicable at the time, a photograph or film of the scene should be taken at a later time determined by the identification officer, if he considers it practicable to do so. As with identity parades the suspect or his solicitor (friend or appropriate adult) should be given details of the first description of the suspect by any witnesses to be present. They should also be allowed to view any material released by the police to the media for the purpose of recognising or tracing the suspect, provided it is practicable and would not unreasonably delay the investigation.

7.161   The location of the group identification is a matter for the identification officer, though he can take into account representations from the suspect, his solicitor, friend or appropriate adult. The place should be one where other people are passing by, or waiting around informally, in groups which the suspect can join and be seen by the witness as part of the group. Examples given in Annex C include people leaving an escalator, pedestrians walking through a shopping precinct, passengers in railway or bus stations waiting in groups or standing in queues. If the group identification is to be held covertly the choice of location is limited. If he is free on bail the witness can be placed at a point along a route taken by the suspect or on a bus or train on which he travels. The appearance of the other persons cannot be controlled, but in selecting the location the identification officer must consider the general appearance and number of persons likely to be present and there must be a reasonable expectation that, from time to time, persons of a broadly similar appearance to the suspect, as well as the suspect, will be seen by the witness. As with other identification procedures, a group identification need not be held if, because of the unusual appearance of the suspect, none of the locations which it would be practicable to use satisfies the above requirements which are necessary for a fair identification.

7.162 If a suspect unreasonably delays joining the group, or having joined the group deliberately conceals himself from the sight of the witness, the identification officer may treat this as a refusal to co-operate (Annex C 30). If the witness identifies someone other than the suspect, an officer should inform that person and ask if he is prepared to give his name and address. There is no obligation on the part of the person to do so. There is no duty to record the details of other members of the public present in the group or at the place where the procedure is conducted (Annex C 31). When the procedure has been completed the identification officer must ask the suspect if he wishes to make any comments on the conduct of the procedure (Annex C 32) (and record any such comments). If the suspect has not already been told, the identification officer must tell the suspect of any identification made by the witnesses.

Group identification with the consent of the suspect (Annex C, paras 13-17)

7.163 A suspect must be given a reasonable opportunity to have a solicitor or friend present (if a juvenile or mentally disordered suspect, the appropriate adult must be present and if a foreigner an interpreter). If any of these are present they may be concealed from the sight of the persons in the group which they are observing if the identification officer considers that this facilitates the conduct of the identification. As with a parade, officers conducting witnesses to a group identification must not discuss it with the witness, nor disclose whether a previous witness has made an identification. It is the responsibility of the identification officer to ensure that witnesses do not communicate with each other about the case or overhear others who have already seen the suspect in the group, on that occasion see the suspect, or on that occasion see or be reminded of any photograph or description of the suspect or be given any other indication of his identity. Anything said to or by the witness during the procedure regarding the identification should be said in the presence and hearing of the identification officer and, if present, the suspect's solicitor, friend, appropriate adult or interpreter for the witness. Witnesses will be brought to the location of the group identification one at a time. Immediately before he views the group the witness must be told by the identification officer that the person he saw may or may not be in the group and if he cannot make a positive identification he should say so. How this is to be done will depend on whether the group is moving or stationary.

Moving group (Annex C, paras 19-24)

7.164 When the group in which the suspect is to appear is moving, for example leaving an escalator, paragraphs 20 to 24 of Annex C apply. These provide that if two or more suspects consent to a group identification, each should be the subject of separate identification procedures which may, however, be conducted consecutively on the same occasion. Thus all can be at the bottom of an escalator and sent up at intervals with a different group of people. As with a parade the identification officer must tell the witness to observe the group and ask him to point out any person he thinks he saw on a relevant occasion. If he does so, and it is practicable to do so, the officer should arrange for the witness to take a closer look at the person he indicated and ask him whether he can make a positive identification. If this is not practicable the officer should ask him if he is sure that the person he has indicated is the relevant person. The witness should continue to observe the group for a period which the identification officer reasonably believes is necessary in the circumstances for the witness to be able to make comparisons between the suspect and persons of a broadly similar appearance. Once the witness has been informed of the procedure in accordance with paragraph 21, he should be allowed to take any position in the group that he wishes.

Stationary group (Annex C, paras 25-29)

7.165 Where the group in which the suspect is to appear is stationary, for example a queue, paragraphs 26 to 29 of Annex C apply. If two or more persons consent to a group identification, each should be the subject of separate identification procedures unless they are broadly of the same appearance, when they may appear in the same group. Where separate group identifications are held, the groups must be made up of different people. The suspect may take any position in the group he wishes. If there is more than one witness the suspect must be told, out of the sight and hearing of the witness, that he may change his position in the group. The identification officer must ask the witness to pass along or among the group and to look at each person at least twice, taking as much time and care as is possible in the circumstances, before making an identification. When he has done this the officer must ask him whether the person he saw on an earlier relevant occasion is in the group and to indicate any such person by whatever means the identification officer considers appropriate in the circumstances. If this is not practicable he should be asked to point out any person he thinks he saw on the earlier relevant occasion. If he does make an identification the officer should, if practicable, arrange for the witness to take a closer look at the person he has indicated and ask him if he can make a positive identification. If that is not practicable he should be asked how sure he is that the person he has indicated is the relevant person.

Identification without the suspect's consent (Annex C, paras 34-36)

7.166 Covert group identification held without the suspect's consent should so far as is practicable follow the rules for group identification with consent. Paragraph 35 states that the suspect has no right to the presence of a solicitor, friend or appropriate adult given the covert nature of the identification. If the group identification takes place in the street or other public place this must be so but if the procedure is to be conducted covertly in the police station the appropriate adult and a solicitor may be present, but of course they need not be informed of the intention covertly to hold a group identification. Any number of suspects may be identified at the same time.

Identification in a police station (Annex C, paras 37-39)

7.167 Group identification should only take place in a police station for reasons of safety, security or because it is impracticable to hold them elsewhere. Where it does take place in a police station it may take place either in a room equipped with a one-way screen, eg the identification suite, or anywhere else in the police station the identification officer considers appropriate. Any of the additional safeguards applicable to identification parades should be followed if the identification officer considers it practicable to do so in the circumstances.

Identification involving prison inmates (Annex C, paras 40-41)

7.168 A group identification involving a prison inmate may only be arranged in prison or at a police station. Whether in prison or a police station the arrangements should follow those for a group identification in a police station set out at Annex C, paras 37-39, above para 7.167. If in a prison other inmates may participate but the inmate suspect should not be required to wear prison uniform unless all the other participants are wearing the same uniform.

Documentation (Annex C, paras 41-43)

7.169 If requested, a copy of the photograph or video film taken in accordance with paras 8 and 9 Annex E must be supplied to the suspect or his solicitor within a reasonable time. If the photograph or video film includes the suspect, it must be destroyed or wiped clean at the conclusion of the relevant criminal proceedings unless the person is prosecuted or cautioned for a recordable offence. A record of the conduct of the group identification must be made on the forms provided and must include:

(a) anything said by the witness or suspect about any identification or the conduct of the procedure; and

(b) any reasons why it was not practicable to comply with any provisions of the code governing the conduct of a group identification.

IDENTIFICATION BY CONFRONTATION (CODE D, ANNEX D)

7.170 Identification by confrontation is the least satisfactory means of identification and may be arranged only if a video identification, identification parade and a group identification have proved to be impracticable for any reason. It will be recalled that there is an order of preference and any attempt to short-circuit the system by, for example, releasing the suspect so that he may be confronted by a witness, is likely to be met with exclusion of the identification evidence (*R v Nagah* (1990)). Confrontation does not require the suspect's consent and must be carried out in accordance with Annex D. Force may not be used to make the suspect's face visible to the witness. This provides that the identification officer is responsible for the conduct of a confrontation. Before it takes place the officer must tell the witness that the person he saw may or may not be the person he is to confront and that if he cannot make a positive identification he should say so. As with the other identification procedures the suspect or his solicitor must be provided with details of the first description of the suspect by any witness who is to attend the confrontation. They should also be allowed to view any material released by the police to the media for the purpose of recognising or tracing the suspect, if practicable and to do so will not unreasonably delay the investigation.

7.171 The suspect should be confronted independently by each witness, who shall be asked, 'Is this the person?' If the witness identifies the person but is unable to confirm the identification, they shall be asked how sure they are that the person is the one they saw on an earlier occasion. The confrontation must take place in the presence of the suspect's solicitor, friend or interpreter unless this would cause unreasonable delay. (If an appropriate adult is involved he should also be present.) The confrontation will normally take place in a police station, either in a normal room or in one equipped with a one-way screen, the latter only being used if the suspect's solicitor, friend or appropriate adult is present or the confrontation is recorded on video. In *R v Joseph* (1994) the Court of Appeal held that the evidence obtained by confrontation in the precincts of the trial court should have been excluded notwithstanding that the defence had asked for it and the trial judge had intimated that he would be unlikely to exclude the result if it went against the defence.

Identification by photograph and pictures (Code D and Annex E)

7.172 The showing of photographs and identikit and other types of pictures to a witness is a well-recognised method of trying to identify offenders (eg *R v Palmer*

(1914)). The practice was covered in detail by the Home Office Circular 109/1978. Annex D to Code E replaced and largely repeated the instructions of the Circular. The preamble to the Circular repeated the words of the Report of the Departmental Committee on Evidence of Identification, Cmnd 338, 1976, para 5.91:

> 'The object of showing a group of photographs to a witness is to test his ability to pick out the photograph, if it is there, of the person whom the witness has said that he has seen previously on a specified occasion. Every precaution should be taken to exclude any suspicion of unfairness or erroneous identification.'

7.173 When showing photographs to witnesses, two different situations must be distinguished: first, the situation in which the police are seeking to identify a suspect; and second, the situation in which they have a suspect under arrest. In the second situation the procedures already discussed can be used so that witnesses can identify the suspect as the person they saw in the relevant circumstances. Photographs or pictures should not be shown to witnesses in these circumstances (Code D 3.3, Note 3F emphasises that the admissibility and value of identification evidence will be compromised if potential witnesses view any photograph other than in accordance with Code D). This section is concerned with the first situation, when the police are looking for the perpetrator of a crime. Here, the showing of photographs, or the use of identikit or photo-fit or similar pictures, may be necessary in order to identify a suspect who is not yet known to the police. It may be necessary to go further and seek the help of the public in identifying the criminal by releasing videos or photographs to the national and local media or broadcast them on television programmes such as 'Crime Watch' or 'Crimestoppers'.

Identification by photograph (Annex E)

7.174 When photographs are used, they will usually be ones which were taken and retained by the police of an individual following his arrest on a previous occasion. The procedure for taking these photographs, both with and without the person's consent, is dealt with in Code D 4 (see para 7.103, post). A duty of confidence may arise when police take a photograph of a suspect at a police station without his consent; but when that photograph is used reasonably for the prevention and detection of crime, the investigation of alleged offences or the apprehension of suspects or persons lawfully at large, the police have a public interest defence to an action for breach of confidence. Thus in *Hellewell v Chief Constable of Derbyshire* (1995) the plaintiff, who had 32 convictions, 19 of these for theft, had no cause of action when police released his photograph to local traders, not for public display but so that members of staff could recognise persons causing trouble in the area.

Procedure

7.175 An officer of at least sergeant rank (as opposed to inspector in relation to identification parades) supervises the showing of photographs, whilst any officer or police employee can actually show them to a witness. The officer must confirm that the first description of the suspect given by the witness has been recorded before the witness sees any photographs. If he is unable to confirm this he must postpone the showing. (Annex E, Note 3). Only one witness at a time should view the photographs, not fewer than 12 at a time and as far as possible of a similar type, and he should be kept apart from other witnesses and given as much privacy as possible. He must be told that the person he saw may or may not be there. The witness must not be prompted or guided in any way when shown the photographs but must be left to make any selection without help. Some searches will involve the witness looking at standard albums. Where, on the other hand, the police have a suspect in mind, his photograph should be mixed in with others of close resemblance. None of the photographs used shall be destroyed, whether or not an identification is made, since they may be required for production in court. A record should be kept of the photographs shown and any comment made by the witness. The photographs should be numbered and a separate photograph taken of the frame or part of the album from which the witness made an identification as an aid to reconstituting it.

7.176   If the witness positively identifies a suspect from a photograph, photo-fit or identikit, these shall not be shown to other witnesses (unless the person in the photograph etc has been cleared by the police). Instead, all the witnesses should, if possible, be asked to attend an identification parade or other identification (see above). In *Connolly v Dale* (1995) C was arrested for murder and the defence sought to interview witnesses, most of whom lived in a hostel. The police had yet to take witness statements from them and required some of them for an identity parade. The police warned against showing photographs and the manager of the hostel refused the defence inquiry agent access to the hostel on the instructions of the police. The Divisional Court held that the police were in contempt of court in preventing defence access to witnesses. It was accepted that the purpose of the police in preventing access to witnesses was to protect the integrity of the identification parade which would be contaminated if photographs of the accused were shown to them. The police relied on s 51(3) of the Police Act 1964, obstruction of the police, to justify their action but their Lordships said that, in their judgment, the actions of the solicitor and inquiry agent in attempting to identify potential alibi witnesses, even though by showing photographs of him they might contaminate the proposed identity parade, could not amount to wilful obstruction, the word 'wilful' importing a requirement of mens rea and a requirement that the act be done without lawful excuse, neither of which was present.

7.177   If a witness attends a parade, the fact that he has previously been shown a photograph or picture must be revealed to the accused and his lawyer. The reason for this is to alert the defence to the prejudice which may be caused to the accused at trial if it is revealed to the jury that he was identified by police photographs, thus implying that he has a criminal record. For this reason the fact that photographs have been shown to the witness should not be revealed by the prosecution but they should inform the defence of their existence and leave it to them to decide whether the jury should be informed of the fact (*R v Wright* (1934); *R v Lamb* (1980)). Exceptionally the prosecution may disclose the fact to the jury. Thus in *R v Bleakley* (1993), D was charged with robbery of a newsagent. A shop assistant identified him from police photographs and subsequently at an identification parade. The day before the parade D went into the shop and tried to speak to the witness, who avoided him. At trial it was suggested that the assistant had identified D at the parade because he had seen him in the shop the day before. The trial judge ruled that evidence of the identification by photograph could be given to rebut this suggestion. The Court of Appeal held that this was a correct ruling.

7.178 In recent years photo-fit and identikit pictures have been devised to help a witness to reconstruct a suspect's face. In 1988 the Government approved a computer-based system called E-fit, a computer programmed with various facial features taken from photographs which the operator can use to produce a picture of the suspect on the screen. They are admissible as evidence (*R v Cook* (1987); *R v Constantinou* (1989)) but it is desirable that a jury be warned as to their accuracy along the lines of *R v Turnbull* (1977) (see the powerful commentary attached to Constantinou). The same principles apply to an artist's sketch made on the instructions of a witness. The court in Cook put them in the same category as photo-fits and in *R v Smith (Percy)* (1976) a sketch was admitted in evidence on the basis that the witness was directing the hand of the artist and it was her sketch made through the hands of the artist.

Identification by video recordings and surveillance cameras

7.179 Video recordings are increasingly being made which show the commission of a crime or some event connected with the investigation of crime, the recording either being made by television companies in the course of collecting news, by the police who may video an observation of premises, a car chase or the holding of an identification parade or other form of identification. In addition there are now many thousands of premises and public places constantly being surveyed by camera, which record all activity within their field of vision (British Telecom are installing fingertip-size cameras in telephone boxes which are triggered when attempts are made to break into the cash box – The Times 23 April 1994). All of these are seen as real evidence and admissible to prove the truth of the events depicted. The tape may then speak for itself and normally no evidence is admissible to explain or interpret it. Thus a camera in a store may pick out D taking goods from the shelf and secreting them about his person. A witness may not give evidence of his opinion that this act amounts to theft, that is for the jury to decide. There are, however, exceptions, as follows.

The maker of the tape-recording or an eye-witness

7.180 If a witness has himself made the video recording, he can authenticate it, confirm when and where it was made, produce it in evidence and describe what he saw by reference to it. A person who is on the video recording may similarly give evidence of what he saw by reference to it. These witnesses may be asked to look at the tape and describe what is happening, or to identify particular persons on the tape. This is not opinion evidence but direct evidence of what they saw or that they recognise the person(s) on the video.

Identifying persons on the video known to the witness

7.181   Where the identity of a person on the video recording is in dispute a witness who knows him may give evidence identifying him as the defendant. Thus in *R v Grimer* (1982) a security officer saw a video recording of a theft taking place and recognised the defendant whom he knew. This evidence was held to be admissible to identify the defendant as the thief. In *R v Fowden and White* (1982) the Court of Appeal rejected the argument that it was for the jury to determine the question of identity holding that there was no reason in principle why a witness should not be called to identify someone he knows shown in a video recording. In that case the witness knew the defendant from another shoplifting case a week later which made it impossible for the defence to test the accuracy of the identification without prejudice to the accused; the evidence should not then have been admitted. However, in *R v Caldwell and Dixon* (1993) where two police officers had jointly viewed a video recording and claimed to recognise D, the Court of Appeal said that the fact that the police officer's knowledge comes from the fact that the defendant has a criminal record cannot operate to prevent the officer identifying D from a video recording. To do so would be unfairly to reward those with a criminal record. In *R v Jones* (1994) video cameras were installed in a public house following a violent assault, and the appellants were identified from the videotape recorded on the following evenings. The Court of Appeal held that Code D had no application to this form of identification. There is, however, as much danger of a wrong identification in witnesses viewing video recordings as there is in any other form of identification. Recognising this the Court of Appeal in *R v Caldwell and Dixon* (1993) recommended that procedures be instituted for regulating identification from video recording. The court pointed out that there is an analogy between this form of identification and the showing of photographs. Until such procedures are instituted it would be wise to adopt and adapt the procedures in Code D, Annex D whenever this form of identification becomes necessary. In the context of the Caldwell case one of the suspects had been arrested just before the officers viewed the recording of the robbery. They claimed to be unaware of this and at the very least procedures should be in place to ensure that suspects or arrested persons are not seen before an identification is made and police officers should view the recording separately and come to their conclusion without help from each other or anyone else.

Identifying persons on the video who are not known to the witness

7.182   Expert evidence may be admissible to identify persons shown on a video recording, possibly with the assistance of computer enhancement of the video. In *R v*

Stockwell (1993) the Court of Appeal upheld the use of expert evidence relating to 'facial mapping' in order to enhance the value of poor-quality video images. In *R v Blenkinsop* (1995) police identified D as one of a number of anti-hunt demonstrators who attacked the home of a kennel huntsman, from a video film and on various 'still' photographs taken at the scene. In dismissing D's appeal against conviction the Court of Appeal held that when a jury is invited to conclude that the person shown in the photograph or video recording was the defendant whom they had seen, the full Turnbull warning was inappropriate. There was, however, a general and invariable requirement that the jury should be warned of the risk of mistaken identification, and the need to exercise particular care in any identification they make for themselves. This applies to identification by witnesses who claim to know the person in the photograph or video recording, as well as to identification by those who do not. In the Blenkinsop case the police had seen D at the demonstration and later identified him as a participant in the violence. In Caldwell and Dixon (above) the officers knew the defendants from their previous contact with them, but in either case a mistaken identification is a real possibility. *R v Turnbull* is considered at para 7.91, ante.

VOICE IDENTIFICATION

7.183 Until recently there was little authority on voice identification but there is now a trio of cases on the subject. In *R v Robb* (1991) evidence from a phonetics expert and that of a police officer that he recognised the voice of the defendant as that of the person who made ransom demands on the telephone was properly admitted and there was no unfairness. In *R v Deenik* (1992) the appellant was charged with the unlawful importation of drugs. A female customs officer impersonated the wife of his co-accused, after the co-accused had been found in possession of a radio pager which received calls from a London call box. The officer had a number of conversations with a man whose voice was later identified by her as that of the appellant. He was arrested at the call box in question and she listened in while he was being questioned by other officers. The defence argued, unsuccessfully, that this evidence was unreliable in the absence of safeguards analagous to those which apply to visual identification and should be excluded. The Court of Appeal held that the evidence was properly admitted and that analogies with Code D and visual identification were of little value. However, in *R v Knowles* (1993), an unreported case, the Court of Appeal appears to have recognised that the dangers involved in voice identification are similar to those involved in visual identification by holding that in a case depending wholly or substantially on voice identification, the same general principles should apply as in visual identification. In *R v Johnson* (1995) the victim of an attempted rape and robbery identified J as her assailant following a voice identification procedure arranged after J's arrest which suggests that voice identification is beginning to be seen as part of the identification procedures in appropriate cases. See *R v Blenkinsop*, above, and *R v Turnbull*, discussed at para 7.91, ante.

HANDWRITING

7.184 The comparison of handwriting samples in criminal cases is governed by s 8 of the Criminal Procedure Act 1865:

'... comparison of disputed writing with any writing proved to the satisfaction of the judge to be genuine shall be permitted to be made by witnesses; and such writings, and the evidence of witnesses respecting the same, may be submitted to the court and jury as evidence of the genuineness or otherwise of the writing in dispute'.

7.185 In *R v Ewing* (1983) it was made clear that the prosecution must first prove the genuineness of the allegedly genuine document beyond reasonable doubt. Second, they must prove beyond reasonable doubt that the document with which it is compared was written by the same person who wrote the genuine document. The word 'witness' in s 8 includes lay and expert witnesses. The common law rule is that evidence that the handwriting on a particular document or documents is that of a particular person may be given by lay witnesses who are familiar with the person's handwriting or by an expert (*R v Derrick* (1910)). The expert need not have attained his expertise in any particular way; it is a matter for the court to decide whether he has sufficient skill and knowledge (*R v Silverlock* (1894)). *R v Tilley* (1961) suggests that whenever disputed handwriting is an issue expert evidence should be called to assist and given that the dangers of wrongly attributing writing to a person are similar to the dangers of a wrong identification it seems sensible to seek expert analysis. Disputed documents will often have to go before the jury and where they do the jury should be warned against making their own comparisons (*R v O'Sullivan* (1969)) though it is recognised that it is not possible to prevent them doing so. One may note that s 76(4) (Art 74(4)) provides that parts of an excluded confession are admissible to prove that the accused person writes in a particular way.

FINGERPRINTS (S 61, ART 61)

7.186 Identification by fingerprints can serve two purposes. The first and by far the more frequent usage is to identify the accused so that a record of his antecedents can be prepared for the court. The second is to detect the offender by, for example, comparing prints left at the scene of the crime with national records or with prints taken freshly from the suspect. PACE permits fingerprinting: The provisions for taking fingerprints are contained in ss 61 (with or without consent), 54 and Annex F.

7.187 Section 61 provides that except as provided by in the section no person's fingerprints may be taken without the appropriate consent. Fingerprints may be taken with consent provided that:

'(3) The fingerprints of a person detained at a police station may be taken without the appropriate consent (ss 3):

(a) if an officer of at least the rank of inspector authorises them to be taken; or
(b) if –
    (i) he has been charged with a recordable offence or informed that he will be reported for such an offence; and
    (ii) he has not had his fingerprints taken in the course of the investigation of the offence by the police.'

7.188 Subsection (3A) provides that where a person charged with a recordable offence or informed that he will be reported for such an offence has already had his fingerprints taken as mentioned in s 61(3)(b)(ii), that fact shall be disregarded for the purposes of that subsection if:
(a) the fingerprints taken on the previous occasion do not constitute a complete set of his fingerprints; or
(b) some or all of the fingerprints taken on the previous occasion are not of sufficient quality to allow satisfactory analysis, comparison or matching (whether in the case in question or generally).

7.189 Under sub-s (4) an officer may only give an authorisation under sub-s (3)(a) if he has reasonable grounds:
(a) for suspecting the involvement of the person whose fingerprints are to be taken in a criminal offence; and
(b) for believing that his fingerprints will tend to confirm or disprove his involvement or will facilitate the ascertainment of his identity (within the meaning of s 54A).

7.190 Under sub-s (4A) the fingerprints of a person who has answered to bail at a court or police station may be taken without the appropriate consent at the court or station if:
(a) the court, or
(b) an officer of at least the rank of inspector,
authorises them to be taken.

7.191 A court or officer may only give an authorisation under sub-s (4A) if:
(a) the person who has answered to bail has answered to it for a person whose fingerprints were taken on a previous occasion and there are reasonable grounds for believing that he is not the same person; or
(b) the person who has answered to bail claims to be a different person from a person whose fingerprints were taken on a previous occasion.

7.192 An officer may give an authorisation under sub-s (3)(a) or (4A) orally or in writing but, if he gives it orally, he shall confirm it in writing as soon as is practicable.

7.193 A person's fingerprints may be taken without the appropriate consent under the following circumstances (sub-s (6)):
(a) he has been convicted of a recordable offence;
(b) he has been given a caution in respect of a recordable offence which, at the time of the caution, he has admitted; or

(c) he has been warned or reprimanded under s 65 of the Crime and Disorder Act 1998 for a recordable offence.

7.194 In a case where by virtue of sub-s (3) or (6) above a person's fingerprints are taken without the appropriate consent :

(a) he shall be told the reason before his fingerprints are taken; and

(b) the reason shall be recorded as soon as is practicable after the fingerprints are taken.

7.195 Subsection (7A) provides if a person's fingerprints are taken at a police station, whether with or without the appropriate consent:

(a) before the fingerprints are taken, an officer shall inform him that they may be the subject of a speculative search; and

(b) the fact that the person has been informed of this possibility shall be recorded as soon as possible after the fingerprints have been taken.

7.196 Subsections (8)-(9) provide:

'(8) If he is detained at a police station when the fingerprints are taken, the reason for taking them and, in the case falling within subsection (7A) above, the fact referred to in paragraph (b) of that subsection shall be recorded on his custody record.

(8A) Where a person's fingerprints are taken electronically, they must be taken in such a manner, and using such devices, as the Secretary of State has approved for the purposes of electronic fingerprinting.

(8B) The power to take the fingerprints of a person detained at a police station without the appropriate consent shall be exercisable by any constable.

(9) Nothing in this section –

(a) affects any power conferred by paragraph 18(2) of Schedule 2 to the Immigration Act 1971, section 141 of the Immigration and Asylum Act 1999 or regulations made under section 144 of that Act; or

(b) applies to a person arrested or detained under the terrorism provisions.'

7.197 Two preliminary points should be noted:

(1) the expression 'fingerprints' includes palm prints (s 65, Art 53; for a definition of palm, see *R v Tottenham Justices, ex p ML* (1985));

(2) categories (b)-(d) confer powers on the police. Consequently, if the person resists the taking of the prints, the police can use reasonable force (s 117, Art 88).

Procedure

7.198 In non-consensual cases, reasonable force may be used to obtain the fingerprints (s 117, Art 88) and details must be kept of the circumstances which required force and those present. The person must be told:

(i)   the reason for taking the prints and the reason must be recorded (in the custody record if he is in detention (s 61(7), (8));

(ii) that they may be the subject of a speculative search and the fact he has been told must be noted on the custody record (s 61(7A), (8)).

7.199   He must also be told of the possibility that the prints will be destroyed in due course, if he is not prosecuted or not proved to have committed the offence (Code D 3.23, see further paras 7.226-7.232, post and s 64 in relation to the destruction of fingerprints and samples).

TAKING OF SAMPLES (ss 62-64, Arts 62-64, Code D 5)

7.200   (Articles 62-64 of the NI Order are mostly identical to ss 62-64, so only section references will be used unless they differ.) It is sometimes necessary for the police to take forensic samples from a person's body in order to check on that person's involvement in an offence. The most obvious instance is the breathalyser in road traffic cases. Power to take samples in these cases lies in s 8 of the Road Traffic Act 1988, which makes the refusal to supply a sample of breath, blood or urine in drink-driving cases an offence. Sex offences are a less frequent but similarly relevant area (eg swabs taken to detect semen or vaginal traces). The samples under discussion here include blood, urine, semen, teeth impressions, saliva, hair and scrapings from beneath fingernails. PACE, which considerably extended the common law powers of the police to take samples, draws a distinction between non-intimate samples, which can be taken against the person's will, and intimate samples, which cannot. The sanction against refusal to supply the latter is the power of the court to draw the inference of guilt. Partly in the light of experience of the operation of these provisions and partly to take account of the onward march of technology, in particular the development of DNA profiling, PACE required amending. The RCCJ, 1993, made a number of recommendations (Chapter 2, paras 25-38) and, as has been so often the case, the Government took up all the recommendations that the police should have new powers but were less enthusiastic about the recommended safeguards. Sections 62-65 of PACE, as amended by the Criminal Justice and Public Order Act 1994, ss 54-58, govern the taking and retaining of samples (Arts 61-64 and Art 53, as amended by the Police (Amendment) (NI) Order 1995, Arts 8-13).

Intimate samples (s 62, Art 62)

7.201   The following terminology is employed in s 65 (Art 53):

"'intimate sample" means -
(a) a sample of blood, semen or any other tissue fluid, urine, or pubic hair;
(b) a dental impression;
(c) a swab taken from a person's body orifice other than the mouth ...'

7.202   One significant change made by the CJPOA 1994 to the definition of samples is the 'demotion' of saliva and swabs from the mouth from being intimate samples to non-intimate samples (bringing England and Wales in line with Northern Ireland (PACE (NI) Order 1989, Art 53) and, correspondingly, the search of a mouth is no longer an intimate search (s 65 and Art 53). Conversely, dental impressions, having previously been treated as intimate samples only by virtue of Code D 5.1, have now been given statutory confirmation of this status by s 58(2) of the 1994 Act which amends s 65 of PACE (Art 53).

7.203   Intimate samples can only be taken from persons in police detention if:
(i)   an inspector or higher rank authorised it; and
(ii) he had reasonable grounds for suspecting the person to be involved in a recordable offence; and
(iii) he had reasonable grounds for believing that the sample would confirm or disprove that person's involvement in that offence; and
(iv) that person (and/or his parent or guardian where appropriate, see s 65) gave his written consent (s 62(1), (2)).

Recordable offences

7.204   The power to take intimate samples, which had previously been limited to suspected involvement in serious arrestable offences, is now greatly extended to include the broader category of recordable offences (see para 2.108, ante). This means that offences such as assault and most burglaries, which had previously been excluded from the power, will now be subject to it and the range of offences in which samples can be taken is equivalent to that for taking fingerprints, the difference being, at least in respect of intimate samples, that written consent must be obtained. Indeed, the objective is to create a data bank of DNA profiles of all those convicted of recordable offences similar to that which exists for fingerprints.

7.205   A new sub-s (1A), has been inserted into s 62 by s 54(2) of the 1994 Act, which provides a power to take an intimate sample from persons who are not in police detention, but from whom at least two non-intimate samples have previously been taken in the course of investigating an offence, for the same means of analysis and which proved to be insufficient. The taking remains subject to authorisation from at least an inspector (on the grounds listed in para 7.203, ante), and the written consent of the person. This amendment is directed at persons who have been previously arrested and detained, during which time they may not have been asked to provide an intimate sample, or having been asked, refused to do so, but from whom non-intimate samples had been obtained, which were found to be insufficient, either in quantity or quality, for the particular form of analysis they were subjected to, such as DNA analysis (Code D 6.2 (b), Note 6B). In Northern Ireland, the provisions in Art 62 shall apply to persons who have been arrested under s 41 of the Terrorism Act 2000 and the taking of a sample may only be authorised if the officer is satisfied that it will assist in determining whether the person has been involved with committing, preparing or instigating acts of terrorism. Where persons are not in police detention they will probably have either been remanded in custody or released on bail. Provisions which enable the police to exercise the power to take samples when the suspect is not in police detention are contained in a new s 63A which was inserted into PACE by s 56 of the Criminal Justice and Public Order Act 1994 (Art 63A of the 1989 Order which is inserted by the Police Amendment (NI) Order 1995) (see para 7.217, post).

7.206   The inspector who makes the authorisation need not be independent of the investigation but the spirit of s 62 demands that considerable effort be made to find an independent officer. The authorising officer must have reasonable grounds to 'suspect' the person is involved in the offence, but reasonable grounds to 'believe' that the taking of an intimate sample 'will tend to confirm or disprove' the person's involvement ('believe' connotes a higher degree of certainty than 'suspect', (see paras 2 83-2.92, ante), but 'tend to' reduces the effect of this). Samples can of course be used to clear a suspect, eg a genital swab taken from a suspected rapist.

Consent

7.207   The requirement of consent in both s 62(1) and (1A) provides a stumbling block. An intimate sample cannot be taken without the person's consent, and this is unlikely to be given willingly. A sanction lies in s 62(10) which states that proper inferences can be drawn from a refusal to consent without good cause (Sch 11 of the CJPOA 1994 having repealed the corroboration provisions in this subsection), but the fact that inferences may be drawn is no substitute for positive proof of guilt or innocence. 'Good cause' for refusing consent could include, apart from guilt, belligerence (eg of a parent at the proposal to take a sample from his child), drunkenness, religious objection (eg of a Jehovah's Witness to the taking of a blood sample), physical fear (eg of a pregnant suspect at the thought of a genital swab), or simply a belief in innocence coupled with indignation at the police request. Whether the reason amounts to a 'good cause' for the purpose of s 62(10) will be judged by the court or jury. The inferences may be drawn when determining whether to grant an application to dismiss the case (under s 6 of the Magistrates' Court Act 1980 – transfer for trial; s 6 of the Criminal Justice Act 1967 – serious fraud; or Sch 6, para 5 of the Criminal Justice Act 1991 – violent or sexual offences involving a child) or whether there is a case to answer and/or at trial (s 62(10)).

Procedure

7.208   Before the person is asked to provide the intimate sample, he must be formally told of the authorisation to take it (the authorisation itself being given either orally, eg over the telephone, or in writing, but if given orally it must be confirmed in writing as soon as possible), the grounds for it, the nature of the offence involved and that a refusal to do so without good cause might harm his case if it comes to trial. He must also be informed that any sample taken may be the subject of a speculative search against other samples held by the police and be reminded of his right to free legal advice (s 62(5), (6), (7A)(a), Code D 6.8 Note 6E). Documentation is very important in the taking of intimate samples. Thus, where one is taken, a record must be made of the authorisation and grounds for it, together with the fact that written consent was given (s 62(7), (7A)(b), Code D 6.2, 6.10-6.12). Dental impressions may only be taken by a registered dentist. (On the use of dental impressions voluntarily surrendered by a dental practitioner, see *R v Singleton* (1995) at para 4.64, ante.) Most other intimate samples may only be taken by a registered medical practitioner, the one exception being a urine sample, which may be taken by a constable (s 62(9), as amended by s 54(4) of the 1994 Act). If, as in most cases, clothing has to be removed and is likely to cause embarrassment, no person of the opposite sex (other than the practitioner or nurse) must attend, nor should there be any unnecessary bystander present. Since a sample is taken with consent, there is no need for constables to attend to restrain the person. Consequently only the medical practitioner and one constable (to record what has taken place) need attend. If the person is a juvenile or is mentally disordered or mentally handicapped he can request an adult of the opposite sex to be present and, in the case of a juvenile unless he specifically objects and the adult agrees, an appropriate adult (see paras 7.248–7.250, post) must always be present when the clothing is removed (Code D 6.9). Although the person must be in police detention, the sample need not be taken at a police station. D can be taken to a hospital where the medical practitioner can take the sample.

7.209   The police powers to take intimate samples and to undertake intimate searches may well coincide in relation to the same suspect. The contrast between the powers can be summarised as follows:

	Intimate search	*Intimate sample*
Power	Consent or authorisation by the police	Consent and authorisation by the police
Object	To find weapons or serious drugs	To find evidence of a recordable offence
Searcher	Medical practitioner, nurse or constable	Medical practitioner

Non-intimate samples (s 63, ART 63)

7.210   These are exclusively defined by s 65 (Art 53):

"'non-intimate sample" means -
(a) a sample of hair other than pubic hair;
(b) a sample taken from a nail or from under a nail;

(c) a swab taken from any part of a person's body including the mouth but not any other body orifice;

(d) saliva;

(e) a footprint or a similar impression of any part of a person's body other than a part of his hand'

7.211 Categories (b) and (c) can include traces of explosives, drugs, blood or semen. Category (e), although not expressly excluding dental impressions, must do so by implication since they are now defined as intimate samples. Fingerprints and palm prints are also covered separately by s 61 (see paras 7.96-7.101, ante).

7.212 Non-intimate samples may be taken in two situations:

(a) with the suspect's consent, in which case the suspect may give the appropriate written consent (for 'appropriate' see s 65 and Code D 2.12); or

(b) where the suspect does not consent if:

(i) a person is in detention and an officer of at least the rank of inspector authorises the taking;

(ii) that authority may only be given if the officer has reasonable grounds for suspecting his involvement in a recordable offence; and

(iii) he has reasonable grounds to believe that the sample will tend to confirm or disprove the person's involvement in the offence; or

(iv) a person has been charged with or informed that he may be prosecuted for a recordable offence and has not given a non-intimate sample or if he has done so that sample has proved insufficient or unsuitable for analysis; or

(v) if a person has been convicted of a recordable offence (s 63, as amended by s 55 of the CJPOA 1994 and Art 11 of the Police (Amendment) (NI) Order 1995).

7.213 (iv) and (v) put the taking of non-intimate samples on a par with the taking of fingerprints without consent and, since consent is not required, reasonable force may be used to obtain the sample (s 117, Art 88, Code D 6.7, Draft NI Code 5.11). If force is used, a record must be made of the circumstances and those who were present at the time. As with fingerprints, these new powers apply to any offence and not, as previously, only the offence under investigation. As with the taking of intimate samples, where the person is not in police detention there is a power to require the person to attend at a police station so that the sample may be taken (see para 7.217, post).

7.214 The procedure for taking non-intimate samples is found in s 63 (Art 63). Where a sample is taken either with or without the suspect's consent, before it is taken he must be informed that the sample may be the subject of a speculative search, and the fact he has been so informed must be recorded on the custody record. Where it is proposed to take a sample without the person's consent, the taking must be authorised by an officer of at least the rank of inspector, the authorisation being given either orally or in writing, but if given orally it must be confirmed in writing as soon as possible. The person must be informed of both the authorisation and the grounds for it, which will include the nature of the offence for which the person is under suspicion.

Where a sample is taken without the person's consent, the authorisation and the grounds for giving it must be recorded on the custody record as soon as practicable after it was taken. Where the sample is taken from a person who falls within (iv) or (v) above, prior to the taking, he must be told of the reason for taking it and the reason must be recorded on the custody record as soon as practicable after the sample is taken. Unlike the procedure for taking intimate samples, in respect of non-intimate samples, there is no requirement to remind the suspect about his entitlement to legal advice or warn him that, if consent is refused, the police may consider using reasonable force to obtain the sample. It is suggested that a warning be given in these terms. Samples of hair (other than pubic hair), may either be cut or plucked (s 63A(2), Art 63(10), added by Sch 9, para 39 of the CJPOA 1994) giving effect to the decision in *R v Cooke* (1995), but, where the sample of hair is plucked (eg when it is required for the purposes of DNA analysis), the person must be given the opportunity to express a preference as to which part of the body the hairs should be taken from. Hairs that are taken for these purposes should be plucked individually unless the person prefers otherwise, and no more should be taken than the person taking them considers to be reasonably necessary for a sufficient sample (Code D Note 6A).

FINGERPRINTS AND SAMPLES: SUPPLEMENTARY PROVISIONS

7.215   The provisions of ss 62(1A) and 63A were originally inserted by the Criminal Justice Act 1994 ss 54 and 55 and amended by the Criminal Procedure and Investigations Act 1996, s 64 and the Criminal Justice and Police Act 2001, s 81(1). They relate to the taking of fingerprints and samples at a place other than a police station, and the checking of fingerprints and samples against existing police records (defined as a 'speculative search').These sections have the effect of broadening the circumstances when samples may be taken and extending to prisons and mental hospitals the places where they may be taken.

7.216   Section 62(1A) provides that an intimate sample may be taken from a person who is not in police detention but from whom , in the course of the investigation of an offence, two or more non-intimate samples suitable for the same means of analysis have been taken which have proved insufficient provided that an officer of at least the rank of inspector authorises it to be taken and if the appropriate consent is given. The authorisation may only be given if he has reasonable grounds for suspecting the involvement of the person from whom the sample is to be taken in a recordable offence and for believing that the sample will tend to confirm or disprove his involvement. The procedures in relation to the keeping of records etc are to be found in s 62(3)-(12) and are identical to those in respect on intimate samples taken whilst the person is in police detention (see para 2.208).

7.217   Section 63A also creates a power for a person not in police detention to be required to attend a police station for the purpose of providing a sample. He must have been charged with or informed that he will be reported for a recordable offence or convicted of a recordable offence and either not had a sample taken or the one which was taken was found not to be suitable for the same means of analysis, or the sample proved insufficient (s 63A(4)). There is a deadline of one month from the date that the person was told that he would be charged or reported or one month from the date the officer was informed the sample was insufficient . The person must be given at least seven days' notice but the police can direct the time at which or between what times he should attend (s 63A(6)). Failure to attend can result in arrest (s 63A(7)).

7.218 Section 63(3) gives power to take samples in prison and s 3 of the Criminal Evidence (Amendment) Act 1997 has extended the power to take non-intimate samples to persons in psychiatric hospitals.

7.219 Section 63A(1) provides that where a person has been arrested on suspicion of being involved in a recordable offence or has been charged or informed that he will be reported for a recordable offence the fingerprints or samples or information derived from any power conferred by PACE may be checked against:
(a) other fingerprints, samples or information held by or on behalf of any relevant law-enforcement authorities or which are held in connection with or as a result of any criminal investigation ;
(b) information derived from other samples of the information is contained in records which the person carrying out the check has access and which are held by any relevant law-enforcement agency.

7.220 A relevant law enforcement agency means:
(a) a police force;
(b) the National Criminal Intelligence Service;
(c) the National Crime Squad;
(d) a public authority (other than those at (a)-(c) above) with functions in any part of the British Islands which consist of or include the investigation of crimes or the charging of offenders;
(e) any person with functions in any country or territory outside the United Kingdom which either corresponds to those of a police force; or otherwise consist of or include the investigation of conduct contrary to the law of that country, or the apprehension of persons guilty of such conduct;
(f) any person with functions under any international agreement which consists of or include the investigation of conduct which is unlawful under the law of one or more places, is prohibited by the agreement, or contrary to international law, or the apprehension of persons guilty of such conduct.

7.221 The reference to a police force in sub-s (1A) refers to all UK police forces maintained under the relevant Police Acts and the Metropolitan and City police forces, Ministry of Defence and police forces of the Armed Services, British Transport Police, Jersey, Guernsey and Isle of Man police forces.

7.222 These provisions were intended to place on a statutory footing previously informal procedures which were of doubtful legality and to give recognition not only to the proliferation of law enforcement agencies but also to the increasingly international nature of criminal investigation.

DNA databases

7.223   The main purpose behind the new s 63(3A), which allows non-intimate samples to be taken from persons charged with or informed that they may be prosecuted for a recordable offence, or from persons convicted of such an offence who have not previously given such a sample, is not to obtain evidence in respect of those offences but to build up a database of samples which will be used in other investigations as is currently done in relation to fingerprints. The Royal Commission on Criminal Justice found it

> 'proper and desirable to allow the police to take non-intimate samples (eg saliva, plucked hair, etc) without consent from all those arrested for serious criminal offences whether or not DNA evidence is relevant to the particular offence, and [we] so recommend'. (Report, Ch 2, para 35)

7.224   Section 63(3A) goes further than that recommendation, applying to recordable offences rather than 'serious' offences, but this is understandable given that the power to take fingerprints in the same circumstances also applies to recordable offences. Section 63(3B) authorises the taking of such samples without consent when the person has been convicted of a recordable offence, but the section does not authorise the taking of samples from persons convicted before these provisions come into force. Home Office Circular 16/95 issues guidance on the management and compilation of the National DNA Database and procedures for the taking, profiling and analysis of samples and their destruction where relevant.

7.225   The usefulness of such samples in the investigation of other offences is demonstrated by the decision in *R v Kelt* (1994). D was arrested in 1988 in connection with a murder and a blood sample was lawfully taken under s 62. An informant told police that D was involved in an armed robbery in 1987. Comparison was then made with blood found on money bags at the scene of that armed robbery which implicated D in it. He was convicted of the robbery and his appeal against conviction, based on the use of the sample in the investigation of another offence, was dismissed (but see *R v Nathaniel* (1995) where the defendant's appeal was allowed but has been superseded by the provisions of s 64: see para 7.228 below). Provision is made for a 'speculative search', the checking of fingerprints, samples or information obtained from samples from a person arrested on suspicion of being involved in a recordable offence, against those contained in records held by or on behalf of the police or held in connection with or as a result of an investigation of an offence (s 63A(1), inserted by s 56 of the 1994 Act, Art 12 of the 1995 Order).

Destruction of fingerprints and samples (s 64, Art 64)

7.226   The general principle concerning the retention and destruction of fingerprints, palm prints, intimate and non-intimate samples taken by the police during the investigation of an offence was until recently, fairly straightforward: they must usually be destroyed, as soon as practicable, unless the person is found guilty of or is cautioned for the offence for which they were taken. Provisions concerning fingerprints and other samples are found in s 64 (Art 64), which has been amended to take account of provisions in the Criminal Justice and Public Order Act and the Criminal Justice and Police Act 2001.

7.227 Under s 64(1A) where fingerprints or samples are taken from a person in connection with the investigation of an offence the fingerprints or samples may be retained after they have fulfilled the purpose for which were taken but they may only be used for purposes related to the prevention or detection of crime, the investigation of an offence or the conduct of a prosecution.

7.228 Amendments were made to s 64 following the House of Lords ruling in *R v B, A-G's Reference (No 3 of 1999)* (2001), the effect of which was to encourage the police to hold DNA samples unlawfully. The amendment applies retrospectively so that samples which ought to have been destroyed may now be retained.

7.229 The amended provisions of s 64 were unsuccessfully challenged in *R (S) v Chief Constable of South Yorkshire* and *R v Marper v Chief Constable of South Yorkshire* (2002). The Court of Appeal, confirming the Divisional Court's ruling, held that there was a pressing social need for the Art 8 restriction and its imposition was proportionate.

7.230 DNA evidence is vitally important in the detection of crime , the RCCJ noted police arguments for legal provisions covering 'frequency databases',

> 'which are necessary for giving estimates of the likelihood of a DNA sample matching a sample in the database... . The police argue that DNA databases should not be confined to samples from convicted persons. We see no objection to the retention for data base purposes of any DNA samples obtained by the police in the course of their investigations provided that these are kept by an independent body.' (Report, Ch 2 para 36)

7.231 The Royal Commission stressed that if samples of those who were not convicted or cautioned were to be retained, it should be for statistical purposes only and strong safeguards should exist 'to ensure that such samples can no longer be linked by the police or prosecution to the persons from whom they were taken'. There is no provision for the independent body. 'Strong safeguards' are conspicuously absent in the Act.

7.232 A further argument for keeping all the samples was raised during the passage of the Bill. This was a technical one and concerns not only the samples, but the information derived from them. Seemingly, technical difficulties might arise during the processing and analysis stage, whereby a number of different samples, all of which have been processed in the same 'batch' and subjected to individual analysis, appear in a combined computer record and print-out. Thus, amongst the data which apparently cannot be separated into individual records, will appear samples and information which will lead to the conviction of some and the innocence of others. 'It is not technically feasible to keep separate the records of those who have been convicted while destroying the records of the innocent' (HC Standing Committee B, 3 February 1994, col 524). This may provide the justification for s 64(3B) which concerns the information derived from analysed samples. Where s 64(3A), above, does not apply, and the sample itself is destroyed under (1), (2) or (3) above, the information derived from the sample may be retained, although again, it shall not be used in evidence against the person entitled to its destruction, nor for the purpose of investigating any offence.

PHOTOGRAPHS (CODE D 5)

7.233 Like fingerprints, photographs are primarily used to establish the identity of the person arrested, so as to make sure that the correct person appears in court and, where appropriate, the correct criminal record is produced to the court. Photographs may, however, also be used for the purposes of identifying and detecting offenders by, for example, showing them to witnesses of a crime (see paras 7.172-7.78, ante).

7.234 This section deals with the provisions governing the power to take photographs of those who have already been arrested, which are contained in the Act and Code D. Thus, Code D 5.12 provides that photographs of an arrested person may be taken at a police station only with his written consent or without consent if his consent is withheld or it is not practicable to obtain consent (for example if he is drunk or would attempt to thwart the taking of photographs). In either case he must be told the reason for taking it and that it will be destroyed unless the circumstances in para 7.235 below apply. He must be told that he may witness the destruction or he will be given a certificate confirming it has been destroyed if he so requests within five days of being cleared or informed that he will not be prosecuted. He must also be warned that if he significantly alters his appearance between the taking of the photograph and any attempt to hold an identification procedure this may be given in evidence if the case comes to trial (see *R v Byrne and Trump* (1987)).

7.235 A record must be made as soon as possible of the reason for taking a photograph without consent and of the destruction of any photographs (Code 5.16). Force may be used to take a photograph if it is established that the detainee is unwilling to co-operate sufficiently to enable a photograph to be taken and it is not reasonably practicable to take the photograph covertly (Code D5.14). Any photograph, negative or copy taken must be destroyed if the person:
(a) is prosecuted and cleared unless he has a previous conviction for a recordable offence; or
(b) has been charged but not prosecuted (unless he admits the offence and is cautioned or has a previous conviction for a recordable offence) (Code D 4.4).

7.236 The above does not require the destruction of copies of a police gazette in which photographs of wanted persons are circulated (Note 4B).

TERRORISM OFFENCES

7.237 Section 64(7) provides that none of the provisions relating to the destruction of fingerprints or samples applies to persons detained under the Terrorism Act 2000 therefore none of the provisions amending this section applies to such persons. Paragraph 62 of Sch 10 of the 1994 Act amends the POT Act to incorporate the provisions of ss 62 and 63 of PACE, which regulate the taking of intimate and non-intimate samples, and the new definition of intimate and non-intimate sample (see para 7.288(e), post).

PHYSICAL CONDITIONS OF DETENTION

7.238   Section 8 of Code C sets out the physical arrangements which must be made for the detention of persons at police stations. Some of these provisions (eg adequate heating of a cell in winter, regular meals) will be more important than others when it comes to determining whether oppression or irregularity has been used for the purposes of ss 76, 78 (Arts 74, 76). In designated police stations the facilities should meet Home Office requirements. It is at the smaller non-designated stations that physical conditions are likely to pose most problems, though this is tempered by the limited time a person can be kept there. Each cell must be 'adequately heated, cleaned and ventilated' (Code C 8.2) and have dimmed night-time lighting so that the suspect can sleep and the jailer can check on his condition at the prescribed hourly intervals. Bedding should be clean and of reasonable standard (especially if the person is likely to be detained for a lengthy time, eg under the prevention of terrorism legislation), and toilet and washing facilities must be available. The cell will not, however, be comfortable. The risks of damage being caused to fittings and of suicide and self-mutilation mean that the furnishings of cells are spartan. Confinement in a cell will usually suffice for an unruly suspect, but occasionally his violent or unpredictable (eg through drugs) behaviour will require handcuffs. Special care is required when considering the use of handcuffs if the suspect is mentally handicapped or mentally disordered. If practicable no cell should contain more than one person. An unexpected inrush of arrested persons may make this impracticable, as may congestion at local prisons which forces a police station to accommodate persons on remand and thus cuts down the number of cells available for arrested suspects. As for prisoners on remand, the authority for their detention is the Imprisonment (Temporary Provisions) Act 1980. The Prison Act and Rules apply and not the PACE Code. If double occupancy of a cell is unavoidable, the custody officer should take care to place similar types together (and not, for example, to put an elderly first-time female shoplifter with an experienced prostitute). A juvenile should not be placed in a cell unless there is no other secure accommodation available and he can only be properly supervised in a cell, or the conditions in a cell are considered more comfortable than what other secure accommodation there might be (Code C 8.8). An interview room nearby might suffice, but placing him in the charge room in view of passing prisoners is unsatisfactory and the absence of a room proximate to the jailer will necessitate a cell. In that case, the door can be left unlocked unless the juvenile's behaviour dictates otherwise. If a juvenile is placed in a cell, the reason must be noted and he must not share it with an adult (though he could with other juveniles). If clothing has to be removed from the detained person (for forensic or other investigative purposes, or for hygiene or health or cleaning purposes) adequate replacements must be supplied, a record made, and, most importantly, the person must not be questioned until the clothing has been offered to him. If thin, standard, disposable clothing is offered, adequate heating of the cell and interview room must be ensured.

7.239   Each detained person should be visited hourly and those who are intoxicated at least every half an hour (Code C 8.10; the NI Draft Code equivalent states 15 minutes) when they should be roused and spoken to (even if asleep, lest, for example, they choke on vomit). Code C Note 8A suggests that juveniles and others at risk (the mentally ill and those whom the police suspect may hurt themselves) should be visited more frequently. (This is a provision of the NI Draft Code rather than simply guidance as it is in England and Wales.) Limited police resources and congestion in the charge room should not be allowed to prevent this good practice, particularly since 17 deaths occurred in police stations excluding those within the Metropolitan Police District in 1994 (HOSB 13/95; 15 in both 1993 and 1992), some of which may have been avoided had more frequent checks taken place. Occasionally a person's behaviour may be so threatening (eg he has already tried to kill himself) that an officer will have to sit in permanent visual contact with him. Where a custody officer has any cause for concern about a suspect's condition, he should seek medical treatment. Two light meals and one main meal along with drinks should be provided, if possible at recognised meal times, in any 24-hour period, drinks on reasonable request should be offered and special dietary or religious needs (eg fasting during Ramadan) should be met as far as practicable. The latter can often be supplied, at their expense, by the suspect's family or friends. The police surgeon may issue, or be approached for, instructions about diet. All meals must be noted. Daily outdoor exercise, especially for those detained to the maximum of 96 hours, should be offered, but shortage of supervisory officers or of physical facilities may rule this out. A detainee must be given at least eight hours' rest in any 24-hour period. This should only be delayed or interrupted if there are reasonable grounds to believe that a failure to do so would put others at risk of harm, property would be lost or damaged or it would unnecessarily delay the suspect's release from custody or prejudice the investigation. Alternatively the suspect, his appropriate adult or legal adviser may so request, but any such interruption which occurs would not be taken into account in the overall time allocated for rest (Code C 12.2).

7.240   Once again the importance of accurate documentation as to the person's detention and any complaints he has made must be stressed, for a court may subsequently be called upon to decide whether a confession has been obtained improperly (ss 76 and 78, Arts 74, 76), and the person's surrounding conditions and treatment may, for example, amount to, or contribute to, a finding of oppressive conduct by the police. In this context of record-keeping the custody officer assumes the overall supervision of detained persons. In some designated stations the cell and charging areas are proximate, enabling him to check detainees himself. In others he may also be station sergeant and in charge of an operations room in another part of the building, dividing his time between the two. The regular observation and treatment of detainees are then left very much in the hands of junior officers, or civilian detention officers. Indeed, in busy stations one officer may be delegated mainly to watch the wall charts (ie a board listing the detention, review, meal and other times for each prisoner). Any complaint about the person's treatment (which may come from him or his representative or an officer who is concerned about him) must be passed urgently to an officer of at least inspector rank who is unconnected with the investigation (Code C 9.1). Given the implications for the possible exclusion of evidence and the lodging of an official complaint, the complaint should be investigated quickly and as thoroughly as possible in the time available. If physical violence is involved or alleged, the police surgeon must be called (Code C 9.1). Much will depend on whether the detainee's representations are interpreted by the custody officer as a 'complaint' for these purposes. The custody officer may well be able to resolve minor grievances at once (eg replace a light bulb, allow D to wash) with no harm to the detainee's interests, especially if the latter's solicitor is consulted and agrees. But even here it behoves the custody officer to make a note, in the custody record, of the problem and of the action taken.

The ill

7.241 The treatment and questioning of persons who are ill should be distinguished from the provisions governing forensic examinations (see ss 62, 63). The inevitable controversy which surrounds the death or injury of those in police custody, and problems over the admissibility of evidence which can flow from alleged maltreatment during police custody, mean that medical treatment should be readily sought by the custody or interviewing officer if he has the slightest doubt about the detainee's fitness. Consequently, the provisions of Code C 9 err very much on the side of caution in counselling early medical assistance. The moral for the custody officer is to 'play safe'. Where the detainee shows no sign of sensibility or awareness and in other urgent cases (eg extensive bleeding), he should immediately be sent to hospital or attended by the first available doctor. A police surgeon should otherwise be called immediately when a detained person

'(a) appears to be suffering from physical illness or a mental disorder; or
(b) is injured; or
(c) [Not used]
(d) fails to respond normally to questions or conversation (other than through drunkenness alone); or
(e) otherwise appears to need medical attention' (Code C 9.2).

7.242 The Codes provide a little assistance in determining the role of the police surgeon in non-forensic matters. Their advice, for example, should be sought on medical and dietary matters; on the issue of fitness for interview where drink or drugs are involved; they must supervise the administering of medication and controlled drugs and will give directions regarding infectious diseases (Code C 8.6 and 9.6; Note 12B; 9.5 and 9.3 respectively). There is no requirement to assess fitness for detention, yet Robertson (1992), found that doctors who were called to see suspects who were injured and/or drunk would almost always do so. What is more, he found that the criteria used by different doctors in assessing fitness for interview, whilst being adequate, did vary. However, in the absence of formal guidelines it is suggested that if any doubt exists about the suspect's fitness for interview, it should be postponed, and if need be, the suspect bailed to return at a later date. The custody officer must arrange for medical treatment immediately, whether or not the person asks for it and whether or not he has just received non-hospital treatment elsewhere (eg he has been given first aid at the scene of the crime, or en route to the station). These last two points are critically important for, if the person's condition deteriorates during police custody or his condition affects his interview, police conduct and the admissibility of a confession are very likely to be challenged. The symptoms of illness may become apparent when the person reaches the station and the custody officer performs the preliminary formalities (see para 7.07, ante). The officer may be helped in identifying medical problems if the suspect carries either medication relating to or documentary evidence of their illness (eg an identity card or bracelet specifying it). The custody officer should seek to ensure that the person is fit to be interviewed. The interviewing officer should also be made aware of any medical conditions affecting the suspect. He may also be able to detect signs of mental illness or mental handicap. The dangers of allowing unsupervised interrogation of these persons are well known (see the Report into the case of Maxwell Confait (1977)). Indeed, concern over the interrogation of the mentally handicapped led to the enactment of s 77 of PACE (see para 7.269, post). The difficulties of detecting mental disorder (see para 7.264, post) and of distinguishing it from intoxication are self-evident. The custody officer must be alert to the possibility and err in favour of summoning medical advice whenever the detained person appears to be mentally disordered or disturbed. If a person has been taken to a police station under the authority of s 136 of the Mental Health Act 1983 (see further para 7.271, post), a doctor's presence will again be necessary unless it is clear that an assessment of the person under the Act can be made promptly by a doctor and social worker. Special caution is needed in cases of apparent intoxication through drink. On the one hand, a blow to the head, shock, forms of epilepsy or mental illness, the lack of, or taking of, prescribed drugs, or a diabetic condition, may prompt signs of intoxication and conceal the real diagnosis. On the other hand, in cases of genuine intoxication, the custody officer should not allow the person to be left alone for lengthy periods. Indeed, guidance from the Home Office states that, where the person is still incapable of understanding the charge against him after four hours of detention, the police surgeon should be called. In cases of doubt the police should always call for medical advice (Code C Note 9B). The police surgeon should also be consulted in all cases involving prescribed or controlled drugs. The former should only be administered once medical approval has been given. If controlled drugs have to be taken (withdrawal from these may cause both harm to the suspect and produce unreliable evidence), the police surgeon must personally supervise (Code C 9.5). Personal supervision may be carried out over the telephone and provided the custody officer and the police surgeon are satisfied that no individual is at risk of harm or injury, the detained person may administer the controlled drug himself. If there is any doubt, the police surgeon should attend and any consultation must be recorded on the custody record.

7.243 Other cases may arise where the person's health appears to the investigating or custody officer to have deteriorated since his arrival at the police station, or where the person or his representative lodges a complaint about police misconduct. If the person's health deteriorates whilst being questioned, the interview should, it is suggested, be terminated at once, the reasons noted on the interview record and the opinion of the custody officer sought. If the symptoms appear to flow from police misconduct (eg a physical assault in the cell, or the undue use of force in restraining a suspect), then a police surgeon (Code C 9.1) or, if unavailable, another doctor or hospital treatment should, it is suggested, be sought. Occasionally the detained person will have drugs with him which he says have been prescribed by a doctor, or he may claim that they have to be collected from his home (eg for a heart condition, epilepsy). In both cases a police surgeon (or appropriate health care professional) should be consulted before the medication is taken (Code C 9.9).

7.244 Once medical assistance is deemed necessary, it should be obtained without delay, even if this means that the questioning of a person has to be interrupted. The obvious recourse for advice is to the police surgeon. If he is unavailable or cannot attend quickly, a local and readily available general practitioner should be called (each station should therefore have a list of such contacts). In cases of emergency or apparent urgency, hospital treatment is the answer. If an infectious disease appears to be involved, quarantine steps must be taken (Code C 9.3). Home Office Circulars on the proper treatment of known or suspected sufferers of AIDS and hepatitis B have been produced (Nos 113 of 1992 and 48 of 1989 respectively). Whilst sensible precautions are essential (eg special care in a search of the person so as to avoid being punctured by a syringe in a coat pocket), victimisation of the suspect or oppressive conduct can have serious implications for the admissibility of evidence under ss 76 and 78 of PACE (Arts 74, 76).

7.245 Code C Note 9A suggests that medical advice need not be called for 'minor ailments or injuries which do not need attention'. Certainly a headache cured by the custody officer's offer of an aspirin would qualify, but the definition of 'a minor ailment' may prove more problematic, particularly if the person concerned considers it needs medical attention. Where doubt exists about the extent of the ailment or injury, the police surgeon should be called and, irrespective of his attendance, details should be carefully noted in the custody record.

7.246 When the detained person requests medical treatment or examination, the police surgeon (an estimated 1,500 to 2,000 doctors are employed as police surgeons) should be called in all cases. An independent examination may also be allowed at the person's own expense. Although this provision is couched in discretionary terms (Code C 9.4), it is clearly in the interests of the police that such examination be permitted. The examination by either police surgeon or other doctor need not be delayed pending the arrival of the other. If the detained person has to take medication, the custody officer assumes responsibility for its safe-keeping and availability (Code C 9.5). In keeping with the rest of the Act and Code, written records must be compiled of, inter alia, any request for a medical examination and any medical directions given to the police (Code C 9.7-9.8). The custody record can conveniently be used if the person is under arrest and a police surgeon will usually enter his findings here although a general practitioner of the suspect's own choice need not do so because of the confidentiality with his patient (Code C Note 9C). However, in either case where findings are not entered on the custody record, it must show where they are recorded, for they may become necessary at subsequent legal proceedings. As to the availability of these records, they qualify as excluded material under s 12 of PACE, and can only be used in proceedings with the consent of the patient. Alternatively, the doctor might exceptionally be subpoenaed to give evidence as to his diagnosis.

Special categories

7.247   There are some categories of people who are recognised as vulnerable and for whom PACE has made special provision. They include juveniles, people with learning disabilities (referred to in the Code and hereinafter, to maintain consistency with the provisions, as mentally handicapped) and those suffering from mental disorder, and people with a visual, hearing or speech impairment (Code C 1.4-1.6). The most critical initial task is to ascertain whether the detained person falls within one of these special categories. Sometimes the circumstances of the arrest or their behaviour on the way to the police station will alert the arresting officer, who will inform the custody officer of any concerns. In other cases, the custody officer will be alerted by the manner in which responses are given whilst carrying out the preliminary formalities, or the presence of particular types of medication found in their possession. Sometimes the vulnerability will be obvious (eg the blind; but even here care must be taken in observing the person lest someone with a serious visual impairment – though not blind – is missed). For others the chance to write may help (eg to reveal that he cannot speak or to communicate his nationality in some written form). Others still may be determined in response to direct questions (eg date of birth) and indeed it has been suggested that part of the onus of identifying vulnerabilities should rest on the suspects themselves (Gudjonsson, 1993). Once a suspect has been identified as falling within one of these categories, a third party is required to attend at the police station to assist him. In the case of someone who is deaf, or cannot speak or understand English, an interpreter must be called (Code C 3.6), whereas if the suspect is blind or cannot read, someone with an interest in him, provided he is not involved in the investigation, must be present to check any documentation (Code C 3.14). The onus of calling third parties lies on the custody officer, and the courts have taken a strict view of non-compliance (see para 7.264, post).

Appropriate adults

7.248   In the vast majority of cases, the third party will be an appropriate adult, who must be contacted if the suspect appears to be 16 or younger or is mentally handicapped or appears to be mentally disordered (Code C 3.9). For the purposes of the Code, if someone is mentally incapable of appreciating the significance of any question asked or answers given, he shall be treated as being mentally handicapped or mentally disordered (Code C 1.4). An appropriate adult must be informed as soon as practicable of the suspect's whereabouts and the reasons for his detention and should be asked to come to the police station to see him (Code C 3.9). Neither solicitors nor lay visitors who are present at the police station in their respective capacities may act as appropriate adults (Code C Note 1F, although in Northern Ireland a solicitor may act as an appropriate adult if there is no other 'responsible adult available' Draft Code C Note IE). The custody officer must explain to the suspect that the appropriate adult is there to assist and advise him and that they are entitled to meet in private at any stage (Code C 3.12). This information need not be told in the presence of the appropriate adult, but the spirit of PACE requires that it is, for otherwise any impact it may have will be diluted. Brown, 1992 found that whilst private consultations with juveniles were usual, explanations to appropriate adults of their role were rarely given. The appropriate adult is entitled to see the suspect's custody record on arrival at the police station, or as soon as practicable thereafter (Code C 2.4). He will be able to see from this when the suspect was detained, what condition he was in on arrival at the police station, what medication, if any, he had on him and whether a legal adviser has been contacted. This information may help the appropriate adult assess the suspect's physical and mental condition which may affect what advice is given, particularly if the suspect is not already known to the appropriate adult. There is no obligation on the custody officer to inform the appropriate adult of his entitlement to see the custody record, but it is suggested that it is good practice to do so.

7.249 Cautioning a suspect and informing him of his legal rights must be carried out whilst both he and the appropriate adult are present or repeated when the adult arrives. If either has to be repeated, this must be done in D's presence (Code C 3.11 and 10.6). The information to be provided consists of the grounds of detention, the right of notification of arrest, the rights to free legal advice and to consult the Codes of Practice, written notices of these rights and other rights in custody, the right to contact diplomatic representatives where relevant, and the caution. This is especially important because the juvenile or mentally disordered suspect may not fully appreciate the significance of his legal rights and the appropriate adult would be able to advise in this respect, indeed the request for legal advice may come from either the suspect or the appropriate adult (Code C 3.13). However, it is important to note that D must be told of his right to legal advice at the outset. The custody officer should not delay telling him until the appropriate adult arrives, or delay securing legal advice, if requested, providing Annex B does not apply (Note 3G). Research indicates that delays do exist between receiving requests and acting upon them (Brown, 1992). Where legal advice is not required, the custody officer should ask the suspect and appropriate adult for their reasons for waiving the right, and record them on the custody record in accordance with Code C 6.5 (see para 7.61, ante). However, due to the particular difficulties faced by vulnerable suspects, and the fact that neither they nor the appropriate adult may be sufficiently aware of its importance, the Home Office Appropriate Adults Review Group Report,

1995, recommends that whenever the need for an appropriate adult is identified, a legal adviser should also be called. It is permissible for a solicitor to take instructions from a third party provided that they are confirmed by the client as soon as possible. Where legal advice is required, the provisions concerning the right to legal advice contained in Code C 6 apply (Code C 3.13). Where a suspect does require legal advice, he should be given the opportunity to talk privately with his legal adviser without the appropriate adult being present, should he so wish (Code C Note 1EE). This provision enables a full and frank discussion of the suspect's legal position to take place in the knowledge that the information disclosed will be treated as confidential and subject to legal privilege. Currently, information passed between suspect and appropriate adult is not covered by legal privilege. In the case of social workers, where 'there is clear evidence of serious danger to the client, worker, other person or the community, in other circumstances judged exceptional' (British Association of Social Workers' Code of Ethics), the social worker is entitled to disclose information obtained without the suspect's consent and this has occurred where suspects have made admissions of guilt. To guard against this, social workers are encouraged to inform suspects of this point at the initial meeting (BASW: The Social Worker as Appropriate Adult under PACE, pp 44-45) and the Law Society issued guidance recommending that a solicitor's initial interview with his client should be in the absence of the appropriate adult (Law Society Gazette, 19 May 1993, 'Legal Practice' pp 41-42). The RCCJ recommended that a rule be formulated which governs the status of information passed between appropriate adult and suspect (RCCJ Report, 1993, Recommendation 73) and the Home Office Appropriate Adults Review Group Report 1995 recommends that the information be confidential and the relationship between suspect and appropriate adult be a privileged one.

Interviews

7.250   Whilst juveniles and those who are mentally handicapped or mentally disordered are capable of giving reliable evidence, some amongst these groups, due to their age, inexperience and state of mental well-being, might provide misleading information or unreliable and self-incriminating statements in order to secure their release. They may seek the approval of the interviewing officer and offer incorrect or inaccurate information which they believe the officer wants to know, without appreciating the long-term effect of their actions. It is with this in mind that Code C 11.14 stipulates that, whether suspected or not of an offence, they should not be interviewed or asked to provide or sign a written statement in the absence of an appropriate adult unless the urgent situations provided for in C 11.1 and Annex C apply (see paras 8.25 -8.27, post). The adult has to be told (or reminded if he regularly fulfils the role) that his presence is needed to:

(1)   provide advice to the person being questioned;
(2)   observe the conduct of the interview and the fairness of the proceedings;
(3)   facilitate communication with the interviewee.

7.251 He should be told that he is not there simply to act as an observer, which means he should intervene where necessary in order to carry out his role (Code C 11.16). Without a full understanding of the role, these last two points together can easily lead the adult to become, wittingly or otherwise, the ally or agent of the interviewing officer and increase the pressure on the juvenile. Tape-recording can reduce the risk but may not reflect the pressure of an adult's physical presence, however it will offer some safeguards and D's lawyer should listen to the tape rather than relying on the interview record (ie a written, police summary of the tape, see para 8.28, post). Research indicates that appropriate adults rarely intervene, and where intervention does occur it is likely to be against, rather than in support of, the suspect (Evans, 1993; see also Dixon, 1990; Irving and Mackenzie, 1989). In the majority of cases, those who attend as appropriate adults at least for juveniles are members of the suspect's family (Brown, 1992) who are likely either to be overawed by the criminal process or put pressure on the individual to confess. In *R v Jefferson* (1994), a father who robustly intervened in interview and encouraged his son to tell the truth did not fail in his duty as an appropriate adult (although in this case the son made no admissions), but if the intervention is such that it might render any subsequent confession unreliable, it may be excluded under s 76. Informing appropriate adults of their role is a requirement of Code C 11.16. It must be good practice to do this on their arrival at the police station and to repeat the information at the start of any interview at which an appropriate adult is present. Interviews in the absence of an appropriate adult may exceptionally take place outside 'a police station or other authorised place of detention' in the circumstances provided for in Code C 11 and Annex C discussed at para 8.34, post.

7.252 Appropriate adults are additionally required to read and sign any interview record (Code C 11.9), to be present during an intimate search (unless D objects – see para 7.43, ante), to be present at any time D is cautioned (this should be repeated if first done in their absence) (Code C 10.6). If they are present whilst a review is being carried out under s 40 (see para 6.157, ante) they are entitled to make representations on D's behalf (Code C 15.1). This depends on:

(a) the adult being present – he may not have been contacted yet or he may have gone home, in which case he should, it is suggested, have been forewarned of any pending review; and

(b) whether he is able to formulate such representations – a lawyer is likely to have better prospects.

7.253 It is suggested that he and preferably a lawyer also be present throughout any exchange between D and the police at this stage. If D is to be charged or may be prosecuted, the appropriate adult must be present as the charge is read to him and must also be given a written notice of the particulars of the offence (Code C 16.1 and 16.3). Once charged or told that a prosecution may follow, the police may wish to confront D with a statement or interview record concerning someone else (eg an accomplice). Code C 16.4 requires that a copy of the statement or sight of the record be given to the appropriate adult.

Juveniles

7.254   The largest category for which special provision is made is juveniles. It covers any person who appears to be under 17 (s 37(15), Art 38(14)). Thus, if a person refuses to give his age or the officer doubts the one given and the officer assesses the person as a juvenile, he must treat him as such unless and until evidence to the contrary is produced (Code C 1.5). Brown (1992) found that 17 per cent of all those detained by the police were under 17, and in some areas the figure was considerably higher. As for a juvenile under the age of ten, he has by law no criminal liability and so cannot be detained. If he is arrested in the belief that he is older (as to which see para 5.43, ante) or if he is taken to the station voluntarily or for his well-being, it appears to be the practice in some forces for the custody officer to complete the essentials of a custody record, but thereafter the juvenile's return home must normally be arranged. Alerting the local authority's social services should be considered if the custody officer is concerned for the juvenile's physical or moral well-being (the authority may decide to exercise its supervisory powers under the Children Act 1989: under that Act 'child' means a person under the age of 18) and, in a clear case of danger to the juvenile, the police themselves have the power under the 1989 Act (s 46) to remove a juvenile and, after liaison with the authority, place him in safe accommodation (see para 6.29, ante). If, but for the presumption of doli incapax, a child would have committed a serious offence, such as homicide, the urgency to involve the social services is self-evident since they may seek a care or supervision order on the basis that the child is beyond parental control (s 31(2)(b)(ii) of the Children Act 1989).

INITIAL ACTION

7.255   Where a juvenile has been arrested, the custody officer must take all practicable steps to identify the parent, guardian, local authority (where relevant) or other person responsible for the juvenile's welfare and tell that person of the arrest, the reasons for it and where the juvenile is being held (see para 6.28, ante). The person responsible for the juvenile's welfare will usually be the appropriate adult (above) and will also be asked to attend the station in that capacity. He will not always be the appropriate adult (eg the juvenile does not want his parent to be involved, the parent is implicated in the offence, the parent refuses to attend the station) with the result that the custody officer has two duties:

(a)   to identify and notify the person responsible for the juvenile's welfare; and
(b)   to identify, notify and call the appropriate adult (further defined below).

7.256   Even if the conditions for delaying notification of arrest (s 56(5), Art 57(5)) or legal advice (s 58(8), Art 59(8)) apply, this should not stop the custody officer from taking steps to contact the person responsible for the juvenile's welfare and the appropriate adult (Code C, Annex B, Note B1).

7.257   In the case of juveniles, the term 'appropriate adult' is defined as follows:
(i)   parent or guardian (including a local authority if the child is in care or being looked after under the Children Act 1989); or

(ii)   a social worker; or

(iii) a responsible adult aged over 18 (not a police officer or police employee) (Code C 1.7).

7.258   In some cases the parent will be incompetent to act as an appropriate adult because of a low IQ (see *R v Morse* (1991)) or other mental health problem, but the issue of competency may depend upon his ability to fulfil the role of appropriate adult at the time of the interview (see *R v W* (1994)). In many more cases he will be incompetent through lack of experience and/or knowledge of police procedures. Any person, including a parent (or guardian), who is implicated in the offence as perpetrator, victim or witness or has received admissions from the juvenile, should not act as an appropriate adult (Note 1C). Similarly, where the juvenile and parent simply do not get on with each other (see *DPP v Blake* (1989)) or they are living apart and the juvenile does not wish him to attend, the parent should not be asked to do so. Section 34(2) of PACE (Art 38(2)) places a duty on the custody officer to inform the parents of an arrested juvenile of the fact that he has been arrested (see para 6.11, ante). It follows that while the juvenile may not wish them to be informed they must be. However, a parent does not have to be the appropriate adult and if the juvenile is adamant that he does not want one of them, it is suggested that he should be asked to nominate some other adult whom he knows or in whom he trusts. In many cases the parent will not wish, or be able, to attend and the custody officer should proceed to seek another appropriate adult. This may prove to be very difficult. Solicitors or lay advisers who are present at the police station in a professional capacity may not act as appropriate adults (Code C Note 1F). Custody officers might contact social services emergency duty teams, although with a lack of resources, particularly at night-time, availability may be limited and social workers might not necessarily be trained for the role of appropriate adult and may face a conflict of interest over issues of confidentiality (see Littlechild, 1995). In some areas, volunteer appropriate adult schemes have been set up, some of which provide training for those who volunteer. The presence of such schemes will greatly alleviate the problem where appropriate adults are otherwise hard to find. Failing these alternatives, the juvenile should be asked to name an individual. This may be a person who has looked after him, or a relative such as an adult sibling, or neighbour or community figure in whom the juvenile can trust.

7.259   If the juvenile is in local care, the authority will be the appropriate adult and so, if he is suspected of stealing from the children's home where he lives, a social worker unconnected with the home should be called. Similarly, if he has admitted the offence to a social worker, it is in the interests of fairness that another social worker act as appropriate adult (Code C Note 1D). However, where a social worker does withdraw, it should not be assumed that an admission has been made. Brown, 1992, found that the police were successful in 97 per cent of cases in obtaining an adult to act and that of these 66 per cent were parents or relatives, 28 per cent were social workers, and 6 per cent other responsible adults. If an appropriate adult cannot be contacted or cannot attend the station within a reasonable time, the custody officer may have to consider releasing, or charging the juvenile and/or releasing him on bail, for there are many steps in the investigative process which cannot be accomplished without an adult's presence (see para 7.248, ante).

7.260   In addition to the requirement for an appropriate adult, PACE also seeks to ensure that certain actions (eg the taking of an intimate sample) can only be done to a juvenile with an 'appropriate consent', which must be written and which s 65 defines as follows:
- for juveniles between 14 and 17 – consent of juvenile and parent or guardian (including a local authority if the child is in care: s 118);
- for juveniles below 14 – consent of parent or guardian (as defined above).

Where the appropriate adult is someone other than those listed, the appropriate consent cannot be given.

7.261   A juvenile should not be held in a police cell, unless there is no other way of guaranteeing his security, or the cell is considered to be more comfortable than alternative secure accommodation within the police station (Code C 8.8). If he is, the reason must be recorded and he must not be kept there with a detained adult. Few stations possess rooms, other than cells or interview rooms, that can be used to detain juveniles. Often the interview rooms, which could be used for juveniles, are physically apart from the cell area, thus making security impracticable. Occasionally there will be spaces in the secured cell area where a juvenile can be allowed to roam within reason and under the supervision of the jailer but in busy stations this will be impossible. Much too will depend on the age and character of the juvenile. Very often an ordinary cell will have to be used and perhaps relabelled as a juvenile room. Wherever he is kept, he should be visited more regularly than other detained adults (Code C Note 8A). Once charged, if he is to be detained, the juvenile should normally be transferred to local authority accommodation (s 38(6) of PACE, Art 39(6); the authority being under a duty to provide such accommodation, s 21 of the Children Act 1989). A juvenile may only be kept in police detention in the following circumstances.
(a)   The custody officer certifies that it is impracticable to transfer him to local authority accommodation, and specifies why this is so. In assessing practicability, the officer is not entitled to take into account the juvenile's behaviour (unless it falls within (b) below), the nature of the offence, nor the fact that the local authority does not have any available secure local accommodation (overtaking the decision of *R v Chief Constable of Cambridgeshire, ex p Michel* (1991) and see further at para 6.28, ante).
(b)   Where secure accommodation is not available, the officer considers that keeping an arrested juvenile, aged 12 years or more, in alternative local authority accommodation would not provide sufficient protection from the risk that he may cause the public serious harm (s 38 as amended by s 24 of the CJPOA 1994; Code C 16.6 and Note 16B).

7.262   Two further points about juveniles can be noted. First, Note 11C indicates that a juvenile should only be arrested at school if it is unavoidable, and where this arises, the head teacher (or nominee) must be informed. Furthermore, a juvenile may only be interviewed at school in exceptional circumstances, and only then with the permission of the head teacher (or nominee) (Code C 11.15). If exceptional circumstances exist, and whilst the Code does not refer to them, it may be assumed that the circumstances must be those found in Code C 11.1 (para 8.34, post), ideally the parents and, if different, the appropriate adult should attend the school. They can sometimes be notified in advance of the police arrival at the school, but these school interviews are by their nature urgent ones and, if the offence is not against the school, a teacher can act as the appropriate adult (see further discussion on this point at para 8.25, post). If the offence is against the school, the juvenile should be arrested if there is sufficient evidence and questioned elsewhere, or asked to attend the station, or interviewed at home or some other place known to him. Second, if the juvenile is a ward of court and the police wish to question him, they can do so without informing the High Court (*Re R and G (minors)* (1990)). The temporary carers of the juvenile will then be under a duty to inform the court if anything significant is likely to occur to the juvenile (eg he is to be prosecuted and a custodial sentence is likely on conviction).

The mentally disordered and mentally handicapped

7.263   For the most part, the Act and Codes treat the mentally disordered and mentally handicapped in a similar way, although the problems suffered by each stem from significantly different causes. In respect of those suffering from mental disorder, two situations must be distinguished. In the first a suspect becomes involved in the investigation of a criminal offence. In the second a person is brought into a police station by the police under their Mental Health Act powers (see paras 7.271-7.280, post). In either case, the Government's policy of keeping those with mental health problems within the community as far as possible, is likely to lead to an increase in the number becoming involved with the police.

Treatment of mentally disordered and mentally handicapped suspects

7.264   The police treatment of those with mental health problems is a highly sensitive and occasionally notorious area. Indeed the Report into the death of Maxwell Confait was one of the reasons for the Royal Commission on Criminal Procedure which preceded PACE. The Act has very little to say in the area but the Code contains a number of provisions which the courts will generally interpret strictly (see *R v Morse* (1991); *R v Cox* (1991); *R v Kenny* (1994)). The cardinal requirement of the Code is that, if an officer suspects that a person is mentally disordered or mentally handicapped, he must treat him as such (Code C 1.4). Unfortunately it does not provide precise definitions of either term. 'Mental disorder' is a generic term used throughout Code C (Note 1G) and is defined by s 1(2) of the Mental Health Act 1983 as 'mental illness, arrested or incomplete development of mind, psychopathic disorder and any other disorder or disability of mind'. 'Mental handicap', on the other hand, is defined by s 77(3) of PACE as relevant to a person who 'is in a state of arrested or incomplete development of mind which includes significant impairment of intelligence and social functioning'.

Thus the term 'mental disorder' appears to include 'mental handicap' although the Code notes that whilst treating the two conditions similarly, they are different (Code C Note 1G). A more understandable approach may be to recognise that people in either category might display similar symptoms, albeit from different causes, but that the special need for protection will arise in either case. Code C 1.4 confuses matters further by including that a person 'mentally incapable of understanding the significance of questions put to him or his replies' shall be treated as mentally disordered or mentally handicapped. The Code's addition, whilst lacking any definition, is, however, useful in putting the police and especially the custody officer on alert. It presumably includes someone whose IQ is sufficiently low as to make his interrogation of dubious value, whilst not being so low as to be mentally handicapped. The arresting officer may be able to spot the existence of a mental disorder or handicap from the circumstances of the arrest or on the journey to the station, but very often it will be the custody officer who, during the opening formalities, is best placed to detect them. Even so, the decision is a difficult one. Psychiatrists regularly disagree over the meaning of mental disorder, yet police officers are expected to recognise it without any diagnostic training. Research indicates that a significant number of suspects detained in police custody are mentally ill or otherwise disturbed during interview (Irving, 1980; Irving and McKenzie, 1989) and a sizeable proportion of others would have IQ levels below the national average (Gudjonsson et al, 1990). This latter research indicates that between 15 per cent and 20 per cent of adult suspects were sufficiently vulnerable as to justify the presence of an appropriate adult yet the police had only called one in 4 per cent of cases. Without specific training, difficulties in identifying mental disorder will inevitably be encountered. In a fairly common situation, incoherence through drunkenness or drugs could easily mask a mental disability. However, the Code is clear: if there is any suspicion of mental disorder or handicap, the person must be treated as such and a failure to do so may result in the exclusion of evidence through the application of ss 76-78 (Arts 74-76). Identification is clearly important because the courts take an objective approach with regard to the defendant's state of mind as it actually was when the confession was made, irrespective of any belief on the part of the police at the time that the person was of average mental ability (*R v Everett* (1988)).

TREATMENT DURING DETENTION

7.265 The policy of PACE towards mentally disordered or mentally handicapped suspects is that various procedures can only be performed if an 'appropriate adult' is present. These procedures, which apply equally to both mentally disordered and mentally handicapped suspects as well as juveniles, have been outlined in paras 7.248–7.253, ante, where the role of the appropriate adult was discussed and should be referred to regularly. In respect of the mentally disordered or mentally handicapped suspect, the appropriate adult is defined in Code C 1.7(b) as:

(i) a relative, guardian or other person responsible for the suspect's care or custody;

(ii) a person experienced in dealing with the mentally disordered or handicapped (eg a specialist social worker or a social worker approved for the purposes of the Mental Health Act 1983, but not a police employee); or

(iii) some other responsible adult aged 18 or more, but not a police employee (eg a neighbour, priest, or schoolteacher).

7.266 Category (iii) should only be sought in the absence of (i) and (ii). Code C Note 1E suggests that someone with training and experience in mental health issues may be better suited than a relative to act as an appropriate adult, but if the suspect prefers the familiarity of a relative to someone unknown to him, his preferences should be respected where possible. More practically it may be impossible for D to identify a person in (i), so that category (ii) has to be used. Many of the problems concerning the availability of appropriate adults and how they fulfil their role which were identified in connection with juveniles (para 7.248, ante) will apply with mentally disordered and mentally handicapped suspects. Indeed, it is arguably more important that the individual is able to convey the nature of the proceedings and provide support to a suspect whose state of mental well-being is likely to be more fragile and potentially more volatile than that of most juveniles.

7.267 It has already been noted (para 7.263, ante) that those with mental disorder and mental handicap are treated similarly throughout the Code. One significant difference lies in the requirement to call a police surgeon which applies only to those who appear to be suffering from a mental disorder (Code C 9.2(a)), presumably in recognition of the fact that those who are mentally handicapped do not per se need medical treatment. If it appears to the custody officer that D suffers from a mental disorder he must immediately call a police surgeon or, in emergency, send D to hospital or call a medical practitioner (Code C 9.2), whether D requests it or not. Due to the immediacy requirement in the Code, the task of calling the police surgeon will take precedence over the summoning of an appropriate adult, but, having summoned medical help, the custody officer must then identify and contact an appropriate adult as soon as possible, explain the situation and ask him to come to the station (Code C 3.9) or go to the hospital if D has been sent there. Police surgeons, usually with a background of general practitioner work, have had little or no training in identifying mental disorder, yet they are now being required to determine whether a mental disorder exists and to assess the suspect's fitness for detention and fitness for interview. Robertson, 1992, noted that the role of the police surgeon has changed considerably over the last decade with over 80 per cent of their current work involving examinations of prisoners, yet specific training has, until recently, been sadly neglected. This is particularly so in the area of mental health. In the absence of such training, assessments of mental disorder are likely to be haphazard. It is suggested that until it is clear that all police surgeons have received training in this area, if the initial suspicion of mental disorder is sufficient to call a police surgeon to examine the suspect, it must also be sufficient to call an appropriate adult. Research indicates that this does not always happen, even if the custody officer knows or believes the suspect to be mentally disordered (Bean and Nemitz, 1995 and Palmer and Hart, 1996).

7.268 Where an intimate or strip search takes place, an appropriate adult of the same sex as the suspect must be present, unless the latter specifically asks for a particular adult of the opposite sex instead. Strip searches may only take place in the absence of an appropriate adult in urgent cases where the suspect or others are at risk of serious harm (Annex A(B) 11(c); see para 7.15, ante). Regarding the issue of consent, the Act is silent and does not provide a definition as it does in respect of juveniles in s 65 (para 7.260, ante). Where the consent of a person is required before certain procedures are carried out (eg taking an intimate sample), the consent of a person who is mentally disordered or mentally handicapped is only valid if it is given in the presence of an appropriate adult (Code D 1.11). Careful consideration should be given before any decision is made to use handcuffs to restrain mentally disordered or mentally handicapped suspects who are detained in a cell (Code C 8.2) and they should be visited more regularly than other detained adults (Code C Note 8A). The physical treatment of mentally disordered suspects in particular calls for caution since their behavioural response to detention is likely to be unpredictable, leading in an extreme case to suicide or an attempt at self-mutilation. If the latter is suspected (something may be known of D's background), D should, if practicable within the station, be kept in a cell within easy sight of the custody or other officer or at least in a cell with ready access for officers, and regular inspections should be made of him. Home Office Circular 66/90, which is concerned with provision for mentally disordered offenders, sets out existing legal powers and recommends that careful consideration be given to diverting mentally disordered offenders from the criminal justice process where a prosecution is not in the public interest. To further these aims, it suggests that effective liaisons be developed between the police and health and social services to ensure that treatment and/or support is available for those who are mentally disordered, whether or not they are prosecuted. Home Office Circular 12/95 encourages inter-agency working in this area and offers suggestions on how this might best be achieved.

CONFESSIONS

7.269   A second significant difference in the treatment between mentally disordered and mentally handicapped suspects is concerned with the admissibility of confession evidence and lies within the Act rather than the Code. In both cases interviews or the signing of statements may only be conducted in the presence of an appropriate adult (Code C 11.14), unless an urgent interview can be authorised by a superintendent or higher rank (see para 7.133, ante). Given the evidential dangers, an urgent interview must be regarded as highly exceptional and highly undesirable (Code C, Annex C, Note C1) (and for examples of how not to interview those with mental health problems, see *R v Delaney* (1988); *R v Lamont* (1989); *R v Moss* (1990); *R v Paris, Abdullahi and Miller* (1992)). Indeed, it was the adverse publicity given to the police following the interrogation of some mentally handicapped suspects (principally the Report into the death of Maxwell Confait (1977)), which led to s 77 (Art 75), a provision which gives greater protection at the trial stage specifically to the mentally handicapped. Thus, where the case against D depends wholly or substantially on a confession by him and the judge is satisfied:

(i)   that he is mentally handicapped; and

(ii) that the confession was not made in the presence of an independent person (s 77(1)(b)),

7.270 the judge must warn the jury that 'there is a special need for caution before convicting the accused in reliance on the confession', and must explain why the need arises. If it is a summary trial, magistrates must treat the case as one in which there is a special need for caution before convicting the accused on his confession (s 77(1), (2)). The definition of 'mentally handicapped' is given in s 77(3) and should be distinguished from the wider concept of mental disorder. In *R v Ham* (1995) the Court of Appeal held that a finding of mental handicap must be based on medical evidence, applying the statutory test, and it was inappropriate for a trial judge to rely upon suggested assumptions by police officers and a general practitioner as to the defendant's mental state. Section 77(3) also defines 'independent person' so as to exclude a police officer or person employed for, or engaged on, 'police purposes'. 'Police purposes' are defined by s 64 of the Police Act 1964 and include special constables, police cadets and civilians employed by the force (eg a telephonist, or a matron employed to look after female prisoners). It is probable that the 'independent person' in the Act and the appropriate adult in the Codes of Practice were intended to be one and the same person. However, the position is far from clear. Unlike the Codes which preclude a solicitor or lay visitor, present at the police station in that capacity, from being an appropriate adult (Code C Note 1F and see para 7.131, ante), s 77(3) contains no such equivalent limitation as regards the independent person. One explanation for this might be that s 77(3) has not been amended in subsequent years, as the Codes have been in this respect, but the case of *R v Bailey* (1995) suggests that the two roles are different. Here the court held that a confession by a mentally handicapped person to a friend was not made in the presence of an 'independent person', since such a person would not be independent to the person confessing (as opposed to independent from the police investigation). This seems to place the 'independent person' in a different category from the appropriate adult required by the Codes, since if a friend is not independent for these purposes, clearly a relative cannot be either. Clearly the current position demands clarification. Section 77 does not require corroborative evidence in support of the confession, but merely a warning as to the special need for caution, although where the interview was conducted in the absence of an independent person and there is corroborative evidence, the warning need not be given (see *R v Campbell* (1995), but the third party here was, somewhat confusingly, described as an appropriate adult). As regards a confession obtained from the mentally disordered (as opposed to handicapped), in the absence of an independent party, corroboration is similarly not required but is highly desirable. When combined with the exclusionary terms of ss 76 and 78 (Arts 74, 76) the result is that evidence obtained from either mentally disordered or mentally handicapped suspects by maltreatment or breaches of PACE and the Codes will usually be excluded by ss 76 and 78 (*R v Everett* (1988); *R v Delaney* (1988); *R v Kenny* (1994)), and s 77 therefore serves a very limited, supporting role for those confessions which are allowed to proceed for the jury's consideration (see para 8.141, post).

Persons detained under the Mental Health Act 1983

7.271   Under s 135 of the Mental Health Act 1983 (Art 130 of the Mental Health (NI) Order 1986) a magistrate can issue a warrant authorising the police to remove a mentally disordered person to a place of safety for up to 72 hours. Under s 136 (Art 132 of the Order) a mentally disordered person who is found in a public place to be in immediate need of care or control can be taken by a constable to a place of safety for up to 72 hours, in order that he be examined by a medical practitioner and a social worker who is approved to work in this area, and that arrangements be made for his future treatment and care. Implementation of s 136 is governed by a local policy agreed between the social services, the health authority and the police. As the Code of Practice on the 1983 Act, issued by the Department of Health (1990) under the authority of s 118 of that Act, states, 'the aim of the policy should be to secure the competent and speedy assessment by a doctor and an approved social worker of the person detained' (para 10.2). 'Mental disorder' is defined by s 1 of the 1983 Act (see para 7.264, ante) and must be distinguished from mental handicap. Where a person is detained under the Mental Health Act and brought to a police station, the custody officer should organise expert advice (below). Although 'place of safety' in ss 135 and 136 includes a police station, ideally it should be used rarely and even then temporarily. As the Department of Health in its Memorandum on the 1983 Act remarked (para 291), '[o]nly in exceptional circumstances should a police station be used as a place of safety'. If it is, the patient 'should remain there for no longer than a few hours while an approved social worker makes the necessary arrangements for his removal elsewhere …'. The problem lies in finding a hospital which is physically able to accept the patient and willing to admit him on the recommendation of the intervening constable. Furthermore, there is no legal duty on a hospital immediately to accept a person detained under s 136. Hence the police station is a more common first port of call than is desirable, in spite of the likelihood that such a person will have exhibited some bizarre or unusual behaviour in a public place so that mental disorder will be a ready conclusion for the constable and especially the custody officer. Those detained under s 135 are less of a problem since the police are shielded by a magistrates' warrant and provision for treatment at a hospital or other health centre is more likely to have been planned before the warrant was sought.

7.272   A person brought to a police station under s 135 or s 136 has not been arrested for an offence but, by virtue of s 137(1), is deemed to be in legal custody. The Mental Health Act is silent as to his treatment there but Code C 1.10 includes him within its provisions, except those relating to reviews and extensions of detention. Thus, if such a person is questioned about an offence those provisions relating to questioning, cautioning, tape-recording, etc are relevant, as are those on the rights to legal advice and to notify an outside person. Furthermore, the Code of Practice (2nd edn, 1993) on the 1983 Act advises (para 10.6.b) that the local social services and an appropriately qualified doctor should be contacted immediately and that the local policy (above) should have formulated procedures for establishing such contact. That same Code suggests (para 10.11) that the detained person should be given the same information about his Mental Health Act rights and status as if he had been admitted to a hospital. A written notice would suffice from the police point of view, and a clearer explanation could be left for the social worker to impart. As regards the person's physical treatment, the checking of his property and possible removal of clothes (such as a belt, shoelaces) are clearly important lest he try to harm himself or others (Code C 4, see para 7.26, ante); as are those relating to his conditions of detention and physical comfort (Code C 8, see para 7.238, ante). If an assessment by a doctor of a s 136 patient can be arranged 'without undue delay' (Code C 9.2), the custody officer need not call a police surgeon (as he must do for mentally disordered suspects, see para 7.263, ante). It is suggested that this 'delay' be interpreted most strictly. The maximum length of detention under the Mental Health Act is 72 hours and, unlike PACE, the purpose is not for questioning about an offence but for medical assessment. Thus, periodic reviews of the patient are not required by statute. However, bearing in mind the DSS instruction above, the encouragement in Code C 3.10 to organise the patient's assessment as soon as possible, and the patient's physical and mental well-being, it is prudent for a custody officer to organise regular reviews of his custody. Once the patient has been assessed and a decision made about his care, custody at the station ceases since the purpose of s 136 is exhausted. The process may take quite some time since the approved social worker has to explore the patient's family and psychiatric background and may have to arrange for his compulsory admission to hospital (in which case the police have the power to convey him there: s 137 of the 1983 Act). In practice great efforts are made to persuade the person to enter hospital on a voluntary rather than compulsory basis. Throughout the patient's custody the custody officer should complete the appropriate form (not a custody record since there has been no arrest for an offence) signifying that he is and has been in custody under s 136 so that the person's legal status is clear (Rogers and Faulkener, 1987, found that in 36 per cent of referrals to hospital the requisite form was not used, suggesting that there might be a confusion between s 136 cases and 'voluntary' referrals).

Hearing impairment

7.273 If a suspect appears to be deaf, or so hard of hearing that the custody officer doubts whether communication will be effective, in addition to handing the suspect the written notice of rights, an interpreter must be called to ensure that he is fully informed of these rights (Code C 3.6). Similarly, where legal advice is requested an interpreter must be present (Code C 13.9) and an interview cannot take place in the absence of an interpreter unless the suspect gives written agreement or the conditions for an urgent interview in Code C 11.1 or Annex C apply (Code C 13.5). Where the person is charged, if an interpreter is not already present, one must be called as soon as possible to explain the nature of the offence and any other information provided by the officer (Code C 3.10). The biggest problem facing the treatment of a deaf suspect is often finding an interpreter, a task which the custody officer must fulfil as soon as is practicable (Code C 3.6) and every attempt should be made to explain that one will be provided at public expense (Code C 13.8). If the suspect is unable to recommend one, local social services departments may have lists of qualified interpreters who are skilled in both sign language and lip-reading techniques and have experience of police procedures. The Council for the Advancement of Communication with Deaf People, which examines and sets standards for sign language interpreters, also keeps a register of interpreters who are trained and qualified to meet these standards (see further 'Legal Action', June 1995). Code C 13.9 states that a police officer may act as interpreter, but not when legal advice is being obtained and only in other situations if prior written agreement is obtained from the suspect (or the appropriate adult, if relevant) or where an interview is tape-recorded in accordance with Code E. However, in most circumstances, a contemporaneous written record should be compiled. (For the use of tape-recorders in the interviewing of the deaf, see para 8.27, post.) If an interpreter has to be called, he should be asked to read any record of interview and sign to confirm its accuracy (Code C 13.7). In most cases it is D who will need an interpreter but if the appropriate adult, called to attend the interview of a juvenile (or, it is suggested, mentally disordered or mentally handicapped suspect), is hard of hearing, an interpreter should be called unless the adult agrees in writing to the interview or the conditions for urgent interviews apply (Code C 13.6).

Visual impairment

7.274   For the blind or those with seriously impaired vision (including a suspect whose glasses have been broken or mislaid), the normal fear of being in a police station is likely to be exacerbated and custody officers should be alert to this. The presence of a third party (eg a solicitor, friend or relative or the appropriate adult if relevant) is required, first, to assist D in the comprehension of documents such as the notice of his rights (there being no requirement in the Codes for a Braille copy to be available) and, second, with D's consent, to sign any documents (principally the custody record) on his behalf (Code C 3.14). The presence of such a person will help counter any subsequent allegation of oppression or unreliability (s 76, Art 74) or unfairness (s 78, Art 76) and Code C 1.6 plays safe by requiring the police to treat any person in custody who appears to be blind or seriously visually handicapped as such.

The illiterate

7.275   The illiterate and semi-literate constitute a large category of detained persons for whom the provision of written notices is pointless and to whom the custody officer should therefore pay attention in orally communicating and explaining their rights under Code C 3.1. A solicitor, relative, or other third person can fulfil a useful role in explaining documentation (Code C 3.14). The use of tape-recording helps during interview, but where a written statement is taken from D the interviewing officer should read it over carefully and slowly to him (especially if a third party is not present) before asking him to make his mark (Code C 11.10). If the detainee disagrees with the record, his views on any inaccuracies must be recorded and the officer must certify what happened on the interview record.

Foreign citizens (Code C, s 7)

7.276 Code C does not apply to the following people, who are likely to be foreign citizens, when they are detained in custody:

(a) those who have been arrested for the purpose of having fingerprints taken under s 3(5) of the Asylum and Immigration Appeals Act 1993; and

(b) those served with a notice of detention under the Immigration Act 1971,

although the treatment and detention conditions in the Code should apply as a minimum standard.

7.277 For the initial treatment of foreign citizens who are detained under all other powers, two categories must be distinguished.

(a) Convention countries – The United Kingdom has signed bilateral consular conventions with a number of countries and as soon as the suspect, D, has identified his nationality (eg by word or production of a passport), the custody officer can check the list in Code C Annex F, to see whether it is a bilateral convention country. If it is, the relevant consulate must be informed of D's detention as soon as practicable. The only exceptions are when D is a political refugee or is seeking asylum. In these cases, only at D's express request may the police inform his diplomatic representative. In order to discover whether these exceptions apply, the police must wait until D's wishes are ascertained (eg via an interpreter) and must not go ahead and inform. On the other hand, if D's wishes for not informing the consulate do not concern his political status (eg he is embarrassed, he fears that his country will send him home), the police have no option under the Code – the consulate must be told (however, the sanction for failing to do so will be diplomatic rather than legal, since D is hardly likely to complain nor is a court likely to exclude any evidence).

(b) Non-convention countries – Citizens of these countries must be told as soon as practicable of their right to have their consulate informed of their whereabouts and the grounds for their detention. Again the custody officer must wait until D's wishes are ascertained before contacting the consulate, for D may not wish, for whatever reason, to exercise the right (eg he may have been arrested for demonstrating against his embassy), but where contact is desired, it must be made as soon as possible.

7.278 The only difference between (a) and (b) is that in (a) the consulate must be told about D's detention (unless the asylum exception applies), whereas in (b) the onus lies on D to ask for it to be told. The following provisions are common to each category.

7.279 Any foreign citizen (including those from the Republic of Ireland) may communicate with his diplomatic representatives at any time (Code C 7.1). The most convenient, initial method will be by telephone but physical visits to him are clearly included within 'communicate' and consequently this means that there is a right for him to be visited at any time (eg during an interview). This right of communication is unqualified (even if the criteria in s 56(5), Art 57(5) – delay in notification of arrest – are satisfied). Thus, even if the police suspect that communication will alert embassy staff and thereby thwart their investigation, it must be allowed. However, the suspect should only be told of this right of communication 'as soon as practicable'. Delay may be caused by, for example, waiting for an interpreter or if large numbers are arrested (eg during a demonstration), by waiting for a custody officer to deal with him. But 'practicability' should not be stretched to cover delays in the investigation, for the test is practicability of the notification procedure and not practicability of the investigating officers.

7.280   As soon as a diplomatic representative arrives at the police station (whether called out by D or not) he must be allowed to talk to D out of the hearing of the police. This applies even if a reason for delaying notification of arrest or legal advice exists under Annex B (Code C Note 7A). On the other hand, the police are not prevented from questioning D whilst the diplomat is being informed or before he arrives at the station.

7.281   The following points should also be noted.
(i)   The foregoing provisions only apply to those in police detention (ie under arrest). Those who are at a police station voluntarily have of course the unqualified right to leave and they may demand consular contact as a condition of their co-operation with the police.
(ii)   The provisions are independent of the right of notification of arrest (s 56, Art 57) but the latter may be lawfully delayed (see para 7.51, ante).
(iii)   In keeping with the general emphasis on documentation, the custody record should state when D was informed of his consular rights and the fact of any communication with his diplomatic representative.
(iv)   If D claims diplomatic immunity, verification will usually be required from a consular official and the Foreign Office.
(v)   If D seeks political asylum or refugee status, the case should be handled sensitively and the Refugee Unit at the Home Office notified. Consular contact should then only be established in the very rare case when D gives his full and informed consent.

Interviews with non-English-speakers

7.282   If the detained person does not understand English and the custody officer is unable to communicate with him, an interpreter will be needed. For the more common languages a police force should have a list of appropriate interpreters. For some forces (eg those covering a port) the list should be extensive. If difficulties arise, the local Community Relations Council or an ethnic minority or refugee organisation may be able to help or the community liaison officer may have some contacts. For the more unusual languages a local educational institution or hospital (which will face similar problems of communication and have their own contacts) can be tried. It is most important that a list of willing and qualified interpreters be prepared since the need for one may arise urgently (eg a terrorist or kidnapper detained and questioned about the location of a bomb or hostage). Indeed, some interpreters will become regular employees at a station (they are paid for by the police and this must be explained to the detainee: Code C 13.8). A competent police officer can act (except when the detainee is receiving legal advice) if the detainee expressly agrees (Code C 13.9). The interpreter must be called as soon as practicable (Code C 3.6), but in the meantime the custody officer should give D a written notice of his rights if one is available in his language. Stations should have a book containing the notices in several languages and the appropriate page can be shown to, or photocopied for, the suspect. This list of languages, however, is very limited, but should include the main ethnic minority and principal European languages. Exceptionally D may be interviewed before the interpreter arrives if the conditions in Code C 11.1 or Annex C are satisfied (see para 8.34, post), but the usefulness will obviously depend on the degree of communication possible.

7.283 Since an interpreter may telephone or write a letter on the detainee's behalf, a problem of security can arise, especially with an untried interpreter. As for security during interview (ie whether the interpreter is conveying the correct information to and from the detainee), the use of tape-recorders is essential. A more frequent problem will be the competence of the interpreter in understanding and conveying technical terms to the detainee (including the notification of his rights under Code C 3.1-3.2). At the end of the interview, the interpreter should be asked to certify the accuracy of the written or taped record (Code C 13.3, 13.7).

Immigration cases

7.284 Where the police are involved with the investigation of immigration offences, they may be acting under their own powers (in which case PACE and the Codes of Practice apply) or more normally they will be assisting the Immigration and Nationality Department of the Home Office. If the latter, immigration officers will usually assume responsibility for the detention of an immigrant under the authority of the Immigration Act 1971. When immigration officers are working at a police station, they are instructed to apply the relevant aspects of the Codes of Practice (even though they are not legally bound to, s 67(9) of PACE only applying to a person 'charged with the duty of investigating offences'). To this effect a special Code of Practice has been issued by the Immigration Service with the following points. In addition to the usual PACE rights (eg access to legal advice) this Code suggests (para 4.1) that 'consideration should also be given to advising a person that he can contact a representative of an immigrant welfare organisation'. Even if a police officer has already cautioned the detainee, the immigration officer should do so before he conducts an interview (Immigration Code 6.3). If the immigration officer wishes to question the detainee after he has been charged, the custody officer should be consulted.

Prison interviews

7.285   The police may need to interview a prison inmate for a variety of reasons, eg where he requests it or where it is believed that he has useful information about criminal offences. Liaison with the prison service is essential and the police must bear in mind the pressures on it. A record of prison visits should be kept by the police service and authorised by a senior officer (chief inspector). A distinction needs to be drawn between a compulsory interview (the police have reasonable grounds for suspecting D of an arrestable offence) and a 'voluntary' interview (the police do not suspect D but want information from him). In the latter, D has the right to refuse an interview. The Prison Service Circular Instruction (10/1989) states that the spirit of the PACE and Codes of Practice provisions must be observed and that the prisoner should be treated no less favourably than if he were being interviewed at a police station. A notice summarising the prisoner's rights must be handed to him before the interview begins and he

> 'must be allowed ample time to read it thoroughly. If he or she has difficulty in reading it, or appears to have difficulty in understanding it, the notice should be read, and if necessary explained fully. When you are satisfied that the notice is understood, the inmate should be asked to complete the section below to indicate whether or not he or she wishes to consult a solicitor: and then to sign it' (preamble to the notice, issued by the Prison Service).

7.286   The benevolence of this instruction is tempered by para 4 of the notice which explains that, where the police have reasonable grounds for suspecting an arrestable offence, they may put questions to the prisoner and he is 'required to remain in their presence while they do so'. The notice includes an explanation of the entitlement to legal advice. The temptation may be for the police on the day of the interview to dissuade the prisoner from exercising it on the grounds that contacting a solicitor will cause undue delay. Hence it is important for the interviewing officer to liaise with the prison beforehand to see if the prisoner wants legal advice. However, there is no obligation on the police to do this (advance notice of an interview may jeopardise the usefulness of the interview) and so in practice notice of the right to legal advice will often be given as the interview commences. If the prisoner is to be asked about involvement in offences, it will qualify as an 'interview' for Code C purposes (see Chapter 8) and thus, if facilities exist, an interview should be tape-recorded. If not, a contemporaneous written record should be made. The importance of the proper recording of interviews has been regularly emphasised by the courts and failure to do so usually leads to the exclusion of the evidence.

Terrorism provisions

7.287   The rights under s 56 (Art 57), to inform a third party of detention, and under s 58 (Art 59), to legal advice, are qualified if the person is detained under 'terrorism provisions'. This phrase means the provisions of s 41(1) of Terrorism Act and any provision of Sch 7 of that Act conferring a power of arrest or detention, and 'terrorism' has the meaning assigned to it by s 1 of that Act (s 65 of PACE 1984 (Art 2 of the 1989 Order)). It encompasses the detention of:

(a) persons who are arrested on suspicion of having committed a variety of 'terrorist' offences; and

(b) persons at a port of entry in order to examine whether they have infringed the terms of the Act.

7.288 Detention in both categories is limited to 48 hours but in both categories such detention may be extended on application to the Home Secretary for a further five days(Sch 8). The Act is not confined to terrorism involving Northern Ireland, but extends to 'international' terrorism (eg Palestinian terrorists detained in the UK). However, the 'international' terrorist must be liable to criminal proceedings in the UK or to deportation. The Act is not intended to catch a person involved in terrorism abroad, but who is acting lawfully in this country. Under the 2000 Act it is illegal to enter into, or otherwise be concerned in, any arrangement whereby money or other property is made available to a person for terrorist purposes or to a proscribed organisation (s 10(1)(c)). It is also illegal to deal with and facilitate the retention or control of terrorist funds (s 11). The safeguards contained in PACE 1984 and Codes of Practice apply, with modifications, to persons detained in England and Wales under the Terrorism Act 2000, as do the same safeguards in the PACE Order 1989 for those detained in Northern Ireland, although the Northern Ireland Codes of Practice do not apply to the detained terrorist. Some of the statutory provisions have been restricted and the following qualifications apply when a person is detained under the terrorism legislation.

(a) Search of the person – Section 43 of the Terrorism Act 2000 permits a constable to stop and search a person for 'any document or other article which may constitute evidence that he is a terrorist. The extensive powers of stop and search under s 1 of PACE (Art 3 of the PACE Order) do not permit such a search, though other stop and search powers may apply, eg s 47 of the Firearms Act 1968. The search power under s 15 is not, as PACE (Order) power is, limited to places where the public have access. It may be exercised anywhere. This power is also wider than that under s 54 of PACE (Art 55 of the PACE Order). The latter powers only apply when a person has been arrested whereas s 15 is a power to search in order to determine whether the person may be arrested. See also the power to stop and search vehicles and persons under s 43 of the Terrorism Act, discussed at para 3.78, ante.

(b) Right to have someone informed when arrested – The Jellicoe Report (Review of the Operation of the Prevention of Terrorism (Temporary Provisions) Act 1976 (1983)) recommended (para 135) that refusal of the right to communicate the fact of arrest should only arise in the rarest of cases. The European Commission of Human Rights (Case of McVeigh (1983)) requires similarly that a special case be made out for refusal, otherwise Art 8(1) of the European Convention is infringed (right to family and private life). In addition to the normal reasons for denying notification of arrest (s 56(5)) two further 'special cases' apply to those held under terrorism provisions. They follow the recommendations (Nos 24, 25) of the Jellicoe Report. Thus, notification will be refused if:

    (i)   it will prejudice the gathering of information about terrorists; or

   (ii)   it will alert others and thereby 'make it more difficult' to prevent terrorism and arrest terrorists (Sch 8, para 8(4) of the Terrorism 2000 Act). (Nothing in Art 57 of the PACE (NI) Order (the equivalent to s 56) applies to a person detained under the terrorism provisions (Art 10).)

The breadth of these additional qualifications is self-evident. Whether their terms stray too far for the European Convention remains to be seen. Refusal of notification may last up to 48 hours from arrival at a police station or any other premises; 'premises' refers to the fact that persons detained under terrorism provisions may be held on board a ship or vessel or other place specified by the Secretary of State (s 30(12)(c)). A crucial qualification to the foregoing is that the Prevention of Terrorism Act applies to 'international' terrorists. Thus, if foreign or Commonwealth nationals are detained, the right to notify their diplomatic representatives arises and this cannot be delayed without a breach of the Code of Practice (see further para 7.157, ante). For example X, a foreign national, is arrested for murder. His embassy must be informed at once and its representative must be allowed to see X, though the police may question X until the representative arrives.

(c)   Right to legal advice – As with (b), this right may be delayed for a maximum period of 48 hours, as opposed to the general limit of 36 hours. Three further grounds for delaying access to legal advice operate in addition to the general ones in s 58(8) of PACE are contained in Schedule 8 of the Terrorism Act 2000. These are identical to those in para (b) above.

    Schedule 8 para 9 of the Terrorism Act contains a provision whereby an assistant chief constable can order that access to legal advice will take place in the presence of a 'qualified officer'

    The qualified officer must be of at least inspector rank, must be in uniform and, in the opinion of the authorising officer, should have no connection with the case (Sch 8, para 9(4)) The subjective nature of the last criterion will enable a realistic interpretation so that, for example, an officer who has merely collated information concerning the case could be employed. Whether he will be able to detect secret messages from the overheard conversation is another matter. He could tape-record the conversation for later analysis. The provision has more to do with deterrence than detection.

(d)   Review of detention – The detention of a person detained under s 41 must be reviewed as soon as practicable after the beginning of the detention and thereafter at not more than 12-hourly intervals. (The 'relevant time' in relation to an arrest under s 41 of the Terrorism Act 2000 is the time of arrest wherever it takes place in the UK. The review officer can only authorise continued detention if he is satisfied that one of the conditions set out in para 23 of Sch 8 applies . Review of detention pending removal from the territory and of examination without detention must similarly be carried out immediately the detention or examination begins and thereafter at not more than 12-hourly intervals. (The 'relevant time' in relation to port detention or examination is the beginning of the detention or examination.

The detention or examination can only be continued if the review officer is satisfied that steps taken to remove the person or to complete the examination are being carried out diligently and expeditiously. The review officer in each case must be an officer who has not been directly involved in the matter in connection with which the person is detained or examined. In the case of a review of detention carried out in the first 24 hours of detention, the review officer must be an officer of at least the rank of inspector. Thereafter he must be an officer of at least the rank of superintendent (Sch 8, para 24). As with review of detention under PACE and Order, provision is made for postponement of a review, for representations about detention, for informing the detainee of his rights under ss 56 or 58 of PACE 1984 (Arts 57 and 59 of the PACE Order), and for recording the outcome of a review (Sch 8, paras 28). Paragraph 25 contains a provision similar to that contained in s 40(11) of PACE 1984 (Art 41(11) of the PACE (NI) Order 1989) to cover the situation where the review officer is of a rank lower than a superintendent and a higher-ranking officer then gives directions which are at variance with the duty of the review officer (see paras 6.35 and 6.69, ante).

(e) The taking of intimate and non-intimate samples is dealt with in Part 1 of Sch 8 of the Act to enable the taking of intimate and non-intimate samples, in accordance with the provisions contained in s 62(1) to (11) and s 63(1) to (9) of PACE (see paras 7.200 et seq, ante), where the authorising officer is satisfied it is necessary to do so in determining whether the person concerned has been involved in committing, preparing or instigating acts of terrorism, or whether that person is subject to an exclusion order under the Act. The taking of samples may also be authorised where the officer has reasonable grounds to suspect the person's involvement in offences referred to in s 40(1)(a) of the Terrorism Act 2000 (involving exclusion orders, membership and resources of proscribed organisations or contributions to acts of terrorism), and a belief that taking a sample would confirm or disprove that suspicion. The terms 'intimate' and 'non-intimate' samples have the meaning given to them under s 65 of PACE.

(f) Other exceptions – The extended periods of detention permissible under the terrorist legislation were preserved (s 51(b) of PACE), as were the powers (1) to search an arrested person who has been arrested not for an offence but for examination (s 32(10)), and (2) to retain fingerprints for the purpose of gathering intelligence (ss 61(9)(b) and 64(7)(b)). The various requirements in the Codes of Practice (eg Code A 4.5, Code C 2.6) for officers to record their names are replaced in cases of detention under the Terrorism Act by a duty to record the officers' warrant numbers.

8 The questioning of suspects

INTRODUCTION

8.1 The questioning of persons assumes such importance in the detection of crime and the proper conviction of offenders that special provisions govern it in PACE (ss 76-78, Arts 74-76 of the NI Order) and have been developed in the Code of Practice C (Code C). Breach of these provisions is more likely and more regularly to be met with the exclusion of evidence than in any other area of police powers. Article 6 of the European Convention on Human Rights which guarantees the right to a fair trial must also be complied with in relation to the questioning of suspects. A number of its provisions which have been considered in relation to the right of silence and inferences and the right to legal advice are dealt with in this chapter.

SUMMARY

8.2 There are two overriding, but difficult, principles to apply. First, as soon as an officer has grounds to suspect that a person has committed an offence and wishes to question him, he must caution that person if the answers or failure to answer may be given in evidence to a court in a prosecution. Second, an interview with a suspect, which is questioning after caution about involvement in an offence, will normally take place in a police station after arrest where the suspect will have all the protections of PACE and Codes C and E, including access to legal advice and the recording in written or taped form of the interview. Thus the situation in which an officer suspects D of an offence and eventually arrests him and takes him to a police station may be charted as follows:

Suspicion (1)	Reasonable suspicion (4)	Arrest	Police Station (5)
(2) Caution	Arrest followed by caution		Police detention
(3) Questioning - is an interview if the answers, or failure to answer, may be given in evidence in a prosecution	After the decision to arrest no interview, unless Code C11.1 applies, until D is in police station		Interview in accordance with Code C11 and Code E

8.3   There are four important stages leading up to an arrest:
(1)   police suspicion of a person, D,
(2)   the cautioning of D,
(3)   the questioning of D, and
(4)   D's arrest if the suspicion is confirmed and has a reasonable basis.

8.4   If D is caught red-handed, all four will coincide. If D is stopped, questioned and arrested in the street (or attends the police station voluntarily, is questioned and then arrested), the sequence will be (1), (3), (2) and (4). The difference between (2) and (3) can be narrow and difficult to distinguish. For example, if a police officer does not suspect D and merely asks him what he saw or knows of an incident, neither (2) nor (3) applies. If anything, D is only a potential witness. If then the constable suspects that D was involved and asks him questions about his suspected involvement, (2) and (3) arise, an 'interview' develops (see below), and it must be recorded. If the officer begins to suspect that D is involved, (2) also arises. It will be readily appreciated that such analysis, of what may be a rapidly developing conversation, is far easier to conduct on paper than in the street. However, the point is important in practice for Code C contains frequent references to both principles (2) and (3), whilst the courts have been concerned to prevent circumvention of the intended framework for questioning with its built-in safeguards and particularly energetic in requiring the proper recording of interviews, which Code C requires 'whether or not the interview takes place at a police station' (C 11.5).

8.5   The requirement in Code C 10.1 that

'a person whom there are grounds to suspect of an offence must be cautioned before any questions … are put to him regarding his involvement or suspected involvement in that offence if his answers or his silence … may be given in evidence to a court in a prosecution';

together with the definition of an interview by Code C 11.1A as 'the questioning of a person with regard to his involvement or suspected involvement in a criminal offence which, under para 10.1 of Code C, must be carried out under caution';

together with the requirement in Code 11.1 that

'Following a decision to arrest a suspect must not be interviewed about the relevant offence except at a police station or other authorised place of detention'

unless delay would be likely to produce the consequences set out in Code C 11.1, indicates that the questioning of a suspect on the street after caution but before arrest can amount to an interview. Given the low level of reasonable suspicion which justifies an arrest (see para 5.07, ante) such interviews should be very brief. When interviewed following an arrest any significant statement or silence which occurred before arrival at the police station must be put to the suspect for confirmation or denial (Code C 11.4A). If it is denied it may still be used in evidence but its evidential value is reduced. A further dimension is added by the provisions of the Criminal Justice and Public Order Act 1994 (CJPOA 1994) which, provided that where a person is at an authorised place of detention, he has been allowed an opportunity to consult a solicitor, permits a court or jury to draw proper inferences:

(a)   from the suspect's failure on being questioned after caution but before charge to mention any fact later relied upon at his trial (s 34);

(b)   if at trial he declines to give evidence; or from his failure or refusal to do so (s 35);

(c)   from his failure to account for objects, substances or marks on his person, clothing or in the place where he was arrested (s 36); and

(d)   to explain his presence at a place at or about the time when the offence was committed (s 37).

8.6   (a), (c) and (d) are relevant here, for the refusal or failure to answer questions put during an interview prior to arrest or during an interview post-arrest may trigger one or more of these provisions.

CAUTIONING AND INTERVIEWING

Cautions

8.7   Code C 10.1 requires that:

'A person whom there are grounds to suspect of an offence must be cautioned before any questions about an offence or further questions, if the answers provide the grounds for suspicion, are put to them if either the suspects answers or his silence (ie failure or refusal to answer a question or to answer satisfactorily) may be given in court in a prosecution. He therefore need not be cautioned if questions are put for other purposes, for example, solely to establish his identity or his ownership of a vehicle or to obtain information in accordance with any relevant statutory requirement (see 10.9) in furtherance of the proper and effective conduct of a search (for example to determine the need to search in the exercise of a stop and search power or to seek co-operation while carrying out a search) to seek verification of a written record in accordance with paragraph 11.13 when examining a person in accordance with the Terrorism Act 2000, Sch 7, and the Code of Practice for Examining Officers issued under that Act, Sch 14, para 6.'

8.8   An interview is the questioning of a person regarding his involvement or suspected involvement in a criminal offence or offences which, by virtue of para C 10.1 is required to be carried out under caution (Code C 11.1A). Following a decision to arrest, interviews should only take place at a police station where all the safeguards and requirements of PACE and Code C apply.

8.9   The caution, amended in the light of the provisions of the Criminal Justice and Public Order Act 1994, is in the following terms:

'You do not have to say anything. But it may harm your defence if you do not mention when questioned something which you later rely on in court. Anything you do say may be given in evidence' (Code C 10.4).

8.10   It will be seen that cautions and interviews are inextricably linked by the above provisions. A caution is required before asking questions if the answers or failure to answer may be given in evidence and an interview is such questioning.

8.11   A number of points call for discussion.
(1)   The trigger for a caution is grounds to suspect of an offence while the threshold requirement for an arrest is reasonable grounds to suspect of an offence. Note 10A introduced in the 2003 Code states: 'There must be some reasonable, objective grounds for the suspicion, based on known facts or information which are relevant to the likelihood that the offence has been committed and that the person to be questioned, committed it.' In *R v Rouf* (1999) the Court of Appeal required that the suspicion be reasonable before a caution was necessary. However, it is stressed that Note 10A is a 'Guidance Note' which is technically of a lower status than the Code itself but the line between Code 10.1 and note of guidance 10A is indeed a fine one. Nonetheless a caution is required at an earlier stage than arrest, stage (1) of the four stages suggested above. Thus, questioning of a suspect on the street before arrest or of a suspect who voluntarily attends a police station must be under caution. However, there must be grounds for suspicion before the need for a caution arises. It is not enough that the officer is suspicious or has a hunch or is relying on his sixth sense (*R v Shah* (1994)). If such questioning is under caution and is about the suspect's involvement or suspected involvement in an offence, it is an interview. If no decision to arrest has been made that interview need not take place in a police station, though it must be recorded. Once a decision to arrest has been made there should be no further questioning under caution in order to obtain evidence, whether positive or negative, until the person has been taken to a police station and detained without charge. A further caution is required upon arrest for an offence unless it is impracticable to do so because of his

condition or behaviour at the time or he has already been cautioned immediately prior to his arrest in accordance with Code C 10.1 above (C 10.3,10.4). It follows that questioning outside a police station should only be such as to raise the suspicion to reasonable suspicion but may nevertheless amount to an interview if the answers, or failure to answer, may be given in evidence to a court in a prosecution. In *R v Okafor* (1994) customs officers deliberately failed to caution after finding cocaine in D's luggage, so as to avoid the possibility that he might realise that he had been detected and not lead customs officers to any accomplice. The trial judge exercising his discretion under s 78 of PACE admitted evidence of the conversation between D and customs officers after finding the heroin despite the breaches of Code C (D should have been cautioned, it was an interview which should have taken place in a police station after arrest when D had been informed of his rights). The Court of Appeal held that no questions about the offence should have been asked after the heroin had been found, the conversation should have been excluded, but the appeal was dismissed, the proviso to s 2 of the Criminal Appeal Act 1968 being applied. It is useful to contrast this case with the Court of Appeal's reasoning in *R v Nelson and Rose* (1998), the facts of which are similar. In this case the court held that the evidence should have been excluded because the officer suspected that an offence had been committed and the fact that the dependant had a sufficient opportunity in subsequent interviews to exercise an informal and independent choice as to whether she should report or retract what she had already said resulted in dismissal of the appeal.

(2) A suspect must be cautioned only if questions are put to him regarding his involvement or suspected involvement in that offence if his answers, or his failure or refusal to answer satisfactorily may be given in evidence to a court in a prosecution. This appears to anticipate a degree of knowledge of the law of evidence which is not possessed by the ordinary constable for not everything a suspect says or fails to say is admissible evidence though it is popularly believed that anything said in the presence of the suspect is admissible. The reality is more complicated, as the discussion at para 8.16(8), post, indicates. In *Westminster City Council v Cinquemani and Zanelli* (2002) the defendants were charged with unlicensed street trading. A council enforcement officer saw people eating and drinking outside the premises. The first defendant introduced himself as the manager and admitted he was responsible for the tables on the footway. He was not cautioned, since the officer had had grounds to suspect the defendant as soon as he became aware that he was the manager there had been a breach of Code C10.1, and the evidence was excluded.

(3) A caution is not required when questions are being put for purposes other than the use of the answers in evidence. Examples given in Code C 10.1 include questions put solely for the purpose of establishing identity or ownership of a vehicle or in the furtherance of the proper and effective conduct of a search, such as the need to determine the need to exercise stop and search powers or seek co-operation while carrying out a search. This is fine as far as it goes but there is a thin line between questions which have no evidential value and those that do. For example,

in *R v Cohen* (1993), where the court considered the previous definition of 'interview' which included the phrase about the proper and effective conduct of a search, it was held that questions put to a suspect in his home after controlled drugs had been found which were directed at establishing to whom they belonged and whether they were for personal use or for sale, did not constitute an interview. However, if the person accepts that the drugs belonged to him and that they were for sale, those answers, or now, in the right circumstances, the failure to answer, could be given in evidence in court. There is at the point when drugs are found suspicion that C has committed an offence. The answers to the questions can provide reasonable cause to believe that he is guilty of an offence and positive answers, or now a failure to answer followed by a defence at trial that the drugs were not his, may be used in evidence. If a caution is required at the outset the questioning would amount to an interview as now defined by Code C 11.1A. (One may note that it is sufficient that the answers or failure to answer 'may' be given in evidence.) It is easy to see that a search of premises when the suspect is present could require a caution and subsequent questioning become an interview: see *R v Keane* (1992) and *R v Khan* (1993) in which s 30(10) of PACE (Art (32(13)) (discussed at para 5.174, ante) was relied upon to justify a delay in taking the arrested person to a police station in order to search their premises. The Court of Appeal warned against using the subsection to circumvent the safeguards provided by Code C (and see para 6.108(a), ante). Questions may be asked which assist in the proper and effective conduct of the search but there is a thin line between such questions and questions which go to D's involvement in the offence for which he has been arrested and become an interview. There were breaches of the Code in these cases, none of which justified exclusion, but the Court warned against using the subsection to circumvent the safeguards provided by Code C. Code C 11.1 adds emphasis to this warning.

A decision which was favourable to the police is *R v Parks* (1993). The officers stopped D, who was driving his father's car containing what proved to be the proceeds of a number of recently committed burglaries. The officers were not aware that the burglaries had been committed and after dealing with road traffic offences they noticed stereo systems, some tapes and other goods on the back seat. A number of questions were asked about the ownership of these items and damage to the ignition system which they had noted. When the boot was opened they saw a video recorder, two television sets and other property. A further fifteen questions followed, most concerned with the ownership of the property but some about his movements that day. Only then did the officer arrest D on suspicion of theft of the property and car and caution him. The trial judge accepted that the officer did not initially suspect that the property was stolen; that it was only just before the caution that the officer suspected that an offence had been committed, therefore when there were grounds to suspect an offence the caution was given. One can accept that it was only just before that point that the officer had reasonable suspicion to justify an arrest but he must surely have suspected an offence at a much earlier stage and should, it is submitted, have cautioned much earlier. It does not, however, follow that the questioning, which was largely aimed at determining whether the property was owned by D, amounted to an interview. The Court of Appeal considered *R v Weekes* (1993) and accepted that if the answers to exploratory questions at the roadside give rise to a well-founded suspicion, what started out as an inquiry could become an interview. The Court had reservations as to whether in this case it was, but even if it was it was 'only just an interview' and as such was not a significant and substantial breach of the Code. A later series of questions after arrest at the police station while the car was being searched, a number of which were also aimed at determining to whom the property belonged, clearly was an interview and should have been contemporaneously recorded. However, the Court accepted that the trial judge correctly exercised his discretion not to exclude it. *R v Maynard* (1998) goes the other way: where officers asked specific questions of the appellant which were designed to ascertain criminal liability and where there were reasonable grounds to suspect an offence such that she had been arrested, no interview should take place.

(4) In practice the duty to caution will often coincide with the moment of arrest. The revised caution is not particularly appropriate to the arrest stage. While the warning that anything he says may be used in evidence may prevent him blurting out some damaging remark, the warning that his failure to mention any fact later relied upon at trial may damage his defence is of no effect except possibly as a warning of things to come which few suspects will understand.

(5) The more difficult case is where a person who is not under arrest has been answering questions about a crime, at a police station as a volunteer or elsewhere, and a stage is reached where the officer begins to suspect that the person was involved in the crime. A caution is required at that point but his natural inclination is to continue the questioning without the interruption of a caution and the deterrent effect which it and being told that he is not under arrest and is not obliged to remain as required by Code C 10.2 may have on a talkative suspect. In the absence of a contemporaneous record, it may be impossible for a court to judge whether the stage for cautioning was improperly passed – hence the value of recording interviews (see below). A similarly difficult situation arose in *R v Purcell* (1992). D escaped from police trying to arrest him for rape. He was at large for 12 months using an alias when he was arrested on suspicion of burglaries, which he admitted and was then cautioned. In the interview he allegedly blurted out his real name and said he was wanted for something really bad. The officer said, 'What is it?' and D said, 'I'm ashamed. I done a rape … I'm so ashamed.' The interview about the burglaries proceeded and when it was finished the officer referred back to this conversation. D said he did not want to talk about it. The officer then read a note of what D had said and D appeared to read it before he signed it. The officer was permitted to give evidence of this conversation at D's trial for rape. On appeal following conviction it was argued that D should have been cautioned before being asked what he had done. The Court of Appeal held that there was no breach of the 1985 Code (which in this respect is virtually the same as the 1995 Code) the question 'What is it?' not being asked for the purpose

of obtaining evidence which may be given to a court in a prosecution. In these circumstances the officer arguably did not suspect that D had committed an offence when he said he was wanted for something really bad, therefore there was no need to caution before seeking more information. It does, however, demonstrate how thin the line is between seeking more information which may give rise to suspicion of an offence, and asking questions the answers to which may be given in evidence.

(6) In the case of a 'volunteer' (ie a person not in police detention) being questioned at a police station, the officer must not only give the caution when the requisite suspicion arises, but must also tell him that he is not under arrest, he is not obliged to stay and that, if he does, he can obtain free and independent legal advice (Code C 3.21). Again the tone and context of delivery are likely to influence the impact of this message, but if properly delivered this is a formidable safeguard to the citizen. One may also note that s 29 of PACE (Art 31) requires that a volunteer be informed at once that he is under arrest if a decision is taken by the constable to prevent him from leaving at will. Code C 3.21 requires that a caution must then follow unless he has already been cautioned immediately prior to his arrest. Code 11.1 also comes into play at the point when a decision to arrest is made. No interview is to take place after that decision unless one of the three conditions set out in the Code applies. The fact that the person is already at a police station does not, it is submitted, mean that questioning can continue. Once arrested the person should be taken before the custody officer and processed in the same way as any other arrested person. Any further questioning will then take place in accordance with Codes C 11 and E.

(7) It is not clear from the wording of Code C 10.1, which refers to 'grounds to suspect of an offence' and questions about 'that offence' whether a re-caution is required each time a new offence is suspected. The length of time since the previous caution was given is relevant. In *R v Oni* (1992), a decision on C 10.1 of the first Code of Practice which in this respect is similar to the second and the current C 10.1, O, who had been seen to throw a cigarette out of a car, was asked whether it was cannabis. When he said it was, he was cautioned. A search of the car revealed heroin and cash and O was questioned about this without a further caution. Less than two minutes had elapsed between caution and further questioning. O's appeal against conviction, based on the failure to re-caution, was dismissed: the Court of Appeal was of the view that the earlier caution was apt to cover the later questions. There was no breach of the Code; even if there had been the trial judge had correctly exercised his discretion under s 78 having taken into account the fact that O did not give evidence and had suffered no prejudice from the lack of a second caution. Perhaps one may here draw an analogy between this situation and the requirement of a caution on arrest which is required by C 10.3 'unless: (b) he has already been cautioned immediately prior to arrest in accordance with paragraph 10.1 above'. 'Immediately prior' would include a two-minute interval and possibly up to ten minutes but it would be wise to err on the side of cautioning before questioning about new offences if more than ten minutes have elapsed

since the last caution. This proposition is supported in *R v Miller* (1998) where an hour had lapsed since the previous caution. A further caution should have been given, not least because of the anxiety a person might feel which would could cause him to forget the rights of which he had been informed earlier.

(8) When a person is arrested, a caution need not be given if it is impracticable (eg D is intoxicated, or violently resists arrest) or if one has already been given immediately prior to the arrest (Code C 10.4(b)); eg questioning of a person raises sufficient suspicion to warrant a caution at 5.30pm, a few questions later and there is enough evidence to arrest him at 5.40pm. A second caution is unnecessary.

(9) If a caution is given to a juvenile or the mentally disordered, it must be given initially in the presence of the appropriate adult or repeated when he arrives (Code C 10.12).

(10) When a person's detention is authorised by a custody officer at a police station, the suspect is given a written notice of his rights and the notice repeats the caution (Code C 3.2).

(11) There is no specific provision requiring a caution before a person makes a voluntary statement not in response to questioning, for example in *R v Pall* (1992) D, who was on bail awaiting trial, was served with statements of a co-accused. He was later arrested for further offences and after a short interview about those offences D, having been told that he could not be questioned about the earlier offences with which he had been charged, wrote his own statement which, in part, contained admissions to the earlier offences. His appeal, based on the failure to caution him, was dismissed, it not being unfair in the circumstances to admit the statement. However, the court said that Annex D to Code 11 properly interpreted applied to such a situation. Code C 16.5 requires an abbreviated caution where a person is questioned after charge in the limited circumstances permitted by that paragraph but does not specifically deal with the above situation. Again one should err on the side of cautioning in the abbreviated form, since s 34 of the CJPOA 1994 applies to questions under caution before charge, and follows Annex D.

8.12   The wording of the caution ('You do not have to say anything. But it may harm your defence if you do not mention when questioned something which you later rely on in court. Anything you do say may be given in evidence') seems straightforward. Minor deviations from the wording are acceptable provided the sense of the caution is preserved. Note for Guidance 10C permits the officer to explain it in his own words if it appears that the person does not understand what it means. This can be a difficult task for the officer. He may explain that the person does not have to answer his questions but that a refusal to offer any explanation or other information now which may be used at trial in his defence later, may mean the court or jury will not believe what he says. That may be possible in an interview room but there will be few opportunities for such explanation on the street. The danger in putting it more positively by, for example, suggesting that his co-operation will reflect well on him at trial, is that it may be seen as inducing an unreliable admission or confession leading to its exclusion under s 76(2)(b) of PACE. If there is a break in questioning, the interviewing officer must ensure that the suspect is aware that he is still under caution on resumption (Code C 10.5). The simplest way is a reminder that he is still under caution and this will usually suffice if the break is short (eg the officer being called to consult a colleague or to answer a telephone, or the suspect visiting the lavatory); but even here an intelligent suspect will benefit from a repetition of the caution, especially if he is unrepresented. Certainly longer breaks warrant repetition of the caution; and re-commencement of an interview will also require a reminder of D's right to free legal advice if he is unrepresented (Code C 11.2).

Interview

8.13

'An interview is the questioning of a person regarding his involvement or suspected involvement in a criminal offence or offences which, by virtue of paragraph 10.1 of Code C, is required to be carried out under caution.

Procedures undertaken under section 7 of the Road Traffic Act 1988 do not constitute interviewing for the purpose of this code' (see *DPP v Rous* (1992)) (Code C 11.1A).

8.14   At the outset one must be aware that the Code definition, unlike a statutory definition, is merely a guide and the courts will have the last word. There was much criticism by the courts of the previous definition and it would be surprising if the present definition escapes judicial criticism. The importance of determining what is and is not an interview lies in the aim and purpose of Code C, commonly known as the 'anti-verballing provisions'. In *R v Hunt* (1992) Steyn J, after outlining the potential scope for miscarriages of justice in the false attribution of incriminating statements to persons in custody and the role of Code C in blocking off loopholes to prevent such verballing, said:

'The extent to which the provisions [of Code C] are effective will therefore crucially depend on how extensive or restrictive a meaning is given by the courts to the ordinary English word "interview" read in the context of PACE and Code C.'

8.15   Clearly the word must be restricted to the context in which it is used – 'the questioning of a person regarding his involvement or suspected involvement in a criminal offence or offences'. In other words the police must suspect a person and have cautioned him before any questioning of him may become an interview for Code C purposes. Even then not all questioning becomes an interview. Only questions the answers to which (or the failure to answer or satisfactorily answer) may be given in evidence before a court in a prosecution are elevated to the status of an interview. Sometimes it will be clear that questioning is an interview; eg D is stopped in the street and an offensive weapon is discovered, clearly any questioning about the offence of possession of such a weapon will be an interview (see *R v Foster* (1987)). This narrows the term down but still permits a very wide interpretation. Thus, in *R v Matthews* (1990) the Court of Appeal took the view that:

'Normally any discussion or talk between a suspect or prisoner and a police officer about an alleged crime will amount to an "interview", whether instigated by the suspect, or prisoner or a police officer.'

8.16 See *R v Okafor* (1994) where customs officers, having found cocaine in a snail stew brought into the UK by D, further questioned him without caution about his acquisition of the stew without telling him that cocaine had been found. This was held to be an interview which should have been excluded. See also *R v Rowe* (1994) where it was held that three meetings at a prison between police officers and D, a convicted prisoner, at which questions were asked about other offences with which he was later charged, were interviews which should have been contemporaneously recorded as required by Code C 11.5 (as to interviews in prisons see para 7.285, ante).

8.17 The case law on the meaning of 'interview' has established the following – an interview requires a meeting between an officer and a suspect and the asking of a question or questions, so that a concealed tape-recording of D's conversations with another person in a police cell or with his family in an interview room will not amount to an interview (see *R v Jelen and Katz* (1989); *R v Shaukat Ali* (1991); *R v Bailey and Smith* (1993) (not unfair to admit the evidence in these cases but cf *R v H* (1987)); it can take place outside the police station (*R v Maguire* (1989)); the suspect need not be talking to the investigating officer (*R v Sparks* (1991)); it can qualify as an interview even if the officer genuinely believes that he is only having an informal chat, ie the conversation is viewed objectively by the court and, if it decides it is an interview, the officer's belief or motives are irrelevant (*R v Sparks* (1991) and see *R v Weerdesteyn* (1995) where a 'chat' with a suspect after his arrest and interview was held to be an interview); it should not be given a restricted meaning (*R v Matthews* (1990); *R v Sparks* (1991)); it must involve a person whom the police suspect of an offence (*R v Grier* (1989)); it is 'a series of questions directed by the police to a suspect with a view to obtaining admissions on which proceedings [can] be founded', per Bingham LJ in *R v Absolam* (1989): the 'series of questions' can be quite short (16 in *R v Fogah* (1989), 3 in *R v Manji* (1990), 2 in *R v Cox* (1993) and only one in *R v Ward* (1993)); the subject matter and the likely evidential effect of the answer, or failure to answer, is the crucial factor, not the length of the conversation; the questioning must relate to the suspected offence (*R v Absolam* (1988); *R v Matthews* (1990); *R v Pullen* (1991); *R v Marsh* (1991)); it would appear to require a two-way process (*R v Younis* (1990)) so that if a suspect 'blurts out' an admission unprompted it is not an interview. *R v Menard* (1995) took the same view of the situation in which D, while detained at a police station, asked to see officers without suggestion, invitation or inducement, and volunteered information which the officers recorded for their own records. It was said that questioning is the hallmark of an interview but the court warned against any attempt to disguise as an information-gathering exercise what is in reality an interview. This, together with the limitations of these decisions, should be noted. No questions were asked; if any were asked in that situation, even to clarify what D had volunteered, it could become an interview. The decision of the Court of Appeal in *R v Maguire* (1989) may be doubted in the light of the amended Code provisions. The suspect there had been arrested and confessed en route to the police station. The Court agreed with the trial judge that questions near the scene of a suspected crime designed to elicit an explanation and legitimate reason for the suspect's conduct did not amount to an interview. Yet Maguire had already been arrested and any subsequent questions about the offence or the circumstances of it can be double-edged, eliciting an explanation of guilt or innocence, and the reality is that in such circumstances the questioning is usually more concerned with establishing guilt than innocence. A different, and it is submitted, a more correct view of a similar situation was taken in *R v Hunt* (1992). There the defendant was found to be in possession of a flick knife. He ran off and was arrested. In the police car he was asked why he had the knife. The Court of Appeal held that the question and subsequent answer was an interview. Any post-arrest questioning about the crime must be an interview even if the answers appear to be inadmissible in evidence. Thus an innocent explanation, if true, should mean no prosecution. If untrue it might lead to a prosecution and may be admissible as an out-of-court lie under the principles set out in *R v Lucas* (1981). It may also give rise to an inference under s 34 of the CJPOA 1994. More therefore depends upon the answer, or lack of one, than the question. See, for example, *R v Gordon* (1995). D was asked for the knife with which he had stabbed the deceased. He replied, 'I haven't got it'. When police found it under his bed he said, 'All right, that's the one'. His appeal against conviction was upheld because of a misdirection and the failure to give a Lucas direction. Had such a direction been given D's defence of self-defence could be rebutted by the lie if there was no other credible explanation for his lie other than to cover up his guilt. In this respect the apparently exculpatory answer is of as much evidential significance as the incriminatory admission.

Summary

8.18   In summary, for an interview:
(a) the police must suspect that an offence has been committed;
(b) the police must suspect D of involvement, for otherwise any conversation with a member of the public, eg a witness, would qualify;
(c) if D is a suspect and is cautioned the question(s) must be about his involvement in the suspected offence. So, for example, questions aimed at discovering his identity or matters unrelated to the offence is not an interview within Code C.

The rare case in which an offender immediately owns up before any questions can be put to him would not be an interview in the absence of any questions (see *R v Younis* (1990); *R v Menard* (1995) (any such spontaneous utterances must in any case be noted and D asked to sign the record of them, see Code C 11.13));
(d) it follows from (a) and (b) that all questioning about the offence after caution amounts to an interview and after arrest such interviews should normally take place in a police station.

8.19 In *R v Ward* (1993) one question put to a person who had been arrested having been found hiding near a crashed and stolen car, was held to be an interview. In *R v Cox* (1992) two questions to D after his arrest were an interview being directed at his involvement in the offence for which he had been arrested, the answers to which could have been given in evidence. Though a decision under the previous definition of 'interview', note should be taken of the court's conclusion that the concept of an 'interview' had to be judged against the intended framework for questioning of suspects taken as a whole, ie a decision to arrest, followed by an arrest, taking the arrested person to a police station, notifying him of his rights, consultation with a solicitor, followed by an interview. Any attempt to undermine the intended framework by on-street or in-car questioning on the way to a police station is likely to be met with the sanction of exclusion of any answers or failure to answer. In *R v Goddard* (1994) D's conviction for possession of heroin was quashed because the trial judge had failed to exclude evidence of a conversation between D and a police officer after his arrest and caution about three wraps of heroin he had thrown away at the scene of the arrest. The post-arrest questioning as to what the wraps contained and how much heroin they contained, which elicited incriminating replies, was clearly an interview which should have been carried out in the police station after D had been informed of his rights.

8.20 The most difficult practical problem lies in determining when conditions (a) and (b) above are satisfied. Take the following situation (and cf the facts in *R v Maguire* (1989) and *R v Park* (1994)): a police officer hears the sound of breaking glass, approaches the scene and D runs round the corner into him. The glass in a pavement advertising hoarding is broken.
(i) After identifying D the officer, P, asks him what he has been up to. D replies, 'Nothing'.
(ii) P says, 'What's all this broken glass about?' D says, 'I had an accident.'
(iii) P, 'What sort of accident?' D explains, but
(iv) on further questioning D admits to having broken the glass deliberately.
(v) P puts the offence of criminal damage to him and asks for clarification.
(vi) D confirms his admission and says he did it because his girlfriend had walked out on him.

8.21 On any interpretation stages (v) and (vi) constitute an interview (which must be recorded). However, one interpretation of the first sentence of Code C11.1A, is that the interview begins at stage (i) when P has grounds to suspect (no more) that D has committed an offence. A caution must be given at this stage and if the questioning is about D's involvement in the offence the questioning thereafter would amount to an interview. But the better view is that the questions up to (iv) are not about his involvement in an offence, rather they seek to establish whether an offence has been committed. More complicated cases can be imagined. It is not difficult to decide what is an interview after the event with the benefit of hindsight but police officers have to make a decision in often difficult circumstances, before they start asking questions. The reality of policing and the need for common sense require some leeway for the police to make preliminary inquiries without the encumbrance of note-taking (which the trial judge and Court of Appeal in Park (1994) seemed to accept). Since the Code provisions are not binding on the court, and any significant statement or silence must be put to the suspect so as, in effect, to be part of a later interview, some flexibility should be possible (cf *R v Park* above). As Bingham LJ was prompted to remark in *R v Marsh* (1991):

> '[I]t is plainly desirable that these provisions [the Code] should not become so highly technical and sophisticated in their construction and application that no police officer, however well intentioned and diligent, could reasonably be expected to comply with them. There has to be a reasonable commonsense approach to the matter such that police officers confronted with unexpected situations, and doing their best to be fair and to comply with the Codes, do not fall foul of some technicality of authority or construction.'

8.22   It is submitted that the current position is that in view of the wording of Code C11.1A pre-arrest questioning will constitute an interview unless the officer is able to satisfy the court that at the relevant time he had been involved in a criminal offence – the intention of the officer in asking the question is not relevant; only whether there was suspicion of involvement in an offence or not is the primary consideration.

Intelligence interviews

8.23   It has become common practice to question detainees ostensibly to gain intelligence about the activities of criminals or criminal methods. Sometimes such questioning takes place 'off the record' and the provisions of Code C are not fully complied with; on rarer occasions the tape recording of the questioning takes place. The admissibility of evidence obtained during 'intelligence' interviews may fall to be considered by the courts in which case the normal admissibility criteria, including the operation of s 78, applies.

8.24   In *R v Howell, Harns and May* (2003), following *R v Drury and Clark* (2002), the verballing provisions were held to apply. The defendants were members of the Flying Squad who were convicted of conspiracy to steal and doing acts tending to prevent the course of justice. Certain police officers, who were themselves under investigation, were invited to give evidence for the prosecution. The interviews were not contemporaneously or properly recorded nor signed by the 'suspect'. The Court of Appeal held that the evidence was admissible – both PACE and the CPIA applied.

Juveniles and the mentally disordered

8.25   The definition of an interview appears to create a difficult problem for the police dealing with juveniles and the mentally disordered on the street. Code C 11.14 states:

> 'A juvenile or person who is mentally disordered or otherwise mentally vulnerable must not be interviewed regarding their involvement or suspected involvement

in a criminal offence or offences, or asked to provide or sign a written statement under caution or record of interview, in the absence of an appropriate adult unless paragraphs 11.1, 11.8 to 11.20 apply.'

8.26   Code C 11.15 further bars interviews with juveniles at their places of education except in exceptional circumstances and then with the agreement of the principal or his nominee.

8.27   Police officers must be particularly on their guard in questioning such persons suspected of criminal offences. The suspected juvenile etc must be cautioned but questions should then be confined to matters of identification or establishing whether an offence has been committed and other non-evidential questions (see further para **7.262**, ante). It is hoped that the courts will see the obvious need for some flexibility given the difficulty in determining when the answer to a question may be given in evidence, but the courts have made it clear that the presence of an appropriate adult is an important safeguard for this vulnerable group and will not tolerate any attempt to deny this group that protection. It must be emphasised that this is not a bar to questioning juveniles etc, but is a bar to interviewing them without an appropriate adult being present. This indicates the importance of keeping the definition of an interview in mind. Questions designed to identify the person, to establishing whether he is a juvenile, mentally disordered or handicapped, whether an offence has been committed and whether there are reasonable grounds to suspect that the person committed it, are permissible, albeit under caution once there are grounds to suspect him. At that point there are grounds for arrest and thereafter no further questions should be asked until the formal interview in the presence of the appropriate adult. Even then it is possible that the bona-fide pre-arrest questioning to establish grounds for arrest could become an interview. One must then rely on the good sense of the court and hope that where it is 'only just an interview' (cf *R v Parks* (1994)) it will not lead to exclusion of any evidence thus obtained.

Custody and review officers

8.28   Others involved in the detention process can easily fall foul of the Code's provisions regarding cautions and interviews. For example, the exchange between the arresting officer, custody officer and prisoner on being brought to a police station could easily become an interview, see for example *R v Oransaye* (1993). Code 3.4 seeks to avoid such problems by requiring that the custody officer notes on the custody record any comment a person may make in relation to the arresting officer's account but shall not invite comment. If he authorises the person's detention he must inform him of the grounds as soon as practicable and in any case before the person is questioned about any offence. Any comment made by the person in respect of the decision to detain must be noted but again no comment invited. The custody officer shall not put specific questions to the person about his involvement in any offence, nor in respect of any comment made in response to the arresting officer's account or the decision to detain, lest it constitute an interview as defined above. Code C 15.6

applies the same constraints on the exchange between a review officer and a detainee lest they too become an interview. He should hear the representations, note any comments if the decision is to continue detention, but he shall not put specific questions to the person about his involvement in any offence, nor in respect of any comment made on the decision to detain further (see para 6.137, ante).

Cautions, interviews and undercover operations

8.29   Undercover operations can present difficulties in this context. Clearly a caution at the point of suspicion would destroy the operation. On the other hand, to permit questioning unchecked would undermine the intended protection of the Code and expose persons to the danger of verballing which it seeks to prevent. In *R v Christou and Wright* (1992) undercover police officers set up shop in order to recover stolen property and collect evidence against the thieves and handlers. Cameras and tape-recorders recorded the transactions. Most conversations involved bartering but the officers also engaged in banter and asked questions consistent with those expected of a shopkeeper prepared to deal in stolen goods. This evidence was admitted at the trial of C and W, who were convicted. Their appeal, based on the argument that the recorded conversations were wrongly admitted, was dismissed. The Court of Appeal made it clear that Code C applied to suspects not in police detention and was intended to protect those who in their unequal position were vulnerable to abuse or pressure from police officers. The situation at the shop was very different. The appellants were not being questioned by police officers acting as such; conversations were on equal terms. The Code was not intended to apply in such circumstances. However, it would be wrong for police officers to adopt or use an undercover pose to facilitate the asking of questions about an offence uninhibited by the requirements of the Code and with the effect of circumventing it. (See also *R v Maclean and Kosten* (1993) and *R v Cadette* (1995) in which Customs and Excise officers used subterfuge to obtain evidence, not unfairly.) This last point was taken up by the Court of Appeal in *R v Bryce* (1992). There an undercover police officer contacted a man by telephone and after a short conversation arranged to meet him with a view to buying a stolen Saab 900S motor car. The defendant arrived in a Saab. He told the officer that the alarm had been deactivated and the coded stereo radio removed. In response to the officer's question D said that it had been stolen two or three days ago and said he was stealing two a week and asked whether the officer would be interested in others. At that point he was arrested and cautioned. He maintained his silence during interviews in the police station but when the tape was switched off the officer claimed that D then said he would tell him what had happened but he did not want it recorded. He then was said to have made damaging admissions. He denied these at trial but the trial judge admitted all the conversations. Quashing his conviction Lord Taylor LCJ said that the series of questions by the officer clearly offended against what their Lordships had said in Christou and Wright. It was blatantly an interrogation with the effect, if not the design, of using an undercover pose to circumvent the Code. The questions went directly to the issue of guilt, were hotly disputed and there was no contemporaneous record. The interview at the police station was a classic example of a suspicious sequence of total denial or refusal to comment, followed by an alleged confession off-tape, followed by a denial that the conversation took place, which had given rise to suspicions of verballing. The earlier case of *R v H* (1987) may now be seen as an attempt to circumvent the Code provisions. H had been arrested and interviewed about an alleged rape which he denied. He was released on police bail and the alleged victim was persuaded to speak to him on the telephone. The recorded conversation was excluded (see commentary [1995] Crim LR 232).

8.30   In *R v Smurthwaite and Gill* (1994) both defendants had been convicted of soliciting murder having solicited an undercover police officer posing as a contract killer. In dismissing their appeal the Court of Appeal considered the wider question of what evidence is admissible when a police officer acts as an agent provocateur. While that was not in itself a defence the fact that the evidence was obtained by such an agent or by a trick, while not requiring a judge to exclude it, was not irrelevant to the question whether the judge should, in the exercise of his statutory or common law discretion, exclude it. The Court should have regard to the following (not exhaustive) factors.

(i)   Was the officer acting as an agent provocateur in the sense that he was enticing the defendant to commit an offence he would not otherwise have committed?

(ii)   What was the nature of the entrapment?

(iii)   Did the evidence consist of admissions to a completed offence, or the actual commission of an offence?

(iv)   How active or passive was the officer?

(v)   Was there an unassailable record of what happened, or corroboration?

(vi)   Had the officer abused his role to act as an interviewer?

8.31   The officers in this case were not true agents provocateurs and the defendants had made all the running throughout; the evidence was then correctly admitted.

Recording of interviews outside the police station and/or comments on arrest

8.32   Regardless of the venue, any interview between a police officer or person investigating a criminal offence and a suspect must be both recorded, and recorded accurately (Code C 11.7(a)). Failure to do so has been a regular basis for the exclusion of evidence and for disapproval by the judiciary (see *R v Absolam* (1988), and *R v Matthews* (1990)). This is unlikely to be a problem when interviews are conducted at police stations and tape-recorded, but can be problematic if not so conducted. Code C 11.10 requires that the person interviewed (and the appropriate adult and/or solicitor if present) be given the opportunity to read the interview record and to sign it as correct or indicate in what respects it is inaccurate. If the interview takes place outside the police station before arrest, or after arrest in the emergency situations envisaged by Code C 11.1, the record will be in the officer's notebook. Code C 11.13 further requires that a note be made of any comments made by a suspected person, including unsolicited comments, which are outside the context of an interview but relevant to the offence. The effect of a failure to do so depends on whether the breach is seen as significant and substantial, which itself may depend on whether what was said were mere comments, more substantial comments or an interview. Thus in *R v Courtney* (1995) Customs and Excise intercepted two parcels of herbal cannabis addressed to one M. An officer posing as a postman delivered the parcels to the address. When asked C said he was not M but had to sign for it. He opened the parcel and was then arrested. A note was made of the earlier comments but it was not shown to C. This was held to be a breach of Code C 11.13 but was not significant or substantial and the note was admitted. However, in *RSPCA v Eager* (1995) E was interviewed in her home by RSPCA inspectors who recorded the interview in the car outside giving E no opportunity to read it or sign it as correct. This was seen as a significant and substantial breach of the Code.

8.33   To complicate matters it has been held that showing the suspect the note of an interview for verification is itself an interview (*R v Townend* (1989)). However, seeking verification of unsolicited comments would not be an interview. It is probably far easier to seek verification of everything noted before arrest and after arrest, whether or not an interview, at the beginning of the formal interview and incorporate it into the taped interview. Code C 11.4 requires that any significant statement or silence which occurred before arrival at the police station be put to the suspect after caution at the beginning of an interview and that he be asked whether he confirms or denies the earlier statement or silence and whether he wishes to add anything. A 'significant' statement or silence is one which appears capable of being used in evidence against the suspect, in particular a direct admission of guilt, or a failure or refusal to answer a question, or to answer it satisfactorily, which might give rise to an inference under Part III of the CJPOA 1994, considered below paras 8.42-8.59. If the verification process is not done on tape the suspect should be asked to endorse the record with words such as 'I agree that this is a correct record of what was said' (or not said in the case of a failure to answer questions) and to add his signature. In the event of disagreement the officer should record the details of the disagreement and again ask the suspect to read it and sign that he has accurately recorded the disagreement. Any refusal to sign should also be recorded (Note of Guidance C 11.E). In Khan (2000) the defendant was stopped driving whilst disqualified, it was alleged he said, "It's not stolen, I am disqualified". This was a significant statement and should have been put to the defendant for his agreement. If the suspect is represented his solicitor should be made aware of the previous statements before any interview; this is perhaps more necessary in the case of a failure to answer questions if reliance is likely to be placed at trial on the drawing of inferences (see the discussion below, paras 8.42–8.59).

Interviews outside the police station in an emergency

8.34   If D is arrested outside a police station for any offence he must not usually be interviewed about the offence until he arrives at the station (Code C 11.1). Conversations in the police car are to be avoided.

8.35 There are three exceptions which correspond to three of those justifying delay in the notification of arrest, s 56(5) (Art 54(5)), and in the access to legal advice, s 58(8) (Art 56(8)), where delay in questioning may
(a) lead to
    (i) interference with, or harm to, evidence connected with an offence;
    (ii) interference with, or physical harm to, other people, or
    (iii) serious loss of, or damage to property
(b) lead to alerting other people suspected of committing an offence but not yet arrested for it; or
(c) hinder the recovery of property obtained in consequence of the commission of an offence (Code C11.1).

8.36 (a) could include questioning for the sake of a hostage's safety or to try to prevent an accomplice from disposing of blood-stained clothes; an example of (b) would be to ascertain from D the rendezvous for a gang of burglars, who will only proceed to the hoard of property once each member has turned up at a pre-arranged spot; (c) would allow questioning to prevent accomplice robbers from making off with the proceeds (eg to ascertain the best place for a road check, or the likely ports of entry to alert). The exceptions are both narrow (the police cannot in theory ask a man, found 'with a smoking gun', the question 'what happened?') and flexible for, unlike ss 56 and 58, there is no requirement of authorisation by a senior officer. Operational requirements may mean that it is the arresting officer who decides whether one of the exceptions applies and whether he can continue to question D. As soon as he has enough information to avert, or at least to be in the position to try to avert, one of the aforementioned risks, then questioning must cease until the suspect reaches the station. Apart from risking an official complaint and disciplinary action, an officer who manipulates these exceptions and questions unnecessarily runs the real risk that any statement elicited from D will be excluded at trial. If D is interviewed (as explained in para 8.32, ante) outside a police station but not arrested, or at least interviewed prior to arrest, the interviewing officer must compile an interview record in his pocketbook or on the forms provided for this purpose or in accordance with Codes of Practice E or F. (Code C 11.5(b)). This must recount various formalities (eg the place, time, persons present; see Code C 11.5(b)) and then either a verbatim record of the conversation or an accurate summary. It must be timed and signed by the officer. All records should be compiled contemporaneously unless (a) the officer thinks this would be impracticable, or (b) it would interfere with the interview (Code C11.5(c)). Both are capable of wide interpretation (eg a record is impossible whilst D is dressing and showing the police around his home, or whilst the police fear D may escape, see *R v Parchment* (1989); or a record would spoil the flow of the interview; and note that there is no requirement in (b) of 'serious' or other extreme 'interference') but there are some limitations. First, in (a) the condition is impracticability not inconvenience, so whereas torrential rain would render it impracticable in the street, the proximate protection of a doorway or police car would render it practicable. If a record is not made during the course of the interview it must be made as soon as practicable thereafter. Second, the onus is on the officer to establish (a) or (b) (see *R v Delaney* (1989) where no attempt to prove it seems to have been made). Third, the reason for invoking (a) or (b) must be recorded in his pocketbook (Code C 11.9) and this reason can then be unhurriedly tested at trial. Fourth, unless impracticable, D should be asked to read and sign the record as correct or indicate in what respects it is inaccurate (Code C 11.11). The record of each interview should be offered to the suspect for him to sign or indicate where he disagrees, 'unless it is impracticable' (Code C 11.11). This last phrase can only apply in extreme situations such as the interviewee being taken ill before the record is shown to him. In normal circumstances a record can always be offered to D, however late in the day and whether he chooses to receive it or not is up to him. If D cannot read or refuses to read, the officer should read the record to him (C 11.11) and if an appropriate adult or solicitor or, it is suggested, an interpreter is present during the interview, he too should be asked to read and sign the record.

8.37   Importantly, interviewing in any of the above circumstances should cease once the relevant risk has been averted or the necessary questions have been put in an attempt to avert that risk.

Interviews inside the police station

8.38   As a preliminary to a discussion of the recording of interviews, it is worthwhile citing the views of the Lord Chief Justice in *R v Canale* (1990):

> 'The importance of the rules relating to contemporaneous noting of interviews can scarcely be over-emphasised. The object is twofold: not merely to ensure, so far as possible, that the suspect's remarks are accurately recorded and that he has an opportunity when he goes through the contemporaneous record afterwards of checking each answer and initialling each answer, but likewise it is a protection for the police, to ensure, so far as possible, that it cannot be suggested that they induced the suspect to confess by improper approaches or improper promises. If the contemporaneous note is not made, then each of those two laudable objects is apt to be stultified.'

8.39   If a person attends voluntarily at a police station to answer questions as a suspect, Code C is very relevant. As a suspect he will soon have to be cautioned and warned of his rights (Code C 3.5 and see para 8.7,ante); an 'interview' will be involved and need to be recorded. Also if a person is brought to a station under arrest, he will receive a caution and reading of his rights (see Code C 3.1 and para 7.14, ante). Moreover, each interview or re-commencement of an interview at a police station must be prefaced by the interviewing officer reminding the person of his right to free legal advice (Code C 11.2). Although the same reasons for not making a contemporaneous record apply (Code C 11.5(c), impracticability or interference with the course of the interview), the chief difference from interviews outside the station is that a verbatim record is always practicable in a station either in writing or more commonly on tape when the provisions of Code E also apply. As for the former, this will arise in interviews for summary offences (which do not have to be taped), and interviews for indictable offences which cannot be taped (because of mechanical failure, lack of machines, or wish of the suspect). The record must contain certain formalities (Code C 11.7), must be offered to D and his legal representative (and appropriate adult where relevant) for perusal and signature, and any refusal to sign must be recorded (C 11.11 and 11.12). If the suspect has made any significant statement or silence before his arrival at a police station, at the beginning of the interview the interviewer must, after caution, put it to the suspect and ask him whether he confirms or denies that previous statement or silence and whether he wishes to add anything. (As to what is a 'significant statement or silence' see para 8.54 post.)This will be recorded and form part of the interview record which will be shown to the suspect at the end of the interview. In addition a written record must be made of any comment made by a suspected person, including unsolicited comments, which are outside the context of the interview and he should be asked to acknowledge it by signature (para 11.13). The Code does not require such comments to be put to the suspect before any interview, unless 'significant', but it may be difficult at what is an early stage of the investigation to determine what is and what is not 'significant', therefore it may be prudent to put all comments to the suspect at any formal interview and obtain further confirmation of it. PACE and Code C does not provide for an 'off-the-record' interview, such a conversation after arrest and caution will amount to an 'interview' (*R v Woodall* (1989)) and each interview must be recorded contemporaneously, unless it is impracticable or it would interfere with the conduct of the interview (Code C 11.7). It is possible to argue that D's insistence can satisfy either exception. However, a summary of the interview must be made (para 11.7(c)) and made as soon as practicable after the interview ends (para 11.7) and then shown to D (para 11.11; this requirement again applies 'unless impracticable' but this is to no avail for, having made the summary, it can hardly be impracticable to show it to D. The fact that he does not like it is irrelevant.) Thus, it is suggested that the interviewing officer must in turn insist upon a contemporaneous note being made (the presence of a legal adviser may help and it would be quite proper for the interview to be suspended whilst advice is taken). If D is adamant, he has to be told that a record will be subsequently made. D should then be asked to read and sign it, or at least to read it. If he refuses, the document should still be served on the defence (see *R v Matthews* (1990)). It is unlikely to be of great evidential value if D refuses to give evidence at trial. If he does, then it can be used to show consistency or inconsistency (provided that the court admits the statement, ie that it is a reliable record of what he said). One must distinguish between an interview 'off the record' which is not permitted, and a spontaneous statement made at a private meeting requested by the suspect without any pressure or inducement from the police which, in the absence of questioning, is not an interview – see *R v Younis* (1990) and *R v Menard* (1995).

Silence and denials of the accused

8.40 In *R v Gilbert* (1977) the Court of Appeal held that the trial judge was wrong to invite a jury to draw adverse inferences against an accused who, despite being interviewed by the police and making a statement, failed to mention that he had acted in self-defence until trial. Lord Dilhorne said:

> '... A right of silence is one thing. No accused can be compelled to speak before, or for that matter, at his trial. But it is another thing to say that if he chooses to exercise his right of silence, that must not be the subject of any comment adverse to the accused.... . Our task is to apply the law as it now is; and in the light of the authorities to which we have referred, in our opinion the judge in asking the jury to consider whether it was remarkable that, when making his statement, the accused had said nothing about self-defence, fell into error and misdirected them.'

8.41   The Criminal Justice and Public Order Act 1994 changes the law along the lines of changes introduced in Northern Ireland by the Criminal Evidence (Northern Ireland) Order 1988. The first sentence in the above quotation remains true, but it is no longer the law that a jury cannot be invited to draw an inference from the failure to mention a fact when being interviewed by the police which he later relies upon at trial. Section 34 of the 1994 Act makes provision for the drawing of proper inferences in such circumstances. Also of relevance is s 36, which provides for the drawing of proper inferences from the failure to account for objects, substances or marks in certain circumstances; and s 37 which permits such inferences to be drawn from the failure of the accused to account for his presence at the scene of the offence. Perhaps the most controversial provision, s 35, which permits proper inferences to be drawn from the failure of the accused to give evidence, is properly the subject of textbooks on the law of evidence and will not be dealt with here.

The failure to mention facts when questioned or charged (Art 3 of the Criminal Evidence (Northern Ireland) Order 1987)

8.42   The 1987 Order is not identical to ss 34-38 of the 1994 Act but is in the same terms and has the same basic purpose.

8.43   Section 34 begins:

> '(1) Where in any proceedings against a person for an offence, evidence is given that the accused -
> (a)   at any time before he was charged with an offence, on being questioned under caution by a constable trying to discover whether or by whom the offence had been committed, failed to mention any fact relied on in his defence in those proceedings; or
> (b)   on being charged with the offence or officially informed that he might be prosecuted for it, failed to mention any such fact,
> being a fact which in the circumstances existing at the time the accused could reasonably have been expected to mention when so questioned, charged or informed, as the case may be, subsection (2) below applies.'

8.44 Subsection (2) provides that where the subsection applies -

'(a) a magistrates' court in deciding whether to dismiss a charge in the course of proceedings with a view to transfer for trial to the Crown Court;

(b) a judge in deciding under s 6 of the Criminal Justice Act 1987 whether to dismiss a charge of serious fraud, or under para 5 of Schedule 6 to the Criminal Justice Act 1991 to dismiss a charge of violence or a sexual offence involving a child;

(c) the court in determining whether there is a case to answer; and

(d) the court or jury, in determining whether the accused is guilty of the offence charged,

may draw such inferences from the failure as appear proper.

(2A) Where an accused was at an authorised place of detention at the time of the failure, subsections (1) and (2) above do not apply if he had not been allowed an opportunity to consult a solicitor prior to being questioned, charged or informed as mentioned in subsection (1) above.'

8.45 Subsection (2A) was inserted by s 58 of the Youth Justice and Criminal Evidence Act 1999. The effect of the amendment, necessitated by the judgment of the European Court of Human Rights in the case of *Murray v United Kingdom* (1996), is to prohibit the drawing of an inference where the suspect has not been allowed an opportunity to consult a solicitor. The equivalent provisions in the Criminal Evidence (Northern Ireland) Order 1988 were the subject of the decision of the court and were amended by the Criminal Evidence (Northern Ireland) Order 1999, Art 36. An 'authorised place of detention' is either a police station or another place prescribed for the purpose by the Secretary of State. The prohibition on inferences operates whether or not the accused was lawfully denied an opportunity to consult with a solicitor, for example under s 58 of PACE. If, however, the suspect denies the opportunity when it is offered he cannot rely on the protection of sub-s (2A), nor do they apply after a consultation has taken place even if the solicitor is not present during interview.

8.46 This provision explains the need for the new caution and the introduction in that caution of the phrase, 'But it may harm your defence if you do not mention when questioned something which you later rely on in court'. Section 34 and Art 3 are clearly aimed at the ambush defence of the kind used in *R v Gilbert* (above). Research for the Royal Commission on Criminal Justice (1993) (RCCJ Research Study No 10, Chapter 5) suggested that the 'ambush defence' is comparatively rare and occurred in only 5 per cent of trials studied. Despite rejection by the RCCCJ and the earlier Royal Commission on Criminal Procedure (Cmd, 8092, 1981) and widespread opposition from within the legal profession the provisions were implemented as part of a package of measures. Dennis (2002), in a partial review of the jurisprudence, argues 'that a combination of the Strasbourg jurisprudence on Article 6 of the European Convention on Human Rights and increasingly restrictive interpretation by the English courts has resulted in marginalisation of s 34' and 'when inferences from silence in the police station are

518 The questioning of suspects

possible at all, they provide no more than support from an existing (clear) prima facie case.'

8.47 A suspect retains the right to remain silent during questioning and the right to silence is a discrete and closely related right to the privilege against self-incrimination. This means that the courts have stated that these provision should not be 'construed more widely than the statutory language requires' (per Lord Bingham at p 181 in *R v Bowden* (1999)). In *Averill v United Kingdom* (2001) this proposition was supported by the ECHR.

8.48 Before more detailed consideration of s 34 is undertaken it will be useful to outline the respective agendas of the interviewer and the legal advisor.

Conditions for operation of s 34

8.49 Lord Bingham laid down the following conditions that had to be met before s 34 could operate:
(1) there had to be proceedings against a person for an offence;
    The provision only applies in criminal proceedings.
(2) the failure to answer had to occur before a defendant was charged;
    The wording is such that inferences may not be drawn after charge; in order to draw inferences the prosecution must prove that the defendant knew of the relevant facts at the time of interview (*R v B (MT)* (2000). In *R v Nickolson* (1998) it was held that no inference could be drawn by an accused's failure to give an explanation as to how the victim's nightdress had come to have a semen stain on it, where the police had not known and, therefore, not questioned him about it.
(3) the failure had to occur during questioning under caution by a constable or other person within s 34(4);
    The failure to mention relevant facts must occur 'on being questioned under caution' or 'on being charged'. It is clear that if there has been no caution there can be inference but if the defence respond to questioning by submitting a prepared statement which does not take account of a particular fact then inferences may be drawn (*R v Dervish* (2002)).
(4) the questioning had to be directed to trying to discover whether or by whom the offence has been committed;
    In *R v Pointer* (1997) the police had conducted an undercover operation where it was alleged that officers had tried to purchase drugs from the appellant. Since the interviewing officer considered there was sufficient evidence for a successful prosecution before the interview he could not have been trying to discover whether or by whom an offence had been committed and therefore the conditions of s 34 were not satisfied. This should be contrasted with *R v Elliott* (2002) where the court held that, even though the officer believed there was sufficient evidence to charge, it would not be inappropriate to interview in order to give the suspect an opportunity for an innocent explanation to be given.

(5) the failure had to be to mention any fact relied on in the person's defence in those proceedings;

The Court of Appeal held that this requirement involves two questions. Firstly, is there some fact which the defendant has relied on in his defence; and, secondly, did the defendant fail to mention it when he was being questioned. If a defendant gives or calls evidence about a fact then he relies on it in his defence but it is also possible for the provision to bite even if evidence is not called. To hypothesise about facts put in evidence has been held not to be relying on a fact (*R v Niclolson* (1998)) and merely putting the prosecution to proof is unlikely to be treated as relying on a fact; but cross-examination of prosecution witnesses which involves asserting the existence of facts may be. A positive suggestion put by counsel as opposed to questions intending to probe will be reliance on a fact (*R v Webber* (2004)).

(6) the fact that the defendant failed to mention had to be one which in the circumstances existing at the time of the interview, he could reasonably have been expected to mention when so questioned.

The 'time' must be the time at which he failed to mention the fact and the 'circumstances' are those existing at that time. The court must have regard to the 'actual accused with such qualities, apprehension, knowledge and advice as he is shown to have had at the time' (*R v Argent* (1997)). This will cover such factors as the level of intelligence of the suspect, the complexity of the evidence, the manner of police interviewing and disclosure.

8.50 The purpose of the s 34 provisions is to obtain an early disclosure of a suspect's account; there may be a host of reasons why a suspect will not be forthcoming. For example, he may be frightened, tired, ill, suspicious of the police, unable to understand what is going on and so on. Additionally he may have received legal advice not to give his account (see para 8.69 post).

8.51 One must distinguish between the failure to mention a fact and later relying on it at trial and simply remaining silent without such reliance. Silence of itself adds nothing to the prosecution case. Section 38(3) of the 1994 Act (Art 2(4)) makes it clear that a person cannot be convicted, nor a case to answer made out or a case transferred to the Crown Court, solely on an inference drawn under s 34 (Art 3) or any of the other provisions of the Act. There must therefore be evidence which persuades the court or jury beyond reasonable doubt that the accused is guilty as charged. Inferences drawn under s 34 (Art 3) then have a negative effect in that they undermine the defence based on the unmentioned facts. If the prosecution do not adduce evidence sufficient to prove their case beyond reasonable doubt, inferences drawn under s 34 cannot bridge the gap. A similar point was made by Lord Lowry in *C (a minor) v DPP* (1995) in restoring the common law presumption that a child between the ages of 10 and 14 is doli incapax. He pointed out that in order to obtain evidence outside the commission of the offence upon which one could find that the presumption had been rebutted, the prosecution had to rely upon interviewing the suspect, having him psychiatrically examined or calling evidence from someone who knew the child well. After explaining the effect of s 34 he went on to say that he could not see how this provision could avail the prosecution on the issue of guilty knowledge. Positive evidence is required.

8.52   One must further distinguish between failing to answer or giving an equivocal answer, and telling a lie. A lie can be corroboration of the prosecution evidence if:

(a)   it is deliberate;

(b)   it relates to a material issue;

(c)   the motive for the lie is a realisation of guilt and a fear of the truth (but the jury must be reminded that there are other innocent reasons for telling lies); and

(d)   the statement must be shown to be a lie by evidence other than that of the witness to be corroborated (*R v Lucas* (1981)).

8.53   There may well be an overlap between the use of lies as evidence and reliance on s 34. If D lies about his presence at the scene of the crime, saying he was elsewhere, and later at trial seeks to give an innocent explanation for being at the scene, he has failed to mention a relevant fact later relied on and s 34 (Art 3) may operate. However, if the prosecution prove that he lied and was at the scene and D then admits the truth and seeks to explain his presence, it may be questioned whether he has relied on that fact in his defence. In any event the evidential effect is much the same. If, following a Lucas direction, the jury conclude that he lied to hide his guilt, there is then positive support for the prosecution case; if s 34 (Art 3) is relied upon there is negative support in the sense that D's statements may be disbelieved.

Significant statements

8.54   At the beginning of any interview carried out at a police station, the interviewing officer, after cautioning the suspect, must put to him any significant statement or silence which occurred before his arrival at a police station, and must ask him whether he confirms or denies that earlier statement or silence and whether he wishes to add anything (Code C 11.4). 'A significant statement or silence' is defined as:

> '… one which appears capable of being used as evidence against the suspect, in particular a direct admission of guilt, or a failure or refusal to answer a question or to answer it satisfactorily, which might give rise to an inference under [s 34] of the CJPOA 1994'.

8.55   This procedure is designed to prevent any allegation of verballing, whether positive, by ascribing to the suspect a statement he did not make, or negative, by ascribing to him a failure to answer. There can be few more significant statements than an admission of guilt and the basis for the admissibility of such statements is to be found in s 82(1) of PACE (Art 70(1)) which defines 'confession' to include 'any statement wholly or partly adverse to the person who made it … whether made in words or otherwise'. Thus, if D is asked whether he used the knife shown to him to stab V and he nods in response, the nod can be interpreted as an affirmative reply and is a confession within the section, not a failure to answer. Statements often come in a mixed form, partly inculpatory and partly exculpatory. While strictly speaking the exculpatory parts are not admissible in evidence, the House of Lords has ruled that out of fairness to the accused the whole statement should be put before the jury, though the judge should point out that the incriminating parts are likely to be true, whereas excuses do not carry the same weight (*R v Sharp* (1988)). It follows that the entire statement should be put to the suspect. While out-of-court statements of a self-serving nature designed to set up a defence, such as a statement by the accused charged with murder two days after the offence that his defence would be that it was an accident (*R v Roberts* (1942)), are not admissible, such statements made by an accused in response to police questioning cause much difficulty. If, for example, an accused told a police officer at the scene of a killing that it was an accident, that statement, though hearsay, may be admissible as an exception to that rule as part of the res gestae. Alternatively it is evidence which should be admitted at his trial, not as evidence of the facts stated, but as part of the general picture. If D gives evidence to that effect then his statement to the police is evidence of consistency. Exculpatory statements, if they can be proved to be a lie, may also be evidence which supports the prosecution case. Thus if D on being asked where he was on the night of a burglary says, 'I was at my girlfriend's all night', that is an alibi and not a significant statement as defined by Code C. But if this proves to be a lie, the fact that he said it and that it was a lie can, subject to *R v Lucas* (1981) (see point (5) above), be given in evidence against the accused. While therefore such a statement need not be put at the beginning of an interview as required by Code C 11.2A, it should be put to him at some stage in the interview.

8.56 Identifying significant silences can be even more difficult. One must bear in mind that statements include gestures of assent or dissent. Thus a vigorous shake of the head in response to the accusation, 'Did you attack V?' is a statement of denial (see below point (9)), not a failure to answer, and it is only a failure to answer, or to answer satisfactorily, which can lead to inferences being drawn under s 34 (Art 3). On the other hand, if D on being asked 'Why did you attack V?' shrugs and says 'I don't know', that may be an unsatisfactory answer which could result in an inference being drawn under s 34 (Art 3) if D puts forward a defence of self-defence at trial. Note also that significant silences are only relevant if D has been cautioned, whereas a statement may be significant if made before caution.

8.57 Section 34(5) states that the section does not:

'(a) prejudice the admissibility in evidence of the silence or other reaction of the accused in the face of anything said in his presence relating to the conduct with which he is charged, in so far as evidence would be admissible apart from this section; or

(b) preclude the drawing of any inference from any silence or other reaction of the accused which could properly be drawn apart from this section'.

8.58 At common law a statement made in the presence of an accused, even one which reasonably calls for some explanation of denial from him, is not evidence against him or of the facts stated save so far as he accepts the statement, by words or otherwise, so as to make it, in effect, his own. If he accepts the statement in part only, then to that extent alone does it become his statement (*R v Christie* (1914)). The failure of an accused to reject an accusation made when the parties are on equal terms can, in the right circumstances, be some evidence that he admits the truth of the accusation but the person is under no obligation to comment when informed by a police officer that someone else has accused him of a crime (*Parkes v R* (1976); *R v Chandler* (1976); *Hall v R* (1971)). Once a person has been cautioned that he need not say anything his failure to respond cannot be seen as an acceptance of what was said so that it becomes evidence against him. Subsection (5) preserves the common law in this respect, but there is now some obligation to comment imposed by s 34 (Art 3).

8.59   Section 34 (Art 3), unlike ss 36 and 37 (Arts 5 and 6), applies in relation to questioning by persons charged with the duty of investigating offences or charging offenders as it applies to questioning by constables, and in sub-s (1) 'officially informed' means informed by a constable or any such person (s 34(4)). The phrase 'charged with the duty of investigating offences or charging offenders' repeats the use of that phrase in s 67(9) of PACE which applies Codes of Practice to such persons. The section applies to constables attested as such whether a member of a police force maintained for a police area or statutory police forces such as British Transport police and Ministry of Defence police whose officers are constables and need not rely on sub-s (5). Others persons who are not constables to whom the section will apply include Customs and Excise officers, investigators employed by the Federation against Copyright Theft (FACT) and commercial investigators employed by companies to investigate offences committed by employees, but not DTI Inspectors and Immigration Officers (see para 2.37, ante). Arguably it will not apply to those who voluntarily agree to abide by the Codes of Practice, for example the RSPCA – see *RSPCA v Eager* (1995). The agreement to abide by the Codes has meant that the courts do not have to decide whether they are bound by them but unless and until it can be shown that they are charged with the duty of investigating offences or charging offenders s 34 will not apply to them.

Section 39 authorises the Secretary of State to apply the provisions to the armed services.

The accused's failure to account for objects, substances or marks (s 36 of the CJPOA 1994, Art 5 of the 1987 Order)

8.60   Section 36 (Art 5) provides as follows:

'(1) Where
(a)   a person is arrested by a constable, and there is -
    (i)   on his person; or
    (ii)   in or on his clothing or footwear; or

    (iii) otherwise in his possession; or

    (iv) in any place in which he is at the time of his arrest,

    any object, substance or mark, or there is a mark on any such object; and

(b) that or another constable investigating the case reasonably believes that the presence of the object, substance or mark may be attributable to the participation of the person arrested in the commission of an offence specified by the constable; and

(c) the constable informs the person arrested that he so believes, and requests him to account for the presence of the object, substance or mark; and

(d) the person fails or refuses to do so,

then if, in any proceedings against the person for an offence so specified, evidence of those matters is given, subsection (2) below applies.'

8.61 Subsection (2) permits the drawing of such inferences as appear proper by magistrates, judges, court and jury in the same circumstances as in s 34(2).

8.62 The section is extremely wide and is made even wider by sub-s (3) which provides that sub-ss (1) and (2) shall apply to the condition of clothing or footwear as it applies to a substance or mark on the shoes or clothing. The fact that shoes are scuffed may be seen as a mark under sub-s (1) or condition under sub-s (3) but the fact that clothing is torn is more the condition of the clothing. 'Object' can include anything used in the commission of an offence or something which is the proceeds of an offence, eg a knife or stolen goods. 'Substance' can include blood, semen, an accelerant such as petrol in a case of arson or simply mud found on a suspect's shoes. 'Mark' will include a finger- or palm print found on an object or scratches on the face but note that the section does not apply where finger- or palm prints are found at the scene of the crime. What inferences can properly be drawn will depend upon the exact circumstances but one may note that under this section it is the failure to account for evidence which the prosecution will have presented to the court. Thus if V was murdered and the prosecution prove that D's clothing was splattered with blood which forensic evidence proves conclusively was that of the victim then, at the very least, D is proved to have been at the scene of the murder. If there is other evidence that he struck the fatal blow, the jury may well be satisfied of his guilt. The failure to account for the presence of the blood on his clothing leaves the prosecution evidence unchallenged and the only proper inference is that the prosecution contention that he killed V must be accepted. Whether this is an innovation may be doubted. Subsection (6) permits the drawing of other inferences which could have been drawn apart from this section and in the above circumstances a jury would have reached the same conclusion without the aid of s 36 (Art 5). On a charge of murder the fact that V's blood was found on D's clothing is circumstantial evidence pointing to his guilt. By itself it is not enough to convince a jury beyond reasonable doubt. His failure to account for the presence of the blood adds weight to that evidence but will still not be enough to convince a jury of his guilt. Other positive evidence of his involvement will be required. Section 36 (Art 5) adds little if anything to the common law and in the majority of cases will add little to the prosecution case.

8.63 There is a possibility of overlap between s 36 and s 34 where, for example, D is asked to explain the presence of blood on his clothing and makes no comment but provides an innocent explanation at trial. A double inference may then be drawn.

8.64 As with s 34 (Art 3) there are a number of built-in limitations.

(1) The section applies only where a person is arrested by a constable. Subsection (1)(a)(i) clearly applies only to the time of arrest, as does sub-s (1)(a)(iv) which specifically says so. Arguably sub-s (1)(a)(ii) and (iii) can apply to objects etc found some time after arrest. Thus blood-stained clothing worn by the suspect on arrest or found after a search of his home under s 32(2)(b) of PACE (Art 34(2)(b)) following his arrest there, are within s 1(a)(i) and (iv). However, such clothing which has been discarded by the suspect and which is found some time after his arrest, or which is found before his arrest, may be of great evidential significance if it is linked to him but will only trigger the section if either:

   (a) the clothing is proved to be the accused's and sub-s (1)(a)(ii) is interpreted broadly (D is arrested, it is his clothing and there is no requirement that he actually be wearing them at the time of the arrest); or

   (b) the clothing is found in circumstances in which it is in his 'possession' which could include his home, the boot of his car, or at his girlfriend's home but not a rubbish skip.

   The phrase 'any place where he is at the time of arrest' in sub-s (1)(a)(iv) would appear to exclude the finding of clothing following an arrest in the street and a search of his premises under s 18 of PACE (Art 20) but in those circumstances sub-s (1)(1)(a)(iii) 'otherwise in his possession' may be relied upon.

(2) The constable must 'reasonably believe that the presence of the object etc may be attributable to the participation of the person arrested in the commission of an offence …'. This high standard is discussed at para 2.03 but the phrase 'may be attributable' waters it down somewhat.

(3) Section 36 (Art 5) applies to 'an offence specified by the constable' (s 1(1)(b)) and sub-s (2) applies only in proceedings 'for the offence so specified' which may not necessarily be the offence for which D was arrested. Thus if D is stopped and searched under s 1 of PACE and a blood-stained knife is found in his possession which the constable reasonably believes was used in a serious wounding, the section may operate to permit a proper inference to be drawn if he is charged with wounding but not if he is charged with possession of an offensive weapon. There are alternative verdicts available on a charge of wounding but the fact that D is charged with an offence under s 18 of the OAP Act 1861 and s 20 of that Act in the alternative does not prevent the operation of s 36 (Art 5).

(4) The suspect will have been cautioned after arrest and will, unless Code C 11.1 applies, be interviewed in a police station. He will have been cautioned a number of times but sub-s (4) provides that sub-ss (1) and (2) will not apply unless the accused was told in ordinary language by the constable (that is the constable who has the reasonable belief required in sub-s (1)(b) above) when he requests the suspect to account for the presence of the object, substance or mark under sub-s (1)(c) what the effect of this section would be if he failed or refused to

comply with the request. The form of caution is set out at Code C 10.5B which requires that the suspect be told by the interviewing officer, in ordinary language:

(a) what offence he is investigating;

(b) what fact he is asking the suspect to account for;

(c) that he believes this fact may be due to the suspect's taking part in the commission of the offence in question;

(d) that the court may draw a proper inference if he fails or refuses to account for the fact about which he is being questioned; and

(e) that a record is being made of the interview and that it may be given in evidence if he is brought to trial.

'Ordinary language' suggests that legal technicalities should be avoided in describing the offence, which may be one of a number of possible offences. Therefore a description of the facts such as 'at (time and date) jewellery was stolen from Park Jewellers Ltd in the High Street by a man using a knife' may be preferable to legally defining the offence. By analogy to the formal caution the phrase 'proper inferences may be drawn' may be replaced by 'you may harm your case if you fail or refuse to account ...'.

Some forces have adopted a policy of giving this five-step caution after the question has been asked and the response given. Two reasons are given: first, it would be oppressive to give the warning first; and second, giving it could prevent unsolicited comments. It is submitted that this policy is misguided. It can hardly be oppressive to do that which is required by law for the protection of the suspect, and ss 36(4) and 37(3) make it clear that the warning must be given 'when making the request' for an explanation. A refusal or failure to answer a request for an explanation without the statutory warning cannot be the subject of any inference.

Where, despite the fact that a person has been cautioned, failure to co-operate may have an effect on his immediate treatment, such as being detained if he refuses his name and address, or his refusal to provide particulars and information in accordance with a statutory re-quirement, for example, under the Road Traffic Act 1988, may amount to an offence or make him liable to arrest, he should be informed of any relevant consequences and that they are not affected by the caution.

(5) Section 36 (Art 5), unlike s 34 (Art 3), applies only to constables and designated investigators and not to other bodies who are charged with the duty of investigating or charging offences and to whom the Codes of Practice apply, with the exception of officers of Customs and Excise to whom the section is applied by sub-s (5).

(6) Section 38(3) (Art 2(4)) applies to prevent transfer for trial to the Crown Court, a case to answer, or conviction of an offence solely on an inference drawn under s 36 (Art 5).

The accused's failure to account for his presence at the scene of an offence (s 37 of the CJPOA 1994, Art 6 of the 1987 Order)

8.65 Section 37(1) (Art 6)

'Where -
(a) a person arrested by a constable was found by him at a place at or about the time the offence for which he was arrested is alleged to have been committed; and
(b) that or another constable investigating the offence reasonably believes that the presence of the person at that place and at that time may be attributable to his participation in the commission of the offence; and
(c) the constable informs the person that he so believes, and requests him to account for his presence; and
(d) the person fails or refuses to do so
then, in any proceedings against the person for the offence, evidence of these matters is given, subsection (2) below applies.'

The section is similar to s 36 (Art 5). Subsection (2) permits proper inferences to be drawn in exactly the same circumstances as in s 36 and this section does not apply unless the accused is told what the effect of the section will be in ordinary language (sub-s (3)). The special warning set out in Code C 10.5B applies to this section as it does to s 36 (Art 5). Like that section this section applies only to constables and Customs and Excise officers (sub-s (4)) and it does not preclude the drawing of other inferences which could be properly drawn apart from this section. Section 38(3) also applies to this section.

8.66 The wording of s 37 (Art 6) makes it clear that unlike s 36 (Art 5), this section only applies to the offence for which D was arrested. It is also clear from sub-s (1)(a) that the section only applies where the constable who finds the person at the scene of the offence also arrests him. This could cause problems when a number of officers are searching the scene of an offence and constable A finds D who makes off before he can be arrested. If he is arrested by another officer after a short chase the section does not apply unless 'found' is broadly interpreted to apply so that constable B can be said to have found D at the place of the offence. That may well be possible if D is still at or near the scene when arrested but not if he makes his escape and is arrested a mile away by another constable who was not at the scene. If in the above circumstances the officer who finds D at the scene arrests him some days after he got away, the section applies, there being no limit on the time between being found and arrested. There may of course be other difficulties such as identification of D. The section is also confined to the situation in which D is found by a constable. Thus if D is found on premises by a security guard, escapes and is later arrested, the section does not apply. If D is detained by the guard who calls the police, the section may apply if D can be said to be found by the police who respond to the call. As sub-s (1)(b) makes clear, the arresting officer need not be the investigating officer, eg a uniformed constable arrests D and turns him over to a CID officer, but the investigating officer must reasonably believe that D's presence at the place and time may be attributable to D's participation in the commission of the offence, and that officer must inform D, and give the special warning under Code C 10.5B, and request him to account for his presence. (As with s 36 (Art 5) the requirement that the constable 'reasonably believes', discussed at para 2.03 is watered down by the words 'may be attributable'.)

8.67 Like s 36 (Art 5) this section may add little to the existing position. If D is found in the early hours of the morning in an alley at the rear of burgled premises some short time after the burglary, his presence there cries out for explanation. If there is other evidence linking him to the burglary, his failure to explain his presence strengthens the prosecution case against him. Assuming that the prosecution present a case capable of persuading the jury beyond reasonable doubt that D was the burglar, D's failure to explain his presence at the scene leaves the prosecution case unanswered. Section 37 (Art 6) has the effect of highlighting this. It cannot, as s 38(3) (Art 2(4)) makes clear, lead to D's conviction solely because he failed to explain his presence. There must be other evidence and the inference drawn by the jury serves to strengthen and confirm that evidence. In this respect it is a mistake to speak of an inference of guilt from the silence of the accused, whether under this or any of the other provisions of the 1994 Act: it is the evidence which proves guilt, the silence serves to add weight and support to that evidence.

8.68 There is also a possibility of overlap between this section and ss 34, 36 and 37. Thus if D is found near the scene of a burglary in possession of property stolen from the premises and refuses to explain his presence or his possession of the property, and at his trial he puts forward an innocent explanation for both, all three sections may apply.

Legal advice

8.69 Legal advice to remain silent is now capable by itself of preventing an adverse inference. This issue has been considered both by the domestic courts and the ECHR in case of the Condrons. The Court of Appeal (*R v Condron and Condron* (1997)) stated that legal advice to remain silent cannot by itself prevent an adverse inference being drawn under s 34, otherwise the purpose of the provision would be defeated. Legal advice is a relevant consideration to be taken into account by a court in deciding whether the defendant could reasonably have been expected to mention the fact relied on at that time. Whether the advice is correct is not a matter for the court who are simply concerned with whether the defendants conduct is reasonable in all the circumstances. If the defendant wished not avoid an inference being drawn, he or his solicitor may have to state the reason for the advice. In *R v Roble* (1997) the Court of Appeal stated that good reasons for such advice might be that the interviewing officer had disclosed little or nothing of the nature of the case so that the solicitor cannot usefully advise his client or due to the complexity of the material or the period of time since the alleged offence. When the ECHR considered the Condron case (*Condron v United Kingdom*) it stated that the fact that an accused had been advised by his lawyer to remain silent must be given 'appropriate weight' by the domestic court as there may be good reason for such advice. In *R v Betts and Hall* (2001) the Court of

Appeal stated the effect of *Condron v United Kingdom* was that it is not the quality of the legal advice but the genuineness of it. If he has no answer or no satisfactory answer the defendant cannot hide behind the legal advice. Some investigators operate on a 'phased' or 'managed' disclosure of information to the suspect and his legal advisor and in these circumstances it may be appropriate for the suspect to remain silent until full disclosure has been provided. The provision of a prepared statement on behalf or the suspect may not be sufficient to prevent inferences being drawn. (*R v Howell* (2003) and see Cape and Luqmani (2003)). Investigators are well advised to remember that the role of the solicitor is not simply to give information to clients, nor to point out alternatives but to 'protect and advance the legal rights of his client' (Code C Note 6D) – the solicitor has professional obligations to advise a client in their best interests.

Manner of questioning

8.70   PACE (Order) and Codes of Practice offer some guidance on the physical conditions in which interviews should take place (see below), but, apart from counselling against using oppressive tactics to obtain confessions (Code C 11.3) leaves the method of questioning to the interviewing officer. The advent of tape-recording exposed deficiencies in the techniques of questioning and persuaded the police to devote more training to the subject. HO Circular 7/1993 introduced a national training package on investigative interviewing which all forces have taken up (see A Guide to Interviewing and the Interviewer's Rule Book, Central Planning and Training Unit 1992). The PEACE approach to interviewing may, in time, put an end to the totally unprofessional method of interviewing disclosed by the case of *R v Paris, Abdullahi and Miller* (1992) (dubbed the 'Cardiff Three'). The seven principles of investigative interviewing set out in that circular bear repeating.

(a)   The role of investigative interviewing is to obtain accurate and reliable information from suspects, witnesses or victims in order to discover the truth about matters under police investigation.

(b)   Investigative interviewing should be approached with an open mind. Information obtained from the person who is being interviewed should always be tested against what the interviewing officer already knows or what can reasonably be established.

(c)   When questioning anyone a police officer must act fairly in the circumstances of each individual case.

(d)   The police interviewer is not bound to accept the first answer given. Questioning is not unfair merely because it is persistent.

(e)   Even when the right of silence is exercised by a suspect the police still have the right to put questions.

(f)   When conducting an interview, police officers are free to ask questions in order to establish the truth; except for interviews with child victims of sexual or violent abuse which are to be used in criminal proceedings, they are not constrained by the rules [of evidence and procedure] applied to lawyers.

(g) Vulnerable people, whether victims, witnesses, or suspects, must be treated with particular consideration at all times.

8.71 The original Code C (12A) contained a statement that:

'The purpose of any interview is to obtain from the person concerned his explanation of the facts, and not necessarily to obtain an admission.'

8.72 In *R v Oliphant* (1992) it was argued by the defence that the officers in that case were wrong in setting out to obtain admissions by exhorting D to tell the truth. The trial judge appeared to agree but Woolf LJ observed that this unrealistic view requires modification. Provided that officers have an open mind and are prepared to listen to an explanation, which may not amount to an admission, and provided they comply with PACE and Codes, there is nothing wrong with setting out to get a suspect to admit involvement in an offence. The importance of testing answers against what is known or can reasonably be established cannot be overstated, particularly if the suspect is vulnerable. Principle (d) is supported by the comment of Lord Taylor CJ in *R v Paris, Abdullahi and Miller* (1992) and *R v L* (1994) though in the former case the repeated questioning went much too far.

8.73 The evidential requirements for the admissibility of a confession at the trial stage play a major part in dictating the style of interrogation. Thus, the questioning of detained persons must not be 'oppressive' or such as otherwise to lead to unreliable evidence (s 76) or to an unfair trial (s 78). These principles (see further paras 8.43-8.54, post) apply to persons under arrest and therefore in detention, but are not confined to the police station. So, for example, questioning in the police car or at the scene of a crime must not be oppressive. This concept is considered in more detail later but has been held to include 'hectoring and bullying' the suspect (*R v Paris, Abdullahi and Miller* (1992)). As to the 'reliability' principle, this essentially excludes a confession made 'in consequence of anything said or done' which was likely to render it unreliable (s 76(2)(b)). As for s 78, the courts have shown a readiness to use it in the context of confessions. It is clear that the ways in which a detained person has been questioned and treated during the questioning will be crucial evidence as to whether the interviewing officer has breached PACE or Code. The rules governing the giving of cautions and what is an interview, if breached, can also lead to exclusion under s 78; as can the provisions regarding access to a solicitor or the presence of an appropriate adult during the questioning of juveniles and the mentally disordered or handicapped. The protective nature of these provisions should be noted. They are designed to ensure that confessions are reliable evidence and to exclude the possibility that statements, or a failure to answer, which are attributed to the accused were actually said, or not said; hence they are dubbed the 'anti-verballing provisions', and the recording requirements considered above underpin these provisions. Custody officers play an important role in ensuring that the various procedural guidelines (eg as to the provision of refreshments) and the various statutory duties placed on them as regards documentation are complied with. Additionally in many police stations the custody area will be continuously monitored by video cameras to ensure fair treatment and to avoid false allegations of mistreatment.

8.74   Since the custody officer watches over all detained persons, his permission must be obtained before a person is handed over to another police officer for questioning or to accompany him, for example, to the suspect's premises which are to be searched (Code C 12.1). Most requests for access to the person in custody will be in order to question him. The custody officer should ask the officer for a report on the state of the investigation and the reason for the questioning. He should be particularly alert lest a person be questioned when there is already sufficient evidence to charge him. If a suspect has been arrested by another police force or outside the country, complex provisions (s 41; see para 6.108, ante) operate to give the police a reasonable time to transport him to the interested police force before the 'detention clock' begins. If he is questioned about the offence by the arresting force, the 'detention clock' begins on his arrival at the police station in that force area, thus reducing the time available for investigation in the other area. Accordingly, Code C 14.1 states that no questions may be put to him about the offence while he is in transit between the two police forces, except in order to clarify a voluntary statement he has made. However, questions directed towards clarification of a voluntary statement amount to an interview and the better advice would be to refrain from any questioning until the arrested person has arrived at the police station where it can be done in a formal interview in the presence of a solicitor, if required, and on tape.

Physical conditions of the interview

8.75   Before a detainee is interviewed the custody officer is required, in consultation with the officer in the case and appropriate health care professionals, to assess whether or not the person is fit enough to be interviewed. (Code C 12.3. and Annex G). In so doing the officer must have regard to the risks to the persons physical and mental state if the interview took place and determine what safeguards are needed to allow the interview to take place. The custody officer *must not* allow an interview to take place if he considers it would cause significant harm to the detainee's physical or mental state. This does require the careful exercise of judgment and the custody officer must be guided by the appropriate health professional. Vulnerable persons will always be at risk and may not be interviewed except in accordance with the requirements of Code C paras 11.15 to 11.20.

8.76   Whenever possible the interview must take place in interview rooms which are properly heated, lighted and ventilated (Code C 12.4). The person must not be forced to stand. There is no limitation on the number of officers who may attend, but:
(1)   the officer in charge must ensure that each interviewer identifies themselves to the person;
(2)   he should be aware of the possibility that too many may be seen as oppressive.

8.77   In any 24-hour period, the person must be allowed at least eight hours' continuous rest, preferably at night and free from travelling, questioning, or any other interruption by police officers in connection with the investigation concerned. The rest period should not be interrupted or delayed, except at the request of the person, his appropriate adult or his legal representative. Delays following such a request and any action required to be taken under s 8 of Code C (conditions of detention), or in accordance with medical advice, do not constitute an interruption requiring a fresh rest period. However, the rest period can be interrupted or delayed by the police if there are reasonable grounds to believe that allowing the normal rest period would:

(i)   involve a risk of harm to persons or serious loss of, or damage to, property;
(ii) delay unnecessarily the person's release from custody; or
(iii) otherwise prejudice the outcome of the investigation (Code C 12.2).

8.78   Code C is silent as to who should hold these beliefs but it is suggested that it is consistent with his overall responsibilities for detained persons for the custody officer to reach this decision and for him to record the reasons in the custody record. In calculating the time of the rest period, the 'relevant time', usually the time of arrival at the police station (see paras 6.108, ante), is the starting time, unless the person is a 'volunteer' when the period of 24 hours runs from the time of his arrest rather than the time of arrival at the police station (Code C 12.2). Breaks in interviewing should occur at 'recognised meal times'. Shorter breaks will take place about every two hours unless the interviewing officer has reasonable grounds to believe that one or more of the grounds set out in Code C 12.7, which are identical to those set out above justifying delay in rest periods, apply. These grounds are sufficiently broad to entitle ready delays of short breaks. For example, a person in detention has eaten breakfast by 7.30am. Lunch is due at 12.30pm. Breaks from interviewing for coffee or tea at 9.30am and/or 11.30am can be postponed if the officer believes that the suspect is about to confess and thereby clear up the investigation. The sanctions against improper denial of breaks are:

(1)   the duty to record the grounds for the denial (Code 12.11), and
(2)   the possibility that wrongful denial may be used to attack the admissibility of any confession obtained.

Duties of the interviewing officer

8.79   The interviewing officer is responsible for the detained person's or volunteer's welfare during the interview. He is the officer who approaches a superintendent or higher rank for authorisation to refuse the suspect access to legal advice or to press ahead with questioning even though the person is, for example, drunk or mentally ill. Above all, he must return the person to the custody officer and account for his treatment of the person to him. If in the course of an interview a complaint is made concerning the provisions of the Code, it must be recorded and reported to the custody officer (Code C 12.9). He in turn reports it to an inspector or higher rank who is unconnected with the investigation (Code C 9.2). If there is the slightest suggestion that the suspect has suffered physical injury, the police surgeon must be summoned at once. Good practice suggests that a medical examination will be advisable in any event. The interviewing officer must also ensure that the interview is properly recorded, either on tape or by a contemporaneous written record. (The latter may be compiled by him or another officer.)

Urgent interviews

8.80   The questioning of the intoxicated, juveniles, the mentally ill or handicapped, those unable to understand English and the deaf is generally prohibited until the detained person sobers up or an appropriate adult or interpreter arrives. However, an officer of at least superintendent rank can authorise questioning to take place if he 'considers that delay will lead to the consequences set out in para 11.1 of Code C' (see para 8.34, ante) (Code C, Annex C 1(a) to (c)). There are of course dangers that some police officers will use the excuse of urgency to question suspects, who in normal circumstances would not be interrogated without precautions. There are three safeguards against this possibility. First, the questioning is to last only as long as the reason for urgency exists. Second, the grounds for the questioning must be recorded as must any answers. Third, the interviewing officer should be aware of the near certain exclusion of any answers at trial if questioning is seen as a blatant attempt to take advantage of the person's condition and to deny him the safeguards normally available.

Tape-recording of interviews

8.81   The tape-recording of interviews in a police station with suspects alleged to have committed indictable or either-way offences (other than terrorism offences) is now routine. Code of Practice E (Code E hereafter) governs its operation.

8.82   Much of Code E is devoted to the security of tapes so as to guarantee a complete and accurate record of police interviews. This helps to protect both parties by providing an effective safeguard for the rights of suspects and reducing challenges to the admissibility of prosecution evidence. As indicated above the advent of tape-recording has obliged police forces to consider and review their training for interviews and for officers to prepare themselves more thoroughly for them. HO Circular 7/1993 announced the availability of a national training package on investigative interviewing which most forces have taken up to a greater or lesser extent (see para 8.70, ante). The provisions of the Criminal Justice and Public Order Act 1994 which permit proper inferences to be drawn from a failure to disclose and explain, add a further dimension to interviewing and underline the need for proper planning. The Royal Commission on Criminal Justice (1993) found that 70 per cent of suspects did not ask to see a solicitor. Many of these involved minor offences but the proportion of solicitors present at taped interviews, which involve the more serious offences, is higher and will continue to rise. Solicitors who attend police stations will be receiving better training and this must be matched by improvements in police interviewing techniques and better preparation.

Use

8.83 Once a person has been cautioned for an indictable offence or either-way offence, the general rule is that any interview with him at a police station, including any permitted questioning after charge and statements made by others put to him after he has been charged, must be tape-recorded (Code E 3.1). The exception to this is for those arrested under s 41 or detained under Sch 7 of the Terrorism Act 2000 about which a separate Code of Practice exists and Code E does not apply.

8.84 The custody officer may authorise the interviewer not to tape record the interview in the following circumstances:

- A suitable interview room or tape-recorder is unavailable and the custody officer has reasonable grounds to authorise the interview without delay (Code E 3.3(a)). This is likely to be the most used exception, especially since police force budgets will restrict the number of equipped interview rooms at designated stations and since there will probably be none at non-designated stations. It is suggested that the 'reasonable grounds' justifying a non-taped interview should be the same as those under Code C 11.1 which justify an interview outside a police station or of vulnerable suspects under Code C, Annex C.
- It is clear from the outset of the detention that no prosecution will ensue (Code E 3.3(b)) (eg D will be cautioned, D is detained under the Mental Health Act 1983 and will be dealt with outside the criminal process). It should be noted that Code C does still apply to them (Code C 1.10) so that, inter alia, a written record must be compiled of any interview, but Code C 1.12 does not apply the Code to the four categories of persons listed there and Code E does not therefore apply to them (Code E 1.4).

8.85 In all such cases the interview must be recorded in writing in accordance with Code C 11, and the custody officer must make a note in specific terms of the reasons for not tape-recording. As the Code points out the decision not to tape-record may well be the subject of comment in court and the authorising officer may have to justify his decision (Code E, Note 3K).

8.86 The police have the option to tape interviews for summary offences. Physical resources will often preclude this in busy stations and most of such offences (eg routine vagrancy or drunkenness offences) are totally unsuited to the paraphernalia of tape-recording. However, if the resources are available and the investigation is controversial (eg likely summary offences surrounding public disorder), the police are best advised to play safe and record. Moreover, there are many cases where they cannot be sure at the outset whether the investigation will lead to charges on indictment. Thus, it is suggested that wherever the custody officer/interviewing officer has reason to believe that the case presents special or potentially contentious aspects, tape-recording should be considered. Another suitable category is the 'volunteer' who agrees to attend for interview in connection with a complicated (eg fraud) or controversial investigation.

8.87   As indicated above the central concern of Code E is the integrity and security of tapes. A number of points may be highlighted.

(1)   If the suspect is deaf or there is doubt about his hearing ability, a contemporaneous written note of the interview should be taken as well as the tape-recording (Code E 4.4).

(2)   If the suspect objects to the interview being tape-recorded before or during the interview or during a break in it, the interviewing officer must explain that the interview is being tape-recorded and that the Code requires that those objections be recorded on tape, when they have been recorded, or the suspect refuses to have them recorded, the tape-recorder may be turned off having stated on tape that he is doing so and why. The interview must then be contemporaneously recorded in writing in accordance with Code C 11. However, the officer may proceed with a taped interview if he considers it reasonable to do so (Code E 4.5). This decision may be the subject of comment in court (Code E, Note G) but since it is as much for the suspect's benefit as for the police, the possibility of such comment should not cause concern.

(3)   The requirements of Code C, other than those relating to contemporaneous written records, apply to all tape-recorded interviews. The treatment of the suspect, meal breaks, refreshment breaks and periods of rest are therefore the same, as are requirements for the presence of an appropriate adult, interpreters or legal advisers. Code C is paramount and nothing in Code E shall be taken as in any way detracting from it (Code E 1.3).

(4)   The suspect must be cautioned on tape before the interview commences in the terms set out in Code C 10.4, and he must be reminded of his right to free and independent legal advice and that he may speak to a solicitor on the telephone as set out in Code C 6.5. If he does not want legal advice he should be asked for his reasons, which should be recorded. If he wants legal advice he may not be interviewed or continue to be interviewed until he has received it unless one or more of the provisions of Code C 6.5 apply. After a break in questioning the officer must ensure that the suspect is aware that he remains under caution and be reminded of his right to legal advice. If he then decides he wants legal advice the interview must not continue unless Code C 6.5 applies.

(5)   Any significant statement or silence which occurred before the start of the tape-recorded interview must be put to the suspect at the start of the interview. The special warnings required by ss 36 and 37 of the CJPOA 1994 must be given before he is asked to explain the presence of objects etc or his presence at the scene of the crime (see paras 8.54(8), 8.17 and 8.18, ante), though this need not be at the start of the interview. Code E 4.3E restates the provision in Code C 10.5C which requires that the suspect be informed where failure to co-operate will result in consequences such as detention if he fails to provide his name and address, which are unaffected by the formal caution (see para 8.17(4), ante).

(6)   At the end of a taped interview, the master copy is sealed with a master tape label in the suspect's presence and treated as an exhibit in accordance with force standing orders. The label should be signed by the interviewing officer, the suspect and any third party present, eg the appropriate adult and/or legal adviser though

the Law Society advises solicitors not to sign the tape. If the suspect refuses to sign, an inspector, or if not available the custody officer, shall be called into the interview room and asked to sign the label. (In terrorism cases the officer's warrant or other identification number should replace the signature Code E 4.15.) The suspect must be given a notice explaining the use which will be made of the tape-recording and the arrangements for access to it, and that a copy will be supplied as soon as practicable if the person is charged or informed that he will be prosecuted. The second tape is used as a working copy (eg to prepare a record of the interview, to make further copies) and should also be kept securely, for otherwise the master tape will have to be used with all resultant inconvenience. Code E 6 deals with security of tapes and emphasises the need to account for them on the same basis as any other evidential material (Code E 6.1). Importantly no police officer has authority to break the seal on the master tape. If it becomes necessary to do so it must be done in the presence of a representative of the CPS and the suspect or his legal adviser must be given a reasonable opportunity to be present. If either is present they must be asked to reseal and sign the master tape label. If either refuses or are not present the CPS representative should do so (Code E 6.2). Where no criminal proceedings result the arrangements for breaking the seal set down in standing orders in force should be followed.

Record of the taped interview

8.88 If a case is to be pursued (either by further investigation or referral to the Crown Prosecution Service, CPS) the most difficult, yet crucial, and always time-consuming, task for the investigating officer is to prepare a written record of the interview known as the record of taped interview (ROTI). In a study of the recording of interviews Baldwin (RCCJ Research Study No 2 (1992)), found a bleak picture in which even the most progressive forces failed to produce good-quality records of interviews. Nevertheless, with the exception of a small number of police forces who involve civilians, it remains the almost impossible task for police officers to produce an accurate and impartial summary of the taped interview. This must be made in accordance with national guidelines approved by the Secretary of State (Code E 5A – see Annex A to Home Office Circular 26/1995 the following points must be contained in the summary :

(a) the need to include a failure to answer questions adequately, or at all and any failure to account for any object, substance or mark found at the time of arrest, or a failure to account for his presence at a place, at or about the time the alleged offence occurred – see paras 8.54–8.18, ante; and

(b) where the accused is aged between 10 and 14 years, the need to rebut the presumption that he did not appreciate that what he was doing was 'seriously wrong' which, as indicated in *C (a minor) v DPP* (1995) requires positive evidence – see para 8.16(4), ante.)

8.89 A detailed Practice Direction (Criminal Proceedings: Consolidation) [2002] 1 WLR para 43 governs the relationship between the CPS and the defence on such matters as agreeing the record of interview and editing the tape. It is designed to facilitate agreement prior to trial or at least to narrow down the scope of any disagreement, thus avoiding unnecessary adjournments and reducing court time. If the defence wish to challenge the tape, the interviewing officer must be called to prove it in evidence. He should listen to the tape beforehand and he can then testify as to its accuracy (*R v Rampling* (1987)). Research (Baldwin – RCCJ Research Study No 2) suggests that few lawyers listen to the tape but instead rely on the ROTI which is likely to be faulty or misleading about 50 per cent of the time:

> 'There is in the author's view no effective substitute for lawyers involved in a criminal case taking the time to do this in a much higher proportion of cases than happens at present' (Baldwin p 22).

8.90   The tape itself or the agreed record of taped interview attached to the officer's written statement are the real evidence before the court and the jury should ordinarily be permitted to hear them. The tape is an exhibit like any other and, if they wish, they may also listen to it after retiring (see the guidance on this offered by the Court of Appeal in *R v Emmerson* (1990)). In Rampling the transcript was not seen as evidence but as a 'mere convenience'. Paragraph 27 of the Practice Direction regards it as evidence but the trial judge still has a discretion as to whether the jury should be shown copies of any transcript or be permitted to take it with them when they retire. If only part of the tape is played in court and the jury has a full transcript, they should be permitted to hear the whole tape on retiring (*R v Emmerson* (1990)). (See further *R v Riaz* (1991); *R v Aitken* (1991); and *R v Tonge* (1993).)

Transcript

8.91   Expense and time require that the transcription of tapes be kept to a minimum. It may be needed for internal use so as to help the police to pursue an investigation (eg in a complex fraud case where several interviews need to be cross-checked, or where a review of the investigation is necessary, or where the interview is so detailed that the preparation of a transcript is easier than a ROTI); or for external use by the CPS (eg to assess a case, or to prepare it for prosecution) or by the defence. In this last case the police can make the transcript and charge for it. Whether they do so or not, the defence, if legally aided, may apply for legal aid or, if not aided, to the court clerk to see if the expense of a transcript is a legitimate one for the purposes of costs (Guidelines, para 33). Whichever side sees fit to require a transcript, it should be made available to the other (unless the defence has prepared one and disclosure would harm the defence), and wherever possible duplication of the preparation of transcripts should be avoided (Guidelines, paras 34-35).

Visual recording of interviews – PACE 1984. s 60A

8.92   Code of Practice F has been issued by the secretary of state:

Charge

8.93 The general rule is that questioning shall cease when the police believe that there is sufficient evidence to launch a successful prosecution (Code C 16.1). This means not simply sufficient evidence to charge the person and take him before a court (a prima facie case), but sufficient evidence to ensure a conviction. In most cases the interviewing officer will reach this decision, but in some the custody or more senior officer may decide, for example, on a review of the detention. There are two qualifications to this process. First, the interviewing officer should ascertain whether D 'has said all that he wishes to say about the offence' (Code C 16.1). Liberally interpreted this could permit the police to coax D into conversation well beyond the spirit of the Code (eg to 'top and tail' a confession). The requirement of contemporaneous recording of the interview (Code C 11.5) or tape-recording is the crucial safeguard against this; and the courts have shown themselves very willing to exclude evidence of a confession if there has been a significant and substantial breach of the Code. Second, if D is detained for more than one offence, he need not be brought before a custody officer until these requirements have been satisfied for each offence. Once the stage has been reached of having sufficient evidence to prosecute, the suspect will be transferred to the custody officer. Thereafter:

(a) the custody officer will, if he agrees, charge the person or administer a formal caution or notify the person of prosecution;

(b) the person will be cautioned again;

(c) if charged, he will be given a written notice specifying particulars of the offence (including its precise legal description), the name of (or number in terrorism cases) the officer in charge of the case, details of the police station, and the reference number of the case. The notice is prefaced by a repetition of the Code C 10.4 caution, since this is the last chance he has to mention some fact later relied upon at trial (Code C 16.3).

8.94 In most cases questioning the suspect will then cease. However:

(a) the suspect may decide to make a written statement (see below);

(b) the police, if they have not done so already, may confront the suspect with a statement or written record or tape of an interview with another person (or read it to him). The suspect (and any appropriate adult) must be warned that he does not have to say anything but that anything he does say may be given in evidence (the old caution because s 34 CJPOA 1994 applies up to charge but not beyond), and must be reminded of his right to legal advice. The interviewing officer should not say or do anything to invite any reply but should 'sit back' and wait for any reaction (Code C 16.4);

(c) questioning can continue (after the old caution has been given and he has been reminded of his right to legal advice), if:

   (i) it is needed to prevent harm or loss to some other person or to the public. For example, D is charged with kidnapping but has not yet revealed where the hostage is;

(ii) it is needed to clear up ambiguities in the suspect's earlier statements;

(iii) it is in the interests of justice that the accused be confronted with information that has come to light since he was charged (or told of possible prosecution). 'Interests of justice' can include the saving of court time and expense. For example, a person who is protesting innocence or who refuses to speak, but who has been charged, can be confronted with the statement of another accused or a witness which prejudices him (Code C 16.5).

8.95 Details of all charges and the response of the accused to them must be recorded. Similarly, if questioning takes place after charge, the exchanges with the accused must be fully and contemporaneously recorded (Code C 16.7-16.8).

After charge

8.96 Once a person has been charged, the custody officer must decide whether to release him, on or without bail, which may now be conditional (s 38), or to continue the detention and therefore make arrangements for the accused to appear before a magistrates' court (s 46; for discussion of ss 38 and 46, see paras 6.26-6.33, ante).

WRITTEN STATEMENTS (CODE C, ANNEX D)

8.97 If a person, detained or otherwise, wishes to make a statement, he may write it himself or an officer can do so on his behalf. If he writes it himself, he is asked to write first that he is making the statement voluntarily and that he understands the meaning of the caution. This is of particular importance in the light of the new caution with its reference to harm to his defence if he fails to mention a fact later relied upon at trial. He should then be allowed to write freely. Since people are usually unacquainted with the discipline which a narrative requires, the officer can tell the person what matters are relevant and whether what he has written is ambiguous. Since any amendments will appear on the statement as insertions, the officer must take care lest his interruptions be subsequently construed as improper pressure. If the officer is to write the statement, the suspect must similarly be asked to acknowledge his consent and understanding of the caution. The officer must then record every word, including any question and answer designed to clarify the meaning of the statement. On completion, the person is asked to read, amend where necessary, and sign the statement, including a declaration that, inter alia, he has given the statement freely (Annex D6). If he refuses, for whatever reason, to read and/or sign the statement, that fact shall be recorded after the officer has read the statement to him and asked him to change his mind (Annex D7).

CONFESSIONS

8.98 One of the most important common law exceptions to the rule against hearsay is the informal admission (ie an incriminating statement made by a party to proceedings).

It is admissible as evidence of the truth of its contents on the basis that a person is likely to be telling the truth when he says something against his own interest. At common law when such an admission was made by an accused person before his trial and to a person in authority (usually the police), it was known as a confession. It can range from a full, signed admission of guilt, to an incriminating comment and to a mixed statement containing admissions and exculpations. If this last example occurs, the whole statement should be put in evidence, though the judge may point out to the jury that the incriminating parts are likely to be true, whereas the excuses may not carry the same weight (*R v Sharp* (1988) followed in *R v Grayson* (1993) and *R v McCleary* (1994)). The modern test for the admissibility of a confession is contained in s 76 of PACE 1984; Art 74 of the PACE (NI) Order – the sections are in the same terms and to avoid repetition s 76 should be taken to include Art 74.

Definition

8.99

'"Confession" includes any statement wholly or partly adverse to the person who made it, whether made to a person in authority or not and whether made in words or otherwise' (s 82(1), Art 70(1)).

A confession may be made orally, in writing, by conduct or any other way of communicating information. Thus if D accepts, by word or conduct, eg he nods assent, an accusation made by the victim of a crime, then to the extent that he has accepted it, the statement becomes his own (*R v Christie* (1914)). Section 82(1) clearly covers an accused who re-enacts a crime on videotape (cf *Li Shu-Ling v R* (1989)). By confining the definition to 'adverse' statements, s 82(1) does not cover exculpatory statements. So if, after being threatened, D makes such a statement in which, for example, he sets up a false alibi and later at his trial puts forward another inconsistent defence, the prosecution can adduce the previous statement and cross-examine D on it since it is not a confession and does not have to satisfy the test of admissibility for confessions. On the other hand, a plea of guilty is within the definition. Thus, if D pleads guilty but is later permitted to change his plea to one of not guilty, the prosecution may have to satisfy the test of admissibility before the previous plea is admitted. Even if it is admissible, the trial judge may exclude it in the exercise of his discretion to ensure a fair trial if the plea was entered when D was unrepresented or on a mistaken view of the law. Though usually made to the police a confession may be made to anyone, friend, relative or spouse. The only difficulty with confessions made to a spouse is that a spouse is a compellable witness in only a limited number of cases (see s 80 of PACE).

Purposive confessions

8.100   In *R v Z* (2003) the Court of Appeal considered the meaning of adverse in s 82(1). Z had been convicted of aggravated burglary. At trial he unsuccessfully claimed he had acted under duress. During his detention at the police station he had an 'off the record' conversation with a police officer during which he said that was not prepared to make a statement for fear of reprisals. Evidence was given of the conversation which demonstrated inconsistency with his defence at trial. Counsel for the appellant sought to have the conversation excluded by arguing that it constituted a confession. It is likely that, if it had been accepted as such, the evidence would have been excluded. Basing its reasoning on s 3(1) of the Human Rights Act 1998 that courts must construe legislation in a manner which is compatible with Convention rights together with dicta of the ECHR. In *Saunders v United Kingdom* the court reached the following conclusion

> 'he question arises : at what time is the judgment, whether a statement is or is not a confession, whether it is or is not adverse, to be made ? Sat-Bhambra indicates that the decision is to be made at the time of the statement; but prima facie one would have thought that the test is to be made at the time when it is sought to give the statement in evidence. That is, to our mind, confirmed by the underlying rationale of s 76.'

The effect of this is that a court must look to the purpose to which the courts put a statement rather than to the intent with which that statement was originally made.

Admissibility of confessions

8.101   Section 76(1) provides that:

> 'In any proceedings a confession made by an accused person may be given in evidence against him in so far as it is relevant to any matter in issue in the proceedings and is not excluded by the court in pursuance of this section.'

8.102   'Proceedings' means criminal proceedings, including courts martial (s 82(1)), therefore s 76(1) applies to all such proceedings. However, in *R v Beckford* (1991) the subsection was held to apply only to confessions tendered by the prosecution.

The test for admissibility

8.103   Section 76(2) states:

> 'If, in any proceedings where the prosecution proposes to give in evidence a confession made by an accused person, it is represented to the court that the confession was or may have been obtained:
> (a) by oppression of the person who made it; or
> (b) in consequence of anything said or done which was likely in the circumstances existing at the time, to render unreliable any confession which might have been made by him in consequence thereof,
> the court shall not allow the confession to be given in evidence except in so far as the prosecution proves to the court beyond reasonable doubt that the confession (notwithstanding that it may be true) was not obtained as aforesaid.'

8.104 The words 'where the prosecution proposes to give in evidence' confine the section to confessions which have not yet been put in evidence. If a confession is admitted but later in the course of the trial evidence suggests it was or may have been obtained in breach of the section, s 76 (Art 74) is not applicable (neither is s 78 (Art 76) which uses similar terms) and the common law discretion must be relied upon (*R v Sat-Bhambra* (1988)). The onus lies initially on the defence to 'represent' to the court that the confession is or may be inadmissible. 'Represent' means more than raising a suggestion during cross-examination (*R v Liverpool Juvenile Court, ex p R* (1988)). It requires the defence to produce sufficient evidence to raise a doubt and convince the court that further investigation into the confession is warranted. This should not be a difficult task. It is not necessary to raise a prima facie case against admissibility. Instead it is sufficient for the defence to suggest that the confession 'was or may have been obtained' in breach of s 76. The suggestion may often appear on the face of the custody record (eg by revealing prolonged periods of questioning, an improper denial of entitlements under PACE) or from the content of the interview record. Alternatively it may require the production of witness statements and witnesses (principally the accused). Usually the defence will intimate their intention to the prosecution at the outset and the issue can be dealt with early in the prosecution's case. This means that D is entitled to a ruling on the matter before, or at the end of, the Crown's case and this enables him to organise his defence accordingly (*R v Liverpool Juvenile Court, ex p R* (1988)). If D does not raise the issue during the prosecution's case, he can do so later, although the damage of letting the jury hear the confession will have been done. Alternatively, and rarely, the court may raise the issue of its own motion and call upon the prosecution to satisfy the court of its admissibility (s 76(3)).

8.105 The words 'the court shall not allow the confession to be given in evidence' make it clear that if the prosecution fails to prove beyond reasonable doubt that the confession was not obtained in breach of s 76(2)(a) or (b) the trial judge has no discretion; he must exclude the confession.

8.106 The admissibility and relevance of a confession are questions of law to be decided by the judge whereas weight is a question of fact for the jury. In a magistrates' court, the bench is involved in both questions but, if the confession is ruled inadmissible, it must of course perform the difficult task of removing the alleged confession from its mind when deciding guilt. Even if the confession is admitted, the defence may still raise the issue again before the jury by, for example, cross-examining police officers as to the detail of the interrogation which led to the confession. For the jury has to determine the weight, if any, to be given to an admissible confession and it is possible, on hearing how the confession was obtained, that the jury will take a different view of the confession to that of the judge and disregard it or give it little weight.

8.107 Once s 76 is raised, a voir dire, or trial within a trial, must normally be held (*R v Millard* (1987); *R v Liverpool Juvenile Court, ex p R* (1988)). This includes summary trials. The defence can of course give evidence at the voir dire but D cannot be compelled to testify (*R v Davis* (1990)). On a voir dire the sole issue for the court is the admissibility of the confession. It may be declared inadmissible even if it is true, the section being more concerned with how it was obtained. This is understandable when oppression is used but less so when the issue is the likely reliability of the confession. The fact that it is true is the best measure of its reliability but the truth is not in issue at the voir dire. Thus, evidence led, or cross-examination conducted, by the prosecution designed to show that the confession is true is irrelevant to the issue of admissibility (*R v Davis* (1990); *R v Cox* (1991)). To complicate matters further, in determining the voir dire it is permissible for the judge to take into account evidence he has already heard in the trial and he is not confined to the voir dire evidence (*R v Tyrer* (1989)). This however runs the risk of the judge deciding on the truth of the confession (as opposed to its admissibility) by believing an earlier witness's evidence given during the trial. There are two stages involved in the admissibility decision – first to discover the facts (eg did the officer hit or bully D?), second, to decide whether those facts satisfy s 76 (or s 78 which is the alternative means of excluding a confession).

8.108   A crucial factor in deciding the admissibility of a confession under s 76(2) is the availability of a full record of the suspect's treatment during custody and of his interview. The custody record may be critical evidence of proper procedural compliance (see *R v Trussler* (1988)). Similarly, the absence of a contemporaneous record of the interview deprives the court of the full picture and makes it more difficult for the prosecution to prove beyond reasonable doubt that the confession was not obtained in breach of sub-s (2)(b) (eg *R v Delaney* (1988)). This burden may be even more difficult to discharge where the police have acted properly but other circumstances suggest unreliability. For example, in *R v Harvey* (1988) D and her lover X were arrested for the murder of Y. X confessed to the crime in front of D and on the next day D also confessed. X died before trial. At D's trial it was established that she was of low intelligence and suffered from a psychopathic disorder. Two psychiatrists testified that D might have confessed 'to protect her lover in a child-like attempt to try to take the blame'; the Crown was unable to prove beyond reasonable doubt that D's confession had not been obtained because she had heard X confessing (s 76(2)(b)) and D was acquitted.

8.109   In spite of several causes celebres in recent years involving the quashing of convictions based on false or unreliable confessions and calls to emulate the Scottish system, the Royal Commission on Criminal Justice (1993) rejected a requirement of corroboration of a confession as a condition of admissibility. However, in practice, there have been sufficient examples to caution courts against the ready acceptance of confessional evidence alone and to remind the police and Crown Prosecution Service of the desirability of supporting evidence (see principle (b) of the Principles of Investigative Interviewing, para 8.70, ante). A confession may be admitted if it is 'relevant to any matter in issue in the proceedings' (s 76(1)) (most obviously as regards the offence charged, but also in relation to other conduct, eg as evidence of the accused's disposition where the court has decided to allow such evidence). Subject to the rule of relevance a confession may be used as evidence of any matter, including any matter favourable to its maker, though the evidential value of self-serving extracts from a confession may be slight and the judge may well comment on its lack of weight (see *R v Sharp* (1988); *R v Grayson* (1993); and *R v McCleary* (1994)). Since an accused is generally neither competent nor compellable for the prosecution, an out-of-court statement by D1 against his co-accused, D2, who is being jointly tried, is inadmissible as evidence against D2 (unless D1 ceases to be a defendant where, for example, the prosecution offers no evidence against D1 or files a nolle prosequi in relation to D1).

8.110 If a confession is excluded under s 76 (or s 78) because of breaches of the Codes of Practice, subsequent interviews, in which the confession is repeated, will also be inadmissible if they stem from the original one. For otherwise s 76 can be flouted by subsequent compliance with the rules (*R v McGovern* (1990); *R v Blake* (1991); *R v Ismail* (1990); *R v Wood* (1994)). It is a question of fact and degree in each case as to whether a later unobjectionable interview should be excluded. Much will depend upon the objections raised to the earlier objectionable interview and whether those objections were of a fundamental and continuing nature. Thus in *R v Conway* (1994) D alleged that during a visit to his cell he had been promised that if he admitted the offence he could go home to his sick mother. There was no record of the visit in the custody record, no caution was given and no note of the conversation was made. He then confessed in an interview some 20 minutes later. The prosecution did not seek to rely on the interview in the cell but D sought to exclude the later interview. The trial judge's decision that there was no oppression or unreliability was overturned on appeal. The cell interview would have been excluded as unreliable and there was nothing in the intervening 20 minutes to suggest that the effect of the earlier breaches had ceased to have any effect on D. In *R v Neil* (1994) police took a witness statement from D in which he admitted giving a knife to the man who stabbed the deceased and then drove him from the scene. He was then arrested, cautioned and kept in custody overnight before being interviewed as a suspect when he made the same admission. The witness statement was excluded under s 78 but the second interview was admitted. D's appeal was allowed. D had no opportunity to seek legal advice before being interviewed as a suspect and may well have felt bound by the admissions in the earlier statement.

8.111 Other factors may come into play which suggest that the breaches were not cured by the time of a later interview. Thus in *R v Wood* (1994) D, who was of limited mental capacity, was charged with manslaughter of a child by striking him a heavy blow. During an interview with no solicitor, no caution and no contemporaneous record he admitted striking the boy on the day previous to his death. In a second properly conducted interview he repeated this. The medical evidence agreed that the blow which killed the boy had been delivered on the day of his death, not the previous day. This in itself suggested unreliability and the absence of a record of the earlier interview made it impossible for the prosecution to prove that the second interview was not tainted by the first. Occasionally it may be possible for the Crown to prove no connection between them (eg D is oppressed and confesses. He is released on bail but returns to the station with his lawyer and confesses; cf *R v Gillard and Barrett* (1990) in relation to s 78 or, as is suggested in the commentary to Conway, if D had seen a solicitor in the period between the breaches and had been made aware of his rights and that the earlier interview did not count.)

Criteria for admissibility

OPPRESSION (S 76(2)(A), ART 74(2)(A))

8.112   The defence may represent to the court that a confession 'was or may have been obtained by oppression of the person who made it'. This reflects the views of the Criminal Law Revision Committee (11th Report) and of the Royal Commission on Criminal Procedure – that society's abhorrence of methods of investigation amounting to oppression should be signalled by the automatic exclusion of a confession obtained thereby, even if the confession turns out to be true. It also reflects the late development of the common law, which first established oppression as a ground of inadmissibility of confessions in *Callis v Gunn* (1963). This was then incorporated, but not defined, in the revised Judges' Rules of 1964.

8.113   Section 76(8) offers a non-exhaustive definition of the term, based in part on Art 3 of the European Convention on Human Rights:

> '"oppression" includes torture, inhuman or degrading treatment and the use of threat of violence (whether or not amounting to torture)'.

8.114   'Torture' is the most severe form of oppression and, according to a resolution of the United Nations in 1975, 'constitutes an aggravated and deliberate form of cruel, inhuman or degrading treatment or punishment' (Resolution 3452). It suggests a systematic and premeditated course of action rather than a spontaneous act of violence. The Shorter Oxford English Dictionary defines torture as 'the infliction of excruciating pain, severe or excruciating pain of body, anguish, agony' and, given the courts' predilection for giving words their ordinary dictionary meaning (see *R v Fulling* (1987) below), this may be preferred. However, the terms of s 76(8) are well known to international law (eg Art 5 of the UN Declaration of Human Rights 1948) and it is suggested that guidance can and should be sought from that jurisprudence. Thus in the 1984 United Nations Convention against Torture and Other Cruel, Inhuman and Degrading Treatment or Punishment, it is defined as 'any act by which severe pain or suffering, whether physical or mental, is intentionally inflicted on a person for such purposes as obtaining from him or a third person information or a confession' (Art 1). 'Inhuman treatment' has been described by the European Commission of Human Rights as covering 'at least such treatment as deliberately causes severe suffering, mental or physical' (The Greek Case (1969)). In *Ireland v United Kingdom* (1978) the European Court of Human Rights described the interrogation techniques (prolonged wall-standing, hooding, subjection to white (ie high-pitched) noise, deprivation of sleep, and rationing of food and drink) employed by the UK Government in Northern Ireland as 'degrading' because they were 'such as to arouse in their victims feelings of fear, anguish and inferiority capable of humiliating and debasing them and possibly breaking their physical or moral resistance' (see also *Soering v United Kingdom* (1989)). As to 'violence', it is clear that psychological as well as physical acts are included.

8.115 However, since s 76(8) is not an exhaustive definition, subtle distinctions between its terms are unnecessary and it serves simply to illustrate the type of conduct outlawed by s 76. Indeed the expansive view of oppression taken by the Court of Appeal in *R v Fulling* (1987) has meant that the narrow terms of s 76(8) are virtually redundant. For in Fulling the dictionary meaning of oppression was adopted, viz:

'Exercise of authority or power in a burdensome, harsh, or wrongful manner; unjust or cruel treatment of subjects, inferiors etc; the imposition of unreasonable or unjust burdens.'

8.116 Such a wide definition more than embraces s 76(8) and extends oppression well beyond that partial definition. The Lord Chief Justice also added this gloss:

'We find it hard to envisage any circumstances in which such oppression would not entail some impropriety on the part of the interrogator.'

8.117 He implicitly adopted the trial judges' ruling that '"oppression" means something above and beyond that which is inherently oppressive in police custody and must import some impropriety, some oppression actively applied in an improper manner by the police'. The requirement of impropriety initially focuses the court's attention on what the investigator has done rather than on the effect of his conduct on the suspect (s 76(2)(b) more naturally encompasses the latter, see below). In this sense the approach is an objective one. However, the word 'wrongful' in the dictionary definition must be understood in the context of the rest of the definition, particularly the words 'burdensome' and 'harsh' which precede it. Otherwise any breach of the Code may be seen as wrongful and could amount to oppression. Tricks, such as covert tape-recording of a suspect, do not therefore amount to oppression (*R v Parker* (1995)). 'Impropriety', in the Lord Chief Justice's gloss, would seem to be a synonym for 'wrongful' as used in the definition. Thus *R v Davison* (1988) contained a catalogue of improprieties. Not all of them (eg improper denial of a solicitor) amounted to oppression, but failure to release D and to re-arrest him as PACE required meant that his detention was unlawful for nine hours. This then qualified as the exercise of powers in a wrongful manner (per the Fulling test) and was capable of amounting to oppression. The prosecution then had the burden of proving that the confession was not obtained by oppression, which it was unable to do.

8.118 One implication of *R v Fulling* (1987) concerns the method of questioning. It is hard to describe lies or tricks practised on a suspect (eg *R v Mason* (1987), where D was falsely told that forensic evidence had been found linking him to the crime) as falling within the dictionary definition of oppression approved in Fulling. Moreover, as the very facts of the case indicate (D was told that her lover had been having an affair with another woman for the past three years and that woman just happened to be in the cell next to D), the making of true statements will not often constitute oppression. However, they may exceptionally do so; for example, if D is unaware that her mother is near to death and the police tell her this in order to put pressure on her to confess, this deliberate misuse of the truth could amount to 'harsh' or 'improper' treatment (per *R v Fulling*) and therefore oppression. The abuse of power is essential. Thus in *R v Miller* (1986), a pre-PACE Act decision, D, a paranoid schizophrenic, confessed to killing his girlfriend. The confession contained delusions mixed with facts. A psychiatrist testified that the questioning had triggered delusions. The judge's decision that the questioning was not oppressive, not being designed to induce delusions, was upheld by the Court of Appeal and doubtless would not be oppressive under the present law, but may be within sub-s (2)(b) (see below).

8.119   Certainly persistent, heavy-handed or bullying questioning interspersed with misrepresentations could qualify. For example, in *R v Beales* (1991) a confession extracted during a 35-minute interview was excluded because the officer had invented evidence against D and forcefully confronted him with it, repeatedly misrepresented D's answers and 'hectored and bullied [him] from first to last'. In *R v West (Timothy)* (1988), there was oppression when the interviewing officer interrupted the suspect on a large number of occasions before he had finished his reply, often vigorously and rudely with a raised voice, and used obscenities to indicate that he was lying. It was clear to the court that the officer had made up his mind that D had committed the offence and would continue to question until he admitted this. More clearly oppressive was the conduct of the interviewing officers in *R v Paris, Adullahi and Miller* (1992) (dubbed 'The Cardiff Three'). There the officers shouted at one suspect and told him what they wanted him to say despite his denying involvement some 300 times. The suspect was of low intelligence, which made such questioning more obviously oppressive. It is, however, a matter of degree whether aggressive and hostile questioning amounts to oppression. It is more likely to be so if the suspect is a weak or vulnerable person. Much will depend on the particular circumstances and the character of the person being questioned. Thus in *R v Seelig* (1992) the Court of Appeal held that the trial judge was right in determining whether there was oppression to take into account the fact that Seelig was an experienced merchant banker, intelligent and sophisticated. (See also *R v L* (1994) which indicates that other factors, such as the weakness of the case against D apart from the confession and the initial failure to allow access to a solicitor, must be considered, rather than concentrating solely on the hostile questioning. There the questioning was not oppressive nor likely to induce unreliability.)

8.120   The availability of a tape-recording (as in Beales, West and Paris, Abdullahi and Miller) will be crucial in helping a court to decide whether the questioning has reached a degree of impropriety to be called oppressive. Lord Taylor LJ was clearly shocked after listening to the tape-recording of the interview with Miller and expressed the view that short of physical violence it was hard to conceive of a more hostile and intimidating approach by police officers to a suspect. However, the Fulling definition of oppression means that extreme and improper conduct is required and that the style of questioning will more often fall for consideration under s 76(2)(b), but where it falls short of oppression it will not necessarily be regarded as likely to render any confession unreliable; it remains a matter of degree and the circumstances, including the characteristics of the suspect, are all important.

8.121   The following additional points on s 76(2)(a) can be noted.

(1)   The confession must have been obtained by oppression. If D confesses before being subjected to oppressive treatment, s 76(2)(a) does not apply. More realistically, there may be occasions when the police have used oppression but the accused confesses for other reasons unconnected with it (eg after a night in a cell, following oppression, when he decides to get the 'matter off his chest' and save further anxiety to his family). However, the defence will in all probability raise the issue of oppression and it will be extremely difficult for the prosecution to rebut the alleged causal connection between the police conduct and the confession.

(2)   A confession, which a court decides was, or may have been, obtained by oppression, must be excluded, even if it is true. For example, D is severely beaten up by enraged bystanders, neighbours, and confesses to serious sexual offences against young children. The oppressive and improper conduct need not emanate from the police (despite Lord Lane's reference in Fulling to impropriety on the part of the interrogators) and D's confession will be excluded and, unless supported by other independent evidence or testimony (often unavailable in such cases), the prosecution will fail. Similarly if D is punished by an IRA punishment squad and told to confess to his crimes. (If not within sub-s (2)(a) it would be within sub-s (2)(b).)

(3)   D can be oppressed by the use of threats or violence against others (eg a spouse, children or close friends) of which he is aware. Such psychological pressure can overlap with the question of reliability (see s 76(2)(b) at para 8.122, post) and can be excluded on that basis as well.

(4)   Since oppression must be the consequence of some improper conduct by the oppressor(s), acts the unintended consequence of which is oppressive are probably not within s 76(2)(a) unless they are improper acts. Proper acts which cause a person to be oppressed are not within s 76(2)(a) but may be within s 76(2)(b).

(5)   If a confession is obtained by oppression, the things said or done will also render the confession unreliable under s 76(2)(b) (though that subsection need not be relied upon). However, things said or done which do not amount to oppression may nevertheless render the confession unreliable under s 76(2)(b) (ie the greater (2)(a) includes the lesser (2)(b) but the lesser does not necessarily include the greater).

(6)   Since physical injury is the clearest form of oppression, medical evidence assumes particular importance. Medical examination, preferably by the suspect's own doctor, should be readily allowed at the conclusion of interrogation and to avoid subsequent allegations of brutality, the police should be alert to the need for medical examination before the interrogation, especially if the person arrives at the police station already bearing bruises (see paras 7.241).

(7)   It should be remembered that 'oppression' is not confined to conduct which took place at the police station. Questioning or conduct that occurred at the time of arrest or while the person was being conveyed to a police station may be similarly relevant. In any event, the court will wish to hear an account of the whole proceedings which took place between the police and the accused before deciding whether there has been oppression.

RELIABILITY (S 76(2)(B), ART 74(2)(B))

8.122   A confession will be inadmissible if it

'was or may have been obtained ...
(b) in consequence of anything said or done which was likely, in the circumstances existing at the time, to render unreliable any confession which might be made [by the person] in consequence thereof' (s 76(2)(b)).

8.123   A number of preliminary points should be noted.
(1) As with sub-s (2)(a) once it is represented that the confession was or may have been obtained in circumstances of unreliability the burden passes to the prosecution to prove beyond reasonable doubt that it was not so obtained.
(2) The trial judge must initially determine the likelihood of unreliability but the jury will also do so subsequently and, in order to avoid the embarrassment of a jury in effect overruling the judge by reaching a different conclusion, on the issue of admissibility the judge is concerned not with the actual confession but with any confession D might have made in consequence of what was said or done.

> 'On this scheme the judge should imagine that he was present at the interrogation and heard the threat or inducement. In the light of all the evidence given he will consider whether, at the point when the threat was uttered or the inducement offered, any confession which the accused might make as a result of it would be likely to be unreliable' (CLRC, para 65).

(3) The phrase 'anything said or done' in s 76(2)(b), which replaced the reference to threats or inducements in the CLRC's version of the subsection, is extremely broad in scope. It can certainly encompass conduct which amounts to oppression under s 76(2)(a), but stretches well beyond that. It can include threats or promises or the holding out of some hope of advantage directed towards the accused which was a key feature of the previous common law. Everything said or done before and during the period of detention must be considered; the whole picture rather than selective parts of it. Thus in *R v Barry* (1991) D was interviewed over two days. On the first day he was told that it would be beneficial to him to assist the police to recover certain property. On the second day he was interviewed and confessed. The judge's conclusion that the statement on the first day had no effect on the confession made on the second day, was rejected by the Court of Appeal. The Court set out the necessary steps under sub-s (2)(b).
- The first step is to identify what was said or done and this should include everything said or done.
- The next step is to decide whether what was said or done was likely to render a confession unreliable; all the circumstances should be taken into account. The test is hypothetical. However, in *R v Bow Street Magistrates' Court, ex p Proulx* (2001) The Divisional Court held that this does not mean that the subject matter or nature of the confession can be disregarded. The word 'any' extends to 'any such' or 'such a' confession as the defendant has made.

• Finally, the judge should ask whether the prosecution had proved beyond reasonable doubt that the confession had not been made as a result of what was said or done.

In the context of this case the promise of some benefit on the first day was something said which had to be taken into account. It was likely to render any confession made unreliable and the fact that D had some time to think about it made it more, rather than less likely that he would be influenced by it. This is not to say that something said or done cannot be rendered ineffective by time. Much depends on what was said or done and the particular circumstances. A connection, or causal link, must be established between what was said and done and the obtaining of the confession and a delay between what was said or done and the obtaining of the confession may weaken that connection (see para 8.110, ante).

(4) Something said or done can also embrace conduct which is directed towards a person other than the accused but which is designed or is likely to make his confession unreliable (for example, a threat or suggestion that official action will be taken against D's family unless he confesses). It has been held that the phrase does not refer to things said or done by the accused but must be something external to him which then raises the possibility of unreliability. Thus, self-inflicted drug addiction which could prompt D to agree to anything in order to get bail and to feed the addiction will probably not suffice (*R v Goldenberg* (1988); *R v Crampton* (1990)). This reasoning is questionable since s 76(2)(b) also refers to the 'circumstances existing at the time' and the fact that the police proceed to interview a suspect in circumstances of drug withdrawal is arguably something 'said or done' which is likely in those circumstances to render any resulting confession unreliable. It does not matter that the police are unaware of D's difficulties since it has also been held that s 76(2)(b) is tested on an objective basis (see *R v Everett* (1988) where the police thought that D was of average mental age but he was subsequently shown at trial to have a mental age of an eight-year-old) and the fact that the police interviewed D in good faith does not make potentially unreliable circumstances reliable. A less emotive case is where D is required by a medical condition to take drugs which (either by taking or not taking them) then affect his mental abilities, or where D is of low intelligence, or suffering side effects from pregnancy (see *R v McGovern* (1990)). If the police are aware of this but proceed to interview, s 76(2)(b) could apply (and possibly sub-s (2)(a) if they seek to take advantage of the condition – see *R v Miller* (1986), para 8.46, ante). If they call the police surgeon (as Code C 9.2 and Note 9B recommend) and he approves the interview, or if they interview unaware of the medical conditions, the Crampton and Goldenberg cases say that s 76(2)(b) is inapplicable. The argument above suggests that the emphasis of the subsection lies on the objective determination of a confession's reliability (see *R v Everett* (1988)), that D's self-inflicted condition is a relevant circumstance to consider, and that D should be allowed to raise the issue. Whether he succeeds is another matter (though he is helped by the burden of proof lying on the prosecution). One may further note that the mentally disordered and mentally handicapped must be interviewed in the presence of an appropriate adult whose role is not simply that

of observer. He is there to advise the suspect; to see whether or not the interview is being conducted fairly and properly and to facilitate communication (Code C 11.16) (see paras 7.248–7.252, ante). The absence of an appropriate adult may then be something done which in the circumstances is likely to result in any confession made being unreliable (see para 8.53, post).

(5)   Section 76(2)(b) says 'anything said or done'. Does this include an omission? Although the point has not been considered directly, an affirmative answer can be deduced from the cases (eg *R v McGovern* (1990) – failure to allow access to a solicitor; *R v Cox* (1991) – absence of appropriate adult; *R v Doolan* (1988) – failure to caution and record interview).

(6)   'Anything said or done' may include the use of hypnosis. Hypnosis as a method of questioning suspects is unlikely to be used by the police, though the defence may see some benefit from it. There is no definitive evidence of the usefulness of hypnosis and the majority of scientific and medical opinion is opposed to its use. The view of the Home Secretary is that:

> '[A]s hypnosis may be a fallible and limited instrument for obtaining reliable evidence; as evidence so obtained is likely to be inadmissible; and as it carries a risk of longer-term harm to the subject, its use should be discouraged.' (Home Office Circular No 66/1988)

The Director of Public Prosecutions goes further and states that:

> 'Under no circumstances should suspects or persons implicated, however slightly, in the commission of the offence in question be considered for hypnosis' (Home Office Circular No 66/1988).

One must agree with the opinion expressed in that Circular that there is a serious risk that any confession obtained by the use of hypnosis would be inadmissible under s 76 or excluded under s 78. If hypnotherapy is to be used the procedural guidelines laid down in the Home Office Circular must be followed.

8.124   The most obvious external event which is 'said or done' is the conduct of the police. However, this need not emanate from a police officer, see for example *R v Harvey* (1988), see para 8.40, ante. Other conduct external to the police would include a threat by a father to a son that the latter had better tell the truth or he will be beaten (cf *R v Cleary* (1963), a promise by employer to employee that, if the latter 'owns up', the former will not sack him, or a threat by headmaster to pupil that unless the latter tells the truth to a police officer, he will be disciplined).In *R v M* (2000) the conduct was that of a solicitor who lent voluble support to the police but not, as in *R v Wahab* (2002) where the confession was made after advice from a solicitor. It can be argued that the phrase 'anything said or done' implies something out of the ordinary, for the proper exercise of normal police powers and procedures, as set out by Parliament, can hardly be allowed to trigger s 76(2)(b). However, in contrast to oppression (see *R v Fulling* (1987), above), no impropriety on the part of the police is required under s 76(2)(b), see for example *R v Harvey* (1988), para 8.40, ante (see also *R v Morse* (1991)). It is submitted that this is the correct approach – the emphasis of s 76(2)(b) lies on the reliability or otherwise of the confession and not the propriety of police conduct per se. The absence of bad faith may be of some slight value in tipping the scales in favour of the prosecution and admissibility, since proper conduct is less likely to make the confession unreliable (see *R v Maguire* (1989)). Conversely, even where the police have clearly misbehaved (eg *R v Sparkes* (1991) – failures to caution D and to keep a record of interview), that need not affect reliability.

8.125   Section 76(2)(b) encourages the defence to raise the issue of 'likely unreliability' in many more circumstances than were possible under the previous law. A narrow dividing line can separate legitimate police responses from illegitimate ones. The common sense and restraint of the court are the safeguards against abuse of this defence and against simple statements, such as 'I think that it would be better all round if you made a clean breast of it', leading to the exclusion of a confession.

8.126   Section 76(2)(b) could also include something which is properly 'said or done'. Code C 11.3 advises:

'If the person asks the officer directly what action will be taken in the event of his answering questions, making a statement or refusing to do either, then the officer may inform the person what action the police propose to take in that event provided that action is itself proper and warranted.'

8.127   Such a reply, however 'proper and warranted', may nevertheless be challenged at trial by the defence and be held to exclude a consequential confession if it is considered 'likely' in the circumstances to render the confession unreliable. For example the officer replies to a young woman of a nervous disposition with no previous convictions,

'The ground on which you are being detained is that it is necessary to detain you in order to obtain evidence by questioning. If you provide that evidence, you will be released on bail pending a decision whether or not to prosecute.'

8.128   If then a confession is seen as the way out of a very unpleasant situation, what was said may lead to exclusion under s 76(2)(b). (But not if the reply raises a self-induced hope – *R v Goldenberg* (1988) and see *R v Weeks* (1995) where the officer's statement that unless D told the truth and told them what they wanted to hear he would remain in custody was seen as a threat, albeit a statement of fact.) A police officer faced with the direct question, 'What action will you take if I make a statement?' should consider carefully his response. If he replies in 'proper and warranted' terms (if necessary after advice from a senior officer) and the interview is taped and/or witnessed by a third party (preferably a solicitor), the prosecution's task of satisfying s 76(2)(b) should be straightforward. As a further safeguard, it should be made clear to the suspect that decisions in respect of his release or detention will be taken by the custody officer and not by the investigating officer.

8.129   The value of misbehaviour, from the defence point of view, is that the gravity of any and each breach of PACE and the Codes is more likely to influence the court towards exclusion (eg *DPP v Blake* (1989); *R v Trussler* (1988)), as is the type of breach which can be described as significant or substantial, ie those which are more likely to affect the reliability of a confession. The police conduct can clearly include the physical treatment of D. For example, in *R v Trussler* (1988) the denial of a rest period, as prescribed in Code C 12.2, was a crucial factor leading to exclusion under s 76(2)(b). To this extent, the category overlaps with oppression in s 76(2)(a) but goes further by covering that conduct which lacks the gravity of oppression but which still has, or is likely to have, an effect on the particular suspect such as to produce an unreliable confession.

8.130   Two other broad categories of police conduct which attract s 76(2)(b) can be noted:

(a)   denial of D's protective rights; and

(b)   the method of questioning.

Denial of D's protective rights

8.131   It is not every breach of PACE which may affect the reliability of confessions. Thus in *R v Sparks* (1991) a failure to caution and to record the interview were breaches of Code C (and may be dealt with under s 78, see below), but were held not to be likely, without more, to affect reliability (cf *R v Doolen* (1988)). But there are some provisions in the Code C which are designed to protect the accused against himself, especially the vulnerable accused, and breach of which may influence the reliability of what he said. These provisions concern the physical presence of an adviser for the suspect. The most obvious is a lawyer. So in *R v McGovern* (1990) the police conducted a hasty interview at which D became emotionally upset. No lawyer was present to intercede, halt the interview, advise D, and thereby reduce the risk of unreliability. For vulnerable groups of suspects the presence of an 'appropriate adult' is crucial (see Code C 11.14). Thus in *R v Cox* (1991) D's IQ was lower than 99.6 per cent of the population and he was suggestible. Yet he was questioned, contrary to Code C, in the absence of an appropriate adult. The latter's presence was an essential prerequisite for reliability. Moreover, the appropriate adult must be capable and not totally incompetent. (See *R v Morse* (1991) where the father was of very low intelligence and virtually illiterate; but see *R v W* (1994) where W's mentally ill mother acted as an appropriate adult. The police were not aware of the illness and the ruling that there was nothing to suggest unreliability in the confession was upheld on appeal. See para 7.138, ante.) The use of tape-recording goes some way to discovering such cases. Conversely, the absence of a contemporaneous record of the interview will help the defence to raise doubts in the trial judge's mind – another reminder to the police of the necessity of recording interviews.

8.132   Failure to allow access to a solicitor will not necessarily lead to likely unreliability. If the suspect is vulnerable, a juvenile or mentally disordered, it may do so and almost certainly will do so if coupled with a failure to provide an appropriate adult (*R v Moss* (1990)). Despite being described as a 'fundamental right' (*R v Samuel* (1988)) the wrongful absence of a solicitor is seldom considered under sub-s (2)(b) when the suspect is an adult though s 78 is often relied upon. There the character of the accused is important; the suspect who 'knows the ropes' is not prejudiced by the absence, whereas a naive suspect may well be. However, the absence of a solicitor in such a case may well produce an unreliable confession. For example, in *R v Sanusi* (1992) a confession made by a foreigner with no knowledge of our legal system was excluded under s 78 because he was wrongly denied access to a solicitor. Similarly in *R v Beycan* (1990). Both cases should have been dealt with under s 76(2)(b) but demonstrate the tendency to ignore s 76 in favour of s 78 so that the courts are being asked to exercise discretion to exclude what is likely to be an inadmissible confession under s 76.

8.133 The recording provisions of Code C are designed to protect the accused against abuse by verballing. If then the police fail to record the interview or to show him it for approval and D disagrees with the officer's recollection of the record, he is saying, bluntly, that the confession is untrue (eg *R v Waters* (1989); *R v Doolan* (1988)), ie the police have fabricated or misrepresented the confession. The failure to record, coming after the confession was made, cannot be something said or done within sub-s (2)(b) but the thing done which is alleged is the making up of a confession, or the doctoring of it. Whether this is so or not, the failure to record deprives the prosecution of evidence which might be used to rebut the allegation.

8.134 The failure to caution D will also not inevitably trigger s 76(2)(b). D would have to show an extra ingredient which suggests that what he said is unreliable.

Method of questioning

8.135 In so far as the questioning becomes burdensome and oppressive s 76(2)(a) comes into play (eg *R v Beales* (1991) where the police repeatedly misrepresented the evidence against D and bullied him), but s 76(2)(b) clearly extends further. It is thus sensible for the defence to plead both (this may encourage a court, as in *R v Beales*, to decide that even if s 76(2)(a) does not apply, the lesser s 76(2)(b) does). How far then does s 76(2)(b) extend? The key lies in deciding whether what was 'said or done' was likely to render a confession 'unreliable'. This requires the court to look carefully at the circumstances of the particular suspect and then for the prosecution to prove beyond reasonable doubt that nothing was said or done which was likely to produce an unreliable confession. Clearly the method of questioning may produce an unreliable confession in that the suspect may speak for a variety of motives other than that of telling the truth (eg he wants to protect someone; he simply wants to leave the police station and is prepared to say anything, in the hope of retracting it later; he is suggestible and seeks to please his interrogator; he becomes confused and mistakenly incriminates himself; he is persuaded to speak because of promises or threats made to him). In *R v Fulling* (1987), the Lord Chief Justice decided that the following definition of oppression (cited with approval in *R v Prager* (1972)), was insufficient for s 76(2)(a) but suggested that some of it could fall within s 76(2)(b):

'… questioning which by its nature, duration or other attendant circumstances (including the fact of custody) excites hope (such as the hope of release) or fears, or so affects the mind of the subject that his will crumbles and he speaks when otherwise he would have stayed silent'.

8.136   This does of course put the court (and initially the prosecution) in a very difficult position in trying to fathom D's motives for speaking. It is easier if D falls within a group identified by PACE and the Code as 'vulnerable' (eg juveniles). Such persons may be suggestible or readily manipulated, with the consequence that certain styles of questioning are likely to produce unreliable confessions. In relation to the mentally ill or handicapped, the prosecution can face an uphill task. Thus, In *R v Delaney* (1988) the interviewing officer had throughout suggested to D that he really needed psychiatric help, and that if he owned up, people would help him. The officer played down the criminal offence and falsely aroused D's hopes of treatment. As the Lord Chief Justice put it, 'He might, by the same token, be encouraging a false confession.' In a less extreme case, the evidence, or speculation, of psychiatrists or psychologists as to the likely effect of police conduct on D could readily sow sufficient seeds to raise a reasonable doubt (see also *R v Harvey* (1988)). As for the 'ordinary' suspect, the court must consider all the circumstances of the interrogation and what was said by the police, or any other relevant person (eg parent, friend, co-accused, or even a solicitor who suggests that the evidence is stacked against the accused and that a confession and guilty plea will result in a lesser sentence); and the likely effect of what was said on the mind of the accused taking into account his characteristics. This requires an understanding of the pressures which a police station can engender. As the Lord Chief Justice observed in 1981:

'Very few confessions are inspired solely by remorse. Often the motives of an accused are mixed and include a hope that an early admission may lead to an earlier release or a lighter sentence. If it were the law that the mere presence of such a motive, even if prompted by something said or done by a person in authority, led inexorably to the exclusion of a confession, nearly every confession would be rendered inadmissible. This is not the law. In some cases the hope may be self-generated. If so, it is irrelevant, even if it provides the dominant motive for making the confession. In such a case the confession will not have been obtained by anything said or done by a person in authority. More commonly the presence of such a hope will, in part at least, owe its origin to something said or done by such a person. There can be few prisoners who are being firmly but fairly questioned in a police station to whom it does not occur that they might be able to bring both their interrogation and their detention to an earlier end by confession' (*R v Rennie* (1982); cf *R v Goldenberg* (1988)).

8.137   In some cases the evidence of persistent questioning and misrepresentation by the officer may be clear enough to suggest a state of confusion or hopelessness on the part of the suspect such as is likely to produce unreliable statements (see *R v Beales* (1991)). What about tricks or misrepresentations practised on the suspect? For example, D is told, falsely, that his voice has been recognised on a tape (*R v Blake*

(1991)) or that forensic evidence links him to the crime (*R v Mason* (1987), and cf the facts of *R v Kwabena Poku* (1978)). In the right circumstances, this could induce D falsely to confess (eg he hopes to exonerate himself later, he feels there is no option but to concur with the interrogator, he tries to exculpate himself but incidentally incriminates himself). The difficulty is that deceptions which suggest that there is conclusive evidence of guilt may lead to a reliable confession, rather than an unreliable one. In Blake the trial judge found unreliability within s 76(2)(b), in Mason sub-s (2)(b) was not argued, s 78 being preferred. In other cases of deception in undercover operations such as *R v Christou and Wright* (1992) and *R v Smurthwaite and Gill* (1994), and other deceptions such as covert bugging of cells (*R v Shaukat Ali* (1991); *R v Bailey and Smith* (1993)) or houses (*R v Khan (Sultan)* (1994)) the emphasis has been on reliability as a condition of admissibility and, reliability being established, s 76(2)(b) did not come into play.

8.138   Further examples of things said or done which the defence can raise under s 76(2)(b) include:
(i)   a threat to charge the person with a more serious offence or with more offences unless he makes a statement (see the facts of *R v Howden-Simpson* (1991));
(ii)   a promise to charge him with a less serious offence or not to prosecute at all, if he confesses;
(iii)   a promise to 'put in a good word for him at the trial or before the prosecuting solicitor';
(iv)   a promise to take another offence into consideration at the trial rather than prosecute him separately for that offence (cf *R v Northam* (1967));
(v)   a threat to, or promise not to, prosecute the accused's spouse or mistress or other close relation (cf *R v Middleton* (1975)), the more remote the relationship, the less likely it is that there will be a causal connection between the threat/promise and the making of the confession;
(vi)   a threat to inform a third party unless the accused confesses, eg to inform his wife of a charge of indecent assault, or his employer of a shoplifting allegation;
(vii) a threat to prosecute D on a charge unrelated to the one under investigation or to inform another agency about a prosecution (cf *Customs and Excise Comrs v Harz and Power* (1967)).

8.139   Where investigating officers use a suspect to make contact with others in ways which might incriminate the suspect, as in *R v De Silva* (2003) where a suspect denied knowledge of his possession of drugs but was persuaded to cooperate with the investigating officers in making a series of telephone calls to enable the arrest of others, the evidence of his co-operative conduct should have been excluded as a confession rendered unreliable by the inducement (or under s 78 ante).

Facts discovered as a result of an excluded confession

8.140   Section 76(4) (Art 74(4)) deals with the admissibility of evidence discovered as a result of an improperly obtained confession.

(1) Section 76(4), (5) and (6) (Art 74(5) and (6)) tackle the following problems. If a confession is declared to be inadmissible, can the prosecution still use evidence discovered as a consequence of that confession and, if so, for what purpose can it be used? For example, if during the investigation of a theft a confession is forced out of D by oppression and he tells the police where they can find the stolen goods, can the prosecution (a) produce the goods at D's trial and (b) link their discovery to what D told the police? The CLRC 11th Report 1971 unanimously recommended an affirmative answer to (a) and, by a majority, to (b). PACE opted for a half-way house. On the one hand, the prosecution can use in evidence 'any facts discovered as a result of the confession' even if the confession is itself inadmissible (s 76(4)(a), Art 74(4)(a)). On the other hand, proof that those facts were discovered as a result of a wholly or partly inadmissible confession is not admissible (s 76(5) and (6), (Art 74(5)(6)), unless the accused himself gives evidence that they were so discovered (s 76(5), Art 74(5) endorsing *R v Berriman* (1854)). The policy underlying this latter rule is that it is unfair for the inadmissibility of a confession to be negated by the admissibility of the 'fruits of the crime', unless the accused so chooses. This must be right where confessions are obtained by oppression but less supportable when unreliability is involved given that the finding of the stolen goods where D said they would be is a good indication of reliability. Be that as it may, in the example cited above, the law is that the prosecution can produce the stolen goods at trial but cannot show that they were discovered as a result of D's confession, unless D in examination in chief or cross-examination admits that he told the police where to find them. Note that where only a part of a confession is excluded, perhaps one interview out of a number, evidence found as a result of the admissible part is admissible (s 76(6)(b), Art 74(6)(b)).

(2) Those parts of a confession which are relevant as showing that the accused 'speaks, writes or expresses himself in a particular way' are admissible for that purpose (s 76(4)(b), Art 74(4)(b)). The object of this exception is illustrated by *R v Voisin* (1918) where the body of a murder victim had been found alongside a piece of paper bearing the words 'Bladie Belgiam'. The accused was asked by the police to write 'Bloody Belgian' and he happily wrote 'Bladie Belgiam'. This evidence was held to be admissible. *R v Voisin* did not involve an involuntary confession but it will be noted that s 76(4)(b) (Art 74(4)(b)) can apply even if the confession was improperly obtained and therefore inadmissible. In a modern-day example, D, suspected of spraying graffiti, was asked to write the sprayed words 'Mr Brown is a homosexual'. He wrote, as had the graffiti artist, 'Mr Broun is a homeosexal'. The limitation is that the confession can only be used to identify the characteristics mentioned in the subsection and not to establish the truth of anything said or written or to show that the accused had some special knowledge which only the offender could have had. If the accused has written his own confession which is excluded that may be used as a sample of his handwriting where relevant. If D is charged with kidnapping and the victim states that the kidnapper spoke with a local accent and stammered, non-incriminating parts of D's excluded tape-recorded

confession can be used for voice comparison. (See *R v Robb* (1991) and *R v Deenik* (1992) for the admissibility of voice recognition evidence by a non-expert such as a police or customs officer, discussed at para 7.183, ante.)

Confessions by the mentally handicapped (s 77 of PACE, Art 75 of the NI Order)

8.141   Section 77 of PACE (Art 75) provides that where the case against the accused depends wholly or substantially on a confession made by him and the court is satisfied:
(a)   that he is mentally handicapped; and
(b)   that the confession was not made in the presence of an independent person,
the court shall warn the jury that there is a special need for caution before convicting the accused in reliance on that confession.

8.142   Code C 11.15 provides that no interview with a mentally disordered or mentally handicapped person should take place unless an appropriate adult is present. The independent person referred to in s 77 must be independent of the person to whom the confession is made, thus a confession to a friend is not to an independent person *R v Bailey* (1995). It follows that this section should apply only in exceptional circumstances since any confession made in the absence of an appropriate adult is likely to fall foul of s 76(2)(b) and be excluded as unreliable – see for example *R v Moss* (1990) where a mentally disordered person was interviewed nine times over a long period before confessing. The trial judge admitted the confession and gave a s 77 warning but the Court of Appeal thought it should have been excluded under s 76(2)(b). There the Court of Appeal suggested that the section was directed at two types of cases:
(1)   where the interview had been in the emergency circumstances envisaged by Code C 11.1; and
(2)   where the interview was in breach of Code C 11.15 but consisted of not more than one interview over a short period.

8.143   The second of these may be doubted, there being no reason why an appropriate adult should not be present. In practice a prosecution is most unlikely when the prosecution case depends 'wholly or substantially' on a confession obtained in the circumstances envisaged by s 77. There will usually be other evidence taking the case outside the section – see for example *R v Campbell* (1995). In *R v McKenzie* (1993) D, a mentally disordered man with a personality disorder, was convicted of two offences of manslaughter and two of arson. The prosecution case on the manslaughter charge depended almost entirely on his unsupported confession while the arson charges were supported by other evidence. Quashing the convictions for manslaughter the Court of Appeal held that, where D suffers from a 'significant degree' of mental illness and the case against him depends wholly upon confessions which are 'unconvincing to the point where a jury properly directed could not convict upon them' then the trial judge, assuming he has not already excluded the confessions, should withdraw the case from the jury. The confessions were unconvincing because they lacked the incriminating details which would have made them reliable and because D had confessed to 12 other killings which no one believed he had committed. There was also the possibility that he had confessed to ensure that he stayed in the secure hospital where he was detained. Similarly in *R v Wood* (1994), decided before the decision in McKenzie, where D, with a verbal IQ of 76 and a reading age of nine, admitted striking the deceased child the day before his death but the agreed medical evidence was that the blows which killed the child were inflicted on the day of the death.

8.144 The effect of these decisions is that cases are unlikely to proceed on the basis of a confession from a mentally disordered person unless it contains incriminating details of a kind only the guilty person would know or it is supported by other independent evidence. This highlights the need to test the accused's admissions or confession against the known facts and to do what is reasonable to establish the reliability of what has been said – a sensible precaution in most cases but an essential requirement where vulnerable suspects are involved (see further para 7.249, ante). There is nothing in the authorities which limits or defines the particular form of mental or psychological condition or disorder (*R v Walker* (1998)); the importance is whether the confession is unreliable, not the diagnostic label (*R v Roberts* (1998)).

Confessions and s 78 (Art 76)

8.145 (NB: For brevity 's 78' will be used throughout.) It was initially thought that s 76 provided a strict regime for the admissibility of confessions and if the prosecution succeeded in discharging the burden of proof under that section there was little room for discretionary exclusion and it was doubted whether s 78 would apply to confessions. These doubts were not shared by the courts and in *R v Mason* (1987) the Court of Appeal made it clear that s 78 did apply to confessions. While its use was justifiable in that case it has been relied upon to exclude confessions in many cases in which its use was less justifiable and in circumstances in which s 76 appeared to be more appropriate. For example, in *R v Howden-Simpson* (1991) the interviewing officer told the accused that he would be charged with two offences only if he confessed. If he did not, many charges would be brought. This is precisely the sort of threat or inducement with which s 76(2)(b) was intended to deal. The trial judge considered and rejected it. The Court of Appeal went further and decided that s 78 should have been relied upon to exclude the confession because the officer had indicated what action he would take if D did not confess, in breach of Code C 11.3. Similarly, in *R v Fogah* (1989) a juvenile was questioned in the absence of an appropriate adult. The latter's presence is required by the Code C 11.14, partly in order to protect the vulnerable D from making unreliable admissions, yet the court used s 78 to exclude them. The correct vehicle for handling this type of case is, it is submitted, s 76(2)(b) and in relying on s 78 the Court may, in effect, be excluding inadmissible evidence which is not the function of s 78 (see Ralph Gibson LJ in *Halawa v FACT* [1995] 1 Cr App Rep 21 at 33). It is sensible to see ss 76 and 78 as a series of hurdles (see Birch [1988] Crim LR 95) over which the prosecution can be made to jump and which should be approached in order unless it is obvious that one or more does not apply. The first hurdle is oppression under s 76(2)(a). As indicated above this requires serious impropriety and it will rarely be the case that the prosecution fails to clear this hurdle. The second hurdle is s 76(2)(b). Since this requires no impropriety, includes anything said or done in the particular circumstances which include the personal characteristics of the accused and can often be evidenced by breaches of the Code, it is an extremely broad hurdle made more difficult by the requirement that the prosecution prove beyond reasonable doubt that the confession was not obtained in breach of that subsection. If the prosecution succeed in discharging that heavy burden there is the third hurdle of s 78. Though often labelled 'unfairness', the section requires that the judge be persuaded that in all the circumstances, including those in which the evidence was obtained, the admission of the evidence would have such an adverse effect of the fairness of the trial that the court ought not to admit it. Under s 78 it is for the defence to raise sufficient evidence to persuade the court that the challenged evidence would have this adverse effect on the fairness of the trial which means that they have to clear this lesser hurdle before the prosecution have to clear the larger hurdle of rebutting that evidence.

8.146   In deciding whether to rely on s 76 or s 78 (or both since it is clear law that they may be used by the defence consecutively (*R v Alladice* (1988))) one must examine all the circumstances in which the confession was alleged to have been made, including the relevant characteristics of the accused. The following guidelines are suggested.

(a)   If there is serious impropriety which may be oppressive within the Fulling definition s 76(2)(a) should be relied upon in the first instance.

(b)   If the impropriety amounts to something said or done (or not done) which was likely in the circumstances to lead to an unreliable confession, s 76(2)(b) should be relied upon.

(c)   If what is said or done does not involve police impropriety, or is not said or done by the police (cf *R v Harvey* (1988)), but is nevertheless likely to lead to an unreliable confession, s 76(2)(b) should be relied upon.

(d)   If the manner in which the confession was obtained does not amount to something said or done but is nevertheless likely to lead to an unreliable confession; or is something not done after the confession was made, eg no contemporaneous record, or record not shown to the accused, which puts a question mark on the accuracy of the recording, and therefore the reliability, of the confession, s 76(2) does not apply and s 78 must be relied upon.

(e)   If the manner in which the confession was obtained does amount to something improperly said or done but which is not likely in the circumstances to lead to an unreliable confession, eg *R v Mason* (1987) where the deception induced a truthful and therefore reliable confession, s 78 must be relied upon. (One may note that under s 78, unlike s 76, the truth of the confession can be relied upon to demonstrate the reliability of the confession, but the fact that it is true does not mean that admitting it will not have an adverse effect on the fairness of the trial.)

(f)   There are some circumstances in which Code C cannot apply in its entirety, eg undercover operations. Here the courts are more concerned with the reliability of any statements made than the conduct of the police. If there is an unassailable record of what was said and done, or evidence supporting its reliability, it is unlikely that the courts will see the police conduct as likely to lead to an unreliable confession, see for example *R v Smurthwaite and Gill* (1994); *R v Dixon and Mann* (1994); *R v Khalid Latif* (1995), and are also unlikely to exercise their discretion under s 78. (In the case of Colin Stagg, 14 September 1994, evidence was excluded at first instance under s 78 and/or at common law. On either basis Ognall J was satisfied that the conduct of a fair trial demanded the exclusion, because it was obtained by a trick in which the accused was manipulated and attempts were made to incriminate him by deceptive conduct. However, the evidence may be seen as lacking in the reliability demanded by the above cases and in so far as it amounted to a confession could have been excluded under s 76(2)(b).)

(g)   Other tricks like covert bugging of cells or other places, or setting traps to catch thieves, appear to be acceptable if the resultant evidence is reliable, as it usually is in such circumstances. This too may be seen as something done which was not likely to lead to unreliable confessions therefore s 76(2)(b) does not apply and s 78 is unlikely to apply, see for example, *R v Jelen and Katz* (1989); *R v Bailey and Smith* (1993); *Williams v DPP* (1993); *R v Christou and Wright* (1992).

(h)   In a number of recent cases the Court of Appeal has expressed the view that once the judge had decided that there was nothing to require the exclusion of a confession under s 76, it was difficult to see why the evidence should have been excluded under s 78 (see *R v Weeks* (1995) and *R v Campbell* (1995)). As the commentary to the latter case says,

> 'Admissible confessions are often excluded; but the fact that the confession passes the s 76 test certainly suggests that, prima facie, its admission would not have an adverse effect on the fairness of the proceedings.'

This supports the three-hurdle approach suggested above.

8.147   When s 78 is raised, the court has a discretion as to whether to hold a voir dire (*Carlisle v DPP* (1987)). How it should exercise that discretion is unclear. If, as it often will be, the confession is the central plank of the prosecution's case, its admissibility should be argued early on in the trial and in a voir dire and may be coupled with an application to exclude under s 76. Hodgson J in *R v Keenan* (1990) distinguished three situations in which the appropriate procedure may vary:

(a)   where evidence of police irregularity is plain for all to see (eg on the custody record) and the prosecution will concede and argument follows as to whether the confession evidence should be excluded under s 78;

(b)   where there is prima facie evidence of irregularity and the prosecution seeks to justify it and argue against exclusion – the defence may wish to call evidence, occasionally even the defendant himself; and

(c)   the comparatively rare case where the alleged breaches can probably only be established by the evidence of the defendant himself.

8.148 Hodgson J also posed the problem that, in determining the effect, if any, of the evidence on the fairness of the trial under s 78, if objection is taken early on in the trial, the judge is unlikely to know D's likely defence and is in a difficult position to decide whether admissibility of the evidence will adversely affect the fairness of the proceedings. The answer, it is suggested, is to require more from the defence at the voir dire. Indeed, if D's case is thin, the onus lies on him (see below) to establish the unfairness, if necessary by giving evidence (see the commentary to *R v Rajakuruna* (1991)).

8.149 When magistrates are faced with an application to exclude evidence under s 78, the magistrates must deal with it when it arises or leave the decision until the end of the prosecution case, including the disputed evidence (possibly the better course given that the issue under s 78 is to be determined 'having regard to all the circumstances'), with the objective of ensuring a trial which is fair and just to both sides (*Halawa v FACT* (1995)).

8.150 Unlike s 76 (Art 74), there is no direction in s 78 as to the burden and standard proof. In most cases the defence will raise the issue, though there is nothing to prevent the court doing so of its own motion (cf s 76(3), Art 74(3)). Unless D objects, the prosecution 'proposes to rely' on the evidence (s 78), therefore D must clearly raise s 78 and point to some evidence to suggest that the admission of the evidence would have such an adverse effect on the fairness of the trial that it ought not to be admitted. Sometimes this will be readily apparent (eg *R v Mason* (1987)), in other cases D will have to produce evidence. But, as will be seen, misconduct by the police is not the criterion for s 78; the defence must go further and suggest to the court that the fairness of the proceedings will be adversely affected if the confession is admitted. Once this evidential burden has been discharged, the task falls then to the prosecution to rebut the alleged adverse effect on the fairness of the trial. As to the overall burden of proof, on a strict reading of s 78 (and in contrast to the express instructions of s 76) it is suggested that the burden of proof lies on the defence – they must convince the court to such an extent 'that it appears to the court' that s 78 is satisfied. If this is correct then the standard is the civil one (partly because of the word 'appears' and partly in line with the general rule of evidence that a burden of proof on the accused is to be discharged to the balance of probabilities). In seeking to rebut the case presented by the defence the prosecution would appear to have to persuade the judge beyond reasonable doubt. The cases have not yet squarely confronted these issues and there are indications that (see the commentary to *R v Keenan* (1990)) an evidential burden lies initially on D and that, if the legal burden lies anywhere, it is on the prosecution (see also *R v Beveridge* (1987); *Vel v Owen* (1987)). The following preliminary points can be noted.

(1) Section 78 only applies to the evidence on which the prosecution proposes to rely. This means that in a jury trial it must be argued before the evidence is given. On summary trial it may be argued at that point or at the end of the prosecution case including the disputed evidence (*Halawa v FACT* (1995)).

(2) The evidence must adversely affect the fairness of 'proceedings' and these are defined (s 82(1), Art 76) as criminal proceedings (thus including a court-martial).

(3) Though it is the adverse effect on the fairness of the proceedings which concerns the court, the whole of the investigatory stage is open to scrutiny.

(4) Section 78 is quite separate from the common law power to exclude confessions (s 82(3), *R v Sat-Bhambra* (1988), see further at para 8.69, post) though that too is concerned with the fairness of the trial (*R v Sang* (1980)).

(5) In one of the earliest decisions on PACE it was decided by the Court of Appeal that s 78 applies to confessions and that they are not the sole preserve of s 76 (*R v Mason* (1987)).

(6) The relevant confession has usually been made to the police but this is not essential. Section 78 can be used to try to exclude a confession made to others (eg a doctor as in *R v McDonald* (1991)).

(7) One useful supporting role for s 78 is where the prosecution has not used D's confession (because it was obtained in breach of s 78) but D2 proposes to raise it. Since s 76 only concerns a confession which 'the prosecution proposes to give' (s 76(2)), it could be unfair to allow D2 to do so. The s 78 discretion could be used to prevent him doing so.

(8) The court exercises a discretion and this gives the trial judge some leeway. Provided that he interprets PACE and the Codes correctly (no mean achievement) and professes to consider all the circumstances, the chances of a successful appeal are considerably diminished (*R v O'Leary* (1988)). The existence of this discretion means also that it should not be fettered by the erection of rules – each decision rests on its particular facts (cf *R v Canale* (1990) and *R v Gillard and Barrett* (1991)). If an appellate court concludes that the discretion has been wrongly exercised (or not exercised at all), it may be able to put itself in the position of the trial judge and consider whether or how the discretion should have been exercised (*R v Parris* (1988)).

(9) Section 76(4), (5) (see para 8.140, post) is applicable only to a confession excluded under that section. There is no equivalent in s 78; however, it is open to a court to decide that it is unfair to admit evidence found in consequence of a confession which has been excluded under s 78 and to exclude it under that section.

(10) Occasionally a judge has remarked that it is not the court's function to punish/ discipline the police for failure to observe PACE and the Codes (*R v Delaney* (1988); *R v Fennelley* (1989)). However, it is suggested that such reasoning is disingenuous for, no matter how the court expresses it, an inevitable consequence of exclusion of evidence is that the police are disciplined by the collapse of a prosecution. Hodgson J, it is submitted, came closer to the mark in *R v Samuel* (1988) when he described police disciplinary procedures as 'a much less secure method of ensuring compliance' with PACE than ss 76 and 78 (cf the trenchant criticism of police conduct by Lord Lane CJ in *R v Canale* (1990) and more recently of officers of Customs and Excise whose disregard of Code C caused the Court in *R v Weerdesteyn* (1995) some concern).

8.151 The terse terms of s 78 give little help as to their proper interpretation and the courts have displayed a range of approaches. Three general points can be made. First, the section is to be construed widely (*R v Keenan* (1990)). Second, the test is fairness of the proceedings, not fairness to the defence. In other words, fairness to the prosecution and to the court (that it be able to hear all the relevant evidence) must also be considered (*DPP v Marshall* (1988); *R v Quinn* (1990); *R v Kerawalla* (1991)). Third, as Auld J remarked in *R v Katz* (1989):

'The circumstances of each case are almost always different, and judges may well take different views in the proper exercise of their discretion even where the circumstances are similar. This is not an apt field for hard case law and well-founded distinctions between cases.'

8.152 In *R v Oliphant* (1992) the Court of Appeal further emphasised the need to consider the facts of each case against the statutory language of PACE when it said, per curiam:

'It is important, in deciding admissibility of evidence under PACE, not to be diverted by other decisions of the court, often on different facts, from considering the statutory language.'

8.153 Whilst recognising the unpredictable nature of s 78, it is possible to identify factors which have influenced its use. The commonest trigger for the application of s 78 is where the defence can prove that there has been a breach of PACE or the Codes of Practice. In principle, breach of the former should be treated more seriously since the Codes are not binding on the courts (the point was raised but not pursued in *R v Keenan* (1990)), but what should matter is the relevance of the breach to the fairness of the proceedings and, since Codes C and E have far more to say on interrogation procedures than the statute, in practice breaches of the Codes are usually of greater relevance for the reception of confessions. It has been clearly established that not every breach of correct procedures will be greeted with exclusion of evidence. Thus in *R v Walsh* (1989) it was said that a breach of Code C meant that prima facie at least the standards of fairness set by Parliament have not been met and any evidence admitted in such circumstances must have an adverse effect on the fairness of the trial, but this does not mean that in every case of a significant and substantial breach exclusion under s 78 was automatic.

'The task of the court is not merely to consider whether there would be an adverse effect on the fairness of the proceedings, but such an adverse effect that justice requires the evidence to be excluded.'

(See also *R v Keenan* above; *R v Parris* (1989); *R v Waters* (1989); *R v Delaney* (1988).)

8.154 Much depends on the type and extent of the breach. Thus, exclusion is more likely if the breach is flagrant (*R v Canale* (1990), where the Lord Chief Justice found a cynical disregard of the rules governing the contemporaneous recording of interviews) or wilful (*R v Nagah* (1990) where, although D agreed to an identification parade, he was released so that a street identification could more easily be made), and in bad faith (see the remarks by Lord Lane CJ in *R v Alladice* (1988) that a court might find it easier to employ s 78 if bad faith on the part of the police is proved, but in *R v Walsh* it was made clear that breaches which are in themselves significant and substantial are not rendered otherwise by the good faith of the officers concerned). Correspondingly, mistaken conduct on the part of the police carried out in good faith may tilt against the use of s 78 or at least be a neutral factor in the equation (see *R v Clarke* (1989) where the officers did not realise that D was deaf, but the breach of (now) Code C 13.5 could still be considered by the court; *R v Younis* (1990) where the suspect 'volunteered' most of the remarks in the police car and there was no evidence of deliberate police prompting; see also *R v Kerawalla* (1991) where the absence of bad faith was a factor). However, unlike s 76(2)(a), impropriety is not essential (*R v O'Leary* (1988); *R v Samuel* (1988)) and good faith does not remedy a significant breach of PACE procedures. If the procedure is regarded by the court as an important one, it does not matter whether lack of adherence to it was wilful or through ignorance, the effect on the proceedings being the same in either case. See, for example, *R v Walsh* (1989) involving, inter alia, denial of legal advice, omitting to note the reason for not recording an interview contemporaneously, and failure to show D the record of interview. These were regarded as significant and substantial breaches which were not cured by good faith. This case has become the standard reference point for cases involving breach of PACE and the Codes, particularly those involving wrongful exclusion of a solicitor, but, as Woolf LJ pointed out in *R v Oliphant* (1992), the words 'significant' and 'substantial' are not terms of art but are simply offered as guides to ruling out of consideration those merely technical breaches which have no adverse consequences. Similarly in *R v Foster* (1987), the officer failed to appreciate that his brief chat with D in the street was an interview for PACE purposes and therefore did not make a contemporaneous record of it (for a similar mistake by an inexperienced officer, see *R v Sparks* (1991)). This then focuses attention on the type of PACE procedure which has been breached. It should be noted that 'the mere fact that there has been a breach of the Codes of Practice does not of itself mean that evidence has to be rejected' (per Lord Lane CJ in *R v Delaney* (1988)). A link between the breach and fairness to the proceedings must be established (eg *R v Hughes* (1988); *R v Dunford* (1990)). If the PACE procedure is an important safeguard for the suspect, an adverse effect on the fairness of the proceedings is inevitable and that effect is likely to be so adverse that justice demands the exclusion of any evidence thus obtained. Chief of these are the provisions designed to prevent verballing of the suspect (ie concocted admissions) – see *R v Keenan* (1990). Transgression of them often leads to exclusion under s 78 because:

(a) it is unfair to deprive D of his rights (especially legal advice);
(b) it is unfair to the court since it is deprived of a more accurate record of an interview (eg a contemporaneous record);
(c) it is unfair for the criminal process since admission of the confession would allow one side (the prosecution) to win by foul play.

8.155 These reasons appear throughout the cases, though often they are not articulated, especially (c). Indeed sometimes the court, despite what was said in *R v Walsh* (above), having found improprieties, proceed almost automatically to apply s 78 without considering the statutory language (*R v Hughes* (1988)). This category of safeguards is essentially twofold:

(1) provision of legal or other advice; and
(2) the accurate recording of an interview either by a contemporaneous record or by showing D a summary of the interview.

Provision of legal or other advice

8.156 The starting point in this category is *R v Samuel* (1988) where D was interviewed after being improperly denied a solicitor (see further para 7.65, ante). Section 76 was not pleaded before the Court of Appeal but s 78 was, and the Court concluded that denial of 'one of the most important and fundamental rights of a citizen' – legal advice – could well have an adverse effect on the proceedings. This conclusion was assisted by the finding that, if the solicitor had been allowed access, he would probably have advised silence. It emphasises that denial of legal advice per se is not enough. It must also be shown that it produced an adverse effect. (For another early case of improper denial of legal advice, see *R v Smith* (1987).) The point was made again in *R v Alladice* (1988), where a solicitor was wrongly denied access (a clear breach of s 58 of PACE and Code C); the interview was otherwise conducted properly, and the solicitor would probably have reminded D of his right to silence but D, being used to police interviews, already knew that (indeed he exercised it at times during the interview), therefore the solicitor's presence would not have made a difference and there was no unfairness to the proceedings. The same situation was seen in *R v Dunford* (1990), where the improper denial of legal advice was balanced by D's knowledge of his rights and ability to cope on his own. Similarly *R v Oliphant* (1992), where D asked if he could talk to his solicitor, the interviewing officer agreed he could, but D went on to make full and extensive admissions. The trial judge's ruling that the breach of s 58 of PACE and Code C 6.6 was not significant or substantial; the view that the presence of a solicitor would have added nothing to what O knew about his rights, and therefore had no adverse effect on the proceedings, was upheld by the Court of Appeal. In *R v Chahal* (1992) D said he did not want a solicitor and later confirmed this. However, unknown to him his family had instructed a solicitor who attended but was told D did not want a solicitor. His appeal against conviction was dismissed. He was a mature businessman who knew what he was about and had suffered no prejudice. This may be compared with *R v Franklin* (1994), where D initially said he did not want a solicitor. Ten minutes later he asked that his father be informed of his arrest and that he would get a solicitor for him. He was then interviewed twice, having agreed to be interviewed without a solicitor being present, and made admissions. In the meantime D's father had telephoned the police station but D was not told of this, though it was recorded in the custody record. The father instructed a solicitor who attended at the police station but was told that D would not be informed because he did not want a solicitor (see now Code C 6.15 considered at para 7.70, ante). Two further interviews followed at which D was reminded of his right to legal advice but not told that a solicitor had attended. The trial judge admitted the evidence of all four interviews believing he was bound by *R v Chahal*. The Court of Appeal disagreed. There were significant differences between the two cases. In Chahal the solicitor had merely telephoned and C was a mature businessman. In Franklin the solicitor actually attended and D was a young unemployed man who had never been in a police station before. The trial judge had therefore exercised his discretion wrongly, but the case against D was overwhelming and the proviso was applied and the appeal dismissed.

8.157 (For comments on the importance of legal advice, see also *R v Dunn* (1990).) Other cases in which denial of access to legal advice led to exclusion of the confession include:
- *R v Vernon* (1988), where D was not told of the duty solicitor scheme or that a solicitor was on the way;
- *R v Absolam* (1988), where D was not told of his right to legal advice and proceeded to make damaging admissions; and to similar effect *R v Williams* (1989);
- *R v Parris* (1988), where s 58 was wrongly used to delay legal advice; a solicitor's presence would probably have led D to use his right of silence and at the least would have given the court a witness to the interrogation to help it decide between the police and D's version;
- *R v Beycan* (1990), where D was wrongfully denied a solicitor being told 'we usually interview without a solicitor ...' This was particularly unfair since he was a foreigner with poor English and therefore vulnerable. Similarly *R v Sanusi* (1992).

(See Cousens and Blair, *Butterworths Police and Criminal Evidence Act Cases*, Part V for the above and a number of unreported cases involving alleged breaches of s 58 of PACE.)

8.158 The complexity of the offence under investigation may increase the need for legal advice and the adverse effect of its denial (see *R v Guest* (1988), a charge of principal in the second degree to murder; as Ognall J drily observed, an area of law 'not free from difficulty even among experienced criminal lawyers'). The complexity added by ss 34 to 37 of the Criminal Justice and Public Order Act 1994 also increases the need for legal advice in the police station and the adverse effect of the lack of it (see [1995] Crim LR 483). Even the Alladices of this world may not fully appreciate their potential effect.

8.159 The advice need not be that of a lawyer: in *R v Fogah* (1989) D, a juvenile, was improperly interviewed without the protection of an appropriate adult's presence.

Accurate recording

8.160 Examples of a failure to comply with category (2), the accurate recording of an interview, are:
- *R v Canale* (1990), where interviews were not contemporaneously recorded and the reason given on the subsequent record of interview was 'b.w.' (ie 'best way' is not to record an interview contemporaneously) – this 'lamentable attitude' (Lord Lane CJ) towards proper police procedures strongly influenced the Court of Appeal's decision to use s 78;

- *R v Dunn* (1990), where there had been a failure to record a conversation – prima facie a reason for exclusion of it, but this was balanced by the presence of D's legal adviser during the interview.
- cf *R v Matthews* (1989), where D's comments were noted after the interview ended but the note was not shown to her, a clear breach of the Code – the Court of Appeal did not disturb the trial judge's refusal to use s 78, apparently on the basis (or lack of it) that he had considered all the circumstances and his discretion could not be challenged;
- *R v Scott* (1991), where D made an incriminating remark, unprompted by the police, which was noted but not shown to D for his immediate denial or confirmation; instead he was forced to deny it at trial, thus exposing himself to prejudicial cross-examination and this was held to be unfair for s 78 purposes;
- *R v Maloney and Doherty* (1988), where interviews outside and inside the station were not contemporaneously recorded, notes of the interviews were not shown to the suspects and, although they could not read, no lawyer or third party was made available to assist them;
- *RSPCA v Eager* (1995), where E was interviewed in her home by RSPCA inspectors who compiled their record of the interview in their car afterwards giving E no opportunity to read it or sign it as correct.

8.161 Compare *R v Courtney* (1995), where Customs officers intercepted parcels of herbal cannabis and posed as a postman to deliver them to D's address. A note of D's comments on the doorstep was made but was not shown to D. The breach was not significant or substantial and the note was admitted.

8.162 Some cases will involve both categories (1) and (2) – see *R v Walsh* (1989) where legal advice was improperly denied, the interview was not contemporaneously recorded and the eventual record was not shown to D. These were significant and substantial breaches of PACE procedures, and the good faith of the officers could not prevent the application of s 78, the effect on the trial being the same whether the officers acted in good or bad faith (cf to like effect, *R v Williams* (1989)). In contrast, there are many minor provisions in the Code, breach of which will have no effect on the fairness of the trial (eg failure to supply meals and drink on time; *R v Deacon* (1987) where failures to record the time when an interview finished and to allow eight hours' continuous rest were considered by the court but clearly did not weigh heavily); and the courts have frequently remarked that it is not every breach of the Code that will lead to exclusion under s 78 (Keenan; Parris). As suggested in Walsh and subsequent cases the breaches must be significant and substantial to justify exclusion. Those provisions that are mandatory are more likely to be so and to warrant exclusion than those which are directory (*R v Grier* (1989)). Also, there may be an accumulation of minor breaches of procedure which together justify the exercise of the s 78 discretion (eg *R v Moss* (1990)).

8.163 Section 78 has also been used to condemn the tactics and content of police questioning. In fact this was the concern of the first leading case on the section, *R v Mason* (1987). Following an arson attack, D was questioned by the police who, in the absence of other evidence, falsely told him and then his solicitor that D's fingerprints had been found on the bottle used to carry the petrol. D then confessed to his involvement. The Court of Appeal was enraged that D's solicitor had been hoodwinked ('a most reprehensible thing'), thereby affecting the advice he gave his client, and used s 78 to exclude D's confession. This does not mean that deceit practised on D alone is legitimate. On the contrary, the court issued a stern rebuke against such deception but has since distinguished the deception involved in undercover operations (*R v Christou and Wright* (1992); *R v Smurthwaite and Gill* (1994)) and the deception involved in covert bugging of cells or other places (*R v Bailey* (1993); *R v Khan* (1994)). (Bugging a meeting between solicitor and client, which conversation is legally privileged, is likely to be considered even more reprehensible than deceiving the solicitor and lead to the almost certain exclusion of any evidence thus obtained.) This has wider implications and could prevent an interviewing officer from telling D falsely that a co-accused has already confessed and spilled the beans on D. It could be different if the officer truthfully told D that another person or even a lover had already confessed. That might not constitute oppression for s 76(2)(a) (see *R v Fulling* (1987); para 8.114, ante) and, in the light of *R v Mason* (1989), would not trigger s 78, though it may satisfy s 76(2)(b) depending on the impact it may have on the particular suspect and the likely unreliability of anything he says (see *R v Harvey* (1988) and para 8.49, ante). Another example of s 78 in this context is suggested by *R v Howden-Simpson* (1991), where the interviewing officer had told D that if he confessed he would be charged with only two offences, but if he denied it he would be separately charged on a number of counts. Despite being conduct falling squarely within s 76(2)(b) the Court of Appeal suggested that such an inducement could well fall foul of s 78 (see the powerful commentary to the decision in the Criminal Law Review). In *R v Sparks* (1991) the failure to caution (and to record the interview) was a substantial breach of Code C and warranted exclusion of the conversation under s 78. See also *R v Saunders* (1988) where the key component of a caution (that D need not say anything) was omitted. Again, as in Sparks, there was also a breach of the recording provisions for interviews. On the other hand, failure to tell/remind D that he is a 'volunteer' and free to leave (Code C 10.2) is not necessarily a substantial breach (*R v Rajakuruna* (1991)), particularly where D ought to have known that he was a suspect in an investigation.

8.164   The suspect's character and the effect of police conduct on him may be important. If he is of stout disposition, well versed in criminal procedure and able to look after himself in interviews, s 78 may not exercised (see *R v Canale* where D had served in a paratroop regiment; *R v Alladice* where D was well aware of, and in fact used, his right of silence; see also *R v Osman* and *R v Dunford* where D has previous convictions and experience of police interviews). Whereas for a frail suspect, unused to police procedures, breaches of PACE and the Codes may have much greater significance for the fairness of the trial (cf *R v Beycan* (1990) and *R v Sanusi* (1992) where D was a foreign citizen with poor English and no experience of the criminal process). Similarly, the fact that D is mentally disordered or handicapped is a relevant circumstance to be taken into account – *R v Bailey* (1995). The presence of other evidence against D should not affect the decision whether there is unfairness (that aspect is the preserve of s 2(1) of the Criminal Appeal Act 1968, the proviso to which can counterbalance any exclusion of evidence under s 78) – *R v Walsh* (1989). However, where there is enough other evidence to convict D, the court might be more easily persuaded to exclude the peripheral and disputed evidence whilst still allowing the rest to go before the jury (*R v Waters* (1989); *R v Keenan* (1990)). By contrast the absence of other evidence, apart from the disputed area, could be crucial to the fairness of the trial (in *R v Canale* (1990) the disputed interviews were the only effective evidence against D, and see *R v Cochrane* (1988) where the interviews were the only evidence against D and, since s 58 had been transgressed, it was unfair to use them). That other evidence may even be linked to and infected by the disputed area (*R v Beycan* (1990) where it was held that once s 78 excluded admissions at the station, it was unfair to admit statements made in the car en route there). Indeed, as with s 76 (*R v Ismail* (1990), see further para 8.110, ante) an earlier, improper interview may affect a subsequent, proper one such as to warrant the latter's exclusion as well. This may be because the impropriety still influences the later interview, or because the court is determined not to let the police flagrantly flout the rules and then 'get away with it' by obeying them (*R v Canale* (1990)). However, the court, in exercising its discretion, may find that the later interview is not so tainted and can refrain from using s 78 (see *R v Gillard and Barrett* (1990); the distinction between this case and Canale, above, is narrow and seems to depend on the degree of flagrancy of misconduct).

8.165 As has been seen, police misconduct is the most regular reason for exclusion under s 78. This does not mean that fairness to the accused is the criterion for its use. Fairness of the proceedings is the criterion. This means that the trial judge must balance the effect of admitting the evidence on the trial as a whole, including the effect on the prosecution and the public interest in ensuring that all relevant evidence is admitted. Thus, in *R v Hughes* (1988) it was decided that D had genuinely consented to an interview without a solicitor and that balancing the interests of the prosecution and of the defence did not require the use of s 78 (see also *R v Oliphant* (1992)). As the court pointed out in *R v Kerawalla* (1991), the overall fairness of the proceedings has to be judged.

The common law

8.166 Before PACE and Order, a trial judge who found that a confession had been obtained by oppression or as a result of threats or inducements from a person in authority which rendered it involuntary, would exclude it as a matter of law. There was also, it seemed, a discretion to exclude a confession obtained in breach of the Judges' Rules, the precursor of what is now Code C. Whether such a breach rendered the confession involuntary and therefore inadmissible as a matter of law, or whether the judge had a discretion to exclude a voluntary confession obtained in breach of the Judges' Rules, was never very clear, nor was the basis of any discretion to exclude confessions. Section 76 (Art 74) now provides a wider test of the admissibility of confessions.

8.167   So far as non-confessional evidence was concerned the common law was not concerned with how it was obtained but only with the effect that the evidence had on the fairness of the trial. In *R v Sang* (1980) the House of Lords said that there was no defence of entrapment and there was therefore no power to exclude otherwise admissible evidence on the ground that if the offence was committed it was at the instigation of an agent provocateur. Their Lordships accepted that a judge in a criminal trial has a general discretion to refuse to admit evidence where its probable prejudicial effect so outweighed its probative value as to make its admission unfair to the accused, but went on to say that, save with regard to admissions and confessions and generally with regard to evidence obtained from the accused after commission of an offence, the judge has no discretion to refuse to admit relevant and otherwise admissible evidence solely on the ground that it was obtained by improper or unfair means. The common law discretion to exclude applied only to prosecution evidence and was concerned not with how the evidence was obtained but with the effect of the evidence on the fairness of the trial.

8.168   Section 78 now provides a broad discretion to exclude any evidence, including confessional evidence obtained in a manner which while not rendering it unreliable would have an adverse effect on the fairness of the trial if admitted (*R v Mason* (1987)). It is broader than the common law discretion in that it can take into account the manner in which the evidence was obtained in determining its effect on the fairness of the trial but like the common law is concerned with the effect the evidence has on the fairness of the trial. It is narrower than the common law in that it only applies to evidence upon which the prosecution proposes to rely. Neither it, nor s 76, can be exercised to exclude evidence once it has been admitted.

8.169   Section 82(3) of PACE preserves any power of a court to exclude evidence. In the light of s 78 is there any role left for the common law discretion? One use was suggested in *R v Sat-Bhambra* (1988). As indicated above ss 76 and 78 are prospective only but the common law discretion allows the court to remedy earlier unfairness to the accused by excluding a previously admitted confession (after a voir dire D's confession had been admitted, but later on hearing further medical evidence the judge changed his mind). It thus remains as a separate head for excluding evidence but in almost all cases where evidence could properly be excluded at common law it can be excluded under s 78 (see Lord Lane CJ in *R v Delaney* (1988); May LJ in *R v O'Leary* (1988); and *Matto v Wolverhampton Crown Court* (1987)). It may also be the case that where the evidence would not be excluded at common law it will not be excluded under s 78. Thus, in *R v Stewart* (1995), it was argued that evidence of meter tampering, which proved the offence of fraudulent abstraction of electricity, should be excluded under s 78 because of breaches of s 16 of PACE and Code B in the manner in which a warrant of entry under the Rights of Entry (Gas and Electricity Boards) Act 1954 was executed. In dismissing the appeal the Court of Appeal found it unnecessary to decide whether PACE or Code applied, but, even assuming that they did, the Court found no unfairness in admitting the evidence which was there for all to see whether the entry was effected properly or not. This is consistent with the common law's approach to the exclusion of real evidence. There is no question of unreliability, the evidence speaks for itself and whilst its admission may operate unfortunately for the accused it does not operate unfairly.

8.170   Elsewhere it is suggested that the common law has no role to play since ss 76 and 78 have not only supplemented it but have also extended the court's powers to exclude confessions.

Northern Ireland

8.171   In Northern Ireland, Arts 74 and 76 of the PACE Order govern the admissibility of most confessions, but where a scheduled offence (ie a terrorist investigation) is involved, s 8 of the Northern Ireland (Emergency Provisions) Act 1978 (as amended in 1987) takes over (Art 74(9) and Art 76(2)(b) excludes s 8 from the operation of those Articles). The vast majority of cases will be tried on indictment and will be conducted without a jury. In the rare, summary, trial the PACE Order governs. Where the case is tried on indictment and the prosecution proposes to rely on a statement by D, and,

'... prima facie evidence is adduced that the accused was subject to torture, to inhuman or degrading treatment, or to any violence or threat of violence (whether or not amounting to torture), in order to induce him to make the statement,

then, unless the prosecution satisfies the court that the statement was not obtained by so subjecting the accused in the manner indicated by that evidence, the court shall do one of the following things, namely –
(i)   in the case of a statement proposed to be given in evidence, exclude the statement;
(ii)   in the case of a statement already received in evidence, continue the trial disregarding the statement; or
(iii) in either case, direct that the trial shall be restarted before a differently constituted court (before which the statement in question shall be inadmissible)' (s 8(2)).

8.172   The equivalent provision in the PACE Order (Art 74(2)(a)) is much wider since its criterion of 'oppression' has been relatively liberally interpreted by *R v Fulling* (1987). The 1978 Act lacks an equivalent to Art 74(2)(b) and, moreover, the Act's equivalent of Art 76 in the PACE Order is expressed differently, viz the court has a discretion to do one of (i) to (iii) above in respect of a confession 'if it appears to the court that it is appropriate to do so in order to avoid unfairness to the accused or otherwise in the interests of justice' (s 8(3)). This wording is sufficiently close to that of Art 76 to enable courts in Northern Ireland to follow the principled approach of the mainland courts in applying s 78 of PACE.

9 Covert policing

INTRODUCTION

9.1 Marx (1988) distinguishes between four broad categories of police work. First there is work that is overt and non-deceptive. Conventional police work, where the police act in response to reports of crime by victims, witnesses and so on, falls into this category. Secondly there is police work that is overt and deceptive, as where, for example, a suspect is tricked by police officers into providing a confession. Thirdly, police work may be covert and non-deceptive, an example being passive surveillance operations. Finally there is police work that is covert and deceptive, and this is the category into which most undercover operations fall. This chapter is concerned with the third and fourth categories.

9.2 Taylor (2003) has identified a number of reasons for the move by investigative agencies towards techniques of surveillance and covert operations:

- the development of information technologies which provides a new site for policing activities
- the trend away from reactive to proactive policing strategies
- the statutory scheme governing covert operations is less well established than PACE
- surveillance techniques provide high quality evidence tantamount to confessions without the need to interview
- covert operations can bring speedy results.

These factors are also driven by the increasing reluctance of members of the public to give evidence and the growth of organised crime and terrorism which requires law enforcement agents to enhance their investigative capabilities. (See 'One Step Ahead: A 21st Century Response to Organised Crime' (Home Office, 2004))

9.3 There are a number of issues to be considered in deciding whether or not undercover tactics are justified. Marx (1988) suggests the following:

- the seriousness of the crime
- non-deceptive methods have been tried and failed

- undercover activities have been subject to some democratic decision and publicly announced
- the strategy is consistent with the spirit as well as the letter of the law
- the eventual goal is to invoke the criminal justice system so that the deception can be made public
- it is proposed for crimes that are clearly defined
- there are reasonable grounds for concluding that targets are engaged in the commission of equivalent offences regardless of the tactic
- there are reasonable grounds to suspect that a crime will be prevented.

9.4   In the UK these issues had been addressed on a case-by-case basis and a body of common law has developed. These principles were incorporated into the Code of Practice on undercover operations published by the police and customs in 1999 and now largely superseded by the Regulation of Investigatory Powers Act 2000 ('RIPA 2000'). The Association of Chief Police Officers and Her Majesty's Customs and Excise published a number of policy manuals of guidance; these are classed as 'restricted' and now incorporate the provisions of RIPA 2000.

9.5   The legal regulation of police undercover operations is problematic in terms of fair trial values because the veil of public interest immunity, in most cases, denies the defence the opportunity to examine the totality of the investigation. Both inculpatory and exculpatory evidence, it is argued, remains untested by the adversarial trial because the public interest in the detection of crime outweighs the interests of the defendant. In the course of this first section it is intended to describe the operation of public interest immunity in the disclosure regime, to examine the investigative tactics, which attract the procedure, and to identify some of the potential risks to the fairness of the trial.

PUBLIC INTEREST IMMUNITY

9.6   Part 1 of the Criminal Procedure and Investigations Act 1996 contains the procedures for compulsory reciprocal pre-trial disclosure for all cases that are tried on indictment. A voluntary scheme applies to contested summary trials.

9.7   The first stage of the procedure involves disclosure by the prosecutor of material that might undermine the prosecution case (CPIA 1996, s 3). Where this has been done in a Crown Court case, the accused is placed under a duty to provide a defence statement and supporting information (s 5). Where a case is to be tried summarily, the accused may choose to provide this information (s 6). Following receipt of the defence statement the prosecutor must make secondary disclosure of material that might assist the accused's defence (s 7). Sensitive material (see below) is not disclosed at the primary stage nor after the prosecutor has received the defence statement. Section 15 covers material that should not be disclosed in the public interest; the court has a duty to keep the issue under review and the accused has a right to request a review.

9.8   The major criticism of the disclosure procedure prior to the Act developed because of the purported zeal of the court to order disclosure of material relevant to the defence, which the police considered sensitive. This is less likely to happen because of mechanisms contained in the Act and Code. Primary determination of sensitivity is made by the police and is listed in a separate schedule. The code sets out a number of examples of material, which may be considered sensitive. Contained in Code 6.8 of the Code, these are:

'•   Material relating to national security, material received from intelligence and security agencies,

•   material relating to intelligence from foreign sources which reveals sensitive intelligence-gathering methods,

•   material such as telephone subscriber checks which is supplied to an investigation for intelligence purposes only,

•   material given in confidence, material relating to the identity or activities of informants or undercover officers, or other persons supplying information to the police who may be in danger if their identities are revealed,

•   material revealing the location of any premises or other place used for police surveillance or the identity of any person allowing a police officer to use premises for surveillance,

•   material revealing, either directly or indirectly, techniques and methods relied upon by a police officer in the course of a criminal investigation, for example covert surveillance techniques, or other methods of detecting crime,

•   Material the disclosure of which might facilitate the commission of other offences or hinder the prevention and detection of crime, internal police communications such as management minutes, communications between the police and the Crown Prosecution Service,

•   Material upon the strength of which search warrants were obtained, material supplied to an investigator during the course of a criminal investigation which has been generated by an official of a body concerned with the regulation or supervision of bodies corporate or persons engaged in financial activities, or which has been generated by such a body,

•   Material supplied to an investigator during a criminal investigation which relates to a child witness and which has been generated by a local authority social services department or other party contacted by an investigator during an investigation.'

9.9   The Code also allows for especially sensitive material to be excluded from the sensitive schedule and revealed to the prosecutor separately (Code 6.9). Two examples of super sensitive material are given; these relate to material which, if disclosed, might lead directly to loss of life or directly threaten national security.

9.10   The list of sensitive material is extensive. A judge must make any determination as to whether disclosure should be refused because it is not in the public interest, on the application of a prosecutor. The determination is made on the basis of information given to the prosecutor by the police. The question of whether the totality and accuracy of the information is sufficient to justify the application is a matter for each individual judge. Significantly, there is no automatic right for defence counsel to be present at the hearing of the application. In *Rowe and Davies v United Kingdom* (2000), *Fitt v United Kingdom* (2000) and *Jasper v United Kingdom* (2000) the European Court has declared that the use of ex parte proceedings in public interest immunity application proceedings is not per se a violation of Art 6 of the European Convention. The court found that the entitlement to disclosure of relevant evidence is not an absolute right and that there may be competing interests that weigh against the interests of the accused. The withholding of material must be in pursuit of a legitimate aim, and the limitation must be proportionate and no greater than strictly necessary (*Van Mechelen v Netherlands* (1998)).

9.11 The judge must be sure that he has 'sufficient knowledge of the contents of the material before making a ruling on non-disclosure' and that such knowledge might be based on what a prosecutor tells the judge about the information rather than an actual inspection of the disputed material.

9.12 The question for the judge in relation to the immunity claim is whether 'the disputed material may prove the defendant's innocence or avoid a miscarriage of justice.' Material that could have this consequence must be disclosed to the defence and frequently where an order is made the prosecution will discontinue the proceedings. While it is difficult for the defence to contest an immunity hearing the balance will come down in favour of the accused where innocence is at stake. In *Jasper* and *Fitt* the court found for the government by a slim majority and the issues were again considered in *Edwards and Lewis v United Kingdom* (2003). The judge had to decide in an ex parte hearing whether the defendants had been entrapped into committing the offences and, if they had, they were entitled to have the proceedings stayed as an abuse of process. The defence submissions on entrapment were rejected. When the case was considered by the European Court it was noted that the undisclosed evidence in the case related or may have related to an issue of fact decided by the trial judge. It held that the defence should have been in a position to argue their case on the point in full and therefore there had been a breach of Art 6. The court alluded to the possibility that had special counsel been appointed to argue for the defence there might not have been a breach of Art 6.

9.13 Guidance on how to apply the judgment in *Edwards and Lewis* was given by the House of Lords in *R v H and C* (2003). The defendants were charged with conspiracy to supply a Class A drug; at a preliminary hearing the trial judge ruled that unless special independent counsel was appointed to represent the defence at the PII hearing, there was a risk that there would be a breach of Art 6. The Crown successfully appealed against the judge's ruling and the Court of Appeal granted the defendants leave to appeal. The decision took account of the following:

- disclosure by the prosecution of material that may weaken the prosecution case or strengthen that of the defence may be withheld from the defence, if disclosure would give rise to a real risk of serious prejudice to an important public interest

- disclosure of such material should only be withheld to the minimum extent necessary to protect the public interest in question
- if limited disclosure or non-disclosure of the material may render the whole trial process unfair to the defendant, then fuller disclosure should be ordered, even if this leads the prosecution to discontinue the proceedings.

9.14   A template of questions to be asked by judges in reaching decisions on whether or not to order disclosure was formulated. The questions must be addressed in the following sequential order:

(i)   The court must first identify whether the material the prosecution seeks to withhold is material that may weaken the prosecution case or strengthen that of the defence. If the material cannot be so described because, for instance it is neutral or is damaging to the defendant, then it should be disclosed. If it can be so described the golden rule is that disclosure should be made unless other PII considerations prevent it.

(ii)   Next, in determining whether PII applies, the court is to apply the test of whether there is a real risk of serious prejudice to an important, and identified, public interest. If the material does not satisfy that test, then it does not attract public interest and must be disclosed.

(iii)   If the material does attract PII the court must then consider whether the defendant's interests can be protected without disclosure, or whether the disclosure can be ordered to an extent or in a way which will give adequate protection to the public interest in question and also afford adequate protection to the interests of the defence.

(iv)   In considering whether limited disclosure is possible, the court must give consideration to ordering the prosecution to make admissions, prepare summaries or extracts of evidence, or provide documents in an edited or anonymised form.

(v)   If the court is minded to order limited disclosure of this kind, it must first ask whether it represents the minimum derogation necessary to protect the public interest in question. If not, then it must order more disclosure. If, however, the effect of limited disclosure may be to render the whole trial process unfair to the defendant, then fuller disclosure should be ordered, even if this leads the prosecution to drop the case.

(vi)   The issue of disclosure of the case should be reviewed as the trial unfolds, evidence is adduced and the defence advanced.

9.15   In applying these principles the House of Lords made clear that the court should, 'involve the defence to the maximum extent possible, without disclosing that which the general interest requires to be protected, but taking account of the specific defence which is relied on.' The consequence of these judgments is that there will be very few cases in which some measure of disclosure to the defence will not be possible. Special independent counsel are likely to be appointed in very limited circumstances and only after, ' the trial judge is satisfied that no other course will adequately meet the overriding requirement of fairness to the defendant'. Prior to this decision the task of the court had been described as a balancing exercise, weighing the desirability of preservation of the public interest in the absence of disclosure against the interest of justice (*R v Ward* (1993)). The new approach is structured requiring the judge to decide whether or not a failure to disclose might result in the overall fairness of the trial being compromised. The non-disclosure of many aspects of covert policing is essential to its effectiveness.

THE REGULATION OF COVERT POLICING

9.16 Prior to RIPA 2000 the gathering of information via secretive means such as surveillance, listening devices, interception of communications and the use of informants was not subjected to sufficient safeguards and led to a series of embarrassing judgements against the United Kingdom government in the European Court of Human Rights. The turning point of which was *Malone (John) v United Kingdom* which brought about the enactment of the Interception of Communications Act 1985.

9.17 Subsequently a series of piecemeal measures were introduced to cover other areas of authorised secret intrusions, among them the Data Protection Acts 1984 and 1998, the Police Act 1997 and the Intelligence Services Act 1994. Too much reliance was placed on informal non-statutory mechanisms such as Home Office Guidelines (for a discussion, see the 2nd edition of this text).

9.18 The demands of compliance with the European Convention provided the central impetus for change (see *Halford v United Kingdom Hewitt* and *Harman v United Kingdom*). Existing laws were inadequate and did not provide sufficient safeguards against possible abuse by the state. Since the introduction of the Human Rights Act 1998 the Government has sought to avoid future problems by passing the RIPA 2000.

9.19 The purpose of the Act was:

'... to make provision for and about the interception of communications, the acquisition and disclosure of data relating to communications, the carrying out of surveillance, the use of covert human intelligence sources and the acquisition of the means by which electronic data protected by encryption or passwords may be decrypted or accessed; to provide for Commissioners and a tribunal with functions and jurisdiction in relation to those matters, to entries on and interferences with property or with wireless telegraphy and to the carrying out of their functions by the Security Service, the Secret Intelligence Service and the Government Communications Headquarters; and for connected purposes'.

It regulates:

'The use of, a range of investigative powers by a variety of public authorities. It updates the law on the interception of communications to take account of technological changes such as the growth of the internet. It also puts other intrusive techniques on a statutory footing for the very first time; provides new powers to help combat the threat posed by rising criminal use of strong encryption and ensures that there is independent oversight of the powers in the Act.'

9.20   The general scheme of the Act is to seek to provide legality within a framework of accountability. The powers contained in it will be an interference with a person's right to private and family life as guaranteed by Art 8 of the ECHR. The interference will be justified if it is authorised for one or more of the purposes provided for in Art 8(2) and if the action is necessary and proportionate to the ends sought to be achieved

9.21   It is in five parts which provide powers in relation to specific investigative techniques or establishing systems of scrutiny, oversight and redress as follows:

Part I   the interception of communications and the acquisition and disclosure of communications data.

Part II   the use of covert surveillance, agents, informants and undercover officers.

Part III   the investigation of electronic data protected by encryption.

Part IV   independent oversight of the powers in the Act.

Part V   miscellaneous and supplemental matters such as consequential amendments, repeals and interpretation.

9.22   RIPA 2000 does not provide a complete framework for covert investigation and must be supplemented by, inter alia, codes of practice which are issued under s 71, by a series of statutory instruments and by the Police Act 1997 which makes property interference lawful if properly authorised. There are codes of practice on the following:

- interception of communications
- property interference
- covert surveillance
- covert human intelligence sources.

(Part III of the Act was not in force at the date of publication, nor was there a code of practice on encryption.)

PART I: INTERCEPTION OF COMMUNICATIONS

Background

9.23   Part I of RIPA 2000 deals with the interception of communications and the acquisition and disclosure of data; it repealed and replaced the Interception of Communications Act 1985 ('IOCA 1985'). Change was necessary not only because of the human rights impetus, to give effect to the judgement in the case of *Halford v United Kingdom* which established that there was no lawful authority to monitor private telecommunications systems, but also because of the:

> 'extraordinary pace of change in the communications industry which sophisticated criminals and terrorists have been quick to use'

(*Interception of Communications in the United Kingdom – A Consultation Paper* (Home Office, 1999)).

9.24   The Government also wished to provide powers to access communications data, such as itemised billing, which is of significant investigative value.

9.25   According to the Home Office interception represents an indispensable means of gathering intelligence against the most sophisticated and ruthless criminals. The consultation paper evidenced this with statistics which claimed that in 1996/7 the lawful interception of communications by police and HM Customs was instrumental in 1200 arrests, the seizure of nearly 3 tonnes of Class A drugs and 112 tonnes of other drugs with a combined street value of over £600m and the seizure of over 450 firearms. In 1998, 2031 interception warrants and 118 postal warrants were authorised by the Home Secretary and the Secretary of State for Scotland. It is to be noted that both IOCA 1985 and RIPA 2000 made it a criminal offence, subject to certain exceptions, to disclose the contents of interception data or any information, which suggests that interception may have occurred.

9.26   A number of cases had highlighted deficiencies in the IOCA scheme. In *Halford v United Kingdom* , the former Assistant Chief Constable of Merseyside complained that telephone calls made from her office had been intercepted. The ECHR decided that the interception amounted to an unjustifiable interference with her right to respect for private life and freedom of expression contrary to Arts 8 and 10.Employees who made calls on an internal telecommunications system should have a reasonable expectation of privacy. Since domestic law did not regulate the interception of calls made on a private system it could not be said that the interception was 'in accordance with the law' as required by Art 8. *R v Effik* (1994) held that cordless telephone operated through a base system is not part of that public system but is a private system connected to the public system. Accordingly, the interception by the police of telephone conversations on a cordless telephone was not subject to IOCA and therefore the recordings were admissible in evidence.

9.27   The expansion in the communications industry and postal market is indisputable with over 150 telecommunications companies offering fixed line services, mass ownership of mobile phones, the growth in the internet, the development of satellite telephones, international simple resale of call schemes and the removal of the Royal Mail's monopoly on postal services.

RIPA 2000, Pt I: the law

9.28   Attention will now be given to the operation of the interception provisions. RIPA 2000, s 1(1) makes it a criminal offence

> 'where a person intentionally and without lawful authority intercepts, at any place in the UK, any communication in the course of its transmission by means of a public postal service or public telecommunications system'

and intercepting communications on a private system without lawful authority unless the interception is made by a person with a right to control the operation or use of the system (s 1(2), (6). (The interception of a private system incurs civil liability in tort.)

9.29   A postal service is defined as any postal service which is offered or provided to, or to a substantial section of the public in any one or more parts of the UK (RIPA

2000, s 2 (1)). Public telecommunications system is also defined in terms of its provision to the public. The effect of these definitions is to make it irrelevant that a private company may provide the service. Private telecommunications systems are those, which are not public but are directly or indirectly attached to a public system. An office network linked to a public system by a private exchange internal system is within the definition but a self-standing system, such as a secure office intranet, is not.

9.30 An interception of a communication takes place in the UK if it is affected by conduct within the UK and the conduct is either:
(i) intercepted in the course of its transmission by means of a telecommunications system; or
(ii) intercepted in the course of its transmission by means of a private system in a case in which the sender or intended recipient of the communication is in the UK (RIPA 2000, s 2(4)).

9.31 Telecommunications system is defined as 'any system which exists for the purpose of facilitating the transmission of communications by any means involving the use of electrical or electro-magnetic energy' (RIPA 2000, s 2(1). This is taken to include 'any time when the means for which the communication is being, or has been transmitted is used for storing it in a manner that enables the intended recipient to collect it or otherwise have access to it' (s 2(7)). Consequently communications from or to a mobile or portable phone, text messages, email, internet and pagers are included. It is to be noted that stored communications may also be obtained under the authority of a PACE production order or search warrant.

9.32 In the following circumstances an interception will be lawful:
(i) where there are reasonable grounds for believing that both the sender and the recipient consents (s 3(1));
(ii) where one party consents and surveillance has been authorised under Pt II of RIPA 2000 (s 3(2)); known as 'participant monitoring';
(iii) where the interception is by the provider of a postal service for the provision of that service or the enforcement of any enactment of that service (s 3(3)), eg opening a letter to determine the return address; and/or where the intercept occurs for the purposes of s 5 of the Wireless Telegraphy Act 1949;
(iv) where the interception is carried out for the purpose of obtaining information about the communications of a person who is believed to be outside the UK and relates to the use of a public telecommunications system provided to persons in such a country, and the provider of the service is required by the law of the relevant country to carry out or facilitate the interception (s 4(1));
(v) where the interception is authorised by regulations made by the Secretary of State in relation to business communications (s 4(2));
(vi) where the interception is carried out in the exercise of powers conferred under s 47 of the Prison Act 1952 or similar legislation in Scotland and Northern Ireland, or in relation to high security psychiatric hospitals pursuant to any direction given under s 17 of the National Health Services Act 1977 (s 4(4), (5));

(vii) where the interception is carried out in the exercise of powers conferred under s 5 of RIPA 2000 which authorises the issue of interception warrants by the Secretary of State.

9.33   The definition of an interception is provided by s 2(2):

'a person intercepts a communication in the course of its transmission by means of a telecommunication system if, and only if, he-
(a)   so modifies or interferes with the system, or its operation,
(b)   so monitors transmissions made by means of the system, or
(c)   so monitors transmissions made by wireless telegraphy to or from apparatus comprised in the system,
as to make some or all of the contents of the communication available, while being transmitted, to a person other than the sender or intended recipient of the communication.'

9.34   Any attachment of apparatus to the system is a modification of the system (RIPA 2000, s 2(2)) and if the communication is recorded during its transmission to enable others to hear or read it Pt I of RIPA 2000 applies.

Consent of one or both parties to the communication

9.35   Interception will be lawful where both parties consent (RIPA 2000, s 3 (1) (there must be reasonable grounds to believe that both the sender and the intended recipient of a communication have consented to its interception).

9.36   Interception will also be lawful where one party consents and a Part II RIPA 2000 authorisation is in place (this situation could arise where a kidnapper is telephoning relatives or in other circumstances where evidence of crime is being sought and the police wish to record the call. This requires a directed surveillance authority (see para 9.136 post). The failure to obtain a directed surveillance authority in these circumstances may not be fatal to the admissibility of the evidence (*R v Hardy and Hardy* (2003)). In *R v Hammond, McIntosh and Gray* (2002), the Court of Appeal held that where an officer recorded conversations by attaching devices to the telephone or the communications system no interception takes place because no third party is 'involved' and one party (the officer) had consented to the recording. This approach is inconsistent with the statute and suggests that there would be no need for the statutory protection in s 3. For a critique of this and other aspects of telephone interception see Ormerod (2004).

Home Secretary's warrant

9.37   Despite representations by Her Majesty's Inspector of Constabulary during the consultation process on the new provisions, and the position of the ECHR, that supervisory control in this area should be entrusted to a judge (*Klass v Germany*

(1978)), the Government declined to move away from the procedures whereby warrants are issued by the Secretary of State. It is difficult to see how effective scrutiny can be maintained in the light of the number of warrants issued: during the period 1 January-31 December 2001 there were 1,314 warrants and 1,788 modifications issued. (*Report of the Interception of Communications Commissioner* (2001), House of Commons (2002)).

9.38 Under RIPA 2000, s 5 the Secretary of State is empowered to issue an interception warrant which authorises the person to whom it is addressed, by any such conduct as may be described in the warrant, to secure any one or more of the following:

'(a) the interception in the course of their transmission by means of a postal service or telecommunication system of the communications described in the warrant;

(b) the making, in accordance with an international mutual assistance agreement, of a request for the provision of such assistance in connection with, or in the form of, an interception of communications as may be so described;

(c) the provision, in accordance with an international mutual assistance agreement, to the competent authorities of a country or territory outside the United Kingdom of any such assistance in connection with, or in the form of, an interception of communications as may be so described;

(d) the disclosure, in such manner as may be so described, of intercepted material obtained by any interception authorised or required by the warrant, and of related communications data.'

9.39 RIPA 2000, s 6 details those who may apply for an interception warrant application, as by or on behalf of the following:

'(a) the Director-General of the Security Service;

(b) the Chief of the Secret Intelligence Service;

(c) the Director of GCHQ;

(d) the Director General of the National Criminal Intelligence Service;

(e) the Commissioner of Police of the Metropolis;

(f) the Chief Constable of the Royal Ulster Constabulary;

(g) the chief constable of any police force maintained under or by virtue of s 1 of the Police (Scotland) Act 1967;

(h) the Commissioners of Customs and Excise;

(i) the Chief of Defence Intelligence;

(j) a person who, for the purposes of any international mutual assistance agreement, is the competent authority of a country or territory outside the United Kingdom.'

9.40 The application for the issue of an interception warrant on behalf of a person specified in RIPA 2000, s 6(2) must be made by a person holding office under the Crown.

9.41 The application for the warrant must contain the following information:

• background to the operation in question;

- person or premises to which the application relates (and how the person or premises feature in the operation);
- description of the communications to be intercepted, details of the communications service provider(s) and an assessment of the feasibility of the interception operation where this is relevant;
- description of the conduct to be authorised as considered necessary in order to carry out the interception, where appropriate;
- an explanation of why the interception is considered to be necessary under the provisions of s 5(3);
- a consideration of why the conduct to be authorised by the warrant is proportionate to what is sought to be achieved by that conduct;
- a consideration of any unusual degree of collateral intrusion and why that intrusion is justified in the circumstances. In particular, where the communications in question might affect religious, medical or journalistic confidentiality or legal privilege, this must be specified in the application;
- where an application is urgent, supporting justification should be provided;
- an assurance that all material intercepted will be handled in accordance with the safeguards required by RIPA 2000, s 15.

9.42   Before the issue of an interception warrant RIPA 2000, s 5(3) requires the Secretary of State to be satisfied:

'(1) that it is **necessary** on any of the following grounds:
(a) in the interests of national security;
(b) for the purpose of preventing or detecting serious crime;
(c) for the purpose of safeguarding the economic well-being of the United Kingdom; (the information which it is thought necessary to obtain must be information relating to the acts or intentions of persons outside the British Islands);.or
(d) for the purpose, in circumstances appearing to the Secretary of State to be equivalent to those in which he would issue a warrant by virtue of paragraph (b) of giving effect to the provisions of any international mutual assistance agreement **and**

(2) that the conduct authorised by the warrant is proportionate to what is sought to be achieved by that conduct.'

The conduct authorised by the warrant is wide (RIPA 2000, s 5(6)):

'The conduct authorised by an interception warrant shall be taken to include-
(a) all such conduct (including the interception of communications not identified by the warrant) as it is necessary to undertake in order to do what is expressly authorised or required by the warrant;
(b) conduct for obtaining related communications data; and
(c) conduct by any person which is conduct in pursuance of a requirement imposed by or on behalf of the person to whom the warrant is addressed to be provided with assistance with giving effect to the warrant.'

9.43   An interception warrant must comply with the requirements of RIPA 2000, s 8 as follows:

'(1) An interception warrant must name or describe either-
(a)   one person as the interception subject; or
(b)   a single set of premises as the premises in relation to which the interception to which the warrant relates is to take place.

(2) The provisions of an interception warrant describing communications the interception of which is authorised or required by the warrant must comprise one or more schedules setting out the addresses, numbers, apparatus or other factors, or combination of factors, that are to be used for identifying the communications that may be or are to be intercepted.

(3) Any factor or combination of factors set out in accordance with subs (2) must be one that identifies communications which are likely to be or to include-
(a)   communications from, or intended for, the person named or described in the warrant in accordance with subs (1); or
(b)   communications originating on, or intended for transmission to, the premises so named or described.'

9.44   The warrant is issued to the applicant who either gives effect to its provisions himself or acts through any other person as he may require to give effect to the warrant. The latter means a duty is placed on the Communications Service Provider (CSP) to take all reasonably practicable steps to give effect to the warrant (RIPA 2000, s 11(4)and (5)). What is reasonably practicable should be agreed after consultation with the CSP and the government. The CSP must be provided with a copy of the warrant but the intercepting agency is only required to provide the name of the person to be intercepted and the specific schedule which identifies the communications which they are being asked to provide assistance in intercepting. All CSPs are required to provide a reasonable intercept capability and their obligations are set out in the (draft) Regulation of Investigatory Powers (Maintenance of Interception Capability) Order) 2002. It is an offence to knowingly fail to comply with the duty under s 11(4), punishable on indictment to a term of imprisonment not exceeding two years or to a fine, or to both. The Secretary of State may take civil proceedings to enforce the duty (s 11(8)).

Duration, cancellation and modification of warrants

9.45   All interception warrants are valid for an initial period of three months. If renewed, warrants issued on serious crime grounds are valid for a further period of three months, warrants issued on national security/economic well-being grounds are valid for a further period of six months. Urgent authorisations are valid for five working days following the date of issue unless renewed by the Secretary of State. Under RIPA 2000, s 10 modifications may be made to the warrant by the Secretary of State or in urgent cases by a senior official expressly authorised by the Secretary of State. Such modifications may include the addition of a new schedule relating to a CSP; a duty exists to modify a warrant to delete a communications identifier if it no longer exists. The CSP must be advised and the interception suspended before the modification instrument is signed. (Code 4.11). If, at any time before its cancellation date, the Secretary of State is satisfied that the warrant is no longer necessary on any of the grounds falling within RIPA 2000, s 5(3), he is under a duty to cancel the warrant and notify the CSP immediately (Code 4.16, 4.17).

The use of evidence obtained by interception

9.46   The Government's position is if evidence obtained by telecommunications interception were to be admitted in court it would detract from the efficacy of the technique. Sections 15 to 18 of RIPA 2000 governs the revelation at trial of the product and fact of interception.

9.47   RIPA 2000, s 15(1) imposes a duty on the Secretary of State to ensure that there are arrangements in place to meet the requirements of the section and s 16. The principle is that distribution and disclosure of intercepted material and related communications must be kept to the minimum necessary (s 15(2)). Section 15 (3) requires that all copies of any intercepted material must be destroyed as soon as it is no longer necessary to retain them for any of the authorised purposes in s 17. The provisions under ss 17 and 18 of RIPA are intended to limit the use of material gathered from telephone intercepts to 'intelligence' rather than 'evidence'. It is submitted that this is an uneasy and unworkable distinction. Section 17 prevents evidence being adduced or questions asked, assertion or disclosure made or other things done in, for the purposes of, or in connection with any criminal proceedings which discloses or suggests that intercepted communication has taken place. This is subject to s 18 which permits disclosure to a person conducting a criminal prosecution for the purpose only of allowing that person to determine what is required of him by his duty to secure the fairness of the prosecution or to disclose it to a relevant judge where that judge has ordered the disclosure to be made to him alone.

Acquisition and disclosure of communications data

9.48   Chapter II of Pt I regulates access to metered communications data by investigating bodies. It replaced the permissive regime previously justified under the data protection legislation which was of dubious legality. Metering is the collection and retention of information about the use made of telephones rather than the content of the call. Examples of communications data include equipment and location details, telephone subscriber details, itemised bill logs, e-mail headers, internet protocol addresses and information on the outside of postal items. Data of these kinds can be obtained provided it is necessary under any of the grounds listed in para 9.42 (a) to (d) and the following additional grounds (contained in s22 (2) (d) to (h)):

(i)   in the interests of public safety;

(ii)   for the purpose of protecting public health

(iii)   for the purpose of assessing or collecting any tax, duty, levy or other imposition, contribution or charge payable to a government department;

(iv)   for the purpose, in an emergency, of preventing death or injury or any damage to a person's physical or mental health, or of mitigating any injury or damage to a person's physical or mental health; or

(v)   for any purpose specified by order of the Secretary of State.

The grounds are considerably wider than those in sn 5 and have been criticised by the Data Protection Commissioner because they are not subject to prior judicial approval. (Data Protection Commissioner, Briefing for Parliamentarians RIPA: http://www.fipr.org/rip/DPCparlRIP.HTM.2000)

PART II: SURVEILLANCE

9.49   Part II of RIPA 2000 and the Code of Practice relates to covert surveillance, defined as watching or listening with a purpose and involves the observation of an individual, a group or a venue in order to gather information which could be used in evidence. Covert surveillance is defined in s 26(9)(a) as any surveillance which is carried out in a manner calculated to ensure that the persons subject to the surveillance are unaware that it is or may be taking place.

9.50   Covert surveillance comprises four types of activity:
- property interference
- intrusive surveillance
- directed surveillance
- covert human intelligence sources.

9.51   These categories reflect the degree to which privacy rights are infringed based on the principle that the higher the level of intrusion the greater the safeguards necessary for the individual. An authorisation, properly granted, under Pt II will provide lawful authority for a public authority to carry out surveillance.

9.52   Authority to conduct surveillance will only be necessary if private information is likely to be gathered. Private information is defined in RIPA 2000, s 26(10) as including any information relating to a person's private or personal relationship with others.

Conditions applicable to all surveillance authorisations

9.53   The following requirements are applicable to all surveillance authorisations:
1.   The authorising officer must be satisfied that the activities are necessary and proportionate.
2.   Arrangements must be made to minimise collateral intrusion.
3.   Records must be kept of authorisations and reviews.

4.   Combined authorisations may be required .
5.   There must be procedures for the retention and destruction of the product obtained.
6.   Information which might be subject of legal privilege, confidential personal information or confidential journalistic material must be given appropriate consideration.

Proportionality and necessity

9.54   The person granting the authorisation must believe that the authorisation is necessary in the circumstances of the particular case for one or more of the statutory grounds in RIPA 2000, s 32(3) for intrusive surveillance, in s 28(3) for directed surveillance and in s 29(3) for covert human intelligence sources. Once satisfied of the necessity requirement the person giving the authorisation must be satisfied that the surveillance is proportionate to what is sought to be achieved. It is also essential that the authorising officer carries out frequent reviews to ensure the continued necessity and proportionality of the activity. Proportionality is discussed at paras 2.36-2.39 ante.

Collateral intrusion

9.55   One of the factors to be taken into consideration in exercising a judgement about the proportionality of the activity is the risk of intrusion into the private lives of persons other than those who are directly the subjects of the authorisation. Measures should be taken, whenever practicable, to avoid or minimise collateral intrusion and the application for authorisation should include an assessment of the risk of such intrusion. If during the course of surveillance it becomes apparent that there is unexpected interference with the privacy of individuals not covered by the authorisation, the authorising officer must be notified in order that consideration may be given to whether the authorisation should be amended or a new authorisation granted (Code 2.8). The authorising officer is required to take into account the sensitivities of communities in the area where the surveillance is taking place and also consider the activities of other public bodies which could impact on the deployment of surveillance. For examples members of NCS, Customs and Excise and so on should consult with a senior officer within the police force area in which the operation or investigation is to take place and consider the implications of any conflicts which might arise.

Record keeping

9.56   It is essential that accurate records are kept for reasons of accountability and as evidence in criminal or civil proceedings. A centrally retrievable record of all authorisations should be held by each public authority and regularly updated whenever an authorisation is granted, renewed or cancelled. The record should be made available to the relevant commissioner or an inspector from the Office of Surveillance

Commissioners, upon request. These records should be retained for a period of at least three years from the ending of the authorisation and should contain the following information:

- the type of authorisation;
- the date the authorisation was given;
- name and rank/grade of the authorising officer;
- the unique reference number (URN) of the investigation or operation;
- the title of the investigation or operation, including a brief description and names of subjects, if known;
- whether the urgency provisions were used, and if so why;
- if the authorisation is renewed, when it was renewed and who authorised the renewal, including the name and rank/grade of the authorising officer;
- whether the investigation or operation is likely to result in obtaining confidential information as defined in this code of practice;
- the date the authorisation was cancelled.

9.57 In all cases, the relevant authority should maintain the following documentation which need not form part of the centrally retrievable record:

- a copy of the application and a copy of the authorisation together with any supplementary documentation and notification of the approval given by the authorising officer;
- a record of the period over which the surveillance has taken place;
- the frequency of reviews prescribed by the authorising officer;
- a record of the result of each review of the authorisation;
- a copy of any renewal of an authorisation, together with the supporting documentation submitted when the renewal was requested;
- the date and time when any instruction was given by the authorising officer.

Retention and destruction of the product

9.58 Where the product of surveillance could be relevant to pending or future criminal or civil proceedings, it should be retained in accordance with established disclosure requirements for a suitable further period, commensurate to any subsequent review.

9.59 In the cases of the law enforcement agencies (not including the Royal Navy Regulating Branch, the Royal Military Police and the Royal Air Force Police), particular attention is drawn to the requirements of the code of practice issued under the Criminal Procedure and Investigations Act 1996. This requires that material which is obtained in the course of a criminal investigation and which may be relevant to the investigation must be recorded and retained. It is also to be noted that this requirement extends to the possibility that exculpatory information may be gathered which must be disclosed in appropriate circumstances.

9.60 There is nothing in RIPA 2000 which prevents material obtained from properly authorised surveillance from being used in other investigations. Each public authority must ensure that arrangements are in place for the handling, storage and destruction of material obtained through the use of covert surveillance. Authorising officers must ensure compliance with the appropriate data protection requirements and any relevant codes of practice produced by individual authorities relating to the handling and storage of material.

9.61   The heads of the intelligence services, MOD and HM Forces are responsible for ensuring that arrangements exist for securing that only information which is necessary for the proper discharge of their function is retained.

9.62   Normal law enforcement activities in response to complaints of crime or preventative patrols will not, in general, require authorisation, nor will surveillance which is carried out in response to events or circumstances where it is not reasonably practicable to obtain authority and only surveillance carried out covertly must be authorised.

9.63   Observations carried out in high crime areas (hot spots) will not require authorisation unless there is specific information that particular individuals are likely to come under surveillance *and* it is likely that private information will be gathered.

Information subject to legal privilege, confidential personal information and confidential journalistic material

9.64   Information under any of these headings is subject to additional safeguards as follows:
(i)   the authorising officer must take into account the possibility of obtaining such information when considering the necessity and proportionality requirements for the surveillance authorisation
(ii)   if such information is obtained the operation or investigation must be frequently reviewed
(iii)   legal advice should be sought and dissemination must be carefully controlled, in particular to ensure that dissemination does not result in prejudice to any proceedings related to the information
(iv)   the relevant commissioner or inspector must be notified of the information and the circumstances in which it was gathered during his next inspection or visit.

Property interference

9.65   The Police Act 1997 was introduced to provide a statutory scheme for the authorisation by chief officers of police, of the National Criminal Intelligence Service (NCIS), the National Crime Squad (NCS), HM Customs and Excise of operations which include entry on or interference with property (both real and personal) or wireless telegraphy without the consent of the owner. Section 92 provides that:

'No entry or interference with property or with wireless telegraphy shall be unlawful if it is authorised by an authorisation having effect under this Act'

It only covers the installation of devices which could have attracted liability under trespass, criminal damage or unlawful interference with wireless telegraphy, under the Wireless Telegraphy Acts 1949 and 1967. It does not cover devices installed with the consent of the person able to give permission in respect of the premises in question, for example the placing of listening devices in police stations. Authorisation is given under PA 1997, s 93 and rests with the authorising officer who must be a chief constable or equivalent who must believe that:

• it is necessary for the action specified to be taken for the purpose of preventing or detecting serious crime (or in the case of the Police Service of Northern Ireland, in the interests of national security); and

• the taking of the action is proportionate to what the action seeks to achieve.

The authorising officer must take into account whether what it is thought necessary to achieve by the authorised conduct could reasonably be achieved by other means.

9.66 The interference with the property is not constrained to the property of the person directly under surveillance and the section clearly encompasses straightforward bugging as well as placing a tracking device on a car, cloning a mobile phone or entering premises in order to download the contents of a suspect's hard disk. During the period 1 April 2002 to 31 March 2003 there were 2,424 property interference authorisations in England, Wales and Northern Ireland; of those 281 required the prior approval of the Surveillance Commissioner (*Annual Report of the Chief Surveillance Commissioner 2002-03*, House of Commons (2003)).

Authorisation procedures

9.67 The Code contains a number of considerations as follows. Firstly there are issues relating to community sensitivities. Code 6.8 requires any person granting or applying for an authorisation or warrant to enter on or interfere with property or with wireless telegraphy to take account of particular sensitivities in the local community where the entry or interference is taking place and of similar activities being undertaken by other public authorities which could impact on the deployment. In this regard, it is recommended that the authorising officers in NCIS, NCS and HMCE should consult a senior officer within the police force in which the investigation or operation takes place where the authorising officer considers that conflicts might arise. The Chief Constable of the Police Service of Northern Ireland should be informed of any surveillance operation undertaken by another law enforcement agency which involve its officers in maintaining or retrieving equipment in Northern Ireland. This provision is also necessary to prevent disorder and for the safety of the operatives.

9.68 Procedures to ensure accountability and the appropriate level of authority are contained in Code 6.9–6.37. Authorisations will generally be given in writing by the authorising officer. However, in urgent cases, they may be given orally by the authorising officer. In such cases, a statement that the authorising officer has expressly authorised the action should be recorded in writing by the applicant as soon as is reasonably practicable. This should be done by the person with whom the authorising officer spoke (Code 6.9).

9.69   Code 6.10 makes provision for the absence of the authorising officer permitting an authorisation in writing or, in urgent cases, orally by the designated deputy. Where, however, in an urgent case, it is not reasonably practicable for the designated deputy to consider an application, then written authorisation may be given by the following:

- in the case of the police, by an assistant chief constable (other than a designated deputy);
- in the case of the Metropolitan Police and City of London Police, by a commander;
- in the case of NCIS and NCS, by a person designated by the relevant Director General;
- in the case of HMCE, by a person designated by the Commissioners of Customs and Excise.

9.70   Applications to the authorising officer for authorisation must be made in writing by a police or customs officer or a member of NCIS or NCS (within the terms of PA 1997, s 93(3)) and should specify:

- the identity or identities of those to be targeted (where known);
- the property which the entry or interference with will affect;
- the identity of individuals and/or categories of people, where known, who are likely to be affected by collateral intrusion;
- details of the offence planned or committed;
- details of the intrusive surveillance involved;
- how the authorisation criteria (as set out in Code 6.6 and 6.7) have been met;
- any action which may be necessary to retrieve any equipment used in the surveillance;
- in case of a renewal, the results obtained so far, or a full explanation of the failure to obtain any results; and
- whether an authorisation was given or refused, by whom and the time and date.

9.71   Additionally, in urgent cases, the authorisation should record (as the case may be):

- the reasons why the authorising officer or designated deputy considered the case so urgent that an oral instead of a written authorisation was given; and
- the reasons why (if relevant) the person granting the authorisation did not consider it reasonably practicable for the application to be considered by the senior authorising officer or the designated deputy.

9.72   Where the application is oral, the information referred to above should be recorded in writing by the applicant as soon as reasonably practicable.

Notifications to surveillance commissioners

9.73   Where a person gives, renews or cancels an authorisation, he must, as soon as is reasonably practicable, give notice of it in writing to a surveillance commissioner, in accordance with arrangements made by the Chief Surveillance Commissioner (Code 6.14). In urgent cases which would otherwise have required the approval of a surveillance commissioner, the notification must specify the grounds on which the case is believed to be one of urgency.

9.74   There may be cases which become urgent after approval has been sought but before a response has been received from a surveillance commissioner. In such a case, the authorising officer should notify the surveillance commissioner that the case is urgent (pointing out that it has become urgent since the previous notification). In these cases, the authorisation will take effect immediately.

9.75   Notifications to surveillance commissioners in relation to the authorisation, renewal and cancellation of authorisations in respect of entry on or interference with property should be in accordance with the requirements of the Police Act 1997 (Notifications of Authorisations etc) Order 1998; SI 1998 No 3241.

Duration of authorisations

9.76   Written authorisations given by authorising officers will cease to have effect at the end of a period of three months beginning with the day on which they took effect. In cases requiring prior approval by a surveillance commissioner this means from the time the surveillance commissioner has approved the authorisation and the person who gave the authorisation has been notified. This means that the approval will not take effect until the notice has been received in the office of the person who granted the authorisation within the relevant force, service, squad or HMCE. In cases not requiring prior approval, this means from the time the authorisation was given (Code 6.18).

9.77   If at any time before the day on which an authorisation expires the authorising officer or, in his absence, the designated deputy considers the authorisation should continue to have effect for the purpose for which it was issued, he may renew it in writing for a period of three months beginning with the day on which the authorisation would otherwise have ceased to have effect. Authorisations may be renewed more than once, if necessary, and the renewal should be recorded on the authorisation record (see Code 6.27 below). Commissioners must be notified of renewals of authorisations.

Reviews

9.78   Authorising officers should regularly review authorisations to assess the need for the entry on or interference with property or with wireless telegraphy to continue.

This should be recorded on the authorisation record (see para 8.82 below). The authorising officer should determine how often a review should take place when giving an authorisation. This should be as frequently as is considered necessary and practicable and at no greater interval than one month. Particular attention is drawn to the need to review authorisations and renewals regularly and frequently where the entry on or interference with property or with wireless telegraphy provides access to confidential information or involves collateral intrusion.

Cancellations

9.79   The senior authorising officer who granted or last renewed the authorisation must cancel it, or the person who made the application to the Secretary of State must apply for its cancellation, if he is satisfied that the authorisation no longer meets the criteria upon which it was authorised. Where the senior authorising officer or person who made the application to the Secretary of State is no longer available, this duty will fall on the person who has taken over the role of senior authorising officer or taken over from the person who made the application to the Secretary of State or the person who is acting as the senior authorising officer (see the Regulation of Investigatory Powers (Cancellation of Authorisations) Order 2000; SI 2000 No 2794).

9.80   The surveillance commissioners must be notified of cancellations of authorisations (Notifications of Authorisations etc) Order 1998; SI 1998 No 3421). The information to be included in the notification is set out in the Police Act 1997.

9.81   The surveillance commissioners have the power to cancel an authorisation if they are satisfied that, at any time after an authorisation was given or renewed, there were no reasonable grounds for believing the matters set out in Code 6.6 and 6.7 above. In such circumstances, a surveillance commissioner may order the destruction of records, in whole or in part, other than any that are required for pending criminal or civil proceedings.

Authorisation record

9.82   Code 6.27 requires that an authorisation record should be created which records:
- the time and date when an authorisation is given;
- whether an authorisation is in written or oral form;
- the time and date when it was notified to a surveillance commissioner; and
- the time and date when the surveillance commissioner notified his approval (where appropriate).

9.83   The authorisation record should also record:
- every occasion when entry on or interference with property or with wireless telegraphy has occurred;
- the result of periodic reviews of the authorisation;

- the date of every renewal; and
- the time and date when any instruction was given by the authorising officer to cease the interference with property or with wireless telegraphy.

Ceasing of entry on or interference with property or with wireless telegraphy

9.84 Once an authorisation or renewal expires or is cancelled or quashed, the authorising officer must immediately instruct those carrying out the surveillance to cease all the actions authorised for the entry on or interference with property or with wireless telegraphy. The time and date when such an instruction was given should be recorded on the authorisation record (see Code 6.27).

Retrieval of equipment

9.85 Where a surveillance commissioner quashes or cancels an authorisation or renewal, he will, if there are reasonable grounds for doing so, order that the authorisation remain effective for a specified period, to enable officers to retrieve anything left on the property by virtue of the authorisation. He can only do so if the authorisation or renewal makes provision for this. A decision by the surveillance commissioner not to give such an order can be the subject of an appeal to the Chief Surveillance Commissioner.

Cases requiring prior approval of a surveillance commissioner

9.86 In certain cases, an authorisation for entry on or interference with property will not take effect until a surveillance commissioner has approved it and the notice has been received in the office of the person who granted the authorisation within the relevant force, service, squad or HMCE (unless the urgency procedures are used). These are cases where the person giving the authorisation believes that:
- any of the property specified in the authorisation:
  - is used wholly or mainly as a dwelling or as a bedroom in a hotel; or
  - constitutes office premises; or
- the action authorised is likely to result in any person acquiring knowledge of:
  - matters subject to legal privilege;
  - confidential personal information; or
  - confidential journalistic material.

9.87 Office premises are defined as any building or part of a building whose sole or principal use is as an office or for office purposes (which means purposes of administration, clerical work, handling money and telephone or telegraph operation) (Code 6.31).

Authorisations for entry on or interference with property or with wireless telegraphy by the intelligence services

9.88   Before granting a warrant authorising for entry on or interference with property or with wireless telegraphy by the intelligence services, the Secretary of State must:
- think it necessary for the action to be taken for the purpose of assisting the relevant agency in carrying out its functions;
- be satisfied that the taking of the action is proportionate to what the action seeks to achieve;
- take into account in deciding whether an authorisation is necessary and proportionate whether the information which it is thought necessary to obtain by the conduct authorised by the warrant could reasonably be obtained by other means; and
- be satisfied that there are satisfactory arrangements in force under the Intelligence Services Act 1994 or the Official Secrets Act 1989 in respect of disclosure of any material obtained by means of the warrant, and that material obtained will be subject to those arrangements (Code 6.32).

9.89   An application for a warrant must be made by a member of the intelligence services for the taking of action in relation to that agency. In addition, the Security Service may make an application for a warrant to act on behalf of the Secret Intelligence Service (SIS) and the Government Communication Headquarters (GCHQ). SIS and GCHQ may not be granted a warrant for action in support of the prevention or detection of serious crime which relates to property in the British Islands (Code 6.33).

9.90   A warrant shall, unless renewed, cease to have effect if the warrant was under the hand of the Secretary of State, at the end of the period of six months beginning with the day on which it was issued. In any other case, at the end of the period ending with the second working day following that day (Code 6.34).

9.91   If at any time before the day on which a warrant would cease to have effect the Secretary of State considers it necessary for the warrant to continue to have effect for the purpose for which it was issued, he may by an instrument under his hand renew it for a period of six months beginning with that day. The Secretary of State shall cancel a warrant if he is satisfied that the action authorised by it is no longer necessary.

9.92   The intelligence services should provide the same information as the police, as and where appropriate, when making applications, requests for renewal and requests for cancellation of property warrants (Code 6.36).

Retrieval of equipment

9.93   Because of the time it can take to remove equipment from a person's property it may also be necessary to renew a property warrant in order to complete the retrieval. Applications to the Secretary of State for renewal should state why it is being or has been closed down, why it has not been possible to remove the equipment and any timescales for removal, where known (Code 6.37).

Intrusive surveillance

9.94 Applications to carry out intrusive surveillance may only be made by the senior authorising officer of the Police Service or HMCE (RIPA 2000, s 32(6)), ie the Chief Officer, Commissioner/Assistant Commissioners in the Metropolitan Police, in Northern Ireland the Deputy Chief Constable is also authorised and in the National Crime Squad Assistant Chief Constables are included.

9.95 The authorising officer must be satisfied that the authorisation is necessary in the circumstances of the particular case on the grounds that it is:
• in the interests of national security
• for the purpose of preventing or detecting serious crime; or
• in the interests of the economic well-being of the country.

9.96 Authorisations to conduct intrusive surveillance should generally be in writing. In cases of urgency they may be given orally and the applicant is required to make a written statement as soon as is reasonably practicable that the authorising officer has expressly approved the conduct. Under RIPA 2000, s 35 notice must be given to a 'Surveillance Commissioner' and under s 36 the authorisation will not take effect until it has been approved, except where it is urgent and the grounds for urgency are set out in the notice, in which case the authorisation will take effect from the time of its grant. There were 461 intrusive surveillance authorisations given in the period 1 April 2002 to 31 March 2003 (*Annual Report of the Chief Surveillance Commissioner 2002-03*, House of Commons (2003)).

9.97 Intrusive surveillance is defined in RIPA 2000, s 26(3) as covert surveillance that:
a. is carried out in relation to anything taking place on any residential premises or in any private vehicle; and
b. involves the presence of an individual on the premises or in the vehicle or is carried out by means of a surveillance device which consistently provides information which is of the same quality and detail as if the surveillance were conducted by the individual on the premises or in the vehicle.

9.98 Residential premises are defined in RIPA 2000, s 48(1). The definition includes hotel rooms, bedrooms in barracks, and police and prison cells, but not any common area to which a person is allowed access in connection with his occupation of such accommodation eg a hotel lounge.

9.99 A private vehicle is defined in RIPA 2000, s 48(1) as any vehicle which is used primarily for the private purposes of the person who owns it or of a person otherwise having the right to use it. A person does not have a right to use a motor vehicle if his right to use it derives only from his having paid, or undertaken to pay, for the use of the vehicle and its driver for a particular journey.

Information to be provided in applications for authorisation

9.100   Applications should be in writing and describe the conduct to be authorised and the purpose of the investigation or operation. The application should specify:
- the reasons why the authorisation is necessary in the particular case and on the grounds (eg for the purpose of preventing or detecting serious crime) listed in RIPA 2000, s 32(3);
- the reasons why the surveillance is considered proportionate to what it seeks to achieve;
- the nature of the surveillance;
- the residential premises or private vehicle in relation to which the surveillance will take place;
- the identities, where known, of those to be the subject of the surveillance;
- an explanation of the information which it is desired to obtain as a result of the surveillance;
- details of any potential collateral intrusion and why the intrusion is justified;
- details of any confidential information that is likely to be obtained as a consequence of the surveillance.

A subsequent record should be made of whether authority was given or refused, by whom and the time and date.

9.101   Additionally, in urgent cases, the authorisation should record (as the case may be):
- the reasons why the authorising officer or designated deputy considered the case so urgent that an oral instead of a written authorisation was given; and/or
- the reasons why it was not reasonably practicable for the application to be considered by the senior authorising officer or the designated deputy.

9.102   Code 5.13 provides that a case will not normally be regarded as urgent unless the time that would elapse before the authorising officer was available to grant the authorisation would, in the judgement of the person giving the authorisation, be likely to endanger life or jeopardise the investigation or operation for which the authorisation was given. If the urgency has arisen because of neglect or the officer's own making it will not be regarded as urgent.

Duration of the authorisation

9.103   Where the Secretary of State issues an intelligence services authorisation it is valid for six months from the date of issue. If the authority is signed by a senior civil servant, although expressly authorised by the Secretary of State it will cease to have effect at the end of the second working day following the day of issue unless it is renewed by the Secretary of State.

9.104 All other authorisations are valid for three months beginning with the day on which they take effect except for oral authorisations given in urgent cases which will cease to have effect at the end of the period of 72 hours beginning with the time when they took effect.

9.105 Renewals are valid for three months; they will not take effect unless approved by a Surveillance commissioner.

9.106 The Code also requires regular reviews to be undertaken to assess the need for the surveillance to continue. The frequency is a matter for the authorising officer and should be done as frequently as is considered necessary and practicable.

9.107 It is the responsibility of the senior authorising officer who grants or last renews the authorisation to cancel it or apply to the Secretary of State for its cancellation. When the decision is taken to discontinue or where an authorisation is quashed or cancelled by a surveillance commissioner, the senior authorising officer must immediately instruct those carrying out the surveillance to stop all surveillance on the subject(s).

9.108 Directed surveillance is defined in RIPA 2000, s 26(2) as surveillance which is covert, but not intrusive, and undertaken:
a. for the purposes of a specific investigation or specific operation;
b. in such a manner as is likely to result in the obtaining of private information about a person (whether or not one specifically identified for the purposes of the operation); and
c. otherwise than by way of an immediate response to events or circumstances the nature of which is such that it would not be reasonably practicable for an authorisation under Pt II of RIPA 2000 to be sought for the carrying out of the surveillance.

9.109 A total of 26,400 directed surveillance authorisations were given in 2002-03 (*Annual Report of the Chief Surveillance Commissioner 2002-03*, House of Commons (2003)).

9.110 Under RIPA 2000, s 28(3) an authorisation for directed surveillance may be granted by an authorising officer where he believes that the authorisation is necessary in the circumstances of the particular case:
• in the interests of national security;
• for the purpose of preventing and detecting crime or of preventing disorder;
• in the interests of the economic well-being of the UK;
• in the interests of public safety;
• for the purpose of protecting public health;
• for the purpose of assessing or collecting any tax, duty, levy or other imposition, contribution or charge payable to a government department; or
• for any other purpose prescribed by an order made by the Secretary of State.

9.111 The authorising officer must give authorisations in writing, except that in urgent cases, they may be given orally by the authorising officer or the officer entitled to act in urgent cases. In such cases, a statement that the authorising officer has expressly authorised the action should be recorded in writing by the applicant as soon as is reasonably practicable.

9.112   A case is not normally to be regarded as urgent unless the time that would elapse before the authorising officer was available to grant the authorisation would, in the judgement of the person giving the authorisation, be likely to endanger life or jeopardise the investigation or operation for which the authorisation was being given. An authorisation is not to be regarded as urgent where the need for an authorisation has been neglected or the urgency is of the authorising officer's own making.

9.113   Authorising officers should not be responsible for authorising investigations or operations in which they are directly involved, although it is recognised that this may sometimes be unavoidable, especially in the case of small organisations, or where it is necessary to act urgently. Where an authorising officer authorises such an investigation or operation the central record of authorisations (see Code 2.14-2.15) should highlight this and the attention of a Commissioner or Inspector should be invited to it during his next inspection.

9.114   Authorising officers within the police, NCIS and NCS may only grant authorisations on application by a member of their own force, service or squad. Authorising officers in HMCE may only grant an authorisation on application by a customs officer.

Information to be provided in applications for authorisation

9.115   A written application for authorisation for directed surveillance should describe any conduct to be authorised and the purpose of the investigation or operation. The application should also include:
- the reasons why the authorisation is necessary in the particular case and on the grounds (eg for the purpose of preventing or detecting crime) listed in s 28(3) of RIPA 2000;
- the reasons why the surveillance is considered proportionate to what it seeks to achieve;
- the nature of the surveillance;
- the identities, where known, of those to be the subject of the surveillance;
- an explanation of the information which it is desired to obtain as a result of the surveillance;
- the details of any potential collateral intrusion and why the intrusion is justified;
- the details of any confidential information that is likely to be obtained as a consequence of the surveillance.
- the level of authority required (or recommended where that is different) for the surveillance; and
- a subsequent record of whether authority was given or refused, by whom and the time and date.

9.116 Additionally, in urgent cases, the authorisation should record (as the case may be):

- the reasons why the authorising officer or the officer entitled to act in urgent cases considered the case so urgent that an oral instead of a written authorisation was given; and/or
- the reasons why it was not reasonably practicable for the application to be considered by the authorising officer.

9.117 Where the authorisation is oral, the detail referred to above should be recorded in writing by the applicant as soon as reasonably practicable.

Duration of authorisations

9.118 A written authorisation granted by an authorising officer will cease to have effect (unless renewed) at the end of a period of three months beginning with the day on which it took effect.

9.119 Urgent oral authorisations or written authorisations granted by a person who is entitled to act only in urgent cases will, unless renewed, cease to have effect after 72 hours, beginning with the time when the authorisation was granted or renewed.

Reviews

9.120 Regular reviews of authorisations should be undertaken to assess the need for the surveillance to continue. The results of a review should be recorded on the central record of authorisations (see Code 2.14-2.15). Particular attention is drawn to the need to review authorisations frequently where the surveillance provides access to confidential information or involves collateral intrusion.

9.121 In each case the authorising officer within each public authority should determine how often a review should take place. This should be as frequently as is considered necessary and practicable.

Renewals

9.122 If at any time before an authorisation would cease to have effect, the authorising officer considers it necessary for the authorisation to continue for the purpose for which it was given, he may renew it in writing for a further period of three months unless it is a case to which Code 4.25 applies. Renewals may also be granted orally in urgent cases and last for a period of 72 hours.

9.123 A renewal takes effect at the time at which, or day on which the authorisation would have ceased to have effect but for the renewal. An application for renewal should not be made until shortly before the authorisation period is drawing to an end. Any person who would be entitled to grant a new authorisation can renew an authorisation. Authorisations may be renewed more than once, provided they continue to meet the criteria for authorisation.

9.124   If at any time before an authorisation for directed surveillance, granted on the grounds of it being in the interests of national security or in the interests of the economic well-being of the UK, would cease to have effect, an authorising officer who is a member of the intelligence services considers it necessary for it to continue, he may renew it for a further period of six months, beginning with the day on which it would have ceased to have effect but for the renewal.

9.125   All applications for the renewal of an authorisation for directed surveillance should record:
- whether this is the first renewal or every occasion on which the authorisation has been renewed previously;
- any significant changes to the information in Code 4.16;
- the reasons why it is necessary to continue with the directed surveillance;
- the content and value to the investigation or operation of the information so far obtained by the surveillance;
- the results of regular reviews of the investigation or operation.

9.126   Authorisations may be renewed more than once, if necessary, and the renewal should be kept/recorded as part of the central record of authorisations (see Code 2.14-2.15).

Cancellations

9.127   The authorising officer who granted or last renewed the authorisation must cancel it if he is satisfied that the directed surveillance no longer meets the criteria upon which it was authorised. Where the authorising officer is no longer available, this duty will fall on the person who has taken over the role of authorising officer or the person who is acting as authorising officer (see the Regulation of Investigatory Powers (Cancellation of Authorisations) Order 2000; SI 2000 No: 2794).

Ceasing of surveillance activity

9.128   As soon as the decision is taken that directed surveillance should be discontinued, the instruction must be given to those involved to stop all surveillance of the subject(s). The date and time when such an instruction was given should be recorded in the central record of authorisations (see Code 2.14-2.15) and the notification of cancellation where relevant.

Covert human intelligence sources (informants and undercover police)

Background

9.129   Many successful investigations and prosecutions of criminal offences involve the use of an informant. The informant, typically will be a criminal who comes to police notice and is able to negotiate a trade off for information in the form of an indemnity from prosecution or a financial reward. Of necessity these types of individuals operate in a murky hinterland which is only superficially regulated by a façade of rules and principles. The informant must be put into historical context and an understanding of the development of the police is essential. Prior to the creation of the full time uniformed police in the 19th century responsibility for providing information and accusations of criminal conduct and even apprehending offenders, lay with those who were, by definition, members of the civilian community (Radzinowicz, 1956). Prosecution might be taken in the name of the Crown but the modern distinction between 'informer' – the person who supplies information to the police and 'informant' – the person who makes the formal accusation – is blurred. Long before the invention of police forces English law accommodated arrangements for obtaining information from persons who were themselves suspected of participating in criminal offences with others. In *Chitty* (1826), the following quote is to be found:

> 'The law confesses its weakness by calling in the assistance of those by whom it is broken. It offers a premium to treachery and destroys the last virtue which clings to the degraded transgressor. Still, on the other hand, it tends to prevent any extensive agreement among atrocious criminals, making them perpetually suspicious of each other'.

In 1975 an indemnity given to Bertie Smalls, armed robber and police informant par excellence attracted criticism in the Court of Appeal from Lawton LJ:

> 'The spectacle of the Director of Public Prosecutions recording in writing, at the behest of a criminal like Smalls, his undertaking to give immunity from further prosecutions, is one which we find distasteful. Nothing of a similar kind must happen again. Undertakings of immunity from prosecution may have to be given in the public interest. They should never be given by police. The Director should give them most sparingly.'

9.130 Modern practice is to permit those who assist the police and are subsequently convicted with a discounted sentence which reflects their contribution to criminal detection. Such individuals are regarded as essential to law enforcement but are not without risk to the integrity of the trial process.

9.131 The use of informants in criminal investigation has a long history. It is regarded as effective by those in law enforcement and nowadays is not confined to the most serious offences that threaten the fabric of society but has become sufficiently commonplace and sophisticated for it to be a common practice. RIPA 2000 now provides the statutory controls for the use and conduct of informants who are given the somewhat bureaucratic label of covert human intelligence sources (CHIS).

9.132 Essentially the CHIS is a witness who is afforded special status and protection on the grounds of public policy. The transition from witness to CHIS rarely follows a smooth path and presents law enforcement agencies with a multiplicity of ethical and organisational concerns. The RIPA 2000 regime is intended to deal with issues of legality which require a delicate balance of ethical management and control (for a more detailed consideration of associated issues see Billingsley, Nemitz and Bean (2001)).

Definitional issues

9.133   It was not RIPA 2000 alone that served as the catalyst to regularise the use of informants. There were a number if controversies surrounding their use. One such example was the case of Delroy Denton who, while registered by the Metropolitan police as an informant, raped and murdered Marcia Lawes (see *The Guardian*, 16 July 1999). A working party consisting of representatives from the Police Complaints Authority, Metropolitan Police, National Crime Squad and members of community consultative groups was set up in 1997. It made suggestions for minimum national standards to be established which took account of human rights and an assessment of an informant's value that included issues relating to public confidence and the seriousness of the crime. Sir John Hoddinott, Chief Constable of Hampshire, conducted an investigation that did not establish sufficient evidence to prosecute any of the officers involved but revealed mismanagement and illegality.

9.134   Prior to RIPA 2000 the regulation of informants was set out in guidelines. The police defined an informant as:

> 'an individual whose very existence and identity the law enforcement agencies judge it essential to keep confidential and who is giving information about crime or about persons associated with criminal activity or public disorder Such an individual will typically have a criminal history, habits or associates, and will be giving the information freely whether or not in the expectation of a reward, financial or otherwise. (NCIS 1999)'

9.135   Dunnighan and Norris (1996) found that it was not possible to run informants according to the guidelines in existence in 1996. There were a number of risks attached to law enforcement agencies in employing individuals who came within the above definition: there must therefore, be strong evidence of their utility. According to Billingsworth, Nemitz and Bean (2001), 'about one third of all crimes cleared up by the police involve the use of informants'. A typology of informants consisting of the following exists:

- a witness who wishes to remain anonymous
- a person who gives information to crimestoppers
- a confidential source
- a covert human intelligence source (registered)
- the 'supergrass.'

9.136   The witness who wishes to remain anonymous may be able to do so as a consequence of the hearsay provisions in s 23-26 of the Criminal Justice Act 1988 because he is 'in fear'. Those who call crimestoppers to give information about criminal activity always remain anonymous. The 'supergrass' is the derisory name given to those who give Queen's evidence and are given a reduced sentence for their cooperation. It is the overlap between 'confidential contacts' who are not subject to the RIPA 2000 regime and the 'covert human intelligence source' (defined below) which has the potential to circumvent the law. NCIS define a confidential contact as, 'an individual or member of an organization who discloses information to the police from which an individual can be identified and there exists personal, professional or other risks by their doing so'.

The fundamental difference between the two categories is said to be that confidential contacts do not establish or maintain a personal or other relationship *'for the purpose of gathering information.'*

9.137 There is very considerable difficulty in the labelling of sources and investigative agencies will need to exercise great care. It is submitted that there are very fine differences and similar principles will apply however they are labelled. In cases of doubt the RIPA 2000 procedures should be followed.

9.138 Under RIPA 2000, s 26(8) a person is a source if:

a. he establishes or maintains a personal or other relationship with a person for the covert purpose of facilitating the doing of anything falling within Code (b) or (c);

b. he covertly uses such a relationship to obtain information or to provide access to any information to another person; or

c. he covertly discloses information obtained by the use of such a relationship or as a consequence of the existence of such a relationship.

9.139 The definition is drawn in very broad terms. 'Relationship' is not defined and the words 'personal or other relationship' could cover most situations. The purpose of the relationship is to obtain 'information' or 'any information ' which contrasts with the obtaining of 'private information ' in relation to intrusive and directed surveillance. Covert is given the same self-evident meaning as elsewhere in the Act:

'a purpose is covert, in relation to the establishment or maintenance of a personal or other relationship, if and only if, the relationship is conducted in a manner that is calculated to ensure that one of the parties to the relationship is unaware of the purpose.'

9.140 'Use' and 'Conduct' are key terms within the Act and require separate consideration before authorisation The use of a source involves inducing, asking or assisting a person to engage in the conduct of a source or to obtain information by means of the conduct of such a source – this is what the law enforcement agency does in connection with the source. The conduct of a source is any conduct falling within RIPA 2000, s 29(4), or which is incidental to anything falling within s 29(4) – this is what the source does to fulfill the tasking given to him or which is incidental to it.

9.141 There were 5,000 'active CHIS authorisations on 31 March 2003 (*Annual Report of the Chief Surveillance Commissioner 2002-03*, House of Commons (2003)).

Authorisation procedures

9.142 Under RIPA 2000, s 29(3) an authorisation for the use or conduct of a source may be granted by the authorising officer where he believes that the authorisation is necessary:

- in the interests of national security;
- for the purpose of preventing and detecting crime or of preventing disorder;
- in the interests of the economic well-being of the UK;
- in the interests of public safety;
- for the purpose of protecting public health;
- for the purpose of assessing or collecting any tax, duty, levy or other imposition, contribution or charge payable to a government department; or
- for any other purpose prescribed in an order made by the Secretary of State.

The authorising officer must also believe that the authorised use or conduct of a source is proportionate to what is sought to be achieved by that use or conduct (Code 4.8).

9.143 The public authorities entitled to authorise the use or conduct of a source are those listed in Sch 1 to RIPA 2000. Responsibility for authorising the use or conduct of a source rests with the authorising officer and all authorisations require the personal authority of the authorising officer. An authorising officer is the person designated under RIPA 2000, s 29 to grant an authorisation for the use or conduct of a source. The Regulation of Investigatory Powers (Prescriptions of Offices, Ranks and Positions) Order 2000; SI 2000 No 2417 designates the authorising officer for each different public authority and the officers entitled to act only in urgent cases. In certain circumstances the Secretary of State will be the authorising officer (see RIPA 2000, s 30(2)).

9.144 The authorising officer must give authorisations in writing except that, in urgent cases, they may be given orally by the authorising officer or the officer entitled to act in urgent cases. In such cases, a statement that the authorising officer has expressly authorised the action should be recorded in writing by the applicant as soon as is reasonably practicable.

9.145 A case is not normally to be regarded as urgent unless the time that would elapse before the authorising officer was available to grant the authorisation would, in the judgement of the person giving the authorisation, be likely to endanger life or jeopardise the operation or investigation for which the authorisation was being given. An authorisation is not to be regarded as urgent where the need for an authorisation has been neglected or the urgency is of the authorising officer's own making.

9.146 Authorising officers should not be responsible for authorising their own activities, eg those in which they, themselves, are to act as the source or in tasking the source. However, it is recognised that this is not always possible, especially in the cases of small organisations. Where an authorising officer authorises his own activity the authorisation should highlight this and the attention of a Commissioner or Inspector should be invited to it during his next inspection.

9.147 The authorising officers within the police, NCIS and NCS may only grant authorisations on application by a member of their own force, service or squad. Authorising officers in HMCE may only grant authorisations on application by a customs officer.

Information to be provided in applications for authorisation

9.148 An application for authorisation for the use or conduct of a source should be in writing and record:

- the reasons why the authorisation is necessary in the particular case and on the grounds (eg for the purpose of preventing or detecting crime) listed in RIPA 2000, s 29(3);
- the reasons why the authorisation is considered proportionate to what it seeks to achieve;
- the purpose for which the source will be tasked or deployed (eg in relation to an organised serious crime, espionage, a series of racially motivated crimes etc);
- where a specific investigation or operation is involved, nature of that investigation or operation;
- the nature of what the source will be tasked to do;
- the level of authority required (or recommended, where that is different).
- the details of any potential collateral intrusion and why the intrusion is justified;
- the details of any confidential information that is likely to be obtained as a consequence of the authorisation; and
- a subsequent record of whether authority was given or refused, by whom and the time and date.

9.149 Additionally, in urgent cases, the authorisation should record (as the case may be):

- the reasons why the authorising officer or the officer entitled to act in urgent cases considered the case so urgent that an oral instead of a written authorisation was given; and/or
- the reasons why it was not reasonably practicable for the application to be considered by the authorising officer.

9.150 Where the authorisation is oral, the detail referred to above should be recorded in writing by the applicant as soon as reasonably practicable.

Duration of authorisations

9.151 A written authorisation will, unless renewed, cease to have effect at the end of a period of 12 months beginning with the day on which it took effect.

9.152 Urgent oral authorisations or authorisations granted or renewed by a person who is entitled to act only in urgent cases will, unless renewed, cease to have effect after 72 hours, beginning with the time when the authorisation was granted or renewed.

Reviews

9.153 Regular reviews of authorisations should be undertaken to assess the need for the use of a source to continue. The review should include the use made of the source during the period authorised, the tasks given to the source and the information obtained from the source. The results of a review should be recorded on the authorisation record. Particular attention is drawn to the need to review authorisations frequently where the use of a source provides access to confidential information or involves collateral intrusion.

9.154   In each case the authorising officer within each public authority should determine how often a review should take place. This should be as frequently as is considered necessary and practicable.

Renewals

9.155   Before an authorising officer renews an authorisation, he must be satisfied that a review has been carried out of the use of a source. If at any time before an authorisation would cease to have effect, the authorising officer considers it necessary for the authorisation to continue for the purpose for which it was given, he may renew it in writing for a further period of 12 months. Renewals may also be granted orally in urgent cases and last for a period of 72 hours.

9.156   A renewal takes effect at the time at which, or day on which the authorisation would have ceased to have effect but for the renewal. An application for renewal should not be made until shortly before the authorisation period is drawing to an end. Any person who would be entitled to grant a new authorisation can renew an authorisation. Authorisations may be renewed more than once, if necessary, provided they continue to meet the criteria for authorisation. The renewal should be kept/ recorded as part of the authorisation record.

9.157   All applications for the renewal of an authorisation should record:
- whether this is the first renewal or every occasion on which the authorisation has been renewed previously;
- any significant changes to the information in Code 4.14;
- the reasons why it is necessary to continue to use the source;
- the use made of the source in the period since the grant or, as the case may be, latest renewal of the authorisation;
- the tasks given to the source during that period and the information obtained from the conduct or use of the source;
- the results of regular reviews of the use of the source.

Cancellations

9.158   The authorising officer who granted or renewed the authorisation must cancel it if he is satisfied that the use or conduct of the source no longer satisfies the criteria for authorisation or that satisfactory arrangements for the source's case no longer exist. Where the authorising officer is no longer available, this duty will fall on the person who has taken over the role of authorising officer or the person who is acting as authorising officer (see the Regulation of Investigatory Powers (Cancellation of Authorisations) Order 2000; SI 2000 No 2794). Where necessary, the safety and welfare of the source should continue to be taken into account after the authorisation has been cancelled.

Management of sources

Tasking

9.159 Tasking is the assignment given to the source by the persons defined at RIPA 2000, s 29(5)(a) and (b), asking him to obtain information, to provide access to information or to otherwise act, incidentally, for the benefit of the relevant public authority. Authorisation for the use or conduct of a source is required prior to any tasking where such tasking requires the source to establish or maintain a personal or other relationship for a covert purpose.

9.160 The person referred to in RIPA 2000, s 29(5)(a), designated the source handler, will have day-to-day responsibility for:
- dealing with the source on behalf of the authority concerned;
- directing the day-to-day activities of the source;
- recording the information supplied by the source; and
- monitoring the source's security and welfare.

9.161 The person referred to in RIPA 2000, s 29(5)(b),designated the source controller, will be responsible for the general oversight of the use of the source.

9.162 In some instances, the tasking given to a person will not require the source to establish a personal or other relationship for a covert purpose. For example a source may be tasked with finding out purely factual information about the layout of commercial premises. Alternatively, a trading standards officer may be involved in the test purchase of items which have been labelled misleadingly or are unfit for consumption. In such cases, it is for the relevant public authority to determine where, and in what circumstances, such activity may require authorisation.

9.163 It is not the intention that authorisations be drawn so narrowly that a separate authorisation is required each time the source is tasked. Rather, an authorisation might cover, in broad terms, the nature of the source's task. If this changes, then a new authorisation may need to be sought.

9.164 It is difficult to predict exactly what might occur each time a meeting with a source takes place, or the source meets the subject of an investigation. There may be occasions when unforeseen action or undertakings occur. When this happens, the occurrence must be recorded as soon as practicable after the event and, if the existing authorisation is insufficient it should either be updated and reauthorised (for minor amendments only) or it should be cancelled and a new authorisation should be obtained before any further such action is carried out.

9.165   Similarly where it is intended to task a source in a new way or significantly greater way than previously identified, the persons defined at RIPA 2000 ,s 29(5)(a) or (b) must refer the proposed tasking to the authorising officer, who should consider whether a separate authorisation is required. This should be done in advance of any tasking and the details of such referrals must be recorded.

Management responsibility

9.166   Public authorities should ensure that arrangements are in place for the proper oversight and management of sources, including appointing individual officers as defined in RIPA 2000, s 29(5)(a) and (b) for each source.

9.167   The person responsible for the day-to-day contact between the public authority and the source will usually be of a rank or position below that of the authorising officer.

9.168   In cases where the authorisation is for the use or conduct of a source whose activities benefit more than a single public authority, responsibilities for the management and oversight of that source may be taken up by one authority or can be split between the authorities.

Security and welfare

9.169   Any public authority deploying a source should take into account the safety and welfare of that source, when carrying out actions in relation to an authorisation or tasking, and to foreseeable consequences to others of that tasking. Before authorising the use or conduct of a source, the authorising officer should ensure that a risk assessment is carried out to determine the risk to the source of any tasking and the likely consequences should the role of the source become known. The ongoing security and welfare of the source, after the cancellation of the authorisation, should also be considered at the outset.

9.170   The person defined at RIPA 2000, s 29(5)(a) is responsible for bringing to the attention of the person defined at s 29(5)(b) any concerns about the personal circumstances of the source, in so far as they might affect:

- the validity of the risk assessment
- the conduct of the source, and
- the safety and welfare of the source.

9.171   Where deemed appropriate, concerns about such matters must be considered by the authorising officer, and a decision taken on whether or not to allow the authorisation to continue. Public authorities have a duty of care to those who are affected by surveillance, this includes surveillance operatives and covert human intelligence sources. Civil liability may arise if the duty of care is breached. In the context of the duty to a CHIS see *Swinney v Chief Constable of Northumbria Police*

(1997) where the details of an informant were contained in a briefcase which was stolen from a car. Public authorities have a duty 'to take reasonable care to avoid unnecessary disclosure to the general public of the information which X had given to the police.' In *Swinney* there had been no breach of the duty because compared with the duty to suppress crime , the risk of the car being broken into was small and sensible steps had been taken to prevent the theft of the briefcase. Where a CHIS voluntarily wishes to sacrifice his own anonymity he is not precluded from doing so by the principle to public interest immunity (*Savage v Chief Constable of Hampshire* (1997).

Additional rules

RECORDING OF TELEPHONE CONVERSATIONS

9.172   Subject to para 4.174 below, the interception of communications sent by post or by means of public telecommunications systems or private telecommunications systems attached to the public network may be authorised only by the Secretary of State, in accordance with the terms of Pt I of RIPA 2000. Nothing in this code should be taken as granting dispensation from the requirements of that Part of RIPA 2000.

9.173   Part I of RIPA 2000 provides certain exceptions to the rule that interception of telephone conversations must be warranted under that Part. This includes, where one party to the communication consents to the interception, it may be authorised in accordance with RIPA 2000, s 48(4) provided that there is no interception warrant authorising the interception. In such cases, the interception is treated as directed surveillance (see ch 4 of the Covert Surveillance Code of Practice).

USE OF COVERT HUMAN INTELLIGENCE SOURCE WITH TECHNICAL EQUIPMENT

9.174   A source, whether or not wearing or carrying a surveillance device and invited into residential premises or a private vehicle, does not require additional authorisation to record any activity taking place inside those premises or vehicle which take place in his presence. This also applies to the recording of telephone conversations other than by interception which takes place in the source's presence. Authorisation for the use or conduct of that source may be obtained in the usual way.

9.175   However, if a surveillance device is to be used, other than in the presence of the source, an intrusive surveillance authorisation and if applicable an authorisation for interference with property should be obtained.

SOURCES AND UNDERCOVER OFFICERS INVOLVED IN THE COMMISSION OF CRIME

9.176   There are conflicting views as to the legality of the criminal conduct which sources engage in during an 'infiltration'. The deployment of sources who participate in criminal activity with the authority of the law enforcement agency which deploys them is a recognised tactic employed to detect serious crime RIPA does not give authority for such activity but :

Code 1.4 of the Covert Human Intelligence Sources Code of Practice states:

'Neither Part I of RIPA 2000 or the Code of Practice is intended to affect the practices and procedures surrounding criminal participation of sources.'

Where the source has acted in accordance with the terms of the authorisation, the law enforcement agency seeks to rely on its prosecutorial discretion and does not prosecute. There are a number of difficulties with this approach : firstly, it is not the agency's province to decide against prosecution, the discretion is that of the Crown Prosecution Service, secondly the so called authorisation is vaguely worded which means that it likely that the extent of the criminal activity will be covered despite the intentions of the authorising officer and thirdly the deployment of sources in these circumstances may not be in 'accordance with the law;. It is suggested that conduct involving participation authorised in accordance with RIPA will constitute a breach of Art 8. The alternative view is that such conduct is not a breach of Article 8. This is a wholly unsatisfactory situation which should be remedied by the kind of legislation which operates in other jurisdictions (see Queensland Australia – Police Powers and Responsibilities Act 2000).

9.177   Undercover police officers appear somewhat belatedly in Code 4.2:

'a source may include those referred to as agents, informants and officers working undercover'

It follows that undercover officers may also be vulnerable in these circumstances.

Administrative procedures

9.178   The management of sources requires a methodical approach. The attached charts will assist in the administration. It will be noted that a number of sequential steps should be taken in respect of each level of source management. These steps are:

- recruitment – see p 613.
- registration and authority for use and conduct – see p 614.
- application for conduct only – see p 615.
- deployment and cessation – see p 616.
- contact/meetings – see p 617.
- infiltration – see p 618.
- application for infiltration – see p 619.

Recruitment of a potential source

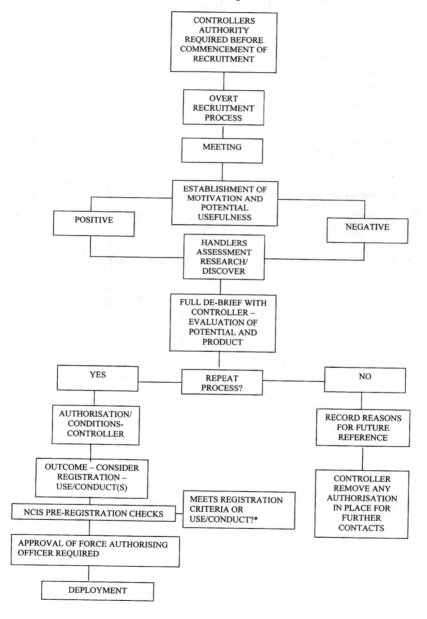

CHIS registration process for use
(and/or conduct)

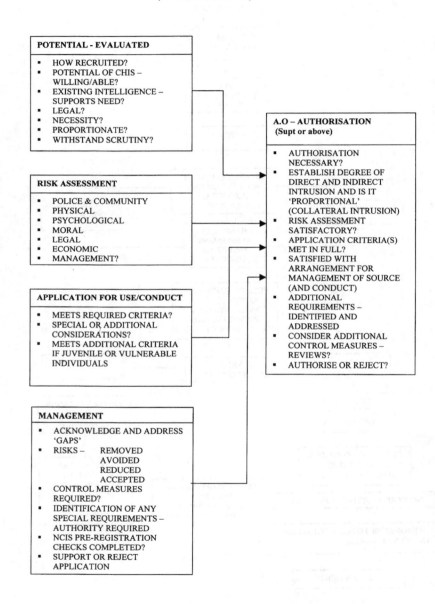

POTENTIAL - EVALUATED

- HOW RECRUITED?
- POTENTIAL OF CHIS –
  WILLING/ABLE?
- EXISTING INTELLIGENCE –
  SUPPORTS NEED?
- LEGAL?
- NECESSITY?
- PROPORTIONATE?
- WITHSTAND SCRUTINY?

RISK ASSESSMENT

- POLICE & COMMUNITY
- PHYSICAL
- PSYCHOLOGICAL
- MORAL
- LEGAL
- ECONOMIC
- MANAGEMENT?

APPLICATION FOR USE/CONDUCT

- MEETS REQUIRED CRITERIA?
- SPECIAL OR ADDITIONAL
  CONSIDERATIONS?
- MEETS ADDITIONAL CRITERIA
  IF JUVENILE OR VULNERABLE
  INDIVIDUALS

MANAGEMENT

- ACKNOWLEDGE AND ADDRESS
  'GAPS'
- RISKS –   REMOVED
              AVOIDED
              REDUCED
              ACCEPTED
- CONTROL MEASURES
  REQUIRED?
- IDENTIFICATION OF ANY
  SPECIAL REQUIREMENTS –
  AUTHORITY REQUIRED
- NCIS PRE-REGISTRATION
  CHECKS COMPLETED?
- SUPPORT OR REJECT
  APPLICATION

A.O – AUTHORISATION
(Supt or above)

- AUTHORISATION
  NECESSARY?
- ESTABLISH DEGREE OF
  DIRECT AND INDIRECT
  INTRUSION AND IS IT
  'PROPORTIONAL'
  (COLLATERAL INTRUSION)
- RISK ASSESSMENT
  SATISFACTORY?
- APPLICATION CRITERIA(S)
  MET IN FULL?
- SATISFIED WITH
  ARRANGEMENT FOR
  MANAGEMENT OF SOURCE
  (AND CONDUCT)
- ADDITIONAL
  REQUIREMENTS –
  IDENTIFIED AND
  ADDRESSED
- CONSIDER ADDITIONAL
  CONTROL MEASURES –
  REVIEWS?
- AUTHORISE OR REJECT?

Application for conduct(s) only

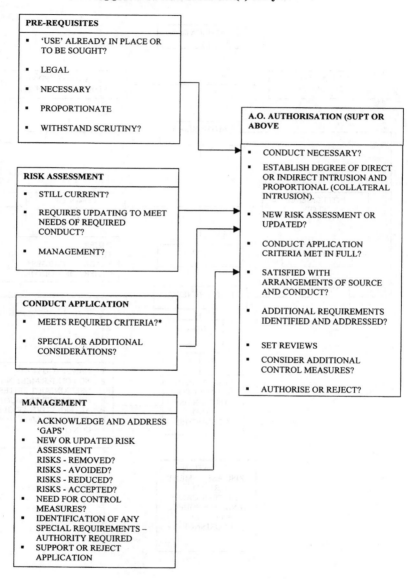

PRE-REQUISITES

- 'USE' ALREADY IN PLACE OR TO BE SOUGHT?
- LEGAL
- NECESSARY
- PROPORTIONATE
- WITHSTAND SCRUTINY?

RISK ASSESSMENT

- STILL CURRENT?
- REQUIRES UPDATING TO MEET NEEDS OF REQUIRED CONDUCT?
- MANAGEMENT?

CONDUCT APPLICATION

- MEETS REQUIRED CRITERIA?*
- SPECIAL OR ADDITIONAL CONSIDERATIONS?

MANAGEMENT

- ACKNOWLEDGE AND ADDRESS 'GAPS'
- NEW OR UPDATED RISK ASSESSMENT
  RISKS - REMOVED?
  RISKS - AVOIDED?
  RISKS - REDUCED?
  RISKS - ACCEPTED?
- NEED FOR CONTROL MEASURES?
- IDENTIFICATION OF ANY SPECIAL REQUIREMENTS – AUTHORITY REQUIRED
- SUPPORT OR REJECT APPLICATION

A.O. AUTHORISATION (SUPT OR ABOVE

- CONDUCT NECESSARY?
- ESTABLISH DEGREE OF DIRECT OR INDIRECT INTRUSION AND PROPORTIONAL (COLLATERAL INTRUSION).
- NEW RISK ASSESSMENT OR UPDATED?
- CONDUCT APPLICATION CRITERIA MET IN FULL?
- SATISFIED WITH ARRANGEMENTS OF SOURCE AND CONDUCT?
- ADDITIONAL REQUIREMENTS IDENTIFIED AND ADDRESSED?
- SET REVIEWS
- CONSIDER ADDITIONAL CONTROL MEASURES?
- AUTHORISE OR REJECT?

*See criteria

Deployment and cessation of CHIS activity

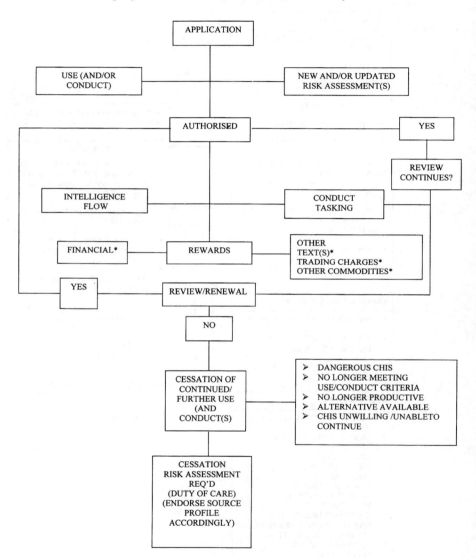

*Risk assessments maybe required according to circumstances

Any contact & meeting of a source

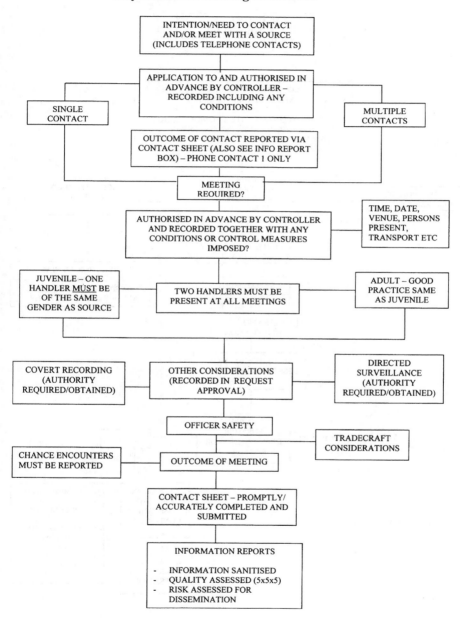

CHIS infiltration

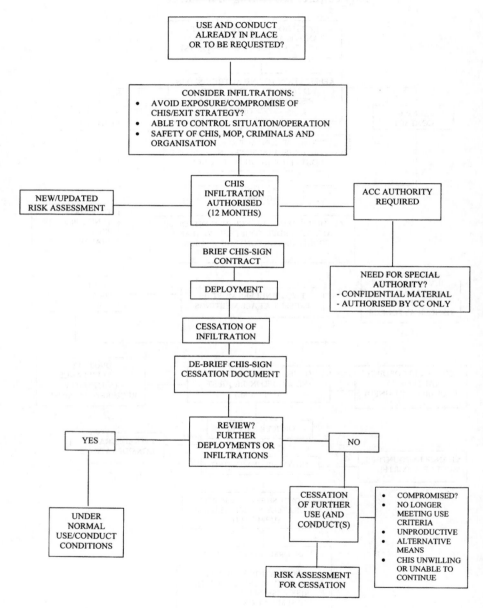

Application for CHIS infiltration

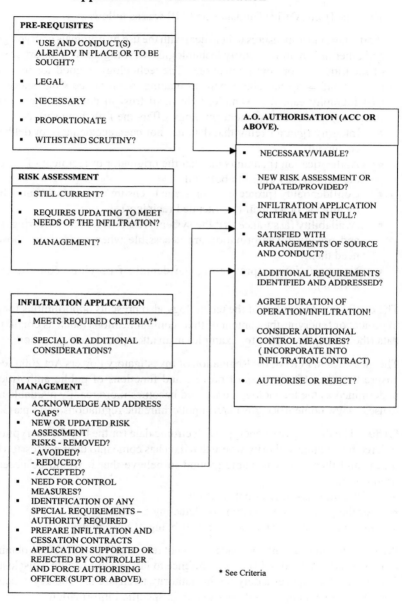

PRE-REQUISITES

- 'USE AND CONDUCT(S) ALREADY IN PLACE OR TO BE SOUGHT?
- LEGAL
- NECESSARY
- PROPORTIONATE
- WITHSTAND SCRUTINY?

RISK ASSESSMENT

- STILL CURRENT?
- REQUIRES UPDATING TO MEET NEEDS OF THE INFILTRATION?
- MANAGEMENT?

INFILTRATION APPLICATION

- MEETS REQUIRED CRITERIA?*
- SPECIAL OR ADDITIONAL CONSIDERATIONS?

MANAGEMENT

- ACKNOWLEDGE AND ADDRESS 'GAPS'
- NEW OR UPDATED RISK ASSESSMENT RISKS - REMOVED?
  - AVOIDED?
  - REDUCED?
  - ACCEPTED?
- NEED FOR CONTROL MEASURES?
- IDENTIFICATION OF ANY SPECIAL REQUIREMENTS – AUTHORITY REQUIRED
- PREPARE INFILTRATION AND CESSATION CONTRACTS
- APPLICATION SUPPORTED OR REJECTED BY CONTROLLER AND FORCE AUTHORISING OFFICER (SUPT OR ABOVE).

A.O. AUTHORISATION (ACC OR ABOVE).

- NECESSARY/VIABLE?
- NEW RISK ASSESSMENT OR UPDATED/PROVIDED?
- INFILTRATION APPLICATION CRITERIA MET IN FULL?
- SATISFIED WITH ARRANGEMENTS OF SOURCE AND CONDUCT?
- ADDITIONAL REQUIREMENTS IDENTIFIED AND ADDRESSED?
- AGREE DURATION OF OPERATION/INFILTRATION!
- CONSIDER ADDITIONAL CONTROL MEASURES? (INCORPORATE INTO INFILTRATION CONTRACT)
- AUTHORISE OR REJECT?

* See Criteria

PART III: INVESTIGATION OF ELECTRONIC DATA PROTECTED BY ENCRYPTION

9.179   The Home Office Guidance on Pt III was as follows:

'Part III provides measures to help deal with the use by criminals of cryptographic and other information security technologies. Cryptography is the art or science of securing data or communications. The technology is good for individuals' privacy and is a vital component in making e-commerce work successfully. Cryptography can, for example, help instil trust in doing business over the Internet. This is because the technology offers the following services:

- Integrity (guaranteeing that data has not been accidentally or deliberately corrupted);
- Authentication (guaranteeing that the originator or recipient of material is the person they claim to be); and
- Confidentiality (protecting a message to ensure its contents cannot be read by anyone other than the intended recipient).
- Availability (assurance that the systems responsible for delivering, storing and processing information are accessible when needed, by those who need them)
- Non-repudiation (preventing the denial of previous commitments or actions).'

The confidentiality aspect of the technology also presents opportunities for criminals to protect or 'encrypt' the content of their communications (such as emails) or stored data (their computer disks, for example) in an attempt to evade detection.

The measures in Pt III of the Regulation of Investigatory Powers Act 2000 seek to help ensure that the effectiveness of powers and functions of public authorities are not undermined as the technology concerned becomes more readily available and easier to use.' (www.homeoffice.gov.uk/crimpol/crimreduc/regulations/part3/part3.html)

9.180   The disclosure of encrypted electronic data (or the key for encryption) can be ordered by a public authority where that data has come into their possession by lawful means and there are reasonable ground to believe that it would be necessary and proportionate:

- in the interests of national security
- for the purpose of preventing or detecting crime
- in the interests of the economic well-being of the country.

9.181   An order can only be made if it is not reasonably practicable to obtain it in any other way (RIPA 2000, s 49). It is an offence to fail to comply with a disclosure notice (s 53) and s 55 imposes a duty on the authority to ensure that the key, when it comes into their possession, is used only to obtain specified information.

9.182   These measure have caused considerable concern. Despite Home Office reassurances the British Chamber of Commerce has stated that they are 'likely to create an environment which will inhibit investment, impede the evolution of e-commerce, impose direct and indirect costs on business and the consumer, diminish overall trust in e-commerce, disrupt business- to-business relationships, place UK companies at a competitive disadvantage, and create a range of legal uncertainties which will place a growing number of businesses in a precarious position.' (www.britishchambers.org.uk/newsandpolic.ict/ripbillssummary).

9.183 Part III was not in force and consultation on the Code of Practice was ongoing at the date of publication.

PART IV: OVERSIGHT

9.184 The Interception of Communications Commissioner must be a person who has held high judicial office and his role is set out in RIPA 2000, s 57t:

*   to keep under review the carrying out by the Secretary of State of the functions conferred on him by ss 7 to 11 of RIPA 2000 and the adequacy of any arrangements made for the purpose of ss 15 and 16 of RIPA 2000.
*   to keep under review the exercise and performance by the Secretary of State of the powers and duties conferred or imposed by or under Ch II of Pt I (the acquisition and disclosure of communications data).
*   to give the Investigatory Powers Tribunal set up under s 65 of RIPA 2000 all such assistance as the Tribunal may require for the purpose of enabling them to carry out their functions under that section.

9.185 The Chief Surveillance Commissioner must also have held high judicial office. His main responsibility is to keep under review the performance of functions under Pt III of the Police Act 1997 and performance of the powers and duties conferred or imposed by or under Pts II and III of RIPA 2000.

9.186 In addition to the Commissioners, a tribunal is established under RIPA 2000, s 65 to deal with complaints under s 7(1)(a) of the Human Rights Act 1998 (proceedings for actions incompatible with convention rights); to consider and determine any complaints made to them, to consider and determine any reference to them by any person who claims to have suffered detriment as a consequence of any restriction or prohibition under s 17; and to hear and determine any other proceedings as may be allocated by order. Section 67 requires the tribunal to exercise merely a form of judicial review. A tribunal will simply state whether the determination is favourable or not. The structure is complex with several different commissioners covering activities that could, logically be the province of a single body. The Government preferred this scheme in order to ensure that expertise prevailed and to maintain, what they considered to be, a higher standard of scrutiny.

Index

[all references are to paragraph number]